# THE AMERICAN CENTURY

## A History of the United States
## Since the 1890s

THIRD EDITION

# THE AMERICAN CENTURY

## A History of the United States
## Since the 1890s

### THIRD EDITION

*Walter LaFeber*
*CORNELL UNIVERSITY*

*Richard Polenberg*
*CORNELL UNIVERSITY*

*Nancy Woloch*

**ALFRED A. KNOPF**   **NEW YORK**

Third Edition
98765432

Copyright © 1975, 1979, 1986 by Newbery Award Records, Inc.

**Library of Congress Cataloging-in-Publication Data**

LaFeber, Walter.
  The American century.
  Includes bibliographies and index.
  1. United States—History—20th century.  2. United States—Foreign relations—20th century.  I. Polenberg, Richard.  II. Woloch, Nancy, 1940—   .  III. Title.
E741.L25  1986    973.9    85-19647
ISBN 0-394-35116-9

Manufactured in the United States of America

Designer: Glen M. Edelstein

Cover: Katherine Von Urban

Cover photo: Peter B. Kaplan © 1984

# PREFACE

The encouraging response to the first two editions of *The American Century* has confirmed the need for a concise but interpretive twentieth-century American history text that offers adequate coverage of the post-1941 period as well as of the years before World War II. We stress economic and urban growth, social and political change, civil rights and liberties, and the growth of the United States into a global superpower. But we also devote special sections to art, architecture, music, dance, theatre, poetry, photography, sculpture, and sports because these topics are of interest to students and offer important historical insights. Further, we give equal attention to U.S. foreign and domestic policies and show how the two are interrelated. To help students understand foreign policy, we include brief analyses of developments in the Soviet Union, Asia, and Latin America.

In this new edition of *The American Century* we have adopted suggestions made by instructors and students. We have thoroughly revised the book to take account of the recent scholarship on the history of women in modern America. This new material has been incorporated in a way that makes the book more balanced and inclusive. We have also added sections on the history of technology (including the space race and computers), and have written an account of developments in the 1980s. Updated chapter bibliographies provide students with a selective guide to the recent literature and to the books we have found most helpful.

We wish to thank the scholars who read the various versions of this book and were unsparing in their comments: Charles M. Dollar, James Hijiya, F. Jack Hurley, Kenneth Jones, Richard S. Kirkendall, Thomas Krueger, Fred R. Mabbutt, Otis L. Graham, Sara Lee Silberman, George Skau, David Trask, and Allen Yarnell. We are indebted to Joanne Florino for preparing the index and instructor's manual. We are especially grateful to the editorial and production staffs of the Random House/Knopf College Department, particularly Christopher J. Rogers, history editor; Niels Aaboe, manuscript editor; Kathy Bendo and Sam Fussell, who researched the photos; and Lester Kaplan, who handled the book's production.

*Walter LaFeber*
*Richard Polenberg*
*Nancy Woloch*

# CONTENTS

# THE AMERICAN CENTURY

## A History of the United States Since the 1890s

### THIRD EDITION

Henry Ford in his first car, 1896.

# 1890s

## The Beginnings of
## Modern America

odern America emerged during a forty-year crisis that began with the Civil War (1861–65) and ended with the war against Spain in 1898. The crisis, which recast every part of the nation's life, climaxed in the 1890s. At the Chicago Columbian Exposition of 1893, Americans celebrated their triumphs in industry and technology while, ironically, enduring the nation's worst economic depression. A young historian, Frederick Jackson Turner of the University of Wisconsin, delivered a speech at this world's fair that helped explain the irony. American social and political institutions, Turner asserted, had been shaped by the vast open lands of the West. According to the 1890 census, however, these lands had finally been settled. Turner concluded: "And now, four centuries from the discovery of America, at the end of a hundred years of life under the Constitution, the frontier has gone, and with its going has closed the first period of American history." Scholars later agreed that Turner overemphasized the importance of the frontier in the shaping of American character, but few, then or since, would deny that a different America was indeed born in the last years of the century. The birth pains were terrifying as well as promising.

## THE SCULPTOR OF MODERN AMERICA: THE CORPORATION

Between 1860 and 1900 no birth was more notable than that of the modern industrial corporation. Barely conceived of before the Civil War, it quickly came to dominate Americans' lives by determining what they possessed, where they worked, and, in general, by producing everything they needed from their baby food to their tombstones.

Before the Civil War, state and national governments had created corporations largely to operate public highways and banks. But shrewd business executives soon realized that merely by obtaining a charter of incorporation from a state government, they suddenly had the right to acquire great sums of capital through sales of stock. At the same time, the liability of each investor was limited to the amount he or she invested. It was like magic. The new creature first appeared to build railroads during the 1850s boom. It was the Civil War, however, that shaped the industrial corporation.

The mammoth armies of the North and South created an immense market that demanded rapid production of goods. Through privately owned corporations, such men as Gustavus F. Swift (meat), Gail Borden (dairy and groceries), and Andrew Carnegie (railways and later steel) got their start by supplying the sinews of war. Equally important, when

Southerners deserted Washington in 1861, unopposed Northern politicians were able to whip legislation through Congress to aid their section's factories. Between 1862 and 1865 members of Congress consequently built a tariff wall insulating American producers against foreign competition, passed bank laws to standardize and liberalize the monetary system, and allowed owners to import cheap labor from Europe. Most striking, Congress simply gave away tremendous amounts of land and mineral resources to corporations that were building the transcontinental railway (completed in 1869) and other transportation systems. By the early twentieth century, the government had given private railway builders free land equivalent to the areas of Maine, New Hampshire, Vermont, Massachusetts, Rhode Island, and much of New York. Some of this acreage held rich deposits of coal, lead, and iron ores.

This was hardly "private enterprise." Corporations obtained incalculable favors from government to develop the country's wealth. An intimate, sometimes questionable, relationship developed between business and government. One member of the House of Representatives observed in 1873 that Congress had become like an "auction room where more valuable considerations were disposed of under the speaker's hammer than in any other place on earth." More cynically, one presidential candidate advised another during the 1870s that businessmen wanted "men in office who will not steal but who will not interfere with those who do." By the 1890s, corporate and national interests were viewed as much the same thing. "After all," one business journal declared in 1895, "the government is the servant of the people." The result was historic: in 1850 the laws had shaped the corporation, but by 1900 the corporation shaped many of the laws.

As the nationwide infrastructure of railways and telegraph lines appeared, the pace of industrial revolution quickened. Except for Western Union and Montgomery Ward, companies that operated across the nation were nonexistent in the 1870s. By 1910, however, they dominated production and distribution. Using the new transportation network, a business could draw raw materials from the Midwest, transform them into processed goods in the East, and sell them nationwide. The isolated, rural, "island communities" of the 1870s became part of an integrated and more homogeneous America. Small local firms suddenly faced competition from giant producers and either copied the giant, merged with it, or were wiped out by it. Local business executives lost ground to distant managers who controlled vast flows of money and goods and so controlled the market.

Such a revolution not only hit the oil, steel, food, and camera industries, but even the making of soap. Before 1870 the soap market was divided among small firms and some European companies. In 1879, however, one small company—Procter and Gamble (P&G) of Cincinnati—accidentally discovered a soap that floated. The discovery, moreover, occurred just as inventors were devising new machinery to mass produce soap. Thus doubly blessed, P&G soon shaped two hundred thousand cakes of Ivory Soap each day. It then pioneered in developing a national advertising campaign and networks of offices to push sales. P&G built a more efficient factory, established a purchasing department to ensure supplies of animal and vegetable fats for the soap, and diversified into salad oils and other soaps. Competitors, such as Colgate, had to develop similar nationwide systems or go under.

In 1880 such firms as P&G, Colgate, Eastman Kodak, American Tobacco, Quaker Oats, Campbell Soup, Pillsbury Flour, and Borden were little known or nonexistent. Twenty years later they were household words and, indeed, some—such as Eastman Kodak and American Tobacco—ranked among the first American multinational corporations by selling their products in such exotic places as Central Europe and China. Little wonder that the President of Columbia University, Nicholas Murray Butler, announced, "In my judgment the limited liability corporation is the greatest single discovery of modern times. . . . Even steam and electricity are far less important," for "they would be reduced to comparative impotence without it."

Inheriting a chaotic and decentralized America, the corporation streamlined and centralized the nation's economic life. It also produced unimagined wealth that marked the beginning of an affluent America. In 1860, 31 million Americans turned out manufactures valued at $2 billion, traveled on thirty thousand miles of railroads, and produced little iron or steel. Forty years later, 70 million people produced manufactures worth $11 billion, used two hundred thousand miles of rails, and overtook Great Britain and Germany to become the world's greatest iron and steel (and soap) producers. The corporation helped create such new cities as Chicago, Atlanta, Kansas City, Minneapolis, and Dallas.

# THE NEW TECHNOLOGY: EDISON, ENERGY—AND SECRETARIES

The new corporation was the child of the new machines. For in the late nineteenth century United States technology, which had lagged behind the British and French, suddenly developed and transformed the world with the electric light, typewriter, telephone, thermionic valve (which made possible radio and later transistors), farm implements, and three revolutionary developments—electricity, automobiles, and airplanes. All of these discoveries and products appeared in the forty years after the Civil War. Samuel Colt, whose pistols were world famous because of their quality and also because they were made from interchangeable parts in an astonishing assembly-line process, perfectly caught the spirit: "There is nothing," he declared in 1854, "that cannot be produced by machinery."

By 1900, however, the "machinery" had grown quite complex. To develop the technology Americans wanted to sell overseas and use in their own homes required two particular ingredients: scientific knowledge and money. The lonely inventor, living on a shoestring, whose sudden discovery changed the world, was becoming rare. Thomas Edison's laboratory, which developed the incandescent bulb in 1879, had by 1901 turned into the General Electric Corporation's laboratory employing hundreds of skilled technicians. The garage where Henry Ford tinkered on his first horseless carriage had become a mechanized industrial complex. Only the corporation could provide the range of management skills and the amount of money needed for developing much of the new technology.

But from the start, government at both the state and national levels was also necessarily involved. The 1862 Land Grant College Act had established new universities, and poured resources into other schools, which were to "teach such branches of learning as are related to agriculture and the mechanic arts." These schools began producing professional engineers who drove the United States to the forefront of world technology. A people that too often is thought of as anti-intellectual actually built its twentieth-century civilization on scientific discoveries and technology that demanded the most rigorous intellectual training and application.

Between 1860 and 1900 the government and the corporation produced goods that changed the face of American society. Before this era, producers could make more goods (and thus more profit) only by adding laborers or finding new sources of power (usually rivers) to run primitive machines. After this era, producers had new machines to do much of the labor and electricity to provide cheap, mobile power. Before this era, many producers were craftsmen who worked at home. After this era most producers worked in centralized, industrial complexes. Before this era the power came from such renewable and relatively clean sources as wind, water, and wood. After this era the sources became nonrenewable and more polluting—coal, oil, and natural gas—as energy consumption in the United States multiplied five times between 1850 and 1900.

The transformation of the business office exemplified the changes. Before 1860 the office usually had a few male employees who with their pens handled a wide range of tasks and acted as both managers and secretaries as they tried to work their way up. Though the managers remained men, by 1900 the office was a large enterprise with many women who performed specific tasks (as typing and filing) with such new machines as the typewriter, which appeared in the 1870s. Women left their homes to become wage earners. With no hope of moving up the corporate ladder, they were the new proletariat of American business. The office was becoming routinized, bureaucratized, and—most important—mechanized and corporatized. And so was much of American society.

The creators of this society naturally believed it was the best of worlds. In 1886 Andrew Carnegie looked at his vast, efficient steel empire and observed, "If asked what important law I should change, I must perforce say none: the laws are perfect."

## BOOM HIDDEN IN BUST

Not all Americans agreed with Carnegie. During the quarter-century following 1873, the country suffered from increasingly severe periods of economic depression. The 1873 panic was triggered by overexpansion and stock exchange corruption. The economic crisis worsened until labor violence erupted in 1877, 1886, 1892, and then sporadically between 1893 and 1895. Overproduction caused this twenty-five-year crisis. Industries and farms produced so much that markets were glutted, prices fell, and both farmers and laborers suffered. Pig-iron production, for example, doubled between 1873 and 1893, while its price dropped from $50 to $13 a ton. Production of cotton, traditionally the nation's leading export, increased more than 50 percent during these years; Americans eventually produced more than the entire world could consume. Some corporations, like some farmers, could not stand the competition and went bankrupt. But others prospered during depressions. Andrew Carnegie's foresight enabled him to build plants cheaply during economic panics and even to buy out competitors. "So many of my friends needed money," he recalled, "I bought out five or six of them. That was what gave me my leading interest in this steel business."

As men like Carnegie learned that efficiency and cost cutting were necessary for survival, they tended to drive others out of business until such vital industries as sugar refining, oil, steel, and tobacco were dominated by only one or two companies. In these fields competition increasingly disappeared. Prices were then determined not by many sellers in an open marketplace, but by a few corporations on the basis of their own costs and whatever return they thought desirable on their investment. Companies banded together to fix prices in "pools" or formed giant combinations known as "trusts," which destroyed competition. To form a trust a number of corporations would join together, giving a group of trustees the power to set prices for all of them. Thus the corporations fixed prices and cut out competition. Their profits skyrocketed. During the 1890s depression, companies rushed to join together for survival. In the early part of the decade dozens of mergers occurred annually. But the figures soared to nearly three thousand between 1897 and 1902. The lone American entrepreneur who made a fortune by competing in an open marketplace would hereafter be a rare phenomenon.

But at the very moment competition was vanishing and opportunity narrowing, belief in the self-made man flourished. Business tycoons helped popularize the idea that success came to those who worked hard and saved their money. "Perseverance is the great thing," said John D. Rockefeller, creator of Standard Oil. "The young man who sticks is the one who succeeds." The view that there was room at the top for all who were virtuous received its most popular formulation in the novels of Horatio Alger. The typical Alger hero, such as "Ragged Dick" or "Mark the Match Boy," began life as a poor orphan. But he was "manly and self-reliant" and through honesty and hard work attained a position of solid respectability with the further assurance that he would "go far." The belief that success resulted from virtue sanctified corporate practices and led to the exaltation of entrepreneurial liberty as the highest social value.

When state or national legislatures tried to control corporations, they were often stopped by the courts. Carnegie might have believed the laws were perfect, but the Supreme Court tried to improve on perfection. It did this by radically changing the idea of "due process," a basic tenet of American law. Before the 1880s due process referred to procedure. For example, the Constitution's Fifth Amendment provides that no person can "be deprived of life, liberty, or property, without due process of law," that is, be subjected to arbitrary arrest, unlawful forfeiture of property, and the like. In 1868 the Fourteenth Amendment strengthened this guarantee by providing that no state government can take away individual rights without due process. This amendment was aimed especially at preventing Southern states from depriving black citizens of voting and other rights. The Supreme Court, however, interpreted it in quite another way.

Between 1886 and 1898 the Court ruled on whether the Minnesota and Nebraska legislatures could regulate railroads in those states. The judges held the state laws invalid, not because the legislatures had violated *procedural* due process in passing the regulations, but because in the Court's opinion the laws were unfair *in substance* to the railroads. The Court asserted the right to decide whether the railway rates were reasonable, instead of deciding, as it had in the past, whether the procedures used in passing the laws were constitutional. Judges thus declared that their own views, rather than those of elected officials, should determine the substance of these particular state laws.

This was potentially an explosive situation, for the Court had put itself above elected officials in order to protect private corporations. Its view was often shaped by Justice Stephen J. Field, who served on the Supreme Court from 1863 to 1897. His beliefs, in turn, had been molded by his experience as an ambitious businessman on the California frontier (where in self-defense he learned the art of shooting to kill without taking the pistol out of his pocket), and from his reading of classical economists who believed an open marketplace existed in which everyone competed equally.

In the *Wabash* case of 1886 the Court struck down an Illinois law regulating railroads that went into other states. The Court declared that since the railway was in interstate commerce, only Congress could deal with it. This decision forced Congress in 1887 to establish the Interstate Commerce Commission to stop such unfair practices as rebates to favored customers. At first the railroads fought the ICC, but shrewd railway lawyers, such as Richard Olney of Boston, adopted different tactics. Olney argued that ICC was inevitable because public opinion demanded it; therefore the railroads should only ensure that their spokesmen controlled the agency. This was one reason why the ICC proved ineffectual; the other was a series of Supreme Court decisions that stripped it of any powers to set fair rates. The same fate paralyzed the Sherman Antitrust Act, passed by Congress in 1890 to outlaw business combinations that tried to monopolize markets or engaged in "restraint of trade" in interstate commerce. The impact of the Sherman Act was so pitiful that it was followed by the spectacular merger and trust movement between 1897 and 1902.

Americans, who have always professed reverence for both efficiency and competition, found by the 1890s that they could not always have both. With the aid of the Supreme Court they chose efficiency. Some critics might tag the corporate leaders of the cut-and-thrust post–Civil War era "Robber Barons." Most Americans, however, were willing to overlook the brutal, often illegal, practices if Rockefeller could deliver cheap, dependable oil for home lamps, or if Cornelius Vanderbilt's New York Central Railroad could reduce the price of bread by cutting transportation costs for flour from $3.45 a barrel in 1865 to only 68 cents in 1885. When writers debated whether Shakespeare or Vanderbilt had contributed more to the human race, Shakespeare inevitably lost.

The Robber Barons helped corrupt politics, undercut laws, and stifle competition, but many people nevertheless agreed with Carnegie's assessment: "It will be a great mistake for the community to shoot the millionaires, for they are the bees that make the most honey, and contribute most to the hive even after they have gorged themselves full." For those Americans who questioned whether they should serve as drones to such queen bees as Carnegie, alternatives seemed quite limited. The crucial question became: what kind of checks could the society produce to limit the corporation's spreading power? Queen bees, after all, are quite brutal.

## THE COLLAPSE OF THE FIRST BARRIER: THE SOUTH, WHITE AND BLACK

Five forces in American society might have made the corporation more responsible: the South, labor unions, organized religion, protest movements, and the political parties. During the 1880s and 1890s each of these either finally accommodated itself to the new industrial America or else was swept aside.

Historically the South had led opposition to the corporation's dominance, for that section had fought for low tariffs, agrarian values, and easy credit. However, Southern resistance halted after the Civil War as Northern capitalists followed Union soldiers into the defeated South, making the area a virtual colony of the North. Spurred by new wealth, cheap labor, and nonexistent taxes, the South doubled the number of its industrial laborers and tripled its investment in manufacturing between 1880 and 1900. By 1900 the region contained half the nation's textile mills. In 1870 one house stood at a rail intersection in Alabama; thirty years later this site, named Birmingham, produced $12 million of manufactures annually and competed with Pittsburgh as leader in world steel production. Yet the South industrialized only as rapidly as the rest of the country. Its spectacular development simply allowed it to keep pace with the North.

Much of the new Southern industry, moreover, depended on Northern capital. Many southerners, known as "redeemers," rushed to make their own fortunes by cooperating with the entrepreneurs from above the Mason-Dixon line. The redeemers sacrificed tax income, thereby sacrificing schools and community facilities, in order to induce industry to build in their towns. One redeemer believed that "it were better for the state to burn the schools" than levy heavier taxes on corporations to pay the state debt. The thirteen Southern states together had less taxable property than the single state of New York and spent $3 million less each year on education than did New Yorkers. In 1900 illiteracy afflicted nearly half of all southerners and more than three-quarters of the section's blacks. State universities in the South were nearly bankrupt. In 1900 Harvard alone received more income than all Southern colleges combined. The institutions that did thrive, such as Vanderbilt in Tennessee and Johns Hopkins in Maryland, depended on Northern funds. Even in higher education, the South was colonized by the North.

The agrarian South did not disappear, but its character greatly changed. The average farm, approximately three hundred fifty acres before the Civil War, shrunk to less than half that acreage afterwards. Meanwhile the number of farms doubled to over a million, one-third of them operated by tenants or sharecroppers for absentee owners. This was hardly an economic base from which the South could challenge the mighty corporation.

Blacks particularly depended on tenant farming or sharecropping. White farm owners preferred former slaves to white workers, for as one owner remarked, "No other laborer [than the Negro] . . . would be as cheerful or so contented on four pounds of meat and a peck of meal a week, in a little cabin 14 by 16 feet with cracks in it large enough to afford free passage to a large-sized cat." During the 1890s, however, race relations underwent a transformation. On the farms blacks saw that tenant farming renewed their slave ties to the land, now without even the relative security that slaves had possessed. When blacks tried to gain employment in the new factories, bloody clashes with whites resulted.

During the late 1880s radical whites attempted to weld together the poor of both races into a class movement that became the Populist party. But redeemers broke up this coalition with racist attacks that first split apart the whites and then turned them violently against blacks. Racism proved stronger than common economic interests shared by both blacks and whites. Lynchings multiplied until they averaged 188 a year during the 1890s. "The government which had made the Negro a citizen found itself unable to protect him," black antilynching crusader Ida Wells-Barnett claimed in 1895. "The white man's victory became complete by fraud, violence, intimidation, and murder." So-called Jim Crow laws were rushed through state legislatures, segregating schools and transportation into supposed "separate but equal" facilities. In 1896 the Supreme Court upheld such laws in *Plessy* v. *Ferguson*. The Court brusquely overrode the lone protest of Justice John Marshall Harlan, who argued that "our Constitution is colorblind." By 1900 black illiteracy was six times as great as that of whites.

When the United States declared war against Spain in 1898, many blacks insisted they be allowed to fight for the liberation of Cubans and Filipinos from Spanish control. After overcoming considerable white opposition, McKinley finally allowed the creation of four black regular regiments and a volunteer force that reached about ten thousand men. The regulars distinguished themselves in Cuba, but when black soldiers returned home they found conditions worse than before. The President would do nothing. The New York *World* published a cartoon showing McKinley studying a map of the Philippines. In the background a figure pulled back a curtain to reveal murders and lynchings of blacks. The caption read: "Civilization Begins at Home."

Most black leaders responded to this crisis by accepting the policies of Booker T. Washington, a black educator. Washington advised acceptance of segregation, stressed the need for nonviolent accommodation to white society, and urged blacks to achieve equality ultimately by means of economic gains, particularly through vocational training. "The opportunity to earn a dollar in a factory just now is worth infinitely more than the opportunity to spend a dollar in an opera house," he observed. Washington hoped that self-help measures would eventually tear down most racial barriers: "In all things purely social we can be as separate as the fingers, yet one as the hand in all things essential to mutual progress." In effect Washington promised that blacks would constitute a docile labor force. "The Negro is not given to strikes," he noted.

Some black leaders dissented. T. Thomas Fortune, a New York editor, founded the Afro-American League in 1890. It protested strenuously against the spread of Jim Crow institutions, but died out within a short time. W. E. B. DuBois, who began teaching at Atlanta University in 1897, also criticized the accommodationist doctrine. He asserted that Washington's emphasis on vocational training cheated blacks of the cultural advantages of a liberal education and deprived them of leaders. But the great majority of black clergymen, professionals, and politicians flocked to Washington's side. His popularity grew when such corporate leaders as Carnegie applauded his policies and when President Theodore Roosevelt asked him to dine at the White House—the first black ever invited as a guest to the mansion. The ensuing antiblack uproar ensured that he was also the last of his race invited to the White House by Roosevelt. By the turn of the century it was impossible for either a black movement led by Washington or a South whose industry and culture were largely dependent on Northern capital to check the new corporation.

## THE COLLAPSE OF THE SECOND BARRIER: LABORERS AND UNIONS

Like the South, the labor movement initially fought the corporation, then accommodated to it. Between 1860 and 1900 the number of industrial workers increased from 2.7 million (or 40 percent of all workers in farms and factories) to 13 million (65 percent). Several union movements attempted to organize laborers after the Civil War but fell victim to racism, the economic depression, and internal political divisions. The continual economic crises after 1873 drove workers to the breaking point, and some organized in small local groups. Nearly 24,000 strikes occurred during the last quarter of the century. Several were especially dangerous.

The general railroad strike of 1877 nearly paralyzed the nation, frightening some Americans into urging a third presidential term for General Ulysses S. Grant because he was the best hope to head off "another French Revolution." Nine years later the Haymarket Riot began when two laborers were killed during a clash with police during a strike in Chicago. At a protest meeting the next night in Haymarket Square a bomb was thrown. Eight policemen were killed. The bomb thrower was never caught, but amid the hysteria the anarchist movement, which preached individual freedom by abolishing all state controls, was conveniently blamed. Four anarchists were hanged; a fifth committed suicide in his prison cell. Haymarket became a symbol to critics of the new corporate system. The riot helped inspire a number of works that fundamentally criticized industrialism, among them Mark Twain's *A Connecticut Yankee in King Arthur's Court* (1889). Twain ends his novel with the free-wheeling Yankee entrepreneur using his industrial ingenuity to kill 25,000 people.

Eugene V. Debs, ca. 1910.

The image of capitalism did not improve in 1892 when strikers at Carnegie's Homestead works in Pittsburgh were fired upon by hired Pinkerton detectives.

The new corporate America was born amidst bloodshed and violence. The terrible depression of 1893–96 worsened matters, as labor uprisings threatened to paralyze many cities. The most serious was a strike against the Pullman Company in Chicago. The trouble began when management sliced wages by 25 percent and fired many workers but refused to reduce costs in the model town of "Pullman," where most employees lived. The American Railway Union, led by Eugene V. Debs, refused to move Pullman coaches. The railroad owners then declared that they would not run trains without those cars, and blamed the union for disrupting transportation. On the advice of Attorney General Richard Olney, President Grover Cleveland obtained an injunction against the strikers and then, over the protest of Illinois Governor John P. Altgeld, sent federal troops into the city. The ostensible reason was to keep United States mail moving, but the effect was to break the strike for the benefit of a private corporation. In 1894 the Supreme Court upheld this use of a sweeping injunction, and Debs went to jail.

Labor's only major success occurred when Samuel Gompers organized the American Federation of Labor in 1886. This union survived the horrors of the 1890s largely because Gompers reached an accommodation with the new corporation. One leader of an earlier, short-lived union had urged his members to become politically active in order to "strangle monopoly." But Gompers refused to identify labor's interests with those of any one political party, choosing instead to work for whichever candidates seemed most friendly at the time. Gompers, moreover, had little desire to "fight monopoly." Instead he tried to counter big corporations with big labor, using union techniques such as strikes and boycotts directly against a particular corporation in order to obtain recognition and benefits. He concentrated on organizing skilled workers along craft lines because he believed that only they could exert much leverage on employers. This policy excluded not only most men in the industrial work force but almost all women factory workers, who tended to hold unskilled jobs. By 1900 the AFL had organized only 3 percent of the nation's nonfarm employees, but it had established the roots for its twentieth-century triumphs. Gompers survived by accepting the corporation and by accepting as well the antianarchist, antisocialist, and, to some extent, the nativist fears of most Americans.

The immigration question proved especially important. Through the mid-nineteenth century the country received over 2 million newcomers each decade, but this number doubled in the 1880s and 1890s. The source of the migration changed from Western Europe to Eastern and Southern Europe, which in turn meant accepting increased numbers of Roman Catholics and Jews. Both old-stock Protestant Americans, who considered the newcomers racially inferior, and segments of organized labor, which disliked the added competition for jobs, favored attempts to restrict immigration. The long-cherished notion that the country could transform immigrants into acceptable citizens through the so-called melting pot of schools and churches began to fade. In 1882 the first exclusion law in American history was passed; it was limited to keeping out Chinese. The nativist sentiment that would prove so powerful was foreseen in 1886 at the dedication in New York harbor of the Statue of Liberty. On the statue's pedestal are inscribed the words, "Give me your tired, your poor, your huddled masses yearning to breathe free." During the ceremonies not one speaker alluded to the inscription but instead emphasized how Americans must go forth to spread liberty to the rest of the world. The speeches symbolized a major change in the nation's history, for the speakers, like Frederick Jackson Turner seven years later, were serving notice that the frontier had closed. Americans were being urged to find new frontiers in other lands.

## FRANK LLOYD WRIGHT: ARCHITECTURE FOR THE OLD FRONTIER AND THE NEW CITY

"American architecture," a critic acidly observed in 1891, "was the art of covering one thing with another thing to imitate a third thing, which, if genuine, would not be desirable." Houses and office buildings were mere boxes, banks resembled Greek temples, government buildings looked like ancient

Frank Lloyd Wright.

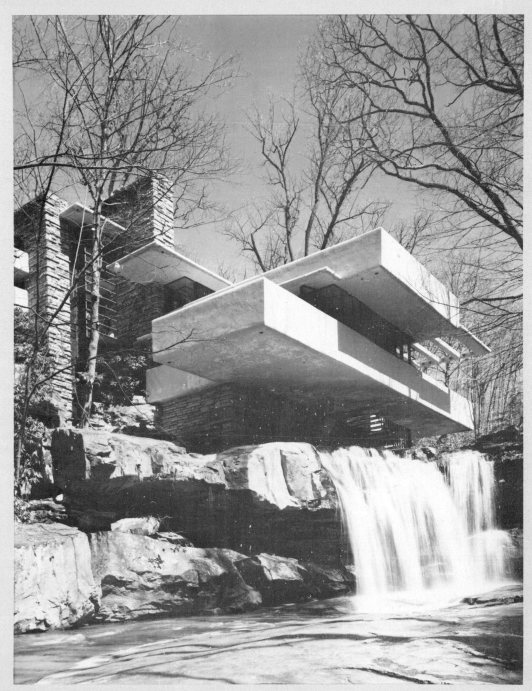

Frank Lloyd Wright: "Falling Water" (1936); Bear Run, Pennsylvania.

THE  SOLOMON  R  GUGGENHEIM  MUSEUM
FRANK  LLOYD  WRIGHT  ARCHITECT

Frank Lloyd Wright: Sketch of the Guggenheim Museum; New York City.

Rome. There was little that could be called an American architecture. Then Frank Lloyd Wright burst upon the scene.

Wright was born in Wisconsin in 1869. His work by century's turn exemplified key American characteristics. Like the Frontier Thesis of Frederick Jackson Turner, Wright's genius emphasized the importance of space and the natural frontier environment in American life. "Intimacy with Nature is the great friendship," he insisted, then built structures that followed the land's contours and harmonized with the environment. His houses were not mere boxes ("more of a coffin for the human spirit than an inspiration," he sniffed), but a "prairie architecture" that would not be "on a hill," but "*of* the hill." Inside, room flowed into room, space into space, like the prairies outside, instead of being artificially separated by walls. These were the first ranch houses. In Wright's plans, they were to be wholly American and also functional for Americans, much as Greek temples were useful for Greeks, but less so for American business executives.

During the 1890s many became frightened that machines would soon strangle the natural environment. Wright, however, saw no conflict between machines and nature. In building his prairie architecture he was the first designer to use products of the industrial revolution that transformed the nation between 1870 and 1900. He innovated with such new building materials as steel, reinforced concrete and, later, plastics. Like Carnegie and Rockefeller, moreover, Wright was an ambitious American entrepreneur, and he hated any governmental interference in either his art or his business. "I believe in the capitalist system," he declared. "I only wish I could see it tried some time."

Yet he was too much of an individualist and noncomformist to be accepted by his countrymen. Scandal plagued him, particularly after he left his wife and children to travel in Europe with the wife of one of his clients. For his new love, he built the ultimate prairie-style house, Taliesen, in Wisconsin. In 1914 a crazed servant killed the woman and six others, then burned Taliesen. Wright rebuilt it, but after the scandal had difficulty obtaining work. Nearly bankrupt in 1929, he was saved by a commission to build the Johnson Wax Company's administration building in Racine, Wisconsin. He then entered his last, greatest period, creating magnificent homes, the entire campus of Florida Southern College, and a radical tubular structure for the Guggenheim Museum in New York City. He rightly considered himself the world's greatest architect, condemning cities that would not take his advice (on Dallas: "Seems to be made of rubber bath-mats"; on Pittsburgh: "Abandon it."). He died at ninety years of age, having completed seven hundred buildings and while working on plans for a mile-high, 528-floor skyscraper that would reach upward like the great trees of his American West. His epitaph was written by a French newspaper editor: "Nothing was ever more deliberately and more profoundly American than the personality and career of Frank Lloyd Wright."

## THE COLLAPSE OF THE THIRD BARRIER: PROTEST MOVEMENTS

Farmers already knew about the closed frontier. Following the 1873 depression, the great American West changed for them from being a promise to a hell. During the next quarter-century wheat and corn sometimes cost considerably more to grow than the price the crops brought on the market. With new machinery and vast lands, farm output soared. From 1860 to 1890 wheat production grew from 173 million to 449 million bushels. In the process, farmers produced so much that they had to rely on exports to other nations to absorb surpluses. But on the world market Americans had to compete with cheap grains from newly opened fields in Argentina and Russia. Terrible winter storms followed by intense heat and drought during the 1880s left many farmers with no crops at all. On particularly brutal frontiers, as in the Dakotas, the isolation and barrenness of rural life took a toll in the form of suicide and mental breakdown. Other agrarians tried to escape to the growing cities.

Some farmers, however, tried to fight. They organized such political movements as the Grange, the Greenback party, and the Populist party. The Populists hoped to improve the farmer's condition by gaining control of the federal government and then using it to regulate the railroads and trusts, provide more credit, impose graduated income taxes, and clean up corrupt politics. Corporate leaders attacked the Populists, and so did many urban laborers who feared that "farm power" might mean higher bread prices. The Populists' demand for government help led to their being labeled "radical" and "socialist." Such terms were beside the point, for corporations had been growing rich from government legislation since the Civil War. The real struggle was over who would use the government.

In 1892 the Populist presidential candidate, James B. Weaver, received more than a million popular, and 22 electoral, votes. The party also elected governors in Kansas, North Dakota, and Colorado. Two years later, in the congressional elections, Populist candidates received nearly 1.5 million votes. That was the peak of the party's power. The last hope for a racially tolerant party that could make important changes in industrial America disappeared when William Jennings Bryan and the Democratic party absorbed most Populists in the 1896 presidential campaign.

Another reform movement also challenged the social values of the new corporation. The women's rights organization began in 1848 at Seneca Falls, New York, when a group of feminists resolved that since "all men and women are created equal," and since men refused them suffrage and thus made them "civilly dead," any law that made women inferior to men would have "no force or authority." In 1869 Wyoming territory gave women the vote. Such a success, however, made slight impact, in part because most women apparently cared little about voting. In Massachusetts, where six hundred thousand women could vote in state elections, only twenty thousand chose to do so. By the 1870s, moreover, feminist leaders attempted to build on the Seneca Falls declaration by urging massive social change that would go far beyond the vote ("that crumb," as one leader termed it): reform of divorce laws, ending of job discrimination, legal equality (in many states married women could not testify in court against their husbands or hold title to property), and a marriage institution in which the partners would be more equal.

Every feminist reform seemed to threaten social stability. When in the 1870s feminist leader Victoria Woodhull urged free love and licensed prostitution, she provided an excuse for all-out attacks on the women's movement. Those attacks frequently linked the feminists to anarchists and strikers as threats to social order. Woman suffrage alone was a threat. Business leaders, even as they transformed the nation, tried to retain the image of a tranquil, stable society that rested on the family and on a clear division of labor within the family. The prospect of women voting brought dire predictions of role reversal, domestic disorder, and social anarchy. In an early debate over the suffrage question, one senator even charged that were women given the vote, they would turn society "into a state of war, and make every home a hell on earth."

The woman suffrage movement split into conservative and liberal factions, then reunited into an organization led by Susan B. Anthony, and later by Carrie Chapman Catt, that dropped demands for drastic reforms in order to gain the vote. To accomplish this, suffragists shrewdly used the arguments of their male opponents: Women were concerned primarily with taking care of the family and consequently should have the vote since their concern for spiritual and traditional values, as opposed to men's money-grubbing, would raise the moral level of politics. But women were also capable of appealing to other prejudices. Suffragists in the South exploited racial fears by asserting that the enfranchisement of white women would ensure white supremacy in the voting booths. Elsewhere, native, white, Protestant women, indignant because they could not vote—whereas male immigrants ultimately could—spoke with disdain of "the ignorant vote." The drive for the franchise thus gained momentum. But in narrowing their program, feminists—like the South, the AFL, and Populists-turned-Democrats—had gone far in accommodating themselves to the America of the industrial corporation. In the end, conflicts in the post–Civil War era revolved not around the question of whether conservatives could carry out a class solution, but around the question of which class would succeed in carrying out a conservative solution.

American socialists never capitulated in quite the same fashion. Neither, however, did they gain many followers. Socialists like Daniel De-Leon, who espoused a straightforward brand of Marxism, had little influence. In the United States, unlike England and Germany, no close bonds ever developed between the socialist movement and organized labor. The socialists who achieved the widest recognition sought to modify Marxist ideology by smoothing its rough and jagged edges. The Christian Socialists, for example, sharply attacked the new corporate order and the suffering it caused, but called for the creation of a cooperative society in the name of traditional Christian morality. They rejected Marx's materialism and his belief in the inevitability of class struggle.

No one carried the attempt to reconcile socialism with American values further than Edward Bellamy, whose best-selling *Looking Backward* (1888) led to the creation of "Nationalist Clubs" across the country. Bellamy's novel described a society in the year 2000 that was organized according to socialist principles, one in which cooperation had replaced competition. But his utopia differed substantially from Marx's. Bellamy did not condone class conflict or assume that the working class was a repository of special virtue. He emphasized change in the United States rather than around the world; he found a place for religious worship in his new order; and he saw the new society developing in a gradual, peaceful way. One character explains: "Evolution, not revolution, orderly and progressive development, not precipitate and hazardous experiment is our true policy... prudence and conservatism are called for." This explains why Abner Doubleday, the supposed father of baseball, could join a Nationalist Club, and why Bellamy found an honored place as an example of the best in American life in the popular *Sweet Home Family Soap Album*.

## THE COLLAPSE OF THE FOURTH BARRIER: CHURCHES

In an earlier America the church had been an outspoken critic of men who sought profit rather than godliness. By the post–Civil War era, however, both Protestant and Roman Catholic leaders in the United States had largely lost their capacity to make fundamental economic or political analyses. "Our churches are largely for the mutual insurance of prosperous families, and not for the upbuilding of the great under-class of humanity," a leading New York City clergyman commented in 1874. American Protestantism's last great theologian, Jonathan Edwards, had lived nearly 150 years before. Church leaders, moreover, confronted not only the complexities of the new industrialism, but an intellectual revolution that transformed every branch of knowledge.

Discovery of the quantum theory in physics demonstrated that energy is not emitted in predictable, continuous steps, but in unpredictable and interrupted stages. This discovery threatened to replace the ordered seventeenth-century world of Isaac Newton with an uncertain, rapidly changing universe that apparently had few if any absolutes. Sigmund Freud's investigations in Austria revealed new, treacherous depths in the unconscious. Such findings triggered the dilemmas that would characterize twentieth-century thought. American novelists, particularly the "naturalist" school led by Frank Norris, Stephen Crane, and Theodore Dreiser, pointed to the brutal side of human nature, stressed that social morality was shaped by industrialism instead of the reverse, and proclaimed that such formerly forbidden topics as sex were too important to be treated with silence.

Some church leaders worked to reconcile the new science and literature with their religious beliefs. The most popular response, however, was the new revivalism led by Dwight L. Moody, who condemned outright Charles Darwin's discoveries that species evolved over the ages and were not created in a particular moment, as the biblical version seemed to indicate. Moody handled such problems by proclaiming that reason was less useful in religion than emotion. His message was particularly well received in college communities. Between 1886 and 1888 Moody and John R. Mott of Cornell organized the Student Volunteer Movement; its modest slogan was "The Evangelization of the World in this Generation." Mott also spearheaded the spectacular growth of the Young Men's Christian Association. Some churchgoers tended to solve their intellectual confusion through sheer activity.

Indeed the entire country seemed to seek activity as an escape from the cataclysms of the 1890s. Bicycling became the rage. Olympic sports grew so popular that Americans won nine of fourteen gold medals in the 1896 games and fourteen of twenty in 1900. Americans also became so adept at boxing that the national champion automatically became the world's champion. It was the era of John Philip Sousa, his United States Marine Band, and rousing marches (such as *Stars and Stripes Forever*), which comforted depression-ridden Americans with rambunctious nationalism. When such emotions eased the nation's entry into war against Spain in 1898, the churches rushed to join. As the *California Christian Advocate* exclaimed, "This war is The Kingdom of God coming!" That news must have surprised Roman Catholic Spain.

By 1900 the church had failed utterly to lessen the oppressiveness or the power of the rampaging industrialism. Its failure was so marked that new organizations, such as the Salvation Army, had developed to aid the human casualties in the urban slums. By 1902 coal mine owner George F. Baer could oppose strikers with the remark: "The rights and interests of the laboring man will be protected and cared for—not by the labor agitators, but by the Christian men to whom God in his infinite wisdom has given the control of the property interests in this country." Few church leaders disputed Baer.

## THE COLLAPSE OF THE FIFTH BARRIER: THE POLITICAL PARTY SYSTEM

Some scholars believe that the last, best hope to check the corporation's rising power was the political system and particularly the choice it provided voters in the 1896 presidential election. This is doubtful. Given the experiences of the social groups and sections discussed above, the issue had been decided before 1896. The triumph of William McKinley over William Jennings Bryan in that year did no more than confirm a prevailing trend. It also established a political pattern that would govern the United States for nearly forty years. In perspective, McKinley and the Republicans won not only a victory but virtual unconditional surrender.

The roaring depression of 1893 was the destroyer. It struck while a Democratic President, Grover Cleveland, and a Democratic Congress held power. The 1894 elections consequently brought about the largest turnover of congressional strength in the nation's history. The Democrats lost 113 House seats; their Capitol Hill leadership was virtually wiped out. In

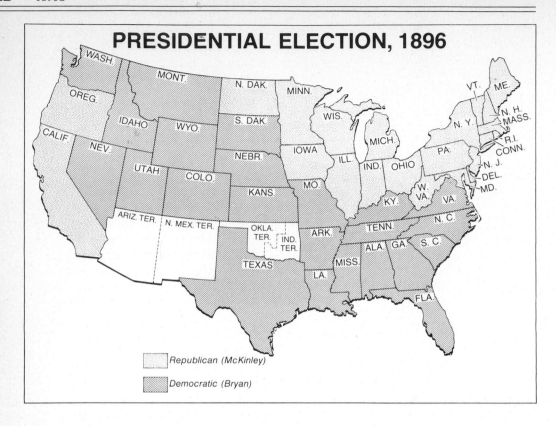

# PRESIDENTIAL ELECTION, 1896

Republican (McKinley)

Democratic (Bryan)

New England only a lone Democratic congressman survived (John F. Kennedy's grandfather, John "Honey Fitz" Fitzgerald), and even such southern states as Texas and Virginia elected Republicans.

Until this point, voters had been able to separate Democrats from Republicans rather neatly. Democrats preached limited government and noninterference in the affairs of individuals, states, and corporations. The marketplace, not the government, was supposed to encourage or regulate the society. As one Democratic leader proclaimed, "We are never doing as well as when we are doing nothing." The Republicans, on the other hand, urged a more active government and greater centralization of power. They used government to erect protective tariffs, give land to railroads, and make the monetary system more efficient for business. Republicans, however, did not plan to use power to reform or regulate. Thomas B. Reed, the 300-pound Republican from Maine who dominated the House of Representatives, dismissed reformers with sarcasm: "One, with God, is always a majority, but many a martyr has been burned at the stake while the votes were being counted." The corporations, therefore, had nothing to fear from Democrats and much to expect from Republicans.

But after the 1894 disaster, Democrats searched desperately for new blood. They found it when Bryan, a former Nebraska congressman, electrified the party's 1896 convention with his "Cross of Gold" speech. He urged increased coining of silver (which was cheaper than gold) to create more money and thereby enable farmers and other depression victims to pay their debts. The proposal found no support from leading businessmen. They feared mixing silver with gold as Bryan proposed would so cheapen the nation's currency that the banking and credit system would sink. They also feared the proposal would be condemned in European money markets that provided large amounts of capital for the building of American railroads, mines, and factories. Nor did urban wage laborers like Bryan's plan, for it could mean they would be paid in cheaper silver dollars and have to pay higher grocery prices.

The Nebraskan also had another major problem. Since the 1840s and 1850s American politics had been increasingly influenced by close-knit, well-organized ethnic and cultural groups (such as the German and Irish) that were concentrated in the cities. These ethnic groups sought to preserve such traditions as beer fests and nonreligious activities on Sunday afternoons. The Democratic party, with its more tolerant view of pluralism and ethnic traditions, offered little interference and these groups had consequently become highly important in the party organization. Bryan was a Democrat, but he represented a largely rural view and constituency, was a "dry" on the burning question of whether alcoholic beverages should be prohibited, and practiced a religious fundamentalism abhorrent to many Roman Catholics and liberal Protestants in the Democratic party. He argued for an activist government that would move decisively in both the society and the economy.

McKinley, meanwhile, transformed the Republican party. Republicans had long been friends of business, but since the antislavery crusade of the 1850s they had also become identified with attempts to impose their own moral and political standards on ethnic groups and newly arrived immigrants. When Republicans preached the evils of alcoholic drink, or the need to reserve Sunday for nothing but quiet meditation, Irish, German, and Jewish immigrants tended to vote Democratic. As a rising star in the political jungles of Ohio, however, McKinley had learned how to moderate such zeal so that he could win votes from ethnic settlements and "wets" in Cleveland and Cincinnati, as well as from traditional Republican rural areas. During the 1896 campaign he blurred the lines between the parties, welcoming the ethnic Democrats, whom Bryan was driving out, while keeping most traditional Republicans. McKinley vowed to end the depression through high tariffs to protect the home market and an unequivocal gold policy to restore confidence in the nation's credit.

The confrontation was perhaps the most dramatic in the country's political history. An unprecedented number of voters turned out to give McKinley a triumph. His administration raised the tariff and then, with the help of rising prices in 1897–98 caused by new discoveries of gold and increased agricultural exports to Europe, the President killed any hope for modifying the currency by having Congress pass the Gold Standard Act. With these issues decided, Americans began staying away from the polls on election day. One-party states became fixtures. Democrats owned the South (especially when blacks were kept from voting after the 1890s), and Republicans controlled much of the Northeast and Midwest. A new era of American politics began, characterized by a diminished concern for elections, little party competition in many states, and Republican power. The new industrialism had little to fear from Washington.

# THE UNITED STATES BECOMES A GREAT WORLD POWER

Not coincidentally, the United States saw its economy mature at the same time that it became a world power. It joined England, France, Germany, and Russia in the great-power class at the moment the Europeans were most imperialistic: between 1870 and 1900 they conquered more than 10 million square miles (one-fifth of the earth's land) and 150 million people. (Imperialism may be defined as one sovereign people subjugating and controlling an alien and formerly sovereign people.) The United States, however, did not join the rush for land, thereby differentiating its empire from that of the Europeans, who sought colonial areas—that is, territory that they could formally control and populate. After the Civil War Americans sought empire primarily for trade, not territory, and preferred to allow native inhabitants to rule themselves under informal United States protection. This was the Americans' "new empire," as it was termed in the late 1890s.

The old empire had developed between the seventeenth century and the 1850s, and had been based on the land conquered by Americans in their march across the continent. This old empire ended with the settlement of the Pacific Coast, the frontier's close, and consolidation of the continent by the corporation. The last act had been a series of vicious Indian wars that climaxed white determination to drive red men from lands in the Dakotas, Oklahoma, and Wyoming that had been given the Indians earlier in the century. These lands had been thought barren, but settlers rapidly encroached upon them after the Civil War, whereupon the federal government concocted devices to expel the Indians. Between 1887 and 1934 they lost to whites about 86 million of their 138 million acres. One Sioux chief asked the obvious: "Why does not the Great Father put his red children on wheels, so he can move them as he will?" When some tribes refused to budge, the U.S. Army appeared. "We must act with vindictive earnestness against the Sioux, even to extermination, men, women and children," General William Tecumseh Sherman proclaimed in the late 1860s. The next quarter-century proved the general not guilty of overstatement. Sherman was especially ruthless, destroying buffalo herds, then attacking Indian camps in midwinter so that he could burn all provisions and thus cause mass starvation. The tribes were exterminated or reduced to begging, and their great chiefs—Geronimo, Big Foot, and Chief Joseph—died or fled, while Sitting Bull, the famous conqueror of Lieutenant Colonel George Custer's cavalry, ended as an exhibit in a circus.

Perhaps the ultimate horror occurred at Wounded Knee, South Dakota, in 1890. After troops disarmed cooperative Sioux, someone fired a rifle. The cavalry opened full fire, then unloaded large cannon, which exploded nearly a shell a second in the defenseless camp. "We tried to run," one Sioux woman recalled, "but they shot us like we were buffalo." At least 150 and perhaps 250 of the original 350 men, women, and children were murdered. This occurred only eight years before the United States sent the cavalry against Spaniards; later it would be used against Filipinos and Chinese. The Indian campaigns sharpened the military's effectiveness. More important, they gave many Americans a rationale for warring against peoples of other colors.

Racism, however, did not trigger American imperialism in 1898. Its taproot lay in the post-1873 depressions and the need to find overseas markets for the overly productive factories and farms. That need became imperative during the strike-ridden days of the mid-1890s, when, in the words of Secretary of State Walter Quintin Gresham, "symptoms of revolution" appeared among unemployed laborers and farmers. Riots and strikes from Brooklyn to Chicago to California were capped by a march of thousands of unemployed (the so-called Coxey's Army) on Washington, D. C., in 1894. The "symptoms" would disappear only with employment, and that required expanded markets. "The prosperity of our people," the Secretary of the Treasury announced in 1894, "depends largely upon their ability to sell their surplus products in foreign markets at remunerative prices."

The United States exported less than 10 percent of its manufactures and about 18 percent of its farm products, but these figures were misleading. Products that formed the economy's backbone heavily depended on external markets: 70 percent of the cotton crop had to be sold abroad, 40 percent of the wheat, 50 percent of the copper, 15 percent of the iron and steel, and even 16 percent of the agricultural equipment. These figures were impressive, but they had also been inadequate, for they had not prevented a quarter-century of depressions. Even greater overseas markets were required. There was, of course, an alternative. Americans could reorient their system, making more equal the distribution of wealth. That alternative was never seriously considered by business and political leaders, who instead preferred greater production and expanded markets. The needed world outlets, however, were coming under the control of the aggressive Europeans. If Americans were to find overseas buyers, they needed the aid of the State Department and perhaps the army and navy. As one prominent Republican observed in 1897, "Diplomacy is the management of international business."

William McKinley in the White House, 1898.

Two business possibilities dramatically opened, one in Asia, the other in Latin America. In 1895 a surging Japan humiliated China in a brief conflict that revealed the loser to be a paper dragon. The humiliation ultimately led to the outbreak of the Chinese Revolution. More immediately, the European powers rushed to carve out areas of China exclusively for their own trade and investment. This flew directly in the face of a half-century American policy, known as the "open door," whose objective was to trade with a whole, sovereign China. United States trade with the Chinese had spiraled upward during the mid-1890s, but the European encroachments threatened to shut off what many Americans believed to be their greatest potential market. McKinley knew that major American interests were deeply endangered, particularly after iron and textile exporters implored him to check the European moves. The President's hands were tied, however, by another crisis ninety miles off the Florida coast.

Since 1868 Cubans had revolted against the domination, corruption, and inefficiency of their Spanish rulers. The United States had barely avoided involvement during the 1870s. The conflict simmered down during the next decade but burst into flames once again in 1895. Under the leadership of José Martí, the Cubans announced the establishment of their own independent government. Several restraints initially kept Americans out of the struggle. For one thing, they feared that intervention might result in their having to annex Cuba, which they wished to avoid because of the racial, constitutional, and political problems that would inevitably arise. As it was, they were experiencing enough difficulty just keeping their own nation together during the 1890s. Moreover, the business community, with which McKinley was in close contact, did not at first want war. The depression finally seemed to be lifting in 1897. Seeing the light at the end of a long tunnel, businessmen feared that the demands of a war economy would threaten the growing prosperity.

In early 1898, however, both restraints disappeared. The first problem evaporated when Americans began to understand that they did not have to govern a free Cuba. They needed only a veto over certain Cuban actions so that, for example, the island could not fall under British power. The inhabitants could otherwise be allowed to govern themselves. McKinley and Congress devised a classic solution in which the United States would enjoy power over, but have little daily responsibility for, the Cubans.

The second restraint disappeared in March 1898, when the business community and McKinley began to fear that a continuation of the Cuban struggle endangered $50 million worth of American investments on the island and, more important, caused uncertainty and unrest in the United States, particularly as Spanish brutality brought outcries among some Americans to free Cuba. A political threat also existed. If McKinley let Cuba fester and uncertainty continue, Bryan might oust the Republicans in 1900 with the cry of "Free Cuba and Free Silver." "Look out for Mr. Bryan," remarked McKinley's top political advisor, Mark Hanna, in February 1898. But, he was asked, would not the Democrats hesitate before offering the nomination again to Bryan? "Hesitate?" Hanna replied, "Does a dog hesitate for a marriage license?"

In late January 1898 McKinley sent the warship *Maine* to Havana to protect the United States property. Two weeks later it blew up, killing more than 250 Americans. The causes have never been determined, but the nation (although not the President) quickly blamed Spain. War sentiment grew, fueled by an increasing fear that United States would not be able to protect its vital interests in China until the Cuban problem was solved. On March 25 a close political advisor in New York City cabled McKinley: "Big corporations here now believe we will have war. Believe all would welcome it as relief to suspense." Two days later the President presented an ultimatum to Spain. The Spanish surrendered to two of the demands by promising to stop their brutalities and to declare an armistice. But they refused a third request to promise eventual independence to Cuba and allow McKinley to act as a mediator in the negotiations. Any Spanish government that accepted that demand would have immediately fallen from power. On April 11 McKinley asked Congress to declare war. Not for the first or last time, Americans concluded they would have to fight abroad in order to have peace and prosperity at home.

## "THE SPLENDID LITTLE WAR"

It would be one of the weirdest and most significant of wars. The first action occurred not in Cuba, but thousands of miles away in the Spanish-controlled Philippines. Six weeks before declaring war, McKinley ordered Admiral George Dewey, the American commander in the Pacific, to take the Philippines should war erupt. Dewey's force was not overly imposing. When it left Hong Kong to fight the Spanish fleet, British naval officials remarked that the Americans were "a fine set of fellows, but unhappily we shall never see them again." Dewey, however, easily blockaded, then smashed a decrepit Spanish flotilla, killing or wounding 400, while only several Americans suffered scratches. The United States had suddenly become a major military power in the Far East as the result of Dewey's victory at Manila Bay.

The campaigns in Cuba were not as spectacular. The American army numbered only 28,000 regulars before the war, and when augmented with 200,000 volunteers it was short of modern rifles, had inadequate medical supplies, ate food that was unfit for human consumption, and wore uniforms designed for duty in Alaska. The War Department proved so ineffectual that McKinley had to fire his Secretary of War amidst a national scandal. America's only salvation lay in the fact that Spain was even more inefficient and corrupt. A broken-down Spanish navy struggled across the Atlantic only to be blockaded in Santiago. American troops overcame the heat and malaria long enough to win the heights overlooking that city. Theodore Roosevelt, who had the good taste to have his uniform custom tailored by Brooks Brothers in New York City, led one charge up the heights, leading the troops directly into the enemy fire. They were saved only by the inability of the Spanish garrison to hit slowly moving targets. Americans held their precarious position for two days, in part because of the heroism of black units. Spain's navy was thus forced out into the harbor and then destroyed easily by the American fleet. Madrid asked for peace.

A war that lasted only three months made the United States a great world power. Americans held a commanding position in Asia and the dominant role in the Western Hemisphere. At home they felt only the exhilaration, for they never had to consider curtailment of their individual liberties or rationing of foodstuffs in order to fight the war. Only 500 Americans died in battle, but four times that number fell victim to diseases. It was an unreal war. One reporter noted that as an American warship shelled a Spanish fort in Cuba, the sailors "whispered and chuckled. . . . Meanwhile from below came the strains of the string band playing from the officers' mess. . . . War as it is conducted at this end of the century is civilized." The horrors of 1873–97 were over, with the new corporate system preserved by what Secretary of State John Hay called "that splendid little war." The conflict that made the nation a great power also, unfortunately, gave war a good name.

## THE PEACE: CLOSING CUBA, OPENING CHINA

McKinley had limited diplomatic objectives. He did not want to copy the Europeans by obtaining a large, expensive, unmanageable colonial empire. After obtaining Cuba, therefore, he allowed the Cubans to write their own constitution but forced them to accept the Platt Amendment passed by the United States Congress. This legislation gave the United States the right to land troops in Cuba to maintain law and order, limited the amount of debt the island could accumulate, and made Guantanamo an American naval base. When Cuba balked at these demands, the McKinley administration summoned Cuban leaders to Washington, courted them with an economic agreement that opened the American sugar market to them on favorable terms, and then threatened that if they would not agree to the amendment the administration would put it into effect by force. By a narrow vote the Cuban Constitutional Convention accepted the amendment. "There is, of course, little or no independence left Cuba under the Platt Amendment," the United States commander in Cuba accurately observed. Supposedly independent, the island would actually be controlled and exploited by the United States for 60 years. The President in addition took Puerto Rico from Spain and made that area an unorganized territory of the United States.

He also acquired the Philippines, but the Filipinos reacted quite unexpectedly. McKinley had decided that they were unprepared for self-government and that if left to themselves they would be victimized by some European power. He did not want all of the islands, only the magnificent port of Manila from which American merchants and warships could develop and protect interests in China. Manila, however, would be threatened if the remainder of the islands fell into European hands. McKinley therefore decided reluctantly that he had no alternative to taking all of the Philippines. As he later explained to missionaries who visited the White House, he had constantly prayed about the problem; then one night a voice told him to annex the Philippines for, among other reasons, "we could not turn them over to France or Germany—our commercial rivals in the Orient—that would be bad business and discredita-

Emilio Aguinaldo, commander of Filipino insurgents.

ble.'' Apparently everyone who had endured the post-1873 depressions knew the horrors of ''bad business,'' even voices. The Filipinos, however, were not impressed. Led by Emilio Aguinaldo, they declared themselves independent and fought 120,000 American troops in a three-year struggle. Two thousand Americans and perhaps as many as 200,000 Filipinos died. The United States used increasingly brutal methods to end the insurrection. After some American troops were massacred, one general ordered the killing of every Filipino male over the age of ten. This order never took effect, but lesser barbarities continued until 1902, when Aguinaldo had been captured and resistance broken.

    At home, anti-imperialist groups, led by conservative businessmen, intellectuals, and some Democrats, organized to blast McKinley's Philippine policy. ''G is for guns/ That McKinley has sent/ To teach Filipinos/

What Jesus Christ meant," went one anti-imperialist poem. But despite financing from Andrew Carnegie and literature written by such figures as Mark Twain, these groups received very little support. Their only victory, if that is the proper word, was preventing Harvard from giving McKinley an honorary degree. In the election of 1900 Bryan tried briefly to gain the support of the anti-imperialists, but he decided to soft-pedal their cause in order to emphasize again the free-silver issue. Nothing could save either the anti-imperialists or Bryan. McKinley and his vice-presidential running mate, Governor Theodore Roosevelt of New York, won a landslide victory larger than the Republican triumph of 1896.

Despite the Philippine bloodshed, the President had scored notable victories including an end to the depression, solution of the Cuban problem, and establishment of the United States as a great power in Asia. The last was particularly important. Using Dewey's victory as leverage, McKinley moved to stop the carving up of China by the Europeans; viewed another way, he sought to keep all of China open to American exporters and missionaries. In 1899 and 1900, Secretary of State John Hay issued two "open-door" notes asking the other powers to promise that they would keep China open on an equal basis to all outsiders; meanwhile Chinese sovereignty would be recognized in all parts of the empire. The other powers, particularly Russia, grumbled, but Hay publicly announced that everyone had accepted the American position. This was not accurate, for the Russians, and later the Japanese, would not agree that China should become a marketplace open to all. They believed that their proximity to the China market gave them—indeed, required that they have—favored position for their own economic and political interests. Hay and McKinley nevertheless insisted that American businessmen and missionaries enjoy an open door to compete for Chinese customers and souls on the same terms as anyone else, even Russians and Japanese. American statesmen would hold to that insistence until the 1940s.

The Civil War and the ensuing economic crisis mark the most threatening forty-year era in United States history, but McKinley's triumph at the end of the dark years gave Americans new optimism and reaffirmed their traditional belief that the nation had a special mission to perform in the world. For the country had not simply survived the terrors of the post-1860 years, but had done great works. It had spawned the corporation, an almost magical instrument for ordering and expanding wealth. With the conquest of Spain and the issuance of the open-door notes, the nation stood on the world stage as one of the great global empires. Frederick Jackson Turner had been proven correct: A new period was indeed opening in American history. With the continental frontier apparently closed, Americans were seeking new frontiers.

In September 1901, McKinley explained why to the Pan-American Exposition in Buffalo, New York. The United States possessed "almost appalling" wealth, the President announced, and must therefore move into the world market to trade: "Isolation is no longer possible or desirable." The next day McKinley was shot by an anarchist. Theodore Roosevelt, a most outspoken expansionist and a student of Turner's theories, moved into the White House.

## Suggested Reading

For the events and legacy of the Civil War era, a superb recent analysis is James M. McPherson, *Ordeal by Fire: The Civil War and Reconstruction* (1982). Excellent overviews of the 1865 to 1900 years include Alan Trachtenberg, *The Incorporation of America: Culture and Society in the Gilded Age* (1982), which has a good bibliography; Robert Wiebe, *The Search for Order* (1968); and Samuel Hays, *The Response to Industrialism* (1957). Leading economic histories include David A. Hounshell, *From the American System to Mass Production, 1800–1932* (1984); Alfred D. Chandler's *The Visible Hand: The Managerial Revolution in American Business* (1977), a prize-winning account; David F. Noble, *America by Design: Science, Technology and the Rise of Corporate Capitalism* (1977); Irwin Unger, *The Greenback Era . . . 1865–1879* (1964); William H. Becker, *The Dynamics of Business-Government Relations: Industry and Exports* (1982); and Mira Wilkins's pioneering *The Emergence of the Multinational Enterprise; American Business Abroad from the Colonial Era to 1914 (1970);* and James B. Gilbert's key work, *Designing the Industrial State . . . 1880–1940* (1972).

On social history, see Robert V. Wells, *Revolutions in Americans' Lives: A Demographic Perspective on the History of Americans, Their Families and Their Society* (1982); Herbert C. Gutman, *Work, Culture, and Society in Industrializing America (1976);* John F. Kasson, *Civilizing the Machine: Technology and Republican Values in America, 1776–1900* (1976); Paul Boyer, *Urban Masses and Moral Order in America, 1820–1920* (1978); David W. Noble, *The Progressive Mind, 1890–1917* (1971); David I. Macleod, *Building Character in the American Boy: The Boy Scouts, YMCA, and Their Forerunners, 1870–1920* (1983); Cynthia E. Russett, *Darwin in America* (1976). Standard is Sidney E. Ahlstrom's magisterial *A Religious History of the American People* (1972). Legal-constitutional studies can begin with Loren P. Beth, *The Development of the American Constitution, 1877–1917* (1971); and several works by J. W. Hurst, including *Law and the Conditions of Freedom in the 19th Century* (1956).

For analyses of the less-privileged groups, Fred Shannon's *The Farmer's Last Frontier* (1945) remains useful; and see Ray Allen Billington, *Frederick Jackson Turner* (1973) for the frontier crisis. The black experience is described in John Hope Franklin, *From Slavery to Freedom* (1974); C. Vann Woodward, *The Strange Career of Jim Crow* (1974); David Gordon Nielson, *Black Ethos: Northern Urban Life and Thought, 1890–1930* (1977); and Louis R. Harlan's prize-winning two-volume biography, *Booker T. Washington (1973, 1983).* On nineteenth-century women's history, see Barbara Welter, *Dimity Convictions* (1976); Catherine Clinton, *The Other Civil War* (1984); Ellen Carol Dubois, *Feminism and Suffrage* (1978); Aileen Kraditor, *The Ideas of the Woman Suffrage Movement, 1890–1920* (1965); Sheila M. Rothman, *Woman's Proper Place* (1978); Margery W. Davies, *Woman's*

*Place Is at the Typewriter . . . 1870–1930;* and Nancy Woloch's overview in *Women and the American Experience* (1984). For a survey of 20th century women's history, see Lois Banner, *Women in America: A Brief History,* 2nd. ed. (1983). The tragedies of the Native American are surveyed in Wilcomb E. Washburn, *The Indian in America* (1975); R. M. Utley, *The Indian Frontier of the American West, 1846–1890* (1984); Dee Brown's best-selling *Bury My Heart at Wounded Knee: An Indian History of the American West* (1971); and Evan S. Connell's colorful and superb book on General George Custer, *Son of the Morning Star* (1984). The South's history is in C. Vann Woodward, *Origins of the New South, 1877–1913* (1951), a classic. Immigration is well covered in Maldwyn A. Jones, *American Immigration* (1960); Oscar Handlin, *The Uprooted* (1951); and John Higham, *Strangers in the Land* (1955). On Haymarket see Paul Avrich, *The Haymarket Tragedy* (1984).

Political histories include R. Hal Williams, *Years of Decision: American Politics in the 1890s* (1978), with a good bibliography; Samuel T. McSeveney's important *The Politics of Depression, 1893–1896* (1972); Lawrence Goodwyn, *The Populist Moment* (1978); and John G. Sproat, *"The Best Men": Liberal Reformers in the Gilded Age* (1968). Important biographies are Lewis L. Gould, *The Presidency of William McKinley* (1980); Nick Salvatore's prize-winning *Eugene V. Debs* (1982); Allan Nevins, *Grover Cleveland* (1933); and Howard C. Livesay, *Samuel Gompers* (1978).

Above all, for references on diplomacy consult R. H. Burns, editor, *Guide to American Foreign Relations Since 1700* (1983). The place to begin on foreign policies is Thomas McCormick, *China Market* (1967), especially on the depression's effect; William Appleman Williams's pioneering *Tragedy of American Diplomacy* (1972); Ernest May, *Imperial Democracy* (1961); David Pletcher, *The Awkward Years* (1963); and Charles Campbell's exhaustive *Transformation of American Foreign Relations, 1865–1900* (1976) with a splendid bibliography. For affairs in Asia, see Warren I. Cohen's overview, *America's Response to China* (1971); Michael H. Hunt, *The Making of a Special Relationship: The U.S. and China to 1914* (1983); and Marilyn B. Young, *The Rhetoric of Empire* (1968). Unique is Emily S. Rosenberg's *Spreading the American Dream: American Economic and Cultural Expansion, 1890–1945* (1982). For the 1898 war and the anti-imperialist debate, see Philip S. Foner's two-volume *The Spanish-Cuban-American War* (1972); David Healy's excellent *The U.S. in Cuba, 1898–1902* (1963), Robert L. Beisner's *Twelve Against Empire* (1985); and Philip S. Foner and Richard C. Winchester, *The Anti-Imperialist Reader* (1984).

Robert C. Twombly's biography, *Frank Lloyd Wright* (1973) is good, but also consult Wayne Andrews, *Architecture, Ambition and Americans: A Social History of American Architecture* (1978).

Suffragist Parade: Mrs. C. Blaney, Mrs. H. M. Wilmarth, and Jane Addams.

CHAPTER TWO

# 1900–1917
## The Progressive Era

An interest in reform has always characterized American history. There have been relatively few periods when at least some people did not want to change society for the better. What has varied over time have been the things people identified as evils, the intellectual justifications and political techniques used to eradicate those evils, the obstacles reformers encountered, and the degree of support they received. Seldom has a larger proportion of the population favored social improvement than during the opening years of the twentieth century, when Americans first tried in a systematic way to control the forces of industrialization and urbanization. Because the United States was becoming a major world power, the successes and failures of the Progressive movement affected not only Americans but people around the world.

## THE REFORM IMPULSE

Although pr___ ___eels of the Populist revolt and sometim___ ___ the two movements differed in ir___ ___ ___oport primarily from farm-___ ___ progressivism won back-f___ ___sses, and had as wide a Po___ ___ s and South Carolina. coun___ ___ ve conditions in the cal an___ ___ attention to politi-on a w___ ___Progressives drew issues, th___ ___roader range of levels that ___ ___ate, and national

Progressi___ ___ ___ ___us success. So many different people ___ ___ ___ings styled themselves "Progressives" that ___ ___ed to lack a clearly defined program. Progressi___ ___ ___urprisingly diverse groups: small businessmen who ___ ___rb on monopolies, and big businessmen who sought to exten___ ___economic influence and eliminate their competitors; native Amer___ans who feared the influx of Eastern European immigrants, and settlement-house workers who appreciated the newcomers' contributions to American culture; Southern whites dedicated to the preservation of Jim Crow, and Northern blacks just as fully committed to its eradication; social scientists who believed that planning held all the answers to human progress, and prohibitionists who imagined that closing the saloons would usher in a new world.

Yet for all its diversity, there was a distinctly Progressive approach to social problems. Progressives saw industrialization and urbanization as potentially disruptive forces. The burgeoning cities and corporations seemed to endanger social stability and to undermine older ideals of individual initiative and equal opportunity. To restore a sense of order, to impose a reasonable measure of control on the forces transforming American life, Progressives used the power of government in an unprecedented fashion. In some respects the concern with democratizing government through direct election of senators, the initiative and referendum, and woman suffrage followed logically from this conviction that government had to play an expanded role. Progressives were optimists, activists, and rationalists. They assumed that society was malleable and they devoted their energies to molding it in the proper way.

## BIG BUSINESS

One major impetus to progressivism was an awareness of the social problems resulting from explosive economic growth. Between 1880 and 1900 the United States took over world leadership in industrial output. Not only did production increase, but it became concentrated in the hands of relatively few corporations and trusts, which often found it both possible and profitable to control market conditions. The creation of the United States Steel Corporation in 1901 symbolized the growth of industry, its consolidation, and its domination of the market. By purchasing Andrew Carnegie's steel interests, J. P. Morgan established the first billion-dollar corporation and controlled 60 percent of steel output. Yet this was only the most spectacular in a series of mergers that took place at the time. By 1904, one percent of American companies produced 38 percent of all manufactured goods.

Recognizing that the existence of mammoth trusts called for a measure of public control, reformers were divided over what course to pursue. Some wished to restore competition by dismantling the trusts, outlawing monopolies, and encouraging small enterprise. Others believed that big business was highly efficient. They saw nothing wrong with trusts so long as the government ensured that the benefits of efficiency were passed on to the public in the form of low prices, and that profits were kept within reasonable bounds. Despite sharp differences of opinion on this matter, Progressives agreed on the desirability of bringing private economic power under a larger measure of public control. Most reformers thought that government should regulate railroad rates, lower the protective tariff, and protect consumers from impure or unsafe products. What distinguished Progressives was less their unanimity on a solution to economic problems than their agreement that unruly economic forces required some form of discipline.

Those most directly affected by the growth of industry were factory workers themselves. Efforts to improve their conditions centered on three issues: compensating workers injured on the job, regulating the hours and wages of working women, and restricting child labor (or what Progressives called "child slavery"). Reformers channeled most of their energies into enacting laws for these purposes at the state level. Not until relatively late in the Progressive era did they turn to federal legislation, and then they met with only partial success. In 1908 a major obstacle to state regulation crumbled when the Supreme Court, reversing an earlier ruling, held in *Muller* v. *Oregon* that fixing a ten-hour day for women did not violate the Fourteenth Amendment's guarantee against deprivation of property without due process. Equally important, the Court based its decision on documentary evidence concerning the harmful social effects of long working hours, thereby accepting a key argument of reformers.

## CITIES AND SLUMS

The United States became more highly urbanized as it became more highly industrialized. Progressivism represented as much a response to one as to the other. Between 1890 and 1920 the number of people living in cities increased by 300 percent, the number of rural dwellers by only 30 percent. Urban population grew by 11.8 million in the decade after 1900, so that by 1910 more than 44 million Americans—45.7 percent of the total population—lived in areas defined as urban by the Census Bureau. The largest cities grew at a spectacular rate: by 1910, 1.5 million people lived in Philadelphia, 2.1 million in Chicago, and 5 million in New York. Not only did big cities grow bigger, but there were also more of them. In 1860 there were nine cities with a population over 100,000; in 1910 there were fifty. This urban expansion reflected a natural increase in population as well as the effect of both migration from rural areas and immigration from Europe.

Because cities grew so swiftly, contained such a diverse population, and furnished some with a chance to acquire fabulous wealth, they were plagued by mismanagement. Investigations into municipal government unearthed officials who took bribes or who, for the right price, granted lucrative gas and street-car franchises to private corporations. Many Americans assumed that for every corrupt official who was exposed, a dozen others continued to operate in darkness. Where city government was not corrupt it often seemed archaic, administratively unable to cope with the needs of modern ubran life. Above all, there was what Jacob Riis termed "the blight of the tenement": dimly lit, badly ventilated slums, jammed with more people than it seemed they could possibly hold. To Progressives the slum was "the great destroyer of individuality" and as such posed a threat not only to the health of its residents but also to the health of the state. "Democracy was not predicated upon a country made up of tenement dwellers," said one reformer, "nor can it so survive."

Progressive solutions for these problems were as varied as the prob-

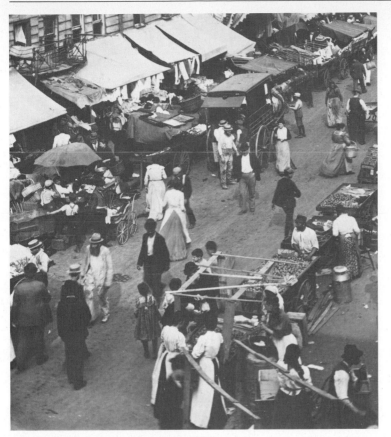

New York City's Hester Street, ca. 1900.

lems themselves. Some reformers concentrated on modernizing and de-politicizing urban government. They favored extending the merit system, streamlining municipal administration, freeing cities from state control, and transferring powers traditionally exercised by mayors to impartial city managers or commissions. Other Progressives, including Samuel "Golden Rule" Jones of Toledo and Tom Johnson of Cleveland, emphasized the benefits of municipal ownership of public utilities. Many reformers sought to tear down slums by enacting building codes that imposed structural and sanitary safeguards. New York City adopted such a tenement-house law in 1901, and other cities followed in its path. Finally, there were those who wished to make the urban environment more civilized through planning. One observer, with the confidence typical of progressivism, predicted that Americans would not always be satisfied "to live in those abominations of desolation which we call our great cities" but would insist on a planned urban landscape, "every part of which shall be in perfect harmony with every other part."

## MORALITY AND DEMOCRACY

Some Progressives wanted to protect Americans not only from the perils of urban and industrial life, but from their own impulses as well. Moral uplift was an important element in reform, and perhaps nothing revealed this relation more clearly than the link between progressivism and prohibition. Not everyone who supported prohibition was a Progressive in politics, but a large number of reformers favored a ban on alcohol and, what is more significant, justified their stance on thoroughly Progressive grounds. Starting with the premise that the saloon functioned as the home of the political boss and a breeding-ground for corruption, reformers concluded that if they ended the sale of liquor they would take a long step on the road to urban reform. Moreover, many believed that liquor caused workers to squander hard-earned wages and neglect their families. A Boston social worker thought that ignoring prohibition was like "bailing water out of a tub with the tap turned on; letting the drink custom and the liquor traffic run full blast while we limply stood around and picked up the wreckage." In this view, prohibition seemed an indispensable weapon in the effort to stamp out poverty.

To achieve any of these goals—business regulation, urban reform, social justice, moral uplift—required, in the view of Progressives, the extension of political democracy. Reformers favored the election of senators directly by the people rather than by state legislatures, and in 1913, after several states had made this change, it was incorporated into the Seventeenth Amendment. Similarly, Progressives endorsed the preferential primary, which gave voters a larger voice in the selection of candidates; most states adopted some variant of this system. Progressives also favored the initiative and referendum. By 1915, twenty-one states had accepted such plans, under which citizens could introduce a measure into the state legislature and vote on it at a general election. Finally, reformers supported woman suffrage, in part because they expected women to vote in behalf of social reform. A litmus-paper test for progressivism might well have involved attitudes toward popular rule.

## WOMEN AND THE PROGRESSIVE IMPULSE

If progressives counted on woman suffrage to provide new votes for social reform, they had good reason. Middle-class women were avid supporters of the progressive agenda. In women's clubs, temperance locals, social settlements, and other reform associations, they committed their energy to urban improvement, moral uplift, and social justice. Such activism not only served progressive ends but bolstered the arguments of suffragists, who based their claim to the vote on the good that women would do for society if they had it.

A great swell of female organization, well under way by the 1890s, laid the groundwork for women's involvement in progressive reform. The first women's clubs, formed after the Civil War, had been devoted to cultural projects. In 1892, when the National Federation of Women's Clubs began, clubwomen decided to "contemplate our own social order" and steered their attention to urban improvement. Contributing to libraries, settlements, and hospitals, they advocated better city services, protection for women and children in factories, and finally, in 1914, woman suffrage. Members of the militant Women's Christian Temperance Union, meanwhile, followed leader Frances Willard's injunction to "Do everything." In addition to campaigning for prohibition, WCTU members became involved in a gamut of causes—pacifism, labor reform, social purity, city welfare work. Many temperance workers were also drawn into the suffrage movement.

While clubwomen and temperance advocates demonstrated what women could hope to accomplish collectively, the city provided a broad arena for their efforts. As the new century began, women created new reform organizations to improve urban life and to serve as bridges between social classes. The National Congress of Mothers (1897) sponsored playgrounds and kindergartens, battled urban social ills, and promoted "all those characteristics which shall elevate and ennoble." The National Consumers League (1899) sought to protect women wage earners in stores and factories and also to insure the safety and cleanliness of products bought by homemakers. The Women's Trade Union League (1903), whose members included women factory employees as well as their middle-class "allies," hoped to unionize women workers. With major bases in New York and Chicago, the WTUL burst into action. In New York's shirtwaist strike of 1909–10, when some thirty thousand garment workers walked off the job, league members masterminded strike publicity and joined waistmakers on the picket line. They protested the infamous Triangle Fire of 1911, when scores of women garment workers, locked in the upper stories of a shirtwaist factory, were incinerated or leaped to their deaths. Since unionization proved difficult, the WTUL supported the passage of protective laws to insure women workers a minimum wage, limit their working hours, and provide safer working conditions. Between 1908, when the Supreme Court voiced approval of such laws in *Muller* v. *Oregon*, and 1917, some twenty states enacted them.

The most significant achievement of progressive women was undoubtedly the settlement house. In 1889, when Jane Addams founded Hull House in Chicago and a group of women college graduates started the College Settlement in New York, they provided an ideal progressive solution to urban problems. By 1900, one hundred settlements existed; by

Victims of the Triangle Fire, 1911.

1905, two hundred; and by 1910, four hundred. Located in the immigrant ghetto, the settlement house responded to neighborhood needs by providing clubs and social services. It answered what Jane Addams called the "subjective need" of young educated women who wanted to contribute to public life. (Men worked in settlements, too, but they were in a minority.) It gratified, in one settlement worker's words, a "thirst to know how the other half lived." The settlement house also became an urban social science laboratory, investigating local conditions and transforming its findings into legislative proposals. Settlement residents supported such reforms as juvenile courts, compulsory education laws, housing laws, factory regulation, and sanitation measures. Finally, the settlement house propelled its leading residents into positions of civic responsibility. Florence Kelley of Hull House moved on to become a state factory inspector, consumer advocate, and lobbyist. Julia Lathrop, another Hull House resident, became the first head of the federal Children's Bureau, founded in 1914.

The suffrage movement was quick to capitalize on the activism of urban reformers, labor advocates, and settlement workers. Hull House leaders such as Lathrop and Kelley spoke at suffrage conventions. Jane Addams, too, served as an officer of the National American Woman Suffrage Association. In her articles and speeches, she argued for the vote by appealing to progressive sensibilities. The complexity of city government, Addams claimed, demanded "the help of minds accustomed to . . . a responsibility for the cleanliness and comfort of other people." Modern urban problems could not be solved by mere business expertise, she argued, but from "the human welfare point of view." When the Progressive party first convened in 1912, it at once endorsed woman suffrage and invited Jane Addams to make a major seconding speech for nominee Theodore Roosevelt. Addams defended her partisanship. When a "great party" pledged itself to protect children, care for the aged, and promote industrial safety, she explained, it was "inevitable that it should appeal to women and seek to draw upon the great reservoir of moral energy so long undesired and unutilized in politics."

The energy generated by progressive reform was reflected throughout the women's movement and ranged across the political spectrum. In the decade before World War I, women established a peace movement. They joined the campaigns against prostitution and "white slavery." College students formed suffrage societies and social service clubs. Progressive educators sought to reform classroom teaching and to promote vocational education. In YWCAs, women reformers offered residences and services to young working women. On the left, women were equally involved. Socialist women contributed to labor reform and suffrage campaigns. IWW organizer Elizabeth Gurley Flynn mobilized workers in the Lawrence and Patterson textile strikes. Anarchist and free speech advocate Emma Goldman toured the nation and voiced her views in *Mother Earth* (1906–18). Decrying the "conventional lie" of marriage and woman's role as "sex commodity," Goldman defended free love, advocated contraception, and called for women's emancipation. Public health nurse Margaret Sanger, following Goldman's example, campaigned for sex education, contraception, and other radical causes. Her short-lived periodical, *The Woman Rebel* (1914), where the term "birth control" was first used, brought her a multicount federal indictment for violation of the obscenity laws. Radical efforts were not necessarily appreciated by the progressive mainstream of the women's movement, which was devoted primarily to woman suffrage and social service, but they contributed to a rising feminist tide.

A most influential feminist of the era was Charlotte Perkins Gilman, who was less interested in the vote than in women's emancipation from economic dependency. In *Women and Economics* (1899) and subsequent works, Gilman denounced the home as an archaic institution that imprisoned women, transformed them into nonproductive consumers, and clogged the wheels of progress. "Only as we think, feel, and work outside the home, do we become humanly developed, civilized, and socialized," she wrote in 1903. To foster women's economic independence and liberate them from the home, Gilman proposed large apartment units, collective housekeeping arrangements, and child-care facilities. Although her ideas diverged from those of mainstream feminism, which tended to emphasize women's homemaking expertise, Gilman's views were admired both within the women's movement and outside it. Progressive America was receptive to all facets of reform.

# SIN AND SOCIETY: THE MUCKRAKERS

In 1907 the sociologist Edward A. Ross published *Sin and Society,* in which he asserted that modern society required a new definition of wrongdoing. The old personal categories of sin, such as theft or murder, failed to take account of new social crime. To Ross, the person who granted railroad rebates was no better than a pickpocket, the person who adulterated food no different from a murderer, the person who employed children on much the same level as a slaveholder. Yet although a new "criminaloid" type had emerged, a suitable moral code had not evolved along with it. "Our social organization has developed to a stage where the old righteousness is not enough," Ross concluded. "We need an annual supplement to the Decalogue." Ross's book never became a best seller, but a group of journalists known as muckrakers popularized a similar message. By documenting the social costs of urbanization and industrialization, the muckrakers helped provide an audience for Progressive reform.

The development of this literature of exposure—Theodore Roosevelt first applied the label "muckraker" and meant it as a term of scorn—reflected technological changes in magazine publishing. In the decade of the 1890s new developments in printing and photoengraving made the publication of inexpensive magazines feasible. As the price dropped from 25 or 35 cents to 10 cents, the magazine-reading public tripled and advertising revenue soared. Not only could writers reach a wide audience, but that audience apparently wanted to read about what was wrong with America. Articles of a muckraking nature began to appear in the 1890s. As early as 1901 *McClure's* published "In the World of Graft," which exposed the alliance between police and criminals in various cities. The author defined certain underworld terms for his readers benefit—"pinch" (arrest), "pull" (influence), "fix" (bribe)—and even thought it necessary to define "graft." A few years later, it is safe to say, Americans would not have needed a definition.

In 1902, *McClure's* circulation was boosted by the start of two major muckraking series, Lincoln Steffens' probe of corruption in municipal government, "The Shame of the Cities," and Ida Tarbell's exposé of the development of John D. Rockefeller's Standard Oil Trust. From 1903 to 1912 nearly two thousand articles in this genre appeared. Virtually no area of American life escaped the muckrakers' attention. They exposed corrupt city officials and United States senators who never cast a vote without consulting business interests. They zeroed in on fraudulent business deals. They described what it was like to live in a slum or work in a sweatshop. The muckrakers told of vermin scurrying around the floors of meat-packing plants: "The rats were nuisances; the packers would put poisoned bread out for them; they would die, and then rats, bread and meat would go into the hoppers together." They depicted workers horribly maimed when factories failed to install safety devices. They threw a harsh light on those who made a living from gambling, liquor, or, worst of all, the white-slave trade—"the recruiting and sale of young girls of the poorer classes by procurers." The muckrakers taught consumers about food adulteration, and about such innocent-sounding patent medicines as "Mrs. Winslow's Soothing Syrup," "Faith Whitcomb's Nerve Bitters," and "Lydia Pinkham's Vegetable Compound," many of which contained habit-forming drugs.

Behind these journalistic assaults rested characteristically Progressive assumptions. Muckrakers went after the inside scoop. They believed that the truth lay beneath the surface, that things were not what they seemed, that, as the historian Richard Hofstadter observed, "reality was the inside story. It was rough and sordid, hidden and neglected." In trying to get to the bottom of things, journalists often sought real-life experiences. Jack London served time in a county penitentiary before he described the brutalizing effects of the prison system. Upton Sinclair worked in the Chicago stockyards before he wrote *The Jungle.* John Spargo recounted his attempt to do a child's work in a coal mine: "I tried to pick out the pieces of slate from the hurrying stream of coal, often missing them; my hands were bruised and cut in a few minutes; I was covered from head to foot with coal dust, and for many hours afterwards I was expectorating some of the small particles of anthracite I had swallowed." Muckrakers usually wrote fact, not fiction; they were concrete; they named names. They spent more time criticizing specific evils than proposing broad solutions.

## THE REFORM IDEOLOGY

The muckrakers, by calling attention to social evils, helped create a climate conducive to reform. Similarly, a group of intellectuals, by developing a new approach to eonomics, law, and history, lowered another barrier to change. This barrier had taken the form of an ideology that rejected state aid for the victims of industrialization and urbanization.

Conservatives, following what they believed to be Charles Darwin's path, reasoned that society, like nature, evolved through a struggle that assured the survival of the fittest. In economics conservatives stressed laissez-faire; in law they worshipped precedent; in history they dwelt on the sanctions for private property written into the Constitution. In each instance society was a captive—of natural law, of precedent, of the past. William Graham Sumner, perhaps the most prominent American social Darwinist, summed all of this up in the title of an essay: "The Absurd Attempt to Make the World Over."

Unlike Sumner, a group of reform-minded sociologists and economists reasoned that the attempt to make the world over was anything but absurd. Rather, it seemed to them the height of common sense. Lester Frank Ward, for example, insisted on drawing a distinction between nature and society: human beings, unlike other species, could control their environment through intelligent planning. In *The Psychic Factors of Civilization* (1893) Ward tried to demonstrate that human progress often resulted from cooperation rather than from competition. A number of economists drew similar conclusions. Richard T. Ely of the University of Wisconsin denied that natural laws governed the workings of the economic system or that laissez-faire was an adequate guide to public policy. Thorstein Veblen, in *The Theory of the Leisure Class* (1899) and other works, pointed to the inefficient and unproductive aspects of the profit system as well as to the waste involved in conspicuous consumption and conspicuous leisure.

During the Progressive era the legal profession often acted as a stumbling block to reform. "The right of property is of divine origin derived by title-deed from the universal creator of all things and attested by universal intuition," intoned a widely used legal text on which a generation of jurists was reared. But at the same time men like Oliver Wendell Holmes, Jr., who was appointed to the Supreme Court in 1903, Louis D. Brandeis, appointed in 1916, and Roscoe Pound of the Harvard Law School, began to transform the law from a bulwark of the status quo into a vehicle for change. Although they would not always be found on the same side of an issue, Holmes and Brandeis shared a similar conception of the relationship of law to society. Holmes believed that "the life of the law has not been logic: it has been experience." If the law was rooted in human history rather than in abstract principles, if people made laws to fulfill their needs, then the law must change as new needs arose. Pound, in "The Need for a Sociological Jurisprudence" (1907), held that law must conform to "the general moral sense" of the community. It could do so by placing a higher value on social justice than on individual property rights. Judges did not, and should not, hand down decisions in a vacuum.

Once legal scholars had reached this point it remained only for Progressives to interpret the Constitution itself as the product of particular social interests. A number of historians did so, but none captured more attention than Charles Beard in *An Economic Interpretation of the Constitution* (1913). Beard shared the Progressive concern with unmasking the "real" forces in history. He attempted to demonstrate that the upper classes, who had not been making out well under the Articles of Confederation, had organized the movement for adoption of the Constitution; that the document lacked widespread popular support; and that "the Constitution was essentially an economic document based upon the concept that the fundamental private rights of property are anterior to government and morally beyond the reach of popular majorities." Precisely the same issue was debated in the Progressive era and, not surprisingly, both conservatives and reformers regarded the book as a tract for the times. William Howard Taft wondered whether Beard would have been happier had the Constitution been drafted by "out-at-the-elbows demagogues, and cranks who never had any money." Conversely, a reformer believed that once Americans realized that the Constitution was "a human document" they would not allow it to stand in the way of necessary change.

Muckrakers and intellectuals played the complementary roles of popularizing and rationalizing reform. Both showed less interest in how society was supposed to function than in how it really did. Both sometimes regarded ideology as nothing more than a cloak for economic interest. When Richard T. Ely said that imaginary natural laws of economics were "used as a tool in the hands of the greedy," he sounded rather like a muckraker dissecting the behavior of unscrupulous businessmen. Journalists and scholars assumed that just as a bad environment made bad citizens, so a good environment could work wonders, for "to upbuild human character in men you must establish for them the right social relations." While they ranged over the political spectrum—from the socialist Upton Sinclair to the rather conservative Oliver Wendell Holmes— their work resulted in a diagnosis of social problems and a theory of state action that provided the underpinning for progressivism.

## NATIVISM VS. THE MELTING POT

In their search for social harmony, reformers discovered no greater sources of dissonance than the twin issues of ethnicity and race. Progressivism coincided with a massive wave of immigration. In the twenty-five years before World War I, 18 million immigrants came to the United States, nearly four-fifths of them from Italy, Russia, Poland, Greece, and other countries in Southern and Eastern Europe. By 1917 one of every three Americans was an immigrant or the child of one. With the nation becoming more urban and industrial, these immigrants, to a greater extent than those who had arrived earlier, settled in big cities and took

Immigrants aboard the S.S. *Westernland.*

jobs in manufacturing. Some left Europe to escape political or religious persecution, some to avoid military service, but most were drawn by the magnet of economic opportunity. Industrialists who needed a supply of cheap labor often encouraged migration. Immigrants themselves wrote home urging their friends to join them. One Polish immigrant reported, "Let nobody listen to anybody but only to his relatives whom he has here, in this golden America."

Many Americans, Progressives among them, believed that the new immigrants were racially inferior and therefore genetically incapable of becoming good citizens. In 1910 this view drew support from the report of a commission headed by Senator William T. Dillingham. The commission, which had spent three years collecting data and expert testimony, concluded that ethnicity provided a reliable guide to one's capacity for Americanization. People from Southern and Eastern Europe, the commission tried to prove, did not assimilate as well as older immigrant groups, but rather committed more crimes and had a higher incidence of alcoholism and disease. A few Progressives, such as Edward A. Ross, rested their nativism squarely on racial grounds, Ross saw new immigrants as "beaten members of beaten breeds" with "sugar loaf heads, moon faces, and goose-bill noses," who "lack the ancestral foundations of American character." He described them in this way: "In every face there was something wrong—lips thick, mouth coarse, upper lip too long, cheek bones too high, chin poorly formed, the bridge of the nose hollowed, the base of the nose tilted, or else the whole face prognathous."

Most Progressives who wished to restrict immigration, however, wanted to do so for reasons of reform rather than of race. A number of reformers believed that immigration injured American workers. Not only did the immigrants depress wages by working for next to nothing, but they retarded the growth of trade unions. Employers understood all too well that a labor force in constant flux, composed of men and women of different nationalities speaking different languages, could not very easily be organized. Progressives often located the source of poverty in the boatloads of immigrants who, with few skills and little prospect of employment, became public charges. Immigrants, said Robert Hunter in *Poverty* (1904), placed an intolerable strain on existing charities and social services. Finally, reformers realized that the immigrants provided the main prop for boss rule in the cities and believed that without immigrant votes political machines would die a natural death.

Although most Progressives appear to have viewed immigrants as their racial inferiors or as impediments to reform, there were some who took a considerably more tolerant position. Either they expressed confidence in America's capacity to absorb the immigrant, or they invoked the concept of a vast melting pot in which all peoples contributed something to a novel American type. In addition, the doctrine of cultural pluralism— that each immigrant group should preserve its own heritage—gained a number of converts. Norman Hapgood, Randolph Bourne, and Horace Kallen, among others, envisioned the United States as a world federation in miniature. "Our dream of the United States ought not to be a dream of monotony," said Hapgood. "We ought not to think of it as a place where all people are alike." Asserting that diversity enriched American culture, Kallen held that each immigrant group could preserve its own language, religion, and culture yet share equally in American life. He favored "a democracy of nationalities, cooperating voluntarily and autonomously . . . an orchestration of mankind."

The settlement-house movement provided the chief means of aiding urban immigrants. The settlement house, once it overcame community suspicion, became the center of civic and social life in the neighborhood. Classes in arts and crafts, playgrounds for children of working mothers, meeting places for labor unions, instruction in homemaking, child care, and English—all could be found at settlement houses. Settlement workers—mostly young, college educated, and middle class—investigated housing and working conditions and fought for the enactment of reform legislation. Jane Addams hoped that by inculcating respect for Old World culture she could effect a reconciliation between immigrants who clung to tradition and their children who often rejected the past in their haste to adopt American ways. The settlements were typically Progressive in their middle-class origins and in their emphasis on urban problems, yet they were atypical in their close involvement with the life of the working poor and their respect for immigrant culture.

## RACISM AND REFORM

Black Americans occupied a more precarious political and economic position than did immigrants, yet attracted even less support from Progressives. Reformers belonged to a generation of white Americans that, for the most part, believed that blacks were by nature lazy, improvident, and incapable of mental discipline. Whatever difficulties the black faced, therefore, derived from hereditary shortcomings. Few Progressives saw any conflict between racial discrimination and social reform. In the South, woman suffragists promised that they would use the vote to maintain white supremacy. In the North, black women sometimes marched in a separate column at the rear of suffrage parades. Settlement houses often set aside segregated facilities, if they provided them at all, for blacks. New York social worker Mary White Ovington, an ally of W. E. B. DuBois, attempted but failed to found a settlement house for blacks; in 1911, she published a pioneer study about the problems of New York's black ghetto for the Greenwich Street Settlement. But few settlement workers shared Ovington's interests or sympathies. One settlement worker described the blacks in Boston as "low and coarse, revealing much more of the animal qualities than the spiritual." Most Progressives would surely have agreed with Theodore Roosevelt who, although he opposed the disfranchisement of blacks, held that "as a race and in the mass they are altogether inferior to the whites."

During the Progressive era most Southern blacks lost the right to vote. In the 1890s three states disfranchised the black. After the Supreme Court ruled in favor of the literacy test in *Williams* v. *Mississippi* (1898), ten Southern states deprived blacks of the franchise. Some set literacy and property qualifications for voting, but added "understanding" and "grandfather" clauses that in effect exempted whites. Propertyless persons and illiterates could vote if they demonstrated an understanding of the Constitution or if they were the lineal descendants of someone who had voted in 1867. Most Southern states enacted poll taxes, which, although not very high, deterred poor blacks and whites from voting. Poll taxes had to be paid well in advance (usually during the spring when farmers had little spare cash) and were cumulative, so as people fell into arrears it became more difficult to catch up. Finally, the South adopted the white primary. Given Democratic control of Southern politics, exclusion from the primaries amounted to virtual exclusion from the political process. These measures had an awesome effect. From 1896 to 1904 the number of black voters in Alabama plunged from one hundred eighty thousand to three thousand; the number in Louisiana from one hundred thirty thousand to five thousand. Southern Progressives defended these measures in part on reform grounds: removing Negro voters, they said, would end political corruption and produce good government. Indeed, one way to stop the stealing of ballots, historian C. Vann Woodward has remarked, was to stop people from casting them.

Nothing better illustrated the connection between racism and reform than the career of James K. Vardaman as Governor of Mississippi (1903–07). Much of Vardaman's program was squarely in the Progressive tradition. He ended the system of convict leasing under which planters brutally exploited prison labor; he increased spending for education and brought

W. E. B. DuBois.

about more effective regulation of railroads, banks, and insurance companies; he sought without success to enact child labor legislation. At the same time, however, Vardaman was a vicious race-baiter. He called for the repeal of the Fourteenth and Fifteenth Amendments, cut expenditures for black schools, and declared that the Negro was "a lazy, lying, lustful animal which no conceivable amount of training can transform into a tolerable citizen." He even offered a thinly veiled excuse for lynch law: "We would be justified in slaughtering every Ethiop on the earth to preserve unsullied the honor of one Caucasian home."

If progressivism could serve as the basis for white supremacy, it also provided W. E. B. DuBois and other black leaders with a model for new strategies of protest. DuBois, who had studied at Berlin and received a doctorate from Harvard, taught at Atlanta University from 1897 to 1910. He served as a spokesman for black intellectuals who rejected Booker T. Washington's program of racial accommodation. DuBois also exhibited a characteristically Progressive faith in the redemptive powers of reason. He assumed that by presenting empirical data about the black's condition he could help persuade white Americans to eliminate racial injustice. In *The Philadelphia Negro* (1899) and other books, DuBois offered a meticulous examination of the conditions under which blacks lived in the hope that his readers would recognize the need to end discrimination. For DuBois, as for other Progressive intellectuals, research was the first step on the road to reform.

But it was no more than a first step. As early as 1905 DuBois attempted to found an organization devoted to the defense of civil rights. Five years later he succeeded in creating the National Association for the Advancement of Colored People, with the goals of abolishing segregation, restoring voting rights to blacks, achieving equal educational facilities, and enforcing the Fourteenth and Fifteenth Amendments. The NAACP had the support of such white reformers as Oswald Garrison Villard, Jane Addams, Lincoln Steffens, John Dewey, and Moorfield Storey, who became its first president. In 1915 the Association filed an *amicus curiae* brief in a Supreme Court test of Oklahoma's "grandfather" clause, which the Court found unconstitutional. With its emphasis on political and legal rights, its belief in educating the public, and its assumption that segregation hindered the free development of the individual, the NAACP accurately reflected the Progressive movement, of which it was part. Perhaps it did so in another way as well: during its first seven years, DuBois was the only black to serve in a policymaking position.

## THEODORE ROOSEVELT

Theodore Roosevelt's standing with historians has undergone mercurial changes. For a decade after his death in 1919 biographers presented his life as an inspiring example of moral rectitude. One author entitled his concluding chapters: "Roosevelt—Not Impulsive," "Roosevelt—Broad-Minded," "Roosevelt—Wonderful Brain." A harsher appraisal emerged in the 1930s and 1940s. Historians began to notice that, beneath all the grand rhetoric, Roosevelt at bottom was a conservative, an opportunist, a militarist, someone who had never grown up. The index of Henry Pringle's Pulitzer Prize–winning biography (1931) contained six entries under the heading "adolescence in manhood." Since the 1950s Roosevelt has been treated with more indulgence. Conceding his faults, scholars have nevertheless concluded that Roosevelt strengthened the presidency, acted as a "skillful broker of the possible," and did more than anyone else "to infuse reform with respectability and . . . to reestablish popular respect for the federal government as an effective instrument for the public weal."

Born in New York of a well-to-do family in 1858, Roosevelt was graduated from Harvard in 1880 and then elected a Republican state assemblyman. A profound personal tragedy struck in 1884 when his wife died of Bright's disease the day after giving birth to a child. Roosevelt sought refuge for a time in the Dakota Badlands but returned to New York and began his climb up the political ladder. In 1889 he became a member of the Civil Service Commission, in 1895 President of the New York City Police Board, and in 1897 Assistant Secretary of the Navy. In 1898, after his service with the Rough Riders in Cuba, he was elected Governor of New York. Two years later the Republican leaders decided to exile Roosevelt to the vice-presidency. Boss Thomas C. Platt said, "Roosevelt might as well stand under Niagara Falls and try to spit water back as to stop his nomination." Roosevelt complained that he would "a great deal rather be anything, say professor of history, than Vice-President," but, like the good party man he was, he went along. In September 1901, with the assassination of William McKinley, Theodore Roosevelt ascended to the presidency.

Roosevelt shared a good deal with the conservatives of his day. He believed in the essential goodness of American institutions and he hated those who wanted to tear down what had taken so long to construct. He always considered the muckrakers overly concerned with the seamy side of life, and throughout his career he denounced Populists, trade unionists, and socialists who threatened the existing order of things. In the 1890s he had noted that "the sentiment now animating a large proportion of our people can only be suppressed as the Commune in Paris was suppressed, by taking ten or a dozen of their leaders out, standing . . . them against a wall, and shooting them dead." The realities of political life in 1901 nourished his conservative instincts. In the White House only by accident, Roosevelt faced a Republican party and a Congress dominated by conservatives. Mark Hanna, a powerful party leader and Senator from Ohio, warned the new President to "go slow."

What set Roosevelt apart from the stand-patters and validated his Progressive credentials was his belief in orderly change. Reform, by perfecting the system, would help to preserve it. "The only true conservative," Roosevelt remarked, "is the man who resolutely sets his face toward the future." Not only did he welcome moderate change, but Roosevelt also thought that the national interest transcended the claims of any particular class, and he assumed that the President had an obligation to act as spokesman for that interest. These beliefs helped shape the response of his administration in four important areas: business, labor, reform legislation, and conservation.

## THE SQUARE DEAL

Despite his reputation, Roosevelt never believed in trust-busting. Combination seemed to him a natural process, but one that required federal supervision to protect consumers. Eventually Roosevelt came to a tacit understanding with some of the biggest businessmen: he would not enforce the antitrust law if they would open their books for inspection and keep their dealings aboveboard. But in some cases Roosevelt considered government intervention necessary. During his presidency the Justice Department instituted forty-four antitrust suits, the most famous of which involved the Northern Securities Company. J. P. Morgan had created this $400-million-dollar holding company through a merger of important northern railroad lines. In 1902 the Justice Department invoked the Sherman Antitrust Act, claiming that the Morgan firm unfairly restrained trade, and two years later the Supreme Court narrowly upheld the government. (Of one dissenter Roosevelt said, "I could carve out of a banana a judge with more backbone than that.") The significance of Roosevelt's move lay less in its impact on the railroad—the ruling merely banned one particular holding company—than in its clear assertion of his willingness to act in behalf of the public interest.

Roosevelt's action in the anthracite coal strike illustrated his skill as a mediator. In 1902, fifty thousand Pennsylvania miners struck for higher wages, an eight-hour day, and union recognition. Management refused point-blank to negotiate. By October, when the fuel shortage threatened homes, hospitals, and schools, Roosevelt called both sides to the White House. Even then the owners refused to talk to the union leaders, whom they considered "outlaws" responsible for "anarchy" in the coal fields. Furious at what he termed their "arrogant stupidity," Roosevelt, without any clear constitutional authority, declared that he would send ten thousand soldiers to the mines, not to break the strike, but to dispossess the operators. If this was a bluff, the owners did not call it. They quickly agreed to the creation of an arbitration commission which, in March 1903, proposed a 10 percent increase in wages (and the price of coal) and establishment of an eight- or nine-hour day, but did not recommend union recognition. Roosevelt did not consider himself a champion of labor—on other occasions he used troops against strikers in Colorado, Arizona, and Nevada—but a steward of the national interest. In his successful campaign against the Democrat Alton B. Parker in 1904, TR said that his behavior in the coal strike afforded both sides a "square deal."

The Square Deal reached a culmination in Roosevelt's second term with the enactment of three major pieces of legislation. The Pure Food and Drug Act of 1905 made it a crime to sell adulterated foods or medicines and provided for correct labeling of ingredients. The Meat Inspection Act of 1906 led to more effective supervision of slaughterhouses, provided for the dating of canned meat, and prohibited the use of dangerous chemicals or preservatives. The Hepburn Act of 1906 authorized the Interstate Commerce Commission to set aside railroad rates on the complaint of a shipper and to establish lower rates. The courts would then pass on the "reasonableness" of commission rulings. This legislation, much of which had attracted public backing as a result of muckraking exposures, broke new ground in regulating business practices.

Yet some businessmen strongly supported these measures. In the case of meat inspection, for example, large packers believed that government supervision would drive out smaller competitors who could not meet the costs of inspection, and would also open the European market by vouching for the good quality of American meat. But those who agreed on the need for regulation could not always agree on the kind of regulation needed. Reformers favored broad supervision and substantial administrative discretion in enforcement. Businessmen favored a narrower kind of regulation and judicial review of administrative rulings. Most of the legislation passed under TR fell somewhere between the two positions, and indeed resulted from his willingness to compromise.

Perhaps no cause was more closely linked to Roosevelt's name than that of conservation. Unlike aesthetic conservationists who wished to save the forests from commercial exploitation, Roosevelt preferred a utilitarian approach to natural-resource development. Roosevelt favored the commercial use of such resources in a controlled and scientific manner. He popularized conservation through several White House conferences and broadened its definition to include coal fields, mineral lands, and oil reserves as well as forests. And he supported the Newlands Reclamation Act (1902), which enabled the proceeds from the sale of western lands to be used for federal irrigation projects. Under Frederick H. Newell, the Bureau of Reclamation undertook work on twenty-five major projects within a few years. Roosevelt created the Forest Service in the Department of Agriculture and made Gifford Pinchot its chief. He appointed an Inland Waterways Commission, which in 1908 submitted a plan for multipurpose river development. Through the use of executive authority, TR created five new national parks, established fifty-one wildlife refuges, restricted the uncontrolled development of coal fields and water power sites, and added 43 million acres to the national forests.

# BOXING: BLACK CHAMPIONS AND WHITE HOPES

Boxing in its modern form originated in England in the nineteenth century. Efforts were made to civilize the sport ("All attempts to inflict injury by gouging or tearing the flesh with the fingers or nails, and biting shall be deemed foul") that culminated in 1867 when John Sholto Douglas, the Marquis of Queensberry, proposed new rules. They eliminated "wrestling or hugging," provided for three-minute rounds (rather than rounds lasting until a knockdown), established a 60-second rest period between rounds, substituted padded gloves for bare fists, barred hitting a man who was down, and warned: "A man hanging on the ropes in a helpless state, with his toes off the ground, shall be considered down." For years, boxing in America was dominated by Irish immigrants, the most famous of whom was John L.

Johnson and Jeffries at Reno, 1910.

Joe Louis and trainer Jack Blackburn in 1936.

Sullivan. But the era of Irish supremacy was interrupted in 1908 when Jack Johnson, a black fighter, won the title.

During the seven years he held the championship, Johnson elicited a response from white America that reflected broader currents of racial tension in the Progressive era. Johnson flouted social conventions, most importantly the injunction against interracial sex. He was often seen with white women, and three of his four wives were white. A black newspaper speculated that his behavior had led directly to the introduction of bills banning interracial marriage in several state legislatures. In any event, a search rapidly began for a "white hope" who might defeat Johnson. It soon narrowed to Jim Jeffries, who had retired unbeaten in 1905. Socialist Jack London joined the cry: "Jeffries must emerge from his alfalfa farm and remove the golden smile from Johnson's face. Jeff, it's up to you!" The fight was scheduled for July 1912. Jeffries's supporters were confident, believing him superior "in both breeding and education." But Johnson won easily and collected $120,000. An outcry then arose against showing films of the fight, for many believed that youth would be "tainted, corrupted, and brutalized by such scenes." Reformers claimed a victory when Congress made it a federal offense to transport motion pictures of prize fights across state lines.

It was another act of Congress, however, that proved Johnson's undoing. The Mann Act (1910) was aimed at the "white slave trade," that is, at those who transported girls across state lines for purposes of prostitution. Given the existing prejudice, Johnson was a natural target. "In Chicago," thundered a Southern congressman, "white girls are made the slaves of an African brute." Johnson was unfairly convicted of violating the law and in 1913, rather than serve a jail sentence, he fled to Canada and then to Europe. In 1915 he lost the title to Jess Willard in a match fought in Havana, Cuba. Johnson later claimed he threw the fight in a vain effort to appease his enemies in the United States. In July 1920 Johnson returned home, surrendered, and was sentenced to a year in the penitentiary. After his release he fought exhibition matches, worked in nightclubs, and developed a vaudeville routine. He died in an automobile crash in 1946.

The next black heavyweight champion, Joe Louis, aroused no such bitter antagonism. Louis held the title from 1937 until his retirement in 1949, and his victories became occasions for celebration in black communities. "Everywhere Negroes marched through the streets, slapping backs, shaking hands, and congratulating each other." Novelist Richard Wright believed that Louis tapped the deepest springs of rebellion in the black community: "Joe was the concentrated essence of black triumph over white." Yet Louis was at the same time ex-

ceedingly popular among whites. He violated no racial taboos and he epitomized good sportsmanship in the ring. In 1938 his crushing first-round defeat of the German fighter Max Schmeling, who supposedly believed in Aryan supremacy, was hailed as a vindication of democracy. When the United States entered World War II Louis enlisted and was frequently cited as a model of patriotism.

Attitudes toward military service affected the career of another black fighter in a much different way. In 1964 Cassius Clay won the heavyweight championship. He then announced his conversion to the religion of Islam and changed his name to Muhammad Ali. His commitment to black nationalism provoked anger among those who favored integration. Former champion Floyd Patterson challenged Ali ("just so I can bring the championship back to America"), thereby becoming what one critic termed "the first black 'white hope' in boxing history." In 1967 Ali refused induction into the army on the grounds of religious objection. He told newsmen, "I ain't got no quarrel with them Viet Cong." Indicted for draft evasion, Ali was stripped of his title and denied a chance to fight until March 1971 when he lost a decision to Joe Frazier. Ali later regained his title, but his most significant victory came in June 1971 when the Supreme Court found that his religious convictions entitled him to a draft exemption.

In Ali's case, as in Jack Johnson's, the heavyweight championship had itself become a focal point of racial tensions and concerns.

## THE NEW NATIONALISM

By the end of his second term Roosevelt did not stand just where he had at the start of his first. Historians have pointed out that Roosevelt, in his last two years in office, called for increased federal controls, taxes on income and inheritances, stricter regulation of railroad rates, extension of the eight-hour day and workmen's compensation, and limitations on the use of injunctions in labor disputes. Roosevelt spoke indignantly about "certain malefactors of great wealth" and condemned the conservatism of the courts. This posture may have reflected Roosevelt's concern over the strength shown at the polls by socialists, his resentment at the effort of businessmen to attribute the economic slump of 1907 to his policies, or his willingness to speak out more boldly since he did not expect to seek renomination. Whatever the reason, Roosevelt had gone far toward embracing the doctrine that came to be known as the New Nationalism.

That doctrine received its fullest statement in Herbert Croly's *The Promise of American Life* (1909). A prominent Progressive who later helped found the *New Republic*, Croly believed that a "morally and socially desirable distribution of wealth" must replace the "indiscriminate individ-

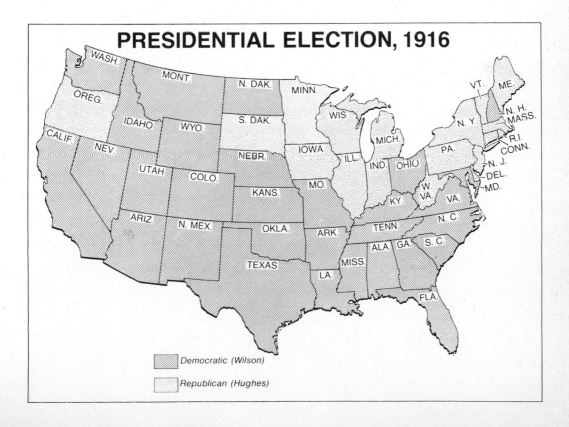

PRESIDENTIAL ELECTION, 1916

Democratic (Wilson)

Republican (Hughes)

ual scramble for wealth." A Jeffersonian fear of positive government, Croly said, had kept American reformers in a strait jacket. To achieve order and rationality they must reject laissez-faire in favor of positive action, competition in favor of concentration, and equal rights in favor of aid to the underprivileged. Croly, who regarded labor as another selfish interest group and opposed the common ownership of property, was not a socialist. But he went as far toward accepting the welfare state as any Progressive when he said: "Every popular government should have, after deliberation, the power of taking any action which, in the opinion of a decisive majority of the people, is demanded by the public welfare."

## TAFT AND THE INSURGENTS

Theodore Roosevelt handpicked William Howard Taft as his successor, but two men could hardly have been temperamentally more unalike. Roosevelt was an athlete; Taft was a ponderous man who in 1904 weighed 326 pounds. Roosevelt was never happier than when stalking a wild animal in the jungle; Taft never wanted to kill anything. Roosevelt had a flair for the dramatic; Taft did nothing to cultivate his public image. Roosevelt loved the rough-and-tumble of politics; Taft hated it. Unlike his predecessor, Taft had made his career in the law and in public administration. He had served as a superior court judge in Ohio, United States Solicitor-General, federal circuit court judge, Governor-General of the Philippines, and Secretary of War. Roosevelt inspired strong feelings, but Taft had a natural instinct for accommodation. One Republican noted that "the trouble with Taft is that if he were Pope he would think it necessary to appoint a few Protestant Cardinals."

As President, Taft helped win important victories for progressivism. He proved to be a vigorous trust-buster. His Attorney General brought twenty-two civil suits, and the courts returned forty-five criminal indictments, for violations of the Sherman Act. In 1911, however, the Supreme Court crippled antitrust enforcement by accepting the "rule of reason." Asserting that the Sherman Act was not intended to prohibit all combinations in restraint of trade, but only those that were unreasonable, the Court made it virtually impossible to prosecute monopolies successfully. In the field of conservation, Taft continued Roosevelt's program by withdrawing additional forest lands and oil reserves. Taft favored the Mann-Elkins Act (1910) which placed telephone and telegraph companies under the jurisdiction of the ICC and authorized the commission to examine railroad rates on its own initiative. He reformed government administration by creating the Department of Labor, establishing a Children's Bureau, and introducing the eight-hour day for federal employees. Two constitutional amendments ratified in 1913—the Sixteenth authorizing an income tax and the Seventeenth providing for direct election of senators—obtained congressional approval during Taft's years in office.

Despite his record, however, Taft gradually lost the confidence of Progressives. Even at the start of his administration, Republicans were divided. Reformers like Senator Robert M. La Follette of Wisconsin and conservatives like Senator Nelson Aldrich of Rhode Island were nominally members of the same party, but disagreed sharply over political and economic policy. Between 1909 and 1912 the division became irreconcilable and the party ultimately split in two. Taft's position on three major issues—legislative reform, trade, and conservation—helped that process along. In each case Taft sympathized with the Progressive position but his political technique, or lack of one, brought him inexorably into the conservative camp.

For many years the Speaker of the House of Representatives had dominated that body. He served as Chairman of the Rules Committee, made all committee assignments, and granted or withheld recognition during debate. Progressive Republicans disliked this arrangement because they considered the power itself inordinate and believed that the Republican Speaker, "Uncle Joe" Cannon of Illinois (whose favorite saying was "this country is a hell of a success"), used his position to subvert reform. Taft was no admirer of Cannon's either, but conservatives threatened to block other legislation if he sided with the insurgents. Taft backed away from the fight and in 1909, when the challenge to Cannon failed, Progressives attributed their defeat in part to Taft's desertion. The revolt later succeeded: in 1910 the Rules Committee was enlarged and the Speaker removed from it, and in 1911 the Speaker lost the right to make committee assignments. But Taft took none of the credit; instead, insurgents regarded him as an ally of the old guard.

Controversies over the tariff drove yet another wedge between Taft and the reformers, both of whom, ironically, favored downward revision. Their differences first emerged over the Payne-Aldrich Tariff of 1909. The bill, to which protectionist Nelson Aldrich had attached 847 amendments in the Senate, effected a modest reduction in the tariff. But it did not go as far as some Progressives would have liked, and they strongly resented Taft's claiming credit for the measure and heralding it as a major reform. Again, in 1911 Taft urged Congress to adopt a reciprocal trade agreement with Canada which would remove tariffs between the two nations. Many midwestern Progressives, who came from dairy and lumber states, feared competition from Canadian imports and opposed this particular form of tariff revision. It passed over their objections but Canada refused to cooperate and the plan died. Republican insurgents and Democrats then enacted three low tariff bills. Taft, claiming that they were politically motivated attempts to embarrass him, vetoed the measures.

A bitter dispute over the activities of Secretary of the Interior Richard Ballinger completed the rupture between Taft and the insurgents. In the summer of 1909 Louis Glavis, an investigator for the Interior Department, informed Gifford Pinchot that Ballinger had, shortly before taking office, apparently profited from aiding a Seattle group in its effort to deliver rich Alaskan coal fields to a large business syndicate. Pinchot brought the accusation to Taft who, after listening to both sides and asking Attorney General George W. Wickersham to investigate, exonerated Ballinger and fired Glavis. Pinchot leaked his side of the story to the press and in January 1910 publicly condemned Ballinger. Taft then dismissed Pinchot, the idol of conservationists, from his post as chief of the Forest Service. From January to June 1910 a joint congressional committee conducted an investigation. It found no proof that Ballinger was corrupt, but it turned up a damaging fact: Taft had asked Wickersham to predate his report so it would appear that the decision to fire Glavis resulted from it rather than from a preliminary verbal report. A generation of reformers convinced itself that Ballinger and Taft had betrayed the conservation movement.

Dissatisfaction with Taft led Pinchot, La Follette, Governor Hiram Johnson of California, and others to create the National Progressive Republican League in January 1911. Designed to push La Follette's candidacy within the Republican party, the League ended by endorsing Theodore Roosevelt's candidacy on a third-party ticket. At first it seemed doubtful that Roosevelt would make the race. He had returned from a hunting expedition to Africa in June 1910 with no thought of seeking renomination and with some hope that Taft could heal the wounds in the Republican party. But in 1911, as his disenchantment with the President grew, Roosevelt changed his mind. Taft's attempt to negotiate arbitration treaties as a means of resolving international disputes peacefully, and his remark that the War of 1812, the Mexican War, and the Spanish-American War "might have been settled without a fight and ought to have been," offended Roosevelt. Taft's decision to bring an antitrust suit against U.S. Steel for its acquisition of the Tennessee Coal and Iron Company in 1907, a merger to which TR had tacitly assented, infuriated the former President.

By the time the Republican convention met in June 1912 the two men, once good political friends, had become bitter personal enemies. If Roosevelt, who had done well in the primaries, was the people's choice, Taft was the convention's. His control of the Republican National Committee and of the party machinery in the South assured Taft's renomination on the first ballot. Reformers walked out in disgust, and in August Roosevelt agreed to run as the candidate of a new Progressive party. His assertion that "every man holds his property subject to the general right of the community to regulate its use to whatever degree the public welfare may require it" summarized the party's platform. His cry to the convention— "We stand at Armageddon and we battle for the Lord"—captured the movement's religious fervor.

# WOODROW WILSON

Republican disunity, however, permitted the Democrats to capture the White House for the first time in twenty years. Their candidate, Thomas Woodrow Wilson, was born in Virginia in 1856, the son of a Presbyterian minister. After being graduated from Princeton (1879), Wilson studied law at the University of Virginia but gave up his practice for graduate work in political science at the Johns Hopkins University. His doctoral dissertation, *Congressional Government*, appeared in 1885. In it Wilson held that American politics, characterized by a powerful but irresponsible Congress and a weak President, was inferior to the Cabinet system that linked the interests of the executive and legislative branches. He then taught at Bryn Mawr, Wesleyan, and finally at Princeton, which named him its president in 1902. There, Wilson encouraged the introduction of small seminars and tried unsuccessfully to abolish the exclusive "eating clubs," which he regarded as anti-intellectual. In 1910 the New Jersey Democratic leaders, considering Wilson a safe but attractive figure, invited him to run for the governorship. He did, and to the bosses' dismay, presided over a reform administration, enacting a direct primaries law, a corrupt practices act, and workmen's compensation. In 1912 Wilson won the democratic presidential nomination on the forty-sixth ballot. That November, with Roosevelt and Taft dividing the normal Republican vote, Wilson, although he received only 41.8 percent of the popular vote, carried forty states and won an overwhelming electoral victory.

His Calvinist training and Southern upbringing helped mold Wilson's political outlook. A devoutly religious man, Wilson believed that God had given the universe a moral structure and had placed men on earth to do His work. Once he cast an issue in moral terms or defined a conflict as one between good and evil, Wilson would no more think of compromising than he would of endorsing only five of the Ten Commandments. One politician noted that Wilson "said something to me, and I didn't know whether God or him was talking." Some thought that Wilson also had trouble telling the difference. His boyhood in the South influenced the President as much as his religious upbringing. Wilson, whose father had owned slaves and served as a chaplain in the Confederate Army, remarked, "The only place in the country, the only place in the world, where nothing has to be explained to me is the South." He later demonstrated his loyalties to section and party by rigidly segregating black and white officeholders in government agencies, and by removing Southern blacks from federal jobs. Like most white Americans, Wilson saw no contradiction between his religious convictions and his racial practices.

In 1912 Wilson campaigned on the slogan of the "New Freedom," which he presented as an alternative to Roosevelt's New Nationalism. The New Freedom, which Wilson worked out in discussions with the prominent Boston attorney Louis D. Brandeis, held that government should intervene in the economy to the extent necessary to restore competition. Unlike Roosevelt, who now viewed antitrust actions as a throwback to the past, Wilson asserted that trusts were inefficient, the product of financial manipulation, and the cause of artificially inflated prices. He would not go on a rampage against trusts but believed that by stripping them of special privileges they would fall of their own weight. Unlike Roosevelt, who favored child-labor legislation and a minimum wage for women, Wilson denounced paternalism. He told a group of workers: "The old adage that God takes care of those who take care of themselves is not gone out of date. No federal legislation can change that thing. The minute you are taken care of by the government you are wards, not independent men." Whereas Roosevelt, in advocating welfare measures, implied that the condition of the poor did not necessarily reflect a failure on their part, Wilson placed the issue squarely on moral grounds: under the rules of free competition an individual's character—as measured by thrift, hard work, ingenuity—would determine the individual's reward.

## ENACTING THE NEW FREEDOM

Once elected, Wilson met with remarkable success in enacting his program. This resulted from a receptive legislative climate as well as from his creative use of presidential authority. In 1913 the Democrats controlled both houses of Congress. With Wilson only the second Democrat to occupy the White House since the Civil War, the party was determined to demonstrate its capacity for national leadership. Moreover, presidents usually receive wide support from newly elected congressmen, and of the 290 House Democrats, no fewer than 114 were first-termers. Wilson used every device at his disposal to corral supporters. He conferred regularly with legislative leaders, enforced party discipline by dispensing patronage, stressed loyalty to caucus decisions and, when he thought it necessary, appealed directly to the people. All of this reflected Wilson's admiration for English government and his belief that the President "must be prime minister, as much concerned with the guidance of legislation as with the just and orderly execution of law." Indeed, it was during Wilson's tenure that, for the first time since Jefferson abandoned the practice, a President delivered his messages to Congress in person.

Within a year and a half of Wilson's inauguration, Congress placed the New Freedom on the statute books. The Underwood Tariff (1913) substantially reduced import duties. During the debate Wilson had publicly denounced the lobbyists who were swarming into Washington to look after their clients' interests. He aroused such a furor that, before voting, senators felt obliged to reveal how the tariff affected their own financial holdings. The act also included the first income tax passed under the Sixteenth Amendment. The tax rose from 1 percent on personal and

corporate income over $4000 to 4 percent on incomes over $100,000. The
Federal Reserve Act (1913), which reformed the banking and currency
system, resulted in part from a congressional inquiry into the "money
trust." The investigation revealed that Morgan and Rockefeller interests
held a tight grip on credit institutions. The act provided for a more flexible
currency and established a measure of public control over private bankers.
It created twelve Federal Reserve Banks that, although privately controlled, also were responsible to a Federal Reserve Board. Finally, the
Clayton Anti-Trust Act (1914) attempted to bolster the faltering attack on
monopoly by prohibiting interlocking directorships and other devices that
lessened competition. The Clayton Act made a gesture toward exempting
labor unions, but the wording remained ambiguous enough so that the
Supreme Court could later rule certain kinds of strikes and boycotts
illegal.

With the passage of this legislation Wilson considered his work largely
done. Ten or twelve years ago, he mused in November 1914, "deep perplexities and dangerous ill humours" had marked American life. "The
country was torn and excited by an agitation which shook the very foundations" of its political and economic system. Those in power were regarded with suspicion, and they in turn mistrusted the people. "There
was ominous antagonism between classes," Wilson admitted. But the New
Freedom promised to turn everything around: it would replace class conflict with harmony, and mutual distrust with confidence. Wilson predicted
that "suspicion and illwill" would fade away and that Americans would
march together toward "a new cordiality of spirit and cooperation." The
New Freedom, he believed, had performed its mission of reconciliation.

Convinced that reform had gone far enough, Wilson wanted to go no
further. The only important Progressive measure he endorsed in 1915,
and grudgingly at that, was the La Follette Seamen's Act. It freed sailors
on merchant ships from a contract system that, in practice, amounted to
forced labor. In other areas Wilson drew the line. He opposed establishing
federally financed credit institutions to provide long-term loans to farmers
on the grounds that this would unduly favor one interest group. He continued to regard federal child-labor legislation as unconstitutional, and
he refused to support woman suffrage. In February 1915 he nominated
five men to serve on a newly created Federal Trade Commission. But
Wilson, in the words of a Cabinet member, regarded the FTC as "a coun-
sellor and friend to the business world" rather than as "a policeman to
wield a club over the head of the business community." For the most part
his appointees interpreted their task in the same way.

Yet by early 1916 Wilson began to modify his position, and he did so
largely because he reassessed the political situation. The Democrats had
done poorly in the 1914 elections, losing two dozen seats in the House
and giving up the governorships of New York, New Jersey, Illinois, and
Pennsylvania. Moreover, the Bull Moose party had begun to disintegrate

after Roosevelt's defeat. Lacking a formal grass-roots organization, beset by financial problems, torn by dissension over its policy toward business, the party met with disaster in 1914, losing virtually every contest it entered. Ironically, the demise of the Progressive party, by raising the spectre of a unified Republican opposition, helped move Wilson toward an accommodation with the Progressive platform. To win reelection, Wilson knew he must make inroads into Roosevelt's old constituency.

This he attempted to do in a number of ways. In January 1916 Wilson nominated Louis D. Brandeis to the Supreme Court, a move that infuriated conservatives and touched off a bitter four-month struggle for Senate confirmation. Wilson also reversed his position on several issues. He supported the Federal Farm Loan Act (1916) which created twelve regional banks to provide long-term, low-interest loans to farmers. Similarly, in July he asked the Senate to approve a child-labor bill that had already cleared the House. His efforts helped pass the Keating-Owen Act (1916), which barred the products of firms employing child labor from interstate commerce. (In 1918 Wilson's earlier fears proved correct when the Supreme Court, in *Hammer* v. *Dagenhart,* found the measure unconstitutional.) Having made overtures to agrarians and social reformers. Wilson turned his attention to labor. He backed the Kern-McGillicuddy Act (1916), which provided workmen's compensation for federal employees. In September, to head off a railroad strike, Wilson urged Congress to pass a law giving the union essentially what it wanted: an eight-hour day for railroad workers in interstate commerce. Congress obliged by passing the Adamson Act (1916). Finally, Wilson moved still closer to the ground Roosevelt had once occupied by supporting the Webb-Pomerene bill (which did not pass until 1918), that exempted the overseas operations of business firms from the antitrust laws.

Wilson's strategy succeeded against a Republican opponent, Charles Evans Hughes, who had himself compiled a reform record as Governor of New York and as a member of the Supreme Court. Campaigning not only on his record of Progressive achievement but also on a pledge to keep America out of the European war, the President won a narrow victory. Wilson received 9.1 million votes to 8.5 million for Hughes, and managed a 23-vote margin in the electoral college. Nearly 3 million more people voted for Wilson than in 1912, including many farmers, workers, and New Nationalist Progressives who approved of the direction his administration had taken in 1916. Also, the peace issue apparently helped Wilson among German-Americans and socialists, and among women in the eleven states—particularly California, Washington, and Kansas—which granted them the vote.

Early in 1917, therefore, most Americans expected Wilson's victory to keep the nation at peace and permit completion of the Progressive agenda. Few had any reason to suppose that, within a few months, Wilson would lead the nation into war. Indeed, World War I would expose many of the limitations of progressivism. In retrospect, the reformers' optimism would seem naive, their apparent dedication to serving the general interest merely a rationalization for preserving narrower class interests. Laws regulating morality would seem self-righteous attempts to impose conformity. The Progressive effort to throw the weight of government on the side of the less fortunate would, to a later generation, appear inadequate or paternalistic. Even the struggle for political democracy might be construed as emphasizing form over content. But during the Progressive era only a handful of critics voiced such doubts. In the years before the war the Progressive faith burned brightly.

## Suggested Reading

Important, but conflicting, interpretations of progressivism are presented in Richard Hofstadter, *The Age of Reform* (1955); Gabriel Kolko, *The Triumph of Conservatism* (1963); James Weinstein, *The Corporate Ideal in the Liberal State, 1900–1918* (1969); Arthur A. Ekirch, Jr., *Progressivism in America* (1974); Richard M. Abrams, *The Burdens of Progress, 1900–1929* (1978); John W. Chambers II, *The Tyranny of Change* (1980); and Lewis L. Gould, *Reform and Regulation: American Politics, 1900–1916* (1978).

The social consequences of industrialization and urbanization are considered in Robert Bremner, *From the Depths: The Discovery of Poverty in the United States* (1956); and Charles N. Glaab and A. Theodore Brown, *A History of Urban America* (1967). For the response of social workers and reformers, see two works by Allen Davis—*Spearheads for Reform: The Social Settlements and the Progressive Movement, 1890–1917* (1968) and *American Heroine: The Life and Legend of Jane Addams* (1973); Roy Lubove, *The Progressives and the Slums: Tenement House Reform in New York City, 1890–1917* (1962); and John F. McClymer, *War and Welfare: Social Engineering in America, 1890–1925* (1980).

Women's involvement in reform movements of the progressive era is examined in William L. O'Neill, *Everyone was Brave: A History of Feminism in America* (1971); Nancy Schrom Dye, *As Equals and Sisters: The Labor Movement and the Women's Trade Union League of New York* (1980); Mary Jo Buhle, *Women and American Socialism 1870–1920* (1983); and Margaret Marsh, *Anarchist Women* (1981).

The theoretical foundations of progressivism are explored in Morton White, *Social Thought in America: The Revolt against Formalism* (1957); Eric Goldman, *Rendezvous With Destiny* (1952); Charles Forcey, *The Crossroads of Liberalism* (1961). Richard Hofstadter, *The Progressive Historians* (1968), evaluates Charles Beard and other academics. For the literature of exposure, see David Chalmers, *The Social and Political Ideas of the Muckrakers* (1964).

Progressive attitudes toward racial and ethnic minorities are considered in Rayford Logan, *The Negro in American Life and Thought: The Nadir, 1877–1901* (1954); David Southern, *The Malignant Heritage: Yankee Progressives and the Negro, 1901–1914* (1968); George Frederickson, *The Black Image in the White Mind, 1817–1914* (1968); Alan M. Kraut, *The Huddled Masses: The Immigrant in American Society, 1860–1921* (1982); Jack Temple Kirby, *Darkness at the Dawning: Race and*

*Reform in the Progressive South* (1972); and Roger Daniels, *The Politics of Prejudice: The Anti-Japanese Movement in California* (1962). For the relationship of Negro protest to progressivism, see Elliott Rudwick, *W. E. B. DuBois, Propagandist of the Negro Protest* (1969); and Charles F. Kellogg, *NAACP, 1909–1920* (1967). The disfranchisement of blacks is discussed in J. Morgan Kousser, *The Shaping of Southern Politics* (1974).

Social and intellectual currents in the Progressive era are considered in Henry F. May, *The End of American Innocence, 1912–1917* (1959). Important monographs on the period include Samuel Hays, *Conservation and the Gospel of Efficiency, 1890–1920* (1959); James Timberlake, *Prohibition and the Progressive Movement, 1900–1920* (1963); Thomas Kessner, *The Golden Door: Italian and Jewish Mobility in New York City, 1880–1915* (1977); and Peter Temin, *Taking Your Medicine: Drug Regulation in the United States* (1980).

For the presidency of Theodore Roosevelt, see two studies by George Mowry: *Theodore Roosevelt and the Progressive Movement* (1947), and *The Era of Theodore Roosevelt, 1900–1912* (1958). Also useful are John M. Blum, *The Republican Roosevelt* (1954), and William H. Harbaugh, *The Life and Times of Theodore Roosevelt* (1961). The standard work on Roosevelt's successor is Henry Pringle, *The Life and Times of William Howard Taft* (1939), but see also Norman Wilensky, *Conservatives in the Progressive Era: The Taft Republicans of 1912* (1965), and Donald E. Anderson, *William Howard Taft* (1973). Five volumes of Arthur Link's *Wilson* (1947–1965), taking the account to 1917, have appeared. A briefer analysis appears in Link, *Woodrow Wilson and the Progressive Era, 1900–1917* (1954). John Milton Cooper, Jr., *The Warrior and the Priest* (1983) is a comparative study of Roosevelt and Wilson.

On boxing, begin with Jack Johnson, *Jack Johnson Is a Dandy: An Autobiography* (reissued 1969); Barney Nagler's story of Joe Louis, *Brown Bomber* (1972); and José Torres, *Sting Like a Bee* (1971), the biography of Muhammad Ali.

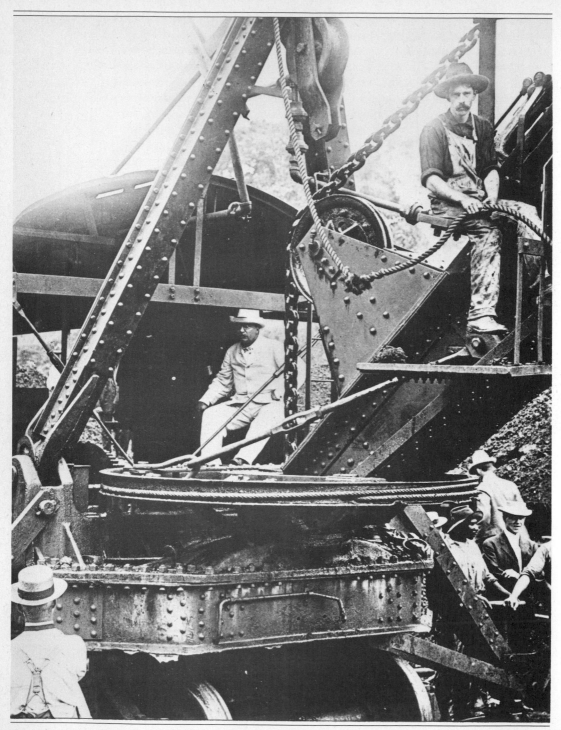

TR at the cutting of the Panama Canal, 1906.

# 1900–1917

## A Progressive
## Foreign Policy:
## From Peace to War

The ideals and policies that Americans adhere to at home determine their ideals and policies around the globe. Between 1900 and 1917 the Progressives exemplified this rule of American history. Dedicated to cleansing the cesspools of the new industrialism in the United States, the Progressives also developed foreign policies to help solve the problems raised by the corporations. And as Progressives searched desperately for order and stability at home amid the industrial revolution, so overseas they used the new American economic and military power in an attempt to impose order in such areas as China, Mexico, and Western Europe.

Many Progressives believed that only in orderly societies could the United States hope to find political cooperation and the long-term markets for the glut of goods and capital its corporations produced. Without such help from foreign friends, unemployment and radical movements could threaten Progressive programs at home. Thus the era began with Theodore Roosevelt trying to make the Caribbean safe from revolution and ended with Woodrow Wilson taking the nation into World War I in order to make the world safe for democracy. These two men hated one another by 1917 (in one of his quieter moments Roosevelt called Wilson a "Byzantine logothete" whose soul was "rotten through and through," largely because Wilson did not lead Americans into war as quickly as Roosevelt wished). Their general foreign policies, however, were quite similar. The most important of the similarities was the determination by each man to create conditions for the overseas expansion of what one observer accurately called in 1908 this "great economic corporation known as the United States of America."

## TR

Theodore Roosevelt once remarked that a man's mission in life could be summed up with the admonition to "work, fight, and breed." He did all three rather well. TR achieved particular success as a fighter in 1898 when his exploits at the victory of San Juan Hill associated his name with militant American expansionism and helped catapult him into the vice-presidency in 1900. After McKinley's assassination in September 1901, Roosevelt assumed personal control of American foreign policy.

The new President's alternatives were analyzed in an article published by his close friend Brooks Adams in the *Atlantic Monthly* in 1901. Adams observed that since 1860 the Republicans had helped create the nation's great industrial complex by passing high tariffs which protected American producers from cheap foreign competition. That complex had become developed, and now the need was to find world markets for its products.

The President would have to choose one of two paths. He could try to lower the tariff as part of a deal in which other nations would reduce their tariffs on American goods. This policy, however, could result in a violent struggle within the Republican party between high- and low-tariff advocates, and might not ensure that other high-tariff nations, such as Germany, would reciprocate by lowering their tariffs to benefit U.S. products. The second alternative was to retain the high tariff, but then (1) to use the powers of the federal government to make American production and transportation so efficient that United States products could compete globally regardless of tariff policy, and (2) to develop a great military force, which would assure American producers that their government could protect their interests in such vital potential markets as China, Latin America, and Africa. Not one to rock his own political boat, and deeply committed to the idea that military force ultimately decided world affairs, Roosevelt enthusiastically chose the second alternative. In this way he hoped to have both political peace at home and expansion overseas.

Roosevelt was clear about the tactics for achieving these goals. To make American producers yet more competitive, he espoused such Progressive measures as the Hepburn Act, which aimed at making the nation's transportation and production more efficient. He wrote Brooks Adams in 1903:

> As you so admirably put it, it is necessary for us to keep the road of trade to the east open. In order to insure our having terminals, we must do our best to prevent the shutting to us of the Asian markets. In order to keep the roads to these terminals open we must see that they are managed primarily in the interest of the country.

Roosevelt also extolled the "strenuous life" of the military, continued the rapid building of the battleship fleet, and built an isthmian canal in Panama so that the fleet could more easily shift from the Atlantic to the Pacific theater. To ensure rapid decision making, and to protect his foreign policy from what he believed to be the provincialism of American domestic politics, he concentrated the power to make decisions in the White House. This drained the power from Congress, a body he believed was "not well fitted for the shaping of foreign policy." And, as did most Progressives, he praised the nation-state as the ultimate arbiter in world affairs. Roosevelt's refused to allow any international agencies to infringe on the nation-state's power.

In formulating his foreign policy strategies, TR distinguished sharply between friendly and potentially threatening nations. Although he had mistrusted the British during the 1890s, Roosevelt now understood that they no longer threatened the United States in Latin America and that the two nations had similar interests in Asia. Anglo-American cooperation, moreover, fitted in with Roosevelt's views of the superiority of the Anglo-Saxon people, who were, in his eyes, destined to "civilize" the nonindustrialized areas of the world. Another partner would be Japan, which Roosevelt believed shared American open-door policies in Asia. Japan was certainly not Anglo-Saxon, but it had become industrialized and efficient, and thus, in the words of Captain Alfred Thayer Mahan (one of TR's close friends and a leading naval strategist), Japan had become "Teutonic by adoption." On the other hand, Roosevelt feared Germany and Russia, the former because its rapidly growing navy threatened British dominion in Europe and Africa, the latter because the Slavs seemed to be the people who endangered Anglo-Japanese-American interests in Asia.

Roosevelt possessed the personality and political power needed to carry out these policies. Above all, he was willing to use the mushrooming American industrial and military power to expand the nation's interest. Roosevelt agreed not with Shakespeare's "Twice is he armed that has his quarrel just," but rather with the version of American humorist Josh Billings: "And four times he who gets his fist in fust."

## "I TOOK THE CANAL"

TR followed Billings's admonition in Latin America. Throughout the late nineteenth century the United States had tried to escape from an 1850 treaty made with England that pledged each nation to construct an isthmian canal only in cooperation with the other. Beset by problems in Africa and Europe, the British finally agreed to negotiate the point. In the Hay-Pauncefote Treaty of November 1901, England gave the United States the power to build and to fortify a canal.

As late as 1902, it seemed that the least expensive passageway could be built in Nicaragua. But a group of lobbyists who had interests in Panama used political pressure and bribes to win congressional support for the Panamanian site then ruled by Colombia. A treaty of January 1903 (the Hay-Herrán pact) gave the United States rights over a six-mile strip in Panama in return for $10 million and a $250,000 annual payment to Colombia. But the Colombian Senate then demanded $25 million. Roosevelt angrily—and ingeniously—announced that if the Panamanians revolted against Colombia, he would keep Colombian troops out of Panama by invoking an 1846 treaty in which the United States had promised Colombia to keep Panama "free and open." The lobbyists gratefully helped arrange the revolution in November 1903, and TR sent a warship to make sure that Colombia would not interfere. He then recognized the new government, gave it the $10 million, and made the new country an American protectorate by guaranteeing its independence. Later Roosevelt bragged, "I took the Canal Zone and let Congress debate." That remark showed little appreciation for Latin American feelings, and even less for the American constitutional system.

# —AND ALSO SANTO DOMINGO

Fomenting revolutions was quite out of character for one as strongly antirevolutionary as TR. More characteristic was his policy in the Caribbean nation of Santo Domingo. The stage was set in 1903 when Great Britain and Germany temporarily landed troops in Venezuela in order to protect the property of their citizens. The resulting uproar in the United States, and the threat that in the future such temporary landings might become a permanent occupation, led Roosevelt to conclude that he could not allow an open door for European force in Latin America. The Europeans informed TR that they did not like sending their military to Latin America, but they would have to do so unless the United States policed the area so that the revolutionary disturbances, and resulting dangers to foreign investors, would not occur.

Roosevelt's opportunity soon appeared in Santo Domingo, a country wracked by dictatorial governments as well as by struggles between German and American business interests. The President initially moved into Santo Domingo, however, not to check European threats to American security, but to fight the inroads that German shipping lines were making on American shippers. State Department officials on the scene told TR that the immediate threat was a revolution that the Germans might use as an excuse to land troops for the enforcement of their business claims.

The President responded by announcing a formula in December 1904 that has become known as the Roosevelt Corollary to the Monroe Doctrine. Any "chronic wrong-doing" might "require intervention by some civilized power," he warned. In the Western Hemisphere the United States would act as this "civilized power," exercising "international police power" to correct "flagrant cases of such wrong-doing or impotence." In early 1905 Roosevelt displayed American strength by sending warships to Santo Domingo. He then made a pact with that country giving the United States control of the customs houses through which the Dominicans collected most of their revenue. In return Roosevelt promised to use the receipts from the customs to pay off the Dominican debts and the foreigners' claims. Although the American Senate refused to consent to this agreement, Roosevelt enforced it by calling it an Executive agreement (that is, an agreement that would last at least through his presidency, but not necessarily be binding on the next president). He had again circumvented the constitutional restraints on his actions, and in 1907 the Senate reluctantly ratified the treaty. The President meanwhile kept warships in control of the waters around Santo Domingo, instructing the naval commander "to stop any revolution." TR hardly solved the Dominican problem. In order to stop recurring revolutions, U.S. troops were periodically stationed in that country through the administrations of the next five American presidents.

The Roosevelt Corollary is important primarily because it committed American power to maintain stability in the Caribbean area. With that commitment, TR once and for all destroyed the ideal of the Monroe Doctrine of 1823, which had aimed at preventing outside forces from controlling sovereign nations in Latin America. Contrary to the principles of 1823—and 1776—New World revolutionaries were no longer necessarily allowed to work out their own nation's destiny. Roosevelt best summarized the results when he claimed that the American intervention would free the people of Santo Domingo "from the curse of interminable revolutionary disturbance" and give them "the same chance to move onward which we have already given the people of Cuba."

Cuba, however, was hardly a good example. In 1906 infighting between the two major political parties threatened to paralyze the island's government. Anti-American factions again surfaced in Havana. Roosevelt thereupon ordered United States troops to land and restore an acceptable government.

## ROOSEVELT LOSES HIS BALANCE

Outside the Caribbean, the President faced a tougher job. In Europe and Asia he had to expand American interests not by unilateral military power but by the delicate game of balance-of-power politics.

During 1905, for instance, Germany challenged France's protectorate over Morocco, and the German Kaiser asked his good friend Theodore Roosevelt to mediate the crisis. Although he had gotten along well personally with the Kaiser, Roosevelt was alarmed by the rapid rise of German naval power, and he was not anxious to help Germany gain an important foothold in northern Africa. After TR finally arranged a conference at Algeciras, Spain in January 1906, France's claims were upheld by nearly every European power attending. The President meanwhile worked through the two American delegates at the conference to ensure that the United States did not come away empty-handed. He gained a pledge from the powers for an open door in Morocco for American and other interests. After World Wars I and II the State Department would use this 1906 pledge as an entering wedge to gain oil and trade concessions in northern Africa for American entrepreneurs.

Roosevelt did not, however, display such surefootedness in the Far East. The focus in that area was on the struggle between Japan and Russia over the Chinese province of Manchuria. In that confrontation, TR much preferred the Japanese. As for China, which was the victim in the struggle, he observed that it was able neither to industrialize nor to militarize; when he wished to condemn an incompetent person, Roosevelt would call him "a Chinese." His racism, combined with his Progressive enchantment with efficiency, led him to view the Chinese less as actors on the world scene than as a people to be acted upon.

Japanese immigrant children, California.

American missionaries and exporters viewed China from the same perspective. Businessmen particularly were watching the development of China. In 1900 they sent $15 million worth of products to the area, in 1902 $25 million, and by 1905 $53 million. The China market was apparently being realized at last. Most of these goods went into Manchuria and North China, that is, to precisely the area over which the Japanese and Russians were struggling. When Japan suddenly struck the Russians with a devastating sneak attack on February 9, 1904, Roosevelt exultantly wrote his son that the Japanese were "playing our game."

But as Japan destroyed the Russian fleet, consolidated its control over Korea and Manchuria, then threatened to invade Siberia, the President had second thoughts. Fearing that a precarious Russian-Japanese balance was being replaced by an aggressive Japanese empire, Roosevelt moved to stop the war by calling on the two belligerents to meet at Portsmouth, New Hampshire in mid-1905. TR was delighted with the conference's work. Japan received control over Korea and in return promised an open door in Manchuria for the United States and the other powers. The Japanese also obtained key Russian bases in Manchuria, vital parts of the Chinese Eastern Railway running through Manchuria, and the southern half of the strategic island of Sakhalin.

The promise of the open door, however, soon proved empty. Such major American exporters as Standard Oil, Swift and Company, and the British-American Tobacco Company found themselves increasingly driven out of Manchuria by Japan. Tokyo's policy was capped in 1907 when Japan and Russia, bloody enemies just twenty-four months before, agreed on a de facto division of Manchuria, with the Japanese exploiting the south and the Russians the north. Roosevelt's first attempt to form a profitable partnership with the Japanese had ended badly.

In 1907 another threat arose to endanger TR's dream of Japanese-American cooperation in developing Asia. Since the 1890s the number of Japanese living in California had leaped from two thousand to nearly thirty thousand. Many of them were laborers who were willing to work more cheaply than Americans. Threatened by what the governor called a "Japanese menace," the California legislature tried to pass an exclusion bill. Anti-Asian riots erupted. Having just defeated a major white power, the Japanese were in no mood to back down before laws that restricted the rights of their citizens to travel, either to Manchuria or to California. Roosevelt temporarily quieted the tumult by working out a deal: California dropped the impending exclusion act and the Japanese promised that in their own way they would voluntarily restrict passports issued to laborers wishing to move to the United States.

## THE FAILURE OF BIG STICK DIPLOMACY

Roosevelt's hope that Japan would manhandle Russia in 1904 had produced not an open door but a one-way street for the movement of the Japanese empire. "I am more concerned over this Japanese situation than almost any other," TR admitted privately. So the man who gave his countrymen the phrase "Speak softly and carry a big stick," decided to send sixteen American battleships on a goodwill cruise to the western Pacific. Congress blanched when it heard of the plan, for it feared that Japan would destroy the fleet with a sneak attack like that launched against the Russians in 1904. Some congressional leaders announced that they would not appropriate money to send the fleet. Roosevelt thereupon bellowed that he had enough money to send the ships to Japan; if Congress wished to leave them there it was Congress's responsibility. Again outmaneuvered by the President—even humiliated—Congress approved the funds. The visit of the Great White Fleet to Japan in 1907 produced effusions of friendship on both sides, but it failed resoundingly to persuade Tokyo officials to retreat in Manchuria.

On the eve of his departure from the presidency, TR made one last attempt to bring the Japanese into line. In the Root-Takahira agreement of November 1908 (negotiated for Roosevelt by his Secretary of State, Elihu Root), the United States and Japan reaffirmed their meaningless pledge to maintain the open door, but in the wording of the agreement, Root accepted Japan's control of South Manchuria. Roosevelt had apparently surrendered to Japan's predominant power.

Apparently, but not quite. While negotiating with the Japanese, Secretary of State Root quietly told the Chinese that the United States would return nearly $12 million of the indemnity that they had paid the United States after American property had been destroyed in China's Boxer Rebellion eight years before. Root said that he was returning the money "unconditionally," which meant that the Chinese could use the money in any way they chose. Root knew, however, that American officials in Asia had already worked out a scheme with the Chinese for a China-owned bank in Manchuria that would have as its objective the undermining of Japanese economic influence. Root was now, in reality, offering to help fund that bank. Because of a political crisis in China, nothing resulted from the American offer, but clearly Roosevelt had decided not to withdraw from Manchuria. He intended to fight it out with Japan.

His gentle encouragement to Japan in 1904 had resulted in cruel policy dilemmas for Roosevelt. But perhaps the greatest irony of the Russo-Japanese war was that, although American Progressives wanted to avoid revolution at all costs, the conflict ignited the Russian Revolution in 1905. The victory of yellow over white also set off unrest in the French empire in Indochina, helped trigger revolutions in Persia and Turkey, and fueled the Chinese revolutionary outbreak of 1911.

Roosevelt never understood that force does not determine who is right, but who is strong. He therefore had been initially pleased with the Russo-Japanese war. TR failed to understand how the chaos and disruption of such a conflict as the Russo-Japanese struggle could produce the revolutionary outbreaks that he and all Americans so dreaded.

## REPLACING BULLETS WITH DOLLARS

Roosevelt's successor, William Howard Taft, was too conservative for most Progressives, but his experiences as Governor-General in the Philippines and as TR's diplomatic troubleshooter in Cuba and Asia had made Taft a practitioner of the Progressives' ardent search for order and stability. He had learned from these experiences that military force had only a limited capacity for solving problems. Taft consequently hoped to use the burgeoning American financial power, instead of the army, as his main foreign policy instrument. He could point to the expansion of American overseas investments from about $800 million at the time of the 1898 war to more than $2½ billion in 1909 as proof that his countrymen were obtaining the power for the economic reordering of the world.

Taft advocated Dollar Diplomacy not because of any special ties to American bankers. He appointed such leading New York corporation lawyers as Philander C. Knox to be Secretary of State and Henry Stimson to serve as Secretary of War, but Taft also thought that "Wall Street, as an aggregation, is the biggest ass that I have ever run across." For this reason, Taft believed that private interests often needed direction from Washington. As State Department officials understood, however, Dollar Diplomacy was not new, but only the financial side of John Hay's open-door policies: Taft would attempt to do with money what Hay had failed to do with diplomacy. The dangers of changing the tactics but not the objectives of policy soon became evident in both Asia and the Western Hemisphere.

## REPLACING DOLLARS WITH BULLETS

Roosevelt's actions in the Caribbean had spread ill will and fear throughout Latin America. Taft wanted a quieter policy, but the full force of Dollar Diplomacy was quickly made apparent in Nicaragua. That nation was the alternate site for an isthmian canal, and a country particularly watched by Secretary of State Knox because of his past associations with extensive American mining interests there. Events began to unfold in 1909 when a long-term dictatorship was overthrown by revolutionaries, including numerous Americans. Knox immediately sided with the revolution. He moved in to control the situation by seizing the customs houses, which were the country's main source of revenue. The Secretary of State urged the new government to pay off long-standing claims to Great Britain by borrowing large sums from American bankers. When Nicaraguans balked at Knox's demands, he dispatched a warship. The agreement was then quickly signed. But the fires of Nicaraguan nationalism had been lit, and the American-controlled government could not maintain order. In 1912 Taft took the logical step required by his Dollar Diplomacy. More than two thousand Marines landed to protect American lives and property and to prevent European powers from intervening to shield the interests of their own citizens.

While the President dispatched troops to Central America, the United States Senate also tried to protect American interests in the area. In 1912 the Senate added the so-called Lodge Corollary to the Monroe Doctrine in reaction to the threat of a private Japanese company obtaining land on Magdalena Bay in Lower California. The Lodge resolution stated that no "corporation or association which has such a relation to another government, not American," could obtain strategic areas in the hemisphere. This greatly extended the compass of the Monroe doctrine, which had previously applied only to foreign governments, not companies. The State Department used the resolution during the next quarter-century to stop the transfer of lands, particularly in Mexico, to Japanese concerns.

## CANADA

The giant neighbor to the north could not be dealt with in such summary fashion. Americans and Canadians had last warred against one another in 1814, but during the 1830s, 1860s, and 1870s conflict had threatened over border incidents. Canada was extremely sensitive to growing American power, particularly since it had discovered that, although it was a member of the British Empire, London officials were anxious to please the United States even when the matter involved conflicting Canadian-American claims. In 1903, for example, Canada had protested Roosevelt's demand that a disputed part of the Alaskan-Canadian boundary be settled in favor of the United States. When both parties agreed to submit the dispute to a jury of "six impartial jurists of repute," TR loaded the jury with his own type of expansionists and threatened to deploy the army if he did not have his way. The British jurist, casting the deciding vote, ruled in favor of Roosevelt and against the Canadians.

The Canadian government had scarcely recovered from this humiliation when in 1911 it signed a long-sought reciprocity trade agreement with the Taft administration. Canadian officials were initially pleased, believing that the pact opened the mammoth American market to their country's raw material producers. But the agreement also made these producers an integral part of the United States industrial complex, a fact noted publicly when a congressional report in Washington likened the treaty to "another Louisiana Purchase." When the Speaker of the House of Representatives added that it would not be long before the American flag would be flying over all the territory to the North Pole, the ensuing uproar forced the Canadian government to call a national election. A new administration came to power, repudiated the reciprocity pact, and passed higher tariffs against United States goods. The annexationist movement was dead, but even the bungling in 1911 could not stop the successful American exploitation of Canada as virtually an economic colony over the next half-century. Taft, of course, would not live to see that result. During his own presidency Dollar Diplomacy had worked no better in the north than in the south.

## CHINA ONCE AGAIN

The results were even worse in China, although in this labyrinth of revolution, power politics, and diplomatic double dealing, Taft and Knox were not wholly to blame. But they certainly made a bad situation worse.

In late 1909 Knox feared that the Chinese would be unable to prevent Manchuria from being carved once and for all into Japanese and Russian protectorates which would exclude American products. Waving the open-door principle, and insisting that the United States must share in the investment opportunities, the Secretary of State proposed a "neutralization" scheme whereby Americans and Europeans would pool their money to help China buy back the key railroads in Manchuria from the Russians and Japanese. This would effectively "neutralize" the area, reopening it to American traders and investors. But Knox had made a blunder of the first magnitude, for when he tried to push his way into Manchuria, he only further united Russia and Japan against all outsiders. The neutralization plan was stillborn.

Apparently learning nothing from the experience, Knox made a second attempt to retain China as a frontier for Americans. In 1910 he insisted that the United States be allowed to participate in an international banking consortium organized by the British, French, and Germans to build railroads in the province of Hukuang. After Washington exerted great pressure, these nations finally allowed American financiers into the scheme, but the Europeans did so reluctantly, for they knew that once outsiders like the Americans entered, Russia and Japan would also demand entrance. This indeed occurred, and the Russians and Japanese proceeded to paralyze the Chinese Consortium so that it could not endanger their own private spheres of interest.

Now that he was faced with the utter failure of Dollar Diplomacy in the Far East, the only remaining tactic left to Taft seemed to be the use of American military force to prop open the gates to Manchuria. But the President knew the United States did not have the military power to scare either Russia or Japan. Theodore Roosevelt had finally seen the light on this score when he wrote privately to Taft in 1910: "Our vital interest is to keep the Japanese out of [the United States] and at the same time to preserve the good will of Japan." The Japanese, TR continued, must therefore be allowed to exploit Manchuria and Korea unless Taft was prepared to go to war. "I utterly disbelieve in the policy of bluff, . . ." Roosevelt railed, "or in any violation of the old frontier maxim, 'Never draw unless you mean to shoot!'" Unfortunately Roosevelt had not followed such a course while he was President, nor did Taft ever consider leaving Manchuria. The mess was left for Woodrow Wilson.

## THE ULTIMATE PROGRESSIVE DIPLOMAT

Woodrow Wilson has exerted a greater influence on modern American foreign policy than any other person in the twentieth century. Richard Nixon, for example, privately remarked in 1968 that "Wilson was our greatest President of this century. . . . Wilson had the greatest vision of America's role." Much like Nixon, Wilson was highly complex, insecure, and driven by ambition. He once recalled that a classmate asked him, " 'Why, man, can't you let anything alone?' I said, 'I let everything alone that you can show me is not itself moving in the wrong direction, but I am not going to let those things alone that I see are going downhill.' "

He wanted to move the world uphill—uphill, that is, to the political and economic system of the United States. The touchstone of Wilson's dealings with other nations was whether these countries were moving rapidly enough in the direction of a democratic, capitalist system. Although he and Roosevelt disliked each other, they did not differ in their conviction that American nationalism was the proper mold for other peoples, especially the nonindustrialized peoples. "When properly directed," Wilson observed, "there is no people not fitted for self-government." He determined to provide the direction, not merely with self-righteousness, but within a framework in which morality, politics, and economics were closely integrated.

Since his objectives were so exalted, Wilson, like Roosevelt, did not worry often enough about the means he used to achieve them. He even told his closest friend and advisor, Colonel Edward House, that lying was perhaps justified if it involved a woman's honor or a matter of public policy. Those categories gave Wilson ample room for maneuver. Politically, his beliefs exemplified the Progressive faith that effective government could best come from an educated elite; to Wilson, this elite sometimes numbered only one man. Even as a young professor of political science he had advocated strong presidential rule that would circumvent the often messy pluralistic politics of the American congressional system. During an explosive crisis with Germany in 1915, he refused to see not only congressmen but even his closest advisors, and communed only with himself for several days. Given the opportunity to exert wide power in foreign policy during the First World War, Wilson set the pattern of the strong, self-sufficient President, largely free of Congress, that has been followed by Franklin D. Roosevelt, Lyndon Johnson, and Richard Nixon. Wilson also exemplified how such powers so often end in disaster.

His policies rested on a crucial belief: The world must look to the United States for its example and, in turn, Americans depended on the rest of the world for their survival. Wilson had been deeply affected by the depression and threats of revolution within the United States during the 1890s. He was therefore open to the influence of Frederick Jackson Turner's Frontier Thesis, which argued that the 1890s crisis could be understood as the terrible result of the closing of America's landed frontier. After four hundred years, Turner had warned in 1893, the United States had lost that frontier. Wilson, who knew Turner personally, paraphrased the Frontier Thesis several years later: "The westward march has stopped upon the final slopes of the Pacific; and now the plot thickens." The world market must act as the new frontier for the American system,

Wilson warned during the 1912 presidential campaign, or disaster impended: "Our industries have expanded to such a point that they will burst their jackets if they cannot find free outlets in the markets of the world."

His genius was an ability to reconcile this need for overseas expansion with his political and moral views. He believed that open markets and capitalism were absolutely necessary for democratic political systems. His famous remark, "Without freedom of enterprise there can be no freedom whatsoever," applied, in his mind, home and overseas. In terms of foreign policy, this view meant that he felt justified in intervening in revolutions in Mexico and Russia because such upheavals threatened to become both antidemocratic and anticapitalist. These revolutions thus gravely endangered what he believed were American needs in the world arena. The meshing of his economic, political, and moral beliefs was perhaps most strikingly phrased by Wilson during his first presidential term:

> Lift your eyes to the horizons of business . . . let your thoughts and your imagination run abroad throughout the whole world, and with the inspiration of the thought that you are Americans and are meant to carry liberty and justice and the principles of humanity wherever you go, go out and sell goods that will make the world more comfortable and more happy, and convert them to the principles of America.

Wilson tied the American need to export its goods, its political system, and its morality in a single package of red, white, and blue.

In encouraging such expansion, he went beyond the acts of previous presidents in two respects. First, he not only used military force to a greater degree, but also utilized it in an attempt to reform entire societies (see below). Second, he employed the powers of the federal government to a greater extent in capturing markets. The Federal Reserve Banking Act of 1913, for example, created new powers that American bankers and industrialists could use in competing for credit and money in foreign money markets. In 1914 Wilson sponsored the creation of a Bureau of Foreign and Domestic Commerce within the Department of Commerce. This bureau sent government agents abroad to be, in the President's words, the "eyes for the whole business community." The Webb-Pomerene Act of 1918 allowed exporters to organize associations for development of overseas trade, associations that previously had been outlawed by antitrust laws. The act ran counter to the supposed Progressive ideal of breaking up trusts, but to the Wilsonians, exploiting overseas markets assumed a higher importance. These markets, after all, could be opened only by American groups large enough to compete with the powerful industrial combines of Europe. The Edge Act of 1919 provided similar privileges for American bankers, and for the same reasons.

In all, it was a beautifully integrated program. The key was restoring vitality and competition at home by exporting goods, political ideals, and morality abroad. The government was to play a central role, creating new agencies and laws for the benefit of various exporters. This was hardly traditional "free-enterprise" capitalism but, as the Progressives understood, the rules of that game had become dangerously old-fashioned with the appearance of the Robber Barons, Populists, and the 1890s crisis. And if Progressive agencies did not do the job, there was always the Marine Corps.

## THE FAR EASTERN MERRY-GO-ROUND

Shortly after entering the White House, Wilson destroyed the China Consortium, which had been established by Taft and Knox, by allowing American bankers to leave the group. This did not signify an American retreat from Asia, however. Realizing that the Consortium was useless in maintaining the open door, Wilson attempted to devise an independent, go-it-alone approach to China that would provide American financial support unfettered by any European or Japanese controls. The President believed that this unilateral approach would build China to the point where Japan and Russia could no longer exploit it at will.

Wilson's first attempt at making his Progressivism work abroad never had a chance to succeed. The Chinese Revolution, which erupted in 1911, made a shamble of his policies, and the approach collapsed when World War I began in August 1914. Japan took advantage of the European struggle to seize German possessions (including the strategic Shantung Peninsula), then tried to impose the so-called "Twenty-one Demands" upon the Chinese. If China had acquiesced, these demands would not only have consolidated the Japanese hold on Manchuria, but also have given them economic and political concessions in China proper. Wilson strongly protested the demands, but it was British pressure and Chinese resistance that finally forced the Japanese to retreat. By 1917, as he prepared to go to war in Europe, Wilson had been ineffective in trying to roll back the Japanese.

During the summer of 1917 he had to come to terms with Japan. In the Lansing-Ishii agreement, Wilson agreed to observe Japan's "special" interests in China, a recognition that actually undercut the open-door principle in Manchuria. In return, the Japanese secretly promised that they would not take advantage of the world war to seek privileges in China that would abridge the rights or property of Americans and the Allied powers. That gave Wilson breathing space, but the lines had been drawn for a showdown with the Japanese after the war.

## ASH CANS AND THE ARMORY SHOW

The New York City Armory art show of 1913 was perhaps the greatest shock American culture felt in the twentieth century. The shock occurred because like all great art, the show, in the words of one observer, was "not only about art but about everything," including "politics, industry . . . and human values." For nearly a century American artists had painted idealized scenes of canyons, rivers, or people. The canyons and rivers had become polluted, and the people changed by industrialism, but the painters nevertheless had continued to draw the old, assuring scenes.

In 1900 a few men determined to change this. They shared a Progressive faith that by stripping away corruption and hypocrisy, Americans would see clearly and then save their republic. Some, like John Sloan and George Luks, worked as illustrators or cartoonists for newspapers, and so were

Inside the Armory.

Duchamp: *Nude Descending a Staircase, No. 2.*

Can School," and excluded them from polite art exhibitions.

In 1912 members of the "Ash Can School" and others excluded by art associations decided to hold an exhibition at the New York City Armory. This time they accompanied their work with recent European painting by Cubists, Expressionists, and Neo-impressionists. These new artists included Van Gogh, Cézanne, and Picasso, the fathers of twentieth-century art, whose pictures often showed unrecognizable or weirdly distorted forms, and were composed of violent, clashing colors. They differed as much from earlier painting as the New York City tenements differed from seventeenth-century English countrysides. Marcel Duchamp's *Nude Descending a Staircase, No. 2* symbolized the show, for the figure was unrecognizable (newspapers ran "Find the Nude" contests), while being dynamic and flowing. One critic called it: "Explosion in a Shingle Factory."

Theodore Roosevelt stormed through the exhibition, according to a witness, "waving his arms . . . pointing at pictures and saying 'That's not art! That's not art!' " But he wrote a moderate review, praising the more traditional American works. That was a misjudgment, for the Europeans overpowered American art. Even the "Ash Can School" called the European paintings too radical. Americans were particularly frightened by the European claim that art was not decoration, but a judgment on Western society and especially the fragmentation of the human spirit resulting from the

outside the dominant art traditions but in positions to witness the social problems. When art organizations refused to show their pictures, eight artists presented their own exhibition in 1908. As the titles demonstrated, these pictures depicted striking new subjects: Sloan's *Sunday, Women Drying Their Hair,* Luks's *The Wrestlers,* Everett Shinn's *Sixth Avenue Elevated [Train] after Midnight.* Some critics condemned them for "exhibiting our sores," denounced them as "The Ash

John Sloan: *Sunday, Woman Drying Their Hair*

industrial revolution. The artist now claimed total freedom to show this world. If the machine created a new environment, and if psychiatrists were discovering hidden motivations, then artists had to be free to show these new worlds in new ways. The Progressive "Ash Can School," European art proclaimed, might be too extreme for Americans, but it, like Progressivism itself, was too conservative to understand the twentieth century.

Such radical art has never been welcome in traditional societies. Nearly three hundred thousand Americans saw the thirteen hundred paintings in New York, Chicago, and Boston, but in Chicago art students burned in effigy the show's organizer as well as a copy of Matisse's *Blue Nude*. The exhibition, however, was applauded by others, especially women whose own drive for equality made them more sensitive to the new art's demands for freedom. The Armory Show shocked the United States into twentieth-century culture, while warning of a breakdown in Western culture itself, a breakdown made real in the horrors of World War I.

## MARINE CORPS PROGRESSIVISM

The open door was also closing in the Caribbean area, where Wilson and Secretary of State William Jennings Bryan vigorously excluded European powers. Wilson sought stability and control in the Caribbean, especially after the Panama Canal opened in 1914 and war broke out in Europe.

In 1914, for instance, Bryan signed a treaty with Nicaragua giving the United States rights to a future isthmian canal, bases on the Pacific, and the right to intervene in Nicaragua to protect these new interests. In Santo Domingo, Wilson mistakenly thought he had averted a revolution by holding an election in 1914. When the new government failed to show its friendship by extending financial favors to Americans, however, chaos

U.S. Marines with wounded Haitian prisoner, 1915.

developed, and Wilson finally sent the Marines in 1916 to control the country. The following year U.S. troops entered Cuba once again, remaining until 1921 in order to protect American-controlled sugar plantations, particularly from attacks by armed Cubans.

But it is Haiti that provides a case study of the tragedy of Wilsonian Progressive diplomacy. Black slaves had successfully revolted against France in 1801, making Haiti the oldest independent nation in the hemisphere except for the United States. In a population of 2 million the vast majority were small independent farmers, and more than 95 percent were illiterate. Politics were controlled by and for an elite, and presidential political life was about as violent as in American politics—between 1862 and 1914 three presidents were assassinated in each nation. Until 1910 the United States had displayed relatively little interest in Haiti. But then the harbor of Môle-Saint-Nicolas became attractive to the growing American Navy, and the Banque Nationale (the key financial institution in the country, controlled by French-German interests) fell into the hands of New York City bankers after a slight push had been given by the State Department.

The American bankers next sought to control the customs houses. Since these provided the government's main source of income, however, Haiti refused. The bankers went to Bryan, giving him false information about the impending dangers of revolution and European control if they did not have their way. The Secretary of State was hardly capable of making his own estimate. Both he and Wilson were largely ignorant of Latin American affairs, and both shared the racism that had influenced Roosevelt's diplomacy; when a New York banker tried to inform the Secretary of State about the language and culture of Haiti, Bryan could only utter with amazement, "Dear me, think of it! Niggers speaking French."

In 1915 the Haitian President was killed by a mob because of his supposed involvement with a mass murder of political opponents. Wilson seized on this disruption as an excuse for landing over three hundred Marines and sailors in July. The Haitian treasury was given to the bankers, while the United States gained control of the customs houses. The State Department succeeded in finding an acceptable president only after promising to use the Marines to protect him from his own countrymen. But still the Haitians fought back with guerrilla warfare in 1915 and again more massively in 1918–19. After Wilson imposed martial law, the American military killed over two thousand Haitians while losing sixteen Marines. In several major actions, Americans slaughtered their opponents rather than take prisoners.

Progressive diplomacy succeeded in tearing up Haiti's society by the roots. A 1918 constitution (written largely by Assistant Secretary of the Navy Franklin D. Roosevelt) legalized American economic interests and the military occupation. The principle of that occupation, which lasted until 1934, was stated by a United States officer in Haiti: "You can never

trust a nigger with a gun." Years later Americans had difficulty understanding why Haitians were impoverished and endured repressive dicta-
tors who received support from Washington.

## THE FIRST TWENTIETH-CENTURY REVOLUTION: MEXICO

Wilson's attempts to apply some of these methods to Mexico ended in
failure. In that nation the President encountered his first twentieth-century revolution, one of those upheavals that, because of their turmoil and
radical redistribution of power, gravely endangered the American hope
for orderly change. United States interests in Mexico were large. With the
help of dictator Porfirio Díaz, Americans had amassed holdings amount-
ing to between 1 and 2 billion dollars. Most of this investment was in
railroads, oil, and mines. During 1910–11 the aged Díaz surrendered to
the superior force of Francisco Madero, but when Madero threatened
foreign economic holdings, opposing forces under the control of General
Victoriano Huerta overthrew Madero. Huerta was strongly supported by
the American ambassador in Mexico City. Then, to the horror of the
ambassador and the world, Madero was murdered by Huerta's forces.

Entering the White House at this point, Wilson refused to accept
Huerta's methods, and his refusal became adamant as it appeared that
British oil interests were supporting the Mexican General. In fact, Wilson
would not recognize Huerta's government, thereby marking a historic
shift in American recognition policy. Before 1913 the United States had
recognized any government that controlled its country and agreed to meet
its international obligations. Wilson now insisted that the government
also be politically acceptable, that is, that it be elected through democratic procedures. The President threw his support to Venustiano Carranza, a military leader enjoying successes in northern Mexico. But when
Huerta did hold elections in late 1913, he himself won the presidency.

Deeply angry, Wilson redoubled his efforts to support Carranza and
cut off British aid to Huerta. Great Britain finally gave in to Wilson amid
the growing shadows of a European war, but only after the President
guaranteed that he would try to preserve British oil holdings in Mexico.
In mid-April 1914, on learning that a German ship was bringing supplies
to Huerta at Vera Cruz, Wilson landed troops to occupy the port. Mexican
cadets opened fire, and over three hundred Mexicans and nineteen Americans were killed. Wilson's display of force, and Carranza's steadily successful campaigns, finally forced Huerta to flee to Europe in August 1914.
When Carranza assumed power in Mexico City, however, Wilson discovered that, like his predecessors, the new ruler would make no deals with
the United States.

The President now searched for an alternative to Carranza and thought

Pershing leads troops across the Rio Grande and into Mexico, 1917; to his left,
Lt. George S. Patton.

that he had found his man in the notorious bandit Pancho Villa. But
Carranza succeeded in isolating Villa, then began preparations for a convention that would issue a revolutionary constitution promising agrarian
reform and the placing of all subsoil mineral rights (such as oil and mines)
in Mexican hands. Outmaneuvered by Carranza and spurned by Wilson,
Villa retaliated with attacks against American citizens, including the
killing of seventeen Americans in Columbus, New Mexico. In March 1916
Wilson insisted that U.S. troops be allowed into Mexico to capture Villa.
Carranza agreed most reluctantly, and was then horrified to discover that
an army of six thousand men under the command of General John J.
("Blackjack") Pershing was marching into his country. As the American
troops penetrated farther south, Carranza finally tried to stop them with
force. Forty Mexicans and twelve Americans lost their lives. Carranza
continued to refuse to listen to Wilson's demands for new elections and
protection of foreign holdings. The President, moreover, now faced the
much greater problem of American involvement in Europe.

   In early 1917 the last American troops left Mexico. Carranza issued
his constitution several months later. Wilson had utterly failed to control
the Mexican revolution. In a larger sense, he had also provided a preview
of how the United States would be unable to cope with later revolutions
in Russia, China, and Cuba.

# AMERICAN ENTRY INTO WORLD WAR I—FIRST PHASE

Wilson's immersion in the revolutions of China and Mexico was unfortunate, particularly since he had little experience in foreign policy before becoming President. His policies tended to emerge from an understanding of the marketplace requirements of the American industrial complex and his personal preferences for the order, stability, and gentlemanly processes that he associated with Anglo-Saxon institutions. As a young professor, he had venerated the British political system. When World War I exploded in August 1914, therefore, Wilson asked the impossible even of himself when he pleaded that the American people be "neutral in fact as well as in name" and "impartial in thought as well as in action." Within a year Wilson told Colonel House he "had never been sure that we ought not to take part in the conflict," especially if Germany appeared to be growing stronger. By that time, the United States was well down the road to war. The American approach to the conflict evolved through three phases.

The first occurred in 1914 and early 1915 when the Allies (Great Britain, France, and Russia) seriously discriminated against American and other neutral shipping by blockading the Central Powers (Germany and Austro-Hungary). The Allies mined shipping routes through the North Sea and forbade neutrals even from trading with other neutrals if the goods traded appeared to be heading ultimately for Germany. After extended negotiations the United States accepted these Allied policies.

Several factors shaped the American surrender. Since 1900 Germany, not England, had been viewed by American officials as the gravest military threat to United States interests in the Western Hemisphere. Once war broke out, moreover, England played on such fears by flooding the American press with stories of supposed German atrocities. The effect of this propaganda has probably been overestimated, but it intensified the sympathy most Americans already felt for England. On the official level, Washington's responses to London were written not by Wilson (who was grieving over the death of his first wife), but by Robert Lansing, Counselor to Bryan in the State Department. A former member of the New York City mercantile community that had strong economic and social ties with England, Lansing did not even pretend to be neutral. He later bragged that he weighted down the American protests with complex legal language that would prolong the dispute until Americans perceived that "German absolutism was a menace to their liberties and to democratic institutions everywhere. Fortunately this hope and effort were not in vain." But Lansing did not wholly have to fabricate a case for England. Judged by traditional international law, most of the British actions were not illegal.

Most important, however, the ultimate recourse against the British acts, short of war, would have been an American embargo on exports to England. This alternative was never seriously considered because, Wilson admitted, an embargo would be "a foolish one as it would restrict our plants." During the summer of 1914 the economy was already depressed. An embargo on exports, even on ammunition and other articles related to war, could gravely affect the American system. When Wilson made this assumption—that is, that the United States had to be able to carry on its large international trade with all the markets the British Navy would allow—he had ceased being neutral. The *Literary Digest* phrased this perfectly: "The idea generally held is that we are not our brother's keeper. We can make and sell what any nation wishes to order. . . . If it happens that only certain nations control the Atlantic, . . . that is not our fault or concern."

By early 1915 Great Britain and France were running short of money to pay for these American goods. During the early days of the war Wilson and Bryan had determined that no loans or credits could be issued by American bankers to either side, for "money was the worst of all contraband" in that it determined all other trade. That policy was completely undercut by the President's determination to keep overseas markets open. By late autumn of 1914 the administration agreed to turn its head away while bankers gave both Germany and the Allies credits, that is, money tagged for specific purchases in the United States. A year later, in August 1915, an intense debate within the Wilson Cabinet ended in permission for American bankers to float a half-billion-dollar loan to the Allies. The lid was completely off. By early 1917 Americans had provided $2½ billion in credits or loans to the Allies, and less than $300 million to the Central Powers. Wilson explained the necessity for this policy in 1916: "There is a moral obligation laid upon us to keep out of this war if possible. But by the same token there is a moral obligation laid upon us to keep free the courses of our commerce and of our finance."

## SECOND PHASE: SUBMARINES

Once Wilson accepted the British blockade, another major obstacle to American trade—German submarine warfare—arose. Unable to compete with British surface naval power by February 1915, the Germans launched a submarine campaign that hardly distinguished among armed ships of war, unarmed merchant ships, and transports carrying civilians. Americans found this relatively new mode of warfare full of horrors. They sharply distinguished between British blockades, in which the English could leisurely search suspected merchant ships, and German submarines, which (because their thin plates and light arms rendered them an easy target), could not surface to ask a ship to identify itself or evacuate civilians before sinking the ship. Nor did the British make Wilson's situation easier when they illegally flew American flags from some of their vessels.

Although the President warned that he would hold Germany to "strict accountability" for any underwater attacks on American shipping, he did little when an American was killed in the sinking of a U.S. tanker ship in March 1915. But on May 15 the British liner *Lusitania* went down with the loss of 1198 lives, including 128 Americans. Historians later discovered that the ship was carrying a large amount of ammunition from New York to London. Even had that been known at the time (and there is evidence the President did indeed know the *Lusitania* was carrying war materiel), Wilson doubtless would have sent the same strong protest to Berlin. When Germany seemed to snub this note, he sent one that threatened war. Secretary of State Bryan resigned over the dispatching of this second note, insisting that if Wilson protested so strongly against submarines, he should also wage a stronger fight against the British blockade, which threatened the Central Powers with starvation. Wilson refused to take that position, nor did the ensuing anti-German sentiment over the *Lusitania* make Americans more neutral. A leading Democratic newspaper editor wrote of Bryan's resignation, "Men have been shot and beheaded, even hanged, drawn and quartered, for treason less heinous." Bryan's departure removed the only relatively neutral member of Wilson's Cabinet. Lansing became Secretary of State.

Although the Germans finally promised not to attack passenger liners, they stepped up their attacks on merchant vessels. In February 1916 many Americans feared that the sinkings would soon pull the United States into war. Congress threatened to pass the McLemore Resolution warning Americans not to travel on belligerent ships, but Wilson waged an all-out effort to kill the measure, vowing that he would never "consent to any abridgement of the rights of American citizens in any respect." It was a brave statement, but his reaction further limited his alternatives. Refusing to restrict the rights of Americans to trade or travel in wartime, he would have to protect those rights.

Germany interpreted the wide support for the McLemore Resolution as proof of the American reluctance to go to war. Berlin did not change this view even after the uproar in the United States over the sensational discovery of German spies in 1915 and 1916 and the continuation of the submarine attacks. Then on March 24, 1916 an unarmed French passenger liner, the *Sussex*, was torpedoed and several Americans suffered injuries. This sinking marked a turning point in Wilson's diplomacy. He demanded that underwater attacks on both passenger and unarmed merchant vessels cease or the United States would have to go to war. Germany responded with the so-called *Sussex* pledge: it would sink no more such vessels until adequate search and safety procedures were carried out, but Germany asked that Wilson also issue a strong protest against the British blockade of Central Europe. The President ignored the German request. In obtaining the pledge, Wilson believed he had scored a significant diplomatic victory.

# THIRD PHASE: MAKING THE
# WORLD SAFE FOR DEMOCRACY

After receiving the *Sussex* pledge, Wilson pushed the submarine problem to the background and concentrated on devising a method of intervening in the war; he hoped to act as a mediator trusted by both sides. As early as 1915, he saw himself as the central figure in reconstructing a postwar world in accord with Progressive principles.

During the early months of the war, Colonel House journeyed twice to Europe in attempts to prepare the ground. House got nowhere with the Germans, who clearly perceived the American's pro-Allied bias; the British and French refused to cooperate because they believed they could win a military victory. In any event, Allied and Central Power peace terms were irreconcilable by late 1915. So much blood had already been shed that a compromise peace was not possible. The President's situation worsened in 1916. The British not only refused to ask for his mediation, but raised American anger by further restricting United States mail, goods, and passengers that had to travel through the war zones. Even House and Lansing became bitter at the British refusal to cooperate with Wilson.

In 1916 the President started out on a course more independent of the Allies. He had carefully laid the groundwork the year before with his "Preparedness" program that started the construction of new warships and armed additional men. In July 1916 he supported legislation for more warships and submarines. As he told House, "Let us build a navy bigger [than Great Britain's] and do what we please." This remark was not in the same spirit as the slogan "He kept us out of war," which Democrats were then spreading across the country to urge Wilson's reelection. But the President did not care for that slogan. During the presidential campaign he warned that Americans must help in the search for peace, for they could not "any longer remain neutral as against any wilful disturbance of the peace of the world." Throughout the year he elaborated on his idea, first revealed in May 1916, when he called for a "universal association of nations" that would carry out worldwide progressivism by creating global free trade, freedom of the seas, and stability through territorial guarantees.

Wilson's hopes for the postwar world became more urgent in June 1916 when the French, British, and Russians met secretly at the Paris Economic Conference to make plans for economic warfare against the United States. The Allies agreed on schemes for government-subsidized industries that would be able to compete against such American giants as U.S. Steel and Standard Oil, and they urged common higher tariffs to choke off American trade. When Wilson and Lansing learned of these agreements they drew up their own economic plans, but equally important, the President increasingly feared what might happen to American interests if the Allied nations won a total victory and then dictated a peace without his mediation. Such a victory could produce an overwhelmingly dominant power (such as Great Britain or Russia), which could dictate a peace that threatened both specific American global interests and, more generally, Wilson's hope for worldwide progressivism.

But the President was given little choice. A month after his reelection, Germany decided to wage all-out submarine warfare, even if such a policy brought the United States into the war. German war aims had grown with the length and bloodshed of war until only a quick military victory could obtain those prizes—neutralization of Belgium, annexation of French territory, naval bases in the Atlantic and Pacific, perhaps even economic reparations from the Allies. The German Navy confidently told the Kaiser, "England will lie on the ground in six months, before a single American has set foot on the continent."

Learning of this decision, Wilson went before Congress on January 22, 1917, in a last dramatic attempt to preserve his role as a neutral broker in the postwar peace. Urging a "peace without victory," the President again urged "not a balance of power" (by which he meant a world comprised of exclusive, closed blocs of nations), but "a community of power" that would be open to all. The Allies responded with cynicism, and on January 31 the German underwater warfare began.

But Wilson continued to stall and would not move to declare war for two months. He feared above all that taking the United States into the conflict would guarantee an overwhelming Allied victory, ruin his own hopes of acting as a mediator, and help ensure the carrying out of the Paris Economic Conference's plans. Wilson worried, moreover, that American entry would decimate the "white civilization" needed to rebuild the postwar world, while allowing the "yellow race—Japan, for instance, in alliance with Russia," to exclude the United States from China. That was an exclusion Wilson swore he would never allow.

The President also encountered determined antiwar opposition led by Republican Progressive Senators Robert La Follette of Wisconsin and William Borah of Idaho. Since 1900 a small band of Progressives had vigorously opposed the use of military intervention by Roosevelt, Taft, and Wilson, particularly since foreign involvements could take the nation's attention off domestic reforms. They now also feared that entry into war could tie Americans into a power structure that would force the United States to support European empires and to fight wars for European, not American, interests. On March 1 the antiwar group suffered a severe defeat with the publication of the Zimmermann telegram. British agents had intercepted and given to Wilson a note written by the German Foreign Minister, Arthur Zimmermann, which proposed to Mexico a Mexican-German alliance. If Mexico cooperated, Germany would help it retrieve the "lost provinces" of Texas, New Mexico, and Arizona, taken from Mexico in the 1840s. Newspapers headlined the telegram, and prowar sentiment flashed to new highs—especially in the Southwest. But despite

Senator Robert La Follette at the opening of Congress, 1917.

this sensation, antiwar voices were not stilled in Congress. Having no illusions that wars necessarily produce peace, 6 Senators and 50 Representatives voted against entering the conflict, while 82 Senators and 373 Congressmen supported Wilson's request for war.

As his nation finally entered the struggle, Wilson tried to preserve part of his status as a neutral by designating the United States an "Associated" power rather than as a full-fledged Allied nation, but this was equivalent to a hope of losing only part of one's virginity. The President went to war because Germany declared submarine warfare against the United States, but equally important, because American economic requirements, which had developed since 1914, left no alternative but to work with the Allies. Wilson rationalized that only by becoming a belligerent could he force Britain and France to open the world to the stabilizing influences of American Progressivism. As he explained privately, he had to participate in the war if he hoped to have a seat at the peace table rather than "shout through a crack in the door." So in April (appropriately, on Good Friday) he asked Americans to go to war to "make the world safe for democracy." Progressive diplomacy had once again ended in the use of military force, this time on a level never before seen in world history. Given the record of 1900 to 1917, too few Americans were asking whether Progressivism was safe for the world.

## Suggested Reading

The indispensable reference work is Richard Dean Burns, editor, *Guide to American Foreign Relations Since 1700* (1983). Start there. Important overviews are John Milton Cooper, Jr., *The Warrior and the Priest: Woodrow Wilson and Theodore Roosevelt* (1983); Lloyd Gardner's essay in Barton Bernstein, ed., *Towards a New Past* (1968); Richard D. Challener, *Admirals, Generals and American Foreign Policy, 1898–1914* (1973); Jerome Israel, ed., *Building the Organizational Society* (1972); and Robert E. Osgood, *Ideals and Self-Interest in America's Foreign Relations* (1953). The two standard works are Howard K. Beale's sweeping *Theodore Roosevelt and the Rise of America to World Power* (1956);' and Walter and Marie Scholes, *The Foreign Policies of the Taft Administration* (1970). For the conflicts in Asia, see Michael H. Hunt, *Manchuria in Chinese-American Relations, 1895–1911* (1973); Jerome Israel, *Progressivism and the Open Door* (1971); and William A. Williams, *American-Russian Relations, 1781–1947* (1952). Caribbean affairs are analyzed in Dana G. Munro, *Intervention and Dollar Diplomacy in the Caribbean, 1900–1914* (1964); but see Lester Langley's fine *The Banana Wars* (1983).

The standard biography is Arthur S. Link's magnificent multivolume study of Wilson; see especially *The New Freedom* (1956) on Mexico and China; and *The Struggle for Neutrality* (1960) and *Campaigns for Progressivism and Peace* (1965) for the entry into war. Two key essays are Lloyd Gardner's *Covenant With Power* (1984); and Martin J. Sklar, "Woodrow Wilson and the Political Economy of Modern United States Liberalism," *Studies on the Left* (1960), pp. 17–47. The Mexican Revolution is well analyzed in Peter Calvert, *The Mexican Revolution, 1910–1914* (1968); and Robert Freeman Smith, *The U.S. and Revolutionary Nationalism in Mexico, 1916–1932* (1972). For a stimulating analysis, see Lloyd Gardner, *Safe For Democracy* (1984). Besides Link and Munro, Caribbean policy is noted in Hans Schmidt, *The U.S. Occupation of Haiti, 1915–1934* (1971); David Healy, *Gunboat Diplomacy in the Wilson Era: The U.S. Navy in Haiti, 1915–1916* (1976), with fresh perspectives on both the Haitian and U.S. sides. Standard accounts of entry into war include Link's work; Ernest May's excellent *The World War and American Isolation* (1959); Ross Gregory, *The Origins of American Intervention . . .* (1971) is a good synthesis; and Kendrick A. Clements, *William Jennings Bryan* (1982).

On art and the Armory show, see: Meyer Shapiro, "Rebellion in Art," in Daniel Aaron, ed., *America in Crisis* (1952); and Milton W. Brown, *American Painting from the Armory Show to the Depression* (1955).

World War I poster.

# 1917–1920

## The Failure of World War I

When Woodrow Wilson addressed Congress in April 1917 he proclaimed that World War I would be fought for the cause of humanity, not for mere conquest. The President and his supporters justified U.S. intervention on the grounds that while Germany stood for reaction, the United States and its allies fought for liberalism. Confident that an American victory would make the world safe for their brand of democracy, Progressives also assumed that at home the war could be conducted in accord with their principles. Progressives had always valued efficiency, harmony, and the search for a "constructive social ideal." Now, many reasoned, wartime mobilization would be entrusted to the very experts in whom they had such confidence. Nagging social conflicts would be swept away in a wave of patriotic unity. The terrible realities of war soon shattered these expectations. Far from making the world safe for anything at all, the war undermined progressivism and unleashed revolutionary forces on an unparalleled scale.

## MOBILIZATION AND REFORM

A month after Wilson's war message, Walter Lippmann (an influential Progressive journalist) remarked that the nation stood "at the threshold of a collectivism which is greater than any as yet planned by the Socialist party." Few Progressives wanted to go quite that far, but most assumed that war would bring with it a substantial amount of economic regulation. Surely, they thought, the need to equip America's troops and provision her allies would allow the government no alternative. Wasteful economic competition would be ended and order would emerge from chaos. In fact, the war did enable Progressives to push through much of their remaining program, not only in the field of economic policy but also with regard to moral uplift and political reform. For a brief, euphoric moment Progressives imagined that the war served their own purposes. "Into a year has been packed the progress of a decade," one reformer exulted in 1918. Only gradually did it become apparent that, whatever the immediate accomplishments, World War I had exacted a frightful toll.

The War Industries Board served as the chief vehicle for directing the production and distribution of war materials. Created in July 1917 and headed after March 1918 by financier Bernard Baruch, the Board embodied several features of the business-government partnership envisioned by New Nationalist Progressives. One wartime administrator even termed Baruch the "supreme interpreter of the national good." Under his guidance the Board performed a variety of functions: it allocated scarce materials, coordinated purchasing, determined priorities, encouraged the development of new facilities, and fixed prices. It also standardized production to effect savings, and it occasionally granted exemption from the antitrust laws to promote efficiency. All of this usually gained the approval of businessmen. Indeed, the Board's central idea was later described as "industrial self-control for patriotic purposes." Patriotism, however, was not all that the Board had going for it. Businessmen cooperated because they respected Baruch (himself a highly successful Wall Street operator), were given a large role in deciding Board policy, and could almost always count on making a handsome profit from war orders.

The Wilson administration experimented with new policies to increase wartime food production. Because European nations relied heavily on American wheat and sugar exports, Food Administrator Herbert Hoover got farmers to bring additional land under cultivation by offering to purchase agricultural commodities at high prices. At the same time Hoover urged consumers to observe "wheatless," "meatless," and "porkless" days, and he also asked grocers to restrict each person's sugar ration to two pounds per month. Hoover ruled that restaurants could not serve bread until after the first course, and insisted that they put out small cubes of sugar rather than sugar bowls. Posters and billboards appeared everywhere with such slogans as "Food Will Win the War," "Serve Just Enough," and "Use All Left-Overs." Conserving food itself came to be known as "Hooverizing." Meanwhile, food exports nearly tripled during the war.

In two additional areas—fuel and transportation—the Wilson administration assumed far-reaching power. The Fuel Administration under Harry A. Garfield helped bring about a substantial increase in coal and oil production, in part by increasing the mechanization of mines. When a coal shortage threatened, Garfield ordered many factories producing civilian goods to close down for a few days and to observe subsequent "heatless" days as a conservation measure. In December 1917, faced with a massive transportation tie-up, the administration took over the railroads. William G. McAdoo, who headed the Railroad Administration, proceeded to integrate rail schedules, limit passenger traffic, modernize equipment, and increase the amount of uniform track gauge. Private owners continued to direct the trains, but as government functionaries they took directions from the Railroad Administration. The owners received a rental fee that guaranteed them a substantial return on their investment.

Besides encouraging these new techniques of industrial control, the war also paved the way for other reforms that Progressives had been demanding for years. For the first time the government interceded on behalf of trade unions. The War Labor Board supported the right of workers to unionize and bargain collectively, and it succeeded in obtaining the eight-hour day in many places. Even the steel industry, in which the twelve-hour day was traditional, adopted a plan under which men continued to work twelve hours but received time and a half for the extra four hours. A newly created U.S. Employment Service helped workers find war jobs. In 1919, the Labor Department established a Women's Bureau to protect the interests of women workers, a major goal of progressive reformers. The government, in addition, took pioneering steps in the fields of social insurance and public housing. The Military and Naval Insurance Act (1917) provided for the retraining of disabled veterans and established a voluntary insurance system under which families of servicemen received federal aid. Finally, a dream of reformers seemed to come true with the initiation of a public housing program for workers who had gone to cities in search of defense jobs in shipyards and munitions plants.

## PROHIBITION AND WOMAN SUFFRAGE

Progressives had always exhibited a keen concern with moral questions, and World War I gave the uplift forces a golden opportunity. Starting with the premise that men in uniform must be protected against veneral disease, social hygienists, with the support of the War Department, launched a successful campaign to shut down brothels in the vicinity of military bases. They adopted the motto "Men must live straight if they would shoot straight." The government's Committee on Women's Defense Work created a department for "Safeguarding Moral and Spiritual Forces" to preserve American purity. Lecturers from the YWCA traveled across the country, warning young women against the hazards of illicit love, attempting to foster "a higher standard of personal conduct and civil cleanliness," and exhorting their listeners to "Do Your Bit to Keep Him Fit." The obsession with cleanliness was sometimes carried quite far. One crusader noted that a boy who joined the army was "swept into a machine that requires cleanliness first, last, and all the time," and consequently became a person with "clean motives and higher desires."

The forces of moral uplift won by far their most important victory with the enactment of prohibition. Although prohibitionists had always put forth a variety of medical, moral, and social arguments, the war provided them with just the ammunition they needed. Since the manufacture of beer required barley, temperance seemed a means of food conservation. Since many brewers were German-Americans, temperance could be equated with Americanism. Since drunkenness lowered the efficiency of defense workers and the potential fighting ability of soldiers, temperance achieved the status of a patriotic necessity. Liquor manufacturers, said William Jennings Bryan, "would, if they could, make drunkards of the entire army and leave us defenseless before a foreign foe."

The year 1917 saw a form of creeping prohibitionism. In May the sale of liquor around military camps was forbidden. In December the alcoholic content of beer was reduced, and Congress passed the Eighteenth Amendment. Even before the Amendment was ratified in January 1919, a Prohibition Act (1918) outlawed the sale of all intoxicating beverages. Elated by their success, some reformers believed that World War I might yet make the world safe for teetotallers. A speaker at an Anti-Saloon League Convention proclaimed, "With America leading the way, with faith in Omnipotent God, and bearing with patriotic hands our stainless flag, . . . we will soon . . . bestow upon mankind the priceless gift of World Prohibition."

Finally the war helped Progressives win the battle for woman suffrage. By the time the United States entered the war women had gained the vote in eleven states. In 1917, however, the House had defeated a constitutional amendment that would have given women the vote, and the suffrage movement seemed stalled. Its forces, moreover, were now divided. A dissident wing, inspired by English suffragists and led by a Quaker, Alice Paul, had broken off to form the "Woman's Party." Attacking the party in power, as English suffragists did, the Woman's Party adopted militant tactics such as picketing the White House, much to the dismay of the majority of suffragists. But war also brought new benefits by enabling the suffrage movement to gain the momentum it had sought for half a century. The incongruity of fighting a war for democracy while denying the vote to half the population—at the very time that women were playing an increasingly essential part in industry—suddenly became too painful. Besides, many claimed that women possessed nuturing qualities of tenderness and mercy that a war-ravaged world desperately required. Even Charlotte Perkins Gilman, a feminist who always stressed the "human qualities" men and women shared, believed that "the basic feminine impulse is to gather, to put together, to construct; the basic masculine impulse to scatter, to disseminate, to destroy." Suffrage leader Carrie Chapman Catt was more pragmatic. In 1917, she announced that she did not know whether the vote was a right, a duty, or a privilege, but "whatever it is, women want it."

In 1917 six states—including New York, Ohio, Indiana, and Michigan—gave the vote to women; in January 1918 the House adopted the suffrage amendment. By then Woodrow Wilson had finally come over to the side of suffrage. He began to define it as a war measure, "an essential psychological element in the conduct of the war for democracy." For a time Southern Democrats, who apparently feared that enfranchising women might set a precedent for protecting the right of blacks to vote, helped block action by the Senate. But in 1919 the Nineteenth Amendment obtained the needed congressional majority and a year later became law when ratified by three-fourths of the states.

# PROPAGANDA AND POLITICS

Although the war smoothed the passage of political, moral, and economic reforms long sought by Progressives, it also led to government actions that conflicted sharply with Progressive values. Perhaps the best example of this was wartime propaganda. More than anything else progressivism meant faith in an informed citizenry and a conviction that government should assist in the educative process. In its search for wartime unity, however, the Wilson administration conducted a massive propaganda campaign, one designed to inspire rather than to instruct. The Committee on Public Information under George Creel published millions of pamphlets, all hammering home the same message: the forces of a peace-loving democracy were pitted against those of a war-crazed autocracy. The Creel Committee recruited seventy-five thousand "Four Minute Men" who, in some 7.5 million speeches at theaters, clubs, and churches, described German atrocities and urged people to buy Liberty Bonds. One pamphlet, written for the CPI by a professor at Stanford University, predicted the consequences of a hypothetical enemy invasion: German soldiers would "pillage and burn," demand huge sums of money, execute anyone who refused to cooperate, and then "look on and laugh" while a priest and minister were "thrown into a pig-sty." "This is not just a snappy story," the author concluded. "Every horrible detail is just what the German troops have done in Belgium and France."

The war injected new issues into politics that badly shook Wilson's electoral coalition. Economic and manpower policies, for example, gave rise to sharp sectional rivalry. Because the administration imposed controls on wheat but not on cotton prices, Democrats representing midwestern wheat growers charged that Wilson unfairly favored the South. Democrats from the South and West called for stiffer corporation taxes and complained that the administration, under the influence of the party's Eastern wing, was coddling war profiteers. Many Southern Democrats opposed Wilson on the issue of conscription. They asserted that volunteers would make better soldiers and that a draft would "saturate the country with undemocratic and liberal influences, with the overbearing spirit of West Point and Annapolis." Although conscription bills passed in 1917 and 1918, with the result that 24 million men registered and 3 million were drafted (along with 1.8 million volunteers), Democrats in Congress were sharply divided.

Not only did the war distort certain Progressive principles and disrupt Wilson's coalition, but it gradually eroded the reformers' confidence in progress, rationality, and order. With the western world in flames, with senseless slaughter occurring daily and national passions aroused beyond all reason, it became increasingly difficult to sustain the old faith in the perfectability of either people or institutions. If this were not serious enough, Progressives' confidence in Wilson's policies and in their own ability to control events was badly shaken by the administration's response to war-time dissent and to the Russian Revolution.

## CURBING DISSENT: WHY

In November 1917 the motion picture *The Spirit of '76,* which depicted various atrocities committed by British soldiers during the American Revolution, played in Los Angeles. The film was seized and the producer indicted under the Espionage Act, for in 1917 England was an ally. The judge conceded that "history is history and fact is fact," but added that the film tended to "question the good faith of our ally, Great Britain." In the case, known as *U.S. v. The Spirit of '76,* he sentenced the producer to a $10,000 fine and a ten-year prison term (later commuted to three years). Although extreme, this was not an atypical case. During World War I the government imposed harsh restrictions on the expression of antiwar opinion; and when official action was not swift enough to suit the public, vigilante groups took matters into their own hands. The targets of repression were radicals who opposed the war, pacifists who opposed all wars, and German-Americans and other immigrant groups who were suspected of having a divided allegiance.

The amount of dissent a nation tolerates in wartime is usually proportional to the internal threat it perceives. In 1917 many Americans felt a keen sense of peril from within because of the nation's very heterogeneity. In the preceding twenty-five years nearly 18 million immigrants had come to the United States, most of them from countries involved in the war. One of every three Americans at the time was either an immigrant or the child of an immigrant. Many people, who imagined that the newcomers retained Old World loyalties, feared that entering the war with a divided populace would destroy the bonds of social cohesion. Wilson himself had once warned of the danger that Americans might be divided into "camps of hostile opinion, hot against each other." For those plagued by fears of disunity, war created a grave threat.

Such fears led to different sorts of defensive reactions. Some tried to extinguish manifestations of German culture: several state legislatures eliminated the "Kaiser's tongue" from school curricula, a few universities revoked honorary degrees bestowed in the past on noted Germans, and a town in Oklahoma even burned German-language books as part of a Fourth of July celebration. These actions went along with a virulent attack on "the German mind" for its "reversions to grossness, coarseness, and bestiality." Others revealed their fears by insisting on a formal observance of patriotic ritual. Mobs often forced people who had criticized the war to buy Liberty Bonds, to sing the national anthem in public, or even to kiss the American flag, presumably with the proper ardor.

For those who were not satisfied with symbolic acts of conformity there remained yet another possibility—joining a patriotic organization. The war led to a blossoming of groups such as the Home Defense League, the Knights of Liberty, the Sedition Slammers, and the Terrible Threateners. By far the largest and most energetic, however, was the American Protective League. With a membership that eventually climbed to two hundred fifty thousand, the League pried into people's opinions and checked on who was buying war bonds. To uncover "slackers," the League stopped men on the street and demanded that they produce their draft cards. Emerson Hough's *The Web* (1919), the League's official history, perfectly conveyed its sense of alarm: "No loyal American was safe. We did not know who were the disloyal Americans. We faced an army of masked men. They outnumbered us. . . ." The League enjoyed quasiofficial status. Its stationery read "Organized With the Approval and Operating Under the Department of Justice of the U.S."; its members received cards identifying them as federal agents; and in May 1918 the Attorney General named it an "Auxiliary to the Justice Department."

In addition to this widespread feeling of insecurity, the behavior of government officials fanned the flames of repression. Woodrow Wilson considered dissent dangerously disruptive, and he regarded the Socialist leader Eugene V. Debs and other antiwar spokesmen as little better than traitors. George Creel, admittedly not the most impartial witness, quoted Wilson to the effect that free speech in wartime was "insanity." Unable to give personal attention to each civil liberties case, Wilson delegated broad responsibility to members of his Cabinet and usually stood by their decisions. Postmaster General Albert Burleson wanted to bar from the mails any publication that criticized the reasons for American entry into the conflict or said anything "to hamper and obstruct the Government in the prosecution of the war." Attorney General Thomas Gregory advised opponents of the war to seek mercy from God "for they need expect none from an outraged people and an avenging government." Gregory boasted that members of the American Protective League were "keeping an eye on disloyal individuals and making reports of disloyal utterances." On occasion Wilson would overrule his subordinates, as when Burleson barred an issue of the liberal journal *The Nation* from the mails. Also, such officials as Secretary of Labor William Wilson and Secretary of War Newton D. Baker held more libertarian views. But usually the Wilson administration cracked down on dissenters with little hesitation.

## SOCIALISTS AND PACIFISTS

It could do so in part because of the nature of the opposition to war. Not only were there relatively few war critics, but most were socialists, anarchists, or members of the Industrial Workers of the World, people on the margins of society who had little political or economic weight and who made convenient targets. The war, in fact, proved disastrous for the Socialist party, which had until then achieved a modest degree of success. In 1912 Debs had polled nine hundred thousand votes—6 percent of the total—in the presidential election. Even in 1916 the party received six hundred thousand votes, elected candidates to office in scores of cities and towns, and reached a wide audience through its press. But when the United States entered the war the Socialists, unlike their European counterparts, kept faith with the ideal of international proletarian solidarity. In April 1917 the party declared that the war benefited only the ruling classes and called on American workers to repudiate the government. It branded the declaration of war "a crime against the people of the United States and against the nations of the world. In all modern history there has been no war more unjustifiable."

This posture weakened the socialist movement for several reasons. Although most Socialists opposed the war, not all party leaders did. A small but influential segment, including Upton Sinclair, Charles Edward Russell, and Jack London, supported Wilson. Some went quite far: Algie M. Simons became Director of the Bureau of Literature of the Wisconsin Loyalty Legion, and John Spargo denounced the antiwar faction for "upholding the impudent claims of the guilty Hohenzollern dynasty." Not only did the war split Socialists into warring camps, but it linked the party in the public mind with treason and thereby robbed it of a good deal of its respectability. Finally, suppression broke the back of the party in some areas. Socialists found their literature barred from the mails, their headquarters wrecked, and their leaders indicted for sedition. Other developments at the time contributed to the party's decline. The Russian Revolution, for example, caused a bitter division between those who wanted to apply Lenin's tactics to the United States and those who, while friendly to the Bolsheviks, denied that it was possible to "transfer Russia to America." But the war itself was crucially important in weakening the Socialists.

Like the Socialist party, the women's movement also divided on the issue of war. Women reformers had long been committed to pacifism. In 1915, a coalition of delegates from women's organizations formed the Woman's Peace party, led by Jane Addams and Carrie Chapman Catt. "As human beings and the mother half of humanity," the party platform declared, women demanded the right to be consulted in national affairs. Once the United States entered World War I, the Peace party splintered and women's pacifist efforts disintegrated. The woman suffrage movement, which supported the war, took the opportunity to prove its patriotic fervor. Clubwomen similarly joined the war effort by selling war bonds and running canteens. A Committee on Women's Defense Work, led by suffragist Anna Howard Shaw, coordinated volunteer jobs. But there were dissidents. Pacifist and feminist Crystal Eastman led a remnant of the Woman's Peace party that campaigned against American policy. Some women socialists maintained their opposition to the war. Members of the Woman's Party continued to demonstrate against "Kaiser Wilson," and when arrested, went on hunger strikes. When Jane Addams persisted in her defiant campaign for peace, dismay quickly turned to damnation. "My dear Miss Addams, believe me you are an awful ass, truly awful," wrote a wartime critic.

For pacifists less resolute than Addams, the war produced a crisis of conscience. In an atmosphere in which an ordinarily tolerant man like attorney Clarence Darrow could remark that "the pacifist speaks with the German accent," and in which conscientious objectors were labeled parasites whose liberties were being preserved by others on the battlefield, it is not surprising that many pacifists recanted. In 1916 the American Peace Society declared that Jesus Christ was a pacifist; in 1917 it backed the war. More than one hundred prominent Quakers announced their "loyalty to the Cause of Civilization, and to the President of the United States."

For those conscientious objectors who stood by their convictions the government made provisions of a sort. The Selective Service Act of 1917 exempted from combat service members of recognized religious sects whose teachings forbade participation in war. These men had to register for the draft and accept induction as noncombatants in the medical, engineering, or quartermaster corps. Of the 24 million registrants, 65,000 requested this classification. Only 21,000 were actually inducted, but fewer than four thousand of them made use of their noncombatant status. The rest apparently took up arms. Approximately five hundred men who refused to cooperate in any way, or whose opposition to the war rested on political grounds and did not qualify them for consideration, were sent to jail; the last was not freed until 1933. In all, the number of conscientious objectors never approached the number of draft dodgers, which the War Department estimated at 171,000.

## CURBING DISSENT: HOW

The Wilson administration launched a three-pronged assault on dissenters. First, it attempted to deport radical aliens. Existing laws already excluded immigrants who favored the forcible overthrow of the government. Immigration acts of 1917 and 1918 tightened these provisions and gave the government additional power to deport aliens who advocated the destruction of private property or who belonged to organizations that worked for revolution. No trial was needed. Deportation could be accomplished through an administrative proceeding. Second, the government dispatched troops to break strikes led by the Industrial Workers of the World in lumber camps in Washington and in copper mines in Montana. The IWW, which had since its creation in 1905 rejected bread-and-butter unionism and called for revolution, made no secret of its opposition to the war. One of its songs, a parody of "Onward Christian Soldiers," included the lines, "Onward Christian soldiers, rip and tear and smite/Let the gentle Jesus bless your dynamite." Claiming that the IWW engaged in sabotage and that it instigated strikes, not to improve working conditions, but to cripple war production, the government threw union leaders into jail and held them for months on the flimsiest of evidence or on no charge at all.

The third and most widely used weapon to curb dissent was prosecution under the Espionage Act (1917) and the Sedition Act (1918). The Espionage Act made it a crime to obstruct military recruitment, and it authorized the Postmaster General to deny mailing privileges to any material he considered treasonous. Under its terms Burleson barred dozens of periodicals, including an issue of *The Masses*, which had a cartoon captioned "Making the World Safe for Capitalism," and an issue of *The Freeman's Journal and Catholic Register*, which cited Thomas Jefferson's opinion that England should grant Ireland independence. Eugene Debs was convicted under the Espionage Act for making a speech that condemned the administration's war policies and its violations of civil liberties. When the Supreme Court upheld his conviction, Debs spent two and one-half years in jail. His comrade, Kate Richards O'Hare, was indicted for allegedly saying that any man who enlisted in the army "would be used for fertilizer" and that women who allowed their sons to enlist were "nothing more nor less than brood-sows." Although she denied having made the statements, O'Hare, a victim of wartime hysteria, served fourteen months in the penitentiary.

In the spring of 1918, as reports of mob violence against radicals reached Washington, the Wilson administration decided to support a Sedition Act in the hope that such a measure would calm public apprehension. After listening to speeches about "pernicious vermin" and "poison dark spreaders of revolution," Congress passed the act. One congressman regretted only that it did not carry the death penalty. The Sedition Act made it illegal to "utter, print, write, or publish any disloyal, profane, scurrilous, or abusive language" about the government, the Constitution, the flag, the armed forces, or even the "uniform of the Army or Navy." Ultimately, more than one thousand persons were convicted under the Espionage and Sedition Acts, including more than one hundred members of the IWW who, President Wilson noted privately, "certainly are worthy of being suppressed."

The Supreme Court ultimately approved these wartime prosecutions. In *Schenck* v. *United States* (1919) a unanimous Court found that a socialist who had mailed circulars to men eligible for the draft, circulars stating that conscription was unconstitutional and should be resisted, had violated the Espionage Act by interfering with the legitimate power of the government to raise an army. Oliver Wendell Holmes, Jr., who delivered the opinion, tried to define the boundaries of permissible speech. The question, Holmes said, "is whether the words used are used in such circumstances and are of such a nature as to create a clear and present danger that they will bring about the substantive evils that Congress has a right to prevent. It is a question of proximity and degree." In *Abrams* v. *United States* (1919) the Court found the Sedition Act constitutional. Jacob Abrams, an anarchist, and several of his friends had distributed leaflets in August 1918 condemning American intervention in the Soviet Union and calling on munitions workers to strike in protest. The government contended that such a strike would also interere with the conduct of the war against Germany. The Court upheld the convictions, but Holmes now dissented, asserting that "the best test of truth is the power of the thought to get itself accepted in the competition of the market."

The suppression of free speech had both predictable and unforeseen consequences. It seriously weakened the radical movement. Indeed, groups were sometimes singled out not only for their antiwar stand but precisely because of their radicalism. For example, the war furnished employers who had always hated the IWW with a patriotic pretext for attacking it. But restrictions on civil liberties also dismayed many Progressives who, though they supported the war, believed that the Wilson administration had gone overboard in curbing individual rights. The crusade for conformity also substantiated the argument of intellectuals, like Randolph Bourne, who rejected all along the notion that war could be directed toward humane ends. War was an inexorable situation, Bourne reasoned, in which the government would do anything it thought necessary to achieve victory. Intellectuals who believed that war could be "moulded toward liberal purposes" were therefore deceiving themselves. The attack on civil liberties, as much as anything else, proved Bourne correct.

## ANOTHER REVOLUTION

If the war profoundly affected Americans, it was because, as Bourne observed, they expected too much from the conflict, not because—as compared with the other belligerents—they sacrificed too much for it. The growing American disillusionment with Russia was an excellent example. In March the Russian people, bankrupt and bled to the breaking point, overthrew the hollow, corrupt regime of Czar Nicholas II. The Czar was replaced with a liberal republic headed by Prince G. E. Lvov. President Wilson welcomed the new government, particularly after Lvov promised to keep Russia in the war whatever the cost. The change of government confirmed Wilson's faith that democracy, not authoritarianism, would shape the future. By summer 1917, however, the war continued to take its murderous toll of the dispirited, inefficient Russian army. The slow collapse of Lvov's regime allowed a corresponding rise in the power

Oliver Wendell Holmes, Jr.

of V. I. Lenin, a Communist leader who had recently returned to Russia from Switzerland. Disillusionment with Lvov's inept policies resulted in July in a new, more conservative regime headed by Alexander Kerensky. The Kerensky government refused to listen to Lenin's demands for withdrawing Russia from the war.

Wilson closely followed these events. He even appointed a special commission to visit Russia during the summer. The commission's report was optimistic, a mood shared by neither Wilson, nor, particularly, by Secretary of State Lansing, who was convinced the Russians were not merely replaying the moderate American upheaval of 1776 but sailing straight into another bloody French Revolution. This view was confirmed on November 7, 1917, when Lenin's Bolsheviks overthrew the Kerensky regime. Wilson's and Lansing's pessimism turned to hatred as Lenin began confiscating private property, radically redistributing political power, proclaiming the need for worldwide revolution, and in March 1918 making peace with Germany. The Bolsheviks "are avowedly opposed to every government on earth," Lansing privately exclaimed. He hoped they would "go to pieces," but doubted this would occur, for "their cry of 'Peace and Land' is popular with the ignorant Russians who have suffered grievously in the past." Wilson's and Lansing's fear of Lenin, however, did not get in the way of their understanding that the Bolsheviks fundamentally challenged Western "political institutions as they now exist and [are] based on nationality and private property," in Lansing's words. Lenin threatened Wilson's entire postwar program. The President did not dismiss this threat by accepting the popular belief that the Soviet leader was an agent installed by Germany to take Russia out of the war. Wilson realized that for the first time he faced a fundamental danger from the left.

His Fourteen Points speech of January 1918—which became one of the famous speeches in American history—was Wilson's first response to Lenin. The President's program was to be both a cure and a preventive for Bolshevism—a cure in that he hoped to offer an alternative program that would win over left-wing parties in Europe, and a preventive in that he planned to create a new world system that would provide immunity against another world war. The key was Wilson's attempt to replace the old balance-of-power diplomacy (that is, a diplomacy dominated by several great powers) with a concert of many nations that he hoped would keep the world system fluid and open to all who could compete. Since the United States was becoming rich and powerful militarily as a result of the war, Wilson also knew that Americans would be able to compete wonderfully well in the world system he was proposing. These two motives, the fear of Bolshevism and the desire for American postwar economic expansion, explained why the Fourteen Points speech demanded open convenants openly arrived at; freedom of the seas in peace and for neutrals in war; the removal of tariffs, trade preferences, and other economic barriers; reduction of armaments; self-determination as a political principle; recognition of a Russia that would be a reasonable neighbor (to Wilson this obviously meant a non-Communist neighbor); and, finally, "a general Association of Nations" that would uphold all of these principles.

Not even Wilson's allies would accept the entire program. At the Paris Economic Conference of 1916, for example, they planned for closed economic blocs that would keep ambitious Americans out of British, French, and Italian markets. Great Britain, France, and Czarist Russia, moreover, had signed secret agreements with Japan and Italy that promised territorial and economic booty from the war if they maintained a common front against Germany. Wilson knew about these treaties because Lenin had gleefully published them. The President also understood that they ran directly against his self-determination principle. In order to keep Japan away from China while American attention was on Europe, Wilson had even neglected several of his own points by negotiating a secret deal with Japan in which the United States agreed to recognize Japan's "special" interests in China. Tokyo officials in turn promised not to use the war as a cover for seizing "special rights or privileges in China." The President knew that this pact (the Lansing-Ishii agreement of November 1917) might later be used by Japan to claim special interests in Manchuria, but Wilson believed that at a postwar conference his own moral stature and his nation's mushrooming economic power would overcome the Allied and Japanese plans. The Bolsheviks, however, were another matter.

## INTERVENING IN THE SOVIET REVOLUTION

Lenin's government seemed to be beyond Wilson's control. As the American humorist Peter Finley Dunne once observed, a revolution cannot be bound by the rules of the game, for it is rebelling against those rules. The President was therefore open to demands by the British and French that he join them in intervening militarily in Russia to overthrow the Bolsheviks and reopen the eastern war front. At first Wilson refused, in part because of opposition from young liberals in the State Department who were led by William Bullitt. A handsome, ambitious, aristocratic Philadelphian, Bullitt argued that Leninism could be destroyed only if Wilson moved farther to the left politically and undercut the Bolshevik program.

The President rejected such advice. He refused to go beyond the Fourteen Points, and in June 1918 agreed to land Americans at Murmansk in northern Russia. The landing was made in cooperation with the French and British troops. The Japanese then moved into Siberia, threatening to control the vital Trans-Siberian railway system while disguising their takeover as "anti-Bolshevism." In July Wilson sent ten thousand troops to Vladivostok in Siberia, then established an American-controlled group to run the railways. He thus assumed responsibility in that far-off part of the world to stand guard against both Japanese and Bolsheviks. Making the world safe for democracy obviously was becoming a big job.

Wilson publicly justified the intervention in Murmansk on military-strategic grounds, but within days the Allied forces were fighting Bolsheviks, not Germans. The American force remained there, moreover, until June 1919, nearly eight months after the war ended. The President excused the Vladivostok operation by arguing that he hoped to help some sixty thousand Czech soldiers, who had been fighting Germany and now apparently wanted to escape through Vladivostok to fight on the Western front. When the Americans landed, however, the Czechs were fighting Bolsheviks. The United States protected the rear of the Czech forces as they waged their battle, and also supported White Russian troops that were trying to overthrow Lenin. The American soldiers remained in Siberia until April 1920.

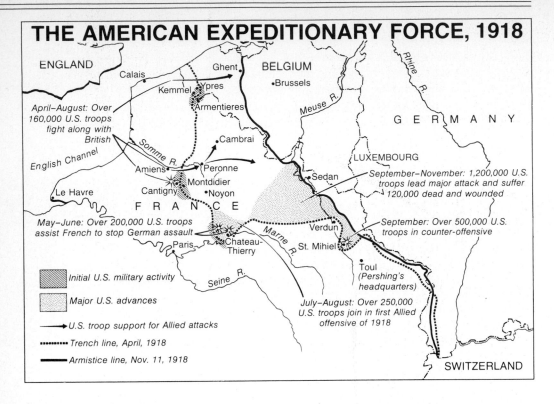

# THE AMERICAN EXPEDITIONARY FORCE, 1918

ENGLAND

Calais

April–August: Over 160,000 U.S. troops fight along with British

English Channel

Le Havre

Ghent

Kemmel Ypres

Armentieres

BELGIUM

•Brussels

Meuse R.

Rhine R.

GERMANY

LUXEMBOURG

Somme R.

•Cambrai

Amiens•    •Peronne

Cantigny  Montdidier
          •Noyon

F R A N C E

May–June: Over 200,000 U.S. troops assist French to stop German assault

Paris

Chateau-
Thierry

Marne R.

Sedan

Verdun

St. Mihiel

Seine R.

•Toul
(Pershing's
headquarters)

September–November: 1,200,000 U.S. troops lead major attack and suffer 120,000 dead and wounded

September: Over 500,000 U.S. troops in counter-offensive

July–August: Over 250,000 U.S. troops join in first Allied offensive of 1918

SWITZERLAND

Initial U.S. military activity

Major U.S. advances

U.S. troop support for Allied attacks

Trench line, April, 1918

Armistice line, Nov. 11, 1918

The interventions made little sense in the overall war effort. They were crucial, however, if Wilson hoped to extinguish the Communist regime and keep Siberia out of Japanese hands. As Secretary of War Newton D. Baker candidly remarked in September 1919, American troops remained in Siberia because withdrawal would leave the area "open to anarchy, bloodshed and Bolshevism." But Wilson failed to overthrow Lenin. The President only worsened an already poisonous relationship between Russia and the West. The President fully realized the dilemma. In 1919 he declared that using troops to stop a revolution was "like using a broom to hold back a great ocean." He nonetheless tried the broom, for as a Progressive dealing with revolution he could see no better alternative.

## THE YANKS IN EUROPE

A central problem for Wilson was that he had to watch closely not only Germans, Bolsheviks, and Japanese but also his European allies. The political relationship with London and Paris, already strained by the Fourteen Points speech, was not improved by the timing and nature of the American military effort.

No major United States force landed in France until eight months after Wilson's war message of April 1917. Not until the spring of 1918 did Americans decisively affect the fighting. But they were then pivotal in turning back a major German offensive just forty miles from Paris. The Americans won a major victory at Chateau Thierry, a triumph that Wilson mistakenly thought would put the French in his debt at the postwar peace conference, and then drove the Germans back along the southern front until Berlin asked for peace in November 1918.

The Yanks had arrived none too early, for throughout 1917 and early 1918 the Allies nearly bled themselves to death. In one offensive alone they expended more than a half million lives to move the battle line several miles. An entire generation of Europeans was being exterminated. Nearly 3 million Allied soldiers lost their lives, probably 10 million people were slaughtered in all, but of this number only 52,000 were Americans. These figures help explain why British and French leaders were so driven by hatred for Germany at the peace conference in 1919, and why they scorned Wilson's pleas for moderation. Such feelings, combined with the President's great reluctance to place American troops under European commanders and his refusal to participate fully in several war-time planning conferences, did not augur well for the peace conference. But then the problems Wilson was enduring at home were also ominous for his postwar plans.

## 1919: RED SCARE

In 1919, as peace came to Europe, industrial warfare flared in the United States. That year more than 4 million workers took part in 3600 strikes. Most of the walkouts had similar causes. Workers who had won union recognition and improved their conditions during the war now attempted to solidify or extend those gains. It seemed essential to do so because wages were lagging behind rising prices, and many workers feared that they could lose their jobs as factories converted back to civilian production. Employers, however, wanted to withdraw many of the concessions made during the war; consequently, they often refused even to negotiate. All of this took place in the wake of the widespread anxiety aroused by the Russian Revolution. Although only a few strikes were led by radicals and none had radical objectives, employers, hoping to capture public opinion, claimed that labor turmoil posed a revolutionary threat.

Two of these disturbances—the Seattle general strike and the Boston police strike—seemed in particular to endanger law and order. In January 1919, when Seattle shipyard workers struck for higher wages, unions throughout the city voted to walk out in support. Although the unions set up a committee that attempted to provide essential health services, many viewed the general strike, in the words of one presidential advisor, as "the first appearance of the Soviet in this country." The government dispatched the Marines, the AFL leadership insisted that Seattle locals return to work, the mayor beefed up the police and issued an ultimatum. Under fierce pressure from all sides the strikers capitulated. Then, in September, policemen in Boston demanded the right to join a union, a right denied them by the police commissioner. A strike followed during which some theft and looting occurred. The reaction was intense. One newspaper declared that "Bolshevism in the U.S. is no longer a spectre"; the President branded the strike "a crime against civilization"; and Governor Calvin Coolidge of Massachusetts proclaimed that there was "no right to strike against the public safety by anybody, anywhere, anytime." The city dismissed everyone involved and recruited an entirely new police force.

In September 1919 the United States also faced the most massive industrial dispute in its history when 350,000 steel workers left the mills. The men, many of whom still worked twelve hours a day, seven days a week, wanted an AFL union recognized as bargaining agent. Indeed, pressure from the rank and file apparently forced the AFL to authorize a strike before it felt strong enough to sustain one. The owners, for their part, welcomed a showdown over the principle of the open shop. Judge Elbert Gary, the president of United States Steel, accurately reflected the opinion of management when he claimed that most workers were satisfied with their conditions, wanted nothing to do with the union, and were being misled by the "coercion, threats, insults or wild promises" of outside agitators. As in Boston and Seattle, charges of radicalism were hurled at the union leaders, particularly at William Z. Foster. A former syndicalist, Foster believed that unions, in achieving one small gain after another, would slowly erode the foundations of capitalism. In this case the union gained nothing at all. By January 1920, its resources exhausted by a long and costly struggle, the AFL called off the strike.

Belief in the imminence of revolution was shared by radicals who often talked and acted as if the United States were about to follow the Russian example. Communists in Chicago, for example, asserted that mass strikes would lead to a "proletarian dictatorship, which will crush the capitalist as the capitalist state now crushes the workers." Moreover, a series of bombings and attempted bombings in the spring of 1919 badly frightened the American people. In April a bomb was sent to the mayor of Seattle. Another, mailed to a Georgia politician, exploded, and the maid who opened the packaged lost both her hands. When the Post Office intercepted thirty-four identical parcels addressed to J. P. Morgan, John D. Rockefeller, and other prominent businessmen, and all were found to contain bombs, headlines blared: "REDS PLANNED MAY DAY MURDERS". In June bombs went off at approximately the same time in eight cities, adding to the fear that these acts were the work not of an individual but of a conspiracy. One of the bombs shattered windows in the home of Attorney General A. Mitchell Palmer.

As Americans felt increasingly threatened by the prospect of violent revolution, they hunted for preventive measures. No fewer than twenty-eight states passed peacetime sedition acts of some sort, under which fourteen hundred people were arrested and three hundred convicted. Legislatures sometimes refused to accept those who held unorthodox views. In November 1919 the House of Representatives refused to seat Milwaukee Socialist Victor Berger. When he won reelection the House again balked at accepting him. In January 1920 the New York State legislature expelled five Socialists, although most of them had held office during the war. States tried to uproot subversive influences by investigating public school teachers and requiring them to sign loyalty oaths. Congress further tightened the immigration laws in 1920 by providing for the deportation of aliens who merely possessed revolutionary literature.

The Red Scare reached its crescendo with the Palmer raids. Shaken by the bombing attempt on his home, Attorney General Palmer came to believe that "the blaze of revolution [is] sweeping over every American institution of law and order . . . burning up the foundations of society." Palmer, with the aid of other officials, worked out policies that effectively deprived radical aliens of due process. The Department of Justice launched surprise raids on the headquarters of radical organizations, seized correspondence and membership lists, detained suspects under astronomical bail, and cross-examined witnesses before they could obtain legal advice. To permit a radical alien to see an attorney before interrogation, J. Edgar Hoover of the Justice Department explained, "defeats the ends of justice." In the first week of January 1920 federal agents, employing these tactics, arrested three thousand alleged Communists in thirty-three cities. Many were imprisoned, although no charges were brought against them; 550 were later deported. Palmer's action violated every civil libertarian principle, but momentarily made him a national hero.

The wartime suppression of civil liberties differed in several respects from the postwar Red Scare. In the former Americans feared subversion, in the latter revolution. The target in 1917 was frequently the German-American; the target in 1919 was often organized labor. But in important ways the two episodes resembled each other. Both occurred because society felt threatened from within, both involved legal and extralegal forms of repression, both exploited anti-immigrant and antiradical sentiments. Each had a crippling effect on the American radical movement, which by 1920 was weak, fragmented, and in disarray. The Palmer raids, no less than wartime intolerance, angered many Progressives who condemned Wilson for permitting, if not actually encouraging, these excesses. By mid-1920 the Red Scare had run its course. With Communism clearly confined to Russia, with labor turmoil and bomb scares at an end, fears began to evaporate. The Wilson administration had won praise for its antiradical stance early in 1920, but had a more difficult time defending its record by the end of the year.

# BASEBALL: SPORT AND BUSINESS

Baseball has been America's National Pastime. It combines raw individual effort with precise team play, compiles masses of figures that excite statistic-loving Americans, has a long tradition that allows fans to link past heroes to the present, and is played during the school-free halcyon days of summer. Its complexity even makes it a favorite of intellectuals ("Baseball is a religion," a distinguished philosopher proclaimed in 1919).

The Sultan of Swat—Babe Ruth.

The game's roots go back to ancient Egypt. Modern American teams appeared in the 1840s, organized—as has been every popular American sport except basketball—by wealthy gentlemen in the Northeast. Nationally popular by the Civil War, the first professional team, the Cincinnati Red Stockings, formed in 1869. The National League appeared in 1876, the American League in 1901, and World Series competition between the two leagues began two years later. Baseball grew quickly at century's turn because of rapid urbanization, new street railways, and, particularly, increased leisure time created by the mechanization of farming and industry.

Equally important, the game was developed by men who viewed it as business, not sport. They organized it along the lines of such corporations as U.S. Steel. A division of labor existed between management and players, with owners monopolizing the athletes through a "reserve clause" that made players the property of a single club. Owners controlled their market by giving each team absolute rights over its own urban area. Supreme Court rulings meanwhile exempted baseball from antitrust laws (a benefit not even U.S. Steel received from the courts). Attendance rose dramatically. The value of some clubs multiplied ten times between 1900 and 1918. Then in 1919 members of the Chicago White Sox (soon tabbed the "Black Sox") were accused of accepting bribes to lose the 1919 World Series.

The sport was severely shaken. But

Judge Landis at opening of World Series, 1923.

three people managed to resurrect baseball so that it became the rage of sportsminded Americans. Kenesaw Mountain Landis, a tough U.S. District Court Judge, was brought in by the frightened owners to clean up the game. He did so brutally, even trying to ban players and owners from attending racetracks (where, Landis believed, lurked shadowy figures who "would sell out the Virgin Mary and their mother.") He ruled baseball until his death in 1944. The second savior was Babe Ruth of the Boston Red Sox and New York Yankees. His twenty-nine home runs in 1919 broke an 1884 record and revolutionized baseball by making it a game of exciting power. Son of a Baltimore barkeeper and a drunk at age eight, Ruth glamorously flouted Prohibition in the 1920s. He ordered the clubhouse boy to discard all letters except "those with checks or from broads." Landis was the puritanical Calvin Coolidge of baseball while Ruth was Babylonian America having an illegal and immoral—but wonderful—time.

The third figure was Branch Rickey, a religious, Ohio-born, sharp-eyed lawyer who developed the "farm system" whereby Major League clubs

Branch Rickey and Jackie Robinson at Dodgers' Florida camp.

developed their own players in minor leagues. This resembled Standard Oil's system of controlling its profitable product from the oil well to the filling station. The devout Rickey would not play ball on Sunday, but liked the player who "will break both your legs if you happen to be standing in his path to second base." His corporate techniques won championships at St. Louis, Brooklyn, and Pittsburgh. In 1947 he forced reluctant owners to allow the first black, Jackie Robinson, to play in the Majors.

Robinson's appearance marked the first of many changes. He was followed by such other black superstars as Willie Mays, Hank Aaron (who broke Ruth's all-time home run record), and Bob Gibson (who struck out more hitters than any other National League pitcher). In 1958 the fabled Brooklyn Dodgers deserted "Flatbush" and became the Los Angeles Dodgers as they made big league baseball a continental sport for the first time. And in the mid-1970s, the courts finally broke the owners' monopoly over their employees.

Players with a specific number of years of experience, the courts decided, could test their worth in the open market. Wealthy clubs, such as the Yankees, were accused of "buying championships" when they won pennants after paying millions to several such stars. These huge sums were made possible by steadily increasing attendance and lucrative television contracts. The sport prospered, but it had been a close call, for in the 1920s baseball had nearly struck out before Landis, Ruth, and Rickey stepped in to save it.

## 1919: BLACK SCARE

The postwar years were marked not only by labor turmoil but also by intense racial discord. In 1919 lynch mobs murdered 78 blacks, at least 10 of whom were veterans. From April to October race riots erupted in 25 cities—including Washington, D.C.; Omaha, Nebraska; and Longview, Texas—and claimed the lives of 120 people. The worst riot, during what came to be known as the "Red Summer," took place in Chicago; it left 38 dead and 537 injured. In truth, race riot was a less accurate term than race war. Marauding bands of whites and blacks, armed with guns and clubs, roamed the streets and hunted each other down. Racial turbulence, like the Red Scare, had its roots in postwar social and economic dislocations. The war had dramatically altered the position of black Americans and raised their expectations. When those expectations clashed with the ingrained prejudices of whites, the stage was set for the Red Summer.

World War I spurred a mass exodus of blacks from Southern farms to

Northern cities. In 1915 and 1916 floods and boll weevils ravaged crops in the cotton belt and forced many tenant farmers off the land. At about the same time, the war opened magnificent opportunities in the North. The demand for industrial labor seemed insatiable as factories were swamped with military orders, workers left their jobs for the army, and the flow of immigration from Europe came to a virtual halt. Black newspapers, particularly the Chicago *Defender,* encouraged migration by playing up the opportunities available to blacks in the North. Labor agents swept through the Southern states attempting to recruit black workers. Some companies even issued free railroad passes to anyone who promised to work for them. From 1916 to 1918, hundreds of thousands of blacks moved North. The black population of Chicago doubled in just four years.

For most, migration had a racial as well as an economic dimension. The letters written by migrants, and their behavior as well, reveal their sense of embarking on a pilgrimage out of bondage and into a promised land. "I am in the darkness of the south," said an Alabama black in explaining his request for train fare to Chicago; ". . . please help me to get out of this low down country [where] i am counted no more thin a dog." A group of blacks from Hattiesburg, Mississippi, on crossing the Ohio River, knelt, prayed, kissed the ground, and sang hymns of deliverance. The North, with its absence of legal segregation, surely afforded some an exhilarating sense of freedom. A black carpenter, who had moved to Chicago, wrote to his brother in Mississippi, "I should have been here 20 years ago. I just begun to feel like a man."

Most blacks genuinely believed that the war would usher in an era of social justice. The NAACP urged blacks to support the war by enlisting and buying bonds, for if they did, whites could no longer ignore their appeals for equality. A similar conviction led W. E. B. DuBois to advise blacks to "close our ranks shoulder to shoulder with our own white fellow citizens and the allied nations that are fighting for democracy." Several concessions made by the Wilson administration bolstered the prevailing optimism. Although the army remained rigidly segregated, the War Department established an officers' training camp for blacks, created a black combat division, and accepted blacks into medical units. The Railroad Administration, while preserving separate facilities for passengers, paid the same wages to white and black workers, and agreed to bargain with a black Pullman union. All this, in the context of 1918, represented progress.

The end of the war, however, disappointed the hopes of DuBois and the others. With the return of millions of veterans, competition for jobs and housing grew fierce. In 1919 blacks discovered that many of their wartime gains were vanishing into thin air. They were again the last hired and the first fired. They still paid the highest rents for the most squalid dwellings. The Wilson administration no longer showed the slightest interest in them. Disillusionment was profound. Nearly four hundred thousand blacks had served in the military, half of them in France where racial distinctions were less important. Then too, blacks who had left farms in Mississippi to work in iron foundries in Chicago were often free to express the bitterness they had formerly concealed. For the first time, a number of black spokesmen openly advocated the use of violence for purposes of self-defense. This heightened race consciousness coincided with heightened fears among whites—fears that blacks would drive down property values or, more generally, forget their "proper place."

The race riots should be viewed against this background of blacks and whites thrown together in cities, of competition for places to live and work, of increased black militancy and corresponding white anxiety. Though no two riots followed exactly the same pattern, there were some similarities. The riots, which usually broke out during a heat wave when tempers were on edge, were often triggered by rumors of an interracial assault. Once the rioting began, the police seldom acted impartially; rather, they treated blacks more brutally than whites. Both sides committed acts of violence. Usually whites were the aggressors, and blacks defended themselves by trading rifle fire with their foes and making sorties

Escorted by a policeman, blacks move their belongings to a safety zone during the race riots, Chicago, 1919.

into white neighborhoods. A few riots lasted a long time. It took thirteen days to restore order to Chicago. Invariably the riots left a legacy of bitterness and led not to mutual understanding but to a hardening of racial animosities.

Some Americans, seeking an explanation for the race riots, alleged that radicals stirred up the black community, and thereby linked the labor and racial turmoil of 1919. The *New York Times* thought it more than coincidental that the race riots in Chicago followed so soon after those in Washington, and guessed "that the bolshevist agitation has been extended among the Negroes." Attorney General Palmer submitted a report that made the point more sharply. Palmer criticized black leaders for their "ill-governed reaction toward race rioting," their "threat of retaliatory measures in connection with lynching," their "more openly expressed demand for social equality, in which the sex problem is not infrequently included," and their "identification of the Negro with such radical organizations as the IWW and an outspoken advocacy of the Bolshevik or Soviet doctrines." The race riots, though, had even less to do with communism than did the strikes. Racial violence, in fact, reflected deep hostility between black and white workers. Yet Palmer's response was understandable. He, like many Americans, was puzzled by the eruption of bitter class and racial antagonism in the aftermath of a war fought, supposedly, to safeguard Progressive principles.

## THE ROAD TO PARIS

The class and racial antagonisms in the United States mirrored those of the world community. If Americans had difficulty handling these problems at home, there was absolutely no hope that they could make the entire world, or even Europe, safe for Progressive democracy. Yet Wilson set out to try.

He immediately ran into a string of disasters. Throughout the war the President had refused to discuss peace terms with the Allies. He feared that such talks could lead to splits that would retard the war effort. He also believed that as the war continued, American economic and military power would give him an increasingly stronger hand. But when he did approach the Allies to discuss the Fourteen Points in late 1918, Wilson discovered that the British adamantly refused to negotiate freedom of the seas (a principle that would protect neutrals against the powerful British fleet). The French insisted on destroying German power regardless of Wilsonian principles. The President's cases were weak, for he had refused to recognize neutral rights on the high seas in 1917–18 and had singled out Germany as primarily responsible for starting the war. After all, such policies had been necessary to sustain the American commitment at home.

On the way to Paris Wilson told his advisors that "the United States was the only nation which was absolutely disinterested" in peace making. Allied leaders knew better, and they comprehended how history had shaped the American position as well as their own. Harold Nicolson, a member of the British delegation to Paris and later a distinguished historian, observed that Americans, like Europeans, had used brutal force to conquer territory in the nineteenth century. Then he asked, "Can we wonder that [Europeans] preferred the precisions of their old system to the vague idealism of a new system which America might refuse to apply even to her own continent?" As Europeans such as Nicolson understood, Wilsonian principles were designed to protect American interests.

The President also informed his advisors that, while he embodied the hopes of all progressive peoples, "the leaders of the allies did not really represent their peoples." This was a colossally mistaken belief. David Lloyd George and Georges Clemenceau, the prime ministers of Great Britain and France respectively, received thumping votes of support at home before the peace conference convened, and both ran on platforms pledging to squeeze every possible *pfennig* and acre out of Germany. Wilson, however, in one of the great American political fumbles, had proclaimed in late October 1918 that patriotism required the election of a Democratic Congress. In a congressional election year the Republicans would probably have gained some seats, but they won a major victory by blasting Wilson for impugning their wholehearted support of the war. Republicans even captured the Senate (49 to 47), the body that would have to ratify Wilson's work at Paris.

Nor did the President ease the situation by naming a peace commission that contained not a single important Republican or senator. This colorless group was designed so that it would raise few problems for the plans of the delegation's leader, Wilson himself. The President decided that no other person could be entrusted with the mission, not even his Secretary of State, whom Wilson once unfairly dismissed as "stupid." In heading the commission, Wilson would have to sacrifice a more detached view of the essentials in order to immerse himself in the time-consuming details of diplomacy. He also gave his political opponents and those who disliked the Fourteen Points a highly visible figure to attack.

All of these political errors, however, are less important in understanding Wilson's failure than are his substantive policies. The Fourteen Points had aimed at two objectives: (1) replacing the European balance of power with a world that was open and free economically and largely self-determined politically, and (2) replacing Lenin's revolutionary program with Wilsonian liberal alternatives. But the President soon learned he could not gain both objectives at once.

## AT PARIS

In the wake of the war's devastation, Communist uprisings appeared in Germany. A Communist government actually controlled Hungary for several months. Threatened left-wing riots in Austria were in part averted by an American warning that food supplies would be shut off if trouble occurred. "We are sitting upon an open powder magazine," Colonel House worried, "and some day a spark may ignite it." By early 1919 Wilson's fear of Bolshevism overshadowed his mistrust of the Western Europeans. He increasingly found himself on their side in a common effort to contain Leninism. He did reject their suggestions that a larger military force be sent to topple the Bolsheviks, but agreed that Lenin should not be invited to Paris. The President allowed William Bullitt to sound out the Soviet leaders, and Bullitt believed he had worked out an agreement with Lenin that the Allies could accept. By the time Bullitt returned from Russia, however, the President refused even to talk with him. Wilson had decided to use pressure, not negotiation, in handling Lenin.

Wilson continued to have faith that Leninism could be conquered through a "slow process of reform." Since it was his League of Nations

The Big Four of 1919: Lloyd George, Orlando, Clemenceau, Wilson.

that would carry out the reform, Wilson, over the vigorous objections of the French and British (who wanted to settle first the precise, strangulating terms for Germany), forced the peace conference to begin in January 1919 with discussions on the League. Within a month the organization was formed. It consisted of an Assembly containing nearly forty nations (but not revolutionary Mexico, Russia, and Germany); a Council, comprised of nine nations with the five permanent seats given to the United States, Great Britain, Japan, France, and Italy; and a Secretariat. Except for procedural matters, most decisions required unanimous consent in the Council.

Article XIV established the Permanent Court of International Justice, which could decide international cases taken to the Court by both parties involved. Article XVI pledged all members to penalize aggressors by cutting off trade and economic aid. It was Article X, however, that Wilson termed "the heart of the covenant."

> The members of the League undertake to respect and preserve as against external aggression the territorial integrity and existing political independence of all Members of the League. In case of any such aggression or in case of any threat or danger of such aggression the Council shall advise upon the means by which this obligation shall be fulfilled.

This wording deserves close study, for in the end Article X contributed to Wilson's doom.

Returning to the United States for a short time in February 1919, Wilson encountered strong opposition to the Covenant from Republicans in the Senate led by Henry Cabot Lodge of Massachusetts. Lodge made public a petition signed by thirty-nine senators condemning the League, six more than the one-third necessary to defeat the pact. This opposition was partly personal. Some Republicans, Lodge and Theodore Roosevelt in particular, hated Wilson, a feeling not lessened by the President's partisan attack on Republicans and his often condescending manner. But the opponents primarily attacked several aspects of the treaty. Article X, they feared, committed Americans to uphold the status quo around the world, pledged the United States to preserve British and French imperial interests, and weakened Congress's power to declare war by providing a nearly automatic American commitment to intervene. The anti-League forces also attacked the lack of a provision protecting America's use of the Monroe Doctrine in the Western Hemisphere, and the failure to exclude domestic questions (such as tariffs) from League authority.

The President was furious with the Senate. "I am going to resume my study of the dictionary to find adequate terms in which to describe the fatuity of these gentlemen with the poor little minds that never get anywhere," he remarked privately. "I cannot express my contempt for their intelligence." Wilson then made a critical mistake. Returning to Paris, he demanded changes in the Covenant—although not in Article X—that would meet some of the Senate's objections. Time that was to have been devoted to drawing up carefully the German Peace Treaty was, at the President's insistence, spent on rewriting the Covenant. Lloyd George, Clemenceau, and Vittorio Orlando, the Italian leader, knew that they had Wilson over a barrel, and consequently gave in to some of his requests only after he gave them much of what they wanted on the German treaty. The President was forced to surrender key parts of his Fourteen Points, particularly those on self-determination and territorial settlements.

As one American official later commented, "One came to Paris when hope was riding high, and each day you could see these hopes just—well, you soon detected that it was a great enormous balloon and gradually all the air was coming out of it. . . . Then there was Russia, a vast black cloud that overhung the whole thing." As the conference wore on and revolution threatened Germany, Hungary, and Austria, the key problem was, indeed, how the Soviet Union could be isolated and Central Europe, particularly a weakened Germany, protected from the virus of communism. Wilson hoped to rebuild Germany so that it would be strong enough to provide its own immunity. Clemenceau, however, and to a lesser extent Lloyd George, determined that Germany must be stripped so that it could never again launch war. Territory taken from Germany was given to France, Poland, and the new independent state of Czechoslovakia. Millions of Germans were therefore wrenched from their native government and placed within the boundaries of other, weaker nations.

Equally important, Germany was saddled with $33 billion of war reparations that had to be paid out of a decimated economy. The French had actually asked $200 billion, but Wilson fought Clemenceau and scaled down the French demands. In return, however, the President and Lloyd George signed a security treaty promising France aid if it were attacked by Germany. The plan thus became clear: to assist a weakened Germany to withstand the onslaughts of communism sweeping in from the east, the peace conference essentially threw out the principle of self-determination, particularly for Germans, in order to build the newly independent states of Poland, Hungary, and Czechoslovakia, which were to act as buffers, or a *cordon sanitaire*, between Russia and Germany. In reality, of course, these states were too weak to stand between two potential giants, so France gave territorial guarantees to the Eastern Europeans by pledging to assist if they were attacked by a third party.

Self-determination was also sacrificed in the Pacific, where the Chinese province of Shantung, formerly controlled by Germany, was claimed by Japan. Wilson initially fought this transfer, but surrendered when the Japanese threatened to leave the League unless they received Shantung. The President did prevent Italy from claiming non-Italian territory along the Adriatic Sea, even though Orlando dramatically walked out of the conference in protest. Finally, Wilson accepted a compromise on the ques-

## CENTRAL EUROPE AND THE BALKANS, 1925

*Territorial changes, 1914–1925*

Germany in 1914

Austria–Hungary in 1914

Territory lost by Russia, 1914–1920

Territory lost by Russia, 1914–1920

tion of Germany's former colonies in Africa and the Pacific that, in actuality, gave France, England, and Japan the complete control they demanded in these areas. He had wanted the League to be responsible for these colonies under a mandate principle. Instead the three Allies divided up the colonies among themselves and pledged only to submit annual reports to the League. Germany was never consulted on these terms, but simply given the hurriedly written treaty in May to sign—or else. The "or else" probably would have been an economic blockade designed to starve the Germans until they did sign. Wilson fought plans for such a blockade, fearing that this would be the quickest way of transforming Germans into Bolsheviks. Berlin officials finally accepted the treaty only after bitterly protesting its terms. One war had finally ended.

## REJECTION

As Wilson returned to do battle with the Senate, he found three groups preparing to fight the Covenant and the peace treaty. One, centering around Lodge and other conservative Republicans, determined to defeat anything Wilson recommended, but focused its objection particularly on the automatic commitment implied in Article X. A second was comprised of such Progressives as Herbert Hoover and Charles Evans Hughes. This group did not personally dislike Wilson (Hoover, indeed, had been one of the President's important advisors at Paris), but attacked Articles X and XVI and was afraid the Covenant would endanger Congress's constitutional control over domestic affairs. A third group, led by Progressive Republicans William Borah of Idaho and Hiram Johnson of California, formed the "Irreconcilables," for they refused to agree to American participation in any international organization resembling the League. They moreover blasted Wilson's refusal to deal with Russia, a policy described by Johnson as "an exhibition of the crassest stupidity." One common thread united the three groups: all wanted to maintain maximum U.S. freedom of action in the world, particularly so Americans could freely exploit their new economic power without having to worry about political restraints.

Wilson's opponents enjoyed a strong position. With the Republicans in control of the Senate, Lodge became chairman of the Foreign Relations Committee, which would first have to act on the Covenant and treaty. As it became clear that Lodge was mustering support, the President attempted to pressure the Senate by embarking on an exhausting speaking tour. After thirty-six formal speeches in three weeks, the 63-year-old Wilson suffered the beginnings of a paralytic stroke on September 26 in Colorado. Desperately ill, he nevertheless angrily stuck to his refusal to compromise with the Senate. When the body added reservations that modified Article X and withdrew approval of Japan's hold on Shantung,

Henry Cabot Lodge, 1921.

Wilson ordered Democratic senators not to vote for the amended Covenant. In November 1919 the League charter, with reservations, was rejected 39 to 55. Four months later it again fell short of the necessary two-thirds needed for ratification, 49 to 35. Twenty-three Democrats, obeying Wilson's orders, ironically joined Irreconcilables in defeating American entry into the League.

The President made one final effort during the 1920 presidential campaign. At first Wilson apparently decided to try for an unprecedented third term, but his illness and realistic Democratic political advisors ended that dream. He then declared the election a "solemn referendum" on the League. Wilson urged the Democratic ticket of Governor James Cox of Ohio and young Franklin D. Roosevelt of New York to support the Covenant strongly. The Democratic ticket equivocated, however, while the Republicans, led by Senator Warren G. Harding of Ohio and Governor Calvin Coolidge of Massachusetts, talked on both sides of the League issue. Harding won overwhelmingly, obtaining 60.3 percent of the popular vote and carrying thirty-seven of the forty-eight states. Foreign policy issues, however, were peripheral, as indeed they have been in nearly every presidential election in the twentieth century. Once elected, Harding clearly stated that he would not push for American association with the League.

Wilson must bear primary responsibility for the American failure to join the League of Nations. His refusal to appoint an important Republican or senator to the delegation, his procedures at Paris, and his unwillingness to compromise with the Senate doomed the Covenant. But in the long run, American participation might have made little difference anyway. The fundamental problem was not the League but the ill-constructed peace, which no organization of mere mortals could have saved. Its treatment of Germany territorially and financially sowed the seeds for the terrible economic depression and the Nazism of the 1930s. The exclusion of Russia, and then Wilson's announcement in March 1920 that the United States would not even recognize the existence of the Soviet government, piled unreality upon unreality. The failure to handle the problems posed by Germany and Russia set off a right-wing reaction not only in the United States, but in Italy, France, Germany, and Eastern and Southern Europe, where the stage rapidly filled with Fascists and National Socialists.

"What gave rise to the Russian Revolution?" Wilson finally queried in 1923, one year before his death. "The answer can only be that it was the product of a whole social system. It was not in fact a sudden thing." The same explanation can also be applied to the appearance of the right-wing forces in the 1920s and 1930s. For the Paris Peace Conference in the end decided not on peace but on vengeance; not on a sanitary Europe but on a *cordon sanitaire;* not on economic justice—for there was little discussion of such issues at Paris—but on a political settlement that would allow economic exploitation; not on an inclusion of all peoples but on an exclusion of many, particularly revolutionary regimes.

The result was best summarized by William Bullitt in Paris after he resigned from the American delegation. He declared that the peace treaty could result only in "a new century of wars." As he left his hotel, Bullitt was asked by reporters where he would go. "I am going to lie in the sands of the French Riviera," he replied, "and watch the world go to hell." He went. And it did.

## Suggested Reading

The most comprehensive work on wartime America is David Kennedy, *Over Here: The First World War and American Society* (1980). For economic policy, consult Robert D. Cuff, *The War Industries Board: Business-Government Relations During World War I* (1943), and Jordan A. Schwarz, *The Speculator: Bernard M. Baruch in Washington* (1981). Propaganda and public opinion are analyzed in George T. Blakey, *Historians on the Homefront* (1970); Carol S. Gruber, *Mars and Minerva:*

*World War I and the Uses of the Higher Learning in America* (1975); and Stephen L. Vaughn, *Holding Fast the Inner Lines: Democracy, Nationalism, and the Committee on Public Information* (1980). On woman suffrage, see William L. O'Neill, *Everyone Was Brave* (1969); and Andrew Sinclair, *The Emancipation of the American Woman* (1965).

For the war's impact on civil liberties, consult William Preston, Jr., *Aliens and Dissenters: Federal Suppression of Radicals, 1903–1933* (1963); H. C. Peterson and Gilbert C. Fite, *Opponents of War, 1917–1918* (1957); and Paul L. Murphy, *World War I and the Origin of Civil Liberties in the United States* (1979). The effect of the war on radicalism is discussed in James Weinstein, *The Decline of Socialism in America, 1912–1923* (1967); and Nick Salvatore, *Eugene V. Debs: Citizen and Socialist* (1983). The Red Scare is well covered in Stanley Coben, *A. Mitchell Palmer* (1963); the labor turmoil in David Brody, *Labor in Crisis: The Steel Strike of 1919* (1965); and racial conflict in William M. Tuttle, Jr., *Race Riot: Chicago in the Red Summer of 1919* (1970).

On foreign policy begin with R. H. Burns, *Guide to American Foreign Relations Since 1700* (1983). An excellent overview of military strategy is Russell F. Weigley's, *The American Way of War* (1973); and a comprehensive analysis of Wilsonian diplomacy is found in Lloyd Gardner, *Safe for Democracy* (1984); and G. Gordon Levin, *Woodrow Wilson and World Politics* (1969). For the peace conference, the following are valuable: Carl Parrini, *Heir to Empire . . . 1916–1923* (1969); Jeffrey J. Safford, *Wilsonian Maritime Diplomacy, 1913–1921* (1978); Lawrence E. Gelfand, *The Inquiry, 1917–1919* (1963); two landmark works by Arno J. Mayer, *Wilson vs. Lenin* (1959), and *Politics and Diplomacy of Peacemaking* (1965). For the Russian problem, different perspectives are provided in Lloyd Gardner, ed., *Wilson and Revolutions, 1913–1921* (1976); George Kennan, *Russia Leaves the War* (1956), and *Decision to Intervene* (1958); William Appleman Williams, *Russian-American Relations* (1952); and John Lewis Gaddis, *Russia, the Soviet Union and the United States* (1978). Wilson's opponents are discussed in William Widenor, *Henry Cabot Lodge* (1981); Ronald Steel, *Walter Lippmann* (1980); Ralph A. Stone, *The Irreconcilables* (1970). Wesley Bagby's *The Road to Normalcy* (1962) analyzes the 1920 election.

The following are "don't miss" books on baseball: Harold Seymour's scholarly *Baseball* (1960), now in two volumes; Robert W. Creamer, *Babe* (1974); Marshall Smelser, *The Life That Ruth Built* (1975); Julius Tygiel's magnificent account, *Baseball's Great Experiment: Jackie Robinson and His Legacy* (1983); and Benjamin G. Rader's superb overview, *American Sports: From the Age of Folk Games to the Age of Spectators* (1983).

Grace Coolidge, Andrew Mellon, and Calvin Coolidge, 1926.

# 1920–1929

## The New Era

Progressivism had appealed to many Americans because it promised stability to a nation experiencing rapid change. By 1920, however, the Wilsonian years had linked reform not with orderly change but with war and revolution. Consequently, Americans in the 1920s turned toward other leaders who invoked traditional values and played on the widespread nostalgia for a simpler, happier past. But Progressivism did not die. If anything, the decade was characterized by a quickening of those forces that were transforming American life—urban and corporate growth, racial and ethnic heterogeneity, concern for social morality, active government, and international involvement. The sharpest conflicts arose not over economic policy or foreign affairs, where something close to a consensus emerged, but over such issues as religion, ethnicity, and morality. Then, in 1929, Americans suddenly entered a chamber of economic horrors that transformed them, their world, and their Progressivism.

## REPUBLICAN POLITICS: HARDING AND COOLIDGE

In 1925 a book entitled *The Man Nobody Knows* climbed to the top of the best-seller list, not because it had great literary merit but because it accurately reflected the prevailing ethos. It was written by advertising executive Bruce Barton, who wanted to dispel the myths surrounding the figure of Jesus Christ. In the gospel according to Madison Avenue, Jesus was the prototype of the modern businessman, indeed the "founder of modern business." A good executive and a regular fellow, He was also an aggressive go-getter. Barton noted that there was no demand for a new religion two thousand years ago. Jesus created one by applying the "principles of modern salesmanship." In deifying businessmen and their values, Barton also preached an ethic of consumption that placed satisfaction above self-denial, luxury above asceticism, and spending above thrift. Presumably one served God not only by following a calling but also by taking advantage of the installment plan. But then He was, in Barton's view, "a great Companion, a wonderful Friend, a kindly, indulgent, joy-loving Father."

This, ironically, might well have served as a description of Warren G. Harding, who won a landslide victory in the 1920 election. A senator from Ohio since 1914 (and the first man ever to move directly from the Senate to the White House), Harding was jovial and expansive, a back slapper who joined as many fraternal lodges as possible. He loved to meet people, had a remarkable memory for faces, and played tennis or golf whenever he could. Harding's chief virtue was that he usually recognized his own limitations, his chief defect that he believed in rewarding old friends with federal jobs. Many of them abused his trust by swindling the government, and when Harding died in August 1923, scandals were erupting on every side. The director of the Veterans' Bureau was convicted of stealing hundreds of millions of dollars; the Attorney General resigned when charged with authorizing the sale of alcohol from government warehouses to bootleggers; and the head of the Alien Property Custodian's Office was found guilty of accepting bribes. The most famous scandal centered around allegations that Harding's Secretary of the Interior, Albert Fall, had leased government oil reserves in Teapot Dome, Wyoming, to private owners in order to line his own pocket. Fall resigned in disgrace and later served a one-year prison sentence.

These revelations, however, did not harm the Republican party, partly because Harding had not been personally involved in the scandals and partly because his successor, Calvin Coolidge, had a reputation for honesty and frugality. A former governor of Massachusetts, Coolidge was a cold, austere individual whose childhood, according to an admiring biographer, was "simple, wholesome and unfurtive." He observed proper protocol, and engaged in no sport more arduous than riding a mechanical horse. His low-key behavior led critics to remark that Coolidge's "ideal day is one on which nothing whatever happens" or to claim that, during his administration, there was "grim, determined, alert inactivity in the White House." But Coolidge's outlook may well have been conditioned by the tragic death of his sixteen-year-old son in the summer of 1924. When Calvin Jr. died, Coolidge recalled, "the power and the glory of the Presidency went with him."

Miles apart in temperament, Harding and Coolidge nevertheless shared similar social and economic views. Both believed that government should foster business enterprise. This meant a hands-off policy in areas where businessmen wanted freedom of action and intervention in areas where they wanted help. "This is a business country," Coolidge remarked, "and it wants a business government." On the other hand, both presidents regarded intervention on behalf of other interest groups as socially undesirable, financially irresponsible, and morally wrong. Such paternalism, Harding warned, "would stifle ambition, impair efficiency . . . and make us a nation of dependent incompetents." This outlook, which governed Republican policies toward business, labor, agriculture, and public power, was also sanctioned by the Supreme Court.

Big business benefited handsomely from Republican rule. Indeed, the *Wall Street Journal* considered Coolidge "sound from every angle." In 1922 Congress enacted the Fordney-McCumber Tariff, which raised import duties to their highest level ever. Harding and Coolidge filled federal regulatory agencies with men who considered it their task to assist the business community. One of them was William E. Humphrey. Appointed to the Federal Trade Commission in 1925, he decided not to prosecute companies that had violated the law so long as they promised to behave in the future. Republicans placed tax policy in the hands of Andrew Mellon, who served as Secretary of the Treasury from 1921 to 1932. Mellon, who resigned from the boards of directors of fifty-one corporations on assuming office, feared that if high taxes deprived the businessman of a fair share of his earnings, then "he will no longer exert himself and the country will be deprived of the energy on which its continued greatness depends." Mellon fought long, hard, and successfully to reduce taxes on inheritances, corporate profits, and the well-to-do. By 1926 Congress had cut the tax rate on an income of $1 million from 66 percent to 20 percent. Mellon received honorary degrees from Pittsburgh, Dartmouth, Rutgers, Columbia, Kenyon, Amherst, Harvard, Yale, and Princeton, the latter noting that "his name bids fair to stand with the greatest masters of finance in modern times."

While business received all kinds of support, organized labor went into eclipse. Union membership fell from 5 million in 1920 to 3.4 million in 1930. This occurred for several reasons: unions had no foothold in industries undergoing the most rapid expansion such as automobiles, rubber, and chemicals; the American Federation of Labor clung to an increasingly obsolete craft structure; employers conducted a vigorous open-shop drive, which included the use of spies and blacklists to block organizers; and several large companies introduced welfare measures—pension, insurance, and stock-sharing plans—that stifled union growth. When walkouts occurred, however, the White House occasionally intervened on the side of management. This happened during the railroad strike of 1922, when Attorney General Harry Daugherty persuaded Harding that the nation faced imminent peril. In Daugherty's view, the workers' support for government control of the railroads "was a conspiracy worthy of Lenin" and raised the possibility that "our time-tables and freight-rates would be made out in Moscow." Daugherty obtained a sweeping court injunction that barred virtually all union activities and proved instrumental in breaking the strike.

Harding and Coolidge rejected any government role either in supporting farm prices or in developing power facilities. At the time agricultural interests supported the McNary-Haugen plan, which authorized the government to purchase farm products at prices above those offered in the world market. The government would export the goods at the world market price, and therefore take a loss. Farmers would reimburse the government from the profits they realized on sales to American consumers at inflated domestic prices. Congress defeated this proposal in 1924 and 1926. It passed the plan in 1927 and 1928, only to have Coolidge veto it as "vicious" and "preposterous" special-interest legislation. Republicans also did their best to extract the government from its involvement in the construction of power facilities in the Tennessee Valley. During World War I the government had built power plants at Muscle Shoals. Harding and Coolidge wished to sell these facilities to private entrepreneurs, but Congress blocked their plans. In 1928 when Congress approved completion of the Wilson Dam and the sale of surplus power, Coolidge killed the measure with a pocket veto.

During the 1920s the Supreme Court mirrored the social philosophy that reigned in the White House. This was hardly surprising, since Harding appointed four judges to the bench, including William Howard Taft who served as chief justice from 1922 to 1930. In a series of decisions concerning organized labor, the Court ruled that unions engaged in certain types of strikes (such as secondary boycotts) were liable to antitrust prosecution, that strict limits could be placed on picketing outside factory gates, and that court injunctions could be used to enforce contracts in labor disputes. The Supreme Court also struck down key welfare legislation. In *Bailey* v. *Drexel Furniture Co.* (1922) the justices ruled against a child labor act passed in 1919 that imposed a 10 percent tax on the profits of firms employing child labor. A majority found that the tax was levied to regulate business practices rather than to produce revenue and therefore was inappropriate. The Court decided in *Adkins* v. *Children's Hospital* (1923) that states could not establish minimum wages for women workers. Since women could now vote, they no longer merited special protection. Chief Justice Taft, although generally content with the Court's performance, nevertheless feared for the future. "The only hope we have of keeping a consistent declaration of Constitutional law," he noted, "is for us to live as long as we can."

## A NEW ORDER: REPUBLICAN ALTERNATIVES TO WILSON'S LEAGUE

In foreign policy as at home, the Harding-Coolidge administrations knew that they could not retreat into isolationism or nostalgia for a pre-1914 world. "There never again will be precisely the old order," Harding declared in 1922. "Indeed, I know of no one who thinks it to be desirable. For out of the old order came the war itself." A new order, constructed and dominated by U.S. economic power, would avert future world wars and revolutions. That power was immense. In 1914 Americans owed the world about $3.5 billion; after they financed the Allies in war, the world suddenly owed the United States $13 billion. Fueled by the new radio, airplane, and especially automobile industries, the booming domestic economy doubled its industrial production between 1921 and 1929. Never had a nation become so rich so fast. That success seemed to confirm superiority in other areas. As *The Ladies Home Journal* trumpeted, "There is only one first-class civilization in the world today. It is right here in the United States." Americans seemed to have the right as well as the power to reconstruct the world.

The new world order was to rest on certain principles. First, military force was to be reduced everywhere. Money spent on rifles was better invested in automobiles so standards of living could rise. The military power required to maintain world stability was to be replaced by a more benign, effective, and profitable economic power. Second, money and trade would be the dynamics of the new order. Americans naturally wanted to set ground rules that played to their own greatest strength in international affairs. Third, economic activities were to be undertaken primarily by private individuals, not governments. If government directed investment and trade, individual rights could disappear and fascism or socialism result. "Constantly I insisted [in the 1920s] that spiritual and intellectual freedom could not continue to exist without economic freedom," Herbert Hoover recalled. "If one died, all would die."

Government's primary responsibility was to ensure that private investment and trade could flow freely into any market. Unfair monopolies were therefore to be broken up, state-controlled enterprises (as in Russia) undermined, and, above all, freedom of enterprise was not to be shackled by such political alliances as Article X of the League Covenant. In 1928, for example, the French again pressed Washington for a political alliance against a revived Germany. Secretary of State Frank Kellogg quickly transformed the request into a meaningless fifteen-nation agreement in which each signatory renounced war, except, of course, for self-defense. The Kellogg-Briand Pact was later laughed at as nothing more than an "international kiss," but most important for Americans it retained their complete freedom of action.

These principles carried on many of the international policies of Roosevelt and Wilson. The most powerful decision makers in foreign affairs were Secretary of State Charles Evans Hughes and Secretary of Commerce Herbert Hoover. Both had long been identified with Progressive programs. They used to the utmost such Wilsonian instruments as the Edge Act and Webb-Pomerene Act, which allowed bankers and industrialists to combine for the exploitation of foreign markets without regard to American antitrust laws.

Hoover emphasized that the key to happiness and prosperity was an "American Individualism," which he defined as "an equality of opportunity." To ensure such opportunity, Hoover, like Wilson, stressed the need for an expanding overseas economy. To exploit global opportunities Hoover also believed that American entrepreneurs should combine in global associations so that they could both compete with foreign cartels and end cut-throat competition at home. One leading American banker caught this policy exactly: businessmen must stop "scrambling amongst each other for the plums which fall," learning instead "by cooperative effort to plant more plum trees that we might share the larger yield." Since Hoover defined the national interest as the interest of business, his Commerce Department blazed the way. Particularly active was its Bureau of Foreign

Secretary of Commerce Herbert Hoover at home with his radio set.

and Domestic Commerce, which during the 1920's quadrupled its budget as it established fifty offices around the world to help businessmen plant new "plum trees" in foreign markets.

The Republicans had helped block U.S. entry into the League of Nations not out of spite or narrow political motives, but because they disliked the restraints imposed by the League on American power. They believed that they had a better idea. Economic individualism and political freedom would join to make a new, just, and lasting order. If they failed, it was because these assumptions were wrong, not because they attempted to retreat into a supposed isolationism.

## THE WASHINGTON CONFERENCE

The first bold stroke of Republican diplomacy appeared when President Harding asked nine major nations to attend the Washington Naval Conference in November 1921. In a brilliantly conceived scheme, Hughes planned to reduce drastically expenditures on warships, dissolve political alliances dangerous to the United States (particularly the Anglo-Japanese alliance, in existence since 1902), and work out an international agreement to maintain the open door to the fabled China market. The last point was crucial, for since 1914 the Japanese, bolstered by their pact with England, had been trying to close the door.

In February 1922 the conference produced three interrelated documents. In the Five-Power pact, the United States, Great Britain, Japan, France, and Italy received respective ratios of 5 to 5 to 3 to 1.7 to 1.7 for the size of their battleship fleets. In reality, the ratios gave Japan naval superiority in East Asia. American naval officers strongly protested the arrangement, but Hughes overruled the Navy with the argument that the ratios also gave the United States dominance in the Western Hemisphere, and England and France control in European waters. Such a realistic division of world power satisfied the Secretary of State.

More important, in return for naval superiority in the Far Pacific Hughes extracted from Japan an agreement to a Nine-Power treaty pledging the maintenance of the open door in China. Clearly the United States was trusting that the Japanese would use their superior power to maintain an open marketplace in China for all nations. Hughes' successes were finally capped by a Four-Power pact that destroyed the Anglo-Japanese alliance, replacing it with an agreement among the United States, Japan, England, and France in which each pledged to respect the others' possessions in the Pacific, and to consult with other powers in the event of aggression in that area.

These three agreements provided the framework for American diplomacy between 1921 and 1941. They marked a triumph for Hughes, for although Japan enjoyed a strong military position, it had pledged itself to the open door. Moreover, after American pressure was applied, the Japanese also agreed to withdraw their troops from Siberia and to surrender Shantung to China. The pressure took the form of a financial arrangement, which had been completed before the Washington Conference convened, between the J. P. Morgan banking house in New York and the Tokyo government. Without that economic leverage on the Japanese, it is doubtful whether Hughes would have wanted to call the conference at all. The deal marked the beginning of a close Tokyo–New York economic relationship.

China attended the conference, complained bitterly about being treated like a bone between dogs, and was then ignored. To Western eyes the Chinese were doubly troublesome, for not only were they weak, but also unstable. In May 1919 the revolution led by Sun Yat-sen's Kuomintang party had accelerated. The major powers refused to recognize the revolutionaries. Americans tried to go on with business as usual, but in 1924 the revolution veered leftward as the Kuomintang cooperated with Soviet Russian agents. Effective economic boycotts and bloody personal attacks were launched against foreign missionaries and businessmen. One Chinese leader warned, "The time has come to speak to foreign imperialism in the language it understands." But with Sun's death in 1925, his mantle fell on Chiang Kai-shek. Chiang completed the Kuomintang triumph in 1927, broke with the Soviets, and greatly moderated the revolutionary program. In 1928 he worked out agreements with the United States and Western Europe that restored China's control over her own tariffs. Beyond this, however, Washington would not go. American Marines remained stationed in three Chinese cities to protect property, and six new U.S. gunboats moved to the Yangtze. A stable, wealthy, cooperative Japan, tied to American interests through the strong bonds of money, was a much preferred partner to a revolutionary, erratic, and poverty-ridden China.

## THE NEW ORDER
## RECONSTRUCTS THE OLD

The Washington Conference also aided American policy in Europe, that most crucial of all diplomatic priorities. Before the war Europeans had taken half of all American exports. Equally important, Latin America and Asia were so interlinked with Europe's economy that until that area was rebuilt the United States could not count on finding steady customers in the less industrialized countries. Some European nations had recovered quickly. Italy was a model after 1922 when Benito Mussolini assumed power. Despite his Fascism, many Americans admired the dictator for embodying their own supposed traits of efficiency, stability, and masculinity; in the words of former Progressive journalist Ida Tarbell, he was the "despot with a dimple." Germany, France, and Great Britain, however, recovered more slowly, and Americans became concerned. "The prosperity of the United States largely depends upon the economic settlements which may be made in Europe," Hughes observed in 1921, "and the key to the future is with those who make those settlements."

Again American economic leverage allowed Hughes to shape such settlements. His fulcrums were the flush New York money market and the $11 billion loaned to Europe during and immediately after the war. The Republicans insisted this money be repaid on American terms, not because their puritan conscience required it, but because these war debts and the European need for capital provided the United States with great power. Washington's attention centered on Germany, for European (and therefore American) prosperity was impossible without a healthy Germany. That nation had been the industrial hub of the continent before 1914, and promised to be so again if properly reconstructed. Moreover, only a stable Germany could protect Europe against the spread of Bolshevism.

Disagreeing strongly with this moderate American approach, France pressed the Germans for high reparations payments until in 1923 they defaulted. When the French Army retaliated by trying to separate the Rhineland from Germany, the German economy went completely out of control. All of Europe was threatened with catastrophe. Hughes cooly stepped into the chaos, convincing J. P. Morgan to join with British bankers in injecting a $200 million loan into the moribund German system. In return, Hughes demanded that Germany be given easier reparation terms. Despite some French objections, the deal was completed at a 1924 conference headed by Chicago banker Charles G. Dawes. The Dawes Plan became the key to rebuilding Europe.

But the results were rather different from what Hughes and Dawes anticipated. When Morgan sold $100 million of securities for the German loan in the United States, the offer was oversubscribed in hours. Americans, rushing to invest in a stabilized Germany, snapped up some 180 bond and stock issues amounting to nearly $2 billion. When some U.S. investors discovered a Bavarian hamlet needing $125,000 for a small municipal project, they talked the village fathers into taking instead a $3 million loan. Dollars were not only flowing into increasingly questionable projects, but were merely moving in a circular fashion: the United States sent money to Germany, which used it to pay reparations to England and France, which in turn sent it back to New York for payment of war debts and interest on loans. One broken link could make the western economies appear to be a row of collapsing dominoes.

Between 1925 and 1929, however, those economies looked less like dominoes than a game of monopoly. During those four years Americans loaned more than $5 billion abroad. By 1928 such giant corporations as Standard Oil of New Jersey, DuPont, Ford, General Motors, and Singer Sewing Machine had invested $3 billion in their own overseas subsidiaries. Americans put another $8 billion into overseas portfolio investments, that is, into stocks and bonds of foreign-owned companies. The State Department welcomed most of these ventures. The rebuilding of Germany, of course, was a primary diplomatic goal. In the Middle East American capitalists bitterly struggled with the British and French for control over the world's greatest oil reserves. The competition ended in 1928 with the "Red Line agreement," in which the giant oil companies divided a large Middle Eastern area, marked on a map with a red pencil, among themselves. Even Russia welcomed capital for developmental projects. Despite its refusal to recognize the Bolsheviks, Washington determined to encourage American businessmen to rush into what Hoover called "an economic vacuum" in order to beat out European entrepreneurs. Hoping that even Soviets could be transformed into capitalists, such American corporations as Ford, Westinghouse, and W. Averell Harriman's ventures invested millions of dollars in Lenin's country. In this area, however, Germany had become a foe, not a friend. Not only did it dominate foreign investments in Russia, but in 1922 the two outcasts publicly agreed to cooperate economically. Secretly they helped rebuild each other's military machine.

Despite the successes in rebuilding Germany, the Middle East, and Russia, Hoover watched the outflow of capital with growing concern. He knew that much of it was going into doubtful enterprises and that other American money, such as that helping Japan develop Manchuria, injured American export interests. United States bankers were following selfish policies that badly hurt other American businessmen. Manufacturers, for example, not only hated the bankers for helping Japanese industry take over former American markets in Manchuria, but also for investing money in bond issues abroad rather than in industrial export enterprises at home. As early as 1922 Hoover had tried to control the bankers by giving the government power informally to approve or disapprove each loan made overseas. The bankers' violent objections, as well as Hoover's own fear of such governmental involvement in private business, ruined the plan. Virtually uncontrolled, the bankers blithely went on, investing in dubious projects until, like lemmings, they nearly self-destructed in 1929.

## THE NEW ORDER IN LATIN AMERICA

American capital was also the key to relations with Latin America. In this area, however, Washington officials were not reluctant to use military force as well to maintain stability. Latin America had so long been counted a United States preserve that when new recruits entered the State Department's Foreign Service School in the mid-1920s, they were told not to expect too much from South Americans; their "Latin temperament" and "racial quality" were weaknesses—although Latin Americans could become "very easy people to deal with if properly managed." A 1924 survey revealed that of the twenty Latin American nations, only six were free of some kind of United States "management." The remainder were either under the Marine Corps or had their finances controlled by New York bankers. With stability assured, United States investments in Latin America more than doubled to $5.4 billion between 1924 and 1929, or at a rate more than twice as great as that in any other part of the world. Much of this went into oil exploration and development. The southern part of the hemisphere was to provide raw materials for the industrial progress of the northern part.

United States officials tried to make Latin America the showcase of American foreign policy. They believed that through cooperation between government and business, the area could produce prosperity and democracy for its peoples and profits for its developers. Hoover's Commerce Department helped investors by coming up with new approaches for building the infrastructure (the highways, communications, and utilities) needed to attract private capital. Such ideas anticipated the Alliance for Progress of the 1960s, and both programs fully understood that undercutting potential Latin American revolutions had to be a paramount objective. "The number of rebellions per capita is highest in those republics where the per capita mileage of highways is lowest," a Commerce Department official announced in 1929. "Romance may have been driven out by the concrete mixer, but the mixer has paved the way for law and order and for better understanding, as well as better business among the far-flung provinces of these sparsely populated commonwealths."

Hoover also tried to help by announcing new political policies. He changed the Wilsonian principle that the only acceptable government was a properly elected regime. Control of the country, a promise to meet international obligations, and the intent to hold elections in the future would now be sufficient to merit American recognition. After becoming President in 1929, Hoover also repudiated the Roosevelt Corollary of 1904–05 and began pulling Marines out of Caribbean nations. Problems did exist, particularly with revolutionary Mexico. The United States had finally recognized the Mexican government in 1923 but continued to object to the Mexican Constitution's Article 27, which provided for national ownership of such subsurface minerals as oil. A heated dispute developed in 1926–27, and it was not helped when the American ambassador accused Mexico of exporting Bolshevism to Central American countries. Wilson's former Secretary of the Interior, Franklin K. Lane, now an attorney for American oil companies, perfectly captured the prevailing view: "When I say that Russia may go her own way and Mexico hers, I say so with a sense that I have a right in [both countries] and also a right to see that they do not go their own way to the extent of blocking my way to what of good they hold." In 1927 a temporary compromise was finally reached on the oil controversy.

A case study of Republican policy took place in Nicaragua. U.S. Marines had occupied that Central American nation since 1912. They had intervened then to stop a rebellion that, in the eyes of Washington officials, threatened North American economic and strategic interests. Of special importance, Nicaragua was a possible site for an interoceanic canal that could rival the U.S. waterway in Panama. North Americans wanted no such competitor. Once the Marines landed, however, they could not leave: when Nicaraguan leaders cooperated with the United States, they became unpopular with their own people and needed protection. In 1925 Coolidge nevertheless decided to pull the forces out. Rebellion immediately erupted. Coolidge thereupon sent back the Marines, but now the situation had changed. A guerrilla leader, Augusto Sandino, fought the Marines successfully from 1927 to 1933. He found increasing support from Nicaraguan peasants who had not benefited from the U.S. occupation. The costly war and growing protests in the United States finally led Hoover to pull the troops out in 1933. But he left behind a new diplomatic invention: a U.S.-trained Nicaraguan National Guard that could replace the Marines in keeping order. In 1934, the U.S.-picked leader of the Guard, Anastasio Somoza, arrested Sandino (who had quit fighting after the U.S. troops left), and murdered him in cold blood. Somoza then made himself dictator. He and his sons ruled Nicaragua as their personal plantation

General Sandino, leader of the Nicaraguan
revolution, 1928.

until 1979 when they were overthrown by anti–U.S. revolutionaries calling themselves "Sandinistas." Such was the forty-five-year legacy of the
Republicans' "New Order" in Nicaragua.

By 1928 hemispheric relationships were becoming badly skewed. The
United States had loaned $2.5 billion and increased exports to Latin
Americans, but when they tried to pay their debts they ran into American
tariff walls that prevented many of their products from entering the
United States. As in Europe, United States investors swamped South
America with dollars; in 1928 Peru received twice as much in loans as it
could legitimately use. Anti-Yankeeism flourished in such conditions. At
the 1928 Inter-American conference, the Latin Americans proposed that
no state had the right to intervene in the internal affairs of another. When
the United States objected, it was joined by only four countries, three of
which were under American control. A year later depression struck. Seven
revolutions erupted in Latin America between 1929 and 1931. Given its
own assumption that a foreign policy's success was measured by the
stability it produced, the Pan American policies of the United States lay
in shambles.

## BESSIE SMITH AND THE BLUES

Thomas A. Edison invented the phonograph in 1877. It did not come into general use, however, until the 1890s, when grooved records replaced cylinders and an inexpensive "gramophone" was developed. Some, expecting that recorded music would discourage spontaneity, asked fearfully whether children put to bed by recorded lullabies would not become "simply human phonographs—without soul or expression?" Despite the skeptics, the popular demand for recordings proved overwhelming. In 1919 more than 2.25 million phonographs were manufactured; two years

"The world in a jug, the stopper in my hand": Bessie Smith, 1923.

Gertrude "Ma" Rainey, 1924.

later, over 100 million records were produced. The first blues recording by a black singer—Mamie Smith's "Crazy Blues"—was released in 1920. It sold extremely well and encouraged record companies to sign other black artists. A large "race market" seemed to exist, particularly among blacks who had migrated to Northern cities during the World War.

Of all the blues singers in the 1920s, none was more popular than Bessie Smith. Born in Tennessee in 1894, she began working with traveling road shows when she was a teenager. For a time she worked with another famous entertainer, Gertrude "Ma" Rainey. In 1923 Bessie Smith made her first recording, "Down Hearted Blues." Columbia Records paid her $125 a side for the record, which sold 780,000 copies within six months. (Throughout her association with Columbia, which lasted until 1931, she never received royalties based on sales but instead was paid a flat recording fee.) In 1925 Bessie Smith organized a traveling tent show, the "Harlem Frolics," which toured in a custom-made 78-foot-long railroad car complete with seven staterooms, kitchen, and bath. Audiences acclaimed her performances and her records sold remarkably well.

The blues idiom had several characteristics. The music was intensely personal. Songs dealt with the singers' own experiences—broken love affairs, natural disasters, tragedy, sorrow. Bessie Smith's own life, while often marked by luxury and extravagance, had its full share of such misfortune. Songs about racial injustice are hard to find, although, it should be added, studios would surely have been reluctant to record them. The blues appealed mainly to the lower classes, for middle-class blacks, and whites, were often offended by the emphasis on gambling, drugs, and sex, allusions to which were usually disguised. "Bought me a coffee-grinder, got the best one I could find," Bessie Smith sang, "So he could grind my coffee, 'cause he has a brand new grind." The blues, finally, was race music. "Race" records were advertised in separate catalogues and sold in stores in black communities. The first black-owned record company, Black Swan, adver-

Cab Calloway

tised: "The Only Genuine Colored Record—Others Are Only Passing for Colored." Bessie Smith almost always sang before black audiences and was booked in black theaters. Only on rare occasions did she perform for whites.

"Cold sober and in a quiet reflective mood": Bessie Smith in 1936.

With the stock market crash of 1929 Bessie Smith's career, and that of many other black performers, went into decline. Record sales nosedived and theater attendance dropped. Increasingly, the radio replaced the phonograph as the chief source of home entertainment. The blues, rough and raw-edged, gave way to the softer sound of "swing." Bessie Smith continued to sing, but she never matched her earlier success. On September 26, 1937, she was fatally injured in an automobile accident outside Memphis, Tennessee. A legend quickly arose that she died after being refused admittance to a white hospital. Although unfounded, the legend provided the basis for Edward Albee's play, "The Death of Bessie Smith." Her Philadelphia grave remained unmarked for over thirty years until in 1970 a plaque was placed on the site. Half the cost was donated by rock singer Janis Joplin as a tribute to a woman who had exerted so important an influence.

# THE POLITICS OF CULTURAL CONFLICT

Social reformers found that the most pressing domestic issues of the decade were precisely those, such as immigration restriction and prohibition, on which they were most bitterly divided. Cultural issues—those relating to ethnicity, morality, and religion—dominated political discourse for several reasons. First, prosperity led to a decline in the relative importance of economic concerns. Indeed, there was a wide area of agreement on these matters between Democrats and Republicans. Second, large numbers of second-generation immigrants became more assertive and demanded a greater share of political power at the national level. The groups that felt themselves being elbowed aside counterattacked. Third, the spread of cosmopolitan mores and values troubled many small town Americans who associated big cities with vice, crime, and immorality. Fourth, the most controversial of the issues, prohibition, assumed new importance simply because it had become the law of the land and could no longer be ignored. Where one stood on such an issue had little to do with one's position on child labor or railroad regulation. It had everything to do with where one's parents had been born, which church one attended (or did not attend), and whether one lived in a village or large city.

Proposals to curb immigration clearly exposed some of these cultural tensions. In 1921, after the arrival of 1.2 million immigrants in just one year, President Harding approved a measure drastically limiting further admission. But this was merely a prelude. In 1924 the National Origins Act sailed through Congress with a huge majority. The Act provided for the annual entry until 1927 of only 164,000 European immigrants under a quota system determined by the composition of the U.S. population in 1890. Under this arrangement the combined quotas for Russia and Italy were less than that for Norway; the combined quotas for Poland and Greece less than that for Sweden. Beginning in 1927 the United States would admit 150,000 European immigrants each year under quotas based on the national origins of the white population in 1920. The measure also barred all Japanese, but set no limits on immigration from Canada, Mexico, or South America. The National Origins Act won broad support from Progressives, including Senators Hiram Johnson of California and George Norris of Nebraska. But urban reformers, whose constituencies included the ethnic and religious groups under assault, expressed dismay at the bigotry of those who had "a fixed obsession on Anglo-Saxon superiority."

If immigration restriction illustrated the divisions among reformers, the experience of the Progressive party in 1924 demostrated their essential weakness. The party was formed by diverse groups uniting out of weakness rather than strength: former Bull Moose Progressives, leaderless since the death of Theodore Roosevelt; socialists, whose movement lay in ruins as a result of the war and the Red Scare; midwestern farmers, resentful over a sharp decline in agricultural prices; and railroad workers, embittered by the Harding administration's role in breaking their 1922 strike. In some respects the Progressive platform of 1924 was a throwback to 1912. It called for public ownership of railroads, the breaking up of monopolies, direct election of the president, and a constitutional amendment barring child labor. The party also favored prohibiting the use of injunctions in labor disputes, promoting public works in time of depression, and imposing high taxes on business profits. To the Progressives and their 69-year-old presidential candidate, Robert M. La Follette of Wisconsin, "that government is deemed best which offers to the many the highest level of average happiness and well-being."

La Follette faced an uphill struggle in his race against Calvin Coolidge and John W. Davis, the conservative lawyer nominated by the Democrats. His opponents, assailing La Follette for having opposed American entry into World War I, branded him a dangerous radical, the candidate of "the Reds, the Pinks, the Blues, and the Yellows." The Progressives, moreover, faced many of the same obstacles that traditionally hamper third parties: lack of funds, absence of grass-roots organization, inability to get on the ballot in every state. Although the American Federation of Labor formally endorsed La Follette's candidacy, labor gave the ticket less support than expected. Similarly, as agricultural prices improved in 1924, farmers' enthusiasm for La Follette waned. In November La Follette obtained 4.8 million votes—under 17 percent of the total—and captured only Wisconsin's thirteen electoral votes. Davis received 8.3 million votes, and Coolidge a whopping 15.7 million. Apparently the Republican slogan—"I like silence and success better than socialism and sovietism"—settled the fate of the reform-minded third party.

During the 1920s a new style of urban reform began to emerge, best symbolized, perhaps, by Democrat Alfred E. Smith and Republican Fiorello H. La Guardia. Smith, the son of Irish Catholic immigrants, epitomized New York City in his manner, accent, and very person. He had worked as a boy in the Fulton Fish Market, honeymooned at Coney Island, served an apprenticeship in Tammany Hall, and then became governor of New York. He was only being candid when he said, "I'd rather be a lamppost on Park Row than Governor of California." La Guardia, who represented East Harlem in Congress from 1922 to 1933, was an Italian-Jewish–American Episcopalian who spoke seven languages and whose wife was a German Lutheran. La Guardia, his biographer has commented, "was a balanced ticket all by himself." Smith and La Guardia supported a broad range of social welfare proposals, but were distinctive chiefly for their stand on cultural issues. Both championed the cause of immigrants. Both openly flouted prohibition. Both served as spokesmen for urban cosmopolitanism in a bitter struggle with rural fundamentalism.

This struggle reached a climax when the Democrats selected Smith as

Governor Al Smith and family.

their presidential candidate in 1928. Smith favored such reforms as public power and McNary-Haugenism, but his contest with Republican Herbert Hoover did not center on economic issues. Smith in fact chose as his campaign manager John J. Raskob, a former Republican and General Motors executive who listed his occupation in *Who's Who in America* as "capitalist." The election turned on the issues of religion, immigration, prohibition, and the city. One New England Protestant reformer expressed the sense of cultural cleavage when she wrote in her diary: "My America against Tammany's. Prairie, Plantation and Everlasting Hills against the Sidewalks of New York!" Given the prevailing prosperity, Hoover was probably unbeatable, but his margin of victory demonstrated the pervasiveness of cultural tensions. Smith received only eighty-seven electoral votes, and 15 million votes to Hoover's 21.4 million. For the first time since Reconstruction, the Republicans broke the Solid South, capturing Virginia, North Carolina, Texas, Florida, and Tennessee. The only consolation for the Democrats was that Smith did extremely well in the nation's largest cities.

## PROHIBITION AND CRIME

Many Americans greeted the advent of prohibition in January 1920 with unwarranted optimism. Prohibitionists had long promised that, given a

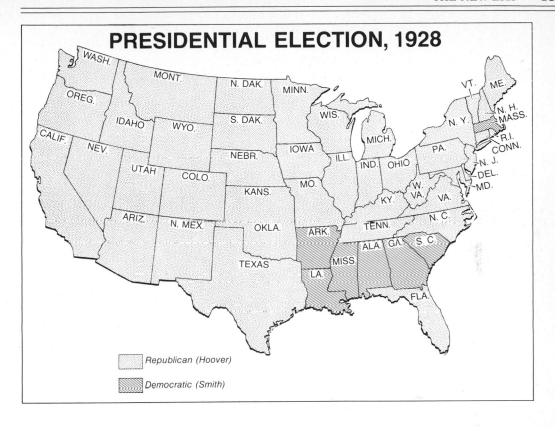

**PRESIDENTIAL ELECTION, 1928**

Republican (Hoover)

Democratic (Smith)

chance, they would eradicate pauperism and improve the condition of the working class. They had also predicted a sudden reduction in crime since "90 percent of the adult criminals are whisky-made." Closing the saloons, many believed, would improve the nation's physical health and strengthen its moral fiber as well, for drys were always saying that liquor "influences the passions" and "decreases the power of control, thus making the resisting of temptation especially difficult." On the day the Eighteenth Amendment took effect, the evangelist Billy Sunday conducted a mock funeral service for John Barleycorn in Norfolk, Virginia. He prophesied: "The slums will soon be only a memory. We will turn our prisons into factories and our jails into storehouses. . . . Men will walk upright now, women will smile, and the children will laugh. Hell will be forever for rent."

Prohibition, however, proved more attractive to some than to others, and the distinction often followed religious, ethnic, and geographic lines. Typically, prohibitionists were likely to be Baptists or Methodists rather than Catholics, Jews, Lutherans, or Episcopalians; old-stock Americans rather than first- or second-generation immigrants. They were more likely to live in small towns, and in the South or Midwest, than in New York,

Boston, or Chicago. Undaunted by accusations that they were narrow-minded fanatics striving to enforce conformity to their moral code, prohibitionists saw themselves as allowing the "pure stream of country sentiment and township morals to flush out the cesspools of cities and so save civilization from pollution." At the heart of the struggle between wets and drys were contrasting cultural styles.

The Eighteenth Amendment, ratified in January 1919 and ultimately approved by every state except Connecticut, Rhode Island, and New Jersey, contained several glaring loopholes. It did not forbid the consumption of intoxicating beverages but only their sale or manufacture. As a result, those who could afford to store up an adequate supply were not terribly inconvenienced. Out of deference to property rights, liquor dealers were permitted a full year's grace in which to wind up their business affairs. The amendment also failed to define the word "intoxicating" or to provide any means of enforcement. The Volstead Act (1920) attempted to remedy these deficiencies: it arbitrarily defined as "intoxicating" any beverage with one half of 1 percent alcoholic content, and it provided rudimentary enforcement machinery.

Yet the task of enforcement proved truly Herculean, particularly in those communities where a majority saw no moral virtue in temperance. There seemed an endless number of ways to evade the law. People smuggled whiskey across the Canadian and Mexican borders, made denatured industrial alcohol palatable by adding chemical ingredients, prepared their own "moonshine" at home in one-gallon stills, falsified druggists' prescriptions, stole liquor reserved for legitimate medicinal and religious purposes in government warehouses, and pumped alcohol back into "near-beer" to give it more of a kick. Those administering the law encountered many difficulties. The Prohibition Bureau, understaffed and underpaid, was the target of a series of attempted briberies. Some evidently succeeded, for one of every twelve agents was dismissed for corrupt behavior, and presumably others were never caught.

For all its inadequacies, the law almost certainly cut down on alcoholic consumption. But people who wanted to continue drinking, and those for whom liquor filled an important psychological need, managed to get around the law. Moreover, the attempt to enforce a moral code to which many did not adhere led to widespread hypocrisy and disrespect for the law. This received formal recognition when the Supreme Court ruled that the government could request income-tax returns from bootleggers. The Court found no reason "why the fact that a business is unlawful should exempt it from paying the tax that if lawful it would have to pay." The memoirs of a leading prohibition agent also testified to the laxity of enforcement. He related how long it took to buy a drink on arriving in different cities: Chicago—21 minutes; Atlanta—17 minutes; Pittsburgh—11 minutes. In New Orleans it took but 35 seconds. The agent asked a cab driver where he could find a drink; the driver, offering him a bottle, replied, "Right here."

Prohibition was associated not only with a cavalier attitude toward the law but also with a more sinister phenomenon: the rise of organized crime. Criminal gangs had existed in the past, but in the 1920s they evidently became larger, wealthier, and more ostentatious. Gangland weddings—and funerals—became occasions for lavish displays of wealth and influence. The 1924 funeral of the Chicago gunman Dion O'Banion included twenty-six truckloads of flowers, an eight-foot heart of American beauty roses, and ten thousand mourners among whom were several prominent politicians. Gangs also became increasingly efficient and mobile as a result of the availability of submachine guns and automobiles. And they grew somewhat more highly centralized, dividing territory in an effort to reduce internecine warfare. Although criminals made money through control of prostitution, gambling, and racketeering, bootleg liquor provided a chief source of revenue.

As organized crime blossomed, new theories arose to account for it. Sociologists at the University of Chicago, for example, argued that criminal behavior did not result from mental or biological inferiority, but represented a logical response to the environment. The gangster, growing up in a climate of lawlessness and graft, was simply a product of his surroundings. In his study of crime in Chicago, John Landesco noted that the gangster developed a self-image that legitimized his behavior. He viewed himself as doing what everyone else in America was doing— seeking wealth and power—but being more open about it. He thought of himself as satisfying a public demand for liquor and other illicit, but essentially harmless, pleasures. He perceived himself as a community benefactor who lent a helping hand to the poor. Indeed, Frank Uale was known as "the Robin Hood of Brooklyn," and "the godfather of 1000 children." A remark attributed to Al Capone summed up much of this rationale: "They call Capone a bootlegger. Yes. It's bootleg while it's on the trucks, but when your host at the club, in the locker room, or on the Gold Coast hands it to you on a silver platter, it's hospitality."

By the end of the decade, opponents of prohibition had successfully turned the tables on its advocates. Once the drys had promised that prohibition would reduce crime; now the wets held prohibition responsible for organized crime and pledged that with repeal, "the immorality of the country, racketeering and bootlegging, will be a thing of the past." Formerly the drys had claimed that prohibition would eliminate poverty; now the wets asserted that the liquor industry could provide needed jobs and revenue to a nation beginning to experience mass poverty in the Great Depression. Prohibition was repealed in 1933. Yet it failed less because it triggered a crime wave or weakened the economy than because it attempted the impossible: to regulate moral behavior in the absence of a genuine consensus that the proscribed behavior was, in any real sense, immoral.

# THE KU KLUX KLAN

In the years following the Civil War, white southerners had organized the Ku Klux Klan to terrorize blacks and prevent them from voting. This early organization passed away with the end of Reconstruction, but in 1915 a new Klan was founded by William J. Simmons. In the early 1920s millions of Americans joined the hooded order, although membership probably never exceeded 1.5 million at any time. Yet the new Klan was not simply a reincarnation of the old. The Klan of the 1920s, although strong in the South, was stronger still in Indiana, Illinois, and Ohio. Perhaps three of every five members did not live in the South or Southwest. The new Klan also was not as heavily rural, but enlisted members in Chicago, Detroit, Atlanta, Denver, and other cities. One of every three Klansmen lived in a city with a population of over 100,000. Finally, the Klan was no longer primarily a white supremacist group. Its chief targets in the 1920s were immigrants and Catholics.

The Klan began its rapid ascent in 1920 when two public-relations experts, Edward Y. Clarke and Elizabeth Tyler, made an arrangement with Simmons that turned the Klan into a highly profitable business venture. To sell Klan memberships they recruited a legion of high-powered salesmen, known as "Kleagles," and adopted shrewd sales techniques. More than one thousand organizers set forth in search of recruits, and since each membership cost $10, of which the Kleagle kept $4, the incentive was rather high. Simmons and the other Klan leaders eventually grew wealthy by taking a rake-off on everything from membership fees to the sale of official robes and hoods. With so much at stake, power struggles inevitably occurred. In 1922 the Klan changed hands. Hiram Wesley Evans, a Dallas dentist, ousted Clarke and Tyler and agreed to buy out Simmons, who held the copyright on Klan regalia. Simmons retained his title but no authority. He later recalled, "Not long after Evans got in I noticed a coldness among all the office help. I didn't have any office to go to. I just sort of had to hang around the place even though my title was Emperor."

The Klan created a world of make-believe by carrying ritual, pageantry, and secrecy to the furthest extreme. Klansmen met in a Klavern, held Klonklaves, carried on Klonversations, and even sang Klodes. They aspired to such high offices as that of "Grand Goblin," "Grand Dragon," and "Exalted Cyclops." They followed a Kalendar in which 1867 was the year 1, and in which awe-inspiring names were assigned to days (dark, deadly, dismal, doleful, desolate, dreadful, desperate), weeks (woeful, weeping, wailing, wonderful, weird), and months (bloody, gloomy, hideous, fearful, furious, alarming, terrible, horrible, mournful, sorrowful, frightful, appalling). Klan members spoke a secret language by forming strange, new words from the first letter of each word in a sentence. Thus "sanbog" meant "strangers are near, be on guard." The symbol "KKK" was exploited to the fullest. An advertisement in a Klan journal offered members a "Kluxer's Knifty Knife," a "real 100% knife for 100% Americans."

Clever organization and secret ritual did not alone account for the Klan's success. It also preached an ideology that appealed to Americans who feared that alien groups were threatening a traditional way of life. Hiram Wesley Evans asserted that blacks could never "attain the Anglo-Saxon level. . . . The low mentality of savage ancestors, of jungle environment, is inherent in the blood-stream of the colored race in America." He regarded Jews as "alien and unassimilable." The Klan was hysterically anti-Catholic. It believed in the existence of a Papal conspiracy to subvert American liberties and blamed Catholics for the deaths of Presidents Lincoln, McKinley, and Harding. Klansmen even suggested that the two antique cannons on the lawn of Georgetown University were pointing at the Capitol for a reason. Racism, anti-Semitism, and anti-Catholicism were all subsumed under a broader fear of the "mongrelization" of America through immigration. As Simmons put it, "The dangers were in the tremendous influx of foreign immigration, tutored in alien dogmas and alien creeds, slowly pushing the native-born white American population into the center of the country, there to be ultimately overwhelmed and smothered."

Klan activities were a strange mixture of benevolence and terrorism. In some cases the Klan functioned primarily as a fraternal organization. Members patronized each other's businesses, helped out in case of sickness or accident, and contributed to various churches and charities. Klansmen attended picnics together and held beauty contests, on one occasion choosing a "Queen of the Golden Mask." But the Klan also set itself up as a watchdog of community morals. It spied on people, reported acts of marital infidelity, attacked "indecent" shows and publications, and promised "to drive the bootleggers forever out of this land and place whiskey-making on a parity with counter-feiting." To uncover every possible scandal, the Klan sometimes tapped telephone wires and intercepted mail at post offices. It punished transgressors by burning crosses outside their homes, ostracizing them, or brutally beating and torturing them. Some victims were immigrants or blacks, other native white Protestants who failed to measure up to Klan standards.

The Klan acquired formidable political power. It helped elect senators in Oregon, Ohio, Tennessee, and several other states. In Texas it elected a senator, held a majority in the state legislature for a time, and controlled Dallas, Fort Worth, and Wichita Falls. The Indiana Klan, under David Stephenson, built a machine that dominated state politics and placed a functionary in the governor's mansion. In Denver a Klansman was named manager of public safety. The Klan's political goals, aside from power for its own sake, were to prohibit immigration, prevent United States entry into the World Court, enforce prohibition, and weaken parochial schools. The Klan put up its own candidates, endorsed others whom it considered friendly, and, above all, sought to prevent the nomination of, or else defeat, candidates such as Al Smith who stood for everything it abhorred.

Despite Smith's defeat, the Klan by 1928 had passed its peak. Torn by internal conflicts between Evans and state leaders, placed on the defensive by politicians who considered it a disruptive force, appeased by enactment of the National Origins Act, the Klan after 1924 began losing members and influence. Then Stephenson was arrested for abducting a young woman, sexually molesting her, and refusing to let her visit a doctor after she poisoned herself. Convicted and sentenced to the penitentiary, Stephenson opened his private files, which exposed Klan lawlessness. Supposedly created to enforce strict moral codes, the Klan could not survive this scandal or the ensuing revelations. By 1930 the organization was everywhere in shambles. Eventually the Klan sold its national offices in Atlanta to a purchaser who, in turn, sold the building to the Catholic Church. Appropriately, it thereafter served as an archbishop's official residence.

## FUNDAMENTALISM AND THE SCHOOLS

In the summer of 1925 the town of Dayton, Tennessee, witnessed an event that symbolized the decade's cultural conflicts. John Thomas Scopes was put on trial for having violated state law by teaching the theory of evolution in the public schools, but the nation's attention was focused on the lawyers for the two sides. Prosecutor William Jennings Bryan was the most prominent spokesman for the traditional values of rural, Protestant America. Defense attorney Clarence Darrow, by contrast, was a skeptic, a relativist, and an agnostic. There seemed no common ground between them. To fundamentalists the theory of evolution was a scientific sham the acceptance of which would erode the moral underpinnings of society. Evolutionists, on the other hand, placed fundamentalists on a par with those who had once refused to believe that the earth revolved about the sun.

Religious fundamentalists believed in the literal truth of the Bible.

The story of Adam and Eve was, in their view, a matter of historical fact. Darwin's theory of evolution, which contradicted the biblical account of Creation, was incompatible with divine revelation and therefore wrong. Many fundamentalists, however, misunderstood Darwin's theory and became easy targets for ridicule. The editor of the *Bible Champion*, for example, discounted the theory of evolution because while visiting a zoo he noted that "the monkeys and apes conducted themselves precisely as he had seen others behave many years ago in his boyhood days. He could see no signs of growing intelligence." Fundamentalists sometimes assumed an overt posture of anti-intellectualism, as when Bryan declared it more important to know the Rock of Ages than to know the age of rocks. Yet if fundamentalists oversimplified Darwin, the theory of natural selection—that evolution occurred through a gradual accretion of useful variations that fit an organism to survive—had by no means been proven. Bryan noted sarcastically that Darwin, in two major books, resorted to the phrase "We may suppose" more than eight hundred times.

Fundamentalists were disturbed by what they considered a breakdown in moral values, and by this they meant everything from "vile and suggestive" motion pictures and dance styles to "unchaperoned automobile riding at night." They attributed this, at least in part, to the popularity of the theory of evolution. By calling the Scriptures into question, Darwin was undermining Christian faith. By emphasizing man's animal nature, he was excusing immoral conduct. In addition, reformers understood that conservatives had taken Darwin's theory, applied it to human society, and concluded that government assistance to the needy violated the natural law of survival of the fittest. Bryan believed that the Darwinian model held that man evolved "by the operation of the law of hate—the merciless law by which the strong crowd out and kill off the weak." If Darwin was not responsible for the uses to which his theory had been put, Bryan nevertheless realized that the application had pernicious results.

Fundamentalist opinion was strongest in the South and Southwest but hardly dominated those regions. During the 1920s, bills designed to prohibit the teaching of evolution were introduced in twenty state legislatures. The measures always encountered stiff opposition and were usually defeated. Only five states—Oklahoma, Florida, Tennessee, Mississippi, and Arkansas—enacted such bills, and even there they were regarded less as weapons of repression than as symbolic expressions of legislative concern. The Butler bill in Tennessee, which led to the Scopes trial, barred the teaching of "any theory that denies the Story of the Divine Creation of Man as taught in the Bible, and [holds] instead that man has descended from a lower order of animals." It passed easily since educators feared that opposing a popular measure might jeopardize state university appropriations. No one took it very seriously. "Probably the law will never be applied," said the Governor on signing it.

It was applied when some acquaintances persuaded Scopes to test the law, and the American Civil Liberties Union agreed to provide legal counsel. No one had interfered with the way Scopes conducted his high school biology class, but he agreed to the trial as a matter of principle. The chief courtroom drama occurred when Bryan took the witness stand and engaged Darrow in a verbal duel over the literal interpretation of the Bible that revealed Bryan's limited knowledge of science. The outcome, however, was a forgone conclusion, for Scopes admitted breaking the law and the judge ruled that evidence supporting the theory of evolution was inadmissible. The jury took nine minutes to find Scopes guilty, and he was fined $100. Offered his old job back, Scopes turned it down to pursue graduate study in geology at the University of Chicago. William Jennings Bryan died five days after the trial ended. Forty-two years later, Tennessee repealed the Butler act.

The furor surrounding the evolution controversy concealed the more subtle pressures exerted on teachers nearly everywhere in the United States. Most Americans believed that the public schools should instill certain values in the young, but usually the sensitive areas involved politics or economics rather than religion. In 1927 Nebraska provided that its teachers emphasize "honesty, morality, courtesy, obedience to law, respect for the national flag, the constitution, . . . respect for parents and the home, the dignity and necessity of honest labor and other lessons of a steadying influence, which tend to promote and develop an upright and desirable citizenry." As Howard K. Beale's investigation *Are American Teachers Free?* revealed, school boards commonly established curricula, selected textbooks, and hired teachers—all with the goal of excluding unpopular ideas. In this sense the antievolution crusade did not represent an entirely atypical effort to restrict what teachers might tell their students. But because it attempted to reassert the validity of an older system of values through legislation, it expressed the cultural tensions that characterized the 1920s.

# THE GARVEY MOVEMENT AND THE "NEW NEGRO"

As cities in America got larger, so too did their black ghettoes. The northward migration of blacks, stimulated by the war, continued into the 1920s. During the decade New York City's black population climbed from 152,000 to 328,000, Chicago's from 109,000 to 233,000. People left the rural South to improve their lives and some undoubtedly succeeded, but large numbers did not. In Harlem and Chicago's South Side they crowded into grimy tenements for which they paid exorbitant rents. In 1927 an investigator said of Harlem that "the State would not allow cows to live in some of these apartments." Most blacks could find jobs only as menial or unskilled workers, and even then took home less pay than their white counterparts. As always, poverty produced chronic ill-health: in the mid-1920s the death rate in Harlem was 42 percent higher, and the infant mortality rate 70 percent higher, than elsewhere in the city.

These conditions made possible the spectacular success of Marcus Garvey and his nationalist doctrine. A Jamaican who came to the United States in 1917, Garvey dreamed of "uniting all the Negro peoples of the world into one great body to establish a country and Government absolutely their own." His Universal Negro Improvement Association claimed hundreds of thousands of followers in the early 1920s, most of them uprooted blacks who had left the rural South for the urban North. Garvey appealed to race pride by glorifying blackness. His paper, unlike other black journals, did not ordinarily accept advertisements for skin-lightening lotions or hair-straightening formulas. Whites, he claimed, had distorted the black past: "When Europe was inhabited by a race of cannibals, a race of savages, naked men, heathens and pagans, Africa was peopled with a race of cultured black men, who were masters in art, science and literature." Garvey also employed pomp and pageantry. His followers wore the resplendent uniforms of the "Knights of the Nile," the "Dukes of the Niger," or the "Black Eagle Flying Corps."

The coin of black pride had a reverse side: distrust of whites. In Garvey's view, "potentially every white man is a Klansman." As competition for jobs and resources increased, he reasoned, whites would become ever less tolerant of black success. The goal of integration, therefore, was a delusion, for the white majority would never accord justice to the black minority. "All true Negroes are against social equality," Garvey wrote, "believing that all races should develop on their own social lines." This could happen if blacks were free to build their own nation in Africa. Garvey did not expect the emigration of all black Americans but rather of a dedicated cadre of trained people. When whites saw that blacks were capable of constructing an advanced civilization of their own, they would learn to respect blacks. A powerful African state would drape a protective mantle around blacks wherever they might live.

Garvey's approach to economics was wholly in keeping with the business ethos of the 1920s. Deeply influenced by Booker T. Washington's self-help program, Garvey asserted that the black worker's only ally was the white capitalist who needed his labor. Blacks should steer clear of white trade unions and, indeed, work for just under union wages because employers would always prefer to hire a white unless there was some incentive to hire a black. In the long run, though, blacks could become autonomous only by developing their own business and commercial establishments. Garvey sponsored several such undertakings, but by far the most important was the Black Star Line, a steamship company de-

A Garveyite and family, 1924.

signed to link the non-Caucasian peoples of the world commercially and to transport repatriates to Africa. It thus united the twin themes of African redemption and black entrepreneurship.

But the Black Star Line was also the immediate cause of Garvey's downfall. The company sold thousands of shares at $5 each to black investors, but it quickly went bankrupt. Lacking managerial experience, Garvey fell victim to unscrupulous dealers who sold him run-down ships at inflated prices. The vessels constantly broke down and failed to pass inspection. The fiasco led to charges in 1922 that Garvey had used the mails to defraud investors. The government was only too happy to prosecute, for it had long regarded Garvey, in the words of the State Department, as "an undesirable, and indeed a very dangerous, alien" who was organizing "all of the negroes in the world against the white people." The trial began in May 1923 with Garvey, who believed himself the victim of persecution, conducting his own defense. He was found guilty and sentenced to five years in prison. In February 1925, when the courts rejected his appeal, Garvey entered the penitentiary. Late in 1927 President Coolidge commuted his sentence and the government deported him as an undesirable alien.

Most other black leaders, who always considered Garvey's ideology dangerous and his movement a threat, seemed relieved by the outcome. The NAACP opposed Garvey because he rejected integration and challenged its authority as spokesman for American blacks. A. Philip Randolph and other socialists placed their hopes in an alliance of black and white workers. They resented Garvey's enmity toward unions, emphasis on black enterprise, and insistence that race was more important than class. Even if Garvey had possessed greater business acumen and received a more sympathetic hearing, his plan still would have foundered. It was easier to talk about black unity than to achieve it. Liberia, seeking to placate France and England, which held adjacent colonies, decided in 1924 not to admit any of Garvey's followers, whom it considered politically unreliable. What had lasting import was his emphasis on race pride. In 1927 the *Amsterdam News* assessed Garvey's influence on blacks in this way: "In a world where black is despised, he taught them that black is beautiful. He taught them to admire and praise black things and black people."

In this respect, Garveyism had much in common with the "New Negro Renaissance," the name given to the work of black poets, novelists, scholars and artists, most of whom lived in Harlem, all of whom were self-conscious participants in a cultural awakening. The person who did most to publicize the movement was Alaine Locke. A Phi Beta Kappa graduate of Harvard, Locke, in 1907, had been the first black Rhodes scholar at Oxford. He went on to study in Berlin and Paris and then became a professor of philosophy at Howard University. In 1925 he published an anthology, *The New Negro*, with contributions by Langston Hughes, Claude McKay, Jean Toomer, Countee Cullen and most of the other writers prominently associated with the Harlem renaissance. Locke believed that the race consciousness cultivated by the urban ghetto was largely responsible for the new literary and artistic awakening. "In Harlem," he wrote, "Negro life is seizing upon its first chances for group expression and self-determination."

Black writers often disagreed sharply over such questions as whether to focus on racial issues or "timeless" concerns ("I want to be known as a poet," Countee Cullen said, "not as a Negro poet"), or whether to portray the seamy side of black life or its more positive aspects. Despite these differences, most of the writers identified with the new Negro renaissance shared common concerns. They emphasized the African roots of black culture and conveyed a sense that American blacks were spiritual aliens, cut off from their native land. They emphasized the dignity of the common people and the importance of the folk tradition. Writers began to use the cadences and idioms associated with spirituals and jazz, and Langston Hughes published a book of poems entitled *Weary Blues* (1925). There were also denunciations of racial injustice, lynching, and segregation. But for all their bitter indignation, these writers, according to historian John Hope Franklin, "were not revolting so much against the system as they were protesting against the inefficient operation of the system. In this approach they proved to be as characteristically American as any writers of the period."

## NEW WOMEN AND THE NEW MORALITY

For women, the decade after World War I was decidedly a new era, though in ways unanticipated by suffragists of the Progressive years. Politically, the decade began on a note of elation. Women were welcomed into the national committees of political parties, women candidates ran for office, and politicians catered to the new "woman's vote." In 1921, Congress passed the Sheppard-Towner Act, the first federally funded health-care plan, which supported maternal and child care services in rural areas. But women's welcome in politics, like the Sheppard-Towner Act, was short-lived. Since women voters did not seem to vote as a bloc or unite behind women's issues, Congress made no further gestures. As progressivism lost momentum, so did the women's movement that had long been associated with it. During the 1920s, feminist energy was dissipated in a prolonged feud over an Equal Rights Amendment, first proposed by the National Woman's Party in 1923. An ERA, its backers claimed, would "secure for women complete equality under the law and in all human relationships." But most women reformers feared that the amendment would harm working women by vitiating protective laws, and loudly denounced it. The ERA, charged Florence Kelley, was "a slogan of the insane."

While arguments over the ERA raged, women's organizations were shrinking, no longer able to mobilize the enthusiasm that once had been generated by the suffrage campaign. Not only was political activism going out of style, but young women of the 1920s seemed to have lost interest in both feminist goals and social causes. "Feminism has become a term of opprobrium to the modern young woman," a 1927 article in *Harpers* claimed. As collective purpose waned, attention turned towards private lives and individual goals. For some "new women" of the decade, this meant a redirection of feminist energy toward jobs, careers, and self-support. A major achievement, claimed journalist Suzanne LaFollette in 1926, was "invading every field that had been held the special province of men." Spectacular breakthroughs drew the most attention, such as former suffragist Amelia Earhart's aviation career. Less spectacularly, large numbers of women were entering the labor force in white-collar jobs and educated women were moving into professional work. During the 1920s, women professionals increased by 50 percent, and the number of married women in the work force rose 30 percent. The new woman of the 1920s wanted marriage and family, *Nation* editor Freda Kirchwey explained, but she also wanted "some way of satisfying her personal ambition."

In popular culture, the new woman of the 1920s was less the ambitious career woman than a younger version, just as assertive and more flamboyant, who was interested in personal independence, primarily of a sexual nature. Americans of the 1920s witnessed a transformation in private life, one that had been building up since the turn of the century. The much heralded "New Morality" (a label affixed by its defenders) was part of a long-term revolution, or evolution, in moral values and sexual behavior that rose into view after World War I and thereafter became a national preoccupation. Symptoms of moral change had been visible before the war, when dance crazes first burst into vogue and issues such as venereal disease were discussed in the press. But then, sexual emancipation was the province of socialists, radicals, and urban sophisticates. Now it was a far more widespread phenomenon that seemed to have taken hold of the entire younger generation, whose antics and attitudes dominated

College students, 1927.

the press. The young and old were as far apart in point of view, an *Atlantic* editorial observed, "as if they belonged to different races."

Behavior, moreover, was changing as dramatically as point of view. "The more sophisticated social life of today," reported Helen and Robert Lynd in their classic study of a Midwestern city, *Middletown* (1928) "has brought with it . . . the apparently increasing relaxation of some of the traditional prohibitions upon the approaches of boys and girls to each other's persons." Such relaxation, they observed, was greatly abetted by the automobile. It also seemed abetted by the media. Movies depicted attractive young women bickering over men, transforming their images with flapper wardrobes, or frolicking in novel locales, such as bathtubs. Newspapers featured pictures of beauty contests that catered to the decade's competitive and exhibitionist instincts. Popular magazines offered advice on "How to Keep the Thrill in Marriage" and best-sellers like *Flaming Youth* (1923), the tale of an adventurous young home wrecker, promised "the truth, bold, naked, sensational." According to social scientists, who now embarked on sexual surveys, middle-class morals were in transition. A pioneer study, by social worker Katherine Bement Davis, of the sex lives of 2200 middle-aged, middle-class women, revealed more sexual activity than readers or surveyor anticipated. Subsequent studies suggested that greater proportions of middle-class Americans were abandoning either premarital chastity or marital fidelity, or both. As all of the 1920s surveys revealed, birth control, though illegal, was widely used, especially among the well off.

The new morality was high on the agenda of cultural conflict, fomenting a battle between liberals and traditionalists. In some quarters, any dent in Victorian repression meant a gain for women. "The Myth of the Pure Woman is almost at an end," declared enthusiast C. V. Calverton, once editor of *The Masses*, a prewar radical vanguard. "Women's demands for equal rights have extended to the sexual sphere as well as the social." Judge Ben Lindsey of Denver, who applauded the younger generation, proposed a new type of "companionate marriage," that would provide a trial run of compatibility and could easily be terminated by divorce. (The divorce rate in 1930 was twice that of pre-World War I.) But traditionalists feared social disintegration and suspected that the new morality was no morality at all. Progressive-era feminists tended to agree with them. Charlotte Perkins Gilman contended that "indulgence" was not necessarily an improvement over "repression" and voiced considerable disgust with the irresponsibility of young women. "It is sickening," she wrote in 1923, "to see so many of the newly freed abusing that freedom in mere imitation of masculine vice and weakness." Contraception, in particular, was an issue that separated prewar feminists from emancipated new women of the next generation. "Your reform is too narrow to appeal to me and too sordid," suffrage leader Carrie Chapman Catt wrote to birth control pioneer Margaret Sanger in 1920.

Margaret Sanger, 1920.

As with much else in the 1920s, the new morality was far less radical a transformation than either proponents or critics believed. Some observers suggested that release from verbal inhibition gave an impression of greater change than actually occurred. Others pointed out that the new morality changed courtship customs but did not challenge traditional goals. According to surveys, young women's newly liberated attitudes were wedded to old-fashioned aspirations. Few were willing to sacrifice marriage for career but hoped rather to attain "a richer and fuller life" with "an all round companion." And they seemed willing, as one young woman put it, "to pay whatever price the companionship costs." The 1920s popularized a new ideal of romantic, companionate marriage, although not the trial run proposed by Ben Lindsey. Women could find fulfillment in traditional domestic roles, now enlivened by a sexual dimension. Some feminists objected to the new emphasis on domesticity. But Middletown readers were more likely to listen to columnist Dorothy Dix who advised wives to join clubs, cultivate worthwhile connections, and strive for upward mobility. "Woman," said Dix, "makes the family status."

Significantly, the birth control campaign, the most radical of prewar reform movements, adapted swiftly to the conservative tone of the decade. Before the war, when Margaret Sanger began her campaign in the 1914 *Woman Rebel*, birth controllers intended to reach a working-class following, end the production of "slaves to capital," and foster proletarian revolution. Since spreading contraceptive information violated federal and state Comstock laws, advocates of birth control were inviting trouble. When Sanger opened a Brooklyn clinic in 1916, she and her colleagues were arrested, tried, convicted, and jailed under New York State Comstock laws. During the 1920s, the laws remained on the books, but the mood of the times—and of the birth-control movement—had changed. After the war, Sanger's organization, the American Birth Control League, became a middle-class reform movement, courting the support of doctors, academics, and eugenicists. Birth-control clinics, now run by physicians, multiplied. And the arguments in favor of contraception changed. Birth control would emancipate women, Sanger asserted, as she had before the war, but it would also produce "more children from the fit, less from the unfit." It would eliminate the diseased and degenerate, rid society of "poverty, mental defects, feeble-mindedness, and other transmissible traits." Capitalizing on its scientific and eugenic thrust, rather than on its radical origins, the birth control movement was able to win the approval of the medical profession and the appreciation of a large segment of middle-class practitioners. A pivot of the new morality, it was able to adjust to conservative times, as Progressive-era feminism could not.

## THE DISCONTENT OF THE INTELLECTUALS

Intellectuals in the Progressive era had been outraged by economic injustice and political corruption. Intellectuals in the 1920s, however, while by no means apologists for Harding and Coolidge, were more often incensed by the materialism and conformity they found at all levels of society. Where the target had once been the crooked politician, now it was more likely to be the narrow-minded puritan who, unable to enjoy life, wanted to make sure that no one else did either. Formerly, intellectuals had drawn up manifestos for social betterment; in the 1920s they were more acutely conscious of the barriers to change, and some lost interest in politics altogether. Three books, all published in 1922, illustrate these themes: Harold Stearns's *Civilization in the United States*, Sinclair Lewis's *Babbitt*, and Walter Lippmann's *Public Opinion*.

The thirty intellectuals who contributed to the volume edited by Stearns examined different aspects of American society and found them uniformly stilted, oppressive, and dull. Stearns himself discovered proof of America's "emotional and aesthetic starvation" in "the mania for petty regulation, the driving, regimenting, and drilling, the secret society and its grotesque regalia." Lives devoted to acquiring material possessions, the contributors believed, were essentially barren and, even worse, marked by hypocrisy. The contradictions between what people said and what they did were so sharp that in practice the moral code "resolves itself into the one cardinal heresy of being found out, with the chief sanction enforcing it, the fear of what people will say." Given this diagnosis, it is not surprising that the book proposed no programmatic solutions. On completing the manuscript Stearns left Greenwich Village for France; other exiles would look down on him sleeping in a Paris café and say, "there lies civilization in the United States."

Of the writers who satirized the values of the business culture, perhaps none did so more effectively than Sinclair Lewis. In George F. Babbitt, Lewis created a figure who personifies boosterism, complacency, and conformity. A small-town real-estate agent, Babbitt is a thoroughgoing materialist whose "symbols of truth and beauty" are mechanical contraptions, who advises his son that "there's a whole lot of valuable time lost even at the U., studying poetry and French and subjects that never brought in anybody a cent." In a speech to his fellow realtors Babbitt defines "the ideal of American manhood and culture" as "a God-fearing, hustling, successful, two-fisted Regular Guy, who belongs to some church with pep and piety to it, who belongs to the Boosters or the Rotarians or the Kiwanis, to the Elks or Moose or Red Men or Knights of Columbus." Vaguely discontented with these values Babbitt finally rebels against them. But finding "nonconformity" hardly more satisfying, Babbitt is disillusioned, and when he is subjected to terrific personal and financial pressure from the community, he gratefully reenters the fold. Lewis's target, therefore, was not Babbitt himself so much as the society that produced him and prevented him from becoming anything else.

Walter Lippmann, meanwhile, expressed profound disillusionment with traditional American political beliefs. Lippmann believed that people thought in stereotypes—"for the most part we do not first see, and then define; we define first and then see"—and therefore irrationally. Democratic theory, he held, had "never seriously faced the problem which arises because the pictures inside people's heads do not automatically correspond with the world outside." Since public affairs were too complex for most people to grasp even if they wanted to, and since most people lacked the time and interest to try, it was not reasonable to suppose that voters would instinctively or intuitively make the right choices. Instead, Lippmann called for "an independent, expert organization for making the unseen facts intelligible to those who have to make the decisions." Social scientists, organized in a network of intelligence bureaus, might perform such a function. Social progress, Lippmann argued, depended not on the old Progressive faith in an enlightened citizenry, but rather on the scientific organization of intelligence.

Many intellectuals in the 1920s assumed a coolly detached stance toward public affairs. "It was characteristic of the Jazz Age," said F. Scott Fitzgerald, "that it had no interest in politics at all." But even those who held themselves most aloof were caught up in the Sacco-Vanzetti case. Nicola Sacco and Bartolomeo Vanzetti, two Italian anarchists, had been

Bartolomeo Vanzetti and Nicola Sacco, 1921.

charged with murder and robbery in 1920, convicted the following year, and sentenced to die. Legal appeals dragged on for six years until, in August 1927, both men were electrocuted. The case stirred immense moral outrage because elementary rules of due process were ignored, the judge was viciously biased, and the Commonwealth of Massachusetts seemed determined to carry out an unjust sentence rather than concede the possibility of error. For a generation of intellectuals, Sacco and Vanzetti came to symbolize all that America was not. In a nation of conformists they were rebels; in a nation of materialists they were "the good shoemaker and poor fishpeddler." They were, it seemed, martyrs crucified by an unfeeling society. If the great majority of Americans followed Bruce Barton in apotheosizing businessmen, most intellectuals followed Malcolm Cowley, who wrote: "March on, O dago Christs, while we/ march on to spread your name abroad/ like ashes in the winds of God."

## THE END OF THE NEW ORDER: 1929

Other Americans had a quite different view of what they had to contribute to the world. "The work that religion, government, and war have failed in must be done by business," an *Atlantic Monthly* correspondent declared in 1928. "That eternal job of administering the planet must be turned over to the despised business man."

One of the great businessmen, not at all despised, was the newly elected President. A multimillionaire mining engineer, Herbert Hoover embodied the success stories of the 1920s. His efficiency, realism, and faith in technology were exemplified when he installed the first telephone on the President's desk. (Before that the Chief Executive had to use a booth in an adjoining room.) He turned to social scientists for programs that would make the society run yet more efficiently and profitably. The roots of the system needed no examination. As Hoover told a crowded Stanford stadium in 1928, "We in America today are nearer to the final triumph over poverty than ever before in the history of any land. The poorhouse is vanishing from among us."

Such economic triumphs of American individualism, moreover, had eradicated the causes of world wars. "It seems to me," Hoover wrote his Secretary of State, Henry Stimson, in 1929, "that there is the most profound outlook for peace today that we have had at any time in the last half century." Most Democrats were forced to agree. When the influential periodical *Foreign Affairs* asked a Republican and a Democrat to discuss their differences on foreign policy in 1928, the Democrat, Franklin D. Roosevelt, could find little of substance wrong with Republican diplomacy.

Hoover and many others fully realized that international stability depended on the strength of the American economy. Since becoming the world's leading creditor during the World War, the United States had dominated the international economy as England had before 1914. That power increased during the 1920s, as the efficient American system exported ever larger amounts of goods. When foreign customers tried to repay with their own goods, however, they encountered walls erected by the 1922 Fordney-McCumber Tariff, which raised average rates on imports to 33 percent. In 1923, United States merchandise exports exceeded imports by $375 million, but by 1928 by $1.1 billion. Profiting handsomely, Americans covered the difference by loaning their dollars to foreigners for the purchase of United States goods, and by investing directly in overseas stocks and bonds. The dollar made the world economy go around.

By 1929, however, the dollar had begun staying home. New overseas investment opportunities did not appear, and a glamorous alternative, the New York Stock Exchange, quickly seduced big and small spenders. In 1924 the *New York Times* industrial average of stocks was 106; by 1928, 331; and during the summer of 1929, it shot up another 110 points. This wild speculation was fueled by "buying on margin," in which an investor bought stocks for a small downpayment while borrowing the remainder at interest rates as high as 10 to 20 percent. The government and the banking community watched this with happy hearts, even encouraging the speculation since they believed the stock exchange rested on a sound American economy.

But that economy was being eaten away by a rash of illnesses. Three became obvious in 1929–30. First, the mass of Americans were too poor to buy the glut of goods being produced. Productivity shot up nearly 50 percent between 1919 and 1929 until the gross national product (the sum of all goods and services produced in the country) reached $104 billion in 1929. But wages did not keep pace. By 1929, 5 percent of the people received one-third of all personal income. As the gap between rich and poor widened, the economy became increasingly unstable. The government refused to consider measures, such as higher income taxes, to make income more equal. Farmers, miners, and textile workers especially suffered. Between 1919 and 1929 farm debt more than doubled. Farmers were further hurt in 1928 and 1929, when their foreign markets, now lacking American dollars, were no longer able to buy large amounts of wheat and cotton. Throughout the decade the rate of bank failures had also been high. In truth, stock prices rested not on a strong economy, but on bankers' loans and on holding companies that had gained control of smaller firms through complex stock manipulations and business hocus-pocus. In October 1929 the stock market suddenly stalled. Excited bankers demanded repayment of their loans, forcing borrowers to declare bankruptcy, disappear, or jump from high buildings. A run on stocks began, and within a month after "Black Thursday," October 24, stock prices plummeted 50 percent. The holding companies proved to be merely paper, for when one of their firms went bankrupt, the rest of the company's properties were also dragged down.

A second illness, the inability of the government to control the economy, next became obvious. Throughout 1927 and 1928 the Federal Reserve System had helped stock speculation with a low interest–easy money policy. When the System tried finally to slow the wild lending, large private banks refused to cooperate. As the stock decline accelerated, eight hundred banks closed in 1930. The government did little to save the banking system. Unemployment of 1.5 million in 1929 shot up to 4.2 million in 1930, further cutting purchasing power. The Federal Reserve System then set lending rates at historically low levels so money would be very cheap. But there were no takers, for there appeared to be nowhere to invest the money profitably. As American capitalism crumbled, the government passed the Hawley-Smoot Tariff in 1930, raising average rates on imports to 40 percent in order to keep out cheap foreign goods.

But the tariff starkly revealed the third illness. The world economy could survive only with the aid of either dollars or American markets. Now both disappeared. Without dollars foreigners could neither buy American goods nor repay earlier loans. As their own economies began to collapse, they too sought protection behind tariff walls that kept out American goods. From 1929 to 1933 world trade dropped 40 percent in value, with the leading exporters—England, Germany, Japan, and the United States—especially hard hit. A domino effect occurred: the American depression caused foreign economies to decline, and the disappearance of these traditional markets for American products in turn worsened conditions in the United States. In trying to cure their own maladies, Americans had instead infected the rest of the world. Meanwhile, President Hoover announced that the economy was basically sound, and a group of Harvard economists declared, "a serious depression . . . is outside the range of possibility."

Actually the world tottered on the edge of catastrophe. The great British economist, John Maynard Keynes, held out little hope: "A general breakdown is inevitable," he privately commented. "America will revert to a Texas type of civilization, France and Germany will go to war." Keynes's conclusions were appropriate, for without a healthy international economy the treaty system, so painfully constructed at Washington in 1922 and in Europe between 1924 and 1929, could not survive. The problem was not that Americans had become isolationist during the 1920s. Indeed, the internationalization of the American system had been so successful that as the domestic economy slowly sank, it dragged the rest of the world down with it.

## Suggested Reading

Useful accounts of American society in the 1920s are William E. Leuchtenburg, *The Perils of Prosperity* (1958); Paul A. Carter, *Another Part of the Twenties* (1977); and Geoffrey Perrett *America in the Twenties* (1982). Republican politics is analyzed in Robert K. Murray, *The Harding Era* (1969); Eugene P. Trani and David L. Wilson, *The Presidency of Warren G. Harding* (1977); and Donald McCoy, *Calvin Coolidge* (1967). For a discussion of labor unions, consult Irving Bernstein, *The Lean Years* (1960); and Robert Zieger, *Republicans and Labor, 1919–1929* (1969).

Three sources are key for foreign policy: R. H. Burns, *Guide to American Foreign Relations Since 1700* (1983); Frank Costigliola's superb *Awkward Dominion* (1985); and Melvyn Leffler's fine *The Elusive Quest* (1979). Useful studies of foreign economic policy are Joan Hoff Wilson's two important works, *American Business and Foreign Policy, 1920–1933* (1971), and *Ideology and Economics: U.S. Relations with the Soviet Union, 1918–1933* (1974). The American role in international conferences is analyzed in Roger Dingman's important *Power in the Pacific: The Origins of Naval Arms Limitation, 1914–1922* (1976). For relations with Asia and Latin America, see Akira Iriye, *After Imperialism: The Search for a New Order in the Far East, 1921–1931* (1965); and Joseph Tulchin, *The Aftermath of War: World War I and U.S. Policy Toward Latin America* (1971). Charles Chatfield, *For Peace and Justice . . . 1914–1941* (1971) analyzes pacifism in this era. And see the important insights in *The Making of the Diplomatic Mind: The Training, Outlook, and Style of United States Foreign Service Officers, 1908–1931* (1975) by Robert D. Schulzinger. On Nicaragua see Neill Macauley's *The Sandino Affair* (1967).

Some of the problems confronting reformers are considered in biographies, particularly Lawrence W. Levine, *Defender of the Faith: William J. Bryan, 1915–1925* (1965); Matthew and Hanna Josephson, *Al Smith* (1970); Howard Zinn, *La Guardia in Congress* (1958); and David P. Thelen, *Robert M. La Follette and the Insurgent Spirit* (1978). Additional information may be found in Clark Chambers, *Seedtime of Reform, 1918–1933* (1963); and David Burner, *The Politics of Provincialism* (1968), a study of the Democratic party.

Cultural conflicts during the 1920s are considered in Don Kirschner, *City and Country: Rural Responses to Urbanization in the 1920s* (1970). On prohibition, see Andrew Sinclair, *Prohibition: The Era of Excess* (1962), and Norman H. Clark, *Deliver Us From Evil* (1976); on the Klan, Kenneth T. Jackson, *The Ku Klux Klan in the City, 1915–1930* (1967), and Charles C. Alexander, *The Ku Klux Klan in the Southwest* (1965). Norman F. Furniss, *The Fundamentalist Controversy, 1918–1931* (1954) discusses Protestant fundamentalism; Ray Ginger, *Six Days or Forever?* (1958), describes the Scopes trial.

The development of black ghettoes is explained in Gilbert Osofsky, *Harlem: The Making of a Ghetto* (1966); Alan H. Spear, *Black Chicago* (1967); and Kenneth L. Kusmer, *A Ghetto Takes Shape: Black Cleveland, 1870–1930* (1976). Contrasting evaluations of the Garvey movement are provided by David Cronon, *Black Moses* (1962); and Theodore Vincent, *Black Power and the Garvey Movement* (1970). For black culture in the 1920s, see Nathan Huggins, *Harlem Renaissance* (1971); and David Levering Lewis, *When Harlem Was in Vogue* (1981).

For women's roles in the 1920s, see Elaine Showalter, ed., *These Modern Women: Autobiographical Essays from the 1920s* (1978); Susan D. Becker, *The Origins of the Equal Rights Amendment: Feminism Between the Wars* (1981); Paula S. Fass, *The Damned and the Beautiful: American Youth in the 1920s* (1977); and David M. Kennedy, *Birth Control in America: The Career of Margaret Sanger* (1970).

The intellectuals' critique of the business culture is recorded in Malcolm Cowley, *Exile's Return* (1934), and evaluated in Frederick J. Hoffman, *The Twenties* (1955). The most famous trial of the decade is assessed in Roberta Strauss Feuerlicht, *Justice Crucified: The Story of Sacco and Vanzetti* (1977). Herbert Hoover's view of the depression is set forth in his *Memoirs,* 3 vols. (1932). Other accounts are John K. Galbraith, *The Great Crash* (1955); Robert Sobel, *The Great Bull Market* (1968); and the relevant portions of William A. Williams, *The Contours of American History* (1961).

On Bessie Smith, see Chris Albertson, *Bessie* (1971); on the blues, Paul Oliver, *Blues Fell This Morning* (1960), and *The Story of the Blues* (1969).

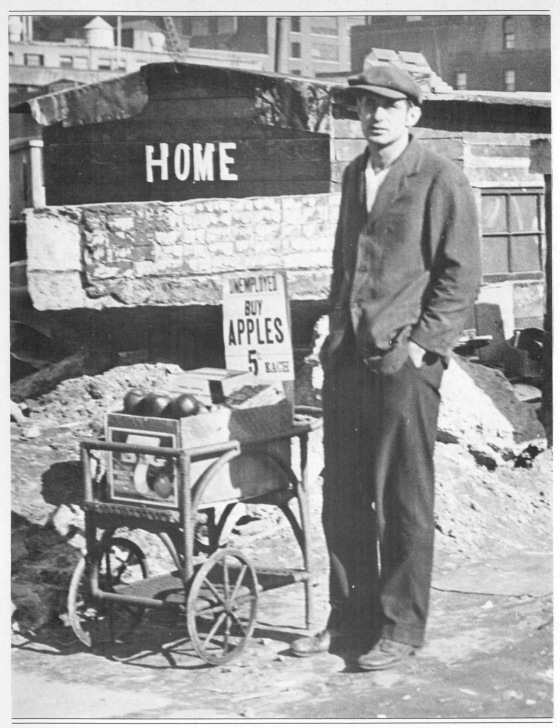

Apple seller, 1932.

# 1929–1936

## Depression
## and New Deal

The Great Depression had a cataclysmic effect on all areas of American life. Producing unprecedented suffering, the economic crisis posed a severe challenge to the prevailing view of the government's social responsibilities. Within a few years that view, which sharply limited the role of government, proved a dismal failure. Yet the fear that disillusioned Americans would turn to revolution on the left, or to dictatorship on the right, proved groundless. Most people favored more moderate change, and that is exactly what the New Deal provided. Franklin D. Roosevelt's first administration erected the foundations of a welfare state. New Deal policies concerning business, agriculture, conservation, labor, and welfare, while benefiting certain interest groups considerably more than others, nevertheless enabled the Democrats to fashion a new political coalition that dominated American politics for several decades.

## HERBERT HOOVER AND THE DEPRESSION

Perhaps no one had ever assumed the office of president with more prestige, or left it so utterly discredited, as did Herbert Hoover. Entering the White House in 1929 as a renowned humanitarian, one who would lead the nation "to the previously impossible state in which poverty in this country can be put on a purely voluntary basis," Hoover exited four years later with his name a synonym for suffering and hard times. People who spent the night on park benches covered by newspapers said they were sleeping under "Hoover blankets." Those who hitched broken-down cars to mules or horses said they were riding in "Hoover wagons." Men who turned their trouser pockets inside out to show that they were empty claimed they were waving "Hoover flags." Hoover had once symbolized the application of scientific intelligence to social problems. By 1932 many considered his refusal to face facts squarely a national scandal.

During the 1920s Hoover had expressed boundless confidence in the potential of American capitalism. In *American Individualism* (1922) he asserted that the American system, by promoting equality of opportunity, permitted the "free rise of ability, character, and intelligence." Yet individualism, he added, by no means required the government to pursue a laissez-faire policy. As Secretary of Commerce under Harding and Coolidge (a position for which he turned down a $500,000-a-year offer as a mining and metallurgical engineer), Hoover endorsed government intervention in the domestic economy. He favored increased spending for public works to create jobs in periods of distress. He supported a constitutional amendment prohibiting child labor. He also advocated the creation of trade associations. By promulgating voluntary codes of business ethics, approved by the government, these associations would allow businessmen to avoid wasteful competition and to pool technical knowledge without violating the antitrust laws. In 1927, when floods ravaged the Mississippi Valley, Hoover brilliantly mobilized state, local, and private resources to aid the victims. Hoover's supporters in 1928 dubbed him "The Master of Emergencies."

As President, Hoover adhered to the same doctrine of limited intervention in battling the depression. Unlike some of his advisors, who recommended a hands-off policy, Hoover believed that government could cushion the impact of the slump. But if he were willing to intervene, he would do so only within clearly defined limits. Hoover never considered legislation a cure-all, for "economic wounds must be healed by the action of the cells of the economic body—the producers and consumers themselves." The government must not unbalance the budget, for that would destroy business confidence; nor should it centralize power in a Washington bureaucracy, for that would erode individual initiative. Instead, the government should encourage voluntary, cooperative action on the part of private citizens and local officials. "Each industry should assist its own employees," the President said. "Each community and each State should assume its full responsibilities for organization of employment and relief of distress." Hoover conceived his task to be largely one of exhortation and coordination, almost as if the depression were a gigantic natural catastrophe, like a flood or an earthquake.

In practice, this program consisted of five parts. First, Hoover summoned business and labor leaders to the White House in an effort to persuade them to maintain wages, keep up production, and proceed with plant expansion. Second, the President stepped up expenditures for the construction of roads, bridges, and public buildings. Federal aid for highway construction jumped from $105 million to $260 million annually, and the number of workers on such projects increased from 110,000 to 280,000. Third, Hoover signed the Hawley-Smoot Act (1930) which substantially raised tariff rates in the hope of protecting American manufacturers and farmers. Fourth, Hoover declared a moratorium on war debts in June 1931. Convinced that economic collapse abroad was prolonging the depression in the United States, Hoover sought to improve the ability of European nations to purchase American goods and thereby stimulate domestic output. Fifth, the President somewhat grudgingly accepted direct aid to big business. Early in 1932 Congress created the Reconstruction Finance Corporation (RFC) in order to assist businesses in financial trouble. In Hoover's last year in office, the RFC loaned $1.78 billion to 7400 banks, insurance companies, railroads, and other institutions.

Some of these initiatives helped, but none succeeded in reversing the downturn. The "conferences for continued industrial progress," as they were called, produced little more than empty promises. Most businessmen simply could not afford to maintain wages or prices while the economy continued to slide downward. The public works program did some good, but even as the federal government was expanding its program, bankrupt states and municipalities were trimming back theirs. Consequently, the total amount spent on such improvements and the total number of men employed declined. The Hawley-Smoot Tariff was an unqualified disaster. European countries, selling less to the United States, retaliated by erecting high tariff walls of their own. The debt moratorium had little domestic impact. Eventually it led to what its critics had feared—a decision by France, England, and most other nations to default on further payments. The Reconstruction Finance Corporation, whose activities were confined largely to bailing out large concerns, was said to dispense a "millionaire's dole."

By the end of 1932 Hoover's policy lay in ruins. Every statistic revealed a startling degree of deterioration. From 1929 to 1933, gross national product fell from $104 billion to $74 billion and national income from $88 billion to $40 billion. Almost every day there were more bank failures: 1350 closed their doors in 1930, followed by 2293 and 1453 in the next two years. Stock prices tumbled precipitously. General Motors had sold for a high of 91 in 1929; in January 1933 it sold for 13. In the same period Standard Oil declined from 83 to 30 and U.S. Steel from 261 to 27. Farmers watched in dismay as their income plummeted by 61 percent. A pound of cotton, which had sold for 16 cents in 1929, brought 6 cents in 1932; a bushel of corn, which had sold for 79 cents, brought 31 cents. Only the number of unemployed workers rose steadily. In 1929, 1.5 million workers—3 percent of the labor force—were jobless. By 1933, at least 13 million workers—25 percent of the total—were idle. An average of 75,000 workers lost their jobs every week for three years.

## THE BREAKDOWN OF RELIEF

Hoover's unwillingness to provide federal relief for the unemployed revealed more clearly than anything else the inadequacy of his approach. The United States in the early 1930s had an unwieldy and anachronistic system of administering relief. Existing agencies were equipped to deal on a temporary basis with individual victims of accident or illness, but not over a period of years with millions of jobless workers. Private charities had small staffs and limited funds; even municipalities often lacked the revenue to make sufficient money available. Only families that had become destitute, that had spent every dime of savings and sold every possession of value, could ordinarily qualify for assistance. Even then, those lucky enough to get on the relief rolls received barely enough for food. Rent, clothing, medical care—all were considered luxuries.

Despite all this, the President vigorously opposed direct federal relief in any form. To his mind it would open a Pandora's box, for it would

cause a sizeable increase in taxes, thereby discouraging private investment; lead to an unbalanced budget, thereby sabotaging confidence in
the nation's credit; and require a gargantuan bureaucracy, thereby jeop-
ardizing states' rights. Above all, the fearful "dole" would undermine its
recipients' moral character, which Hoover took to mean "self-reliance,"
"sturdiness," and "independence." Yet as the situation went from bad to
worse the President was forced to take notice. The agencies he created to
deal with the problem, however, illustrated perfectly Hoover's commitment to voluntary, cooperative action and his conviction that government
could more properly dispense advice than funds.

In September 1930 Hoover set up the President's Emergency Committee for Employment under Colonel Arthur H. Woods. The Committee at
first subscribed to the view that relief was a local function, but by April
1931 even Woods recognized the need for federal involvement. When
Hoover refused to concur, Woods resigned. In August Hoover created the
President's Organization on Unemployment Relief, headed by Walter S.
Gifford of American Telephone and Telegraph. Gifford arranged for a
series of advertisements designed to stimulate charitable donations. But
his group confined itself largely to a cheerleading function, considering
that, as one member put it, "our job is not to raise funds ourselves." By
November Gifford was assuring Hoover that "there is every indication
that each state will take care of its own this winter." Two months later,
testifying before a Senate committee, Gifford confessed that he did not
know how many people were unemployed, how many were receiving
relief, or how much money was available to the states to assist the needy.

While Hoover maintained the fiction that no one was starving, pressure
for federal action mounted in Congress. In June 1932 Congress appropriated $2.1 billion in loans for public works and relief. Hoover vetoed the
measure, but in July he accepted a watered-down version that met some
of his requirements. The Emergency Relief and Construction Act (1932)
provided for loans, not outright grants, to the states of up to $300 million.
To qualify, states had to provide conclusive proof of need, and to receive
further assistance they had to repay the loans within thirty days. The
states themselves, rather than a federal bureaucracy, administered the
program. Finally, loans were made by the Reconstruction Finance Corporation, whose chairman remarked, "I have a very high regard for social
workers, but God forbid they should have the purse-strings." The RFC
guarded the purse-strings very closely: by the end of 1932 it had allotted
less than half the money at its disposal.

Hoover had edged away from his original opposition to any federal
relief whatsoever, but he had moved inches when the situation demanded
he move miles. By late 1932 the rickety relief system was collapsing in
many places. Reports from cities across the country told of funds dried
up and resources exhausted. Toledo: "There is only a commissary available for most families which is distributing the cheapest grades of food

at a cost of six cents per person per day." Chicago: "Some families are being separated, husbands being sent to the men's shelter and wives to the women's shelter." Houston: "Applications are not taken from unemployed Mexican or colored families. They are being asked to shift for themselves." In Philadelphia, families on relief received $4.23 a week; in New York City, $2.39. Tragically, the special precautions taken to aid children revealed how bad things were. The American Friends Service Committee provided free lunches to children in the coal towns of Pennsylvania, West Virginia, and Kentucky. Funds were so limited that the Quakers could distribute meals only to children who were 10 percent underweight. In Oklahoma City, veterans collected discarded food from produce houses and scraps from butcher shops to feed the hungry. "All delicacies (such as figs that had spoiled and canned fruit that had gone a bit sour) were saved for the children."

## THE BONUS ARMY

The long years of hardship apparently left many Americans psychologically numb. No matter how bad conditions were throughout the country, people often regarded their inability to find work or support their families as a sign of personal inadequacy. Yet sporadic acts of protest, sometimes accompanied by violence and lawlessness, eventually occurred. In Minneapolis, several hundred people stormed a produce market, smashed windows, and helped themselves to meat, fruit, and canned groceries. In Dearborn, Michigan, a demonstration by unemployed Ford workers led to a skirmish with the police and four deaths. Unemployment councils in New York City tried forcibly to prevent the eviction of jobless workers from their homes. The Midwest saw the invention of "penny auctions": when banks foreclosed farmers' mortgages and attempted to auction off their possessions, neighbors appeared, armed with rifles, and no one bid more than a penny. The two most important movements of organized protest occurred in the summer of 1932—the Bonus Army and the Farm Holiday Association.

The career of the Bonus Expeditionary Force demonstrated that even the most disillusioned Americans continued to seek improvement within the system rather than outside it. The bonus issue originated in 1924 when Congress, over Coolidge's veto, promised a bonus of several hundred dollars (depending on length of military service) to World War veterans but deferred payment until 1945. By 1932, however, many unemployed veterans wanted to be paid immediately, since they considered the money rightfully theirs and they desperately needed it. When Congress took up a bill providing immediate payment, veterans converged on Washington to lobby for passage. The veterans aroused considerable sympathy, but the Hoover administration believed the case against them to be over-

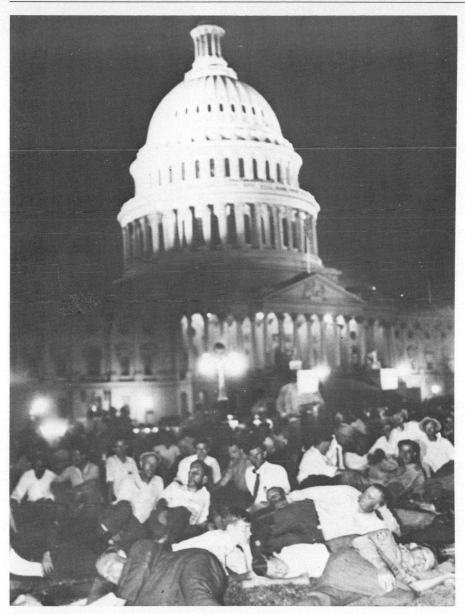

Bonus Army encamped by the Capitol, 1932.

whelming: payment of the bonus would wreck hopes for a balanced budget, give preferential treatment to veterans over other needy citizens, and entitle those veterans who were financially well-off to payment at a time of declining tax revenues.

In June 1932 some 22,000 veterans, led by Walter W. Waters of Oregon, streamed into Washington. They set up camp across the Anacostia River by building shanties furnished from garbage dumps. Many were joined by their wives and children. The Chief of Police of Washington, Pelham D. Glassford, himself a former army officer, provided some funds and provisions. In a sense, the veterans attempted to recreate the life they had known in the army, with its roll calls, discipline, and sense of purpose. One reporter described the march as a "supreme escape gesture . . . a flight from reality—a flight from hunger, from the cries of the starving children, . . . from the harsh rebuffs of prospective employers." Although the House passed the bonus bill, the Senate rejected the measure on June 17 by a large margin. Congress adjourned in July after allocating $100,000 to provide loans for marchers who needed carfare to return home. Only 5160 men took advantage of the offer. The rest, presumably having no homes or jobs to return to, remained.

The presence of the Bonus Army embarrassed and frightened the Hoover administration. The veterans, with their silent, ominous "dead marches" around federal buildings, provided visible proof of hardship in a city where, because so many people worked for the government, the impact of the depression had been muted. Hoover refused to meet with a delegation of veterans, assuming that an interview would only dignify their cause, raise false hopes, and bring even more demonstrators to Washington. In addition, the President came to accept the view that communist agitators had infiltrated the ranks of the Bonus Army. Ultimately the government increased its pressure on the veterans, demanding that they leave an abandoned Treasury Department building in downtown Washington in which some were living. The evacuation led to a scuffle with the police in which two veterans were killed and which provided a pretext for dispersing the Bonus Army itself. On July 28, 1932, General Douglas MacArthur led cavalry and infantry troops, as well as a mounted machine-gun squadron, down Pennsylvania Avenue. With bayonets and tear gas the soldiers drove the veterans out of the business district and across the bridge to Anacostia, and there set fire to the encampment.

The decision to drive the veterans out of downtown Washington was made by Hoover, Secretary of War Patrick J. Hurley, and the District Commissioners, but the decision to pursue them to Anacostia and break up their encampment was MacArthur's alone. Convinced that the Bonus Army was "a bad-looking mob animated by the essence of revolution," MacArthur ignored explicit instructions not to follow the veterans across the Anacostia River. But if Hoover had not ordered this pursuit, he accepted MacArthur's estimate of the revolutionary threat, believed that public opinion would support MacArthur's action, and therefore accepted responsibility for it. To have done otherwise would have required the President to repudiate his Chief of Staff and side with forces he considered subversive. The President thus not only misunderstood what the Bonus Army represented, but also misjudged the public reaction to the government's panicky response. The veterans themselves conveyed something of the bitter public reaction in a ballad entitled "The Prisoner in the White House": "In a cage that is fit for a lion/He moves with the soul of a mouse."

## AGRARIAN PROTEST

Even as the government was driving out the Bonus Army, corn and dairy farmers in Iowa and surrounding states, who could no longer make ends meet, were organizing the Farm Holiday Association. Like the veterans who went to Washington, the farmers wanted Congress to enact special-interest legislation. This took the form of the cost-of-production plan, under which the government would support food prices at a level that would guarantee farmers their operating cost, a 5 percent return on their investment, and a living wage for their operators. The plan would have raised the price of a bushel of oats from 11 to 45 cents, of a bushel of corn from 10 to 92 cents. The farmers, however, attempted to generate pressure on Congress not by camping on the Capitol doorstep but by withholding their products from market, hoping thereby to force prices upwards.

This movement received its greatest support not from tenant farmers or the very poor, but from those who had owned their own land and had done reasonably well before the crash. It was a protest not by the most deprived, but by landowning farmers, those most affected by a spiraling foreclosure rate. In some respects the movement testified to the lasting impact of Populist ideology, although the cost-of-production plan surely went far beyond anything farmers had demanded in the 1890s. Farm Holiday spokesmen characteristically blamed the farmer's difficulties on an international banking conspiracy. They regarded the countryside as productive, the cities as parasitic. The Association's most prominent leader, Milo Reno, who had voted for William Jennings Bryan in 1896, continued in the 1930s to affirm the need to "break the grip of Wall Street and international bankers on our government."

The Farm Holiday Association began implementing its direct-action plan in August 1932. Despite wide support, the plan proved unworkable. Blockading a few markets could not significantly affect overall supply or price levels. Even if prices temporarily rose, they would drop as soon as farmers resumed normal operations. Nor did all farmers wish to cooperate with the strike. As Farm Holiday supporters set up patrols and picket lines, they clashed with farmers seeking to transport their goods to market and with sheriff's deputies attempting to keep the roads open. The resulting violence dismayed the movement's leaders, who called off the strike in September. By then attention was shifting to the presidential campaign and the opportunity to elect candidates who might relieve the distress. In November 1932 Herbert Hoover failed to carry a single rural county in his home state of Iowa.

# JAMES CAGNEY AND THE GANGSTER FILM

In the early 1930s many Americans were troubled by the existence of organized crime, and troubled even more by what they considered its source: the widespread disrespect for the law bred by prohibition, and by the closing of traditional paths to success as a result of the depression. The release of *Little Caesar* in 1931 marked the appearance of a new film genre, the gangster film, that reflected these concerns. The picture's box-office success led to the production of fifty other such films within a year.

The most revealing of these was *Public Enemy*, in which James Cagney played the gangster Tommy Powers. Even as a youngster Tommy was tripping little girls on roller skates. As a teenager he fell in with the wrong crowd and became a thief and bootlegger (although in Cagney's portrayal a rather jaunty, loveable one). As the archetypal gangster, Tommy Powers

Mae Clarke and James Cagney, 1931.

Bogart, Cagney, and Jeffrey Lynn in "The Roaring Twenties."

scorns traditional values, most of which are embodied in his brother, Mike. Tommy Powers cuts through social convention with a scalpel. He sneers at education. When an accomplice asks him to involve Mike in a gangland operation, Tommy replies, "He's too busy going to school. He's learning to be poor." Similarly, Tommy exposes the hypocrisy of war. When Mike returns from military service a hero and accuses his brother of murdering rival bootleggers, Tommy snaps: "You didn't get those medals holding hands with Germans!" Tommy refuses to be domesticated. When his mistress, played by Mae Clarke, gently scolds him and says she

wishes he wouldn't drink so early in the morning, Tommy mimics her savagely: "I wish, I wish, I wish you was a wishing well. Then maybe you'd dry up!" Mashing a grapefruit in her face, he walks out.

In deference to the Hollywood production code—which provided that "the technique of murder must be presented in a way that will not inspire imitation," and that "the use of firearms should be restricted to essentials"—*Public Enemy* opened by stating that it did not intend to glorify the criminal but rather to "depict an environment." There was also a mandatory unhappy ending, in which a rival gang abducts Tommy Powers from a hospital and deposits his corpse on his mother's doorstep. But despite all this, the film's message was plain. Its hero, after all, was a man who thumbed his nose at conventional virtues, and who followed the one career he found open to his talents. The film was reassuring in another sense. For while Tommy Powers disregarded the laws everyone else supposedly observed, his world had laws of its own. The underworld operated according to

J. Edgar Hoover at the Justice Department, 1935.

a clearly defined code, and gangsters dispensed an informal brand of justice by annihilating one another. Moreover, the world of the criminal was encapsulated. The gangster did not injure law-abiding citizens because he moved in a world separate and distinct from theirs.

The image of the police officer in the gangster film was that of a dumb flatfoot, either incompetent, corrupt, or both. Yet with the advent of the welfare state under FDR, crime films changed to reflect the new national mood. As the federal government extended its influence, the image of federal law enforcement was refurbished.

Partly as a result of a massive public relations campaign by FBI Director J. Edgar Hoover, Americans came to regard federal agents as fearless, intrepid, and incorruptible. The circle was not complete, however, until the release of *G-Men* in 1935, staring none other than James Cagney. In the film Cagney joins the FBI to avenge the gangland slaying of a friend. " 'Public Enemy' Becomes Soldier of the Law," read advertisements; "Uncle Sam always gets his man." Now Cagney did his shooting from behind a badge, and, what was even more significant, a federal badge.

## FRANKLIN D. ROOSEVELT

To face Hoover in that election the Democrats nominated Franklin Delano Roosevelt. Born at Hyde Park, New York in 1882, the only child of wealthy parents, Roosevelt had entered Groton in 1896 and Harvard in 1900, and then attended Columbia Law School. In 1910, having practiced law for a time, he entered politics, winning election to the New York State Senate. He strongly backed Woodrow Wilson, whom he later served as Assistant Secretary of the Navy, and in 1920 he ran for vice-president on the Democratic ticket with James M. Cox. In August 1921 Roosevelt, until then a vigorous and athletic man, was struck by poliomyelitis. Years of physical therapy helped somewhat, but his legs remained paralyzed. For the rest of his life FDR wore steel braces, could walk only with assistance, and had to be lifted into and out of automobiles. While FDR adjusted to permanent paralysis, his wife Eleanor threw her energies into Democratic politics in New York State in order to keep the Roosevelt name in the public eye. In 1928 he had recuperated sufficiently to run for Governor. He won by a narrow margin, although Democratic presidential candidate Al Smith lost New York State, and he easily gained reelection two years later. In 1932, recognizing that Hoover's policies had alienated millions, and that the name Roosevelt was "still almost as much a Republican name as a Democratic one," he purposely conducted a vague campaign, promising to end hard times without ever explaining how.

Roosevelt entered the White House in March 1933 with several advantages. With 22.8 million votes to Hoover's 15.8 million, he could claim an undisputed popular mandate. He also had comfortable majorities with which to work in Congress. Democrats outnumbered Republicans 59 to 36 in the Senate, and 313 to 117 in the House. For economic advice Roosevelt could turn to members of his "brains trust," which included Columbia University professors Adolf A. Berle, Rexford G. Tugwell, and Raymond Moley. For political advice the President could rely on Louis Howe—an old friend and supporter—and James A. Farley, whom he made Postmaster General. Roosevelt's Cabinet contained talented administrators, among them Secretary of the Interior Harold L. Ickes, Secretary of Agriculture Henry A. Wallace, and Secretary of Labor Frances C. Perkins. Above all, FDR took office in the midst of a severe national crisis, one he likened to a war. He could depend, therefore, on an extraordinary amount of cooperation from Congress and the public.

## NEW DEAL THOUGHT

New Deal policies were hardly monolithic. People who backed the Roosevelt administration held disparate views: some favored collectivism, others competition; some preferred deficit spending, others a balanced budget. Nor were New Deal programs in different areas always compatible, for they usually reflected pressures exerted by contending social groups. The New Deal also underwent an evolutionary process. Important changes took place between 1933 and 1935, and others occurred between 1935 and 1938. Yet to recognize the complexity of the New Deal is not to deny its unity. Most New Dealers accepted a few broad propositions: that the economy had reached a stage of maturity requiring an unprecedented degree of government intervention; that this must nevertheless be kept within strict confines; and that the test of any policy was how it worked in actual practice.

In a speech to the Commonwealth Club of San Francisco in September 1932 Roosevelt set forth his reasons for believing that the age of economic expansion had ended. In the past, he said, when growth and westward expansion had ensured equality of opportunity, "the business of government was not to interfere but to assist in the development of industry." But all that had changed. Now America's industrial plant was already built if not overbuilt, its last frontier long since closed, and its free land virtually gone. In words that echoed Frederick Jackson Turner's famous speech of 1893, FDR announced: "There is no safety valve in the form of a Western prairie." Under these circumstances, the task of government was no longer the encouragement of productivity but rather "the soberer, less dramatic business of administering resources and plants already in hand, of seeking to reestablish foreign markets for our surplus production, of adjusting production to consumption, of distributing wealth more equitably."

At the same time Roosevelt affirmed that the government owed each person the "right to make a comfortable living." This as well as anything else marked the distance between his approach and Hoover's. For New Dealers, the depression had exposed the bankruptcy of the existing order, characterized by what Tugwell termed its "violent contrasts of well-being, its irrational allotments of individual liberty, its unconsidered exploitation of human and natural resources." The New Deal, Berle noted, brought "a tremendous expansion of the area in which . . . government is prepared to accept responsibility." Roosevelt indeed saw no practical alternative. To rehabilitate the system of private enterprise, government must rescue its victims. Roosevelt feared that a revolution "could hardly be avoided if another president should fail as Hoover has failed."

Of course New Dealers never provided each individual with the right to make a comfortable living, in part because they believed too much intervention to be as dangerous as too little. Conservative critics of the New Deal never tired of pointing out what many reformers admitted from the start: that government intervention posed dangers of its own. Government might easily confuse the demands of highly organized minorities with the general interest of the community and might still more easily discourage individual initiative and enterprise. The task, as the Roosevelt administration saw it, was to strike a proper balance, not swing from one extreme to another. As late as 1939, Thurman Arnold, the head of the Anti-Trust Division of the Justice Department, reasserted the need to follow a middle course: "We do not wish to extend the area of government regulation any further than necessary."

When Arnold declared, "I am not an inspirational preacher," he also conveyed the pragmatic quality of New Deal thought. Roosevelt's followers said they wanted "hard facts," declared it "unwise to lay down too specifically the structure of new things," and even announced that " 'truth' is irrelevant as a test of an economic philosophy." They believed in trying something to see if it worked, discarding it if it did not, and then trying something else. This willingness to improvise, surely a source of strength, nevertheless raised certain problems. For one thing, it was not always clear how long a period was needed to judge whether a program was working or what criteria would be used in making that judgment. For another, new programs attracted support from political interests and developed bureaucratic structures that resisted change. Policies, once instituted, proved less adaptable in practice than they seemed in theory.

## THE BLUE EAGLE

The keystone of the early New Deal was the National Recovery Administration (NRA), created in June 1933. The NRA, rejecting the model of competition, favored business cooperation in partnership with government. Businessmen were permitted to draft codes, subject to presidential approval, that regulated prices and wages and that forbade a broad range of competitive practices. Those participating in such agreements were exempted from the antitrust laws. In addition, the NRA supposedly guaranteed labor the right to organize, and it inaugurated a public-works program to pump money into the economy. This latter function was performed through the Public Works Administration, which FDR placed under Harold Ickes. To head the NRA, however, Roosevelt chose General Hugh Johnson, who had played an instrumental role in the World War mobilization.

Although Congress clothed the NRA with licensing powers, Johnson, fearing that they might not withstand the scrutiny of the courts, attempted to gain voluntary compliance from businessmen. He marshaled public opinion through parades and publicity, and all who took part displayed the NRA symbol—a blue eagle with the slogan We Do Our Part. Just as soldiers used certain insignia to distinguish friend from foe, Roosevelt said, so those fighting the depression "must know each other at a glance." "May God have mercy on the man or group of men who attempt to trifle with that bird," proclaimed Johnson. The codes, he explained, resembled the Marquis of Queensberry rules in boxing. "They eliminate eye-gouging and knee-groining and ear-chewing in business. Above the belt any man can be just as rugged and just as individual as he pleases." By the fall of 1933 every major industry had pledged its cooperation.

But in economics, as in the ring, heavyweights enjoyed a distinct advantage. Many corporate leaders had always disliked what they regarded as excessive competition. They saw nothing wrong with fixing prices, so long as they did the fixing. The antitrust laws had presumably blocked such concerted action, but their suspension provided business leaders with a long-awaited opportunity. As things worked out, big businessmen played the dominant role in drawing up the codes. The NRA, in consequence, generally kept production down and prices up. The codes restricted output by limiting factory hours and banning new plant construction. Similarly, they set minimum prices, prohibited sales below cost, and restricted combination sales, trade-in allowances, credit terms, and other competitive practices.

These policies caused a good deal of dissatisfaction. Consumers resented an arrangement that hurt their pocketbooks, and many small businessmen believed that the codes discriminated in favor of large concerns. Women's organizations, led by the League of Women Voters and the National Consumer's League, protested that one out of four NRA codes discriminated against women by setting lower minimum wages for women workers than for men. At the same time, labor was becoming increasingly dissatisfied because Section 7(a), which was intended to protect the right to organize, was proving insufficient. While it prohibited employers from interfering with their workers' right to join unions and choose bargaining officials, it did not create adequate enforcement machinery or require employers to bargain in good faith. In 1934 Roosevelt appointed a commission, under Clarence Darrow, that investigated the NRA and submitted a highly critical report. The agency's initials, said the disaffected, stood for No Recovery Allowed, or National Run-Around.

The experiment in industrial planning had mixed results. The NRA apparently brought about a measure of economic improvement and, perhaps as important, established the principle of federal responsibility for working conditions. Yet the agency did not live up to expectations, in part because different groups—consumers and workers, large and small businessmen—expected different things of it. There was, in truth, little chance that the NRA could have satisfied all the competing demands made upon it. Having relied so heavily on public support at the outset, the NRA found itself in difficulty when enthusiasm waned. In early 1935 the Senate agreed to extend the NRA for one, not two, years. That May, the Supreme Court brought the troubled flight of the blue eagle to an end.

It did so in the "sick chicken" case. The Schechter brothers, who owned a poultry market in Brooklyn, purchased chickens raised in surrounding states, slaughtered them, and sold them to retailers. In October 1934 the firm was found guilty of violating NRA wage and hour provisions and of selling unfit poultry. The case eventually reached the Supreme Court, which handed down a unanimous opinion. Chief Justice Charles Evans Hughes ruled that the depression did not confer upon the government powers it might not otherwise exercise, that an excessive delegation of legislative powers occurred in the code-drafting process, and that the Schechter brothers were involved in intrastate commerce and therefore outside the scope of federal regulation. Hughes admitted that the chickens had crossed state lines but reasoned that they had come to a "permanent rest"—that is, were killed and eaten—within New York. They therefore were no longer part of a flow of interstate commerce. Through an extremely narrow reading of the Constitution, therefore, the Court declared the NRA illegal.

## TRIPLE A

The New Deal attempted to aid agriculture by helping farmers pay off their mortgages, encouraging inflation to facilitate payment of debts, acquiring foreign markets for farm products and reducing acreage to limit supply. The last, known as the domestic allotment plan, served as the foundation of the Agricultural Adjustment Administration (AAA), which was established in May 1933. Under this plan—which affected wheat, cotton, hogs, tobacco, corn, rice, and milk—farmers signed acreage reduction contracts. In return for curbing output, they received government subsidies. In some respects the AAA was a counterpart of the NRA, for each involved a planned limitation of production under government auspices.

To obtain congressional approval for the AAA, the Roosevelt administration had to beat back proposals of a more extreme sort. The Senate, for example, attached the cost-of-production plan, favored by the Farm Holiday Association, to the measure creating the AAA. But the House, in which party discipline was stronger and White House influence correspondingly greater, rejected the amendment. The Senate also favored massive inflation through remonetizing silver, altering the gold content of the dollar, and issuing greenbacks. The administration finally settled for a compromise that gave Roosevelt discretionary authority, but did not obligate him to devalue the currency. The New Deal began experimenting with currency inflation in the fall of 1933 and continued to do so thereafter, but it never went as far as some congressmen wanted.

The AAA encountered two problems at the outset. George Peek, whom FDR chose to head the agency because of his long association with farm problems, never fully endorsed the idea of production controls. After repeated clashes with others in the administration, he was finally replaced by Chester Davis. A second difficulty concerned the destruction of existing crops. Making agreements to curb future output was relatively simple but did not affect the current harvest. The AAA therefore paid farmers $160 million to destroy one-fourth of their cotton. They plowed up 10 million acres, reducing the crop from 17 to 13 million bales. The administration also induced farmers to slaughter 6 million baby pigs and 200,000 sows. Although farmers received $30 million, and relief agencies distributed the pork to needy families, the extermination led to howls of anguish. "To hear them talk," Secretary of Agriculture Wallace said disgustedly, "you would have thought that pigs were raised for pets!" Roosevelt apparently regarded the matter less seriously than did his critics. He inquired jokingly, "Wouldn't birth control be more effective in the long run?"

The AAA helped farmers who owned their own land, but it often hurt those who did not. Of the 2.86 million tenant farmers and sharecroppers, 1.6 million, many of them black, labored in Southern cotton fields. The AAA policy of reducing farm acreage obviously reduced the need for farm laborers and consequently led to evictions and unemployment. Those tenants and croppers who remained received little. since payments were made only to landowners. They were supposed to apportion the money fairly among their tenants, but seldom did. The Roosevelt administration, believing that the AAA's success hinged on the cooperation of big farmers, would do nothing to jeopardize that support. As Chester Davis noted in February 1936, the elevation of sharecroppers "cannot be forced by the Federal Government to proceed much faster than the rate that the Southern opinion and Southern leadership will heartily support. To try to force a faster pace would merely be to insure violent controversy, lack of local cooperation in administration, evasion and ineffectiveness for the plan."

Not everyone shared this outlook. A number of AAA officials, led by General Counsel Jerome Frank, wished to protect the sharecroppers' position by requiring that planters continue to employ the same workers.

Frank's dispute with Davis eventually forced Wallace to choose between them. Early in 1935 he "purged" the AAA of Frank and those who wanted to make agricultural policy into a vehicle of reform. In July 1935, however, the administration partially appeased Frank's group by supporting the creation of the Resettlement Administration, which took the first, tentative steps toward helping landless farmers acquire their own land and tools. In some cases dissatisfied tenant farmers took independent action. In mid-1934, black and white sharecroppers in Arkansas organized the Southern Tenant Farmers Union. Too frequently, they complained, Roosevelt "talked like a cropper and acted like a planter." When they sang "We Shall Not Be Moved," they were protesting against a New Deal policy that was driving them from the land they worked but did not own.

Despite all this, by 1936 the AAA had succeeded in raising gross farm income by 50 percent, boosting commodity prices by 66 percent, and scaling down farm indebtedness by $1 billion. Then the agency met the same fate as the NRA. In January 1936, in *U.S.* v. *Butler*, the Supreme Court struck down the AAA by a 6 to 3 margin. Justice Owen Roberts, delivering the majority opinion, held that benefits paid to farmers for reducing acreage actually imposed a system of agricultural regulation under the guise of appropriations for the general welfare. In effect, Roberts said, Congress could not stipulate how its appropriations were to be used. In a stinging dissent, Justice Harlan Fiske Stone termed this "a tortured construction of the Constitution." He added that "the power to tax and spend includes the power to relieve a nationwide economic maladjustment by conditional gifts of money." This view New Dealers considered axiomatic for the continued functioning of the welfare state.

## CONSERVATION AND PUBLIC POWER: THE TENNESSEE VALLEY AUTHORITY

Few causes meant more to Roosevelt than conservation. The existing pool of unemployed young men provided an opportunity to unite the functions of forestry and relief, and this the President proceeded to do in the Civilian Conservation Corps (CCC). Within three months after its creation in April 1933, the CCC had enrolled 250,000 young men in their teens and twenties. The volunteers fought forest fires, built water-storage basins, and reseeded grazing lands. They constructed roads, bridges, and camping facilities. They tried to protect trees against blister rust, bark beetles, and gypsy moths. In three years the CCC planted 570 million trees in the national forests. It also showed farmers how to prevent soil erosion. To conserve wildlife, the agency built refuges, fish-rearing ponds, and animal shelters. In September 1935 the CCC reached a high point with five hundred thousand volunteers in more than 2500 camps. The men received $30 per month, of which $25 went directly to their families as part of a relief program.

New Dealers proposed a still more ambitious plan to transform social and economic conditions in the 40,000-square mile Tennessee River Valley. There, Roosevelt said shortly before his inauguration, "we have an opportunity of setting an example of planning . . . tying in industry and agriculture and forestry and flood prevention, tying them all into a unified whole." In May 1933 Congress established the Tennessee Valley Authority (TVA) thereby fulfilling—indeed, exceeding—the hopes of such public-power advocates as Senator George Norris of Nebraska. The TVA promised coordinated, multipurpose development. It not only provided electric power but also prevented soil erosion, helped control floods, allowed for navigation, and experimented with new fertilizers. It meant, FDR said, "national planning for a complete river watershed."

During the 1930s the TVA erected more than twenty dams with a generating capacity of 1 million kilowatts. Consumption of electricity in the region more than doubled. The TVA also cleared a 650-mile channel from Paducah to Knoxville, which greatly stimulated traffic on the river. Inevitably, though, the agency provoked sharp opposition from private electric companies, which took a dim view of government competition. These concerns similarly resented the concept of a federal "yardstick" against which their rates would be measured, arguing, with considerable justice, that TVA costs were not comparable with their own. Wendell Willkie of the Commonwealth and Southern Corporation, a leader of the opposition, branded the TVA "the most useless and unnecessary of all the alphabetical joyrides." Private utilities engaged the TVA in a long series of legal tussles. In February 1936 the agency won breathing room when the Supreme Court, in *Ashwander* v. *TVA*, upheld the government's right to sell the excess energy generated by Wilson Dam. The Court did not finally resolve the broader constitutional question in favor of the TVA until early 1939.

The TVA accomplished a great deal—as much as, if not more than, any other New Deal program—but it never brought about the "designed and planned social and economic order" for which some had hoped. Spokesmen for the agency advocated what David E. Lilienthal, one of its directors, termed "grass-roots democracy." Lilienthal believed that in assuming broad powers, the federal government must not lose touch with local mores and institutions. This required the "decentralized administration of centralized authority." The policy of encouraging local involvement, while helping to secure support, in effect made the TVA responsive to the largest and most influential interest groups. Its agricultural program, for example, was geared to wealthy farmers rather than to share-croppers. Those who had the most extravagant expectations were most unhappy at what they viewed as the TVA's capitulation. Rexford

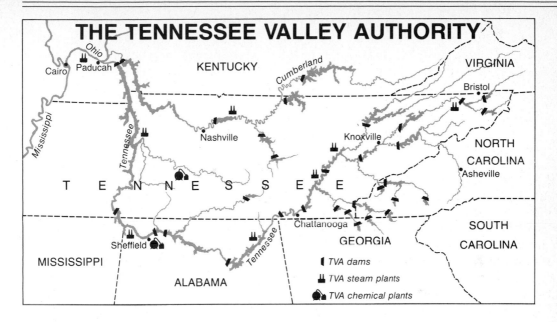

Tugwell said, ruefully, that after 1936 the agency resembled nothing more than a "Tennessee Valley Power Production and Flood Control Corporation." No less than the NRA and AAA, the TVA often catered to the already powerful.

## SOLIDARITY FOREVER?

When Franklin Roosevelt took office, 3 million workers belonged to trade unions, compared to 5 million in 1920. Only one in ten nonfarm workers carried a union card, about the same percentage as in 1910. In the steel, rubber, and automobile industries, unions played virtually no role at all. Thrown on the defensive in the 1920s by the open-shop drive and adverse Supreme Court rulings, labor suffered further losses in the early depression years. Unions found it impossible to keep old members, much less attract new ones, in a shrinking job market. Many workers shied away from union activities for fear of antagonizing employers. After 1933, although the economy slowly revived, the policies adopted by employers and American Federation of Labor officials continued to retard unionization.

The techniques employers used to block organizing drives included hiring spies and private policemen, stockpiling small arsenals for use in case of strikes, and recruiting professional strikebreakers. But in the years 1933 to 1935 employers relied chiefly on the company union, which had the advantage of appearing to comply with Section 7(a) of the NRA without actually doing so. These unions, set up and controlled by employers, lacked any semblance of autonomy. Management expected great things of them. A vice-president in charge of industrial relations at U.S. Steel declared that the union he had just organized would lead to "sound and harmonious relationships between men and management," similar to those prevailing "between a man and his wife." Mr. Dooley had once said that an employer's ideal union was one with "no strikes, no rules, no contracts, . . . hardly iny wages, an' dam' few mimbers." Except for the last point, company unions nicely fitted the definition. By 1935 nearly six hundred of them existed, with well over 2 million members.

The AFL meanwhile was proving itself unequal to—indeed uninterested in—the task of organizing the unorganized, particularly unskilled workers in mass-production industries. With few exceptions, AFL unions followed craft rather than industrial lines. The Federation adhered to the principle of exclusive jurisdiction under which, for example, its metalworkers affiliate had a claim on all metal workers, no matter where they worked or what their own preferences. The creation of industrial unions in steel plants or automobile factories could easily demolish these juristictional rights. To justify their position, AFL leaders insisted that unskilled workers lacked the leverage to bargain successfully, for if they went on strike, employers could easily replace them. The eventual collapse of such old AFL rivals as the American Railway Union and the Industrial Workers of the World supposedly provided iron-clad proof that industrial unionism led up a blind alley.

The Roosevelt administration, unwilling to abandon the NRA concept of a business-government partnership, did little at first to spur union growth. "This is a time for mutual confidence and help," the President said in creating the NRA, but during 1934 capital and labor exhibited little of either. Not only were employers setting up company unions to avoid bargaining in good faith, but labor militancy rose sharply. In 1934, 1.5 million workers went on strike, and industrial violence reached its highest level since 1919. San Francisco longshoremen, Minneapolis truck drivers, Alabama cotton-mill workers—all struck for union recognition and improved conditions, and all clashed with the police or the national guard. Simultaneously, pressure began to mount in Congress, where Senator Robert F. Wagner of New York drew up a measure to make collective bargaining guarantees meaningful. Roosevelt, claiming that the bill needed more study, succeeded in having it shelved.

With the various strands of his labor policy unraveling, FDR finally accepted Wagner's position in the spring of 1935. At the last minute, when the Senate had passed the Wagner Act and the House was about to do so, Roosevelt endorsed it. The Wagner Act (1935) upheld the right of workers to join unions, and created the National Labor Relations Board to conduct shop elections. Most important, the measure substituted the principle of majority rule for that of proportional representation, ensuring that the union winning a majority of votes would represent all the employees. The act prohibited employers from blacklisting workers, refusing to reinstate strikers, engaging in industrial espionage, or setting up company unions. The bill passed by huge margins, in part because many assumed—mistakenly as it turned out—that the Supreme Court would nullify it.

Enactment of this legislation was like a shot of adrenalin to advocates of industrial unionism. A sizeable group within the AFL, led by John L. Lewis of the United Mine Workers, now demanded that the Federation accept industrial unions. Craft unions, Lewis asserted, may have served adequately in the past but were not suited to modern factories, in which technology had erased old craft distinctions. At the AFL convention in September 1935 Lewis presented a plan to allow the chartering of industrial unions. When the delegates rejected his motion by nearly a 2 to 1 margin, Lewis led a walkout. The depth of the disagreement, as well as the hatreds it evoked, was shown when William L. Hutcheson of the carpenters' union called Lewis a "bastard" and Lewis punched him in

Labor leaders: Philip Murray and John L. Lewis.

the jaw. In November Lewis, Sidney Hillman of the Amalgamated Clothing Workers of America, David Dubinsky of the International Ladies Garment Workers Union, and leaders of fledgling unions in the automobile, rubber, and steel industries created what became the Congress of Industrial Organizations. The AFL demanded the CIO's dissolution and, when it refused, suspended and later expelled the unions composing it. Yet in the long run, the split proved a prelude to success, for it enabled labor to take advantage of the spectacular opportunities for organizing unskilled workers provided by the Wagner Act.

## RELIEF AND SECURITY

New Deal policies concerning relief, like those affecting labor, evolved in a halting fashion. This was no fault of Harry Hopkins who, before Roosevelt brought him to Washington to direct relief efforts, had performed a similar function in New York State. Hopkins's approach diverged sharply from prevailing practice. He believed that all needy persons, the unemployed as well as the chronically unemployable, were entitled to receive relief. He favored raising standards to furnish such necessities as clothing and medical care. He also believed that payments in cash rather than grocery slips helped preserve recipients' self-respect. Finally, Hopkins preferred work relief to home relief. The former, while admittedly more expensive, enhanced the individual's feeling that he was a productive member of society; the latter was often degrading. Work relief should, where possible, utilize existing training and skills. Hopkins saw no reason to insist that, as the price of obtaining relief, a teacher or engineer should have to dig ditches.

Hopkins's views regarding eligibility, standards, and programs went far beyond those of the Roosevelt administration and Congress. The first New Deal relief venture—the Federal Emergency Relief Administration (FERA)—showed this clearly. The FERA supervised relief activities from April 1933 to April 1935, except for a six-month period during the winter of 1934. At the outset Congress authorized expenditures of $500 million, half in direct grants to the states and half in matching grants on the basis of $1 for each $3 put up by the states. Administration of the program was left largely in state hands. The matching-grants provision had unfortunate consequences. States, hard-pressed to raise the money necessary to obtain such funds, had either to enact sales taxes, which imposed an unfair burden on the poor, or else cut other expenditures, such as those for education. If providing outright grants for relief broke sharply with existing practice, echoes of Herbert Hoover's policy lingered on in the decision to leave supervision to the states and in the attempt to squeeze yet more money out of them.

In November 1933, with the unemployed facing a long cold winter,

Works Progress Administration artist Isidore Lipshitz.

the administration conceded the FERA's inadequacy and temporarily replaced it with the Civil Works Administration (CWA). The CWA differed from its predecessor in that the federal government administered it and met 90 percent of its cost. The agency also took on some workers who, although unemployed, had not qualified for relief. The CWA offered relatively high wages, paying unskilled workers 40 to 50 cents an hour, up to a maximum of thirty hours a week. Within two months the new agency had put 4.2 million men to work repairing streets, laying sewer pipe, building roads, improving schools and playgrounds, and, as critics always pointed out, raking leaves. By the start of 1934, three hundred thousand women worked for CWA in sewing, canning, and clerical jobs. Undoubtedly some projects were poorly conceived, but most accomplished useful purposes. Many people, particularly in the South, made more from the CWA than ever before in their lives. When employers bitterly complained about this, the CWA in January 1934 reduced working hours and wages. The average weekly wage declined from $15 to $11.50. Then, in April 1934, the administration, worried by the CWA's high cost and controversial nature, canceled the experiment and reverted to the FERA.

Not until April 1935, when it established the Works Progress Administration (WPA), did the New Deal fashion a workable relief program. The WPA only employed those certified as needing relief, but it was federally run, paid good wages, and made room for white-collar and professional workers. At its height, the WPA employed 3 million people a year, and, although starting with an initial appropriation of $4.8 billion, it ultimately spent $10.7 billion over seven years. The WPA included writers' and artists' projects, and also the Federal Theater Project. The latter in 1936 employed 12,500 actors who performed before audiences of 350,000 every week. The WPA never helped all the needy, and it was continually fighting off attempts to slice its budget. Women qualified for federal relief programs only if they were heads of households; over half took sewing jobs. "For unskilled men we have the shovel," a woman WPA official told Eleanor Roosevelt. "For unskilled women we have only the needle." Yet the WPA embodied many of the principles in which Hopkins believed: decent standards, work relief, and utilization of existing skills.

Roosevelt created the WPA in April, endorsed the Wagner Act in May, and in August 1935 signed a third measure—the Social Security Act—which further institutionalized government responsibility for the disadvantaged. The act set up an old-age pension system administered by the federal government and funded by a 1 percent payroll tax. Beginning in 1942 (the date was advanced to 1940) retired workers over 65 would receive $10 to $85 a month, depending on the amount that they had contributed. Those who had already retired would receive pensions to which the government would contribute up to $15 a month. Second, the measure provided for a joint federal-state system of unemployment insurance based on employer contributions. Third, the act authorized federal aid for care of the blind, training of the physically handicapped, and aid to dependent children. Certainly, the Social Security Act had many imperfections: farm workers and domestic servants were excluded from its retirement provisions; state standards for unemployment compensation varied tremendously; and the payroll tax reduced mass purchasing power at the wrong time. The act may not even have amounted to what one Senator termed "a teeny-weeny bit of socialism." It did, however, place another brick in the arch of the welfare state.

## THE NEW DEAL COALITION

Harry Hopkins was once quoted as saying, "We shall tax and tax, and spend and spend, and elect and elect." The remark may have been apocryphal, but it infuriated those who objected to New Deal relief and security policies. Many Republicans asserted, without justification, that social security would require federal prying into the private lives of citizens and would force millions of people to submit to fingerprinting or wear dogtags for identification purposes. Many of these same critics argued, with considerably better reason, that Democrats were attempting to extract partisan advantage from federal relief. Officials sometimes dispensed relief in ways calculated to bolster their political position and occasionally pressured WPA workers into voting a certain way. One Democratic leader privately requested the appointment of administrators who favored "using these Democratic projects to make votes for the Democratic Party."

In 1936, when Roosevelt defeated his opponent Alf M. Landon of Kansas, some Republicans blamed the magnitude of their loss on such unfair tactics. Certainly the dimensions of that defeat were stunning. Roosevelt received 27.5 million votes to Landon's 16.7 million and carried every state but Vermont and Maine. The voters sent only 90 Republicans to the House of Representatives, and left only 16 in the Senate, giving the Democrats the largest congressional majorities since the mid-nineteenth century. The vote revealed a sharp split along class lines, with FDR in effect receiving most of his support from the lower classes and Landon most of his from more prosperous groups. Politics had moved full circle from the 1920s, when cultural tensions had overshadowed economic issues. The Roosevelt coalition embraced Southern whites and Northern blacks, rural dwellers and urban immigrants, middle-class intellectuals and blue-collar workers. In 1936 a person's income and occupation (or lack of one) provided the surest clues to party preference.

The Democratic triumph did not reflect illicit pressure exerted on relief recipients but rather public approval of the programs Roosevelt had instituted. At the time those policies were criticized as inadequate, and in retrospect they may appear even less adequate. In almost every field—business, agriculture, public power, labor, and relief—the New Deal moved cautiously and catered to more powerful groups at the expense of weaker ones. But this should not obscure the improvements in American life, or the changes in the role of government, that had occurred. In 1936 the clearest point of reference was 1932. The inadequacies of Roosevelt's policies, when compared with those of Hoover, did not seem so great after all.

## Suggested Reading

The account most favorable to Hoover's handling of the depression is Eugene Lyons, *Herbert Hoover* (1964); perhaps the most critical is Arthur M. Schlesinger, Jr., *The Crisis of the Old Order, 1919–1933* (1957). Other useful works are Albert Romasco, *The Poverty of Abundance: Hoover, the Nation, the Depression* (1965); Joan Hoff Wilson, *Herbert Hoover: Forgotten Progressive* (1975); David M. Burner, *Herbert Hoover: A Public Life* (1979); Ellis W. Hawley *et al.*, *Herbert Hoover and the Crisis of American Capitalism* (1973). For the crisis of 1932, see Elliot A. Rosen, *Hoover, Roosevelt, and the Brain Trust: From Depression to New Deal* (1977); for the veterans' protest, Roger Daniels, *The Bonus March* (1971) and Donald J. Lisio, *The President and Protest* (1974); for the Farm Holiday movement, John Shover, *Cornbelt Rebellion* (1965).

Important books on Franklin Roosevelt and the New Deal are Frank Freidel, *Franklin D. Roosevelt*, 4 vols. (1952–1973), which covers the period through 1933; William E. Leuchtenburg, *Franklin D. Roosevelt and the New Deal* (1963); James M. Burns, *Roosevelt: The Lion and the Fox* (1956); Arthur M. Schlesinger, Jr., *The Coming of the New Deal* (1959); and Robert S. McElvaine, *The Great Depression: America, 1929–1941* (1984).

The literature on New Deal economic policy is extensive. Robert F. Himmelberg, *The Origins of the National Recovery Administration* (1976), and Ellis Hawley, *The New Deal and the Problem of Monopoly: A Study in Economic Ambivalence* (1966), are excellent accounts. New Deal agricultural programs are evaluated in David E. Conrad, *The Forgotten Farmers: The Story of Sharecroppers in the New Deal* (1965); Sidney Baldwin, *Poverty and Politics: The Rise and Decline of the Farm Security Administration* (1967); and Paul E. Mertz, *New Deal Policy and Southern Rural Poverty* (1978). On experiments in conservation and planning, consult Thomas McCraw, *TVA and the Power Fight, 1933–1939* (1970); and John Salmond, *The Civilian Conservation Corps, 1933–1942* (1967).

For a comprehensive account of workers during the depression, and of New Deal labor policy, see Irving Bernstein, *Turbulent Years* (1970). The sponsor of crucial labor legislation is treated in J. Joseph Huthmacher, *Senator Robert F. Wagner and the Rise of Urban Liberalism* (1968). The welfare programs of the Roosevelt administration are considered in Roy Lubove, *The Struggle for Social Security, 1900–1935* (1968); William W. Bremer, *Depression Winters: New York Social Workers and the New Deal* (1984); Barbara Blumberg, *The New Deal and the Unemployed: The View from New York City* (1979); and Richard D. McKinzie, *The New Deal for Artists* (1973).

On the gangster film, see Robert Warshow's essay "The Gangster as Tragic Hero" in his *The Immediate Experience* (1962); and Andrew Bergman, *We're in the Money: Depression America and Its Films* (1971).

Texas Panhandle, 1938.

# CHAPTER SEVEN

# 1933–1941

## Hard Times:
## Politics and Society

Despite his efforts to combat the depression, and despite the vote of confidence he received in 1936, Franklin Roosevelt by no means succeeded in restoring prosperity during his first or, for that matter, his second administration. Millions of Americans who remained poor and insecure concluded that New Deal policies were inadequate. Some turned to socialism or communism, but more supported men like Dr. Francis E. Townsend, Huey Long, and Father Charles E. Coughlin, all of whom promised instant abundance without a radical alteration of the social order. If some complained that the New Deal was proceeding too slowly, conservatives believed it was traveling at breakneck speed. Limited at first to sniping at New Deal policies, Roosevelt's conservative critics launched a massive offensive after 1937. Faced with mounting hostility in Congress and declining public support, New Dealers went on the defensive. By the end of the decade the Roosevelt administration was devoting most of its attention to national defense and foreign policy, not to domestic reform.

## THE OLD FOLKS' CRUSADE

In 1935 a California congressman arose in the House of Representatives to reflect on the passing of his mother. "She is the sweetest memory of my life," he said, "and the hands that used to feed me and cool my fevered brow now touch me only in my dreams. But if she were living today, . . . that little frail mother of mine . . . would say, "Son, you be good to the old folks, and God will bless you.'" In the year 1935 being "good to the old folks" meant one thing: supporting the Townsend Old Age Revolving Pension Plan. Named for its creator, Dr. Francis E. Townsend, the plan gave birth to a movement whose widespread popularity pointed up the deficiencies of the New Deal and influenced the policies of the Roosevelt administration. Better than anything else, the appeal of the Townsend plan illustrated the devastating impact of the depression on the elderly.

For many elderly people the depression was in fact a nightmare. Many who wanted to continue working could not compete with younger workers. Unemployment among those over the age of 60 climbed to 40 percent. Many who had expected to retire on savings found themselves destitute when the banks failed. Others saw their incomes shrivel as the stock market fell or as private pension plans—often poorly conceived and badly financed—collapsed. Of the 7.5 million Americans over the age of 65, fully half could not support themselves. Some were forced to seek assistance from their children who, given the difficult times that everyone faced, were already experiencing hardship. Others had to apply for public charity even at the cost of sacrificing their self-respect. Only twenty-eight states provided old-age pensions. For the most part they were sadly inadequate, with monthly payments ranging from $7 to $30. In twenty states no pensions of any kind existed.

All these problems were greatly magnified in California, which, as a haven for retirees, had seen its aged population climb from 200,000 to 366,000 during the 1920s. Five times as many people over the age of sixty-five lived in California as in any other state except Washington. Large numbers of retired men and women, separated from their relatives by hundreds or thousands of miles, had no one to fall back on when the depression hit. California's old-age pension plan was defective by every standard. No elderly person with a legally responsible relative able to provide support could receive aid. To qualify for assistance, an elderly person had to go on the relief rolls, sign a pauper's oath, submit to a "needs" test, and accept a lien on any property so that the state could recover part of the cost of the pension upon the person's death. Then, and only then, were the aged eligible for a sum of $22 a month. The system could hardly have been better calculated to deprive the aged of their dignity.

These conditions help explain the overwhelming response to the Townsend plan. Townsend, who had worked as a ranch hand and traveling salesman before becoming a doctor, had gone to Long Beach after the World War. In 1933, at the age of 66, he presented his "Cure for Depressions." Everyone in the country over the age of 60 would receive $200 a month, on two conditions: that they spend the full amount each month, and retire if still employed. This would pump money into the economy, open jobs for younger people, and permit a dignified retirement. The plan would be financed by a national sales tax, later called a transactions tax. Asked why he chose the figure of $200, Townsend explained, "the main reason was so that nobody would come along and offer more." In collaboration with Robert Earl Clements, Townsend set up Old Age Revolving Pensions, Ltd., in January 1934. Within two years seven thousand Townsend clubs with about 1.5 million members had sprung up across the country.

Townsend's appeal derived in part from his standing as a physician, a figure in whom the elderly placed a great deal of confidence. Moreover, Townsend clubs served important social and psychological functions. They sponsored dances, picnics, bazaars, and meetings, all of which tended to counteract the loneliness and isolation that so many elderly people were experiencing. Membership cost only 25 cents, but "special Townsendites" who made larger contributions could join the Townsend National Legion of Honor. Townsend liberally sprinkled his talks with such phrases as "you dear old folks," "dang," and "by gum." The Townsend magazine carried a picture of the doctor alongside that of Lincoln with the caption: "We are Coming Father Townsend, Three Hundred Thousand Strong." The movement also had strong religious overtones. Its motto was "the Townsend plan is religion in action," and its followers were urged to "take up the cross of this crusade" for "God's plan."

The Townsend plan offered a married couple over 60 years of age $4800 a year, at a time when 87 percent of all American families had annual incomes below $2500. Yet the plan won support from many who believed in the values of thrift, hard work, and individualism precisely because it did not seem at all radical. For example, it did not call for deficit spending. The government would collect in sales taxes what it disbursed, and those taxes would not be levied on the rich but on all consumers. The plan required no bureaucracy other than the Treasury Department to make out the checks and the Post Office to deliver them. The plan in no way compromised private property rights. Nor did it imply a "dole." Rather, Townsend viewed the elderly as "Distributor Custodians," entrusted by society to spend $200 a month wisely. Critics, however, doubted the plan's feasibility, pointing out that it would cost $20 to $24 billion a year (or nearly half the total national income), that it would injure the poor through a regressive sales tax, and that it would require a far-flung bureaucracy to see that recipients spent their allotments.

The Townsend movement nevertheless crystallized popular sentiment for old-age pensions and helped move Congress and the administration to support the Social Security Act of 1935. Townsend condemned that measure because it excluded too many people from coverage and provided inadequate benefits. But, limited as it was, the act eroded Townsend's basis of support. His own plan lost on a voice vote in the House of Representatives. New Dealers responded to Townsend's challenge by attempting to discredit his movement. In the spring of 1936 a Senate committee began investigating the clubs in an effort to prove them a financial fraud. The investigators found that Robert Earl Clements had profited handsomely and that Townsend not only exercised absolute control over the clubs but privately referred to the members as "old fossils." (When Townsend refused to testify, he was cited for contempt and sentenced to a year in jail; Roosevelt later commuted the sentence because of Townsend's age.) By the summer of 1936 Townsend's estrangement from the New Deal was complete. Certain that "we shall be able to lick the stuffing" out of both major political parties, Townsend prepared to join forces with other foes of the administration.

## "SHARE OUR WEALTH"

In 1933 Sinclair Lewis published a novel entitled *It Can't Happen Here*, in which a Senator named Buzz Windrip established a fascist regime in the United States. One character described Windrip as "a dictator seemingly so different from the fervent Hitler and the gesticulating Fascists ... a dictator with something of the earthy American sense of humor of a Mark Twain." None doubted that this figure was patterned after Senator Huey Long of Louisiana or that Lewis was asserting that it could indeed happen here. In the highly charged political atmosphere of the 1930s perhaps no one aroused more intense feelings of love and hatred than did the Louisianan. To his supporters, Long had "changed Louisiana from a hellhole to a paradise. He was emancipator. He brought light." To his critics, Long was an unprincipled demagogue. In the summer of 1932 Franklin Roosevelt privately termed him one of the most dangerous men in America.

Born in 1893, Long as a boy had done odd jobs—driving a bakery wagon, carrying water to construction crews, learning to set type—primarily, it seems, to avoid the drudgery of working on his father's farm. His favorite book was *The Count of Monte Cristo*. He later remembered, "That man in that book knew how to hate, and until you learn how to hate you'll never get anywhere in this world." He spent his teens as a traveling salesman and gambler, then borrowed money to attend Tulane Law School, where he crammed a three-year program into eight months and arranged to take a special bar examination. At age 24 Long was elected to the Louisiana Public Service Commission and over the next

Huey Long after Senate filibuster, 1935.

several years gained a reputation for his attacks on the oil and railroad companies that dominated state politics. Although Long cultivated a comical public image, adopting the name "Kingfish" and dubbing his opponents "Turkeyhead" or "Old Trashy Mouth," he was a keenly intelligent man and an astute politician.

In 1928 Long became Governor, and even after his election to the Senate two years later he continued to rule Louisiana very much as he pleased. He dominated the legislature, curbed the press, and built a disciplined political machine. When people protested that he was violating the state constitution, Long replied, "I'm the Constitution around here now." Yet for every one who resented Long's dictatorial manner, there were many who benefited from his reign. He improved the public schools, provided free textbooks, and initiated evening classes for adults; he built new roads, bridges, and highways; he eliminated the poll tax and property taxes on the poor. These reforms helped break down the isolation of the rural poor, provided voters with tangible evidence of his accomplishments, and created jobs for political supporters. Unlike most other Southern politicians, Long did not appeal to white supremacist sentiment. Once he harshly denounced the leader of the Ku Klux Klan: "When I call him a son of a bitch I am not using profanity, but am referring to the circumstances of his birth."

His advocacy of the "Share Our Wealth" program made Long a figure of national prominence in the 1930s. The government, he insisted, must "limit the size of the big men's fortune and guarantee some minimum to the fortune and comfort of the little man's family." To accomplish this, he proposed limiting individual wealth to $3 to $4 million, providing all citizens with a $5000 homestead and a guaranteed annual income of $2500, offering free education through the college level to all whose "mental ability and energy" qualified them, establishing a thirty-hour work week, and financing generous old-age pensions through taxes on the rich. While this would not mean absolute equality, it would remove the most glaring inequalities. "So America would start again with millionaires, but with no multimillionaires or billionaires; we would start with some poor, but they wouldn't be so poor that they wouldn't have the comforts of life." In February 1934, Share Our Wealth clubs began forming; soon there were 27,000 claiming 4.7 million members. The movement's strength centered in Louisiana, Arkansas, and Mississippi.

The Share Our Wealth program went considerably beyond the Townsend plan. Long proposed a more sweeping change in economic relationships and assigned a more prominent role to the federal government than did Townsend. The Louisianan frankly advocated confiscating wealth in order to redistribute income. But in some respects the two resembled each other. Both Long and Townsend were charismatic leaders, both organized clubs that offered members a gratifying sense of personal involvement, and both promised a quick, certain path to good times. In addition, both appealed to those whom the New Deal had helped rather little. Long, who at first supported Roosevelt, broke with him decisively in 1935 on the grounds that the administration was proceeding too cautiously. Never one to hide his ambitions, Long then published *My First Days in the White House* (1935) to explain how he would transform America after his election. He even promised to find a place in his administration for Franklin Roosevelt—as Secretary of the Navy.

Roosevelt considered Long a veritable Pied Piper, leading people astray with spurious and impractical proposals. Nevertheless in June 1935 he moved somewhat closer to Long's position by asking Congress to impose high taxes on inherited wealth, corporate profits, and "very great individual incomes." When the President's message was read, Long declared: "I just wish to say 'Amen.'" Roosevelt's recommendations brought anguished cries from the business community, and by the time Congress finished watering it down, the Wealth Tax Act (1935) barely resembled Roosevelt's original proposal, much less Long's. Even as he borrowed a plank from the Share Our Wealth platform, the President attacked Long by denying him federal patronage, by encouraging the Treasury Department to investigate alleged financial wrongdoing in Louisiana, and by permitting his aides to speak their minds. "The Senator from Louisiana has halitosis of the intellect," said Secretary of the Interior Harold Ickes; "that's presuming Emperor Long has an intellect."

None of this proved very effective. Then, in September 1935, a young doctor, Carl Austin Weiss, assassinated Long and was himself immediately killed by the Senator's bodyguards. With its leader gone, the Share Our Wealth movement came under the control of Gerald L. K. Smith, a minister originally hired to organize the clubs. Smith, who had idolized Long (even wearing suits of clothes his mentor had discarded), appealed to similar hopes and exploited similar grievances. Smith cried: "Let's pull down these huge piles of gold until there shall be a real job, not a little old sow-belly, black-eyed pea job, but a real spending-money, beefsteak and gravy, Chevrolet, Ford in the garage, new suit, Thomas Jefferson, Jesus Christ, red, white, and blue job for every man!" By 1936 Smith, like Townsend, was prepared for a head-on clash with the administration. It came with the blessing of the "radio priest," Father Charles E. Coughlin.

## THE RADIO PRIEST AND HIS FLOCK

Father Coughlin had been assigned to the parish of Royal Oak, Michigan, in 1926. There he conducted a Sunday-morning radio program, "The Golden Hour of the Little Flower," which at first consisted of inspirational readings and devotional messages. But in the early 1930s, with the depression worsening, Coughlin turned to economic and social issues. As he did, his audience grew by leaps and bounds. Each week more than 10 million listeners tuned in Coughlin's sermons. After every broadcast he received hundreds of thousands of letters, and thousands of dollars in contributions. Coughlin enjoyed an unusual latitude in his remarks because he had organized his own radio network after a CBS attempt to censor him in 1931, and because he had the solid support of his superior, Bishop Michael James Gallagher of Detroit.

His position in the Catholic Church goes far toward explaining Coughlin's popularity. Many regarded him, quite literally, as a father, one whose word could implicitly be trusted because it had religious sanction. "For those of us who haven't a material father," said one of his admirers, "he can be our father and we won't need to feel lonesome." Coughlin also set

Doctor Townsend and Father Coughlin, 1936.

forth economic proposals that, if sometimes vague, proved highly attractive. He wanted to reform the monetary system by increasing the amount of currency in circulation, remonetizing silver, eliminating the federal reserve banks, and replacing interest-bearing government notes with non-interest-bearing ones. He also favored nationalizing "those public necessities which by their very nature are too important to be held in the control of private individuals," providing a "just and living annual wage" for all workers, and imposing heavy taxes on the wealthy. "Modern capitalism as we know it is not worth saving," Coughlin said, but capitalism with its abuses eliminated would be very much worth saving.

In 1933 Coughlin, then a staunch Roosevelt supporter, asserted that "the New Deal is Christ's deal." Yet during the next two years he became disillusioned with the President. Coughlin particularly resented FDR's failure to accept monetary management as the key to recovery, his advocacy of United States membership in the World Court, and his opposition to refinancing farm mortgages by issuing millions of dollars in greenbacks. Late in 1934, following the example set by Long and Townsend, Coughlin created the National Union for Social Justice to lobby for his economic program. By mid-1936, having concluded somewhat inconsistently that the New Deal both "protects plutocrats and comforts Communists," Coughlin announced the formation of the Union party. It quickly gained the support of Townsend and Smith. Coughlin expected the party's nominee—William Lemke of North Dakota—to receive 9 million votes, enough to throw the presidential election into the House of Representatives.

During the campaign Coughlin accused "Franklin doublecrossing Roosevelt" of "flirting with Communistic tendencies" and predicted that FDR's reelection would mean "more bullet holes in the White House than you could count with an adding machine." Gerald L. K. Smith blasted New Dealers as "a slimy group of men culled from the pink campuses of America." This rhetoric, however, failed to save the Union party from a humiliating defeat. It received 892,000 votes, under 2 percent of the total. In part this resulted from the party's inability to get on the ballot in several important states or to run a full slate of candidates for local office. In addition, Lemke proved a singularly uninspiring figure. Nor could Coughlin, Smith, and Townsend agree on policy and procedure. Expediency had made them allies, but a good deal of rivalry and suspicion remained. Millions of people who were attracted to economic panaceas would not back a hopeless third-party venture. The kind of support Coughlin and the others enjoyed could not be translated into votes on election day.

Dismayed by the outcome, Coughlin canceled future radio broadcasts but his retirement proved brief. By 1938 he was back on the air with sermons that had taken on a distinctly new tone. Coughlin had employed nativist themes in the past, but never so prominently. He insisted that a conspiracy of international Jewish bankers threatened America. His magazine, *Social Justice,* carried the "Protocols of Zion" (a forgery depicting an alleged Jewish conspiracy to take over the world), termed Hitler's Germany "an innocent victim of a sacred war declared against her nine years ago by the Jews," and honored Benito Mussolini as "Man of the Week." In July 1938 Coughlin founded the Christian Front to combat Communists and Jews. It prepared a Christian Index listing merchants who had pledged to patronize and employ other Christians as a means of curbing Jewish economic power. Coughlin, who had formerly denounced the anti-Catholic nativism of the Ku Klux Klan, ended by stirring up a vicious anti-Semitism.

## THE POPULAR FRONT

During the 1930s the American Communist party gained a fairly wide influence, certainly wider than its membership (which hovered around 50,000) or its voting strength (which fell from 103,000 in 1932 to 80,000 in 1936) would indicate. Party members controlled several large CIO unions including the United Electrical Workers and the Mine, Mill, and Smelter Workers, held responsible positions in the National Labor Relations Board and other government agencies, and gained a firm footing in the American Labor Party in New York State and in other political organizations. Communist doctrines won a large audience among intellectuals. In 1932, for example, fifty-three prominent writers and artists—including Sherwood Anderson, Erskine Caldwell, John Dos Passos, Sidney Hook, Lincoln Steffens, and Edmund Wilson—endorsed the party's candidates, William Z. Foster and James Ford. They explained: "As responsible intellectual workers we have aligned ourselves with the frankly revolutionary Communist Party, the party of the workers."

Nevertheless, the 1930s hardly deserve to be called "the Red decade." The great majority of Americans remained hostile to communism, and most who joined the movement did so only briefly. The party consisted of a small cadre that remained loyal through thick and thin, and others who entered and left as through a revolving door. Surely one reason for this was the party's subservience to the Soviet Union. American Communist leaders consistently followed policies that conformed to Russian interests, not because they were hired Russian agents but because they believed that the needs of American workers were identical with those of the Soviet Union. They equated virtue with the Russian system and either rejected or discounted evidence of Stalinist terrorism. With every shift in party doctrine, those who could not adjust departed.

At first the party followed a line laid down in 1928 at the Sixth World Congress of Communist Parties. Stalin at the time was consolidating his authority and thought that Communist revolutions around the world would assist him by removing unfriendly capitalist regimes. Consequently, Communists in the United States repudiated halfway measures and called for a dictatorship of the proletariat. Communists refused to work through the American Federation of Labor, which they considered hopelessly reactionary, but tried to create their own militant unions. They claimed that Negroes in the black belt constituted a separate nation and therefore should exercise the right of self-determination. They branded Franklin Roosevelt "an abject tool of Wall Street" and condemned the New Deal for striving "to hold the workers in industrial slavery." As revolutionaries awaiting the day of revolution, Communists were equally critical of such reform gestures as the National Recovery Administration and the Wagner Act.

In the summer of 1935 the party dramatically modified its approach. By then Stalin had identified Nazi Germany as the greatest potential danger. Accordingly, he urged Communists to join liberals and socialists in an antifascist popular front. Communists in the United States worked diligently to soften their image. Their leader, Earl Browder, announced that "Communism is 20th-Century Americanism," and traced the party's lineage back to Tom Paine and Thomas Jefferson. The party sought to build bridges to the socialists, took an active role in union organizing, and deemphasized the idea of Negro nationhood. Its view of the New Deal underwent a similar transformation. Communists praised Roosevelt as a progressive and backed almost every one of his proposals. This identification with American values may have reached its height when the *Daily Worker* informed members of the Young Communist League that by selling subscriptions they could "Win a Free Bicycle!" and obtain some "spending money." "Gradually you'll be able to build up a large profitable route," the journal promised.

These popular front tactics exacerbated divisions within the Socialist party. In 1935 Browder invited Socialist leader Norman Thomas to a debate in Madison Square Garden, with the proceeds going to the Socialists. When Thomas accepted, "old-guard" Socialists unjustifiably feared that he was ready to collaborate with the Communists. By 1936 thousands had deserted the Socialist party, whose membership dropped below twenty thousand. Thomas rejected other such overtures and, unlike Browder, kept up a steady attack on the New Deal. Roosevelt, he said, was trying to "cure tuberculosis with cough drops." The New Deal was ignoring the plight of tenant farmers and other dispossessed groups. Planning and capitalism, he added, simply did not mix. To those who urged him to support Roosevelt in 1936 Thomas replied: "The way to get Socialism is to proclaim the Socialist message not to declare a moratorium on it during an election campaign." But his vote—which fell from 903,000 in 1932 to 187,000 in 1936—indicated that the New Deal had neutralized Socialist appeal. Thomas confessed as much. "Roosevelt did not carry out the Socialist platform," he declared, "unless he carried it out on a stretcher."

Communist endorsement of the New Deal during the popular front years reinforced the convictions of those who considered Roosevelt a Red stooge. By 1936 antiadministration newspapers were printing doggerel about "The Red New Deal with a Soviet seal/ Endorsed by a Moscow hand,/ The strange result of an alien cult/ In a liberty-loving land." Generally, New Dealers discounted these attacks, asserting that Communist influence was, and would continue to be, negligible, so long as reform succeeded. Roosevelt also recognized that red-baiting was an old technique for discrediting social change. He was enough of a civil libertarian to want to judge people by how they behaved rather than by what they thought, which books they read, or which meetings they attended. The President evidently viewed Communists as well-intentioned but misguided people who often did the right things for the wrong reasons. Before the signing of the Nazi-Soviet pact, Roosevelt did not consider domestic communism a major threat.

Germany reached that agreement with Russia on August 23, 1939, and went to war with England and France in September. While the pact remained in force—until June 1941, when Hitler invaded the Soviet Union—Communists in the United States completely reversed themselves, scrapping the idea of an antifascist popular front. They opposed American aid to the Allies, claiming that England and France were imperialist nations. They similarly opposed the buildup of defense industries, on occasion calling strikes to disrupt work in aircraft plants. Communists reverted to denouncing Roosevelt as "the leader and organizer of all reactionary forces in the country." The Communist party paid a heavy price for this turnabout. Thousands of members, attracted by the popular front ideology, deserted the party in disillusionment. Many liberals who had cooperated with Communists considered the party's justification of the Nazi-Soviet pact a symptom of its moral bankruptcy. Finally, the party's stance contributed to a Red scare that swept the country after 1939.

## BLACK AMERICANS AND THE NEW DEAL

"People is hollerin' 'bout hard times, tell me what it all about," wailed a 1937 blues recording; "hard times don't worry me, I was broke when it first started out." In singing the blues, surely, people were laughing to keep from crying. The depression had a devastating impact on black Americans, even on those who had never shared in the prosperity of the 1920s. Southern black farmers in the early 1930s scraped by on $300 a year. Of those employed in agriculture, four of every five did not own their land but worked as sharecroppers, tenant farmers, or wage hands. Lacking any security, they often lost their homes as hard times settled over the countryside. In the cities conditions were worse. The unemployment rate for blacks was 30 to 60 percent higher than for whites, in part because of bias in hiring but also because the jobs blacks had held in service occupations were often eliminated. Industries employing large numbers of blacks—such as building construction and bituminous coal—came to a virtual standstill. Desperate whites sometimes resorted to violence to displace blacks. On the Illinois Central Railroad white firemen terrorized blacks, killing ten of them, to get their jobs. Whites also began taking jobs blacks had formerly held as elevator operators, hospital attendants, cooks, waiters, bellhops, maids, and chauffeurs.

To people surviving at a subsistence level, the Roosevelt administration offered a ray of hope, primarily in the form of federal relief. Before 1933, localities administering relief often rejected black applicants, but the New Deal reversed this pattern. In 1935 nearly 30 percent of all black families were receiving some form of aid, and in certain cities the figure approached 50 percent. Proportionately, three times as many blacks were on relief as whites. New Deal programs sought to ensure fair treatment. The Works Progress Administration enabled hundreds of thousands of blacks to weather the depression. In Norfolk, where blacks comprised less than one-third of the population, they accounted for more than two-thirds of the workers on WPA rolls. The Public Works Administration took a pioneering step by introducing nondiscrimination clauses, under which contractors had to pay black workers a fixed proportion of their payrolls, a proportion ultimately reflecting the number of blacks in the labor force. This is not to say that other New Deal agencies never discriminated. On balance, however, blacks received a share of federal assistance in proportion to their numbers if not their need.

If the Roosevelt administration came to the rescue of jobless blacks, it proved less responsive to demands for legal equality and social justice. Little in Roosevelt's background suggested any such concern. He had served under the segregationist Wilson administration in the archsegregationist Navy Department; he made his second home in Warm Springs, Georgia, and apparently never questioned local mores; he accepted "Cactus Jack" Garner, a conservative Texan, as his running mate in 1932 and 1936. As President, FDR maintained that economic recovery, not civil rights, would most effectively aid the largest number of blacks. He believed that New Deal legislation would be lost without the support of Southern Democrats who headed important Congressional committees, and he recognized that civil rights was potentially a source of great friction within his party. As a gradualist and institutionalist, Roosevelt reasoned that only education would finally eradicate racial prejudice. "We must do this thing stride by stride," he said.

Roosevelt took few such strides, however, during his first or second term of office. Despite the angry protests of civil rights groups, New Deal programs in the South followed Jim Crow lines. The Tennessee Valley Authority segregated its work crews, hired only unskilled black laborers, and set up a "model village" that barred blacks. The Civilian Conservation Corps maintained segregated work camps. The National Recovery Administration, which in theory prohibited wage differentials based on race, in practice left loopholes whereby blacks could be paid less. The Agricultural Adjustment Administration's acreage reduction program led to the eviction of thousands of black tenant farmers. The Justice Department refused to prosecute lynchers under a federal kidnapping statute on the grounds that the victims were not taken across state lines for financial gain. Roosevelt branded lynching a "vile form of collective murder" but refused to support an antilynching bill that provided for a federal trial if states failed to prosecute, specified prison terms for members of lynch mobs, and made counties responsible for damages. In 1937, after a mob in Mississippi had set two blacks afire with a blow torch, the House passed the measure. It was filibustered to death in the Senate in 1938 without protest from the administration.

Given this record, the President won a truly astonishing amount of support from black Americans. In 1932 nearly three-fourths of them voted Republican; in 1936, more than three-fourths voted Democratic, and the percentage increased in the years that followed. New Deal relief programs—which primarily aided Northern and urban blacks, who could vote, rather than Southern and rural blacks, who could not—partially, but not fully, explain this shift. Certainly FDR benefited when compared with his predecessor. Having broken the Solid South in 1928, Hoover had hoped to convert white southerners to Republicanism. Unlike Roosevelt, he never even verbally condemned the lynchings that occurred during his presidency. In addition, Roosevelt offered important government positions to such prominent blacks as Mary McLeod Bethune and Robert Weaver. Eleanor Roosevelt and other New Dealers spoke up forcibly on behalf of racial justice. Partly as a result of his wife's prestige in the black community, Franklin Roosevelt received credit for the New Deal's achievements while escaping blame for its shortcomings.

Developments during the 1930s subjected the National Association of Colored People, and the civil rights strategy it advocated, to a severe challenge. The NAACP had always held that blacks could improve their economic position by obtaining the right training, working hard, and persuading white employers to give them an equal chance. It disparaged unified action by black and white workers, declaring it impossible to make an "advantageous alliance with white American labor because of its intense race hatred." In 1935 the organization opposed the Wagner Act, which did not contain a clause preventing discrimination, on the grounds that stronger unions would more effectively freeze out black workers. But the depression caused many members of the NAACP to place their hopes in the labor movement, and their hand was strengthened when the newly formed Congress of Industrial Organizations proved re-

Mary McLeod Bethune and Eleanor Roosevelt, 1937.

ceptive to blacks. Dr. Ralph Bunche and other militants argued that the NAACP should adopt a radical economic platform. In their view, only an alliance of black and white workers could revamp the capitalist system and guarantee a decent living to all.

The NAACP also assumed that civil rights could be secured by lobbying in Congress and by arguing before the courts. Two events during the 1930s, however, weakened confidence in the possibility of ending Jim Crow through political and constitutional means. The first was the failure of the antilynching bill, which the NAACP had helped draft, and to which it devoted a considerable portion of its time, money, and energy from 1935 to 1940. A second event that eroded the gradualist approach was the Supreme Court's decision in *Grovey* v. *Townsend* (1935). The Court held that the Democratic party in Texas—and by extension elsewhere in the South—could exclude blacks from membership and thereby bar them from participating in primaries. The white primary did not violate the Fourteenth Amendment, the Court ruled, since the Democratic party was a voluntary political association whose actions did not involve discrimination by a state. The decision effectively disenfranchised blacks since in one-party areas the only meaningful contests occurred in primaries. The closed primary was an even more effective deterrent to voting than the poll tax or the literacy test.

The NAACP above all prized the goal of integration, yet during the 1930s this too came under fire. Led by W. E. B. DuBois, a number of black intellectuals advocated what one termed "the conscious development of nationalistic sentiment." DuBois, whose stand led to his resignation from the NAACP, continued to oppose forced segregation but saw distinct advantages in voluntary segregation. He asserted: "It is the race-conscious black man cooperating together in his own institutions and movements who will eventually emancipate the colored race." In his autobiography, *Dusk of Dawn* (1940), DuBois described his disenchantment with the view that education would wipe out prejudice. Convinced that racism was rooted in the subconscious and reinforced by economic self-interest, DuBois thought it pointless for a black minority to plead for justice from a white majority. Instead, blacks should set up their own institutions—schools, churches, hospitals, theaters—and a largely autonomous economy founded on socialist principles. DuBois's doctrine, although in some respects reminiscent of Marcus Garvey's, appealed to intellectuals rather than the masses, did not contemplate a return to Africa, and combined economic radicalism with racial nationalism.

DuBois's vision of a cooperative commonwealth never approached realization, as indeed it could not, given the lack of economic resources in the black community. The nearest any sizable group of blacks came to attaining perfect security was in the religious "heavens" of Father Divine. In 1933 Divine, a preacher in Brooklyn and Long Island for more than a decade, moved to Harlem, where he attracted a huge following. Divine opened "heavens"—dormitorylike arrangements where his disciples lived and received adequate food and clothing as long as they worshipped their benefactor (and promised to abstain from sexual relations). His followers believed that Divine was God and that he and they were immortal. Those who died or became seriously ill were said to have stopped believing. Divine, the vast majority of whose followers were black but who also appealed to some whites, created a world in which racial conflict, indeed racial differentiation, no longer existed. He referred only to "people of the darker complexion" and "people of the lighter complexion." The names his disciples adopted similarly revealed their search for order and harmony: "Quiet dove," "Perfect Love," "Sweet Music," and "Keep on Smiling." For thousands of blacks beset by racial, economic, or family troubles, Divine provided a way out, and many remained steadfast in their faith until his death in 1965. During the depression years, when millions followed political messiahs, it was hardly surprising that some turned to a man who claimed he was the True Messiah.

# HALLIE FLANAGAN AND THE FEDERAL THEATER

In 1935, as part of its expanded relief program, the Roosevelt administration initiated various projects to aid unemployed writers, artists, and actors. To head the Federal Theater Project, Harry Hopkins selected Hallie Flanagan, whom he had first met while both were undergraduates at Grinnell College in Iowa. A person of great creative drive and intelligence, Flanagan had gone on to teach drama at Grinnell and win the first Guggenheim grant ever awarded a woman. In 1926 she made a comparative study of European drama and was particularly impressed by Constantine Stanislavsky's Moscow Art Theater. Then she became director of experimental theater at Vassar College where she supervised some of the more imaginative productions of the early 1930s.

Under her guidance, the Federal Theater Project employed an average of ten thousand people a year for four years. Many of its plays had a frank social message. The "living newspa-

Drama in Washington: Hallie Flanagan before the Dies Committee.

per" format, which vividly documented current issues, was well-suited for this purpose. *Triple A Plowed Under* (1936) called for a New Deal for farmers; *Power* (1937) advocated a greater measure of consumer control over public utilities; *One-Third of a Nation* (1938) exposed the poverty and filth of big-city slums. Some productions met with huge popular and critical acclaim. A dramatization of Sinclair Lewis's *It Can't Happen Here* played to 275,000 people in four months; it grossed $80,000 although

Federal Theater Project: *It Can't Happen Here*.

Federal Theater Project: *Macbeth*.

the average ticket was priced at 30 cents. The Federal Theater provided new opportunities for black performers who staged a jazz version of *Mikado,* and, under Orson Welles's direction, a version of *Macbeth* set in Haiti during the Napoleonic era. Members of the children's theater performed *Jack and the Beanstalk* in parks during the summer, and visited hospital wards to teach paralyzed children how to work marionettes.

Throughout its career the Federal Theater faced difficult problems. One concerned the competing demands of relief and art. Some unemployed people, who clearly deserved assistance, claimed to be "actors" even if they had little talent, and Flanagan some-times felt obliged to give them jobs. In addition, disputes arose over the nature of the productions. There was a built-in tension between the desire to appeal to a mass audience (particularly since public response was a means of justifying further appropriations) and the desire to stage avant-garde works that appealed to the actors' and directors' own aesthetic sensibilities. There was yet another hard question: As a government agency, funded by the taxpayers, how far could it safely go in advocating political views? Critics even complained about the production of *The Revolt of the Beavers,* a children's fairytale about exploited beavers who rose against a cruel chief. This, it was said, amounted to "Marxism á la Mother Goose."

The Federal Theater itself became a casualty of sagging New Deal fortunes. In 1939, with Congress anxious to slash relief programs, Flanagan's agency seemed highly expendable. Since most of its employees lived in New York City, Chicago, or Los Angeles, the Federal Theater had a rather narrow political constituency. The agency also came under attack from the Dies Committee for being a "veritable hotbed of un-American activi-

ties." Some congressmen suspected that the performances were obscene. They snickered at such titles as *The Bishop Misbehaves* or *Old Captain Romeo's Four Wives*. Of *A New Kind of Love*, one Republican remarked, "I wonder what that can be. It smacks of the Soviets." In 1939 Congress killed the Federal Theater Project. Hallie Flanagan left to become a Dean at Smith College. Not until 1965 would the federal government again undertake a large-scale program of support for the performing arts.

## WOMEN AND FAMILIES FACE THE DEPRESSION

"Where the folkways and old patterns of conduct are continued—that it is a man's job to support his family—husbands have been nagged and harassed to desperation," a welfare agency officer reported in 1931. "The degradation, the sheer fear and panic . . . have eaten into men's souls." "I did what I had to do," a housewife recalled of the depression years. "I think hard times is harder on a man." "I was going with someone when the depression hit," an unmarried woman remembered. "Suddenly he was laid off. It hit him like a ton of bricks and he just disappeared." "I feel like I was falling down a long dark shaft that has no end," a teenager told his caseworker. "It is both economically unfair and socially unjust to expect me to continue to support my family."

During the 1930s, the depression's impact on family life became a subject of widespread concern. Familiar patterns of courtship and marriage seemed to be falling apart. The marriage rate fell in 1929 and did not start to rise until 1934. Often marriages were postponed until hard times had passed, or simply never occurred. The divorce rate declined, as income fell, but desertion increased. "Mr. Raparka asked [his wife] for money to go to New York in search of a job," sociologist Wight Bakke reported in *Citizens Without Work*. "He has not been heard of since." The birth rate, which had been dropping throughout the 1920s, plunged even further. It fell from 21.3 births per thousand persons in 1930 to 18.4 in 1933. Contraception became more popular, birth control clinics multiplied, and in 1936, a federal court decision made it legal for doctors to distribute contraceptive information and devices, except where prohibited by state law. Depression demands appeared to have succeeded where birth control reformers had not.

Within families that had suddenly slipped downward in economic status, case studies revealed, new patterns of domestic life developed. In some cases, where relationships had always been stable, families simply drew into themselves, curtailing outside activities. "Family members have to do things with and for each other," Eleanor Roosevelt wrote in 1933, "and the result is that the clan spirit grows." In other cases, clan spirit seemed strained to the breaking point. When unemployment struck, disconcerting authority shifts often occurred at home. Depression clearly had a dire impact on those male heads of household who lost their jobs. "Working around the house was not all profit to the unemployed man," sociologist Eli Ginzburg reported. "By taking on feminine duties he widened the breach between the old life and the new. His failure was underlined by the transgression of sex boundaries." In study after study, case analysts described the transformation of former "breadwinners" from family head into "just another member of the family." But women seemed less affected when family income dropped, since they retained much the same roles they had held before depression struck.

In Middletown, the Lynds reported, unemployed men hung about the street, lost their sense of time, and dawdled helplessly. At home, however, "the women's world remained largely intact and the round of cooking, housecleaning, and mending became if anything more absorbing." Domestic routines took on new significance, especially when family survival depended on housewives' frugality. "Making Do" became an important 1930s adage. Women traded depression recipes, restyled old clothes, took in boarders, ran kitchen beauty parlors, and started other household businesses. Older children sometimes contributed to family income if they could find jobs. But wives were most likely to become the family's major new wage earners.

Women's entry into the depression labor force was hardly popular. Once jobs became scarce, widespread opposition was voiced to wives who worked outside the home—and implicitly deprived a male family head of income. Congress prohibited more than one family member from taking a federal service job. State and local governments rejected married women who applied for government posts. In 1931, three out of four school boards refused to hire wives as teachers and many dismissed women teachers who married. The American Federation of Labor urged employers not to hire women with working husbands. Public opinion surveys, such as the new Gallup poll, echoed such injunctions; respondents declared that wives of employed men should remain at home. According to a Gallup poll of 1937, over half of those surveyed agreed that *no* wife should work outside the home.

But despite continued pressure against married wage earners, women were less likely to be unemployed than men and more likely to take jobs for the first time. During the 1930s, the number of working women rose 25 percent and the majority of new workers were married women, precisely those who were urged to remain at home. One reason for this unexpected development was that opportunities for female employment did not contract as much as those for men. The depression's worst impact was on heavy industry—autos, steel, mining—where few women were employed. The sectors that employed many women, however, such as sales, service, and clerical work, were less affected and tended to recover more quickly. Most important, men did not seek jobs in what were considered women's fields. The sexual division of labor that usually handicapped women on the labor market suddenly offered a new measure of protection.

Such protection did not extend to black women workers whose unemployment rates were higher than any other group. It did not affect applicants for federal work relief, where male heads of household were favored. And it rarely helped professional women, whose aspirations were now limited. Career ambitions faded, and so did feminist demands for equal rights and equal opportunity. Still, women's employment record reversed the expectations of depression-era Americans. Denunciations of the working wife were counteracted by both family need and in some cases, new advantages on the employment market. As a result, during the 1930s, women entered the labor force at twice the rate of men.

If the increase of women workers was unexpected, so were the new roles women were called upon to play in social welfare and political life. During the depression, new welfare agencies opened up at all levels of government and social workers were suddenly in demand. Women with expertise in social welfare, moreover, were now welcomed in high-level federal government posts. The leading example was Labor Secretary Frances Perkins, the first woman cabinet member, who had a long career in social welfare. Since the Progressive era, Perkins had worked in settlement houses and for the New York Consumers League. In 1928 she had been appointed state industrial commissioner by FDR. As a cabinet member, she did not expect "to gain anything materially," Eleanor Roosevelt explained in 1933, but "to render a public service to . . . the workingmen and women in their families."

Similar experience in social welfare was evident in the careers of almost all the New Deal's high-level women appointees, such as Florence Allen, the first woman appointed to the Federal Court of Appeals; Ellen Woodward, who headed women's work relief projects under CWA; Mary Anderson, head of the federal Women's Bureau; and Mary W. Dewson, head of the Women's Division of the Democratic National Committee and later a member of the Social Security Board. Like Frances Perkins, these new women office-holders considered themselves social reformers more than feminists. Their brand of politics was widely promoted by Eleanor Roosevelt, who campaigned for women's appointments. "The steady increase of women's influence," she wrote to a friend, "tends to ameliorate bad social conditions." Such influence tended to diminish after 1936, when New Deal receptivity to reform dwindled. But the Roosevelt administration had given women more high-level government jobs than had any previous administration. It also propelled into public view the most politically sophisticated woman reformer ever to live in the White House.

During the 1930s, Eleanor Roosevelt capitalized on a decade of experience in Democratic party campaigns, the League of Women Voters, and other women's organizations such as the Women's Trade Union League. Increasingly influential in New Deal politics, she became a model of activism. In 1933, she began holding her innovative weekly White House press conferences, limited to women reporters. She also defended the interests of unemployed women, supported the establishment of summer work-relief camps for women, campaigned for the end of Washington's alley slums, worked on the federal homestead program, and aided thousands of correspondents who wrote to her in an unprecedented volume of mail. This pace of activity only increased. As political strategist and presidential advisor, Eleanor Roosevelt helped organize the 1936 campaign, served as a spokeswoman for the disadvantaged, and emerged as a forthright liberal, often taking stands to the left of FDR. By defending black pressure groups, pacifists, and the National Youth Congress, she created her own constituency and simultaneously relieved FDR of some pressure from the left. Finally, whether visiting coal mines, testifying to Congress about migrant labor, or campaigning against racial discrimination, she was constantly in public view. By the end of the 1930s, through her press conferences, radio talks, and popular syndicated newspaper column, "My Day," Eleanor Roosevelt had become one of the most prominent figures in public life. Although her role was controversial, her causes were ceaselessly publicized by women reporters who commended her "instinct for civic and social reform" and credited her with "humanizing the New Deal."

## THE CONSERVATIVE RESPONSE

There were, of course, many Americans who did not sympathize with the New Deal and who were distinctly unimpressed by either Franklin or Eleanor Roosevelt. The conservative position—with its reverence for the past, emphasis on man's innate limitations, distrust of the masses, belief in property rights, and quest for social harmony—also had its supporters during the 1930s. The New Deal had overturned traditional ways of doing things, challenged older values, altered the relative power of social classes, and affected certain groups adversely. For all these reasons, some people passionately hated Roosevelt and all he represented. Whereas criticism from the left made its strongest impression during FDR's first administration, criticism from the right was loudest after 1936.

Businessmen constituted one important source of opposition, although sentiment in the business community was never monolithic. Several industrialists endorsed Roosevelt's policies, but organizations such as the National Association of Manufacturers and the Chamber of Commerce consistently fought the New Deal, particularly after 1935. By then, speakers at NAM meetings were talking about the need to rid Washington of "economic crackpots, social reformers, labor demagogues and political racketeers." These critics charged that deficit spending undermined the nation's credit, that the tax on undistributed corporate profits curbed initiative, that the growth of executive power endangered individual liberties, and that the Wagner Act weighted the scales too heavily on labor's side. Roosevelt stirred up class antagonism, businessmen complained, by his unfair references to "economic royalists" who sought control of the government for selfish purposes.

The President believed that business critics failed to perceive the true intent, and effect, of his policies. He compared himself to one who jumped off a pier to save a rich gentleman from drowning; at first the gentleman was grateful, but he later complained bitterly that his silk hat was lost. Whether or not the New Deal rescued the capitalist system, it certainly enabled business to make higher profits than it had under Hoover. Despite all the fuss about fiscal irresponsibility, Roosevelt turned to deficit spending as a last resort, when nothing else seemed to work, and did so reluctantly. Nor did the New Deal redistribute wealth. The share of disposable income held by the rich did not change significantly from 1933 to 1939. Taxes, while higher than in the past, were hardly crushing. Late in the decade they ranged from 4 percent on incomes of $10,000 to 32 percent on incomes of $100,000. "It is the same old story of the failure of those who have property to realize that I am the best friend the profit system ever had, even though I add my denunciation of unconscionable profits," Roosevelt wrote.

In 1934 conservatives created the American Liberty League to mobilize public sentiment against the New Deal. Over the next two years the League enrolled 125,000 members, spent $1 million, and distributed 5 million pieces of literature. To appear nonpartisan it recruited several prominent Democrats. The Liberty League formulated an essentially conservative indictment of the New Deal. It denounced Roosevelt as a dictator, although it had difficulty deciding whether he more nearly resembled a communist or a fascist. It held that the welfare state aided the improvident and unfit at the expense of the hardworking and virtuous and was therefore immoral. It exploited popular reverence for the Constitution and the Supreme Court. Roosevelt's sweeping triumph in the 1936 election, however, discredited the Liberty League, which had found itself in the position of insisting that the people break sharply with the practices of the past four years and dismantle the welfare state. Roosevelt, by contrast, could promise continuity and stability. Only the initiatives he took in 1937, especially his plan to enlarge the Supreme Court, gave conservatives another chance.

# "COURT-PACKING"

At the time of his second inauguration Franklin Roosevelt seemed to stand at the pinnacle of his political career. Yet his second term witnessed a sharp decline in New Deal fortunes. In some ways, the very size of his congressional majorities—the House contained 331 Democrats and 90 Republicans, the Senate 76 Democrats and 16 Republicans—encouraged factionalism and discord. Also, relatively large numbers of Democrats were elected in 1936 from safe districts—that is, by a margin of more than 5 percent—and were therefore less responsive to the wishes of party leaders. But Roosevelt's problem stemmed less from the composition of Congress than from what he wanted it to do. This became apparent in February 1937, when he unveiled his plan to reform the Supreme Court. Asserting that the Court carried too heavy a work load, the President proposed to add an additional justice for each one who did not retire at the age of 70. A maximum of six new positions could be created, and the Court would revert to a smaller size upon the death or retirement of an elderly member.

Several considerations led the President to take this stand. He resented being rebuked by the Court in 1935 for dismissing William E. Humphrey, a reactionary member of the Federal Trade Commission, when in so doing he had followed earlier precedent. The Court, moreover, had struck down crucial reform legislation. It had ruled against the National Recovery Administration and the Agricultural Adjustment Administration, and in June 1936, by a narrow 5 to 4 margin, it agreed that a New York minimum-wage law violated the due process clause of the Fourteenth Amendment. Roosevelt believed that the same narrow reasoning would lead the Court to invalidate the Wagner Act and the Social Security Act, both of which were up for consideration. It also appeared that federal regulation of wages and hours, another item on the New Deal agenda, would not pass the judges' scrutiny even if Congress approved it. Roosevelt believed that the four conservatives on the Court—Willis Van Devanter, George Sutherland, James McReynolds, and Pierce Butler— were busily reading their own political prejudices into the Constitution under a cloak of judicial impartiality.

The President's decision to make an issue of the justices' age, when he really objected to their ideology, offended many, including 80-year-old Justice Louis D. Brandeis. Yet in seeking to enlarge the Court, FDR chose the only course that seemed feasible. He rejected the alternatives—constitutional amendments requiring a two-thirds vote on the Court in order to declare an act unconstitutional, permitting Congress to override Court decisions, or broadening the legislative authority to regulate the economy. Roosevelt did not think for a moment that three-fourths of the state legislatures would approve any of these proposals, and certainly not soon enough to help. Besides, each proposed amendment might create more problems than it would solve. To demand a 6 to 3 vote on the Court would mean little, because five members could persuade another to join them so as to protect the Court's prestige; to permit Congress to overturn rulings would bring judicial review to an end; to broaden constitutional powers would be useless if justices with an Ice Age philosophy continued to interpret those powers. In FDR's view the Court, not the Constitution, needed changing.

The proposal triggered the most bitterly fought dispute of Roosevelt's presidency. Advocates said that the Supreme Court was already "packed" with reactionaries who were frustrating the popular desire for social reform as expressed in the election of 1936. There was nothing sacred about the number nine, they continued, for the Court's size had varied in the past. Legislation that affected millions of people should not stand or fall on the whim of a single judge. Opponents responded that the Court, far from obstructing the New Deal, had invalidated only a few measures, and badly drawn ones at that. Roosevelt had never received a mandate to pack the Court, since he had studiously avoided the subject during the campaign. Finally, they pointed out that Roosevelt's plan would set a dangerous precedent. If a liberal President could restructure the Court to suit his fancy today, what would stop a conservative President from doing the same thing tomorrow?

In the spring of 1937 the plan lost whatever momentum it had when the Court—largely because Justice Owen Roberts switched to the liberal side—upheld the Social Security Act and other vital reform measures. In *NLRB* v. *Jones and Laughlin* the Court sustained the Wagner Act by a 5 to 4 vote. The majority implicitly overturned earlier decisions by holding that the commerce clause was indeed broad enough to cover federal regulation of manufacturing. In *West Coast Hotel Co.* v. *Parrish,* again by a one-vote margin, the Court approved state minimum wage laws. Chief Justice Charles Evans Hughes asserted that "reasonable" regulation, adopted in the interests of the community, by definition fulfilled the Fourteenth Amendment's due-process requirements. In May 1937 Justice Van Devanter's resignation gave Roosevelt his first Court appointment. The administration continued to press a compromise permitting the appointment of one additional justice each year for every member who reached the age of 75. This seemed likely to pass because most senators assumed that Roosevelt would nominate their colleague, Majority Leader Joseph Robinson of Arkansas, to fill the first vacancy. In July Robinson died of a heart attack and the Senate quickly defeated the bill.

The Court debacle injured Roosevelt's standing with Congress and the public, although many who would have broken with him for other reasons merely used the episode as a convenient pretext. The struggle over the Court divided the Democratic party by alienating a number of liberals, aroused widespread distrust of FDR's leadership, and convinced Republicans that their best strategy was to maintain a discreet silence while Democrats battled among themselves. But Roosevelt did not come away empty-handed, for the Supreme Court in 1937 finally put its seal of approval on the New Deal. Roosevelt would make five appointments during his second term—including those of Hugo Black, William O. Douglas, and Felix Frankfurter—and after they took their seats, judicial barriers to the welfare state came tumbling down.

## THE WANING OF THE NEW DEAL

From Roosevelt's vantage point, administrative reform was hardly less important than judicial reform. In 1936 he had appointed a committee to study administrative management. It reported in January 1937, urging Congress to furnish the President with six assistants, expand the civil service system, improve fiscal management, and establish the National Resources Planning Board as a central agency to coordinate government programs. The committee also suggested creating two new Cabinet positions (Welfare and Public Works), changing the name of the Department of the Interior to the Department of Conservation, and giving the President broad authority to transfer agencies, including certain functions of the independent regulatory commissions. In this fashion the committee hoped to find a permanent home for New Deal agencies and provide a suitable administrative apparatus for the welfare state.

But reorganization provoked a storm of opposition when it came before Congress in the spring of 1938. Roosevelt's critics charged that the measure would clamp "one-man rule" on the nation, and succeeded in frightening large numbers of people. After squeaking by the Senate, the bill went down to defeat in the House of Representatives when more than 100 Democrats deserted the President. Congressmen had various reasons for opposing the measure, including a desire to reassert legislative prerogatives, placate pressure groups, and protect their existing channels of access to administrative agencies. The conflict over reorganization resembled the earlier one over the Court in that both measures failed to elicit support from a sizeable constituency, opened Roosevelt to the charge of seeking dictatorial power, divided liberals, and led to stinging presidential defeats. In 1939 Congress passed a mild measure that enabled FDR to establish the Executive Office of the President and to streamline the bureaucracy. But the sweeping changes he favored were not made.

Democratic opposition to Court reform and reorganization crossed sectional lines. But three other measures—relating to housing, wages and hours, and civil rights—divided the Democratic party into rural and urban, Northern and Southern factions. The Wagner Housing Act (1937), which authorized expenditures of $500 million to aid the construction of low-cost units, passed only after Southerners had extracted concessions limiting the appropriation, the number of dwellings to be built, and the cost per family. The Fair Labor Standards Act (1938) similarly catered to the South, which wished to protect its competitive position as a cheap labor market. The measure regulated child labor and established a 40-cent-per-hour minimum wage and forty-hour work week, but it exempted domestic workers and farm laborers, and allowed regional wage differentials. The antilynching bill never had a chance against a Senate filibuster engineered by Southern Democrats. Measures that appealed to the New Deal's Northern, urban constitutency won little support from rural and Southern representatives.

The problems that the New Deal encountered after 1937 went beyond congressional reluctance to enact certain legislation in the form Roosevelt wanted. To a considerable extent Congress accurately reflected the popular mood. Every opinion poll between 1937 and 1939 indicated that between two-thirds and three-fourths of the American people wanted the Roosevelt administration to follow a more conservative course. Although the polls revealed class and party differences, even a majority of Democrats and the poor went along with the prevailing sentiment. In part the New Deal was a victim of the times. FDR's proposals for judicial and administrative reform promised few tangible benefits but seemed rather to demonstrate a lust for personal power just when dictatorships in Europe were arousing a deep suspicion of executive authority in any form. The New Deal declined after 1937 because most Americans did not want to extend it much further.

The administration's response to the recession of 1937–1938 increased this disenchantment with reform. In the fall of 1937 the economy went into a tailspin. Over the next ten months, millions of people lost their jobs. The slump occurred primarily because the administration, in attempting to balance the budget, had cut expenditures sharply. Yet Roosevelt resisted new deficit spending. Unlike the Keynesians, who favored unbalanced budgets in slack periods, FDR believed pump priming appropriate in 1933 "when the water had receded to the bottom of the well" but doubted its worth in 1938 "with the water within 25 or 30 percent of the top." Not until April, when it appeared that economic conditions would ruin the Democrats in the fall elections, did the President listen to advisers who favored additional spending. He then asked Congress to authorize a $3.75 billion relief appropriation. But the damage had already been done. Those who had lost their jobs or whose businesses had failed blamed the Democrats, not the Republicans, and concluded that the time for further innovation was past.

The President suffered yet another reversal in his attempt to purge the Democratic party in the 1938 primaries. Roosevelt fought unsuccessfully to unseat Senators Walter George of Georgia, Millard Tydings of Maryland, and "Cotton Ed" Smith of South Carolina. Many Southerners appeared to resent the President's intrusion into local affairs (what Walter George termed the "second march through Georgia"), while those benefiting most from New Deal relief programs and presumably most sympathetic to the President—blacks and poor whites—hardly participated in Democratic primaries. Opinion polls indicated that even among the unemployed and those on relief a bare majority disliked the White House's intervention. The purge claimed only one victim. John O'Connor of New York City, Chairman of the House Rules Committee, was defeated by a local politician friendly to the New Deal. In the November elections Republicans went on to win a smashing victory: they gained 81 seats in the House and 8 in the Senate. Since all Democratic losses took place in the North and West, Southerners emerged in a much stronger position. For the first time, Roosevelt could not form a majority without the help of some Republicans or Southern Democrats.

Congress assembled in January 1939 and wasted little time in disposing of FDR's program. To demonstrate its resentment at what it judged the attempted politicization of relief, Congress passed the Hatch Act (1939), prohibiting all government employees except a few high-ranking executive branch officials from engaging in political campaigns. The House abruptly cut off funds for the Federal Theater Project, which, because most of its activities centered in a few large cities, was highly vulnerable. The tax on undistributed profits, which businessmen bitterly resented, was repealed outright. Congress also refused to increase expenditures for public housing. When the administration requested $3.86 billion for self-liquidating public works projects, the Senate trimmed the amount substantially, and the House voted not even to consider it. Recognizing how far the pendulum had swung, Roosevelt became more cautious. He opposed efforts to expand federal contributions to the social security program in order to equalize benefits, disapproved proposals for additional deficit spending, and withheld support from a national health bill that would have provided aid for maternity and child care, hospital construction, and "general programs of medical care."

# NATIVISM AND THE APPROACH OF WAR

In the period from 1937 to 1941—years marked first by economic dislocation at home and then by international tension abroad—the United States experienced a sharp upsurge in nativist sentiment. This affected the New Deal because in the minds of some people the Roosevelt administration was playing into the hands of the very groups that seemed to pose the gravest danger—Communists, Jews, and labor agitators. Charges that the President had surrounded himself with dangerous advisors and had embraced an alien ideology were by no means new, but after 1937 they were voiced more frequently and accepted more widely. By 1940 the administration itself had grown concerned enough to crack down sharply on suspected subversives. But it did not succeed in quelling popular fears.

In 1937 workers in the Congress of Industrial Organizations adopted

Sit-down strikes at Chevrolet plant, Flint, Michigan, December 1936.

radical tactics to gain traditional goals of union recognition and improved conditions. Labor's new weapon, the sit-down strike, deeply frightened property-conscious Americans. No fewer than 477 such strikes, involving four hundred thousand workers, took place in 1937, the most important of which was the General Motors sit-down in Flint, Michigan in January. Most Americans assumed correctly that the union's occupation of a factory violated the law, but concluded erroneously that the automobile workers were inspired by revolutionary intent. Two out of every three people favored outlawing sit-down strikes and employing force against the union. "Armed insurrection—defiance of law, order and duly elected authority is spreading like wildfire," protested one group of citizens. Because Roosevelt refused to call out federal troops to evict the strikers he was accused of cringing before the forces of anarchy and disorder.

The popularity of the House Committee on Un-American Activities illustrated the administration's vulnerability to these charges. Created in the summer of 1938 and headed by Martin Dies of Texas, the Committee lashed out at New Deal programs and agencies. Dies insisted that leading New Deal officials hobnobbed with Communists, and during the 1938 campaign witnesses before the Committee attributed subversive leanings to liberal candidates in Michigan, Minnesota, and California. Roosevelt publicly rebuked Dies on two occasions when the Committee behaved in an especially offensive manner. But the President attempted to avoid a direct clash, largely because he knew that the Committee had wide support. In December 1938 a Gallup poll showed that three out of four persons who knew of the Committee approved of its work. Dies came to believe that FDR's "left-wing followers in the government are the fountainhead of subversive activities."

With the outbreak of World War II in September 1939, Roosevelt, himself the target of anticommunist attack, became worried about the possibility of subversion by Fascist agents or by Communists (who were then defending the Nazi-Soviet pact). In 1940 Congress and the administration outdid each other in tracking down potentially disloyal groups. In February, after the Justice Department had decided to prosecute people who had recruited volunteers to fight in the Spanish Civil War (a conflict in which the U.S. was officially neutral), the FBI seized twelve former recruiters in early-morning raids and released them only when the arrests provoked a storm of criticism from civil libertarians. In March, Roosevelt approved the fingerprinting of all aliens applying for visas as temporary visitors, and two months later he authorized the use of wiretaps against anyone "suspected of subversive activities." Congress passed the Smith Act, which required aliens to register, and made it a crime to conspire to teach or advocate the violent overthrow of the government. Congress also required all political organizations subject to foreign control to register with the Attorney General. The government prosecuted Communist leader Earl Browder on the technicality of using a fraudulent passport; he received an unprecedented four-year jail sentence. Attorney General Frank Murphy caught the mood in September 1940. "Unless we are pudding-headed," he said, "we will drive from the land the hirelings here to undo the labors of our fathers."

At the same time, Roosevelt increasingly shifted his emphasis from domestic reform to foreign policy and national defense. By 1940 his chief legislative goal was to obtain approval for assisting England and France. This, given isolationist strength in Congress, required the backing of Southern Democrats. As one conservative Southerner put it, the President had begun "cultivating us in a very nice way." Similarly, FDR's interest in readying plans for economic mobilization in the event of war moved him to mend fences with the business community. In August 1939 he appointed a War Resources Board composed mainly of big businessmen and headed by Edward Stettinius of U.S. Steel. Roosevelt, however, came to fear that the Board's proposals might dilute his own authority in wartime and did not make them public. In May 1940, when he set up a National Defense Advisory Commission to expedite production, he again turned to Stettinius and to William S. Knudsen of General Motors. By 1940 the process of repairing relations with businessmen and Southern Democrats alike was well under way.

New Dealers wasted little time in climbing aboard the defense bandwagon. As early as 1939 the Tennessee Valley Authority noted that it was "developing the power necessary for the large-scale operation of war industries in this well-protected strategic area." By 1940 New Deal bureaucrats commonly justified their programs on the grounds that they contributed to preparedness. The Works Progress Administration undertook projects of military value. The National Youth Administration stressed vocational training programs that were related to national defense. The Civilian Conservation Corps offered drills for its enrollees, provided instruction in reading blueprints, and performed tasks for army posts. All this reflected not only a belief in the worth of such projects but a recognition that they were most likely to receive funding from a stingy Congress.

By 1940 the agenda of American politics had been transformed, with foreign policy replacing reform as the central issue. The presidential campaign that year reflected this change. The international crisis persuaded Roosevelt to seek a third term and gave the Democrats an excuse to nominate him. The Republicans chose Wendell Willkie who, while a critic of many New Deal policies, accepted much of the welfare state. Moreover, as a spokesman for the internationalist wing of the Republican party, Willkie endorsed the main outlines of FDR's foreign policy, refusing, for example, to make issues of aid to England or the peacetime draft. The tense international situation undoubtedly worked to the President's advantage, although Willkie did surprisingly well with 22.3 million votes to Roosevelt's 27.2 million. But during the campaign, Roosevelt made his most famous and, given the events of the following year, his most unfortunate promise: "I shall say it again and again and again: Your boys are not going to be sent into any foreign wars."

## Suggested Reading

There are several good studies of American thought and culture during the 1930s. See especially Richard H. Pells, *Radical Visions and American Dreams: Culture and Social Thought in the Depression Years* (1973); Edwin A. Purcell, Jr.,

*The Crisis of Democratic Theory* (1972); Arthur Ekirch, Jr., *Ideologies and Utopias* (1969); and Charles C. Alexander, *Nationalism in American Thought* (1969). Two more specialized accounts are William Stott, *Documentary Expression and Thirties America* (1973); and R. Alan Lawson, *The Failure of Independent Liberalism, 1930–1941* (1971).

Social ferment during the early New Deal is considered in Arthur M. Schlesinger, Jr., *The Politics of Upheaval* (1960). On the old people's crusade, consult Abraham Holtzman, *The Townsend Movement* (1963). For Long and Coughlin, see T. Harry Williams, *Huey Long* (1969), which provides a wealth of information; Sheldon Marcus, *Father Coughlin* (1973); and Alan Brinkley, *Voices of Protest: Huey Long, Father Coughlin and the Great Depression* (1982). Two useful studies of the Union party are David J. O'Brien, *American Catholics and Social Reform: The New Deal Years* (1968); and David H. Bennett, *Demagogues in the Depression: American Radicals and the Union Party, 1932–1936* (1969). A comprehensive study of the Communist Party is Harvey Klehr, *The Heyday of American Communism: The Depression Decade* (1984).

There are several accounts of blacks and the New Deal, including John B. Kirby, *Black Americans in the Roosevelt Era* (1980); Raymond Wolters, *Negroes and the Great Depression* (1970); Harvard Sitkoff, *A New Deal for Blacks* (1978); and Nancy J. Weiss, *Farewell to the Party of Lincoln: Black Politics in the Age of FDR* (1984). Other useful studies include Dan T. Carter, *Scottsboro: A Tragedy of the Modern South* (1969); Robert Weisbrot, *Father Divine and the Struggle for Racial Equality* (1983); and Michel Fabre, *The Unfinished Quest of Richard Wright* (1973).

For women in the 1930s, see Susan Ware, *Holding Their Own: American Women in the 1930s* (1982) and *Beyond Suffrage: Women in the New Deal* (1981); Lois Scharf, *To Work or To Wed: Female Employment, Feminism, and the Great Depression* (1980); and Jeane Westin, ed., *Making Do: How Women Survived the 30s* (1976).

Conservative opposition to the New Deal is considered in George Wolfskill and John Hudson, *All But The People: FDR and His Critics* (1969); Frank Freidel, *FDR and the South* (1965); Donald McCoy, *Landon of Kansas* (1966); and James T. Patterson, *Congressional Conservatism and the New Deal* (1967). On the Supreme Court see Philippa Strum, *Louis D. Brandeis: Justice for the People* (1984); Michael E. Parrish, *Felix Frankfurter and His Times: The Reform Years* (1982); and Leonard Baker, *Back to Back: The Duel Between FDR and the Supreme Court* (1967). The controversy over executive reorganization is discussed in Richard Polenberg, *Reorganizing Roosevelt's Government, 1936–1939* (1966). Sidney Fine, *Sit-Down: The General Motors Strike of 1936–1937* (1969) is an excellent account of labor turmoil. Information on nativism in the late 1930s may be found in J. Woodford Howard, *Mr. Justice Murphy* (1968); and in Geoffrey S. Smith, *To Save a Nation: American Countersubversives, the New Deal, and the Coming of World War II* (1973). The 1940 campaign is the subject of Herbert S. Parmet and Marie B. Hecht, *Never Again* (1968); see, in addition, Ellsworth Barnard, *Wendell Willkie* (1966).

On the Federal Theater Project, see Jane D. Mathews, *The Federal Theater, 1935–1939: Plays, Relief and Politics* (1967). More general accounts are Malcolm Goldstein, *The Political Stage: American Drama and Theater of the Great Depression* (1974); and John O'Connor and Lorraine Brown, eds., *Free, Adult, Uncensored* (1978).

Pearl Harbor, December 7, 1941.

# CHAPTER EIGHT

# 1929–1941

## The Big Breakdown:
## The United States
## and the World

The depression ripped apart the treaty agreements so carefully built during the 1920s to preserve world peace, for the pacts had utterly depended on a smoothly working economic system. The collapse of 1929 not only destroyed the political arrangements. It created such chaos and disillusionment that fascists and radical leftists replaced moderate governments in such nations as Germany, Spain, and Japan. Extremists did not grasp control in the United States, however. In a remarkable performance Americans continued their allegiance to their traditional economic-political system, even though it was producing the most miserable and inhumane conditions in the nation's history. Franklin D. Roosevelt's foreign policy mirrored that moderation. The President even built his policies around the central belief of the 1920s, for he constantly tried to use international economic solutions, not political or military means, to stop Japanese and German aggression. That approach unfortunately worked no better for Roosevelt than it had for Hoover. The road to Pearl Harbor had been taken between 1929 and 1932. FDR was unable to find an exit from that road, and by 1938 Americans were tragically headed for the dead end of December 7, 1941.

## "MAD DOGS" AND ENGLISHMEN: THE MANCHURIAN CRISIS OF 1931–1932

In June 1931 President Hoover tried to stabilize Western money markets by suggesting a one-year moratorium (or postponement) on the collection of reparations from Germany and war debts from France and England. "Perhaps the most daring statement I ever thought of issuing," as Hoover recalled, it was too daring for the French. They insisted on keeping the hatchet of reparations above German heads. When Paris stalled, the President's policy collapsed. In July the German banking system came apart, then Great Britain's economic system went into a tailspin, the French government fell, and panic struck Europe and the United States. In Asia Japan took its first step toward World War II by invading Manchuria.

The Japanese had been especially hard hit by the depression. Their economy depended on overseas markets, which by 1931 had largely disappeared. Exports to the vital U.S. market, for example, dropped 30 percent in 1930. Japan's liberal government, like liberal regimes elsewhere, was undercut then destroyed by the collapse. By early 1931 dynamic political factions led by ambitious militarists demanded that Japan find its salvation not in the sick Western trading community, but in its own Asian empire. Since 1905 Tokyo had controlled and developed South

Manchuria. North Manchuria, however, was coming under the domination of Chiang Kai-shek's new regime. Chiang and a rapidly multiplying Chinese population even endangered Japanese control of South Manchuria. In September 1931 the Japanese militarists took affairs into their own hands. When a brief skirmish between Chinese and Japanese troops occurred along the South Manchurian railway, Japan's army launched a full-scale invasion of North Manchuria. Tokyo had bloodily repudiated its pledge at the Washington Conference to maintain the open door.

Hoover and Stimson were trapped. Throughout the 1920s American Far Eastern policy had depended on a cooperative Japan, particularly when the only alternatives as partners were a "revolutionary" China and the Soviet Union. Hoover privately remarked he had some sympathy for the Japanese, for they faced a "Bolshevist Russia to the north, and a possible Bolshevist China" to the west. Some officials wanted Japan handled gently because it was holding back the Chinese tide. "The Chinese are altogether too cocky," the American ambassador in London told the Japanese ambassador. "What you people need to do is to give them a thoroughly good licking to teach them their place and then they will be willing to talk sense." The Japanese army's political power also influenced Hoover and Stimson, for they feared that decisive American counteraction would be used by the army as an excuse to capture and mobilize the government for all-out war. In December 1931 the militarists overthrew the civilian regime and accelerated the Manchurian offensive, yet nearly a year later Stimson, who knew that "the situation [in Japan] is in the hands of virtually mad dogs," urged a moderate response so that "the little group of militarists" could not "make us a bogey in the whole matter." Fear of being made the villain would help paralyze Washington officials until Pearl Harbor.

During the next ten years the United States singlehandedly tried to protect its interests in the Far East. China was undependable, Russia too revolutionary, Great Britain hesitant and no longer a Pacific power. The only alternatives were stark: warring against Japan, working out something somehow with Tokyo, or else admitting that the United States had no vital interests in the area. No American President has ever opted for this third alternative. As the Japanese drove deeper into Manchuria in late 1931, Stimson discussed possible economic sanctions (for example, cutting off the considerable American oil and metal exports to Japan), but Hoover refused, fearing that sanctions would inevitably lead to war. The League of Nations investigated the outbreak, indirectly called Japan the aggressor, refused to recognize Japan's establishment of a "Manchukuo" puppet state in Manchuria, and then watched hopelessly as Tokyo responded by quitting the League. Stimson refused to work formally with the League. His main effort was to coordinate an Anglo-American reaffirmation of the Nine-Power pact backed by an increase of military strength in the Pacific. That policy collapsed when the British decided to work through the League while privately trying to appease Japan. From 1931 until Pearl Harbor, London officials, whose primary concerns lay in Europe, would support American actions against Japan only if they were certain the United States would accept the possible consequence of war and be willing to fight Japan virtually alone. Otherwise the British were prepared to make deals with the Japanese, and for that, the United States refused in turn to trust the British.

By early 1932 the United States could take only two steps to threaten the Japanese. Both were taken unilaterally. Stimson announced in January that Washington would not recognize any act (such as Japan's establishment of Manchukuo) that impaired American rights in China by violating the open-door principle. Then in a public letter to Senator William E. Borah (Republican of Idaho), Stimson warned that if Japan insisted on breaking the Nine-Power pact, the United States would not be bound by the Five-Power Treaty limiting navies. Such threats made little impact on the Japanese. They signed a temporary armistice with China in May 1932, digested their conquests, and prepared for further war.

## NEW ORDER TO NEW DEAL

Hoover made one final attempt to put the pieces back together. Between 1930 and 1932 nearly every nation withdrew inside itself, erected tariff walls, and attempted to follow autarchic economic policies. In 1930 the United States passed the Hawley-Smoot bill, the highest protective tariff in its history. A more extreme example of autarchy was Britain's construction of the Imperial Preference system in 1932. Through a series of bilateral pacts, the British government and members of its Commonwealth promised to give one another favored trading privileges, thus largely excluding such third parties as the United States from traditional American markets in Canada, Australia, and South Africa. The United States bitterly fought such policies, not only because they gravely hurt trade, but also because they injected the government into the realm of private enterprise. In 1932 Hoover counterattacked by proposing an international conference in London that would negotiate war debts, reparations, and disarmament. The President hoped that settlement of the debts could be used to pressure England and France into accepting liberal trade policies.

Before the conference could convene, however, Franklin D. Roosevelt moved into the White House. When Hoover and Stimson asked Roosevelt to accept their policies in the Far East and the proposed London conference, FDR agreed not to recognize Manchukuo, but absolutely refused to commit himself on economic issues. During his first eight months in office he rejected Hoover's international approach, most dramatically when he destroyed the London conference by refusing to tie American tariff and monetary policy to any international agreement. Believing that the American economy might be able to resurrect itself if it was not tied to a disintegrating world economy, Roosevelt allowed the war-debt issue to die, took the country off the international gold standard, and began tinkering with the dollar to raise its purchasing power. None of these devices sufficiently spurred the economy. "Yes, it is the zero hour in Washington," critic Edmund Wilson observed in early 1934. "The first splendor of the New Deal has faded. . . . The emergency measures which revived our morale have not achieved all that they have promised."

By the spring of 1934 Roosevelt gave up his experiments and returned to Hoover's assumption that recovery required a booming American export trade. Quite clearly the domestic economy would not further improve without measures—such as some that smacked too much of socialism for FDR's taste—that would radically change the nature of the system. The President's only alternative therefore was to find help outside the system itself, that is, in the world marketplace. Also like Hoover, Roosevelt refused to tie his hands politically. He finally rejected political alliances and the League of Nations in favor of enjoying maximum freedom to trade with anyone, regardless of their political coloring.

Two major differences, however, separated FDR's foreign policy from Hoover's. Roosevelt was dealing with a world rapidly compartmentalizing into closed, government-controlled blocs. Japan's Manchukuo and the British Imperial Preference system, for example, were not open to American competition. More ominously, in January 1933 Adolf Hitler assumed power in Germany. Within three years he worked out exclusive and government-controlled trade arrangements in Europe and Latin America that made it difficult for private American traders to compete.

These developments led to the second distinguishing—if not revolutionary—characteristic of New Deal policy: the government had to involve itself directly, for example by giving subsidies to private businessmen who needed help in the marketplace. Hoover had avoided such direct involvement at all costs, fearing that it would change the nature of the system itself. Roosevelt believed that such danger could be averted. Moreover, he had little choice, for if Americans were to find economic salvation overseas, they could compete against Germans, Japanese, and British governmental policies only if the United States government provided similar aid. That, of course, raised the grave danger that if conflict arose in the marketplace, the governments themselves would be fully involved in the struggle.

The guiding genius behind this policy was Secretary of State Cordell Hull. An ardent Wilsonian, and former congressman from Tennessee who prided himself on complete command of the Tennessee mountaineer's earthy vocabulary, Hull was named Secretary of State because of his influence on Capitol Hill. He was driven by an obsession to reopen the clogged channels of trade. Only when high tariffs, currency manipulation, and the power of state trading enterprises were obliterated, he believed, could individual freedoms be restored and wars averted. For Hull was certain that friction between economic blocs inevitably led to political conflict. He therefore set out to replace such closed blocs with an open, multilateral trading system that had freely convertible currencies (instead of monies manipulated by the state), and which allowed private businessmen to buy and sell anywhere they chose. Hull used this standard of freer trade to judge nearly every diplomatic move he made between 1933 and his retirement in 1944, a standard that led him to condemn Germany in the 1930s, Japan in 1941, and the Soviet Union in 1944. This policy is central to an understanding of why he and FDR came to define these three nations as enemies politically as well as economically.

Between 1934 and 1939 more legislation was enacted in Washington to find markets abroad for American surpluses than in any similar period in the nation's history. Two measures stand out. The Reciprocity Act of 1934 was Hull's pet project. It sharply reversed post-1920 policy by giving

Secretary of State Cordell Hull, Undersecretary Sumner Welles, and Assistant Secretary Adolf Berle at the White House during the beginning of World War II, September 1939.

the President power to reduce or raise tariffs by as much as 50 percent in bargaining with other nations for reciprocal reduction of tariff barriers. The policy also included the unconditional-most-favored-nation principle, that is, that trade favors given to one nation would be automatically given to all others that did not discriminate against American trade. That principle made it impossible for two nations to gang up economically against a third. If used successfully, the Reciprocity Act would be like a giant economic wrecking ball, swinging in all directions to batter down tariff and other state-created barriers that Hull and FDR so hated. Reciprocity pacts with fourteen nations helped accelerate exports between 1934 and 1938 by over a half-billion dollars. Imports, however, lagged; this meant that other nations were not selling enough to Americans to obtain the dollars needed to buy expanded U.S. exports.

As in 1928–29, therefore, a dollar shortage threatened to stunt the growth of the world, and consequently the American, economy. In 1934 Roosevelt established a government-operated Export-Import Bank through which government credits would be made available to foreign customers so they could purchase U.S. exports. Funds to finance foreign trade would now be provided by the government, not just by the private bankers who had proven unequal to the job in the 1920s. American tax dollars were loaned overseas for the purchase of American goods. These acts creating the reciprocity policy and the Export-Import Bank proved so beneficial that both were renewed and expanded during the next half-century.

## AREAS OF SPECIAL INTEREST: LATIN AMERICA AND THE USSR

These economic initiatives were aimed at every corner of the world, but the New Deal selected several areas for special attention. Between 1933 and 1938, Roosevelt and Hull devoted great energy to making North and South America "good neighbors." During those years United States imports from Latin America leaped 114 percent to $705 million, while exports to the south rocketed 166 percent, over $640 million. In 1932 the United States accounted for 32 percent of Latin American trade, but after the reciprocity legislation took effect, Americans enjoyed 45 percent in 1938. Politically FDR continued Hoover's policy of noninterference militarily. A major step occurred at the Montevideo Conference in 1933 when Hull, somewhat against his will, pledged the United States to a clear declaration of nonintervention.

The increased economic leverage was providing Americans with an alternative diplomatic weapon. Cuba provided a classic example. Since 1903 the Platt Amendment had given officials in Washington the right to send troops to Cuba. Control became firmer between 1919 and 1921 when depressed sugar prices ruined plantations and Americans invested heavily, in the "dance of the millions," in Cuban sugar. Throughout the 1920s a dictator protected these interests, but by 1933 the economy had collapsed and left-wing movements challenged the government. After 35 years as an American protectorate, Cuban trade with the United States had dropped 50 percent since 1929, its sugar sold for one-tenth of a cent per pound, and five hundred thousand of its 4 million people searched for work. In September 1933 junior army officers under Fulgencio Batista overthrew the government and put a liberal politician into the presidency.

The regime was indeed too liberal for the State Department, which thought it saw Communists creeping into power. Hull and Under Secretary of State Sumner Welles, a close friend of Roosevelt's, asked FDR to make a show of force in Havana harbor. The President refused. He had a better alternative. In 1933–34 FDR and Batista—who desperately needed economic help—agreed to pump life into the Cuban economy by opening the American sugar market to Cuban cane at prices above the world level. Other foreign-produced sugar was effectively excluded from the United States. The American consumers thus paid extra for their sugar, but Batista lived up to his part of the deal by placing a more conservative president in power in Havana. The policy worked so well that in 1934 Roosevelt felt he could safely repeal all of the Platt Amendment except the section giving the United States the Guantanamo Naval Base. At the same time, Washington also promised to give the Philippines its independence in ten years, but again carefully made economic arrangements to protect American interests on the islands.

FDR pursued the same economic approach toward Russia, but with much less success. After frequent consultation with William Bullitt, who had returned from the French Riviera and Philadelphia to advise him, the President recognized the Soviets in November 1933. He had to overcome strong opposition from the American Legion, the Daughters of the American Revolution, Roman Catholic Church leaders, the American Federation of Labor, and, most important, his own State Department. Hull swore that no deals could be made with a state-controlled economy. He also argued that the Bolsheviks would try, as he believed they had in Cuba during the 1933 revolution, to interfere in American domestic affairs. Roosevelt did, however, receive strong support from businessmen, who argued that the potentially vast Russian market could help rescue Americans from the depression. Political recognition was a prerequisite, the businessmen emphasized, for Russia needed credit to buy goods, and without recognition no private or governmental institution would extend credit.

The Soviets welcomed FDR's initiative, but for very different reasons. They were less interested in trade than in working out a common policy to contain Japan. Since 1931 the Soviets, fearful that Tokyo's militarists would move from Manchuria into Siberia, had desperately searched for friends. One Moscow official remarked that Russia and the United States must join in "breaking [Japan] as between the two arms of a nutcracker."

Within two years after diplomatic relations were resumed, Moscow-Washington relations turned sour. Trade did not prosper because no agreement could be reached on proper credit arrangements. The Soviets became disillusioned when the State Department went out of its way to assure anxious Tokyo officials that recognition was not in any way directed against Japan. Roosevelt and Bullitt, who became the first American ambassador to the Soviet Union, plainly informed Russian leader Joseph Stalin they would make no anti-Japanese alliance. Washington preferred to consider a deal with its old friend Japan than to work with the mysterious, revolutionary Soviets. In 1934 Stalin gave up on the United States, began negotiating with Japan, joined the League, and—too late—reversed his attitude toward Hitler (whom Stalin had dismissed as a fool in 1932) in a last-ditch try at working out anti-Fascist alliances with Eastern and Western governments. Russia and the United States continued to go in opposite directions until they were startlingly thrown together by Hitler in 1941.

## THE FAILURE OF POLITICAL NEUTRALITY

Between 1933 and 1937 the Japanese carefully refrained from further aggression, but tightened their grip on Manchuria. When Roosevelt attempted to help China in late 1933 with wheat, cotton, and airplanes, Tokyo slammed back with the so-called Amau Statement of 1934, which warned that since foreign aid to China could "acquire political significance," Japan had the right to act unilaterally to maintain "peace and order in Eastern Asia." The State Department again reiterated the Nine-Power pact principles for an open door in China, but Japan threw that treaty on the scrap heap by excluding American oil and other interests from Manchuria. By late 1934 Tokyo demanded that the Five-Power principles be changed to allow Japan parity with the American and British fleets. When this was refused, the Japanese withdrew from the agreement and accelerated the building of their navy and fortifications in the Pacific.

In 1936 Tokyo found new friends. During the previous year Mussolini's Italy had suddenly ravaged the small African nation of Ethiopia. When the League and the major powers offered little response, Hitler embarked on his own campaign of aggression. The self-proclaimed Führer, determined to rectify the 1919 Peace Conference's dissection of Germany, marched unopposed to reclaim the Rhineland in 1936. During that summer civil war erupted in Spain between the five-year-old Republic and conservative army-church forces. Within a year Hitler and Mussolini funneled vast aid to help the advancing conservatives while the Republic obtained major help only from the Soviets. Great Britain and France remained on the sidelines of what they preferred to believe was only a civil war, and the United States followed suit. Germany was clearly on the move. In November 1936 the Japanese climbed aboard by signing an Anti-Comintern Pact with Hitler, which secretly called for joint consultation if either party were attacked by the Soviets; both parties promised not to make treaties with Russia. Italy joined the Pact in 1937. The Japanese now had friends and security on their Russian flank if they wanted to move into China or areas to the south.

The United States responded to these developments with a series of neutrality laws. A Senate investigation headed by Gerald Nye, Republican of North Dakota, revealed in 1934–35 that private American bankers had become closely involved with the French and British war efforts during 1915–17. No evidence demonstrated that President Wilson's policies had been directly shaped by the bankers, but the conclusion was too easily drawn that the United States had been shoved into world war by the profit-lust of a few. Congress responded with the 1935 Neutrality Act: When the President declared that war existed, no arms, ammunition, or items of war were to be shipped to any belligerent, and American ships could not transport such supplies to a belligerent. In 1936 Congress passed a second Neutrality Act that prohibited loans to nations involved in war. A year later, in response to the Spanish conflict, other Neutrality Acts forbade Americans from traveling on belligerent vessels and applied these various provisions to civil wars.

But one major change appeared in the 1937 legislation. In response to Roosevelt's anger that the acts tied his hands, and because the damming up of these items threatened vital parts of the country's economy, a "cash-and-carry" provision was added allowing nations to obtain nonmilitary supplies if they paid cash and transported them home in their own ships. Americans, in other words, hoped to avoid wars while making money from them. Obviously the cash-and-carry clause also helped Great Britain and France since in any European war their navies would control the Atlantic. As Japan soon demonstrated, however, the Neutrality Acts were written to prevent the previous war, not the next one.

In July 1937 the Japanese army attacked North China in an effort to build a buffer area around Japan's puppet state of Manchukuo. The Neutrality Acts were useless, for whereas Americans wanted to help China, the Japanese fleet controlled the western Pacific and hence could take advantage of the cash-and-carry provision. Roosevelt tried to escape from the dilemma by refusing to declare that a war existed in Asia. The neutrality provisions consequently did not take effect. He meanwhile desperately searched for ways to aid China.

On October 5, FDR delivered a "quarantine speech" in Chicago, the center of political isolationism. The President talked vaguely about quar-

Japanese troops entering Peking, August 1937.

antining aggressor nations, but offered no specific policies. Historians now believe that a majority of Americans probably supported Roosevelt's call, but the howls of opposition that arose drove Roosevelt and Hull to disclaim any intention of immediate action. The League of Nations, however, picked up the proposal, calling for an international conference to convene in Brussels in November.

Roosevelt was prepared to negotiate with Japan. He instructed the American officials at Brussels to work for the restoration of the Nine-Power pact principles. If Japan would agree to these the United States would discuss economic cooperation with Tokyo in North China but only, of course, within the framework of the open door. The British again dragged their feet, not at all sure that if Japan refused, the President would be prepared to fight. The Soviets offered the United States a security pact against Japan if the Americans and Western Europeans would in turn help fend off Germany. Washington flatly turned this proposal down. The Japanese finally refused even to attend the conference, insisting that the war concerned only themselves and the Chinese. A total failure, the Brussels Conference marked the last major American effort to work collectively to control the aggressors.

In December 1937 Japanese planes attacked an American gunboat, *The Panay*, as it stood guard over Standard Oil tankers in the Yangtze River. Two Americans were killed. FDR strongly protested, and Japan apologized, but the President then tried to take the offensive. In the House he waged a bitter and successful struggle against a constitutional amendment, proposed by Louis Ludlow (Democrat of Indiana), which if passed would have required a national referendum before a declaration of war unless the United States itself was attacked. The following month FDR proposed a 20-percent increase in the fleet and began rebuilding Guam and other Pacific bases.

## THE FAILURE OF THE NEW DEAL

After these small successes the President had to turn from foreign policy to a crisis at home. In early 1937 he believed that the American economy had recovered sufficiently so that some New Deal measures could be cut back. FDR especially hoped to balance the budget, a move that would dry up vast federal monies that had been priming the economy. As Secretary of the Treasury Henry Morgenthau phrased it, "This was the moment, it seemed to me, to strip off the bandages, throw away the crutches, and see if American private enterprise could stand on its own feet." Roosevelt pulled governmental money out too rapidly, however, and like a patient drained of blood, the economy staggered, then collapsed into the most precipitous decline in American history. In nine months industrial production dropped 33 percent, payrolls 35 percent, industrial stock averages 50 percent, profits 78 percent. Only unemployment rose, spiraling upward 23 percent. The domestic New Deal had no other medicines to offer. Roosevelt, one of his Cabinet members noted, "did not know which way to turn." But something had to be done rapidly, for the crisis went beyond economics. Harry Hopkins, one of FDR's closest advisors, declared, "This country cannot continue as a democracy with 10 or 12 million people unemployed. It just can't be done."

Roosevelt's massive spending program on the navy, and later on a 5500-plane air force, provided one response to the crisis. By 1939 defense spending was putting Americans back to work again, although 10 million remained unemployed as late as January 1940. The full-scale war economy of post-1941 would finally solve the terrible economic problems that the New Deal could never remedy.

Another response to the crisis was the traditional hope of finding expanded foreign markets for the vast surplus of American goods. China provided the greatest potential market. "Probably never in its history has China offered greater promise for [U.S.] future trade, industry, and general economic progress," a Commerce Department official told a gathering of American businessmen in mid-1937. "We have built up in China organizations capable of those measures of expansion which are characteristic of American enterprise where very favorable trade conditions permit." The Japanese invasion threatened that dream and more: If the Japanese developed a large cotton industry in North China, then, Secretary of Commerce Daniel C. Roper warned FDR in late 1937, American exports would drop so low as to require "a recharting of the economy of the South and definite Federal production control procedures." Several years later a correspondent of the *New York Times* substituted rubber for cotton but came up with the same conclusion: "The future of China and the future of the United States in Asia may very well be determined by whether or not those rubber tires that roll on the Chinese roads are made in Akron or in Osaka [Japan]."

Secretary of State Hull was caught in the middle of this maelstrom. In 1936 he had been impressed with the advice from John A. Hobson, the great historian of imperialism, that the "last large possibility of maintaining capitalism lies in the Orient." It was doubtful, Hobson continued, that in exploiting this lush market "the Americans will care to play second fiddle to the Japanese, whose character and behavior are so baffling to the Occidental mind." That advice fitted perfectly with Hull's view that an open-door approach, rather than Japanese exclusiveness, was the only method to develop a healthy global trade, world peace, and the American economy. In November 1938, however, Hull suffered a severe setback when Japan proclaimed a Greater Asia Co-prosperity Sphere based on anti-Bolshevism and economic and cultural cooperation through the Far East. It was, Tokyo claimed, an Asian equivalent to the American Monroe Doctrine in the Western Hemisphere. Hull feared that all of Asia would go the way of Manchuria. "In our opinion," he sweepingly declared in late 1938, "an endeavor by any country in any part of the world to establish itself in favor of a preferred position in another country is incompatible with the maintenance of our own and the establishment of world prosperity." That statement requires close study, for it was the cornerstone of American foreign policy.

How to drive Japan from its "preferred position" was the central problem, one compounded by statistics in early 1939 showing Japan to be America's third-largest customer. During a severe depression such trade was not to be lightly discarded for the mere potential of the China market. Japan, moreover, had long been Washington's and London's most dependable ally in the Far East, a bastion against revolution. A war to protect the open door in China, on the other hand, could spawn new revolutions and be bloody as well as long lasting, particularly if the Japanese and Germans coordinated their efforts. "We would like to help China if we knew how, of course," Secretary of Interior Harold Ickes summed up the cruel dilemma in late 1938, ". . . without running the risk of our own involvement in war."

Two alternatives emerged. The first, championed by Hull and his State Department advisors, urged continued effort toward a cooperative policy with Japan. Only then, Hull believed, could traditional multilateral co-operation be maintained for the propping open of the door to Far Eastern markets. He believed that an international trade agreement based on his beloved reciprocity principle would restore economic cooperation and—as Hull's reasoning ran—therefore result in a political agreement. Once brought within such a trade-political network, Japan could find necessary markets peacefully, continue to receive strategic goods from a friendly United States, and quit its iniquitous partnership with Hitler.

A second answer came from Henry Morgenthau and the Treasury Department. He reasoned that Japan's militarists were uncontrollable and too ambitious to settle for a friendly division of the Asian market. Morgenthau urged direct bilateral aid to help China drive back the invader. He bitterly criticized Hull's complicated multilateral, cooperative approach ("while he was discussing it, one country after another goes under.") The Treasury's approach had an added attraction. Such aid could tightly link China to American trade and financial interests rather than allow it to be divided among a number of powers.

Roosevelt at first equivocated between the two alternatives but told Morgenthau in late 1938, "Henry, these trade treaties [of Hull's] are just too goddamned slow. The world is marching too fast." The Secretary of State's approach was also undercut as Japan insisted that only it and China could settle Chinese affairs; third parties were not wanted. Morgenthau won a victory in 1938 when FDR agreed to send a $25 million credit for China's war effort, then a major triumph in July 1939 when Hull finally agreed to terminate the 1911 Commercial Treaty, which governed trade with Japan. FDR was so happy with Hull's acquiescence that he blurted out, "Cordell, I feel like kissing you on both cheeks." Morgenthau next pushed for an embargo on oil, but Hull dug in his heels. No more would be done until Hitler had begun World War II.

# GERMAN AGGRESSION, 1936–1939

**SOVIET UNION**

**LITHUANIA**
Memelland reoccupied, March, 1939
Vilna
Kaunas
SUWALKIE
Memel

**EAST PRUSSIA**

Bialystok
Niemen

**POLAND**
Suwan
Lublin
Warsaw
Bug
Vistula
Cracow
Lvov

**RUMANIA**

**SUBCARPATHIAN RUTHENIA**

**SLOVAKIA**
German protectorate
March, 1939
Bratislava

**HUNGARY**
Budapest

Danzig
POLISH CORRIDOR
Posen

**BALTIC SEA**
SWEDEN

**GERMANY**
Oder
Berlin
Breslau
Dresden

**BOHEMIA** MORAVIA
Bohemia and Moravia annexed, March, 1939
Prague

Vienna
**AUSTRIA**
Austria annexed, March, 1938

**DENMARK**

**NORTH SEA**
Heligoland

Hamburg
Elbe
Bremen

Essen
Cologne
Rhine
Rhineland reoccupied, March, 1936

Sudeten areas annexed, October, 1938

Danube
Munich

**ITALY**

Mainz
SAAR
LUX.

**NETHERLANDS**

**BELGIUM**

**SWITZERLAND**

**FRANCE**

259

# EDWARD R. MURROW AND THE RADIO

"Radio is a recent innovation that has introduced profound alterations in the outlook and social behavior of men," two noted psychologists concluded in 1935. This dramatic view was accurate, even though commercial radio was just fifteen years old. The first national networks were formed in the mid-1920's by the National Broadcasting Company (NBC) and Columbia Broadcasting System (CBS), breakthroughs that led Secretary of Commerce Herbert Hoover to establish a governmental licensing and regulatory agency in 1927. He was concerned that radio be responsible: "It is inconceivable that we should allow so great a possibility for service, for news, for entertainment . . . to be drowned in advertising chatter."

That was a forlorn hope. Radio advertising grew in popularity even during the depression. Albert Lasker, king of the advertising agents, tripled sales of Pepsodent by having the toothpaste sponsor the most popular 1930s program, "Amos n' Andy," in which two white men impersonated black minstrel-show types. Radio standardized habits of living, speech, and taste in a nation once famous for sectionalism and diversity.

Until the 1930s radio broadcast little news. NBC did not have a single daily news series. It believed its job was to entertain the entire family while leaving current affairs to newspapers. Franklin D. Roosevelt changed this with his "Fireside Chats" in 1933. With a voice perfectly suited for the new medium, his broadcasts were so successful that, in the words of a col-

Orson Welles directing the Mercury Theater of the Air.

Edward R. Murrow in London, 1941.

umnist, "The President has only to look toward a radio to bring Congress to terms." As Europe moved toward war, news services increased until in 1937 CBS sent 28-year-old Edward R. Murrow to Europe to establish continent-wide broadcasts. Born in Polecat Creek, North Carolina, he had moved west to study at Washington State College where the nation's first courses on radio were being offered. As Murrow left for Europe, a CBS executive protested, "Broadcasting has no role in international politics," but should limit itself to radioing "the song of a nightingale from Kent, England," a program that had been voted the "most interesting broadcast" of 1932.

Murrow destroyed such illusions. CBS coverage of the 1938 Munich crises was followed hourly by millions. Its effect was noticeable a month later when the network produced Orson Welles's version of "War of the Worlds," a story of invaders from Mars landing in New Jersey. Welles utilized the news bulletin–spot interview techniques used at Munich. Within a half-hour after the program began, New Jersey residents were filling the highways heading out of the state, two Princeton professors had rushed out to study the invaders, and a Pittsburgh woman, crying "I'd rather die this way than that," was stopped before she could take poison. News broadcasting had come of age.

Murrow built a continental staff headed by Eric Severeid and Howard K. Smith. His own most famous pro-

Queen Victoria Station, London, during the "blitz," May 1941.

FDR giving a Fireside Chat, 1940.

grams occurred during Hitler's air "blitz" of London in 1940–41. His rich, quiet, understated voice began each broadcast with "This—is London." He followed with graphic accounts that tried to "report suffering to people [Americans] who have not suffered," by providing eyewitness testimony of bombing ("that moan of stark terror and suspense cannot be encompassed by words"). Murrow pioneered new uses of the microphone, once simply putting it on a London sidewalk while sirens shrieked, antiaircraft guns fired, and people walked to shelters. As the foreign policy debate in Washington intensified, he shrewdly helped the pro-interventionist forces by reporting British belief that Americans were the last hope for democracy, while emphasizing Churchill's greatness and England's bravery. As American poet Archibald MacLeish wrote of Murrow: "You burned the city of London in our houses and we felt the flames that burned it. You laid the dead of London at our doors and we knew the dead were our dead." Murrow brought a new dimension to radio, for he used it to educate and improve society. Even after his death in 1965, his style and ideals shaped news broadcasting.

# THE GHOST OF 1919

As European peace disintegrated after 1935, Roosevelt offered only suggestions for disarmament or economic conferences. Not even the British would accept such proposals. The Conservative government of Prime Minister Neville Chamberlain embraced instead the policy of appeasement, a dirty word during the post-1945 era but not in the 1930s, for it meant adjusting the wrongs inflicted on Germany by the 1919 peace conference. In this sense Roosevelt and most Americans were also appeasers. Like Europeans, they were belatedly conscience-stricken by the harsh penalties pressed on Germany, and so stood paralyzed as Hitler's armies moved into adjoining territories during the mid-1930s. Also like Chamberlain, Roosevelt believed that issues could be compromised with Germany and Italy, especially if done through the personal, private, and manipulative diplomacy that each man preferred to more traditional methods.

When the Munich crisis flared in September 1938, Roosevelt encouraged Chamberlain to talk with Hitler. The President refused to take the side either of the German dictator, who demanded annexation of the Czechoslovak Sudetenland area containing several million Germans, or of the Czechs (supposedly supported by Britain and France), who did not want to surrender their only defensible frontier area. On September 9 Roosevelt angrily made clear to reporters that Americans had no moral commitment to European democracies. Chamberlain finally decided to make a dramatic flight to Munich for talks with Hitler, a decision that would result in Chamberlain's agreeing that Hitler should have his way. FDR wired the Prime Minister, "Good man." A month later Roosevelt told the Cabinet of his "shame" for supporting the Munich agreement and ordered the acceleration of plans for sending war goods to England and France.

The President's disillusionment with Hitler also resulted from Nazi activities in Latin America. German businessmen, including the powerful Lufthansa airline, scored repeated successes in South American markets. An Assistant Secretary of Commerce observed during 1938, "It used to be said that trade follows the flag. Observing world affairs today we might more appropriately say that political ideologies follow trade." As the Germans entered, moreover, traditional U.S. markets disappeared, a loss especially felt during the economic crisis of 1938. Roosevelt responded with increased governmental assistance to American businessmen and also pushed for a common anti-Axis front in the hemisphere. His success was marked in the 1938 Declaration of Lima when all the Inter-American nations agreed to cooperate fully against outside threats. A year later, after war began in Europe, the Americas agreed on a Declaration of Panama, which created a "safety belt" of nearly a thousand miles around the hemisphere in which there were to be no hostile acts by non-American belligerents.

Adolph Hitler, 1933.

By 1940 the only outstanding hemispheric problem was again the Mexican revolution. In March 1938 Mexico finally nationalized all foreign oil companies. Hull blew up, urging quick action against "those Communists down there." The previous U.S. pledges of nonintervention, however, and Roosevelt's fear that a tough policy would turn Mexico toward Japan and Germany, moderated Washington's response. A settlement was finally reached in November 1941 when Mexico agreed to pay $40 million in back claims and establish a committee of experts to settle compensation for the oil companies. In return, the United States helped finance Mexican currency and extended a $30 million Export-Import Bank loan to build a large section of the Pan american Highway from Mexico into Guatemala.

Mexico was restored to the anti-Axis front that the United States was so anxious to forge. In this sense only, Roosevelt's appeasement policy toward the Axis had worked, for it helped forestall war until most of the hemisphere agreed to follow his lead against Germany and Japan.

Otherwise appeasement was a disaster. History catches and controls every decade, and never more tragically than when the 1919 treaty helped paralyze the anti-Hitlerian nations during the 1930s. One nation finally broke away. On August 23, 1939, Stalin signed a nonaggression treaty with Hitler in which they struck an agreement on the division of Poland and the Balkans. Since the Brussels Conference of 1937 Stalin had tried to negotiate a security agreement with France and England. This had foundered on French and British anti-Communist hatreds and the refusal of the Poles and Rumanians to entrust their existence to Russian hands. Stalin had also carried out a gigantic blood purge of his supposed political enemies, which probably exterminated several million Russians. This brutality turned many Westerners, even Communist party members, against the Soviets; a typical American account was entitled, "Stalin, Portrait of a Degenerate," in which he was compared—unfavorably—with "Scarface" Al Capone. Among the victims of the purge were leading Red Army officers. Western officials concluded that in any conflict the decimated Russian forces would be virtually useless. Hitler perceived Russia differently, for a treaty with Stalin would free Germany from the danger of a two-front war. Americans viewed all this incredulously, at first dismissing the Nazi-Soviet pact as a mere "grandstand play" designed by Stalin to frighten the West, then agreeing that there was no difference after all between communism and fascism. The latter fallacy would influence American policymakers during the post-1945 years.

Nine days after the Nazi-Soviet pact, Hitler invaded Poland. England and France, which had guaranteed Poland's boundaries, declared war on Germany. After an impassioned congressional debate, FDR won a modification of the Neutrality Acts. The arms embargo was changed to cash-and-carry in order to help the Allies, but loans remained illegal. Unlike Wilson, Roosevelt never asked Americans to be neutral in thought and deed. He did, unfortunately, insist that his policies would keep the United States out of war even as he was tying the country closer to the Allies.

In November, Russia invaded Finland to obtain strategic areas along the Finnish-Soviet boundary. Despite State Department urgings to do so, Roosevelt refused to break diplomatic relations with Russia, although he placed a voluntary, or "moral," embargo on airplanes and gas ticketed for the Soviets. An important side-effect soon appeared. Spurred by war orders, American employment jumped 10 percent in late 1939 as production rose sharply. The Second World War rescued the economy and between 1940 and 1945 would provide the greatest stimulus the system ever received. In sending that system's products to the Allies and to Finland, however, Roosevelt was giving hostages to the future.

## THE TRIALS OF UNNEUTRAL NEUTRALITY

The German blitzkrieg through Poland was followed by a lull, or "sitz-krieg," during winter and early spring of 1939–40. In May, Hitler suddenly occupied France and the low countries. By June, his forces stood triumphant on the English Channel. Only the British remained to face the Nazis. Winston Churchill, who throughout the 1930s had repeatedly condemned appeasement, replaced Chamberlain and mobilized England for a last-ditch fight. In the Pacific, Japan took advantage of the French and Dutch disasters to make demands on French Indochina and the Dutch East Indies. By September the struggle truly became global, for Japan, Germany, and Italy signed a tripartite mutual assistance pact clearly aimed at the United States. Americans now faced the prospect of a two-front war if they went to the rescue of Great Britain.

Roosevelt and his advisors concluded that Germany, not Japan, posed the gravest threat, and that England must have top priority for war supplies. That policy would continue to govern American actions between 1941 and 1945. Protecting Great Britain, however, also meant safeguarding the European colonial empires in South and Southeast Asia, which produced the vital rubber, oil, and metals for the Anglo-American war effort. Japan, therefore, could not be allowed to strike south. Roosevelt initially responded by proposing an unbelievable building program to construct fifty thousand planes and over a million tons of shipping. In September 1940 he made an Executive Agreement with Churchill that sent fifty United States destroyers to England in return for ninety-nine-year leases to British naval bases in the Western Hemisphere. This act required considerable political courage, for Roosevelt had decided to run for an unprecedented third term and was confronting strong criticism for his earlier aid to England.

The opposition was led by the "America First" group comprised of anti–New Deal industrialists (Henry Ford, Sterling Morton of Morton Salt), old Progressives (Senator Burton K. Wheeler, journalist Oswald Garrison Villard), and public figures who warned of dire military and political consequences should the nation be sucked into the war (flying aces Eddie Rickenbacker and Charles A. Lindbergh, historian Charles Beard). The pro-Allied sentiment was mobilized by the Committee to Defend America by Aiding the Allies. The Committee vowed that it wanted to stay out of war, but argued that this uninvolvement required sending vast aid to nations resisting fascism. It was especially successful in creating public support for the destroyers-bases deal. FDR was also fortunate in that the 1940 Republican presidential nominee, Wendell Willkie, sympathized with the Committee to Defend America and so refused to criticize the President for helping England.

During the campaign FDR stressed that he did not intend to involve the country in war. After the election, however, he stepped up American involvement, often with the public assurance that further involvement would somehow lessen the need for Americans to fight. Roosevelt was trapped. He knew the American system could not long survive in a fascist-dominated world, but he feared making strong public statements because of his estimate of antiwar sentiment, especially on Capitol Hill. When one ardent interventionist urged more action, FDR replied, "Whether we like it or not, God and Congress still live." He consequently committed the United States to the allies while issuing public explanations that fell short of the truth.

Such use of presidential power raised the classic question of whether the ends indeed justified the means. That question could be answered one way in 1941 and in a quite different fashion in the 1960s when Lyndon Johnson used FDR's actions as precedents for his own methods of committing Americans to Vietnam (see Chapter 14). Even in 1941, however, critics led by Charles Beard warned that the question of how Americans went to war was as important as whether they went, for, Beard argued, the misuse of presidential powers could destroy the delicate checks and balances built by the Founding Fathers to protect individual freedom and representative government.

Beard lost that argument. Roosevelt moved rapidly in 1941 against the Axis. In March he pushed Lend-Lease through Congress so that the country could be "the arsenal of democracy" and send vast amounts of goods to England regardless of its inability to pay for the supplies. The act was aimed, FDR said, at keeping "war away from our country and our people." Senator Burton K. Wheeler called Lend-Lease "the New Deal's triple-A foreign policy: it will plow under every fourth American boy." Roosevelt promptly shot back that this was "the rottenest thing that has been said in public life in my generation." But moving supplies to England through Nazi submarine-infested seas of the North Atlantic soon required Roosevelt to send American convoys to protect the supply ships. He ordered such convoying as far as Iceland despite telling a press conference in late May that he had no plans to permit the United States Navy to accompany British vessels. By late summer he ordered American ships to track and report the position of German submarines to British destroyers. When one submarine turned and fired a torpedo at the *Greer*, which had been following the German vessel for three hours, Roosevelt said that the attack was unprovoked and implied that henceforth American ships should feel free to shoot on sight. In November U.S. ships were armed and carrying goods to England. The nation was all but formally at war.

## THE LAST STEP

The formal, constitutional declaration of war ironically resulted from an Asian, not a European, crisis. After Japan threatened Indochina in July

1940, FDR restricted exports of oil, aviation fuel, and scrap metals to Japan. This was a major step, for cutting off Tokyo's main source of these goods could force the Japanese to seize the oil and mineral wealth of South Asia. Yet Tokyo proceeded cautiously. In March 1941 Japan freed itself from the threat of a two-front war by signing a five-year nonaggression treaty with Russia. Hitler was stunned. England had been tougher than expected, and he had failed to reach agreement with Stalin on dividing booty in the Balkans, so Hitler had decided to invade Russia. Despite the Tokyo-Moscow pact, the German dictator struck on June 23 and by early winter had driven to within thirty miles of Moscow. Only the United States remained to keep Japan from taking what it wanted in the Far East.

In July 1941 the Japanese invaded Indochina and Thailand. Roosevelt froze Japanese assets in the United States, thus stopping nearly all trade. Hull had negotiated with Japan throughout mid-1941, but no agreement could be reached on three points: Tokyo's obligations under the Tripartite Pact (Hull wanted Japan to disavow the alliance); Japanese economic rights in Southeast Asia; and a settlement in China. The Secretary of State mumbled to friends that "everything is going hellward," but he refused to give up hope that Japan would be reasonable. Roosevelt supported Hull, restraining Cabinet members, such as Morgenthau, who wanted to have a showdown with the Japanese. The President desperately needed time to build American strength in both the Atlantic and Pacific.

Averting an immediate clash, Hull nevertheless stuck fast to his demands that Japan get out of China, Indochina, and the Tripartite Pact. The Tokyo government of Fuminaro Konoye was reaching the point of no return. American economic pressure was building. Konoye either had to meet Hull's demands and restore normal trade with the United States or remove all restraints and conquer the rich resources to the south. In August Konoye made a final attempt at conciliation by asking Roosevelt to meet him personally to thrash out the problem. FDR was initially attracted, but Hull convinced him the conference would be worthless unless Japan agreed before the meeting to acquiesce to Hull's earlier demands. Konoye naturally refused such preconditions and in early October the military regime of General Hideki Tojo assumed control in Tokyo.

There was one last effort to avert war. In November the Japanese offered to leave Indochina and implied that they did not feel bound by the Tripartite Pact. In return they demanded vast American economic aid. The United States had cracked the Japanese code, so Hull knew that this was the final offer. He rejected it, declaring on November 26 that Japan must in addition evacuate all troops from China and agree to an open-door policy in the Far East. This Japan would not do. The next day Tojo's regime agreed to attack the United States in a surprise raid on the Pearl Harbor naval base on December 7. At no time did the Japanese government harbor any hope of actually conquering the United States.

**JAPANESE EXPANSION, 1937–1941**

Japan and areas under Japanese control before the invasion of China, July 7, 1937

Areas added to Japanese control, 1937 to summer, 1941

Japan hoped that after a large portion of the American fleet was destroyed, Roosevelt would want to avert further conflict and be willing to talk more amicably about China and trade.

Washington officials knew that Japan was preparing to attack, but they believed that the strike would be only against Southeast Asia. Some, such as Secretary of War Henry Stimson (whom FDR had named in 1940 in a bipartisan and pro-Allied gesture), even hoped that the Japanese would attack in the southern Pacific, for the United States would then be justified in declaring war to protect the Philippines. Japan instead struck in the mid-Pacific, crippling American naval forces in a matter of minutes with the worst losses they ever suffered in a single engagement. More than 3500 men lost their lives, and six large battleships and numerous auxiliary vessels settled to the bottom of the Hawaiian harbor.

Pearl Harbor was caught unprepared because of a massive breakdown in military intelligence and communication, not because FDR or Stimson conspired to use the navy as bait so that Japan would attack and thereby enable the administration to take a united country into war. No administration plans to begin a war by losing nearly half its navy. When FDR asked for war against Japan, moreover, he did not think it possible to declare war on Germany, and Hitler remained the primary objective of American policy. Many Americans wanted vengeance on Japan but were not yet ready to become embroiled in Europe. Hitler solved Roosevelt's dilemma on December 11 by declaring war on the United States. He did so in part because he had long promised the Japanese to honor their 1940 treaty, but more importantly because he felt that the United States was already fighting against him without a declaration of war. Hitler's unbounded ego apparently demanded that he, not Roosevelt, take the initiative in the life-and-death struggle. When and whether FDR would have been able to mobilize Americans to fight Hitler without the dictator's declaration of war remain "iffy" questions, as FDR himself liked to call them. That is no doubt fortunate.

The breakdown of intelligence at Pearl Harbor was remarkable. In Washington's last message to the base on December 7, the telegram said nothing about a possible attack on Hawaii, went by slow commercial cable after a delay in transmission through military communications, and was finally delivered to authorities by a Japanese-American on a motorbike nearly seven hours after the strike. It was a symbolic end to the decade. The economic system had broken down by 1931, spawning fascism in Japan and Germany. The Washington Treaty system had consequently broken down, allowing Japan to destroy the open door in Asia. The 1919 peace arrangements had broken down, turning Hitler loose in Europe while Chamberlain and Roosevelt wrung their hands. The American economic system had broken down, leaving the New Deal a failure until it was rescued by war spending. American foreign policy had broken down, leaving Hull uttering platitudes about restoring peace by restoring an international marketplace that had not worked properly since before World War I. The Constitution's checks and balances had broken down, as Roosevelt sent Americans to kill and be killed on the high seas eight months before the formal declaration of war, and while he explained publicly that each step toward war was really a step away from war. After a decade like that, the intelligence breakdown at Pearl Harbor is easier to understand if, like the others, difficult to justify.

## Suggested Reading

Begin with the index and appropriate chapters in R. H. Burns, *Guide to American Foreign Relations Since 1700* (1983). The depression's impact on diplomacy is well analyzed in Charles Kindleberger, *The World in Depression, 1929–1939* (1973). See also Akira Iriye's superb *Across the Pacific* (1967), actually covering the post-1840s era; Henry L. Stimson's autobiography, *On Active Service* (1948); Elting Morison's biography of Stimson, *Turmoil and Tradition* (1960); Raymond G. O'Connor, *Perilous Equilibrium* (1962), a fine study of naval policy through 1930; and for U.S.-Spanish Civil War relations, Douglas Little's superb *Malevolent Neutrality* (1985).

New Deal foreign policy is well surveyed in Lloyd Gardner, *Economic Aspects of New Deal Diplomacy* (1964); Robert Divine, *The Reluctant Belligerent* (1965); Frederick Adams, *Economic Diplomacy: The Export-Import Bank* (1976); and Robert Dallek's *Franklin D. Roosevelt and American Foreign Policy* (1981). For specific topics, see Manfred Jonas, *Isolationism in America, 1935–1941* (1962); Wayne S. Cole's outstanding *Charles A. Lindbergh and the Battle Against American Intervention in World War II* (1974) and Cole's massive *Roosevelt and the Isolationists* (1983); Edward E. Bennett, *Recognition of Russia* (1970); and Bryce Wood, *The Making of the Good Neighbor Policy* (1954). On the Far East see the splendid essays and bibliographies in Dorothy Borg and Shumpei Okamoto, eds., *Pearl Harbor As History* (1973). Useful is Herbert Feis, *Road to Pearl Harbor* (1950), but the best recent work on the entry into war includes Robert Divine's two books, *Franklin D. Roosevelt and World War II* (1969), and *Foreign Policy and U.S. Presidential Elections*, 1940–1960 (1974); James R. Leutze's prize-winning *Bargaining for Supremacy; Anglo-American Naval Collaboration, 1937–1941* (1977); Warren T. Kimball's crucial study, *The Most Unsordid Act: Lend-Lease, 1939–1941* (1969); Roberta Wohlstetter, *Pearl Harbor* (1962); David Reynolds, *The Creation of the Anglo-American Alliance, 1937–1941* (1982); Gordon Prange's invaluable and readable *At Dawn We Slept* (1981), on Pearl Harbor; and Warren Kimball, ed., *The Complete Correspondence of Roosevelt and Churchill*, 3 volumes (1984). On German relations, see Arnold Offner, *America's Appeasement of Germany* (1968), and the broad picture presented in William L. Langer and S. Everett Gleason's standard accounts, *The Challenge to Isolation* (1952), and *The Undeclared War, 1940–1941* (1953), to be used with Charles A. Beard's *President Roosevelt and the Coming of the War* (1948).

For the history of radio news, Erik Barnouw, *History of Broadcasting in the U.S.*, 3 vols. (1966–1970) is standard; and Alexander Kendrick's *Prime Time; The Life of Edward R. Murrow* (1969) is fascinating.

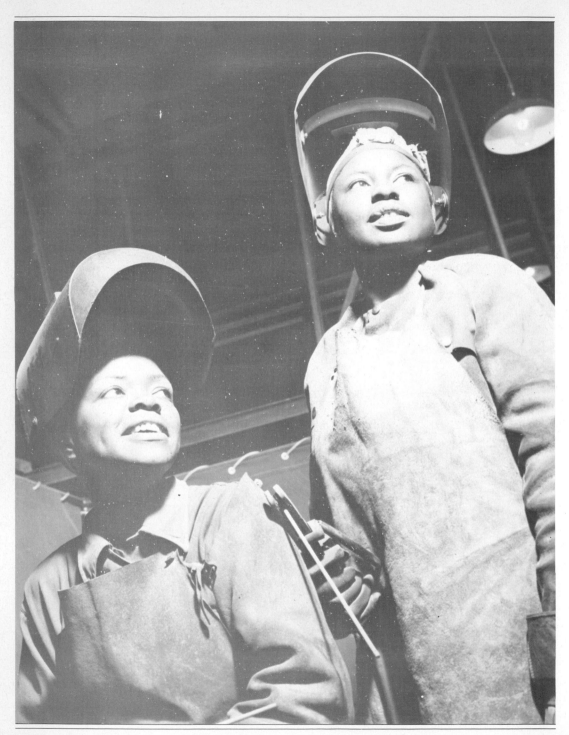

Women welders, New Britain, Connecticut, 1943.

# CHAPTER NINE

# 1941–1947

## War and Peace

World War II severely strained American political, economic, and social institutions. The Roosevelt administration had to devise a program that would release the nation's full productive energies and yet restrain rampaging inflationary forces. The government also had to impose restrictions on the daily lives of millions of people without alienating those upon whom it depended for political support. To a large extent Roosevelt found satisfactory solutions to these problems. Americans were united against common enemies, ones they regarded as the incarnation of evil, and were therefore willing to make certain sacrifices. The war, by producing a high level of prosperity, ensured that those sacrifices would not be too painful. Then, in April 1945, Harry S. Truman assumed the presidency, and four months later the war ended. The accumulated pressures of four years suddenly exploded, threatening to make a shambles of Truman's domestic program. Putting the pieces back together again proved an arduous task.

## IMAGES OF WAR

In 1942 anthropologist Margaret Mead published *And Keep Your Powder Dry,* a study of the way in which American character and values might shape the future conduct of the war. Americans fought best, Mead observed, when they believed that the other side had wantonly provoked them and left them no alternative to war, and when they thought that the struggle was between antagonists of roughly equal strength. In addition, Americans needed to believe in the justice, indeed selflessness, of their cause. A steady succession of military advances, interrupted only temporarily by setbacks, would bolster these convictions. A protracted series of defeats, on the other hand, would call them into question. "To win this war," she said, "we must feel we are on the side of the Right."

Throughout the war years most people felt precisely that way. The attack on Pearl Harbor, widely viewed as proof of Japanese barbarity, enabled Americans to enter the war with more unity than had seemed possible during the bitter struggle between isolationists and interventionists. Most people believed that the war was being waged for "the right of all men to live in freedom, decency, and security," or, as Vice-President Henry A. Wallace put it, to usher in a "century of the common man," in which people around the world would gain political freedom and economic security. One congressman declared: "It is a war of purification in which the forces of Christian peace and freedom and justice and decency and morality are arrayed against the evil pagan forces of strife, injustice, treachery, immorality, and slavery." This was only an extreme statement of a commonly accepted view. "Never in our history," said one observer, "have issues been so clear."

The government did what it could to stimulate a sense of loyalty and unity by channeling civilian energies into war-related tasks. The Office of Civilian Defense (OCD) organized corps of air-raid wardens, fire fighters, auxiliary police, and nurses' aides. The agency maintained that people could, through discipline and self-denial, contribute to an American victory. The OCD gave a "V Home Award" as "a badge of honor for those families which have made themselves into a fighting unit on the home front" by conserving food, salvaging vital materials, buying war bonds, and planting victory gardens. Newspaper, magazine, and radio advertisements also attempted to persuade people to get by with less. B. F. Goodrich asked its customers to conserve rubber tires since "Hitler smiles when you waste miles." The government popularized the slogan, "Use it up, wear it out, make it do or do without." The daily use of certain symbols, particularly the ubiquitous "V" for victory, heightened the sense of shared purpose.

So, too, did the image of the enemy that emerged during the war. In the popular mind, Germany, at least since the time of Otto von Bismarck, had acted as an aggressor nation because of the influence of the Prussian military caste. *Life* magazine described those officers: "They despise the world of civilians. They wear monocles to train themselves to control their face muscles. They live and die for war." Adolf Hitler had seized power with an "insane desire to conquer and dominate the whole world," and had pursued a strategy of piecemeal conquest based on "treachery and surprise" with the ultimate goal of conquering the United States. The Japanese were portrayed as a fanatical people, addicted to the practice of Emperor worship and unconcerned about the sanctity of human life. Racist stereotypes shaped perceptions of the Japanese. *Time* magazine referred to American soldiers at Iwo Jima as "Rodent Exterminators" and noted: "The ordinary unreasoning Jap is ignorant. Perhaps he is human. Nothing . . . indicates it." Similarly, a float in a patriotic parade "showed a big American eagle leading a flight of bombs down on a herd of yellow rats which were trying to escape in all directions."

If Americans viewed the enemy as power-mad, militaristic, and brutal, they saw themselves as just the reverse. Perhaps nothing illustrated this better than reporter Ernie Pyle's best-selling *Here Is Your War*. Ostensibly an account of U.S. forces in Africa, Pyle's book in reality assured civilians that, despite the rigors of war, their fighting men preserved fundamental American virtues. To Pyle, the army was a democratic one: Enlisted men and officers addressed each other by their first names and observed an easy kind of battlefield informality. American soldiers were fierce in combat—"as indestructible as Popeye and as deadly as executioners"—yet they could not resist giving away candy to hungry children, adopting little puppies, or treating captives with consideration. Although the soldiers came from every section of the nation, the cauldron of war had dissolved all religious, ethnic, class, and racial enmities. Democratic, humane, Americans saw themselves as the polar opposites of the goose-stepping Nazis. Even when Americans retreated, Pyle concluded, they did so in an "unretreatlike" way, and then only because they lacked sufficient men and materiel to win. The lesson was plain: If factories turned out more tanks, more machine guns, more bullets, and more airplanes, victory would surely follow.

## THE WAR ECONOMY

The economic problems posed by war differed from those associated with the depression. During the 1930s the Roosevelt administration had attempted to limit productive output, create jobs for the unemployed, and encourage a certain amount of inflation. During the 1940s, however, the government did a sudden turnabout. It endeavored to boost industrial and agricultural production, recruit a sufficient number of workers for defense plants, and hold down wages and prices. The administration sought, wherever possible, to obtain voluntary compliance from businessmen, workers, farmers, and consumers by offering them attractive incentives. But on occasion, when these groups refused to cooperate, it resorted to compulsion.

To supply the massive needs of the Allied forces the government not only induced businessmen to expand their facilities and convert them to war production, but also developed new sources of critical raw materials and doled those materials out in a systematic fashion. At the heart of this managerial effort was the War Production Board (WPB), which Roosevelt created in January 1942 to exercise general control over the economy. Donald Nelson, formerly an executive with Sears, Roebuck and Company, headed the agency. Nelson wanted "to establish a set of rules under which the game could be played the way industry said it had to play it." In this he echoed the sentiments of Secretary of War Henry L. Stimson, who believed that to carry on a war "you have got to let business make money out of the process or business won't work."

The WPB devised various procedures to allow businessmen to combine patriotism with high profits. The government underwrote much of the cost of plant expansion by permitting industry to amortize those costs over a short five-year period, thereby deflating taxable income while inflating earning capacity. The government also invented the cost-plus-a-fixed-fee contract, which guaranteed the military contractor a profit above his costs and removed almost all element of risk from the acceptance of war orders. Firms that entered into pooling arrangements were granted immunity from the antitrust laws provided they first obtained consent by demonstrating how their activities furthered war needs. These policies proved effective. By mid-1942 major producers had converted from civilian to military lines. Industry produced nearly twice as much in 1942 as

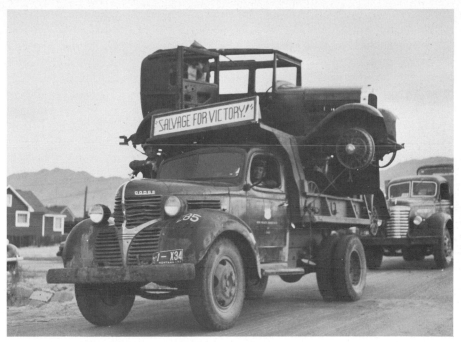

Scrap salvage, Butte, Montana, 1942.

in 1939. As much new industrial plant was built in three years of war as
in the preceding fifteen years. Corporate profits after taxes climbed from
$6.4 billion in 1940 to $10.8 billion in 1944.

In three other ways the government stimulated industrial output. To
compensate for the loss of 90 percent of America's crude rubber supply
when Japan seized the Dutch East Indies and Malaya, a new synthetic
rubber industry was created. The government spent $700 million to con-
struct fifty-one plants, which were leased to rubber companies and operated on a cost-plus-a-management-charge basis. By 1944 annual production of synthetic rubber exceeded eight hundred thousand tons. To
eliminate logjams in production caused by shortages of copper, steel, and
aluminum (all widely used in the manufacture of airplanes, tanks, and
ships), the WPB introduced the Controlled Materials Plan. Under it, each
agency awarding war contracts, such as the War or Navy Department,
presented its materiel requirements to the WPB, which then allotted the
agency a fixed quantity of scarce materials for distribution to its prime
contractors. To prevent transportation bottlenecks from developing, the
government coordinated rail transportation. Unlike World War I, when
Washington had taken over the railroads, a system was devised under
which the railroads submitted to central direction, pooled their resources,

and streamlined their operations. By voluntarily complying, the railroads avoided nationalization.

The policies adopted in recruiting manpower resembled those applied in mobilizing industry. Again, Roosevelt relied heavily on what he termed "voluntary cooperation." At first the demand for labor was filled from the pool of unemployed workers, augmented by women and teenagers entering the job market. But by the end of 1942 high draft calls and twelve-hour factory shifts had exhausted available reserves. The administration made only a feeble attempt to force workers into war-related jobs, however, and finally had to abandon even that. In January 1943 the War Manpower Commission (WMC) issued a "work or fight" order. It eliminated military deferments for everyone, including fathers with dependent children, who held unessential jobs. But this attempt to substitute occupational for familial responsibility as a criterion for deferment aroused a storm of disapproval in Congress, and in December the order was rescinded.

Not until midway through the war did the administration discover a partial solution to the manpower problem. Spurred to action by a dangerously high rate of turnover in aircraft plants and shipyards on the West Coast, the WMC adopted a plan to align production demands with labor supply. Local committees determined how many workers were available; firms in each area could then receive new war contracts only if a sufficient labor supply existed; and a central employment service had to approve new hiring. This plan went into effect in Seattle, Portland, San Francisco, Los Angeles, and San Diego in the fall of 1943 and rapidly spread to cities across the country. It represented a middle stage between voluntarism and compulsion. Workers could not change jobs at will, but were not forced to accept jobs against their will.

# WOMANPOWER ON THE HOME FRONT

One effective solution to the manpower shortage, as the WMC realized by the end of 1942, was "womanpower." Depletion of the male labor pool, loss of 16 million workers to the armed services, rapid economic expansion, and heavy investment in war industry—all created unprecedented need and optimal opportunity for women workers. Accordingly, one of the most dramatic changes of the war years was a vast increase in female employment. Between 1940 and 1945, some 6 million women joined the labor force; the number of women wage earners increased by over 50 percent; and the proportion of women who worked rose from 27 percent to 37 percent. Before the war ended, more than one-third of civilian workers were women.

Although women's numbers rose in all occupational categories (save domestic service), the surge was greatest in defense industry, where female employment increased by a staggering 460 percent. As the male labor pool dwindled, thousands of women moved into jobs in airplane plants and shipyards, steel mills and ammunition factories. They ran cranes and lathes, repaired aircraft engines, cut sheet metal, mined coal, and made parachutes, gas masks, life rafts, instrument panels, and electrical parts. Employers accepted women workers with reluctance rather than alacrity. As late as the summer of 1942, the War Department urged producers to refrain from large-scale female hiring "until all available male labor in the area had first been employed." But by then, few male workers were available. "You're Going to Hire Women," War Secretary Stimson soon told government contractors. By the war's midpoint, "Rosie the Riveter" had transformed the labor force in defense work and other heavy industry. At seven major aircraft plants, the Women's Bureau reported, women's numbers rose from 143 in mid-1941 to 65,000 by the end of 1942. At automobile plants, now converted to war production, one-fourth of workers were women. And in some defense factories, such as Boeing's huge Seattle plant, half the workers were women.

The ramifications of "womanpower" were far-reaching. Protective laws were discarded "for the duration" and working conditions improved. Female geographical mobility increased, as women flocked to war production zones, such as Seattle and Detroit. Occupational mobility increased as well. Women were welcomed into the armed services as WACS, WAVES, and members of the Nursing Corps; one thousand civilian women worked as army pilots, flying noncombat missions. Other new opportunities opened up. Black women were able to leave domestic work for sales and factory jobs, from which they had previously been excluded; older women were able to get work that had been unavailable in peacetime; women professionals found new routes to advancement; and women took half of the new government jobs created by war. Salaries rose across the board, most drastically in war production. For former waitresses and sales clerks, defense work meant a doubling of wages. The age of the female work force rose, as more and more married women took jobs. During the war, three out of four new women workers were wives. For the first time, a majority of the female work force was married.

The sudden demand for female labor was accompanied by equally sudden changes in public opinion and government propaganda. During the depression, opinion polls had reflected antipathy to the working wife; now business magazines praised women's skill at precision work and repetitive tasks. Reversing the policies of the 1930s, when women were urged to stay home, the Office of War Information (OWI) and the WMC joined forces to lure women into defense industry. Wartime advertisements put heavy stress on femininity, glamour, patriotism, and personal relationships. Prospective employees learned that war work could save the lives of male relatives. "Her Man is Out There," read the caption over a picture of an attractive textile worker, now producing uniforms. "Nothing Else Matters." In a popular song, Rosie the Riveter's main concern was her boyfriend, Charlie, a Marine. "Rosie is protecting Charlie, working overtime on the riveting machine," ran the lyrics. OWI propaganda also attempted to fuse women's new work roles in heavy industry with familiar domestic images. War workers were reminded that the overhead crane was "just like a gigantic clothes wringer" and that making ammunition was as easy as running a vacuum cleaner.

Women seemed to appreciate new options for high pay more than OWI similes. "The major inducement is money," a housewife wrote to OWI. "Women like to be out taking part in the world," wrote another. But wartime propaganda was intended to minimize the war worker's challenge to traditional roles. Defense work, it stressed, represented only a temporary response to an emergency, rather than a permanent transformation. And in general, women seemed to make few permanent gains during the war.

They exerted minimal influence over labor policy; the Women's Advisory Committee to the WMC, formed at the end of 1942, had little leverage. Although the National War Labor Board (NWLB) called for equal pay for equal work, women were often classified as (lower-paid) "helper trainees" or "light" workers. As a result, though all salaries rose, the gap between male and female earnings increased. Much ambivalence was voiced about the working mother, "a hazard to the security of the child," according to the Children's Bureau. Concern about high rates of female absenteeism eventually spurred some day-care programs, financed by the Lanham Act of 1941. But only a fraction of working mothers were able to take advantage of them; many remained suspicious of government child care. An additional wartime anxiety was the working woman's impact on family stability. Wartime scarcity of men seemed to encourage hasty courtship, early marriage, and a steep surge in the birth rate. Major concerns were rising divorce rates, juvenile delinquency, illegitimacy, and sexual promiscuity. In war production areas, the government waged special campaigns to curb female "sex delinquency." Most important, new work roles for women *were* only temporary. They were destined to end when the "emergency" did.

In some industries, plans for demobilization of women workers were under way as early as 1943. At the war's end, the female work force rapidly shrank. Defense plants closed or converted to civilian production; all industries prepared to make room for returning veterans. Between layoffs and purges, as in the auto industry, some 4 million women lost jobs between 1944 and 1946. Many war workers expected and accepted such losses; others resented them. "War jobs have uncovered unsuspected abilities in American women," claimed a defense worker who did not want to "return to the kitchen." The public, however, feared that women would replace men in the labor force. Advice literature urged women to relinquish their wartime independence and help returning men adjust to civilian life. Another fear was that women war workers had lost their femininity. "After three months in this land of challenging females," a returning *Stars and Stripes* correspondent wrote, "I feel that I should go back to France."

The wartime demand for "womanpower," in the end, had no lasting impact on the labor force. In 1945, as new opportunities vanished, concerns that arose during the war, over equal pay or child care, vanished too. Daycare facilities shut down; when a bill for equal pay in private employment was proposed, Congress defeated it. But the war still left economic legacies for women. Economic recovery plus veterans benefits spurred the rapid growth of the middle class. The expanding postwar economy, like the wartime economy, soon proved receptive to women workers. By the end of the 1940s, women were once again entering the labor force in unprecedented numbers, though now taking more traditional jobs—sales, service and clerical work. Finally, the war left a legacy of inflation, one that would eventually legitimize the two-income family and the working wife. It was wartime inflation, indeed, that wiped out the depression. But it was also one of Roosevelt's most pressing economic problems.

## FIGHTING INFLATION

Booming industrial production and full employment, combined with a high level of federal spending and a scarcity of consumer goods, created huge inflationary pressures. When someone suggested that "a little inflation would not hurt," the President replied that he was reminded of "a fellow who took a little cocaine and kept coming back for more until he was a drug addict." To curb inflation the administration employed several weapons: wage ceilings, price controls, rationing, taxation, and bond drives. Everyone agreed in principle on the need to check inflation, but no one wanted to come out on the losing end. The administration therefore had a choice: either freeze economic conditions as they stood at the outbreak of the war, and thereby perpetuate certain inequalities; or impose controls selectively, and thereby permit some groups to improve their relative position. The second approach, while perhaps less efficient, was politically more popular and was ultimately adopted.

This was well illustrated by the efforts of the National War Labor Board (NWLB) to halt spiraling wages. In July 1942 the NWLB adopted the "Little Steel" formula, which allowed a 15 percent wage increase to cover the rise in living costs since January 1, 1941. The formula, which applied to all workers, helped those who had not yet benefited from boom conditions. Even labor unions that had already obtained the permissible increase found the formula acceptable. The ruling permitted pay increases through overtime, allowed wage hikes that resulted from the upgrading of job classifications, and affected only cases involving labor-management disputes. Where employers were willing to grant increases—as was often the case, given the labor shortage—they were free to do so. In October 1942 the administration attempted to close this loophole by extending the NWLB's jurisdiction over voluntary wage boosts. When even this proved ineffective, FDR issued a "hold-the-line" order in April 1943. It prevented revision of the Little Steel formula but still allowed exceptions either in extraordinary cases affecting war production or where they were necessary to correct substandard conditions. By the summer of 1943 the government had largely removed wages from the realm of collective bargaining but had still not brought them under ironclad rules.

Regulating the wages workers earned depended, of course, on controlling the prices they had to pay. In April 1942 the Office of Price Administration (OPA) required every merchant to accept as a ceiling the highest price he had charged that March. This general freeze was difficult to enforce and often unfair, for it failed to control the prices of products whose design or packaging had changed, and it penalized dealers who had not already raised their prices. The cost of living continued to creep upward until April 1943, when Roosevelt's hold-the-line order prevented further inflationary rises. Consumer prices advanced by less than 2 percent during the next two years. To a large extent the success of price control hinged on rationing. The OPA introduced ten major rationing programs in 1942, and others followed later. They served different purposes: gasoline was rationed to conserve automobile tires; coffee, to reduce the burden on ocean transport; and canned food, to save tin. The government could not entirely prevent black-market operations—in 1944 one racketeer was found with counterfeit coupons worth 38,000 gallons of gasoline and 437 pairs of shoes—but rationing ensured a reasonably fair distribution of hard-to-get items, and it protected consumers against inflation.

The Roosevelt administration also reduced inflationary pressure by siphoning off excess purchasing power. Wartime taxes imposed heavy duties on the wealthy. The introduction of the withholding system meant that for the first time in U.S. history virtually all wage earners paid federal income taxes and did so out of current earnings. In addition, FDR launched a campaign to sell war bonds, not through the compulsory plan favored by many of his advisors but instead through voluntary purchases. Secretary of the Treasury Henry Morgenthau believed that such an undertaking would "make the country war-minded." He recruited advertising men (who invented such slogans as "Back the Attack") and Hollywood entertainers (who put personal possessions up for auction) to aid in the drive. The voluntary program had mixed results as an anti-inflation measure. Seven bond drives netted $135 billion, but large investors bought most securities, and sales of low-denomination bonds were disappointing.

Even so, 25 million workers signed up for payroll savings plans, and in 1944 bond sales absorbed more than 7 percent of personal income after taxes.

At various times both labor and business challenged the system of economic regulation and left Roosevelt no choice but to intervene. When Montgomery Ward, a huge mail-order concern, refused to grant privileges to a union certified by the NWLB, the President authorized a takeover of the firm. Its head, Sewell L. Avery, shouting "to hell with the government," refused to leave the premises and had to be carried out bodily. Yet on balance the administration succeeded in winning public approval for its policies. This occurred in part because most Americans enjoyed greater prosperity during World War II than ever before and therefore did not find most regulatory measures oppressive. Equally important was the manner in which the administration proceeded. It introduced a coherent system of controls but did so in piecemeal fashion and with a heavy emphasis on inducing the consent of those affected. FDR never used a stick when a carrot would do.

## DR. NEW DEAL MEETS DR. WIN-THE-WAR

World War II solved some of the most serious dilemmas facing social reformers. It brought about full employment and a higher standard of living. It strengthened trade unions, whose membership climbed from 10.5 to 14.75 million. It pushed farm income to new heights and reduced tenancy as landless farmers found jobs in factories. The war also exerted a modest leveling influence. Between 1939 and 1944 the share of national income held by the wealthiest 5 percent of the American people declined from 23.7 to 16.8 percent. In 1944 Congress passed the GI Bill of Rights, a wide-ranging reform measure providing veterans with generous education benefits, readjustment allowances during the transition to civilian life, and guarantees of mortgage loans. Finally, the war seemed to demonstrate once and for all the efficacy of Keynesian economics. Few doubted that soaring government expenditures had produced the boom. In 1943 one reformer noted, "The honest-minded liberal will admit that the common man is getting a better break than ever he did under the New Deal."

Despite all this, the war in many respects weakened social reform and led to profound disillusionment on the part of liberals. In part, this disillusionment derived from a mistaken reading of history. Many reformers, looking back on World War I, remembered only that it had aided their cause by permitting national planning and forgot how it had damaged their movement. In 1943 and 1944, however, liberals detected signs of a conservative resurgence everywhere they looked. Not only did Congress jettison New Deal programs and the administration refuse to support new reform measures, but in December 1943 Roosevelt declared that "Dr. New Deal" had outlived his usefulness and should give way to "Dr. Win-the-War." At that point liberal morale hit rock bottom.

The war obliged reformers to grant priority to military objectives. This often required the setting aside of certain social reforms. Liberals either did not protest or did not protest very loudly when the working day was lengthened to boost industrial output, rural electrification curtailed to free copper for the military, and the antitrust law shelved to permit greater business efficiency. States frequently diluted their child-labor laws so that 14- and 15-year-olds could join the work force and work longer hours. From 1940 to 1944 the number of teenage workers jumped from 1.0 to 2.9 million, and more than 1 million teenagers dropped out of school. "Where a social service doesn't help to beat Hitler, it may have to be sacrificed," observed one reformer. "This may sound tough—but we have to be tough."

Just as the war shouldered aside reforms, so it provided an excuse to abolish various New Deal relief agencies. During 1942 and 1943 Congress—usually with the consent of the administration—snuffed out the Civilian Conservation Corps, the Works Progress Administration, and the National Youth Administration. As a result of job openings in national defense, these agencies' clientele had come increasingly to consist of those last to be hired—blacks, women, and the elderly. Although the agencies tried to justify their continued existence by undertaking projects of military value, they could no longer count on strong backing from Roosevelt. Some reformers urged that the WPA be preserved in case it was needed after the war. But in December 1942, asserting that a national work relief program was no longer justified, the President gave the WPA an "honorable discharge."

As military costs escalated, so too did the federal deficit. Congress became more unwilling than ever to appropriate funds for domestic programs not directly related to the war, and Roosevelt, recognizing this, became reluctant to request such funds. When several Senate liberals introduced a plan to extend social security coverage, liberalize unemployment insurance benefits, and create a comprehensive health-care program, they failed to gain the backing of the administration and stood no chance of winning a legislative majority. Congress not only refused to broaden social security coverage but froze the rate of contributions at 1 percent, thereby postponing a small scheduled increase. The same desire to trim nondefense expenditures led Congress to slash the budget of the Farm Security Administration, an important New Deal agency that had helped marginal farmers purchase land and equipment.

If social welfare schemes stood little chance in wartime, proposals to help those on the lower rungs of the ladder stood even less. Although most Americans enjoyed higher incomes than ever before, not everyone was well off. In 1944 a Senate committee reported that 20 million people "dwell constantly in a borderland between subsistence and privation." Ten million workers—one-fourth of those engaged in manufacturing—received less than 60 cents an hour. Yet the administration opposed granting them an across-the-board wage hike on the grounds that it would increase inflationary pressure. Raising the wages of the lowest-paid would send inflationary ripples through the economy, since to preserve wage differentials, adjustments would be made all along the line. The resulting higher prices would eventually rob the worker of any benefit. Roosevelt believed that in wartime the government could do no more than ensure that the poor were "not ground down below the margin of existence."

The war weakened liberalism in one final respect: it raised issues that threatened to rupture the New Deal coalition. Roosevelt had built that coalition—consisting of blue-collar workers, Southern white farmers, ethnic and racial minority groups, and portions of the middle class—around economic concerns. So long as recovery remained the chief goal, those disparate groups had a good deal in common. But the war subjected this alliance to severe strain. Three sources of division were potentially most disruptive: heightened sensitivity to racial discrimination made it harder to retain the loyalty of both Northern blacks and Southern whites; issues concerning foreign policy and civil liberties affected the political sentiments of ethnic groups; and the need to curb strikes and regulate manpower ran the risk of alienating organized labor.

## CIVIL RIGHTS AND THE SOUTH

If the Democratic party had an Achilles heel, it was the issue of racial justice. During Roosevelt's first two terms the depression had eclipsed racial concerns. New Deal relief programs had proved as attractive to black voters in New York City, Chicago, and Detroit as to white voters in Mississippi, Georgia, and Alabama. But the war spurred blacks to insist more strongly on racial equality. Many believed that the policy of accommodation had backfired during World War I and that a militant posture would be most likely to win concessions from the Roosevelt administration. Claiming that only the end of racial oppression would ensure their backing for the war, black leaders undertook a "Double V" campaign, one that stressed victory in the struggle for equality as well as victory on the battlefield. Yet throughout the war years white Southerners clung tenaciously to the doctrine of segregation. The President, inevitably, was caught in the middle.

The war inspired civil rights groups to develop new forms of protest. In the summer of 1941, A. Philip Randolph of the Brotherhood of Sleeping Car Porters called for a March on Washington to protest against discrimination and "shake up white America." Randolph's movement differed from existing civil rights organizations in important respects: it attempted to mobilize the black masses rather than the middle class, it sought concessions through direct action rather than through court rulings, and it worked for reforms that would benefit northern urban blacks as much as those living in the South. Moreover, Randolph excluded white people from his organization on the grounds that "Negroes are the only people who are the victims of Jim Crow, and it is they who must take the initiative and assume the responsibility to abolish it."

Separatist in structure, the March on Washington Movement was wholly integrationist in objective. It demanded that the President withhold defense contracts from employers who practiced discrimination and abolish segregation in the armed forces and federal agencies. Anxious to have the march canceled, Roosevelt agreed to compromise. On June 25, 1941, he issued Executive Order 8802 providing that government agencies, job training programs, and defense contractors put an end to discrimination. He also created a Committee on Fair Employment Practices to investigate violations. The Executive Order, although it did not provide for integration of the armed forces, was nevertheless hailed by civil rights workers, who concluded "we get more when we yell than we do when we plead."

By 1943 Randolph was advocating disciplined acts of civil disobedience, and the newly created Congress of Racial Equality (CORE) took action along those lines. Founded by pacifists, CORE endeavored to apply the same tactics of nonviolent resistance to the cause of racial justice that Gandhi had used in the movement for India's independence. Unlike the March on Washington Movement, CORE was interracial, but it too stressed direct action and concentrated on the economic aspects of racial injustice. In 1943 CORE sit-ins helped eliminate segregation in movie theaters and restaurants in Detroit, Denver, and Chicago. Most civil rights activity during the war, however, was channeled through the National Association for the Advancement of Colored People. Relying on the traditional means of protest—exposure, propaganda, political pressure, and legal action—the NAACP greatly expanded its membership and influence.

Most Southern whites regarded these signs of increased militancy with mounting apprehension. Committed to the preservation of Jim Crow institutions, whites bitterly resented the charge that their racial beliefs resembled those of the Nazis. A former Governor of Alabama admitted privately in 1944 that the Germans had "wrecked the theories of the master race with which we were so contented so long," but added that the Germans had not dented his own belief in white superiority. Southerners attempted to explain away any evidence of black dissatisfaction as the product of outside agitation. A Memphis, Tennessee newspaper claimed in 1943 that the Southern black "has a care-free, child-like mentality, and looks to the white man to solve his problems and to take care of him. To stir up sullen discontent and misguided hatreds is wrong." During the war a tidal wave of rumors swept the South, culminating in the widely held fear that black women would no longer work as domestic servants but were busily forming "Eleanor Clubs" (named after the President's wife) whose goal was "a white woman in every kitchen by 1943." Because Southerners played a pivotal role in the Democratic coalition, they warned the President to pay attention to their views or else "witness the annihilation of the Democratic party in this section."

In April 1944 a Supreme Court decision abolishing the white primary added to this unrest. The white primary, which effectively disenfranchised blacks in eight Southern states, had withstood several court challenges. But in 1941 the Supreme Court decided that primaries were an integral part of the election process, and in 1944, in *Smith* v. *Allwright,* it ruled that political parties were agents of the state and could not nullify the right to vote by practicing racial discrimination. In an effort to mollify Southerners, the Chief Justice assigned the majority opinion to Stanley Reed of Kentucky. But this did not prevent Democratic politicians or editorial writers in the deep South from construing the decision as part of a broad campaign "to ram social equality down the throats of the white people of the South." Actually, while the decision enfranchised a number of educated, middle-class blacks in large cities, other obstacles to black voting—such as literacy tests and poll taxes—remained as high as ever.

The career of the Committee on Fair Employment Practices (FEPC) illustrated Roosevelt's difficulties in mediating between the conflicting claims of white Southerners and civil rights activists. The FEPC represented an ambitious federal commitment to racial equality, and it succeeded in opening opportunities for some black workers. Yet the agency was hedged about with restrictions. Theoretically the FEPC had jurisdiction over firms holding defense contracts, but it could only act when a worker filed a formal complaint (many workers were unaware of their right to do so), and even then it could not require compliance with its orders but had to rely on moral suasion. The FEPC could, as a last resort, request the cancellation of a defense contract. But war production always took priority over fair employment practices. Nor could the FEPC always count on strong presidential backing. When the railroad unions flouted a directive to grant equal rights to blacks, the case went to Roosevelt, who swept it under the rug by appointing an investigating committee that never reported. Southerners in Congress bitterly denounced the FEPC. It lost half its budget in 1945 and dissolved within a year.

Black workers made sizeable economic gains during the war, usually as a result of manpower shortages. As the labor supply dwindled, many of the traditional barriers to black employment fell. Employers began to relax bars to hiring, and unions found it more difficult to maintain restrictive membership policies. Blacks, who accounted for just 3 percent of all war workers in the summer of 1942, comprised more than 8 percent three years later. The number of skilled black workers doubled, and even larger gains took place in semiskilled positions. Black people by the hundreds of thousands left the farm for the factory in search of opportunity. The government helped in various ways—by hiring more blacks for federal jobs and employing them in higher classifications, by outlawing wage differentials based on race, and by announcing in November 1943 that it would refuse to certify for collective-bargaining purposes unions that discriminated.

The armed forces offered as much resistance to racial equality as had industry, but once again the pressures of war forced a revision in policy. In 1940 military leaders expressed open disdain for black recruits. Blacks could not enlist in the Marines or Air Corps. They could join the Navy only as messmen. They were accepted in the Army but segregated rigidly. The Army maintained that "leadership is not yet imbedded in the negro race," that black soldiers were inferior fighters, and that the military should not serve as a laboratory for social experiments. Only when it became evident that the existing system involved an unacceptable waste of manpower was it modified. The Navy gradually integrated some of its ships, and the Army began the process of desegregating training camps. It also sent black combat units into battle more often but continued to resist integration in war zones except in extraordinary circumstances. By the fall of 1944 there were seven hundred thousand blacks in the armed services compared to 97,000 at the outbreak of war.

The wartime upheaval in race relations sometimes helped trigger deadly riots, especially in overcrowded cities and on Army bases. In June 1943 a violent racial clash engulfed Detroit, leaving thirty-four people dead and seven hundred injured. In such cases, civil rights workers and segregationists usually blamed each other for stirring up trouble. Roosevelt, recognizing that he could not satisfy both sides, generally allowed military needs to dictate his civil rights policy. He supported civil rights advances that contributed to the war and opposed those that seemed to interfere with it. The President summed up his own view in December 1943: "I don't think, quite frankly, that we can bring about the millennium at this time."

## CULTURAL PLURALISM AND CIVIL LIBERTIES

Just as the issue of race affected Roosevelt's hold on blacks and Southerners, so issues concerning foreign policy and civil liberties affected his standing with key ethnic groups. The Democrats had always drawn heavy support from Irish Catholics, Germans, Italians, Eastern Europeans, and Jews. New Deal economic programs solidified this support. But in the 1940s the President faced a growing defection by German-Americans, who had grown increasingly isolationist, Italian-Americans, who feared that harsh terms would be imposed on their homeland, and Polish-Americans, who feared that Roosevelt would allow Russian postwar control over Eastern Europe. Even more serious, Irish-Americans objected to what they regarded as FDR's subservience to Great Britain and excessive collaboration with Russia. Reports to the White House spoke frequently of ethnic group dissatisfaction, of the "anti-Roosevelt sentiment of the Irish Catholics, Italians, and Germans."

To stem this drift away from the Democratic party, the President offered assurances that a vindictive peace would not be sought, praised the loyalty of German and Italian citizens, and took pains to build a good civil liberties record. "We know in our own land," he said in 1944, "how many good men and women of German ancestry have proved loyal, freedom-loving, and peace-loving citizens." During World War I, fearing the danger posed by hyphenated Americans, the nation had stressed assimilation and uniformity. But during the 1940s few were concerned about divided allegiances. Positive values were more often attached to pluralism and ethnic diversity.

Tolerance toward persons of foreign descent was exhibited in several ways. The government placed relatively few restraints on enemy aliens: they could not travel without permission, were barred from areas near strategic installations, and could not possess arms, short-wave receivers, or maps. As the war progressed, however, restrictions were relaxed. Aliens could work in factories with defense contracts if they first obtained permission, and most applications were approved. Citizens of German and Italian extraction encountered little hostility. Spokesmen for the Italian community, testifying before a congressional committee, were treated with kid gloves. Congressmen asked about the nation's baseball idol, who was also an Italian-American: "Tell us about the Dimaggios. Tell us about Dimaggio's father." On Columbus Day in 1942, Attorney General Francis Biddle announced that Italian aliens would no longer be classified as aliens of enemy nationality. "For a long time," Biddle recalled, "I was not permitted to pay for a meal at an Italian restaurant."

Similarly, the Communist party supported the government during World War II and therefore did not find its liberties abridged. Under the leadership of Earl Browder, Communists opposed strikes that might impede production and benefit Hitler's forces. "We have to find out how to make the capitalist system work," Browder said, and this required a willingness to compromise and work for gradual, peaceful change. In 1944 Browder dissolved the party, replacing it with the more informal Communist Political Association. The contrast with the years 1917–18 was stark. During World War I the government had imprisoned Socialist leader Eugene Debs; but in 1942 Roosevelt commuted the sentence of Earl Browder, convicted earlier of passport fraud, in an effort to foster national unity. Under Woodrow Wilson the government had deported radical aliens; but in 1943 the Supreme Court restored the citizenship of a man who had been denaturalized for belonging to the Communist party at the time he swore allegiance to the Constitution.

During World War II the government was more interested in curbing the far right than the far left. The administration persuaded the Catholic Church to silence Father Charles Coughlin, whose magazine, in effect, was asserting that Jews and Communists had tricked America into entering the war. The Justice Department also indicted twenty-six "native fascists" for engaging "in a mass propaganda campaign spreading hatred against the Jews, prejudice against the Negroes, fear of the communists and distrust of our public officials." After courtroom turmoil marred several trials extending over two years, the case was dropped. In 1942 the FBI captured eight German saboteurs who were planning to dynamite railroad terminals and war plants. Roosevelt denied the saboteurs access to the civil courts and arranged a trial by military commission. The Supreme Court, meeting in special session, decided reluctantly that *Ex parte Milligan*—the case in which it had ruled unconstitutional Abraham Lincoln's use of military commissions to try civilians in areas remote from combat—did not apply. Six of the saboteurs were executed and two given long prison terms.

The government provided conscientious objectors with several alternatives to military service. The Selective Service Act (1940) provided that no one should serve as a combatant who "by reason of religious training and belief, is conscientiously opposed to war in any form." Conscientious objectors usually performed noncombatant duties. Perhaps 25,000 men, most of them Quakers and Mennonites, served in the medical corps and related branches of the military. Those who objected to military service in any form could do "work of national importance under civilian direction." Some 11,950 men worked in civilian public service camps, where they engaged mainly in forestry and conservation, building roads, clearing trails, fighting forest fires, and digging irrigation ditches. About five hundred objectors volunteered to be subjects of medical experiments to find cures for typhus, malaria, and other illnesses. Alternatives to the draft, however, did not satisfy everyone. Those whose conscience did not permit them to register with Selective Service, and those whose objection to war rested on political rather than religious grounds, were imprisoned. About 5500 men went to jail, more than three-fourths of them Jehovah's Witnesses who were denied the ministerial exemptions they sought.

Significantly, the only group of immigrants to lose its rights—Japanese-Americans on the West Coast—was politically powerless. Foreign-born Japanese who had migrated before 1924 were barred from citizenship, and most of their children, although born in the United States and therefore citizens, were too young to vote. Japanese-Americans were vulnerable for other reasons as well. They formed a relatively small group, were concentrated in a few states, were largely confined to nonessential

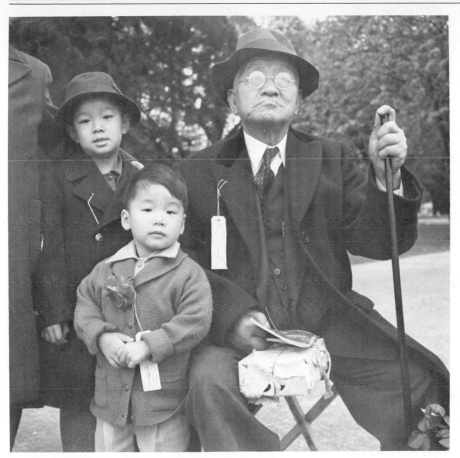

Japanese Americans, California, 1942.

occupations (such as vegetable farming), and could be easily singled out. Powerless and poorly assimilated, Japanese-Americans were the victims of a collective judgment of racial guilt. During the spring of 1942 more than 110,000 people, two-thirds of them citizens, were herded into relocation centers. There most of them remained until 1945.

The decision to relocate Japanese-Americans reflected racial, military, and political considerations. General John DeWitt, who headed the Western Defense Command, expressed a widely held view when he claimed that racial attributes made all Japanese a menace. "Racial affinities are not severed by migration," he said. "The Japanese race is an enemy race." Military leaders believed the Japanese-Americans would commit sabotage at the first opportunity. The absence of any such overt acts was merely taken as proof that an "invisible deadline" was drawing near. Although some undoubtedly believed that military necessity justified relocation, others used the argument as a convenient pretext. Nativist groups had long agitated for Japanese exclusion, and some agricultural interests also expected to profit by the removal of Japanese competitors. West Coast congressmen badgered government agencies, urging drastic action. "There's a tremendous volume of public opinion now developing against the Japanese," DeWitt reported in January 1942. He added that this was the opinion of "the best people of California."

Throughout the war the Supreme Court often defended the rights of unpopular groups. It set aside the denaturalization of a German-born citizen charged with continued loyalty to the Third Reich; it protected a fascist sympathizer who savagely denounced Roosevelt; and it struck down a law compelling schoolchildren to salute the flag. Yet the Supreme Court did not challenge the government's policy toward Japanese-Americans. In June 1943 the Court unanimously held, in the Hirabayashi case, that military officials could impose a curfew that applied only to Japanese-American citizens. In time of war, the Court reasoned, "residents having ethnic affiliations with an invading enemy may be a greater source of danger than those of different ancestry." In December 1944, in *Korematsu* v. *U.S.*, the Court upheld the exclusion of Japanese-American citizens from the West Coast. One of the three dissenting justices branded the decision a "legalization of racism." At the same time, however, the Court ruled that the government could not hold citizens in relocation centers beyond a reasonable time without evidence of disloyal behavior. The decision, though, was handed down a day after the government had revoked the order banning Japanese-Americans from the coast.

## LABOR AND POLITICS

Organized labor was the linchpin of the Democratic coalition. If proof were needed, it was furnished by the 1942 congressional elections. Democrats suffered a severe defeat primarily because war workers who had moved to new states often could not meet residency requirements. The Republicans captured forty-four additional seats in the House of Representatives and nine in the Senate. Roosevelt's policies took account of this dependence on labor. During the war, workers significantly improved their standard of living. Hourly wage rates rose by 24 percent, and weekly earnings (which included overtime) spurted by 70 percent. But as the war progressed, the President was confronted with two politically explosive problems: how to deal with strikes and tighten manpower controls without antagonizing labor.

Late in December 1941 spokesmen for labor and business had agreed to refrain from strikes and lockouts. But the pledge was not legally binding, and workers who suspected that they were being shortchanged ultimately proved willing to violate the agreement. During 1943, 3.1 million men took part in stoppages compared with fewer than 1 million the year before. The most serious was a strike by four hundred thousand members of the United Mine Workers under the leadership of John L. Lewis. Dissatisfied with federal wage controls, miners of bituminous coal refused to accept the decisions of the National War Labor Board. The strike caused severe public indignation. By mid-1943 John L. Lewis had apparently become the most hated figure in the United States. FDR remarked privately that he would be glad to resign as President if only Lewis would commit suicide.

Neither man resorted to such extreme measures. Even though Congress in June 1943 passed the War Labor Disputes Act, making it a crime to encourage strikes in plants taken over by the government, Roosevelt understood that a harsh response—such as an attempt to draft miners or send them to jail—might easily boomerang. Coal could not be mined without the UMW's cooperation, and besides, drastic measures would offend most of organized labor. Roosevelt had to avoid taking any step that might cause labor to close ranks behind the coal miners yet not allow so attractive a settlement that other workers would follow them to the picket lines. The task, one official noted, was "to isolate Mr. Lewis and his assistants from other more responsible labor leaders."

Pulled in one direction by a desire to appease his labor constituency and pushed in the other by public opinion, the President charted a hazardous course between the two. He had the government take over the coal mines but placed them under Secretary of the Interior Harold Ickes, whose relationship with Lewis was reasonably cordial. He appealed to the miners to return to work but permitted bargaining to proceed even while they stayed off the job. He approved a settlement granting the miners a substantial raise, but which did so through a new system of computing working time that did not technically violate hourly wage ceilings. He vetoed the War Labor Disputes Act but requested authority to draft strikers (up to the age of 65) as noncombatants. Roosevelt managed to retain the good will of most labor leaders, who applauded his veto—which was promptly overriden by Congress—and paid little attention to his alternative proposal.

The need to adopt more stringent manpower controls also jeopardized FDR's alliance with labor. In January 1944, faced with a deepening manpower deficit, Roosevelt came out for national service. In its original form this proposal would have placed all citizens, men and women alike, at the government's disposal for assignment to whatever job seemed necessary. Roosevelt favored a less drastic version, but labor detested national service in any form. Union leaders termed the plan a disguised form of "involuntary servitude." In coming out for the measure, Roosevelt had carefully protected himself by insisting that Congress also impose higher taxes on corporations, scale down profits on defense contracts, and authorize effective consumer price ceilings. Congress showed little inclination to do any of these things. Consequently, FDR's advocacy of national service, although it annoyed labor, did not cause many workers to desert the Democratic party.

So successfully did Roosevelt cultivate labor that it provided massive assistance to his 1944 campaign. Inasmuch as two of every three union members considered themselves Democrats, labor knew that a light turnout, such as had occurred in 1942, would be a disaster. The CIO, therefore, set up a Political Action Committee (PAC) that undertook large-scale registration drives and distributed 85 million pieces of campaign literature. On election day, PAC volunteers made telephone calls reminding union members to vote, provided baby-sitters so that housewives could get to the polls, and arranged transportation for those who needed it. The CIO eventually spent $1.5 million, and labor's total contribution to the Democratic campaign—over $2 million—comprised 30 percent of the party's expenditures. Although unions had taken part in past campaigns, never had they done so much for any candidate.

Roosevelt nailed down the labor vote by stressing economic themes. He reminded audiences that the Republicans were the party of Hoovervilles and breadlines, the Democrats the party of collective bargaining and social security. Roosevelt endorsed an Economic Bill of Rights, which recognized each person's right to work at a job that would "provide adequate food and clothing and recreation," to live in a decent home, to receive adequate medical care, to obtain a good education, and to be protected against the hazards of sickness, accident, and unemployment. Ironically, Republican candidate Thomas E. Dewey of New York, although critical of FDR's management of the war, endorsed much of the reform program of the New Deal, at least that portion already on the statute books. He supported social security, unemployment insurance, relief for the needy, and collective bargaining. Some Democrats dubbed him "Little Sir Echo." The 1944 campaign helped place the welfare state beyond the range of partisan dispute.

Roosevelt, although carrying 36 states, won his most slender victory. The President obtained 53.4 percent of the popular vote, compared with 54.7 percent in 1940. He won by a margin of 3.6 million votes as against 5 million in 1940. The key to FDR's triumph was the labor vote in the big cities. In cities with a population over one hundred thousand Roosevelt garnered 60.7 percent of the vote. In seven states with enough combined electoral strength to have reversed the outcome—New York, Illinois, Pennsylvania, Michigan, Missouri, Maryland, and New Jersey—FDR's plurality in the largest city overcame a Republican majority in the rest of the state. The Democrats picked up twenty-two seats in the House and lost one in the Senate. Without the help of the CIO's Political Action Committee, Roosevelt would not have done so well. That help, in turn, reflected Roosevelt's ability to contend with the potentially disruptive issues posed by the war economy.

## MARTHA GRAHAM AND MODERN DANCE

Martha Graham in *Chronicle*.

In the late 1930s and early 1940s a central theme in the work of writers, artists, photographers, composers, playwrights, filmmakers, and dancers was a fascination with America itself—with its history, its folklore, its heritage, and even its geography. This was nicely revealed in Pare Lorentz's documentary film, *The River* (1938), which described the Mississippi's course: "Down the Rock, the Illinois, and the Kankakee/The Allegheny, the Monongahela, Kanawhy, and Muskingum." Appreciation of the values associated with the American past reached a culmination during World War II when those values seemed to offer a hopeful, decent, and humane alternative to totalitarian doctrine. The success of Frank Sinatra's *The House I Live In*—and, even more, that of the Broadway musical *Oklahoma!*—attested to the depth of those sentiments. They were also reflected in modern dance, most notably in the work of Martha Graham.

Born in 1894, Martha Graham had spent her youth in California where, in 1916, she had begun to study dance with Ruth St. Denis and Ted Shawn. She eventually became dissatisfied with the "Denishawn" style, which stressed gossamer motion, oriental pageantry, and silken costumes. Graham was, however, equally dissatisfied with traditional ballet, with its graceful lifts, elegant postures, and classical themes. She sought to develop a new dance vocabulary in which movement was stark and down-to-earth, the costumes simple and severe. One critic noted: "Her idiom of motion has little of the aerial in it, but there's a lot of rolling on the floor." By 1926 she had moved to New York City, organized her own troupe, and given her first recital. Graham infused all

she did with a fierce intensity. One student described her as "all tension—lightning. Her burning dedication gave her spare body the power of ten men."

Graham, who believed that dance should be relevant to contemporary concerns, was by the mid-1930s affirming American values and denouncing fascist brutality. In *Chronicle* (1936) she sympathized with the Loyalist cause in the Spanish Civil War. *American Document* (1938) provided a capsule version of the nation's history—including sections on Puritanism, the Indian, and the Declaration of Independence—ending in what *The New York Times* described as "a final tableau in celebration of democracy." Graham's purpose, noted one critic, was to "bring to bear upon today's perplexities all that was sturdy and upright and liberating in the

*American Document:* "We hold these truths to be self-evident: That all men are created equal."

Martha Graham and Erick Hawkins in *Appalachian Spring*.

American dream." For the first time, Graham used a male dancer, Erick Hawkins, who created something of a sensation by performing bare-chested. For the first time, too, she employed a narrator who, by explaining events, made modern dance forms comprehensible to many who had previously found them mystifying.

Graham's celebration of American values reached a peak in the 1944 production of *Appalachian Spring*, which

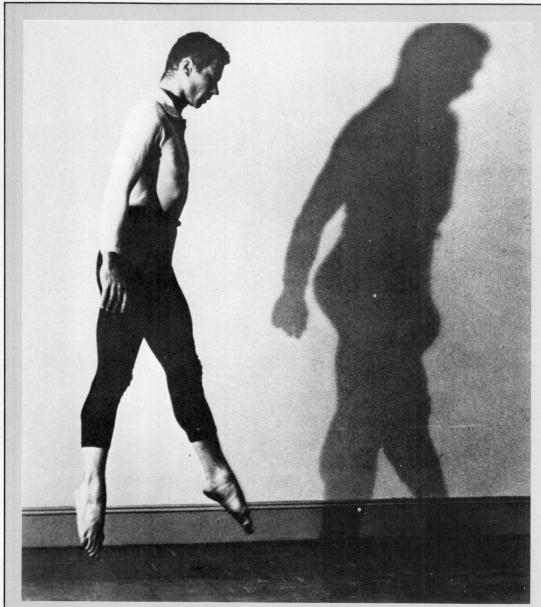

Merce Cunningham rehearsing, 1954.

told the story of the marriage of a young couple in rural Pennsylvania in the mid-nineteenth century. The dance was set in a farmyard, the dancers employed portions of the Virginia Reel, and the music, by Aaron Copland, was based partly on the Shaker hymn, *Simple Gifts*. *Appalachian Spring* vibrated with a spirit of resilience and optimism.

After the war Graham gradually lost her place as the dominant figure in the world of modern dance, but those who replaced her—Merce Cunningham, Paul Taylor—had been her students. She performed for the last time in 1969 at the age of 75, but still remained actively involved in choreography in her nineties. Martha Graham's extraordinary career epitomized one of her maxims: "The only freedom in life is that of the discipline one chooses."

## WAR AND SOCIAL CHANGE

World War II acted as a catalyst for social change. It increased the power of the federal government and of the presidency in an enduring way. During the war the government employed more people and spent more money than ever before. From 1940 to 1945 the number of civilian employees of the government climbed from 1 million to 3.8 million, and

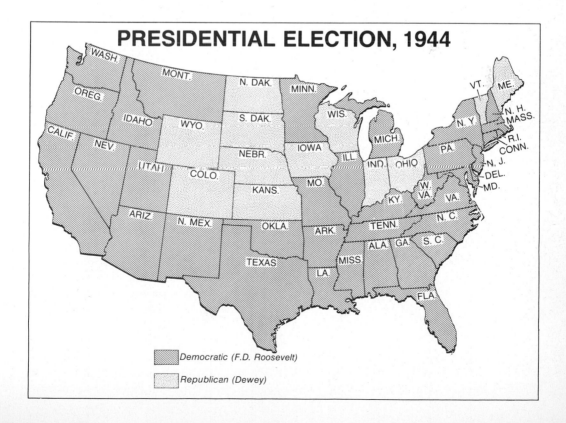

## PRESIDENTIAL ELECTION, 1944

Democratic (F.D. Roosevelt)

Republican (Dewey)

Manufacturing 155 mm. shells, Hammond, Indiana, 1942.

expenditures soared from $9 billion to $98.4 billion. When peace returned the government reduced its operations, but they remained well above prewar levels. The war also accelerated the growth of executive authority and a corresponding erosion of legislative influence. Congress delegated sweeping powers to the President, who in turn delegated them to administrators in war agencies. The big decisions during the war were usually made by men responsible to the President, not by congressional leaders. The Supreme Court, which had in the past scrutinized delegations of legislative authority, refused even to review such cases during the war.

War transformed the economic arrangements under which Americans lived. The huge outlay of funds for military purposes (which at the height of the war reached $250 million a day) enormously inflated industrial capacity. Manufacturing output doubled during the war, and gross national product rose from $88.6 billion in 1939 to $198.7 billion five years later. New industries, including synthetic rubber and synthetic fabrics, came into being. But the desire to obtain the greatest output in the shortest time resulted in awarding a predominant share of military contracts to large corporations and fostering the tendency toward business consolidation. Two-thirds of all military contracts went to one hundred firms; nearly one-half went to three dozen corporate giants. From 1941 to 1943 half a million small businesses disappeared. In 1939 firms with more than ten thousand workers employed 13 percent of the manufacturing labor force, but in 1944 they accounted for fully 31 percent.

Since war contracts were awarded by Army and Navy procurement officers, close ties developed between business and the military. Corporation executives and military officers found that they had much in common, particularly in 1944, when they joined to oppose a plan providing for early reconversion to peacetime production. The military feared that reconversion would lull people into believing the war was already won and adversely affect war production. Large war contractors feared that small competitors who were not tied up with military orders would get a jump on them in manufacturing consumer goods. The mutuality of interest between the two groups was underscored by Charles E. Wilson, who had left General Electric for a top post in the War Production Board. In January 1944 Wilson spoke to the Army Ordnance Association and proposed a long-term arrangement under which business would maintain permanent liaison with the military. This would keep the nation prepared for any future emergency. The military-industrial complex reached maturity later, but it had its origins in World War II.

Just as the war modernized and consolidated industry, so it helped create big agriculture and big labor. Farm population declined by 17 percent from 1940 to 1945 as people left the countryside for jobs in factories and shipyards. But farmers' output and productivity climbed sharply as a result of good weather, increased use of fertilizers, greater mechanization, and the consolidation of small farms into large ones. A million more tractors were in use at the end than at the beginning of the war. Not only did the war hasten the appearance of large-scale, mechanized farming, but it also increased the strength of organized labor. Trade unions attacted millions of members, gained a foothold in new industries, and made collective bargaining accepted practice.

The United States emerged from the war a more highly urban and technological society. The government greatly expanded its role in supporting scientific research and training. Wartime advances in medicine, particularly in the production of penicillin, saved countless lives. Some 12 million men entered the armed sevices, and many later received a college education or technical training under the GI Bill of Rights. More than 15 million civilians moved to new homes. Cities with shipyards, aircraft plants, or munitions factories grew at a staggering rate. Six large cities attracted 2 million migrants; California alone received 1.4 million people. As one observer noted, "the whole pattern of our economic and social life is undergoing kaleidoscopic changes, without so much as a bomb being dropped on our shores."

# TRUMAN'S TROUBLES: THE POLITICS OF INFLATION

On April 12, 1945, a stunned nation heard that Franklin Roosevelt had suddenly died of a stroke at his retreat in Warm Springs, Georgia. Harry S. Truman, who succeeded to the presidency, was quite unlike his predecessor. Roosevelt had been born to wealth and status on a Hudson River estate; the Delano family traced its lineage back to William the Conqueror. Truman came from a family in modest circumstances; like FDR, he had a middle initial, but since his parents could not agree what the S stood for, he had no middle name. Roosevelt had attended Groton, Harvard, and Columbia Law School. Truman, upon graduation from high school, worked as a railroad timekeeper, in a newspaper mailroom, as a bank clerk, and on a farm. After a stint in the Army during World War I, Truman entered the haberdashery business and then took evening courses for two years at the Kansas City Law School. Later, Boss Tom Pendergast of Kansas City chose him to run for county judge and in 1934 picked him for the U.S. Senate. Roosevelt selected Truman as his running mate in 1944 because he was the second choice of each faction in the Democratic party—labor, city bosses, the South—and the only candidate they all found acceptable. Roosevelt seldom made a rash decision; Truman often acted on impulse. Associates usually described FDR as "sphinx-like"; Truman told everyone just what he thought.

Truman, like Roosevelt, had to contend with the problem of inflation but in a different and less favorable context. During the war Roosevelt fought inflation with wage ceilings, price controls, rationing, and taxes. This worked for several reasons: Accepting sacrifices seemed the patriotic thing to do; the system left room for improved living standards; the draft removed millions of servicemen from the consumer-goods market; many were content to save money and pay off old debts. Yet a day of reckoning had to come, and it arrived in 1946, the first full year of peace. Truman endeavored to keep a lid on wages and prices, but he found that people who had postponed buying consumer goods for several years were no longer willing to accept government controls. The longer those controls lasted the more oppressive they seemed. Moreover, Truman faced a legislature that, having taken a back seat during the war, was anxious to reassert its prerogatives.

A battle soon developed over Truman's attempt to preserve the powerful wartime Office of Price Administration. The OPA faced criticism from businessmen who wanted to raise prices and, ironically, from consumers who were tired of doing without certain items. In 1946, responding to these pressures, Congress extended the OPA but stripped it of much authority. Truman recognized that if he signed the measure he would be expected to keep prices down even though the OPA would lack the means of doing so. He vetoed the bill, controls expired on July 1, 1946, and prices skyrocketed. The cost of living index rose six percent in just one month. The administration employed a few stopgap measures to curb inflation but none worked. The consumer price index rose more than twenty-four points from July 1946 to July 1947, compared with less than four points in the preceding year. Prices continued their upward spiral through 1948.

Labor difficulties plagued the Truman administration no less than rising prices. A rash of strikes broke out in 1946 as automobile, steel, electrical, and communications workers walked off their jobs in an effort to win higher wages and consolidate wartime gains. In 1946, 4.6 million workers went on strike, more than ever before in the nation's history. Strikes by railroad workers and coal miners presented especially severe challenges to the administration. In both cases, unions refused to accept arbitrated settlements. Truman, believing that the walkouts jeopardized national security, intervened by taking over the railroads and mines. When the unions persisted the President was furious. He harshly denounced the railroad workers, called for legislation authorizing him to draft strikers, and spoke of the need to "hang a few traitors and make our own country safe for democracy." He sought and obtained an injunction against the United Mine Workers which, after the Supreme Court upheld the President, had to pay a stiff fine. Although both disputes were ultimately settled, Truman's proposal to draft strikers and willingness to use an injunction enraged organized labor.

By November 1946 the various strands in the old New Deal coalition were unraveling, and the Democrats suffered a sharp setback in the congressional elections. Running on the slogan "Had Enough?" the Republicans gained eleven seats in the Senate and fifty-six in the House, thereby capturing control of Congress for the first time since 1928. Democrat J. William Fulbright of Arkansas even suggested that Truman provide the Republican administration the voters obviously wanted by appointing a Republican as Secretary of State (at that time the position next in order of presidential succession) and then resigning from office. Truman did nothing of the sort. Instead, by capitalizing on the behavior of the Republican Congress he began to reconstruct a viable political coalition.

First, Truman made a peace offering to organized labor by vetoing the Taft-Hartley Act in June 1947. Congress had passed the measure in response to postwar labor turmoil and opinion polls that showed two out of three people favoring tighter control of union activities. The bill outlawed the closed shop, banned such union activities as secondary boycotts, provided for an eighty-day cooling-off period before calling a strike if the President thought it would cause a national emergency, barred union contributions to political parties, and required labor officials to sign affidavits attesting that they were not subversive. It also permitted states to pass "right to work" laws outlawing the union shop. (In a closed shop, only union members could be hired; in a union shop, anyone hired had to join the union.) Truman declared the act unworkable, unfair, and arbitrary, but a coalition of Republicans and Southern Democrats easily overrode his veto. Truman's message nevertheless went far toward mending fences with the labor movement.

Next, Truman appealed to religious and ethnic minorities by urging a liberal entrance policy toward refugees. More than 1.2 million "displaced persons," mainly Catholics and Jews from Eastern Europe, were living in camps in American-held zones. Many had been seized by the Germans during the war and used as forced laborers. Others had fled from areas that had fallen under Russian control. Truman admitted 42,000 displaced persons in 1945, and he then urged Congress to revise the immigration laws so as to admit four hundred thousand a year. The old restrictionist argument—that immigrants were dangerous radicals—hardly made sense when applied to people fleeing Communist rule. Yet Congress did nothing in 1947. The following year it passed a lukewarm measure admitting two hundred thousand displaced persons over a two-year period but excluding most Jews and many Catholics. Terming the bill "flagrantly discriminatory," Truman signed it reluctantly.

Finally, Truman attempted to allay any suspicion that his administration was "soft on communism," a theme successfully exploited by Republicans in the 1946 congressional elections. Public opinion polls that year revealed that most Americans considered communism an internal menace. Fear was reinforced when the Canadian government announced that it had broken a Soviet espionage ring and again when the House Committee on Un-American Activities began a new round of hearings into alleged subversion in government. In 1947 Truman responded. The Justice Department instituted deportation proceedings against aliens with communist affiliations and began drawing up a list of subversive organizations. The administration also introduced a comprehensive loyalty program under which all federal employees would undergo security checks. The program was couched in loose, and potentially dangerous, language. An employee could be fired if "reasonable grounds exist for belief that the person involved is disloyal." Those grounds included acts of treason or espionage, advocacy of violent revolution, or "membership in, affiliation with or sympathetic association with" any organization on the Attorney General's list.

These initiatives were closely related to the hardening of Cold War positions. By 1947, as relations with the Soviet Union deteriorated, Americans came increasingly to accept the view (which had earlier been held during the period of the Nazi-Soviet pact) that Russian communism closely resembled German fascism. Both were characterized by purges, concentration camps, secret police, and one-party rule. Both fomented subversion abroad. Both were aggressive and expansionist. Both understood only one thing: force. "A totalitarian state is no different whether you call it Nazi, Fascist, Communist," Truman told his daughter. "The oligarchy in Russia . . . is a Frankenstein dictatorship worse than any of the others, Hitler included." In 1941 the American people had developed an image of Germany that sustained them through four years of hot war. By 1947 they were developing an image of Russia that would prepare them for four decades of cold war.

# Suggested Reading

Wartime domestic policies are analyzed in Richard Polenberg, *War and Society: The United States, 1941–1945* (1972); James M. Burns, *Roosevelt: The Soldier of Freedom* (1970); Geoffrey Perrett, *Days of Sadness, Years of Triumph* (1973); and John M. Blum, *V Was For Victory: Politics and American Culture During World War II* (1976).

Important monographs include David Ross, *Preparing for Ulysses, 1940–1946* (1969), which contains an excellent account of the GI Bill of Rights; Alan Winkler, *The Politics of Propaganda* (1978), which evaluates the Office of War Information; Philip J. Funigiello, *The Challenge to Urban Liberalism* (1978), which explores federal-city relations during the war; and Alan Clive, *State of War* (1979), an account of developments in Michigan.

Women's roles during the war years are examined in Susan M. Hartmann, *The Home Front and Beyond: American Women in the 1940s* (1982); William H. Chafe, *The American Woman: Her Changing Social, Economic, and Political Role, 1920–1970* (1972); and Karen Anderson, *Wartime Women: Sex Roles, Family Relations, and the Status of Women during World War II* (1981).

For the civil rights movement during the war, consult Neil A. Wynn, *The Afro-American and the Second World War* (1975); Herbert Garfinkel, *When Negroes March* (1959); Louis Ruchames, *Race, Jobs, and Politics* (1948); and August Meier and Elliott Rudwick, *CORE: A Study in the Civil Rights Movement, 1942–1968* (1973). Racial policies of the military are analyzed in Richard M. Dalfiume, *Desegregation of the U.S. Armed Forces, 1939–1953* (1969); and racial tensions in Dominic J. Capeci, Jr., *The Harlem Riot of 1943* (1977), and *Race Relations in Wartime Detroit: The Sojourner Truth Housing Controversy of 1942* (1984).

The Supreme Court and civil liberties are discussed in C. Herman Pritchett, *The Roosevelt Court* (1948); Alpheus T. Mason, *Harlan Fiske Stone* (1956); and Sidney Fine, *Frank Murphy: The Washington Years* (1984). Two excellent studies of conscientious objectors are Mulford Sibley and Philip Jacob, *Conscription of Conscience, 1940–1947* (1952); and Lawrence Winter, *Rebels Against War: The American Peace Movement, 1941–1960* (1969). Evacuation and relocation of Japanese-Americans have been explored in Roger Daniels, *Concentration Camps: USA* (1971); Audrie Girdner and Anne Loftis, *The Great Betrayal* (1969); and Bill Hosokawa, *Nisei: The Quiet Americans* (1969). See, in addition, Jacobus ten Broek et al., *Prejudice, War and the Constitution* (1954), and Peter Irons, *Justice at War* (1984).

Government policies concerning labor and manpower are considered in Melvyn Dubofsky and Warren VanTine, *John L. Lewis: A Biography* (1977); Byron Fairchild and Jonathan Grossman, *The Army and Industrial Manpower* (1959); Albert A. Blum, *Drafted or Deferred* (1967); and George Flynn, *The Mess in Washington* (1979). Labor's political role is discussed in Matthew Josephson, *Sidney Hillman* (1952); and James C. Foster, *The Union Politic* (1975).

For the problems confronting Harry Truman, see Alonzo Hamby, *Beyond the New Deal: Harry S. Truman and American Liberalism* (1973); Bert Cochran, *Harry S. Truman and the Crisis Presidency* (1973); Robert Donovan, *Conflict and Crisis* (1977). Two more specialized studies are R. Alton Lee, *Truman and Taft-Hartley* (1966); and Susan Hartmann, *Truman and the 80th Congress* (1971).

Martha Graham's contribution to modern dance is explained in Don McDonagh, *Martha Graham* (1973).

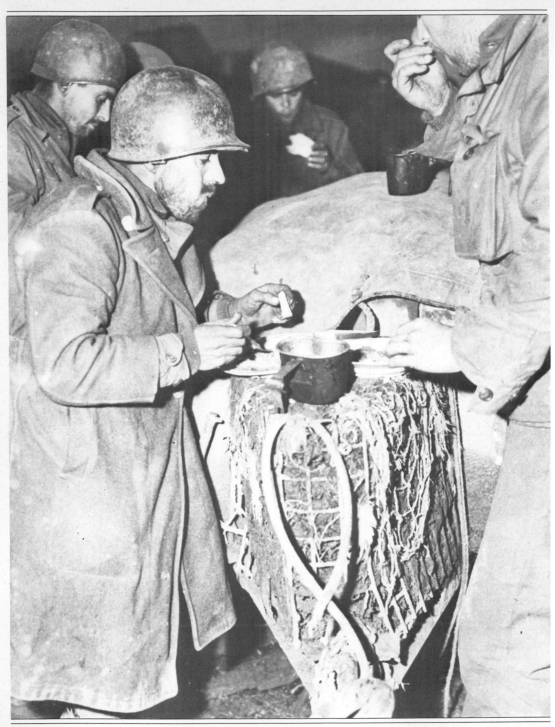

GIs getting their first warm rations after fifteen days of fighting in the Hurtgen Forest, Germany.

# 1941–1947

## One World into Two

On the home front Americans were single minded in their pursuit of victory. On the battlefield they waged campaigns with the same determination. Diplomatically, however, United States policies were divided, even contradictory. On the one hand, the Roosevelt administration sought a united world, devoid of exclusive economic or political spheres, in which open access to all areas could be enjoyed by every nation that could compete. This vision was embodied in the Atlantic Charter of 1941. But on the other hand, Roosevelt had to come to an agreement with his two great allies, Great Britain and Russia, who feared that they had been so weakened by war that they could not compete peacefully against the gigantic American power. The British and Soviets therefore sought their own exclusive spheres of influence. Washington finally made England abandon its policies of spheres, but could never force Stalin to do so. In 1945 FDR, then Truman, finally opted for an open world and so opposed a Soviet sphere of influence in Eastern Europe. The confrontation thus began, slowly at first, then through a series of crises, until in 1947 the Truman Doctrine and the Marshall Plan publicly signaled the beginning of a quarter-century in which the two great powers divided, exploited, and nearly destroyed the world.

# CHURCHILL AND STALIN VERSUS ROOSEVELT

Even before Pearl Harbor, the United States had begun preparing for the postwar peace. The planning took on new urgency on June 23, 1941, when Hitler suddenly invaded the Soviet Union. Except for a brief honeymoon period in late 1933, Russia and the United States had been opponents since the 1890s. The 1941–45 alliance provided only a brief interlude in this history of confrontation. Some Americans thought Hitler could quickly defeat the Soviets. Secretary of War Henry Stimson told FDR that Germany might need no longer than one to three months to conquer Russia. Senator Harry S. Truman, Democrat of Missouri, unfortunately made public his hope that Hitler's and Stalin's forces would bleed one another white on the plains of Russia. Roosevelt took a different course. He ordered immediate aid to Stalin and then began a Lend-Lease program, which by 1945 had pumped $11 billion worth of goods into Russia. He managed to do this despite strong anti-Soviet opposition in Congress. FDR and his top advisors hoped that Russia would stop the German armies, and as the summer passed, it seemed that Russia was succeeding. Churchill had stated the principle on which Roosevelt acted: He would make a pact with the devil himself, the Prime Minister declared, if this would help defeat Hitler.

Roosevelt then focused on another danger. After Hitler's invasion of Russia, Churchill and Stalin had exchanged messages that the State Department feared involved deals on postwar boundaries, possibly even a division of Europe into British and Russian spheres. To clarify this explosive problem, Roosevelt and Churchill secretly met off the coast of Newfoundland in August. In the "Atlantic Charter" issued publicly after the meeting, two key provisions gave the President what he demanded. One clause pledged "respect [for] the right of all peoples to choose the form of government under which they will live." These words applied to victims of Germany and Japan, but they could relate to the Baltic states and to areas of Finland and Eastern Europe that the Soviets had claimed since 1939. The phrase could also mean that parts of the British Empire (such as India and Hong Kong) could leave the Empire—as Washington had long hoped they would.

Another provision of the Charter declared that Churchill and FDR "will endeavor with due respect for their existing obligations, to further the enjoyment of all States, great or small, victor or vanquished, of access, on equal terms, to the trade and to the raw materials of the world which are needed for their economic prosperity." Churchill strongly objected to this clause, for he knew that it aimed at destroying the exclusive British Commonwealth preferential trading system. The Prime Minister yielded only when "with due respect for their existing obligations" was added. But he finally had to lend his endorsement, owing to British dependence on American aid. In February 1942, the United States turned the screws tighter. In return for a long-term Lend-Lease pledge from FDR, the British had to promise to discuss the dismantling of their Imperial Preference system after the war.

Roosevelt and Hull were elated. The key to postwar planning lay in Anglo-American cooperation, for before the war these two powers accounted for half the world's trade. Postwar trade would now be done on American terms, not British. As Hull had long believed, moreover, economic success could be quickly translated into a political triumph. In mid-December, British Foreign Secretary Anthony Eden visited Stalin, who immediately demanded Anglo-American agreement to cutting up postwar Germany and giving Russia control of the Baltic states and a large slice of eastern Poland. Eden refused, arguing that he would have to clear the matter with Roosevelt. Stalin angrily replied, "I thought the Atlantic Charter was directed against [Hitler and Tojo]. It now looks as if the charter were directed against the U.S.S.R." Eden would not budge, but the following month when FDR asked Russia to agree to the Atlantic Charter, Stalin did so only after adding the formal reservation that "the practical application of these principles will necessarily adapt itself to the circumstances, needs, and historic peculiarities of particular countries. . . ." Behind these words lurked the causes of the Cold War: Soviet refusal to allow anyone to claim a right to interfere in Eastern Europe, an area which the Germans had twice used as an avenue to invade Russia during the past twenty-five years.

Roosevelt and Hull had brought the British to heel. Stalin, however, refused to accept the American vision of the postwar world when he added the reservation to the Atlantic Charter. He had given warning.

# ONE WORLD—OR GULLIBLE'S TRAVELS

The central issues of the Cold War were thus in plain view as early as 1942. The question was how FDR and Stalin would deal with them. Washington officials agreed that the most important priority must be a global economic program, resting on Atlantic Charter principles, that would remove the danger of another worldwide depression. Assistant Secretary of State William Clayton put it starkly: if Americans could not be assured of an orderly and secure postwar world, the United States itself would become an "armed camp," living "by ration books for the next century or so." Vice-President Henry Wallace warned that without comprehensive planning, "a series of economic storms will follow this war. These will take the form of inflation and temporary scarcities, followed by surpluses, crashing prices, unemployment, bankruptcy, and in some cases violent revolution." Wendell Willkie capsulized the solution to such dangers in the title of his best-selling book of 1943, *One World*. Willkie's blasts at exclusive spheres (particularly those in the British Empire) led Churchill sarcastically to suggest that Willkie's book be subtitled "Gullible's Travels." But the phrase "one world" said it all: haunted by the ghost of Depression Past, Americans determined to find markets for their inevitable postwar surpluses in a "one world" undivided and indivisible.

Of course this required, as Hull told FDR in early 1942, that the United States oppose any "arrangement which would make the Soviet Union the dominating power of Eastern Europe if not the whole continent." The last part of Hull's admonition was crucial. The Eastern European market itself was not of great importance to Americans, but Soviet control would present a grave danger as a precedent. If Stalin succeeded there, he might use it as a lever to gain influence in the remainder of Europe. If he did forge a private sphere, moreover, his success might encourage the British to repudiate the Atlantic Charter and reestablish their own spheres. Instead of "one world," there would again, as in the 1930s, be a world divided economically and politically. Roosevelt and his countrymen would be back in the dark days of 1938. As Wallace, Clayton, and many others warned, that simply could not be allowed to happen.

In early 1942 Roosevelt tried to bring the Russians around. In one sense his position was weak, for American military forces were inactive in the European theater and retreating in the Pacific. The Japanese mopped up the Philippines, humiliating captured Americans by driving them on a horrible "death march" on the Bataan Peninsula. General Douglas MacArthur, American commander in the Pacific, fled the Philippines to establish headquarters in Australia. The Japanese would not be stopped until mid-year at the gigantic naval battle of Midway, and then in hand-to-hand fighting at Guadalcanal. In Russia, Soviet troops only slowed Hitler's forces. This added to Roosevelt's problems, for Stalin pushed hard for Anglo-American armies to open a second front in Western Europe to relieve the German pressure.

Against this background, Soviet Foreign Minister V. M. Molotov arrived in Washington in May 1942. He wanted to discuss postwar boundaries, but FDR avoided embarrassing conversations by suggesting instead that after the war "four policemen" (the United States, the U.S.S.R., Great Britain, and China) should patrol the world. Molotov and later Stalin readily agreed, for they believed that as a "policeman," Russia would be able to take what it needed in Eastern Europe. This was not at all what Roosevelt had in mind, but the contradictions in the "four policemen" concept would not be faced for another three years. Despite the idea's problems, Roosevelt wanted to avoid discussing specific postwar settlements. Such a discussion could lead to Soviet-American arguments and disillusionment at home. Moreover, the longer he waited, the more financial and military power FDR thought he could bring to bear on Stalin.

A second remark to Molotov had immediate repercussions. Roosevelt promised a second front by late 1942. He probably did this to quiet Molotov on the boundary question. Whatever the reason, Molotov and Stalin were elated. They believed that the Russian people would shortly no longer be alone in engaging Hitler's main forces. But there was no second front in 1942. Churchill killed the plan by refusing to agree that such a campaign could be safely opened so soon.

The Prime Minister instead urged that Anglo-American forces invade North Africa, where the Nazis and their French collaborators, the Vichy French government, held strategic positions in the Mediterranean. Roosevelt realized that Churchill was advancing this plan in part because North Africa had long been vital to the British and French empires, but he finally acquiesced in order to get American soldiers engaged in the European theater. The operation also led Roosevelt into a closer working relationship with the Vichy French. If the Vichyites would cooperate, the invasion might be bloodless and a large part of the French fleet turned over intact to the Allies. This working with Nazi collaborators has since been roundly condemned, particularly after the invasion of November 1942 turned out to be not at all bloodless. FDR survived this mistake, but he could not overcome Stalin's bitterness that the second front had been

INVASION OF HITLER'S EUROPE

Russian front, June, 1944

SOVIET UNION

UKRAINE

• Kiev

• Yalta

BLACK SEA

TURKEY

• Ankara

EASTERN POLAND

P O L A N D

Danzig

Warsaw •

Cracow •

Lemberg •

RUMANIA

• Bucharest

BULGARIA

Sofia •

• Belgrade

SERBIA

CROATIA

HUNGARY

Budapest •

SLOVAKIA

AUSTRIA

Vienna •

HITLER'S GERMANY

Germans surrender at Reims and Berlin, May 7 and 9, 1945

Berlin •

Hamburg •

Essen •

Munich •

Milan •

Bologna •

ITALY

Rome •

Liberation of Rome, June 4, 1944

Cassino

Anzio

Naples •

Salerno •

Allies land in Italy, Sept. 9, 1943

GREECE

Athens

CRETE

ADRIATIC SEA

ALBANIA (IT.)

SICILY

Allies land in Sicily, July 10, 1943

• MALTA (BR.)

M E D I T E R R A N E A N   S E A

L I B Y A

Tobruk

El Alamein EGYPT

• Alexandria

Rommel stopped, Oct. 23, 1942

Tripoli •

TUNISIA

Bizerte •

Tunis •

SARDINIA (IT.)

CORSICA (FR.)

Allies land in southern France, Aug. 15, 1944

Nice

Marseilles

Toulon

VICHY FRANCE

Axis Ally to Nov., 1942; Axis occupied, Nov. 11, 1942

Vichy •

FRANCE

Paris •

Paris liberated, Aug. 25, 1944

Reims

BELG.

NETHER- LANDS

NORTH SEA

SWITZ.

UNITED KINGDOM

London •

Allies land in Normandy, June 6, 1944

SPAIN

Madrid •

PORTUGAL

Lisbon •

GIBRALTAR (BR.)

SP. MOROCCO

FRENCH MOROCCO

Casablanca •

ALGERIA

Algiers •

Allies land in North Africa, Nov. 8, 1942

Axis and annexed areas

Axis allies

Axis occupied

promised—and then repudiated. It almost looked as if Churchill and Roosevelt preferred reclaiming the British and French empires while leaving
Stalin alone to endure the full might of Hitler's armies.

## 1943—TURNING OF THE TIDE

The Grand Alliance was in trouble by early 1943. Roosevelt tried to repair
the damage by asking Stalin and Churchill to meet him at Casablanca in
January. Stalin refused, pleading that the climactic struggle at Stalingrad
required his constant attention. He asked only that the second front be
opened immediately. FDR replied that this certainly could be done in
1943. At Casablanca, however, Churchill once more refused, insisting that
since the Allies were not yet militarily prepared, they instead should move
from North Africa into Sicily and then Italy. FDR again reluctantly acquiesced, but tried to soften the blow for Stalin by announcing that unlike
1918, when the Germans were not thoroughly defeated, the Allies this
time would only accept "unconditional surrender." This sudden announcement was risky, for it threatened to lengthen the war by driving the
German people into a last-ditch resistance. Roosevelt and Churchill were
willing to take that chance in order to placate Stalin. By insisting on
unconditional surrender they assured Russia that although no second
front was in sight, they would nevertheless continue the war until a
defeated Germany would no longer threaten the Soviets.

It was interesting diplomacy, but also increasingly irrelevant. A week
after FDR made his pledge, Russian armies stopped the Germans at
Stalingrad, capturing hundreds of thousands of Hitler's finest troops. By
midsummer the Soviets had regained two-thirds of their lost territory.
Russia had battled 80 percent of Hitler's total force, stopped it and was
now driving it back, doing so without the often promised, but never
delivered, second front. Stalin's need for his western allies was still great,
but dropping markedly. Indeed FDR was becoming the supplicant, for he
wanted the Soviets to promise they would fight Japan after the conclusion
of the European struggle. The military campaigns of 1943 drastically
changed the diplomatic relationships between Russia and her two allies.

And so did a political crisis in Italy. After invading that country, the
Americans and British refused to allow the Soviets to have any influence
in reconstructing the Italian government. Fearful that Stalin would help
Italy's large Communist party gain power. Churchill argued, "We cannot
be put in a position where our two armies [the American and British] are
doing all the fighting but Russians have a veto and must be consulted."
FDR agreed, observing that the Allied military commander, General
Dwight D. Eisenhower, must have complete authority. The Russians were
thus excluded, but at a tremendous cost. For Stalin would repeatedly use
the Italian precedent to justify Russian control of postliberation policies

in Eastern Europe. If the Russians were not to have "access" to Italy as the Atlantic Charter seemed to promise, then, Stalin could argue, the Charter might as well not apply to Eastern Europe either. He was indeed perfectly willing to accept such a division. Stalin believed that each ally had its own security interests. The question was whether the Americans would accept this splitting of Europe into political spheres or try to have it both ways: exclude the Soviets from Italy but insist that the United States have a voice in Eastern Europe. That key issue was becoming sharper.

Churchill, Roosevelt, and Stalin met for the first time at Teheran, Iran, in late November 1943 to bind together the splintering alliance. On the surface, discussions went smoothly. The three men established easy personal relationships, doubtlessly helped along by Churchill's and FDR's firm pledge that a second front would be opened in France within six months. Stalin in turn promised he would fight Japan after Hitler's defeat. FDR himself raised the crucial question of Russia's western boundary, telling Stalin that he "did not intend to go to war with the Soviet Union" over Russian absorption of the Baltic States. A quick agreement was also reached that the Polish-Russian boundary must be moved westward at the expense of Poland.

But the conference floundered on a pivotal question of the Polish postwar government. Since 1940 a pro-western Polish government-in-exile had operated in London, while a pro-Communist Polish regime worked out of Russia. When the London group refused to accept a new Polish-Russian boundary, Stalin would not recognize the group. The hatred burst into the open in mid-1943, when the bodies of 4200 Polish soldiers were discovered in Poland's Katyn Forest. The London Poles immediately— and probably correctly—charged Russia with having slaughtered the men during fighting in 1940. These charges added a tragic dimension to an already explosive problem. The Big Three could not reach agreement on either the composition of a postwar Polish government or a Polish-German boundary. Stalin wanted the boundary moved westward, but Churchill particularly resisted this move on two grounds: it would unduly weaken postwar Germany (a prospect that did not at all displease Stalin), and it would repeat the mistakes of 1919 by giving the Germans a cause for future agression. For the next eighteen months the sore of Poland festered, spreading a cancerous infection within the Grand Alliance.

Two acts of wartime diplomacy had now been played. The first had set the theme with the Atlantic Charter and the British and Russian opposition to its principles. The second act, played out in Italy and Teheran, had brought into the open the dilemmas that would wreck the postwar peace. The third act, which in traditional theater resolves the crises of Act II, would occur with the Yalta conference and its aftermath. Instead of resolving the crises, however, Act III was to become a nerve-wracking, multibillion-dollar, forty-year-long serial.

D-Day: The Normandy Invasion, June 6, 1944.

# ONE WORLD BECOMES TWO: YALTA AND AFTERWARDS

On June 6, 1944, Allied troops under the command of General Eisenhower swept ashore on the Normandy beaches in the largest amphibious operation in history. Led by General George Patton's Third Army, the forces broke through German resistance, liberating Paris in late August and crossing into Germany in mid-September. Devastating air raids hit German war industries, while an unsuccessful attempt to assassinate Hitler in July by some of his closest military advisors indicated the extent of the Nazis' internal weakness. Stalin meanwhile launched a major offensive that conquered much of Eastern Europe in 1944.

Churchill now faced a dilemma. The British had important economic and political interests in Hungary, Yugoslavia, and particularly Greece. The Greek situation was especially sensitive, for that nation bordered the Eastern Mediterranean (one of the so-called lifelines of the British Empire to Egypt and India). But Churchill's attempt to restore the Greek king's power had produced a civil war in which Greek Communists helped the antimonarchical forces. The Prime Minister flew to Moscow and in a dramatic meeting with Stalin worked out, on a half-sheet of scrap paper, a deal that would give Russia control of Rumania and Bulgaria, give Churchill full power in Greece, and divide Yugoslavia and Hungary equally. Roosevelt warned that he would not be bound by this division. But Churchill went ahead, over violent American objections, to quell the Greek civil war with force. Stalin kept his part of the bargain by staying out of that situation and clamping firm control over Rumania.

As they made plans for the Big Three conference scheduled at the Soviet resort city of Yalta in February 1945, gloom was settling over Washington officials. It darkened when in December 1944 the Germans launched a last-ditch counteroffensive that drove a huge bulge into Eisenhower's lines. Only heroics by General Patton and a surrounded American force at Bastogne, Belgium, which delayed the German onslaught by refusing to surrender, finally ended the "Battle of the Bulge." The rapidly advancing Soviets were meanwhile only fifty miles from Berlin. As Roosevelt sat down at Yalta to reconstruct the world, he held few high cards. FDR nevertheless managed to work out agreements on four major problems.

First, the Big Three decided to flesh out a postwar United Nations organization. They had concluded in 1944 that the UN, like the League, would have a Security Council dominated by the four great powers, a General Assembly, a Secretariat, and an International Court of Justice.

Patton, Eisenhower, and U.S. servicemen, Germany, 1945.

At Yalta FDR agreed to give Russia three votes in the General Assembly (in order, so Stalin urged, to offset Great Britain's half-dozen votes of the Commonwealth nations), but only if the United States might, if it wished, also have three votes. Each of the Big Four (U.S., U.S.S.R., Great Britain, and China) would have a veto in the Security Council over substantive issues. Roosevelt had maneuvering room here, for both Stalin and the United States insisted on preserving maximum national power through possession of a veto. The UN, however, would be able at the most to *maintain* the peace. The question at Yalta was whether the Big Three would be able to *construct* a peace.

A second point of discussion offered some hope, for Roosevelt and Stalin quickly settled Far Eastern questions. In return for Russia's promise to fight Japan within three months after Hitler's surrender, FDR secretly agreed that Stalin could have influence in Manchuria, possession of southern Sakhalin and the Kurile Islands (located off the tip of northern Japan), and a lease on the base of Port Arthur. American military advisors, including General MacArthur, had warned FDR that Russian warfare against Japan was necessary if he were to avoid the 1 million Allied casualties that would probably result from an invasion of the Japanese home islands. Given such warnings, and the probability that, once in the Pacific war, Stalin would take by force what FDR had already promised, the Yalta agreements on the Pacific were justified.

A third discussion at Yalta did not end as amicably, for it involved Poland. The Teheran decision on a new Polish-Soviet border was quickly reaffirmed, but again no agreement could be reached on the Polish-German boundary. Stalin wanted the border moved to the Oder-Neisse Rivers, so that Poland would incorporate large areas of prewar Germany. Churchill objected: "It would be a pity to stuff the Polish goose so full of German food that it died of indigestion." (Stalin later provided the necessary medicine simply by removing hundreds of thousands of Germans from the area and giving it to Poland. The West would not recognize the boundary until the early 1970s.)

The major argument, however, centered on the composition of the Polish government. In late summer, 1944, a new controversy had further embittered this issue. When Russian troops drove to the outskirts of Warsaw, Polish underground fighters attacked the Nazis within the city. The Soviet attack then stalled, in part for military reasons, although Stalin was forthright in calling the anti-Soviet underground "a handful of power-seeking criminals." The Nazis then turned and exterminated the Poles. Stalin would not allow American planes to attempt dropping supplies to the underground fighters until it was too late. In January 1945, after the Soviets had finally captured Warsaw, Stalin moved in his own Polish regime as the legitimate government.

Churchill and FDR refused to go along. They finally obtained Stalin's agreement that the government was to be "more broadly based" and "recognized with the inclusion of democratic leaders from Poland itself and from Poles abroad." The new government would hold "free and unfettered elections" as soon as possible on the basis of universal suffrage and a secret ballot. (Such an election would never be held.) Shortly after Yalta, FDR and Churchill exchanged angry notes with Stalin over the meaning of "reorganized." Stalin insisted this meant simply adding a few pro-western Poles to the Communist regime in Warsaw. FDR, however, demanded a complete restructuring of the government. He was on weak ground. At Yalta his Military Chief of Staff, Admiral William Leahy, had remarked that the Polish agreement was "so elastic that Russians can stretch it all the way from Yalta to Washington without technically breaking it." FDR understood, but insisted that this was the best he could do. The President made only one other half-hearted effort to straighten out his policies when he asked Churchill and Stalin to sign a "Declaration on Liberated Europe," which pledged application of the Atlantic Charter principles to liberated countries. Stalin accepted only after inserting an amendment that made the Declaration meaningless.

The failure to reach an agreement on Poland made this issue the "symbol" of the Russian-American conflict. But that struggle increasingly focused on Germany, the fourth question discussed at Yalta. Roosevelt had been torn on this issue. He wavered between fixing the Germans once and for all ("they should be fed three times a day with soup from Army soup kitchens" he commented, and once even mentioned the possibility of mass castration), and rebuilding Germany under tight controls so it could be the core of a healthy Europe. He finally chose the second alternative under strong pressure from Hull and Stimson. They argued that American prosperity depended on a prosperous Europe, which in turn required a rebuilt Germany. That nation, after all, had been the industrial hub of the continent for nearly a century.

To Stalin, however, this policy looked suspiciously like 1919 all over again. "I will not tolerate a new *cordon sanitaire*," he announced pointedly in the spring of 1945. Nor, above all, did he want a united, prosperous Germany as the cornerstone of such a *cordon*. When at Yalta Stalin tried to gain agreement on dismemberment of Germany, FDR and Churchill refused to agree. He then attempted to obtain $20 billion in German reparations (half for the Soviet Union), in order to limit Germany's industry and help rebuild Russia. FDR referred this to a study commission with instructions that the $20 billion figure be only a "basis for discussion."

The disagreement over reparations was a clue to the failure of the Yalta Conference. Stalin had two primary objectives: dismembering German power so that it never again could threaten Russia, and acquiring great quantities of industrial plant to reconstruct the Soviets' own war-devastated economy. Large German reparations would help Stalin gain both objectives. When Roosevelt and Churchill refused to agree on reparations, Stalin faced several alternatives: either obtain large loans and credits from the United States to rebuild Russia quickly, or else impose such absolute control over Eastern Europe (including East Germany) that it would serve as a Russian-dominated buffer zone between Germany and the Soviet Union and also be forced to surrender its industry for Russia's benefit.

Stalin tested the first alternative several times between 1943 and 1946. The critical moment came in January 1945, when Molotov asked Washington for a $6-billion credit. W. Averell Harriman, the American ambassador in Moscow, advised Roosevelt that the Russians "should be given to understand" that financial aid would "depend upon their behavior in international matters." Harriman's advice was accepted. The United States refused to discuss postwar aid to Russia unless the Soviets essentially opened Eastern Europe as the Atlantic Charter asked. This Stalin refused to do.

Within six weeks after Yalta, an iron curtain descended over parts of Eastern Europe. In Rumania, which had been an ally of Hitler, a Soviet official gave the King two hours to establish a government acceptable to the Communists, accentuating his demand by slamming the door so hard that the plaster cracked around the door frame. In Poland, Stalin refused to make radical changes in the pro-Russian government. Amidst this rapid deterioration, Roosevelt died on April 12, 1945. His legacy to Vice-President Harry S. Truman was not a Grand Alliance but the beginnings of the Cold War, caught perfectly by FDR in a comment made privately during his return from Yalta: "The Atlantic Charter is a beautiful idea." It was nothing more.

# TRUMAN

A very different figure now entered the scene. Harry Truman had been a Missouri judge, politician, and United States senator, but he had no experience in foreign affairs. He entered the White House at precisely the time American policy was hardening against the Soviets. Truman was never confronted with the alternatives that Roosevelt had struggled with between 1942 and Yalta. FDR had tried to handle the dilemma—whether to try to enforce the Atlantic Charter or accept political-economic spheres—by delaying until, as in the Polish question, the problem had to be confronted. Truman's temperament was more impulsive and decisive. He disliked delays, preferring to decide on a policy and then make it work. This decisiveness was reinforced by a second influence: his jealousy of, and determination to protect, his presidential powers. This jealousy resulted in part from his realization that he was an accidental President following in the hallowed footsteps of FDR. Truman was adamant in not allowing these circumstances to weaken the presidential powers. This determination easily led him to be tougher than the toughest of his advisors.

Twenty-four hours after entering office, and before he was thoroughly briefed on incredibly complex foreign policies, he told his Secretary of State, "We must stand up to the Russians at this point and not be easy with them." This view was reinforced by advisors—Harriman, Leahy, Secretary of the Navy James Forrestal, Secretary of War Stimson—all of whom harbored deep suspicions about even negotiating with Russia. By late spring Truman was convinced that he might not get "100 percent of what we wanted; but that on important matters . . . we should be able to get 85 percent." He fully realized how American economic and military power, including the possibility of a newly developed atomic bomb, might obtain that 85 percent.

The restraints on Truman were few but significant. The Red Army controlled Eastern Europe and had been the first to reach Berlin. Eisenhower's troops might have raced the Soviets to the German capital, but the American commander wisely calculated that it would not be worth the lives lost. The political division of Germany and Berlin for occupation purposes, moreover, had been determined at earlier conferences. The mighty Russian force, astride the eastern half of Europe, was the most formidable barrier conceivable to Truman's hope for realizing "85 percent."

But the President also had problems at home. Between 1940 and 1944 American industrial production rose 90 percent, total production of goods and services 60 percent. Some place had to be found to sell the products of this system, or else Americans would relive the horrors of the 1930s. Many, particularly the business community, believed that the Soviets could become the great market. "Russia will be, if not our biggest, at least our most eager, consumer when the war ends," predicted the president of the United States Chamber of Commerce in 1944. Pro-Russian sentiment also had such other roots as the propaganda about the valor of "our Russian allies"; the movies sentimentalizing the Soviets (for example, *Mission to Moscow*); and the sanguine statements at the end of the conferences, which failed to mention the deep divisions separating the two nations. These Roosevelt also bequeathed along with an increasingly anti-Russian policy. Truman could not get "tough" with Stalin until Americans were ready to move straight from hot war against a common enemy to cold war against a former ally. Very few were ready to do that in 1945. The President therefore had to educate the country about the "85 percent." He received help from Stalin.

## STALIN

The Soviet dictator, in the words of a fellow Communist who knew him well, combined "the senselessness of a Caligula with the refinement of a

## DIVIDED GERMANY IN A DIVIDED EUROPE, 1946

Moscow•

SOVIET UNION

SWEDEN

Copenhagen•

DENMARK

BALTIC SEA

POLAND

Warsaw•

Oder

Neisse

Berlin

EAST GERMANY

Elbe

Prague•

CZECHOSLOVAKIA

Vienna

AUSTRIA

HUNGARY

Budapest•

Belgrade•

YUGOSLAVIA

RUMANIA

NORTH SEA

Hamburg•

WEST GERMANY

Bonn•

Frankfort•

Rhine

Danube

SWITZERLAND

ADRIATIC SEA

ALBANIA

ITALY

Rome•

NETHERLANDS

Amsterdam•

Brussels•

BELGIUM

LUX.

Paris•

FRANCE

London•

UNITED KINGDOM

English Channel

SPAIN

MEDITERRANEAN SEA

EAST GERMANY

Berlin

Elbe R.

WEST GERMANY

Hamburg

Frankfort

Railroads
Highways
Air routes

Borgia and the brutality of a Czar Ivan the Terrible." Nevertheless, this observer continued, "Viewed from the standpoint of success and political adroitness, Stalin is hardly surpassed by any statesman of his time." Seizing control after Lenin's death in 1924, Stalin became supreme through blood purges. He brutally collectivized Soviet agriculture, ruthlessly shaped Russia into a growing industrial power, and through luck and skill survived the hatreds of both the western powers and Germany between 1931 and 1945. The impact of World War II alone was incalculable: more than 15 million—perhaps 20 million—Russian dead (six hundred thousand civilians starved to death in the battle of Leningrad alone), thousands of cities and villages decimated, agriculture and, to a lesser extent, industry destroyed. During the war, moreover, Stalin knew that his countrymen would fight harder for Mother Russia than for his Communist party, so he loosened some internal controls. But as the Nazi threat disappeared, he quickly reimposed an iron grip. He was Russian power in person.

In an attempt to explain why Stalin would not come to terms with the United States, a few historians have since blamed the dictator's paranoia which, indeed, made him increasingly deranged. This is slippery territory, but several facts are beyond dispute. No foreign diplomat—not even those dealing frequently with him—suggested that Stalin showed any signs whatsoever of paranoia in 1945–46. More important, the substantive issues dividing Russia from the West were more than sufficient to start the Cold War. In the Soviet mind, East–West animosity was natural, for East was communist, West capitalist, and therefore, according to Leninist teachings, conflict was inevitable. Woodrow Wilson and other western leaders had earlier made Lenin appear to be a prophet when they sent troops into Russia. And during the 1930s the Soviets were convinced that the West, particularly at Munich, was trying to drive Hitler to war against Russia. These historical events were little emphasized by Americans after 1945, but they were stamped indelibly on the Soviet mind. Stalin determined that history would not repeat itself, and so he used the Red Army to dismember Germany and clamp his control over Eastern Europe. This was hardly classic communist revolution "from the bottom up." Instead, Stalin imposed control from the top down.

But he did so selectively at first. Hungary, Finland, Bulgaria, and Czechoslovakia remained independent to a considerable extent throughout 1946 and 1947. Eastern Europe did not fall behind the iron curtain with one loud clang but instead disappeared bit by bit as the victim of an escalating Soviet-American argument between 1945 and 1948. Nor did Stalin attempt to overthrow Western European governments during this time. The State Department told Truman in June 1945 that the Russians "are not too greatly concerned about developments in Western Europe so long as the Western European countries do not show signs of ganging up on them." Stalin had broken away decisively from the Marxist-Leninist ideal that world revolution be given top priority. He would settle for "socialism in one zone"—a zone of Eastern Europe, which would protect Russia strategically and help reconstruct it economically. In this zone Stalin would tolerate no intervention. After all, Churchill and FDR had tolerated none in their Italian zone. Consequently, when Truman vigorously urged democratic elections in Poland and Rumania, Stalin blandly replied, "If a government is not Fascist, a government is democratic." But on another occasion he was more candid with Truman: "A freely elected government in any of these countries would be anti-Soviet, and that we cannot allow." He would not complain if the West controlled Italy or Latin America, but, Stalin told the President bluntly, he expected Truman to show similar consideration for Russian interests.

Put simply, Russia's attention focused on Eastern and Central Europe, while America, as a worldwide, expansive economic power, took the entire globe as its province—including the Soviet sphere. For these reasons, the Cold War erupted not over questions in the Americas, Asia, or even Western Europe. It broke out because of American demands in Eastern and Central Europe, that is, in the areas that the Russians were determined to dominate brutally.

## POTSDAM: THE TURN IN AMERICAN POLICY

The Soviets, so Washington officials thought, might not become capitalists overnight, but at least they might tolerate the economic plans that underlay the United States postwar program. "Nations which act as enemies in the marketplace cannot long be friends at the conference table," Assistant Secretary of State William Clayton announced in 1945. When this was applied to Communists and capitalists, Clayton was actually asking for oil and water to mix. Truman was meanwhile demanding at least an 85 percent dissolubility. But the President believed that there was no alternative.

In late April he had a stormy session with Molotov over the Polish issue, which produced only more mistrust. In June Stalin inserted several pro-Western Poles into a government that remained staunchly Communist. Making the best of a bad situation, Truman recognized the Warsaw regime, hoping that over time he could use American financial aid to change the government's policies. The Big Three then concentrated on the conference at Potsdam (on the outskirts of obliterated Berlin) where, it was hoped, German questions would be handled more satisfactorily than had those concerning Poland.

It was not to be. After acrimonious debates, the two central questions of the German-Polish boundary and reparations were lumped together and compromised. Stalin and the Poles received permission to govern part of East Germany de facto (although the area was not formally given to Poland), but Truman in turn required Stalin to accept a reparations package that gave Russia almost nothing out of the German industrial sectors controlled by British and American armies. The United States therefore retained the power to reindustrialize Western Germany (and in late 1945 and 1946 this was accomplished in rapid steps), but at the price of dividing the country. For if Stalin could not get reparations from the West, he would cordon off and exploit East Germany. The deal, therefore, helped ensure the permanent division of Germany.

It also marked a significant turn in American policy. A divided Germany meant a divided Europe. It meant giving up trying to apply the Atlantic Charter principles everywhere. Truman did not fall back immediately. Throughout 1945 and early 1946 his new Secretary of State, James F. Byrnes, worked on peace treaties that would open Eastern Europe, but the Soviets refused to agree. Potsdam was a portent. It demonstrated the abyss separating the Allies on the central issue of Germany, shook Truman with the realization that he would not get his "85 percent" after all, destroyed the hope for an immediately united and open Europe, and, therefore, forced American officials to return to the drawing board and devise new postwar plans.

## CHINA: ANOTHER REVOLUTION AMID THE COLD WAR

At Potsdam, Truman and Stalin did extend earlier agreements on Asian affairs. The Asia that they discussed, however, was changing radically and rapidly. Japan, which had dominated the area for a half-century, reeled from military defeats. In 1944 American forces took Saipan and Guam in bloody fighting, providing bases from which the American air force devastated Japanese cities. Japan's industrial plants suffered (although not nearly as much as the Air Force claimed at the time), but the raids proved especially effective as a terror weapon. In one attack on Tokyo, windswept fires killed more than eighty thousand Japanese.

As Japan tottered, American officials hoped that China might replace the Japanese as the balance-wheel of Asia. Roosevelt pursued this dream, for he clearly realized that if China became dominant in Asia, then it, in turn, would be dependent on American economic and military aid and, he hoped, advice. FDR's schemes even went beyond this. He believed that China and the United States in tandem could dismantle the British and French empires in Asia (including Hong Kong, India, Singapore, Burma, and French Indochina), allow China either to absorb or to police these areas, and then have China and the United States develop them. This vision explains why throughout 1943–44 Roosevelt refused to agree that after the war France should be allowed to re-enter Indochina. The President hoped that this area—comprising Vietnam, Cambodia, and Laos—would be a UN trusteeship area under the day-to-day control of China.

In mid-1944 FDR's dream collapsed when a crisis ripped apart Sino-American relations. The focal point was Chiang Kai-shek, China's leader and the pivot for FDR's plans. Harry Hopkins, Roosevelt's closest advisor, had commented that China could be one of the postwar Big Four, but only "if things go well with Chiang Kai-shek." During the spring of 1944 Chiang's government was gravely beset from two directions. The Japanese launched an attack on South China in an attempt to destroy airfields from which American planes (including the famed "Flying Tigers") were bombing Japan's bases. FDR pleaded with Chiang to throw his armies and American-supplied equipment fully into the battle, but Chiang stalled.

Roosevelt then urged him to name the American commander in China, General Joseph Stilwell, as head of the Chinese armies. Chiang and Stilwell had never gotten along; "Vinegar Joe" condescendingly called Chiang "Peanut" because of his bald head, but also because of his refusal to fight the Japanese. Chiang interpreted FDR's request as an insult and seized the opportunity to throw Stilwell out of the country in September 1944. Roosevelt lost his illusions about China. At Yalta and Potsdam, Americans and Russians settled Asian problems without bothering to consult with the Chinese.

Chiang refused to fight the Japanese because he was saving his troops for the more important struggle with the Chinese Communists. Since 1927 this battle had raged, primarily in the north where Mao Tse-tung's Communist armies had taken refuge after their famous "long march" to escape Chiang's wrath in the mid-1930s. By 1944 Mao had consolidated and expanded his power, gaining support among the peasants (by 1945 he controlled one-quarter of China's population), and effectively fighting guerilla wars against both Chiang and the Japanese.

## THE BOMB

In early 1945 the United States had decided to stick with Chiang and not deal seriously with Mao. By the time of the Potsdam conference in July, however, this policy was insufficient. Stalin's armies would be in the Pacific theater within a month, raising the unattractive prospect that his and Mao's forces might link up in Manchuria. At Potsdam Truman worked diligently to remove that threat. He gained from Stalin the promise that the Soviet dictator would recognize Chiang as the official government of China. After a private lunch with Stalin, moreover, Truman told his advisors he had "clinched" the Russian acceptance of an open door in Manchuria. In return, the President reaffirmed the promises of Far Eastern territory made by FDR to Stalin at Yalta. Truman was elated, but not satisfied. By dropping an atomic bomb on Japan on August 6 and again on the 9th, he tried to end the war as soon as possible, before American troops had to die in an invasion of the home islands and preferably before Russian troops were able to gain control of large chunks of Japanese-controlled territory.

The terrible weapon that Truman now held before the world had resulted from a series of breakthroughs in physics during the interwar era. In 1939 Albert Einstein, the greatest and best-known of the physicists, wrote a simple one-page letter to Roosevelt urging him to begin development of the unknown weapon. Fearful that Hitler might obtain it first, FDR poured $2 billion into the secret Manhattan Project. (The fears were fortunately misplaced; German scientists ran into numerous dead ends and received little understanding from Hitler.) From the beginning, the bomb was built to be used under only American control. FDR evidently saw the bomb as giving him the military power he would need to police the postwar world without having to take the politically unpopular step of sending American armies overseas. At no time did he ever seriously consider sharing the bomb's secrets with Stalin. The President considered it a diplomatic as well as military weapon. Again, Truman fully accepted Roosevelt's policies. Scientists from the University of Chicago protested to Truman that a demonstration on an uninhabited area would be equally instructive to the Japanese and considerably more humane than laying it on a city. The President overruled the dissenters on grounds that the bomb might not work properly, or if it did, it should be used for maximum military effect. Besides, only two bombs could be built by August.

In mid-July 1945, the bomb was successfully tested for the first time. Truman was at Potsdam having difficulty with Stalin, but was greatly "pepped up" by news of the test. The President now began to assume an even tougher position with the Soviets. The Americans, as Churchill privately remarked at Potsdam, "do not at the present time desire Russian participation in the war against Japan." Truman no longer needed or wanted Stalin's help in the Far East. The Big Three urged Japan to surrender unconditionally, including abdication of the Emperor, or face "utter devastation." The Japanese government refused the ultimatum. Hiroshima was obliterated on August 6, killing, searing, and infecting with deadly radiation more than one hundred thousand people. Two days later Russia declared war and invaded Manchuria. On August 9 a second bomb destroyed Nagasaki. The militarists continued to hold out, but the Emperor took the virtually unprecedented step of overruling the government and accepting surrender if the terms did not destroy completely his role in Japanese society. Truman now accepted the condition. World War

Hiroshima, two hours after the atomic blast, two miles from the center of the explosion. The photographer later died of injuries from the explosion.

II was over. It might have ended days before, even before the two bombs were dropped, had Truman earlier accepted the Emperor's role.

The A-bomb had helped end one conflict, and throughout the summer of 1945 Truman, Stimson, and other top officials discussed how it might be used as a negotiating weapon against Russia to preclude a third world war. In June, according to Stimson's diary, he and the President had talked of possible concessions that the bomb might bring from Russia, and Truman "mentioned the same things that I was thinking of, namely the settlement of the Polish, Rumanian, Yugoslavian, and Manchurian problems."

By September, however, Stimson had changed his mind. He warned the President that if the United States refused to cooperate with the Russians in controlling the bomb, but merely talked to them while "having this weapon ostentatiously on our hip, their suspicions and their distrust of our purposes and motives will increase." Truman refused either to negotiate the issue or to use the bomb as an explicit threat against the Soviets. Perhaps he felt that he did not have to, for Stalin well knew that the President had used it without qualms against the Japanese.

## MARGARET BOURKE-WHITE AND PHOTOJOURNALISM

If Edward R. Murrow's radio broad-casts brought the sound of war to Americans, then Margaret Bourke-White's photographs brought them its awful sight. Bourke-White's career had especially prepared her to docu-ment the terrible consequences of modern technology gone berserk. Af-ter graduating from Cornell Univer-sity in 1927, Bourke-White, like many

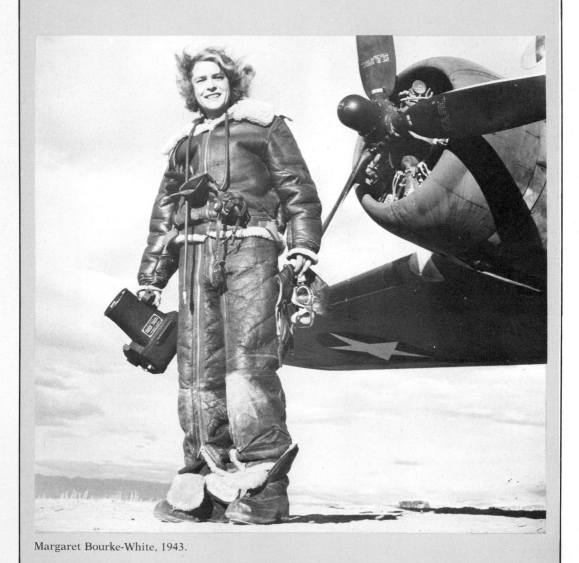

Margaret Bourke-White, 1943.

other artists at the time, became fascinated with the aesthetic of the machine. She photographed industrial plants and equipment for she thought them "sincere and unadorned in their beauty." In 1930, when Henry Luce began publishing *Fortune* magazine—which believed that "any modern estheticism must embrace the machine"—he invited Bourke-White to serve as associate editor and photographer. Not only did she photograph

Churchill sitting for Bourke-White, London, 1940.

examples of American technology, but she also documented military rearmament in Germany and the construction of huge dams and bridges in Russia.

By the mid-1930s Bourke-White had shifted her focus from the triumph of industry to the human anguish it produced. She began to pho-tograph the depression's impact on America: the Dust Bowl, with its parched land and skeletons of dead animals; Southern prisons, with their pot-bellied guards and black chain-gangs; tenant farms, with their tar-paper shacks and emaciated children. She published many of these photo-graphs in *You Have Seen Their Faces*

Stalin smiling for Bourke-White, Moscow, 1941.

(1937), with commentary by Erskine Caldwell (to whom she was married for three years.) Bourke-White was not associated with the Farm Security Administration, which accumulated 200,000 photographs of rural America, but was, in the words of her biographer, "virtually a one-woman FSA photographic project." When Luce introduced *Life* magazine in 1936 Bourke-White became a major contributor. She was instrumental in the development of photojournalism— structured photo-essays that told a logically ordered story.

During World War II Bourke-White was at the height of her creative power. As an accredited Air Force pho-tographer, she observed the assembling of airplane squadrons in England, flew with bombing missions over Africa, and documented American Army operations in Italy. She accompanied General George Patton in his final drive along the Rhine, and so was able to photograph the survivors of the concentration camp at Buchenwald and the charred corpses at the Leipzig-Mochau labor camp. When Patton ordered two thousand German civilians to walk through Buchenwald, Bourke-White photographed them attempting to avert their eyes from the piles of dead bodies. She also photographed Nazi officials who, fearing Allied retribution, had committed

Nazi concentration camp, 1945.

suicide along with their wives and children. Her account of all this appeared in *Dear Fatherland, Rest Quietly* (1946).

After the war Bourke-White photographed people and events in India and South Africa, and, when the Korean War began, she returned to the battlefield. She was one of the first to appreciate the possibilities for aerial photography provided by the newly developed helicopter. Then, during the 1950s, Bourke-White was stricken with Parkinson's disease, an illness that gradually deprived her of the ability to hold a camera steadily. She believed the disease had been triggered by the hardships she had experienced in Korea, but added: "If I had been in a position to make a choice between getting my photographs in the fog, rain and wild mountains of Korea set against the risks involved, I would still choose to get my story—Parkinson's or no Parkinson's." She battled the disease valiantly—a struggle she described in *Portrait of Myself* (1963)—until her death in 1971.

## BACK TO THE 1920s

To drive home his concern over postwar Asia, Truman ordered American planes and troops to help Chiang's forces reach Manchuria ahead of Mao's Communist troops. By the end of 1945, 110,000 American soldiers were in China, many of them in the north. But all this was of no avail. Chiang was unable to consolidate his power, the Russians remained in Manchuria until they took out $2 billion worth of plant and equipment, and American officials failed to work out an agreement between Chiang and Mao.

Truman now turned to General George Marshall, the man primarily responsible for planning and coordinating the entire American military effort during the war. Marshall hoped to find a third faction in China that was "liberal" and middle-of-the-road, then construct a political solution embracing Mao's Communists, Chiang's Nationalists, and the third group. It was hoped that after a period of time Chiang would be able to absorb the third group and subordinate the Communists. During the spring of 1946 Marshall nearly pulled off the miracle, but by summer civil war had reopened.

China was too polarized between reactionaries and Communists to develop any third force. Chiang cared no more for Marshall's telling him—the leader of China—how to run the country than he had for Roosevelt's advice. Marshall reported home that he was confronted by "the incompetence, inefficiency, and stubbornness of the Central government—qualities which made it very difficult to help them." Chiang and Mao, moreover, hated each other. When skirmishes erupted between their forces Chiang decided that with his superiority in men (two to one over Mao's) and firepower (nearly three to one), he could destroy the Communists militarily. Chiang persisted despite Marshall's warning not to try to settle the problem on the battlefield. After initial defeats, the Communists inflicted a series of losses on the Nationalists in mid-1947. Truman privately berated Chiang, but stuck with him to the bitter end. As Admiral Leahy explained the cruel dilemma, "If we break with [Chiang's] Central Government the result will be that we will have no friends in either of the Chinese factions and no friends in China."

But Chiang was past help. In 1947 Washington officials seized the only alternative. They assumed that if Mao won, China would be too chaotic to govern and the Soviets too poor to provide major help. The United States decided to stay out of a situation it could not control. Truman instead turned to Japan to create once again the stability in Asia that Chiang could not provide. In 1947–48 Japanese industrial and political controls were lifted by the American occupation authorities. Stalin did not relish the idea of a revived Japan, but he had nothing to say about it, for the United States had frozen Russia completely out of the Japanese occupation. Japan was on the road back. Truman's approach to Asia smacked of the American policy at the Washington Conference of 1921–22, not of 1943. And it fit in perfectly with the new American approaches in Europe.

## NEW SCIENCE—NEW DANGERS

World War II produced not only the greatest slaughter in history but, ironically, advances in technology and medicine that saved millions of lives and made life more decent for millions of others. Much of the new technology, such as the atomic bomb, or increasing the size and firepower of airforce bombers, aimed at greater and more efficient killing. But Charles Lindbergh, for example, quietly conducted dangerous experiments with new fuel mixtures that eventually doubled the range of warplanes and, later, commercial airliners. Engineers also developed jet propulsion to drive planes not with the old, complex, and less efficient piston engines, but with a great jet of air created by a gas turbine. Before the war, German and British scientists had raced to see who would build the first jet plane. The Germans won one week before World War II erupted, but they could not get planes into operation until 1944. Then American engineers took over. They and the British built jet airliners that, after several disasters, resulted in the Boeing 707. This airplane revolutionized transoceanic flights when it appeared in 1958. Airtime between New York and London was cut in half, to only 6 hours. A new phrase, "jet setters," was born in the 1960s to describe the wealthy who now flew around the world as easily as their grandparents had traveled from New York to Chicago.

Other than atomic energy, no discovery proved more important than penicillin. This miracle drug was first glimpsed in 1889 when European scientists suddenly discovered "good" bacteria that killed "bad," life-threatening bacteria. In 1928 a British scientist, Alexander Fleming, accidentally discovered a broth on which mold *(Penicillium notatum)* grew. This mold possessed new powers to kill bacteria without harming the body's healthy cells. A decade later Americans finally appeared in the story. Only their huge chemical companies had the resources (especially the expensive distilling and fermentation facilities) required to develop penicillin. By 1944 these companies produced enough of the drug to treat all Allied battle casualties so the danger of infection could be dramatically reduced. By 1950, the companies exported enough to meet world demand. The breakthroughs in developing penicillin and sulfa drugs radically changed worldwide health care. Half the drugs used in 1947 had been unknown in 1937.

DDT (dichloro-diphenyl-trichloro-ethane) also became a miracle worker in destroying deadly insects. During World War I more people had died of typhus (carried by lice) than had died of battlefield injuries. But when a typhus epidemic appeared in Italy during late 1943, Allied doctors quickly stopped it by spraying DDT on seventy thousand people in a single day. One expert, Trevor I. Williams, estimates that within the following twenty-five years about 1.5 billion people were for the first time in history free of malaria because DDT destroyed the deadly mosquito carrying the disease. A Swiss scientist had first discovered DDT's powers in 1939 as he worked in the new field of synthesizing chemical agents. (This was the same field that during the 1920s and 1930s had produced the first plastics, synthetic rubber, nylon, and rayon.) Again, however, U.S. plants took the European discovery, then refined and mass-produced it for the world's health, and American wealth.

But there was a flip side. As penicillin and DDT extended life expectancy and reduced infant deaths, world population increased until observers feared that starvation, even political revolution, would result from overcrowding. Others worried that these scientific miracles saved lives only by altering nature's order. For example, animals that fed on mosquito larvae could be endangered when DDT destroyed the larvae. Traces of the deadly drug began to appear in foods eaten by humans. The new sciences of atomic physics, synthetic chemistry, and drugs altered the world by helping the Allies win World War II and by improving living standards, but they also raised new possibilities of destruction.

## CRISES IN THE MEDITERRANEAN—AND AT HOME

There was no peace at the end of World War II. Instead of a world of the Atlantic Charter, Americans witnessed the failure of a settlement in Europe, the refusal of Russia to leave Austria (on the grounds that it was a conquered, not a liberated, state), and Soviet rejection of a plan to control atomic energy on American terms. In February 1946, Stalin warned the Russians that because of the outside threats they would have to revert to rigid state control and make additional sacrifices under new five-year plans. He was tightly closing off Russia and her sphere in Eastern Europe.

Washington buzzed with ominous rumors that Stalin's speech was the "declaration of World War III," since the world could not exist "half free and half slave" any more than it had in the 1930s. In March, former Prime Minister Churchill traveled to Truman's home state of Missouri to announce that "an iron curtain has descended across the continent." He pleaded for a joint Anglo-American atomic force to confront the Soviets, especially since "God has willed" that Anglo-Saxons, not Communists or Fascists, should first have the bomb. Stalin, in reply, compared Churchill's "racial theory" with Hitler's and called Churchill a warmonger. For his part, Truman had no intention of tying American power to a declining England, but he believed, like Churchill, that the Soviets respected only superior strength.

The first test came in Iran during March 1946. During the war the United States, Great Britain, and Russia had occupied Iran to assure a route for the delivery of supplies to the Soviets. The Big Three agreed to leave six months after the war ended. But in February 1946, Russia refused to evacuate its troops, claiming that under western pressure the Iranians were not honoring earlier agreements with the Soviets on oil and security along the Iranian-Russian border. The security issue was of most importance; Stalin did not want to move his troops if the vacuum was filled by British oil and political interests. The United States swiftly reacted. It first took the issue to the United Nations. Then, as Stalin moved reinforcements toward the border, Secretary of State Byrnes issued a warning to stop the troop movement or the United States would take countermeasures. The Russians stopped, settled directly with Iran (on Iranian terms), and withdrew their forces.

Truman had won a significant victory. But the Russians continued to press for advantages and additional security around their southwestern borders, and especially pushed Turkey for a new treaty on the Dardenelles, the vital passage between the Black Sea and the Mediterranean. With American encouragement, including the beefing up of the United States fleet in the Mediterranean, Turkey refused to negotiate. In Greece, the civil war against the British-supported king picked up steam, with Yugoslavia's Communist regime funneling aid to the revolutionaries. The Cold War had expanded from Central Europe through the eastern Mediterranean.

In February 1947 the British suddenly informed the State Department that they could no longer afford to support the antirevolutionary forces in Greece. Decimated by two world wars, England's economy was suffering through one of the coldest and most destructive winters in history.

The British Empire had reached the end of the line. The question became whether the United States would move into the British role. This question was actually academic, for in Iran and Turkey it had already taken the lead. The Truman administration had been waiting for this opportunity.

It was a chance not only to create a long-term anti-Soviet policy. Equally important, Washington officials needed to mobilize the United States for an all-out Cold War effort. This became urgent as they realized that such an effort would cost large sums of money, but that Congress was considerably more interested in budget-balancing and tax-cutting than in another expensive overseas commitment. Somehow, the American people's benign view of world affairs had to be transformed and brought into accord with the tough policies that Washington had actually been following since at least early 1945.

## "SCARING HELL" OUT OF THE AMERICAN PEOPLE

In four stages, Truman encouraged the American people during late 1946 and early 1947 to commit themselves to an anti-Communist crusade. The first stage occurred in September 1946, when Secretary of Commerce Henry Wallace attacked American policies for alienating the Soviets. He urged a more conciliatory approach along economic lines that would open Russia to American goods. Wallace advocated much the same policy that Hull and others had pushed during the war. That approach, however, had not worked. Truman and Byrnes had moved to the next step: political and military confrontation. When Byrnes demanded Wallace's resignation, Truman fired his Secretary of Commerce. Some pro-Wallace support appeared, but of greater significance was the number of former New Dealers (led by a new organization called Americans for Democratic Action) who attacked Wallace as being naive and defended Truman's policies. The President purged the Cabinet of his leading critic and in the process discovered important political support.

The second stage of intensified anticommunism occurred during the 1946 congressional elections. The Republicans scored a stunning victory by capturing both houses of Congress for the first time since 1928. Truman was humiliated; one poll showed his support, which had stood at 87 percent of the electorate in 1945, sinking to only 32 percent. The President, however, turned the defeat to his own advantage. Many of the newly elected senators had advocated tax cuts but had also taken a tough line against subversives at home and abroad. Since Canada had just uncovered a spy ring that had apparently been sending atomic secrets to Russia, attacking subversives promised rich political rewards. Leading members of the Senate's new "Class of '46," including Joseph McCarthy of Wisconsin, John Bricker of Ohio, William Jenner of Indiana, and William Knowland of California, exemplified this Republican line.

Truman tried to undercut their position by proposing a government loyalty program under Executive control that would ferret out subversives in Washington. The President was taking the lead in the hunt for Communists. The loyalty program would not pry the needed monies from a tight-fisted Congress for a major foreign policy offensive. But it did enable Truman to play on Congress's fear of communism. The British retreat from Greece provided the opportunity for the President bluntly to inform Senate and House leaders that this was the moment to put up or shut up.

The third stage of Truman's program was magnificently handled by Undersecretary of State Dean Acheson when, in a private session, he told the congressional leadership that "like apples in a barrel infected by one rotten one, the corruption of Greece would infect Iran and all to the east." Asia Minor, Egypt, and then Europe would be next, as the dominoes would inevitably fall. Believing personally that "we were met at Armageddon," Acheson eloquently concluded that "The Soviet Union [is] playing one of the greatest gambles in history at minimal cost. . . . We and we alone [are] in a position to break up the play." After a stunned silence, the key Republican Senator on foreign policy issues, Arthur Vandenberg of Michigan, admitted that he had been persuaded. But he later warned Truman and Acheson that they would have to "scare hell" out of the American people if they hoped to get necessary public support for their new foreign policies.

Truman did just that with two speeches in the fourth stage of his program. The first address, at Baylor University in Texas on March 6, 1947, provided the classic explanation why Americans must embark on a new crusade. "Peace, freedom, and world trade," Truman began, "are inseparable." "Our foreign relations, political and economic, are indivisible," he stressed. Then: "We must not go through the thirties again." Freedom of worship and freedom of speech are related to freedom of enterprise, for the first two "have been most frequently enjoyed in those societies" hospitable to free enterprise. And "least conducive to freedom of enterprise" is governmental intervention. Yet, the President warned bluntly, unless the world marketplace were quickly reconstructed and opened, even the United States government would soon have to step in to control American society in order to allocate goods and resources. Such governmental intervention "is not the way to peace," Truman concluded. The President's meaning was clear: his administration defined the state-controlled Russian economy as the deadly enemy of American prosperity, and he would do everything possible to save the world on this side of the iron curtain for the American form of "freedom of enterprise." If Americans did not join him, they risked losing all their most precious freedoms.

Six days later he issued the call to action with the "Truman Doctrine" speech. To make the case as forcefully as possible, Truman presented a world divided simply between "free peoples" and areas where "the will of a minority [is] forcibly imposed upon a majority." He included Greece and Turkey in the first group, but unless Congress immediately appropriated $400 million for their aid, they would slide into the second. Only the United States could now save the free world: "If we falter in our leadership, we may endanger the peace of the world—and we shall surely endanger the welfare of our own nation."

The speech "scared hell" out of many people. Senator Robert Taft (Republican of Ohio and the Republican leader) disliked it because "I do not want war with Russia." Doubts existed even within the State Department. Some officials had argued that Turkey, which had been pro-Hitler and was not at all democratic, hardly ranked as a "free people." It shared, moreover, a very sensitive boundary with Russia. But Truman nevertheless decided to use the opportunity in Greece to settle the Turkish crisis. "Turkey was slipped into the oven with Greece because that seemed to be the surest way to cook a tough bird," as one official observed. More generally, the speech was notable because it defined the Communist threat as ideological, and therefore asked Americans to commit themselves against that threat globally. This request has been the most explosive part of the Truman Doctrine, for once the threat was defined ideologically, Americans had to be ready to intervene anywhere in the world where that threat was perceived, regardless of whether the area in question was in fact directly threatened by Russia or, later, China. Later presidents could use the Doctrine as a rationale for American military intervention in Southeast Asia as well as in Europe.

It was "the most fundamental thing that has been presented to Congress in my time," Vandenberg rightly observed, and so Congress wanted to examine the proposal carefully. On March 21, Truman gave it a major push when he issued the Executive Order that set in motion the loyalty program to find Communists in the government. It was the first such program ever established by a President (Congress had earlier legislated the hunts), the first ever established in peacetime, and—most important— the first in which a person could be dismissed for political beliefs. Truman had defined the issue, created a growing consensus, and outflanked congressional opponents. One Truman supporter in Congress chuckled at the trap the President had sprung on Republicans who wanted to fight communism, but not spend money: "Course they don't want to be smoked out. . . . They don't like Communism, but still they don't want to do anything to stop it. But they are all put on the spot now and they all have to come clean." The $400 million was soon appropriated, allowing American military advisors and equipment to aid the Greek government. The revolution finally subsided, however, only after Yugoslavia defected from the Russian bloc in 1948 and quit sending aid to the Greek rebels.

## AVOIDING THE 1930s: THE MARSHALL PLAN

Aid to Greece and Turkey was only a bandage on a large, festering wound that cut to the heart itself, the economy of Western Europe. Confronted with deteriorating economies, the Europeans were responding as Truman feared. A British Labor government, for example, nationalized leading industries, while in Italy and France large Communist and radical socialist factions gained strength. The American economy maintained its pace, but primarily because of a booming $15 billion in exports during 1946. If Europe could not continue to take its share of these exports, the United States would, in the President's words, "go through the thirties again."

The key to the problem was the lack of dollars that Europeans had to spend for American goods. Moreover, they could derive little from their war-ruined economies to sell to the United States in order to acquire dollars. Great Britain, France, Italy, and the Benelux countries needed about $5 billion if they hoped to buy goods from the United States to maintain a minimum standard of living.

In June 1947, the United States announced its plan to save itself and Western Europe. Newly appointed Secretary of State George Marshall offered massive economic aid but attached two conditions. First, the initiative in formulating a long-term program would have to come from the Europeans. They would have to commit themselves. Second, the pro-

Marshall and Molotov, 1947.

gram would have to be cooperative and open. This worked against Russian participation, for although the Soviets attended the first planning session in Paris, they quickly repudiated the Marshall Plan when they saw that they would have to accept American conditions, including the disclosure of Russian economic information. The Soviets claimed that the Truman Doctrine and Marshall Plan had irretrievably divided the world into "two camps." To solidify their own camp, they announced a "Molotov Plan."

The Western Europeans finally asked for $29 billion, but the U.S. cut this to $17 billion for four years, with $5 billion the first year. The figures are revealing, for they show that the decision to give aid was not based merely on anticommunism. More immediately officials planned to provide the $5 billion they had long before calculated as the amount needed to keep American exports to Europe at necessary levels. When the aid was distributed, moreover, it went not primarily to Italy or France, where the Communist threat was most immediate, but to Great Britain and Germany, the potential industrial powerhouses for Europe. The Plan was publicly explained as part of the fight against communism, which it was to the extent that officials believed that poverty and unemployment in Europe would produce radicalism there and perhaps even in the United States. Most important, however, the Plan aimed at averting a repeat of the 1930s by rebuilding the great market for American products and molding Western Europe into a long-term partner.

The United States had emerged from World War II as the greatest power in world history. Its incredible economic plant, monopoly of atomic energy, and success as the world's oldest republic seemed to indicate that Americans were truly embarked on an "American Century," as *Life* magazine proclaimed in 1941. But by 1947 the American Century, like FDR's description of the Atlantic Charter, was only a "beautiful dream." By then the Truman administration had shifted from trying to create a free world (particularly in China and Eastern Europe) to rebuilding nations this side of the iron curtain. The Marshall Plan seemed an intelligent, manageable, and limited plan for maintaining "freedom of enterprise" in the West. On the other hand, the Truman Doctrine proposed world-wide ideological and even military warfare. Truman had beautifully built a public consensus around both.

It now remained to be seen which road Americans would choose: the path that was more modest and whose terminus could be clearly seen, or the one that required commitment without an apparent limit of dollars, energy, and perhaps even lives. As the ancient Greeks understood, the essence of human tragedy is choice. But then they too discovered this after it was too late.

## Suggested Reading

Begin by consulting R. H. Burns, ed., *Guide to American Foreign Relations Since 1700* (1983). Military strategy and decisions are well analyzed in Ronald H.

Spector, *Eagle Against the Sun* (1984); Russell F. Weigley, *The American Way of War* (1973); and Kent R. Greenfield, *American Strategy in World War II* (1963). Wartime diplomacy is detailed in Christopher Thorne's fine *Allies of a Kind: The United States, Britain and the War Against Japan 1941–1945* (1978); Herbert Feis, *Churchill, Roosevelt and Stalin* (1967); and Raymond G. O'Connor, *Diplomacy for Victory: FDR and Unconditional Surrender* (1971). More specific problems are well treated in Mark A. Stoler, *The Politics of the Second Front . . . 1941–1943* (1977); and Robert Divine's analysis of the domestic side, *Second Chance: The Triumph of Internationalism* (1967). Important interpretive studies include John L. Gaddis, *U.S. and Origins of the Cold War, 1941–1947* (1972); George C. Herring, Jr., *Aid to Russia, 1941–1946* (1973); Thomas Paterson, *Soviet-American Confrontation* (1974); Gabriel Kolko, *The Politics of War, 1943–1945* (1967); Joyce and Gabriel Kolko, *Limits of Power, 1945–1954* (1970); Diane Shaver Clemens, *Yalta* (1970); and Daniel Yergin, *Shattered Peace* (1977). The essays in Thomas Paterson, ed., *Cold War Critics* (1971); and Ronald Radosh, *Prophets on the Right* (1975) examine the dissenters. The best detailed analysis of the politics surrounding the atomic bomb is Martin J. Sherwin, *A World Destroyed* (1975).

For excellent overviews on the eruption of Cold War, 1945–1947, see Robert J. Donovan's biography of Truman, *Conflict and Crisis . . . 1945–1948* (1977); Lloyd Gardner, *Architects of Illusion* (1970); Richard Freeland, *The Truman Doctrine and Origins of McCarthyism* (1971); Athan Theoharis, *The Yalta Myths, 1945–1955* (1970); Joseph M. Jones's inside account, *The Fifteen Weeks* (1955); George Kennan, *Memoirs, 1925–1950* (1967); and Dean Acheson's autobiography, *Present at the Creation* (1970). Important background is in Ralph B. Levering, *American Opinion and the Russian Alliance, 1939–1945* (1976); Lawrence Wittner, *American Intervention in Greece, 1943–1949* (1982); Terry Anderson, *The U.S., Great Britain and the Cold War, 1944–1947* (1981); Michael B. Stoff, *Oil, War,* and *National Security, 1941–1947* (1980).

For the era's economic policies, see Richard N. Gardner's splendid *Sterling-Dollar Diplomacy* (1956); for its Latin American affairs, David Green's *The Containment of Latin America* (1971); for its Asian affairs, Akira Iriye, *The Cold War in Asia* (1974); Michael Schaller, *The U.S. Crusade in China, 1938–1945* (1979); and Kenneth E. Shewmaker, *Americans and the Chinese Communists, 1927–1945* (1971). Of special value is Trevor I. Williams, *A Short History of Twentieth-Century Technology* (1982).

Theodore Brown has done a definitive study in *Margaret Bourke-White, Photo Journalist* (1972).

General Douglas MacArthur.

# CHAPTER ELEVEN

# 1947–1952

## The America
## of the Cold War

Two events in March 1947—the announcement of the Truman Doctrine and the institution of a federal loyalty program—set the tone for American foreign and domestic affairs in the Cold War era. For a time Truman managed to turn Cold War tensions to his own advantage, winning reelection in 1948 and forming the North Atlantic Treaty Organization in 1949. With the outbreak of the Korean War in June 1950, however, the Truman administration became a victim of its own policies. In the President's view the North Korean attack closely resembled the fascist aggression of the 1930s, but he found that waging a long, limited war imposed strains on society quite unlike those of World War II. Those strains—political, economic, social, and military—nourished a mood of hysteria in which the Truman administration could itself be charged, by Senator Joseph McCarthy and others, with being "soft on communism" at home and overseas.

## CRISIS DIPLOMACY: 1947–1948

With the Truman Doctrine, the Marshall Plan, and the Molotov Plan, the world divided into what the Soviets called "two camps." Undersecretary of State Dean Acheson later observed that by 1948 the Truman administration had concluded that negotiations with Russia were useless, for "the world of the last half of the twentieth century was, and would continue to be, a divided world. The [decision] was to make the free—that is, the non-Communist–dominated—part of that divided world as secure and flourishing as possible." In 1947, Acheson wrote that because negotiations were not successful, "we must use to an increasing extent our second instrument of foreign policy, namely economic power," to protect the "free" world. The Marshall Plan indicated how the tremendous American economic strength would be used to create a postwar world on American terms. As Truman liked to put it, he was "tired of babying the Soviets."

The Republican-controlled Congress passed the $400,000,000 Truman Doctrine appropriations for Greece and Turkey but proved extremely reluctant to legislate the nearly $12 billion, four-year program that Truman was asking for the Marshall Plan. Secretary of State Marshall and other officials warned that without the Plan the American economy would lose its European markets, then shrivel. This decline, Marshall predicted, "would drive us to increased measures of government control." Such threats did not move Congress, for it believed that lowering taxes and encouraging private investment to go overseas would do the job. The administration vainly retorted that there was not enough time for such solutions and that private investors would not help until government monies rebuilt the infrastructure (roads, communications, banking facilities) of Western Europe. Congress refused to budge. Then came Czechoslovakia.

Although the Czechs survived as an independent people in 1945, their geographical position (bordering on both Russia and West Germany) forced them to be cautiously neutral in 1946. The Czech Communist party's power grew steadily, however, and by 1947 American diplomats had given up hope of bringing the nation into the West's camp. No one was prepared, though, for the sudden demand by Czech Communists in March 1948 for key government posts nor for the threat that this demand would be enforced by the Red Army, then camped on the border. The government surrendered. Foreign Minister Jan Masaryk, long a hero in the West because of his opposition to Nazism, fell to his death from an upper-story window. The Communists claimed that he committed suicide. Truman and many other Americans believed that the Czech leader had been murdered. Whatever the cause, Russia was tightening its grip in response to the challenge of the Truman Doctrine and Marshall Plan. Like Acheson and Truman, Stalin also neglected negotiations. He relied instead on the Russian Army. Rumania fell under complete Communist control in February; Czechoslovakia followed; then non-Communist leaders in Bulgaria, Hungary, and Poland either disappeared or fled to the West.

Truman, comparing these events to those that had triggered world war in 1939, rapidly moved to a tougher military position which had long been urged by Secretary of Navy James Forrestal and other officials. Forrestal was the most fervent anti-Communist of the President's close advisors. He became especially powerful in mid-1947 when Truman named him the first Secretary of Defense. In the new position Forrestal was head of all the military services, now centralized in the Department of Defense. A former investment banker, Forrestal had entered government service early in World War II and soon issued scathing warnings about postwar cooperation with Stalin. As he wrote to a friend in 1944:

> Whenever any American suggests that we act in accordance with the needs of our own security he is apt to be called a goddamned fascist or imperialist, while if Uncle Joe [Stalin] suggests that he needs the Baltic Provinces, half of Poland, all of Bessarabia and access to the Mediterranean, all hands agree that he is a fine, frank, candid and generally delightful fellow who is very easy to deal with because he is so explicit in what he wants.

Events after 1945 strengthened Forrestal's fears. He concluded that the United States and Russia would conflict politically, militarily, ideologically, and spiritually around the globe. To support this conclusion, he arranged that American diplomat George Kennan be brought back from the United States Embassy in Moscow so that Kennan could work out a long analysis of Soviet intentions that verified Forrestal's suspicions. Published in mid-1947 under the mysterious pseudonym of "Mr. X," Kennan's "The Sources of Soviet Conduct" concluded that two factors—Communist revolutionary beliefs and Stalin's need to create an external enemy as an excuse for tightening his dictatorship over the Russian people—made Russia like a "toy automobile" that, when wound up, would move inexorably onward until it struck a superior force. Some Americans disputed this view. Walter Lippmann, the nation's most respected journalist, argued that traditional national interests, not a vague revolutionary mentality or Stalin's personal needs, governed Soviet policy. Therefore, Lippmann concluded, sincere negotiations could end the Cold War by reconciling Russian and American national interests. Forrestal, however, found Kennan's analysis exactly suited to his own views and urged Truman to build the worldwide counterforce needed to stop the toy automobile. With the fall of Czechoslovakia, the President publicly advocated Forrestal's arguments.

On March 17, 1948, just seven days after Masaryk's death, Truman appeared before Congress to deliver a tough speech that urged restoration of selective service, universal military training for all young men (long a pet Forrestal project), and immediate passage of the Marshall Plan. A frightened Congress rushed the Plan through, although the legislators moved more slowly on the draft and rejected universal military training. But the President had gained a triumph, and, as in the case of the Truman Doctrine, had done so by frightening Congress, this time with claims that Stalin had monstrously subjugated another nation without any provocation from the United States. Americans were being conditioned to respond instantly whenever Truman rang out the Forrestal-Kennan version of Soviet policy. And Stalin was giving Truman ample opportunity to do so.

## STALIN'S RESPONSE: THE BERLIN BLOCKADE

The Marshall Plan aimed at rapidly rebuilding Western Europe for two purposes: to make it a market for American farms and factories and to erect a bastion against Soviet expansion. To accomplish these objectives, the reconstruction of West Germany was necessary, for Germany had been the industrial core of Europe. Unless West Germany rebuilt there was little chance Western Europe could recover. The West Germans, however, suffered from inflation in early 1948, primarily because they had printed paper money in such volume that the currency had become almost worthless. In the weeks following the Czech crisis, the United States decided to cure West Germany's economic ills with drastic surgery. The Truman administration pushed for a currency reform program that would replace the bad money with new, better-supported bills. Despite Soviet objection that this had not been discussed with them, the program went ahead without their approval. Then in June 1948 the Western allies asked West Germany to form a Federal Republic, that is, an independent nation comprised of the American, British, and French occupation zones. The new nation, which would include West Berlin (located deep within the Soviet zone), would be rebuilt and closely tied to the West through the Marshall Plan.

These moves directly threatened Stalin's plans to keep Germany so weak that it could never again threaten Russia. At the same time, he was challenged from within the Soviet bloc itself. Yugoslavia's Communist leader, Josip Broz Tito, broke with Stalin, rooted out Russian attempts to assassinate him, and declared Yugoslavia a Communist but independent state. Tito had complete control of the nation, and his army was strong enough to make Russian troops pay dearly if they attempted to invade. "Titoism" became a new, hopeful sign to the West. The United States soon sent aid to the Yugoslavs.

Confronted with these threats in Germany and Yugoslavia, Stalin retaliated by trying to squeeze the West out of Berlin, thus removing that listening post within the Russian zone and weakening the entire Western position in Europe. In 1945 the Allies had made only oral agreements

Berlin airlift, 1948.

about the right to use railroads and highways through the Soviet zone to reach West Berlin. On June 24, 1948, the Russians stopped all surface traffic into West Berlin. The city stood isolated.

Truman correctly viewed Stalin's action as a challenge to American policy toward all of Germany. The President had three alternatives: pull out; use force to open access to Berlin, perhaps starting World War III in the process; or fly over the blockaded routes with supplies. Truman never seriously considered the first point. When the question arose in a Cabinet meeting, he interrupted to say, "There [is] no discussion on that point, we [are] going to stay, period." But he wanted no war and so followed the last alternative. The 2.5 million West Berliners required four thousand tons of food and fuel every day. With a massive airlift that landed a plane almost every minute of the day and night in the small West Berlin airport, the West soon delivered more than twelve thousand tons each day. For more than three hundred days pilots flew through impossible conditions, with some losing their lives in crashes during bad weather, in order to carry out "Operation Vittles." West Berlin held on, and in the early summer of 1949 Stalin agreed to lift some of the road blockades.

The President's tough responses to the Greek, Czech, and Berlin crises won support at home. So also did his foreign policy in the Middle East. Since 1945 hundreds of thousands of Jews, many of them survivors of Nazi concentration camps that had become slaughterhouses, flooded into Palestine. For many decades Palestine had been British controlled, but since 1917, London officials had intimated that someday the territory could become the homeland that Jews had sought for centuries. As the Jews moved into Palestine, they met bitter resistance from Arabs already settled on the land. After a bloody conflict, the Jews proclaimed their new nation on May 14, 1948.

Fifteen minutes after the announcement, Truman recognized the new state of Israel. He did so over vigorous opposition from Cabinet advisors (particularly Forrestal) who feared recognition would turn the rich oil-producing Arab states against Washington. British Prime Minister Clement Attlee and other Western Europeans, who were utterly dependent on Arab oil, also opposed Truman's action. The President nevertheless listened to his political advisors. He acted because of his great admiration for what the Jews had accomplished in Palestine, but his recognition also assured Jewish political support in the 1948 presidential election. Attlee later observed, "There's no Arab vote in America, but there's a very heavy Jewish vote and the Americans are always having elections."

Whatever Truman's motivation, his handling of foreign crises during 1947–48 accelerated his triumphant run for the White House. In Europe Stalin had been especially helpful in this regard. Truman's closest political advisor told him that there was "considerable political advantage to the administration in the battle with the Kremlin."

## DR. KINSEY AND SEX RESEARCH

In 1938 Alfred C. Kinsey began offering a course on marriage at Indiana University. Trained at Harvard as a zoologist, and a specialist in the behavior of the gall wasp, Kinsey had been teaching biology at Indiana for nearly two decades without causing a ripple. This abruptly changed when he introduced his new course. Dismayed at the lack of scientific evidence concerning human sexual behavior, Kinsey set out to compensate by taking the sexual case histories of anyone willing to cooperate. Kinsey assembled this data with the same compulsive care he had once devoted to collecting gall wasps, and soon found that people were volunteering information faster than he could transcribe it. By January 1948, when *Sexual Behavior in the Human Male* appeared, Kinsey's staff had accumulated more than five thousand case histories. Supported by a small grant from the Rockefeller Foundation, the Institute for Sex Research ultimately acquired 17,500 case histories, although it never reached Kinsey's goal of one hundred thousand.

Viewing himself as a scientist,

Dr. Kinsey conducting an interview, 1948.

Kinsey attempted to exclude all moral judgments from his work. He trained interviewers to ask direct questions, telling them that "evasive terms invite dishonest answers." One of his associates recalled: "We also never asked *whether* a subject had ever engaged in a particular activity; we assumed that everyone had engaged in everything, and so we began by asking *when* he had first done it." Kinsey presented his findings in cold, clinical language: 86 percent of American males had engaged in premarital sexual intercourse, 37 percent had on some occasion engaged in homosexual activity to the point of orgasm, and 40 percent had carried on extramarital affairs. Kinsey concluded that existing laws were violently at odds with prevailing practices, that, indeed, better than nine of every ten American men at some time in their lives engaged in some form of sexual activity punishable as a crime. The book, in many respects, was a resounding plea to end this hypocrisy by bringing public moral codes into line with private behavior.

The report was hailed by most psychologists and sociologists. One writer even claimed that Kinsey had done for sex "what Columbus did for geography." But many criticized Kinsey's methodology, pointing out that his statistical sample was drawn too heavily from underworld characters (because it was easy to obtain their

Drs. Masters and Johnson using dolls to illustrate their findings, 1970.

case histories), and that his interview technique did not allow for faulty recall. Others believed that Kinsey took an overly mechanistic approach. Lionel Trilling, professor of English at Columbia University, attacked the report for assuming that "the whole actuality of sex is anatomical and physiological" and thereby ignoring emotional and affective considerations. Yet the book proved amazingly popular. It went through six printings in ten days, sold one hundred thousand copies in three months, and remained on the bestseller list for twenty-seven weeks.

In 1953 Kinsey published a sequel, *Sexual Behavior in the Human Female.* He claimed that since "the anatomic structures which are most essential to sexual response and orgasm are nearly identical in the human female and male," any dissimilarities in response reflected psychological and hormonal rather than physiological differences. Kinsey also reported "a marked, positive correlation between experience in orgasm obtained from premarital coitus, and the capacity to reach orgasm after marriage," and he found that women took part in premarital and extramarital affairs more often than was commonly supposed. The second report triggered even sharper criticism than the first, partly because of the double standard concerning sexual behavior but also because of the growing conformity in the nation. One congressman denounced the book as "the insult of the century against

Dr. Ruth Westheimer providing sex counseling to viewers during her cable-television program, "Good Sex." On hand to help her field live call-in questions is actor Burt Reynolds.

our mothers, wives, daughters, and sisters," and a clergyman feared it "will in time contribute inevitably toward Communism."

In 1954, frightened by this public outcry, the Rockefeller Foundation (under its new president, Dean Rusk) cut off further support for Kinsey's Institute. The man who had no difficulty probing the most intimate details of a person's behavior was virtually incapable of asking wealthy individuals for money. Bitter and disillusioned, Kinsey died in 1956 at the age of 60. His

work, however, paved the way for many others, most notably William H. Masters and Virginia E. Johnson. Their books, *Human Sexual Response* (1966) and *Human Sexual Inadequacy* (1970), reported the results of laboratory experiments that measured the physiological changes in the human body during all phases of sexual stimulation. Yet their volumes, which also made the bestseller lists, caused little commotion, partly because Kinsey's pioneering work had made sex research respectable.

## COLD WAR POLITICS: THE 1948 ELECTION

In 1948 Truman's Fair Deal program combined two features: promises to bolster American defenses against the perceived Communist menace and an expansion of New Deal benefits. On the domestic front, he appealed for civil rights legislation, federal aid to education, national medical insurance, power development in river valleys, increases in unemployment compensation and the minimum wage, higher taxes on corporations, and lower taxes on just about everyone else. Truman did not expect the Republican Congress to enact these measures, but he recognized that, in the words of one advisor, recommendations "must be tailored for the voter, not the Congressman." On the other hand, the Truman administration stepped up its attack on suspected subversives. Early in 1948 the Justice Department arrested a dozen aliens who belonged to the Communist party and instituted deportation proceedings against them. The Attorney General also drew up a list of subversive organizations. None of these groups had an opportunity to contest their listing, and most then experienced difficulty in renting meeting halls or recruiting members.

Yet despite Truman's brand of liberal anticommunism, Democratic prospects in 1948 appeared bleak. When the party convention met that summer newsmen reported that delegates looked like "mourners," that caucus rooms resembled "weeping chambers," and that the affair reminded them of a "wake." The *New York Times* observed: "The delegates drank bourbon, scotch, and rye as if it were so much embalming fluid— and with about the same effect." The reasons for such pessimism were apparent. The Republicans had captured Congress in 1946, and in the past when the party out of power had won control of Congress in an off-year election—Republicans in 1894, Democrats in 1910, Republicans in 1918, Democrats in 1930—it had gone on to victory in the next presidential election. Even worse, the Democratic party seemed to be coming apart at the seams. Henry Wallace was leading a defection on the left into the Progressive party, and Strom Thurmond a defection on the right into the States' Rights Democratic party.

Henry Wallace announced his willingness to run on an independent ticket in December 1947. In the year since he had left the Cabinet, Wallace's differences with Truman had sharpened. Wallace considered the President too cautious in defending the civil liberties of radicals and the civil rights of blacks. But the major source of disagreement concerned foreign policy. Where Truman regarded the Soviet Union as inherently aggressive, Wallace believed that Soviet moves often came in response to an American military buildup. Where Truman condemned Soviet control of Eastern Europe, Wallace held that Stalin had legitimate reasons for establishing a political sphere of influence in that area, provided that such a sphere remained open to American trade and investment. Wallace maintained that the American plan for controlling atomic energy was bound to be unacceptable to the Russians. He criticized the Marshall Plan for turning Western Europe into a "vast military camp," and believed that universal military training would persuade people of the inevitability of war. Fearing that "we are whipping up another holy war against Russia," Wallace accepted the Progressive party nomination in the summer of 1948.

"We're on the march. We're really rolling now," Wallace told a friend after a speech before 32,000 cheering admirers. But his candidacy, itself a product of the Cold War, soon became a casualty of that conflict. Wallace was widely denounced as a Communist dupe, in part because American Communists backed his candidacy, in part because he refused to repudiate their support, and in part because his views concerning the Soviet Union often coincided with the Communist party line. The Americans for Democratic Action, a group of anti-Communist liberals, claimed that the Progressive party represented "a corruption of American liberalism" for it had "lined up unashamedly with the force of Soviet totalitarianism." Wallace drew his following, Democrat Lyndon B. Johnson of Texas chimed in, from "the sallow, deluded lunatic fringe that bores and scavenges like termites eating away at the foundations of a strong building." Wallace, a devout man who never subscribed to the Communist position, failed to repudiate Communist backing, although to have done so might well have helped his candidacy. He probably believed that the number of votes to be gained was not worth the price—that is, contributing to what he considered anti-Communist hysteria.

Even had a majority of Americans not come to believe that Communists ran the Progressive party, events in Europe—particularly the coup in Czechoslovakia and the Berlin crisis—would surely have undercut Wal-

Henry A. Wallace campaigning, August 1948.

lace's candidacy. As it was, the Progressives suffered a disastrous defeat. Wallace received only 1.1 million votes, or 2.4 percent of the total. The party received no electoral votes, and elected only one member, Vito Marcantonio of New York City, to the House of Representatives. Wallace made his best showing in New York, where he obtained 8 percent of the vote, and in California, where he received 5 percent. Nor did the Progressives have the murderous impact on the Democrats that had been predicted. Although Wallace garnered enough Democratic votes to deprive Truman of three states—New York, Michigan, and Maryland—his candidacy also acted as a lightning rod for anti-Communist sentiment. Wallace, not Truman, became the target, with the result that the Democrats could solidify their hold on voters, particularly Irish Catholics, motivated by such sentiment.

Just as the Progressive party hurt Truman in some respects and helped him in others, so the States' Rights Democratic party cost Truman electoral support in the South but strengthened his position with black voters in the North. The States' Rights party (labeled "Dixiecrats" by some and "Dixiebrats" by others) was created when the Democratic convention narrowly adopted a civil rights plank calling on Congress to support the President in guaranteeing blacks political and economic equality. A number of Southern delegates stormed out, called a convention in Birmingham, Alabama, and nominated J. Strom Thurmond, Governor of South Carolina, for the presidency. The Dixiecrats did not imagine that Thurmond could win. Rather they believed that his campaign would teach the Democrats not to take the South for granted and that it would possibly throw the election into the House of Representatives, where some sort of bargain might be struck with the Republicans.

The Dixiecrats bitterly criticized every attempt by the federal government to ensure racial justice. "We stand for the segregation of the races and the racial integrity of each race," they proclaimed. Proposals to outlaw the poll tax, to permit federal trials of lynch-mob members, to provide economic opportunity for blacks—all were said to violate states' rights. Attempting to turn Cold War rhetoric back on the Truman administration, Dixiecrats denounced the Fair Deal for its "totalitarian" features. The Fair Employment Practices Committee, Thurmond noted, was "patterned after a Russian law written by Joseph Stalin about 1920, referred to in Russia as Stalin's 'All-Races law.' " Although the party gained support chiefly for its stand on race, it also attracted Southern conservatives who had held a grudge against the welfare state since the late 1930s but had lacked a political vehicle for expressing their displeasure.

Dixiecrats and Progressives stood at opposite poles on the issue of civil rights. Wallace was assailed by Southern whites for his vigorous advocacy of racial equality and his refusal to speak before segregated audiences. Nevertheless, the two parties faced problems that were in some respects analogous. Just as Wallace failed to win the backing of most liberals, so Thurmond found that many Southern politicians, even those who shared his outlook, would not risk forfeiting their patronage and seniority by abandoning the Democratic party. Both candidates found the electorate enormously reluctant to "waste" a vote on a third party. Progressives and Dixiecrats wanted to bring the Democratic party around to their way of thinking, but their withdrawals proved only that the Democrats could win without them. Thurmond, like Wallace, polled 1.1 million votes, or 2.4 percent of the total. He carried four states (Mississippi, South Carolina, Louisiana, and Alabama), but by freeing the Democrats from the stigma of Southern racism he also simplified Truman's task of appealing to black voters. Blacks provided the Democrats' margin of victory in the crucial states of California, Illinois, and Ohio.

At the Republican convention, delegates were confident of victory. But the defection of the Progressives and Dixiecrats silenced two guns in the Republican arsenal. Republican candidate Thomas E. Dewey—who, according to one observer, sought the presidency "with the humorless calculation of a Certified Public Accountant in pursuit of the Holy Grail"—hardly made the most effective use of the weapons still at his disposal. Dewey often spoke in generalities, emphasizing national unity and avoiding harsh personal attacks. He did so for several reasons: his sharp criticism of Roosevelt in 1944 had not paid off; public-opinion polls all declared him an easy winner if he did not alienate voters already committed to the Republicans; and growing international tensions meant that voters might resent sharp attacks on Truman. Confident of victory, Dewey spent much time campaigning for other Republican candidates in states that were not crucial to his own election.

The same polls that helped convince Dewey to pull his punches persuaded Truman to wage a bare-knuckled campaign. The Democrats emphasized welfare state liberalism but also exploited anticommunism. Truman endeavored to resurrect the Roosevelt coalition by promising to extend the Fair Deal and by charging that Dewey's election would usher in a depression as surely as did Herbert Hoover's. Truman peppered his speeches with references to "Republican gluttons of privilege," "bloodsuckers with offices on Wall Street," who had "stuck a pitch fork in the farmer's back" and had "begun to nail the American consumer to the wall with spikes of greed." Truman not only denounced the Progressive party as a Communist front. He also claimed that Communists supported the Republican party "because they think that its reactionary policies will lead to the confusion and strife on which communism thrives." The Republican party was, therefore, at the same time a spokesman for "powerful reactionary forces" and an "unwitting ally of the Communists in this country."

Truman's strategy paid rich dividends in November 1948. The pollsters made the dual mistake of ending their interviews a few weeks before election day and assuming that the "undecided" vote would divide evenly. But many voters changed their minds at the last moment, and Truman won a disproportionately large share of the undecided vote. "I talked about voting for Dewey all summer, but when the time came I just couldn't do it," said one farmer. "I remembered the depression and all the good things that had come to me under the Democrats." Truman received 24.1 million votes to Dewey's 22 million. The Democrats, by picking up seventy-five seats in the House of Representatives and nine in the Senate, regained control of Congress. Having successfully navigated

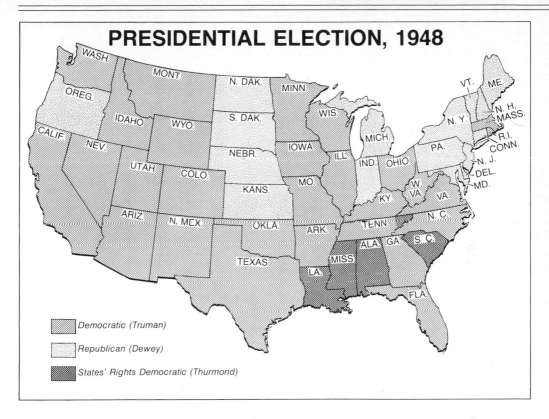

# PRESIDENTIAL ELECTION, 1948

Democratic (Truman)

Republican (Dewey)

States' Rights Democratic (Thurmond)

the rapids of Cold War electoral politics, it remained for Truman to guide his Fair Deal program through Congress.

## THE FAIR DEAL: CIVIL RIGHTS

What Truman managed to do, however, was to extend and codify New Deal measures already on the statute books. Congress accepted his recommendations to expand three programs, all sorely in need of modernization: social security benefits, considerably increased, were extended to 10 million people; the minimum wage was raised from 40 to 75 cents an hour; and the federal housing program was further developed. The National Housing Act (1949), a modest measure calling for the construction of 810,000 low-cost units over a six-year period, won bipartisan support in the Senate. The bill was cosponsored by a Northern liberal Democrat (Robert Wagner of New York), a Southern conservative Democrat (Allan Ellender of Louisiana), and a conservative Republican (Robert Taft of Ohio). Where the New Deal had been innovative, the Fair Deal was more often imitative.

But Congress rebuffed Truman when he attempted to go beyond New Deal initiatives in agricultural policy, federal aid to education, health insurance, and civil rights. In 1949 Truman proposed the Brannan plan for agriculture, which would have substituted an "income support standard" for the concept of farm parity and would have limited the payments available to large, corporate farmers. When organized farm groups denounced the plan, Congress defeated it. The President's $300 million aid-to-education bill was strangled in the House Committee on Education and Labor, whose members were hopelessly divided on the issue of aid to parochial schools. Similarly, Truman's program for health insurance and medical care never got to the floor of Congress. Although the plan allowed patients to choose their own physician and hospital, leaving doctors free to participate or not, it was widely and inaccurately condemned as socialized medicine. The American Medical Association hired an advertising agency to manage its campaign against the measure. "Would socialized medicine lead to socialization of other phases of American life?" asked a leaflet distributed by the doctors. The answer: "Lenin thought so." Fair Deal programs stood no chance where they antagonized entrenched interest groups, offended influential congressmen, or could be labeled communistic.

Of all these Fair Deal setbacks, however, none was more revealing than the defeat of civil rights. That Harry Truman should have been the first President to support such legislation was surely ironic. Although Missouri was one of the slave states that did not secede from the Union in 1861, Confederate sentiment was strong, and Truman's family had favored the Southern cause. His uncle had fought in the Confederate army. Years later his grandmother had expressed dismay when she first saw young Harry in his National Guard uniform, remarking, Truman recalled, "that it was the first time a blue uniform had been in the house since the Civil War, and she said please not to come in it again." Truman described his mother as an "unreconstructed rebel" who, when visiting her son at the White House, warned that if he put her up in the room with Lincoln's bed, "I'll sleep on the floor." Truman observed, "she was just the same Mama she had always been." Yet as Senator from Missouri, Truman supported civil rights measures, and as President, he did so even more strongly.

This reflected not only his own convictions, but also his recognition of the importance of the black vote. Large numbers of blacks had migrated north and west during World War II. Strategically located in such states as Illinois and California, they exerted more political leverage than ever before. The more evenly balanced the Republicans and Democrats, the more influential the black vote. Truman's victory in 1948, when he received close to 70 percent of that vote in large cities, illustrated this. His pluralities in the black wards of Los Angeles, Chicago, and Cleveland enabled him to carry California, Illinois, and Ohio. In addition, Cold War requirements influenced Truman's policies. Since Soviet propagandists never failed to exploit racial discrimination in the United States, Truman argued that such discrimination alienated millions in Africa and Asia. The achievement of racial justice, therefore, could strengthen American diplomacy.

The administration took action on a number of fronts. First, the President appointed a Civil Rights Commission whose report, in October 1947, called for an end to segregation in every area of American life and recommended that steps be taken to implement political, economic, and social equality. Truman endorsed the report, although his own legislative proposals did not go nearly so far. Second, Truman issued executive orders in July 1948 designed to end discrimination in governmental hiring and to eliminate segregation in the armed forces. Third, the Department of Justice filed briefs in support of groups challenging the legality of segregated housing, education, and transportation. In October 1949 one such brief argued that " 'Separate but equal' is a constitutional anachronism which no longer deserves a place in our law." Finally, Truman asked Congress to pass legislation creating a Civil Rights Division in the Department of Justice with authority to protect the right to vote, providing harsh penalties for members of lynch mobs, abolishing the poll tax in federal elections, and setting up a Fair Employment Practices Committee with the power to prevent discriminatory hiring.

Southern Democrats made mincemeat of this legislative package. They threatened a filibuster that would bring the Senate to a standstill. Senate rules required approval by two-thirds of the total membership (sixty-four votes) to close debate. Liberals attempted to amend the rules so as to permit cloture either by a simple majority or by two-thirds of those present and voting, but they met with no success. Southern Democrats also held crucial committee posts by virtue of seniority. A subcommittee of the Senate Judiciary Committee had authority over the antilynching bill; it was headed by James Eastland of Mississippi (who believed that Truman's endorsement of the Civil Rights Commission report "proves that organized mongrel minorities control the Government"). A subcommittee of the Senate Rules Committee was responsible for poll tax legislation; it was headed by Mississippi's other Senator, John Stennis. Southerners ultimately offered a compromise: an FEPC with no enforcement powers, an antilynching bill giving jurisdiction to the states rather than the federal government, and a constitutional amendment outlawing the poll tax that would require approval by three-fouths of the states. Truman rejected the deal.

The Supreme Court proved more responsive to demands for racial justice than did Congress. In *Shelley* v. *Kraemer* (1948) the Court held that state courts could not enforce restrictive housing covenants. These covenants, under which a group of homeowners agreed not to sell or lease property to non-Caucasians, played an important part in maintaining

Grant Reynolds and A. Philip Randolph testifying before Senate Armed Services Committee, 1948.

residential segregation. In St. Louis, 5.5 square miles were closed to blacks; in Chicago, 11 square miles were off limits. If a non-Caucasian family—black, Asian, or American Indian—moved into a home in a restricted area, a state court would issue an injunction requiring it to leave. Those who favored covenants reasoned that homeowners had the right to protect their neighborhood against "elements distasteful to them" and that covenants, as private agreements, did not violate the Fourteenth Amendment's ban on discrimination. The NAACP, which argued the other side, held that court enforcement of the covenants constituted state action within the meaning of the Fourteenth Amendment. In May 1948 the Supreme Court, by a 6 to 0 vote, accepted the NAACP's reasoning. The decision allowed homeowners to make convenants but not seek injunctions to enforce them. The ruling by no means removed all the obstacles to integrated housing, but it removed one of them.

If the restrictive covenant decision vindicated the NAACP, A. Philip Randolph's campaign against segregation in the armed forces proved the worth of a more militant approach. In the spring of 1948 Randolph demanded integration of the military, first through legislation and then, when that failed, through an executive order. Insisting that blacks would not fight for democracy abroad if they did not enjoy it at home, Randolph threatened a massive civil disobedience campaign. "I personally pledge myself to openly counsel, aid and abet youth, both white and Negro, to quarantine any Jim Crow conscription system." Asked if this did not border on treason, Randolph replied, "we are serving a higher law than the law which applies to the act of treason." On July 26, 1948, after protracted negotiations with Randolph, the President issued Executive Order 9981, asserting that equality of treatment and opportunity for all members of the armed services would be effected "as rapidly as possible." Randolph expressed satisfaction, and Truman later set up a committee to implement the new policy. The Navy and Air Force quickly agreed to integrate. The Army, however, raised one objection after another until in January 1950 it finally accepted a plan of gradual integration. The plan suddenly moved into high gear when American soldiers landed in South Korea.

## NATO: MULTIPURPOSE MILITARISM

In early 1949, fresh from his triumphs over the Republicans at the ballot box and over the Russians in West Berlin, Harry Truman was at the peak of his powers. Some leading Senators even believed that the Cold War had been "won." But Truman determined to march on, using these victories to consolidate American power in Western Europe. In early 1949, after close consultation with Senate leaders, the President asked for a military alliance between the United States and Western Europe. Called the North Atlantic Treaty Organization (NATO), it became the first United States political tie with Europeans since 1778, when a treaty with France enabled the American revolutionaries to survive.

Truman urged this major break with the American past for several reasons. American officials worried that the Marshall Plan was not working as effectively as they had hoped because of widespread fear among Europeans, and among United States investors, that Russia could swarm over Western Europe at will. Such fears were much overdrawn. Half the transportation of the standing Russian army was still pulled by horses. U.S. experts concluded that Stalin would not chance a major war for at least fifteen years. Truman's new Secretary of State, Dean Acheson, nevertheless observed that "economic measures alone are not enough," for their success depends "upon the people being inspired by a sense of security." One would not work without the other. Not for the first or last time in their history, Americans had to make a military commitment in order to gain economic benefits. But NATO also vastly increased American leverage in Western Europe. The European armies required American supplies, and the United States would be in a position to exact political

Harry S. Truman and Dean Acheson in 1955.

and economic concessions in return for providing the supplies. The European armies, moreover, were ultimately dependent on the American atomic bomb. As Truman's closest military advisor noted, in case of war with Russia, United States plans were "completely dependent upon full use of atomic bombs for success." Again, the United States held the high card and could ask Europeans to cooperate with its policies in return for atomic protection.

Secretary of State Acheson eloquently took the lead in urging the new policies. He became Truman's chief foreign policy spokesman. Acheson took that role from Forrestal, who had resigned from the Defense Department and then committed suicide after his fears and suspicions of communism deepened until he became mentally ill. The son of an Episcopal minister and a graduate of Yale, the elegant, mustachioed, subtle, and brilliant Acheson was a conservative who believed that the American future depended on close cooperation with Europe. To build this community, Acheson determined to deal with Russia only on American terms, which, given Stalin's views, meant not dealing with Russia at all. Acheson similarly dismissed public opinion at home: "If you truly had a democracy and did what the people wanted," he later declared, "you'd go wrong every time." As Secretary of State, he initially handled Congress as successfully as he had during the crises of 1947. His only allegiance was to Truman, a man completely different in appearance, background, and nearly every other respect except their common mistrust of Russia and their mutual desire to enhance presidential power. An associate of Acheson recalled that the Secretary once looked over a speech drafted for Truman, then "said with that magnificent manner of his: 'You can't ask the President of the United States to utter this crap.'" Demanding a typewriter, Acheson pecked out his own draft of the speech. It was clear who made foreign policy in Washington. When the bubble burst, Acheson would be a highly visible target for his enemies.

## THE BURSTING OF THE BUBBLE: 1949–1950

Creating NATO marked the high point of American postwar policy. In April 1949 twelve nations (United States, Canada, Great Britain, France, Italy, the Netherlands, Belgium, Norway, Denmark, Iceland, Portugal, and Luxembourg) pledged that each would consider an attack on one as an attack on all and that each would respond as it deemed necessary, including the possible use of force. But within six months a series of events rocked the Truman administration.

Overseas the Soviets exploded an atomic bomb and China fell to the Communist forces of Mao Tse-tung. American officials knew that the Russians would have the bomb soon, but few expected it this early. Similarly, the fall of Nationalist leader Chiang Kai-shek in China had been expected, but the actual Communist proclamation of victory shocked Americans. Acheson correctly argued that the United States had no power to stop the Chinese Communists unless millions of American boys were sent to fight, and this not even the most vocal supporters of Chiang Kai-shek were willing to urge. The only hope had been Chiang himself, but despite American advice and $2 billion of aid between 1945 and 1949, his regime had become so corrupt and inefficient that it could not save itself. As Acheson phrased it, Chiang's armies "did not have to be defeated; they disintegrated." The fact remained that the world's two largest nations were Communist, and one of them had the atomic bomb. Senate Republican leader Arthur Vandenberg said it best: "This is now a different world."

Truman also faced dangerous conditions at home. The American postwar depression, which many prophesied and everyone feared, seemed to be approaching. Unemployment figures of 1.9 million in 1948 shot up to 4.7 million, or 7.6 percent of the labor force, by early 1950. The Marshall Plan helped keep the economy buoyant, for almost every dollar appropriated by Congress had to be spent by Europeans in the United States for American goods. (This would be the case with nearly every dollar of the $100 billion Congress appropriated for "foreign aid" during the next quarter-century.) The Plan, however, would last only several more years. When Congress stopped spending these monies—that is, when Americans had to return to a peacetime economy with more "free enterprise" and less government spending—the nation could find itself in conditions resembling the 1930s. Republican congressional leaders who had followed Truman in a bipartisan spirit began to have second thoughts. The administration became fair game for political attacks.

As the nation settled down into a winter of deep discontent, Truman and Acheson prepared to counterattack. The President ordered a complete review of American policy. The review was completed in April 1950 and termed NSC-68 (National Security Council Paper No. 68). This document set American Cold War policy for the next twenty years. It assumed that only the United States could save Western Europe and Japan, which, along with North America, constituted the globe's great industrial centers. The United States would have to take the lead, letting its friends simply follow (much as satellites revolve around a primary planet, as NSC-68 phrased it), while Americans reorganized the "free world." According to NSC-68, reorganization meant militarization, and that, in turn, meant that the United States would soon have to accept a $50 billion defense expenditure instead of the $13 billion budgeted for 1950. Such spending would of course also pump up the deflating domestic economy.

Even as Truman planned a massive escalation of military strength he and Acheson responded cautiously to developments in Asia. While refusing to recognize the Chinese Communists immediately, throughout early 1950 the Secretary of State maintained that the real danger to China came from Stalin's desire to control all Communists, including Mao, and not from Washington. United States trade with China continued into late 1950. In January 1950 the President's military advisors concluded that the island of Formosa (to which the Chiang regime had fled) would shortly fall to Mao's troops, and the United States should not lift a finger. Acheson clearly was flirting with the idea of recognizing the Chinese Communists. The flirtation cooled only after the Chinese seized United States property, mistreated American citizens, and signed a friendship pact with Stalin in February 1950.

At the same time, Acheson took steps to ensure that Japan would replace China as the American outpost in Asia. As early as 1947, when Washington officials saw the hollowness of Chiang's regime, they had encouraged Japan to rebuild more rapidly than the 1945 surrender terms allowed. Following this lead, United States businessmen trooped into the promising Japanese market, increasing their investment from $96 million in 1946 to nearly $500 million in 1949. With Japan recovering and an independent government at work in Tokyo in 1949, the question became how the United States could be assured that Japan would stay on Washington's side for the indefinite future. This question became pressing when China fell, for Japan had looked to China for decades as a market and source of raw materials. If something was not done, the Japanese might well fall into the Chinese Communist orbit.

Acheson's answer was a NATO-like device for Japan: the United States and Japan would sign a treaty ending American occupation but allowing United States military bases to remain. While the Japanese themselves would not possess a large military establishment, their islands would become an American outpost on Russia's Asian rim. Stalin did not care for this. As early as 1947 the Soviets had warned against any "intention to restore the economy of Germany and Japan on the old [pre-1939] basis provided it is subordinated to interests of American capital." Acheson had done much more, making Japan both an economic and military outpost. Faced with NATO to the west and long-term American military bases on his eastern flank, Stalin decided to act.

## KOREA: JUNE 1950

His opportunity lay in Korea. That nation had been divided along its 38th parallel between American and Russian forces in 1945 in order to facilitate the surrender of Japanese troops. After the surrender, however, neither power would leave. Korea was too vital, for whoever controlled it also controlled strategic entrances to Japan, China, and the Soviet Union itself. Russian troops finally retreated in early 1949 but left behind a Communist North Korean government possessing a strong Soviet-equipped army. The United States exited from South Korea several months later; it left behind strongman Syngman Rhee and an army primarily useful for eliminating Rhee's political opponents.

Acheson believed that Rhee's troops and the American presence in Japan sufficed to protect South Korea. On January 12, 1950, the Secretary of State spoke at the National Press Club in Washington, defining the American defense perimeter in the Pacific as running from the Aleutians through Japan to the Philippines. That was the same defensive line that General MacArthur had agreed to in 1949. Acheson carefully added, however, that any aggression against Korea would be opposed by the United Nations. That statement alone would not serve to make Stalin quake in his boots. For his part, Stalin had little to lose and much to gain. His North Korean allies were eager to attack southward to reunite their country. A successful invasion could endanger Acheson's attempt to rebuild Japan. It would also show Mao, with whom Stalin was having difficulties over Sino-Russian border and economic problems, that Russia remained the dominant Communist power. Stalin could accomplish all this, moreover, without any direct Soviet involvement in the attack.

On June 25 North Korean troops moved across the 38th parallel.

Truman quickly responded. On June 27 he sent in American air and naval forces. When these proved insufficient and South Korea faced certain defeat, he ordered United States combat troops into battle. Meanwhile Acheson obtained the support of the United Nations. On June 27 the UN resolved that its members should help repel the aggressors so that "peace and security" could return to the area. Angry over the American refusal to allow the Chinese Communists into the world organization, the Russians had been boycotting UN sessions and were not present when Acheson rushed the resolution through. The struggle against North Korea was to be fought by a UN army under General MacArthur.

But this was misleading. The United States actually controlled operations through MacArthur, and the UN simply followed Truman's lead. Americans contributed 86 percent of the Naval power, more than 90 percent of the air support, and, along with the South Koreans, nearly all the combat troops. The President made these drastic decisions, moreover, without going before Congress to ask for a declaration of war as the Constitution required. He termed the struggle a "police action," not a war, hoping that this would limit the conflict before it expanded with atomic weapons and Russian participation. The President merely consulted and informed congressional leaders, of whom only Senator Robert Taft, the Ohio Republican, raised major objections. This procedure was clearly unconstitutional and later, when the war went badly, proved to be a political error as well, for it left Truman exposed to bitter partisan attack. The President's decision set a precedent for the later Kennedy-Johnson-Nixon commitment of American troops to Vietnam, a commitment again taken without a congressional declaration of war.

## CHANGING "CONTAINMENT" TO "LIBERATION": THE U.S. ON THE OFFENSIVE

Truman and Acheson used the Korean War as an opportunity to take the initiative against communism not only in Asia but in Europe too. The remaining months of 1950 were the most active and crucial ones in the Cold War. During this time the President decided to change his policy of "containment," as defined in the 1947 Truman Doctrine, to the more active policy of actually trying to liberate a Communist-controlled area. Several motivations shaped the new approach. The war gave Acheson a perfect opportunity to build great military bastions in Asia and Europe as he had long desired. After all, he could argue, if the Communists struck in Korea, they might strike anywhere. In a larger sense, the war was the chance to put the global ideas of NSC-68 into effect. Driving back communism would also silence growing criticism at home. These critics, whom Acheson acidly called "primitives" and "animals," attacked the administration for merely containing, instead of eliminating, communism. Truman and Acheson used the Korean War as a springboard to launch a world-wide diplomatic offensive.

In Asia this offensive included the first full-fledged American support to Chiang Kai-shek's rump regime on Formosa. Truman sent the Seventh Fleet to protect Chiang and signed large-scale economic and military aid pacts. By August 1950, the United States had bedded down with Chiang to establish a new American military outpost on Formosa. In Southeast Asia, Acheson agreed to help France reimpose its control over the Indo-chinese peoples in May, a month before Korea erupted. By midsummer the United States sent large military assistance and a military mission to aid the French. Here lay the beginning of the American involvement in Vietnam. Acheson also hurried plans to sign the Japanese security treaty, doing so over strong objections from the Soviets and also from such friends as Australia and New Zealand, who feared the threat of a revived Japan.

**CONFLICT IN KOREA, 1950–1953**

The Secretary of State similarly took the diplomatic offensive in Europe. He used the Korean crisis as the opportunity to achieve goals that had been impossible to gain earlier because of opposition from allies and the Congress. Above all, Acheson determined to lock West Germany firmly to the West by rearming it and integrating the new German forces into NATO. France and England voiced strong opposition to any revival of German militarism, but Acheson refused to listen. Simultaneously, Truman, again without consulting Congress, tied the United States closer to Western Europe by stationing American troops on European soil. Both moves were completed despite strong congressional opposition. In 1949 Acheson had told Congress, "We are very clear that the disarmament and demilitarization of Germany must be complete and absolute." At the same time, he had guaranteed that there would be no Americans assigned to NATO duty without the assent of Congress. The shifting Cold War, especially the new Soviet atomic bomb, changed Acheson's mind. The United States commitment to Europe was fixed for at least the next thirty-five years. Truman meanwhile increased defense spending until in 1952 it reached $50 billion, the figure envisioned by NSC-68.

Finally, Truman and Acheson decided not only to stop the North Koreans but to drive them back until all Korea was liberated. Such a triumph would teach Stalin a lesson, silence the critics at home, insure Japan's position, and put the United States on the border of Communist China itself. In July and August the tragic decision was taken to cross the 38th parallel. In September, General MacArthur made a brilliant landing at Inchon, trapping thousands of Communist troops. By late October, the UN forces were marching through North Korea towards the Yalu River, which separated Korea from China. At this point the Chinese issued blunt warnings that UN troops should not approach the Yalu. Acheson was not concerned. "Everything in the world" was done to assure China that its interests were not endangered, he later observed. "And I should suppose there is no country in the world which has been more outstanding in developing the theory of brotherly development of border waters [like the Yalu] than the United States."

This was an absurd statement. Such "brotherly development" of the Yalu was precisely what Mao determined to prevent. The Chinese wanted no help from the world's most powerful nation, particularly when that nation seemed intent on placing great military forces on China's border. In late November Mao's armies swarmed southward across the Yalu. Large units of American and South Korean troops were surrounded, killed, or left to freeze to death in a bitter winter. By late December the UN forces had fled south across the 38th parallel before MacArthur could counterattack. The war then turned into a bloody stalemate. More than 140,000 Americans were killed or wounded and more than 1 million South Koreans. Most of the casualties were suffered after Truman ordered UN forces to liberate North Korea.

The casualties were only part of the high price Americans paid for the administration's 1950 diplomatic offensive. The immense and rapidly mounting war expenditures skewed the nation's economy, infecting it with inflation and labor strikes. A renewed military-industrial alliance fattened on the defense budget, which, in turn, distorted the economy while wasting irreplaceable resources. Abroad, Americans discovered that their friends held serious doubts about U.S. stability. These allies found German rearmament so repugnant that it would be delayed for four years. Others feared a revived Japan. Some refused to follow Acheson's policy of aiding French colonialism in Southeast Asia. All were concerned how the United States might use its incredible power, particularly its atomic weapons.

The Truman administration was also on the defensive at home. Despite the President's assurance that communism could be contained and even driven back, communism had not only survived, but large numbers of American boys were being slaughtered in Korea. The administration and indeed the entire liberal tradition it claimed to represent were embattled. The struggle at home reached a peak in early 1951, when the President, in his words, reached "a parting of the way with the big man in Asia."

## TRUMAN AND MacARTHUR

In April 1951, for the first time in twenty years, baseball fans booed the President of the United States when he threw out the ball to open the Washington Senators' season. For, a few days before, Truman had relieved General Douglas MacArthur of his command of United Nations forces in Korea. That action released a tidal wave of sympathy for the general, who, on his return to the United States, received a hero's welcome. When MacArthur concluded a speech to Congress by quoting an old army ballad—"old soldiers never die, they just fade away"—and then added, "like the old soldier of that ballad, I now close my military career and just fade away, an old soldier who tried to do his duty as God gave him the light to see that duty," it seemed as if the applause would never end. The Truman administration, however, regarded MacArthur as an ambitious and dangerous man, one who wanted to subvert civilian control of policymaking and plunge the United States into nuclear war. Privately, members of the President's staff revealed their bitterness by composing an imaginary tour schedule for the general: "Burning of the Constitution. Lynching of Secretary Acheson. Twenty-one atomic-bomb salute. Three hundred nude D.A.R.'s leap from Washington Monument."

The basis of the conflict between Truman and MacArthur had existed in 1950 but was concealed because American forces had been successful until late in the year, and the administration, in deciding to cross the 38th parallel, in effect had endorsed MacArthur's goal of eliminating the Communist government in North Korea. Once Chinese forces intervened, however, the options available to the United States narrowed considerably: it could either accept a stalemate or risk nuclear war. Truman chose the first alternative and MacArthur the second. The two men, therefore, rapidly moved toward a showdown. In January 1951 MacArthur demanded permission to blockade China, bomb military and industrial targets across the Yalu River, use Chinese nationalist troops in Korea, and allow Chiang Kai-shek to attack the Chinese mainland. When Truman rejected all of this, MacArthur took matters into his own hands. In March he publicly threatened to destroy China if it did not concede defeat, and he stated that there was no substitute for victory. Truman then recalled him.

MacArthur not only repudiated the very concept of limited war but also disagreed with the administration's strategic priorities. As commander of United States forces in the Pacific during World War II, MacArthur had declared: "Europe is a dying system. It is worn out and run down. . . . The lands touching the Pacific with their billions of inhabitants will determine the course of history for the next 10,000 years." But the Truman administration regarded Europe, not Asia, as the key to containment. Provoking a war with China, as MacArthur seemed ready to do, would antagonize the nations of Western Europe and jeopardize the NATO alliance. By draining off the American forces and channeling them to the Pacific, such a conflict would weaken European defenses. When General Omar N. Bradley, speaking for the Joint Chiefs of Staff, asserted that an attack on China would involve the United States in "the wrong war, in the wrong place, at the wrong time, and with the wrong enemy," he left little doubt as to what he considered the right war, the right place, the right time, and the right enemy: a war waged to defend Western Europe against Soviet domination.

That General Bradley defended the Truman administration was of crucial significance. The conflict between Truman and MacArthur, often interpreted as one between civilian and military interests, actually involved sharp disagreement within the military. This, in turn, reflected the development of ties between the armed services and government that emerged during World War II and grew firmer during the Cold War. The Truman administration, indeed, often asked military men to fill policy-making posts in government; by 1948, 150 officers held such positions. The Joint Chiefs of Staff fully endorsed Truman's decision to recall MacArthur. So, too, did General George Marshall, who served as Secretary of State (1947–49) and Secretary of Defense (1950–51). "The S.O.B. should have been fired two years ago," Marshall commented. On the other hand, almost all the field commanders in Korea backed MacArthur. (The lone exception was General Matthew Ridgeway, and Truman selected him to replace MacArthur.) The military establishment's support of the President's Korean policy helped him ride out the storm created by MacArthur's dismissal.

# LIMITED WAR AT HOME

The Korean War did not require the same level of economic regulation as World War II. Since military operations occurred on a limited scale, the armed forces absorbed a relatively small proportion of industrial output and consumer goods were plentiful. Inflationary pressures, strong during the first nine months of war, subsided in the spring of 1951. World War II had produced gargantuan deficits, but the government showed a budgetary surplus in 1951 and 1952. Even so, the administration took a number of steps to control inflation and encourage production: it limited credit purchases by requiring larger down payments, restricted new housing starts, and liberalized amortization for costs incurred in plant expansion. The President established an Office of Defense Mobilization, issued an order designated to hold the line on prices and wages, and took possession of the railroads when workers threatened to strike for higher wages. Truman bitterly assailed the union leaders for acting "like a bunch of Russians," but the workers eventually won most of their demands, and the government returned the lines to private owners.

The Supreme Court's response to the President's seizure of the steel mills illustrated the problems encountered in regulating the economy during a limited war. In March 1952 a federal wage panel concluded that steel workers deserved a raise, but the companies refused to grant the increase unless the administration approved a sizeable price increase. When the administration refused, the steel firms rejected a wage hike, and the union called a strike. Truman could have invoked the Taft-Hartley Act and ordered an eighty-day cooling-off period, but he did not want to employ the law against workers with a legitimate grievance or risk alienating organized labor. Instead he seized the steel mills, citing as justification the existence of a national emergency, the importance of steel production in wartime, and his implied powers as Commander in Chief. The case rapidly moved to the Supreme Court, which, in *Youngstown Sheet and Tube Co.* v. *Sawyer* (1952), ruled against the President by a 6 to 3 margin. The majority held that the President had no constitutional authority to order the seizure and that in bypassing the Taft-Hartley Act he had ignored "the clear will of Congress." Chief Justice Fred M. Vinson, speaking for the minority, cited precedents under Abraham Lincoln, Woodrow Wilson, and Franklin Roosevelt for granting the President a broad range of discretionary authority in wartime. Obeying the Court, Truman then returned the steel mills to their owners and, when the union struck, refused to intervene. The strike lasted nearly two months and ended with the workers obtaining their raise and the administration reluctantly granting the steel companies their price increase.

Despite the limited nature of the mobilization, the Korean War greatly bolstered the American economy. Expenditures for purchasing armaments and other equipment, constructing bases, and meeting military payrolls rose sharply, from slightly more than $13 billion in the year ending June 1950 to slightly under $60 billion in the year ending June 1953. Although the percentage of gross national product devoted to national security never approached the World War II level (43.1 percent), it nevertheless rose from 6.4 percent in 1950 to 14.1 percent in 1953. As government spending created millions of new jobs, unemployment dropped to its lowest level in years. Federal expenditures, together with special tax incentives, encouraged industries to expand their productive facilities. From 1950 to 1954, steel capacity increased by 24 percent, electrical generating capacity by 50 percent, and aluminum capacity by 100 percent. Finally, the government began to stockpile petroleum, chemicals, and scarce metals to protect itself against shortages in the event of a long war. By 1954 it had acquired more than $4 billion worth of critical materials.

The Korean War also led to a doubling of the size of the armed forces and, more important, to the construction of the hydrogen bomb. Truman had authorized development of the H-bomb in January 1950, but little progress was made in the next six months, and doubts about the bomb's feasibility persisted. The outbreak of the Korean War removed several obstacles to its completion. The national emergency convinced a number of scientists who had refused to work on thermonuclear weapons to put aside their moral qualms and also made it possible to justify testing within the continental United States for the first time since 1945. The war allowed Truman to pump billions of dollars into the bomb project; the Atomic Energy Commission eventually employed 150,000 people. Tests in May 1951 proved the technical feasibility of a thermonuclear weapon. Finally, the first H-bomb was detonated over the Pacific on November 1, 1952, its 10.4 megaton explosion obliterating the uninhabited island of Elugelab. Russia, which had required four years to duplicate the American atomic bomb, obtained its hydrogen bomb only one year after the United States test.

If the Korean War had the effect of accelerating the development of bombs and weapons, it had a similar effect in desegregating the armed services. By mid-1950 the Navy and Air Force had taken long strides toward desegregation, But the Army, although it had yielded to administration pressure to abolish racial quotas on enlistments, still maintained separate black and white units. Yet segregation led to a wasteful duplication of facilities and an inefficient use of manpower. Moreover, the tendency to assign black units to noncombatant duties meant that whites suffered a disproportionate share of casualties. When white troops experienced heavy losses in the early days of the war, field commanders in Korea broke with existing policy and used black soldiers as replacements. In March 1951 the Pentagon announced the integration of all training facilities in the United States. A few months later the Army received a preliminary report from a team of social scientists emphasizing the advantage of integration and denying that it would damage morale. The Army then announced that it would integrate its forces in Korea and the Far East. Later it extended this policy to troops stationed in Europe. By the end of the Korean War, nearly all black soldiers were serving in integrated Army units.

# CIVIL LIBERTIES UNDER SIEGE

The Korean conflict intensified the growing fear of Communist subversion, a fear that partly fed on the actions of the House Committee on Un-American Activities. In 1947 the Committee sought to prove that Communists had infiltrated the motion-picture industry. Several writers and producers who refused to answer questions concerning their political affiliations were jailed for contempt, and Hollywood adopted a blacklist barring the employment of anyone who failed to cooperate with congressional investigators. In 1948 the Committee stalked bigger game: Alger Hiss, president of the Carnegie Endowment for International Peace, who was charged with perjury for denying that, while working for the State Department in the late 1930s, he had given classified papers to a Communist party member for transmittal to the Soviet Union. After his first trial resulted in a hung jury, Hiss was convicted of perjury in January 1950. By 1949 the Committee was looking into espionage by scientists who had allegedly passed secret information about the atomic bomb to Russia. The Korean War, coming on the heels of all this, had a chilling effect on civil liberties. That effect could be measured by the behavior of Congress, the President, and the courts.

Three months after American troops landed in Korea, Congress passed sweeping legislation to curb subversive activities in the United States. The Internal Security Act (1950) made it unlawful to conspire to perform any act that would "substantially contribute" to establishing a totalitarian dictatorship in the United States. The measure required members of Communist organizations to register with the Attorney General, barred them from employment in national defense, and denied them the right to obtain passports. The act imposed stringent controls on immigrants, aliens, and naturalized citizens. It blocked the entry of those who had belonged to totalitarian organizations, provided for the deportation of suspected alien subversives, and permitted the government to revoke the naturalization of those who joined a subversive group within five years of acquiring citizenship. Finally, the act authorized the President, in the event of war or invasion, to detain persons if there were "reasonable grounds" to believe that they might conspire to commit espionage or sabotage. This provision, first put forth by Senate liberals as a substitute measure, was, ironically, added to all the other features. On September 22, 1950, Truman vetoed the bill, declaring that it would "strike blows at our own liberties" by moving toward "suppressing opinion and belief." Congress very easily overrode the veto.

The President's blistering veto of the Internal Security Act did not prevent him from narrowing the rights of government employees under the federal loyalty program. At its inception in March 1947 this program provided for dismissal from federal employment in cases where "reasonable grounds exist for belief that the person involved is disloyal." But the Loyalty Review Board, which supervised the program, found it difficult to discover such evidence. It therefore favored a procedure that would take account of individuals "who are potentially disloyal or who are bad security risks." In April 1951 Truman issued a new executive order providing for dismissal from federal employment in cases where "there is a reasonable doubt as to the loyalty of the person involved." In effect, the burden of proof now fell on employees who, to keep their jobs, had to dispel all doubts. Since those doubts might rest on nothing more substantial than associating with persons considered to be Communists, attending meetings to raise money for suspect causes, or even subscribing to radical publications, the burden was a heavy one.

At the same time that the new loyalty program went into effect, a jury in New York found Julius and Ethel Rosenberg guilty of conspiring to commit espionage. The Rosenbergs were charged with having plotted to arrange for the transfer of atomic secrets to the Soviet Union during World War II. Ethel Rosenberg's brother, who had worked as a machinist on the Manhattan Project, testified that he had transmitted such information and received cash payments; the alleged courier supported this account. The defense denied everything, insisting that the entire story was a fabrication. On April 5, 1951, in handing down a death sentence, Judge Irving Kaufman attempted to tie the case to the Korean War. By helping Russia obtain the atomic bomb, he asserted, the couple had caused "the Communist aggression in Korea, with the resultant casualties exceeding fifty thousand. . . . We have evidence of your treachery all around us every day—for the civilian defense activities throughout the nation are aimed at preparing us for an atom bomb attack." Appeals dragged through the courts for two agonizing years, with the Rosenbergs protesting their innocence to the end, although their sentence would have been commuted to life imprisonment had they confessed. They were electrocuted on June 19, 1953. Even many who considered them guilty regarded the sentence as barbaric.

In June 1951 the Supreme Court moved with the prevailing tide by upholding the constitutionality of the Smith Act. Passed in 1940, the Act made it a crime to conspire to teach or advocate the forcible overthrow of the government. In 1949 Eugene Dennis and ten other Communist leaders had been found guilty of violating the Act, and the following year the Court of Appeals had sustained their convictions. In *Dennis* v. *U.S.* (1951) the Supreme Court approved the Smith Act by a 6 to 2 vote. Chief

Justice Fred M. Vinson wrote the majority opinion. To prove the American Communists presented a clear and present danger to the United States, Vinson pointed to the formation of a "highly organized conspiracy" with "rigidly disciplined members," the "inflammable nature of world conditions," and the "touch-and-go nature of our relations" with Russia. Justices Robert Jackson and Felix Frankfurter, both of whom rejected this line of reasoning, nevertheless concurred with the majority on other grounds. Justices Hugo Black and William O. Douglas dissented. Affirming the value of free speech, Douglas denied that American Communists, whom he termed "miserable merchants of unwanted ideas," posed an immediate threat. He also expected that "in case of war with Russia they will be picked up overnight as were all prospective saboteurs at the commencement of World War II." The Dennis decision cleared the way for the prosecution of other Communist leaders. Nearly one hundred of them were indicted in the early 1950s.

The Internal Security Act, the revamped loyalty program, the trials of alleged spies, the Smith Act prosecution—all trespassed to some extent on civil liberties. Of these measures, Truman's loyalty program undoubtedly affected the largest number of people. Yet of the 4.7 million jobholders and applicants who underwent rigid loyalty checks by 1952, only about ten thousand failed to gain clearance. Most of them quietly resigned or withdrew their applications; 560 people were actually fired or denied a job on the grounds of security. The Korean War's impact on civil liberties, however, would not stop at this point. With the emergence of Senator Joseph McCarthy, open season was declared on liberals. The Truman administration itself became the quarry.

# McCARTHYISM

Joseph McCarthy, elected to the Senate as a Republican from Wisconsin in 1946, had a meteoric career in the early 1950s. Although he first achieved notoriety in a speech at Wheeling, West Virginia, a few months before the Korean War broke out, and although he remained a powerful political force for some time after the war ended, McCarthy's appeal derived largely from his success in exploiting the frustrations involved in waging a limited war. McCarthy declared at Wheeling that the United States, at the end of World War II, had been the most powerful nation in the world; but by 1950 it had "retreated from victory" and found itself in a "position of impotency." One thing alone, McCarthy said, was responsible: "the traitorous actions" of high government officials in the Roosevelt and Truman administrations. This explanation, as deceptive as it was simple, set the tone for all that McCarthy did and for much of what went by the name of McCarthyism.

There was nothing new in the charge that Communists had infiltrated government. What distinguished McCarthy was his assertion that the most eminent and reputable Democrats were serving the Communist cause by waging a "caricature of a war" in Korea. To McCarthy, Secretary of State Dean Acheson was the "Red Dean of the State Department," "the elegant and alien Acheson—Russian as to heart, British as to manner." Similarly, the Wisconsin Senator believed that General George Marshall had been hoodwinked into aiding "a great conspiracy, a conspiracy on a scale so immense as to dwarf any previous such venture in the history of man." Again, Democratic Governor Adlai E. Stevenson of Illinois "endorsed and could continue the suicidal Kremlin-directed policies of the nation." McCarthy even found a trace of grim humor in the situation. "I do not think we need fear too much about the Communists dropping atomic bombs on Washington," he remarked savagely. "They would kill too many of their friends that way."

McCarthyism meant more than wild attacks on the Truman administration. It also signified a climate of all-embracing conformity. Many people became afraid to voice unpopular views or even to express controversial opinions. The drive to conform was sometimes carried to ludicrous lengths. One state required professional boxers and wrestlers to take a non-Communist oath before entering the ring. Efforts were made in Indianapolis, Indiana, to remove such "controversial" works as *Robin Hood* (whose indiscretion was stealing from the rich and giving to the poor) from public-school libraries. Names themselves often took on great significance: the Cincinnati Reds were solemnly renamed the "Redlegs," and a face powder known as "Russian Sable" was marketed as "Dark Dark." Dearborn, Michigan, crowned a "Miss Loyalty" at a beauty pageant complete with loyalty oaths. Not everyone surrendered to this mood, but pressures for ideological conformity in America have seldom been stronger than during the early 1950s.

McCarthyism was also closely identified with the use of heavy-handed tactics. McCarthy presented himself as a rough-and-tumble fighter; his supporters affectionately termed him "Jolting Joe," "The Wisconsin Walloper." Never far from the surface was the suggestion that the Truman administration was infested with moral, as well as ideological, perverts. The Senator, wrote one admirer, "learned that the State Department was literally crawling with so-called 'men' who wore red neckties and sometimes women's clothes—who wanted other men for lovers instead of women." McCarthy's allusions to homosexuality among government employees were hardly more circumspect. He referred to "those Communists and queers" in the State Department who wrote "perfumed notes." McCarthy insisted that the war against communism must be fought with brass knuckles, not kid gloves. The tactics he employed—from the juggling of statistics concerning the number of alleged security risks in the State Department to the browbeating of witnesses—seemed entirely legitimate to his followers.

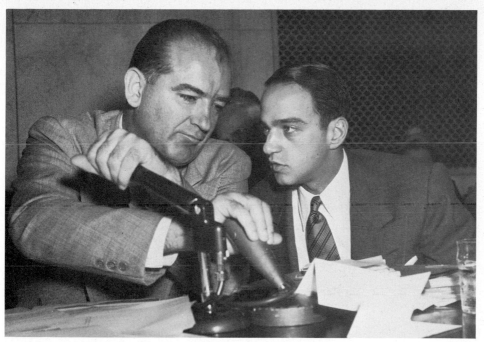

Senator Joseph McCarthy (1) and his aide, Roy Cohn, 1954.

Different critics saw in McCarthy the embodiment of their own worst fears. Socialists, who feared the intrigues of reactionary capitalists, regarded McCarthy as an agent of Texas oilmen and other new millionaires who wanted to impose a fascist order on the United States. Liberals, who feared the introduction into politics of moral issues that could not be resolved through a process of give and take, thought that McCarthyism represented such an issue. They believed that the Senator played on status resentments of middle-class ethnic groups, especially the Irish and Germans, who, having achieved a measure of economic security, were seeking to prove their Americanism by attacking a social elite. A few conservatives believed McCarthy expressed the masses' hatred of aristocratic privilege and excellence. One asserted: "McCarthyism is the revenge of the noses that for twenty years of fancy parties were pressed against the outside window pane."

Support for McCarthy closely followed political, religious, and occupational lines. The Senator won more backing from Republican than from Democratic voters, more from Catholics than from Jews, more from Baptists and Lutherans than from Congregationalists and Episcopalians, and more from blue-collar workers than from white-collar professionals. McCarthy also exploited his position in the Senate. Even though some Republican Senators found his methods abhorrent, few dared to criticize him openly, because they either feared antagonizing him or recognized his partisan value. Moreover, the Senate customarily permits its members broad latitude, relying on tradition or unwritten rules to ensure discretion. McCarthy also manipulated the mass media with great success. He developed techniques for monopolizing headlines that kept his name before the public even when his allegations had no substance.

That McCarthy could have charged the Democrats with treason, and that anyone could have taken those charges seriously, seems, in retrospect, incredible. In the years 1947 to 1952 the Truman administration had built up Western European economic and military strength through the Marshall Plan and NATO, faced down the Russians in Berlin, taken stern measures against radicals at home, developed the hydrogen bomb, and fought a war against Communists in Korea. Nevertheless, Truman erred in supposing that the American people would be willing to make the terrible sacrifices war required without being convinced that the government was doing everything in its power to win that war. In the past, although war had sometimes been used as an instrument of diplomacy, it had always been presented as a crusade: to free Cuba in 1898, to make the world safe for democracy in 1917, to establish the four freedoms in 1941. When McCarthy asserted that the United States was "engaged in a final, all-out battle between communistic atheism and Christianity," when MacArthur claimed that "there is no substitute for victory," they were speaking the kind of language Americans had customarily spoken when waging war. If Truman was correct in believing that in the nuclear age only limited war was feasible, then his opponents were surely correct in recognizing that limited war provided them an unequalled political opportunity. They would make the most of that opportunity in the 1952 election.

## Suggested Reading

For Henry Wallace and the Progressive party see Norman Markowitz, *The Rise and Fall of the People's Century* (1973). In *Democrats and Progressives* (1974), Allen Yarnell discusses the election of 1948. On the Dixiecrats, see Robert A. Garson, *The Democratic Party and the Politics of Sectionalism, 1941–1948* (1974). The Truman administration's civil rights program is explored at length in William Berman, *The Politics of Civil Rights in the Truman Administration* (1970); and Donald McCoy and Richard Ruetten, *Quest and Response* (1973). For the Supreme Court's decision on restrictive covenants, see Clement Vose, *Caucasians Only* (1957). James Patterson's biography of Robert Taft, *Mr. Republican* (1972), assesses an important critic of the Fair Deal.

The political consequences of the Korean War are considered in John Spanier, *The Truman-MacArthur Controversy* (1959); Richard Rovere and Arthur M. Schlesinger, Jr., *The MacArthur Controversy and American Foreign Policy* (1965); and Maeva Marcus, *Truman and the Steel Seizure* (1977). Contrasting views of the

Truman administration's position on civil liberties are presented in Alan D. Harper, *The Politics of Loyalty, 1946–1952* (1969); Athan Theoharis, *Seeds of Repression: Harry S. Truman and the Origins of McCarthyism* (1971); and David Caute, *The Great Fear: The Anti-Communist Purge under Truman and Eisenhower* (1978). The Supreme Court's decision upholding the conviction of Communist party leaders is analyzed in Michal R. Belknap, *Cold War Political Justice* (1977); the decision's impact is discussed in Joseph R. Starobin, *American Communism in Crisis, 1943–1957* (1972). On Alger Hiss, see Allen Weinstein, *The Hiss-Chambers Case* (1978); on the Rosenbergs, Walter and Miriam Schneir, *Invitation to an Inquest* (1983), and Ronald Radosh and Joyce Milton, *The Rosenberg File* (1983). Important studies of the junior Senator from Wisconsin are David Oshinsky, *A Conspiracy So Immense: The World of Joe McCarthy* (1983); Thomas Reeves, *The Life and Times of Joe McCarthy* (1982); Michael O'Brien, *McCarthy and McCarthyism in Wisconsin* (1980); Edwin R. Bayley, *Joe McCarthy and the Press* (1981); and Richard M. Fried, *Men Against McCarthy* (1974).

For foreign policy, the key reference source is R. H. Burns, ed., *Guide to American Foreign Relations Since 1700* (1983), easy to use; excellent overviews are Robert J. Donovan's two-volume biography of Truman, see especially *Tumultuous Years, 1949–1953* (1982); John Lewis Gaddis, *Strategies of Containment* (1982); Ronald Steel, *Walter Lippmann and the American Century* (1980); Gregg Herken's fine *The Winning Weapon: The Atomic Bomb in the Cold War, 1945–1950* (1982); Dean Acheson, *Present at the Creation* (1972); while Adam Ulam surveys Soviet views in *Containment and Coexistence* (1973). Two books by Ronald Radosh are important: *American Labor and U.S. Foreign Policy* (1969), and *Prophets on the Right* (1975).

On the China issue, important work includes Dorothy Borg and Waldo Heinrichs, eds., *Uncertain Years: Chinese-American Relations, 1947–1950* (1980); Nancy B. Tucker, *Patterns in the Dust, 1949–1950* (1983), good on the China Lobby; Robert M. Blum, *Drawing the Line* (1982); and William W. Stueck Jr., *The Road to Confrontation: American Policy Toward China and Korea, 1947–1950* (1981). For the Korean War, two studies are indispensable: Bruce Cumings, ed., *Child of Conflict: The Korean-American Relationship, 1943–1953* (1983); and Bruce Cumings, *The Origins of the Korean War, 1945–1947* (1981). MacArthur gives his side in his *Reminiscences* (1964). The final chapters of Ronald Pruessen's *John Foster Dulles: The Road to Power* (1982) are important for the politics as well as diplomacy.

On the Kinsey Reports, see Wardell Pomeroy, *Dr. Kinsey and the Institute for Sex Research* (1972); and Paul Robinson, *The Modernization of Sex . . . Kinsey, Masters, Johnson* (1976).

Levittown, Long Island, 1958.

# 1952–1957

## Eisenhower and the American Consensus

Dwight David Eisenhower, reared on the Kansas frontier and the plains of West Point Military Academy, became famous as the commander of Allied forces in Western Europe during World War II. In 1952, campaigning for the presidency as a spokesman for traditional American values, he offered reassurance and hope to a people soured by the trials of the Cold War. Within two years of his election, the Korean War had ended and Joseph McCarthy had fallen from power. Americans then settled down to enjoy the piping prosperity that they believed they so richly deserved. It was, one critic observed, a classic case of "the bland leading the bland." Yet appearances deceived, for beneath a placid surface society was in ferment. At home, pressures were building that later would produce the massive civil rights movement. Abroad, the United States approached the Suez crisis of 1956, the turning point of the Cold War. Not even the smiling, waving golfer in the White House was always what he seemed. Widely perceived as passive and even deferential, Eisenhower, behind the scenes, employed presidential power in an energetic and assertive fashion.

## THE SUBURBAN SOCIETY

The most distinctive demographic development in the United States at mid-century was the expansion of the suburbs. During the 1950s, the population of "standard metropolitan statistical areas"—defined by the Census Bureau as places containing a city with at least fifty thousand inhabitants—jumped from 95 to 120 million. That growth took place primarily in the suburbs. Central cities grew by 11 percent, from 54 to 60 million, while suburbs grew by 46 percent from 41 to 60 million. Much of the urban growth in the South and West, however, occurred through the extension of cities' boundaries to incorporate suburban tracts instead of through an increase in the existing population. In the North and Midwest this kind of expansion was uncommon. From 1950 to 1960, fourteen of the fifteen largest cities in the nation experienced a population decline even as their suburbs underwent a population explosion: New York City's suburbs grew by 58 percent, Chicago's by 101 percent, Detroit's by 131 percent, and Cleveland's by 94 percent.

Suburban development depended, in the first instance, on the expansion of the automobile industry and the construction of new highways. The postwar years were boom years for American car manufacturers. Passenger car output rocketed from 2 million in 1946 to 8 million in 1955, and registrations jumped from 25 million in 1945 to 51 million in 1955. For nearly all suburbanites, the automobile was a necessity; indeed, by 1960, nearly one-fifth of suburban families owned two cars. At the same time, states and municipalities built or improved many thousands of miles of new roads. The federal government made an essential contribution. The Interstate Highway Act of 1956 provided for the construction of 41,000 miles of express highways at a cost of more than $100 billion. The new roads made it easier to commute and made it more feasible to commute over much longer distances.

The government aided suburban growth in other ways as well. The Veterans Administration offered to insure the mortgages of former servicemen on highly advantageous terms. More than 3.75 million veterans bought homes under VA programs that, typically, required only a token down payment and provided long-term, low-interest mortgages. The Federal Housing Administration also insured millions of mortgages, giving preference, in all instances, to buyers of single-family, detached dwellings. Those who wanted to buy a home in the suburbs could therefore count on a much more favorable response from federal agencies than those who wished to purchase an older home. Insuring mortgages in the central cities, the VA and FHA believed, represented a much higher risk, and a risk not worth taking. Government programs tipped the balance in favor of middle-income buyers, those looking at homes in the $7,000 to $10,000 range, and those seeking a suburban location.

The burgeoning suburbs began to lure commerce and industry from the cities. The trend toward plant relocation meant that employment in trade and manufacturing declined in the nation's largest cities and rose dramatically in the suburbs. The appearance of giant shopping centers also heralded the economic transformation of suburbia. At the end of World War II there were only 8 shopping centers; by 1960 the number had risen to 3840. In a three-month period in 1957, no fewer than 17 regional shopping centers opened for business, leading one observer to note that "at times it seemed they must be coming off a hidden assembly line."

The migration from cities to suburbs was predominantly a migration of whites; black Americans characteristically moved from farms to cities. In the decade of the 1950s, the twelve largest central cities lost 3.6 million whites and gained 4.5 million nonwhites. By 1960 more than half the black population, but only one-third of the white, resided in central cities. In the suburbs, however, whites outnumbered blacks by a ratio of more than 35 to 1. The number of blacks residing in the suburbs did increase, from 1 million in 1950 to 1.7 million in 1960, but most of that increase occurred in older, all-black communities. Few blacks bought homes in the new, postwar suburban tracts. Either they could not afford to do so or they were excluded by real estate brokers who would not show them homes, bank officers who would not grant them mortgages, or suburban zoning ordinances that artificially boosted home construction costs in order to restrict entry.

The word *suburbia* brought to mind images of small children, and with good reason. The 1950s saw an unusually high marriage rate and a truly extraordinary increase in the birth rate. The postwar "baby boom" crested in 1957, when the fertility rate reached the highest level since the government first began to compile statistics in 1917. At the rate prevailing in 1957, a group of one thousand women could be expected to give birth to 3767 children. At the same time, improvements in medical care led to a steady increase in life expectancy. In 1954, for the first time in American history, life expectancy for white men and women reached 70 years. (Black men and women could expect to live an average of 64 years.) The rapid increase in the over-65 age bracket led one enterprising publisher to market a magazine designed exclusively for those preparing to retire. During the 1950s the population of the United States increased from 152.3 to 180.6 million. That represented an annual growth of 1.7 percent, the highest rate of change in four decades. Far from worrying about scarcity or overpopulation, most Americans confidently assumed that growth would trigger further economic expansion. As one business periodical happily proclaimed: "More People: It Means New Trade, Good Times."

## DOMESTIC IDEALS IN POSTWAR AMERICA

"No job is more exacting, more necessary, or more rewarding than that of housewife and mother," journalist Agnes Meyer wrote in the *Atlantic* in 1950, and the decade that followed seemed to support her claim. Affluence and suburbanization shaped the aspirations of postwar women. When pollsters George Gallup and Evan Hill surveyed the views of "The American Woman" for the *Saturday Evening Post* in 1962, they had reason to conclude, after 2,300 interviews, that "few people are as happy as a housewife." Indeed, 96 percent of the women surveyed declared themselves extremely happy or very happy, though most wished that their daughters would marry later and get more education. "The suburban housewife was the dream image of the young American woman," Betty Friedan would write in 1963. As wife, mother, homemaker and consumer, "she had found true feminine fulfillment."

The domestic ideals that flourished in the 1950s were part of a larger phenomenon, a surge of postwar upward mobility, and part of the prevalent national mood, a turning away from public affairs toward private goals and family life. "Togetherness," a *McCall's* slogan of 1954, meant early marriages, large families, and "sharing a common experience." The accompanying article described a young suburban couple who "centered their lives almost completely around their children and their home," while the father served as "a link with the outside world." The homemaker's role, though more limited, was imbued in the press with higher purpose. Her presence in the household provided security for other family members in a changing world that seemed increasingly full of unstable if not threatening elements. "Two World Wars and a depression have uprooted family life and created a nationwide turmoil," Meyer told her *Atlantic* readers. "The mounting divorce rate, the appalling number of youthful crimes, the deliberate neglect of children in many homes, and the looseness of sexual morality among young and old—these are only some of the inescapable signs of a decaying moral structure in areas for which women have a prime responsibility."

When questioned about their aspirations in moving to the suburbs, women in New Jersey's Levittown cited more personal, material goals—privacy, freedom, comfort, roominess, quality of life, and a chance to enjoy a "normal family role, being a homemaker." They also looked forward to "furnishing and decorating the home." If women's roles as consumers increased in the postwar decade, this was hardly a surprise after the deprivations of the 1930s and the scarcities of the war years. During the 1950s, the median family income almost doubled. Stores were now full of electrical appliances that had been unavailable during the war, from electric mixers to dishwashers, and a gamut of new products from aluminum foil to room deodorants. Postwar consumerism was abetted by an eightfold expansion of consumer credit and by advertisers' ingenuity in tapping the growing household market, where women made three out of four family purchases. "It's nice to be modern," a young housewife told a postwar survey of women's attitudes towards electric appliances. "It's like running a factory in which you have the latest machinery." Advertisers stressed the psychological dimensions of purchasing. "Just as producing once served as an outlet for social tension," reported a 1957 study of consumer motivation, "now consumption serves the same purpose."

While higher incomes provided a dramatic rise in living standards, the baby boom evoked new interest in child rearing. This paved the way for the extraordinary success of Dr. Benjamin Spock's *Baby and Child Care* (1946). No child-rearing manual had ever been published at so propitious a time or geared to such a boom market. During the late 1940s and 1950s, Dr. Spock's book sold over a million copies a year. Though widespread in appeal, his message was directed toward the new suburban family, where each child could be expected to have its own room, and where mothers could be expected to devote full time to answering their children's needs. Parents seemed to appreciate Dr. Spock's upbeat tone and down-to-earth manner. "You make me feel as if I were a sensible person," one mother wrote. Most of the voluminous correspondence Dr. Spock received also managed to recreate his cheerful tone, even when children refused to eat vegetables or speak in sentences, or got caught in pieces of household machinery. But parents were often unable to meet the demands of "permissive" child rearing. Some letters were from physicians with practices too busy to pay attention to their own children, from parents who accused

Homemakers shopping for household appliances, 1956.

Refreshments being served to YMCA father-son group, 1956.

themselves of "selfishness," from couples who found child care "an unbearable drain," and from guilt-ridden mothers who reproached themselves. "I know that a lot of my problem is personal," one mother wrote.

Although early marriage, "togetherness," and child rearing appeared to be the dominant themes of women's lives in the 1950s, the decade also witnessed other developments. One was the massive expansion of higher education that followed World War II. Between 1940 and 1960, the percentage of college-age Americans that went to college more than doubled. The proportion of women attending college fell during the late 1940s, when the GI bill sent millions of veterans back to school, but the educational gender gap was only temporary; during the 1950s, women began to catch up in percentages. Going to college, now a middle-class perquisite, seemed to have no noticeable impact on the domestic goals of most women college students in the postwar era. "The average college girl views her future through a wedding band," the *New York Times* reported. But colleges remained relative enclaves of equality, and they also prepared thousands of alumna for eventual entry into the labor market.

The decade of domesticity, paradoxically, was one in which the contemporary female work force took shape. Between 1940 and 1960, the number of women in the work force doubled. By 1952, 2 million more women were at work than during World War II. The postwar woman worker, moreover, was likely to be married, middle class, and middle aged; during the 1950s, women from middle-class families entered the labor market at a higher rate than any other segment of the population. Since second incomes were now needed to maintain middle-class family status in an inflationary economy, wives, not older children, became the major supplementary wage earners. The needs of the labor market also changed. Economic expansion increased the demand for low-paid, qualified workers in service jobs, sales jobs, and especially office jobs. Elementary school teachers were needed to accommodate the baby boom population. The pool of young, single women, usually the mainstay of the female labor force, had diminished, due to low birth rates in the 1920s and 1930s. Postwar employers therefore turned to the older, married white collar worker. By the early 1960s, one worker in three was a woman, one out of three married women worked, and three out of five women workers were married. Significantly, during the 1950s, women's numbers rose over 40 percent in many occupations, from professional work to clerical work. Equally significant, as a government commission concluded, "Most jobs that women hold are in the low-paid category." Postwar women provided an inexpensive and available new labor pool.

The contradictions between domestic ideals and women's new roles in the labor force would not emerge until the mid-1960s. During the postwar years, most Americans, women included, were relieved to be done with the war and out of the depression, and looked forward to enjoying the benefits of the 1950s—security, prosperity, and unprecedented social mobility.

## THE MOOD OF THE FIFTIES

During the 1950s, many social critics diagnosed American society as suffering from a terminal case of conformity. The suburbs, they claimed, best illustrated the symptoms. In *The Organization Man* (1956), William F. Whyte described an emerging group of Americans, primarily middle-class junior executives, who accepted "a belief in 'belongingness' as the ultimate need of the individual." Organization men and women, Whyte reasoned, found their natural habitat in the new suburbia, with its emphasis on participation in community affairs, sociability for its own sake, and conformity to group values. To residents of Park Forest, Illinois, for example, the lack of privacy was itself a virtue. "I never feel lonely, even when Jim's away," beamed one young woman. "You know friends are near by, because at night you hear the neighbors through the walls." Suburban public schools stressed life adjustment and relied on peer-group disapproval to maintain discipline. "The teacher strives not to discipline the child directly but to influence all the children's attitudes so that as a group they recognize correct behavior."

Whyte concluded that the organization man "is not only other-directed" but "is articulating a philosophy which tells him it is the right way to be." David Riesman had first discussed the concept of "other-direction" in *The Lonely Crowd* (1950), one of the most influential books ever written by an American sociologist. Riesman argued that Americans were in the process of moving from an inner-directed to an other-directed society, one in which the peer group replaced parents as the dominant source of authority and in which those who failed to conform experienced anxiety rather than guilt. If the typical nineteenth-century American had a system of values implanted early in life which thereafter acted as a psychological gyroscope, then twentieth-century Americans had built-in radar systems tuned to the sounds around them. Riesman detected the emergence of this other-directed personality chiefly "in the upper middle class of our larger cities." The children's story *Tootle* epitomized the new view. Tootle was a little engine who was taught to "always stay on the track no matter what" and who, when he strayed off the track to frolic in the fields, was pressured into returning. "The children who read Tootle," Riesman said, "are manipulated away from rebellion and taught the lesson of obedience to signals."

As sociologists found evidence of conformity in the American present, historians discovered evidence of consensus in the nation's past. Many historians in the 1950s minimized conflict and emphasized continuity. David Potter's *People of Plenty* (1954) held that material abundance—the product of "human ingenuity, human initiative, human adaptability, and human enterprise"—had shaped American character. Potter admitted the existence of some inequality (although the word *poverty* did not appear in his index) but noted that social inequality violated the nation's most cherished ideals. He concluded that "in every aspect of material plenty America possesses unprecedented riches and . . . these are very widely distributed."

Unprecedented affluence and the broad acceptance of middle-class liberal values meant that American society had escaped the bitter class antagonism that had plagued Europe, or so argued Louis Hartz in *The Liberal Tradition in America* (1955). Daniel Boorstin asserted that Americans had always shown a lack of interest in ideology. They had been concerned, rather, with finding practical solutions to everyday problems. That, to Boorstin, constituted "the genius of American politics." In the view of these historians, the American past was as free of doctrinal clashes as of widespread suffering or sharp class rivalry.

Boorstin believed that this historical tradition fitted Americans "to understand the meaning of conservatism." During the 1950s a group of self-styled "new conservatives" attempted to clarify that meaning. They reiterated the importance of religion, tradition, hierarchy, property rights, and the organic conception of society. The conservatives pointed to their own "sense of human limitation and frailty, as opposed to the megalomaniac faith in limitless progress through mass-movements and material reforms." They continued in varying degrees to oppose the expansion of the welfare state, which they thought rested on the dangerous premise that "justice is identical with equality." If anything identified the new conservatives it was their assault on "relativism," that is, on the unwillingness of society to uphold correct moral values and stamp out evil ones. This idea was carried furthest, perhaps, in William F. Buckley's *God and Man at Yale* (1951). Buckley, then a recent Yale graduate, condemned the university for hiring professors who caused students to doubt Christianity and the virtues of free enterprise. Buckley claimed that a private university had the duty to inculcate the values held by its financial backers. Professors who did not wish to teach those values, of course, had the right to seek employment elsewhere. The book went through five printings in the first six months of publication.

## REPUBLICANS ON THE POTOMAC

In Dwight Eisenhower the American people found a figure who perfectly suited their mood. In the 1952 campaign Eisenhower exploited the issues identified by the formula "$K_1C_2$"—Korea, communism, and corruption. Of the three, Korea was the most critical. By the fall of 1952 slightly more than half the electorate regarded the war—or, more accurately, how it might be ended—as the single most important issue. Democratic candidate Adlai E. Stevenson of Illinois fully endorsed Truman's war policies, even suggesting that the nation brace itself for years of additional sacrifice. "The ordeal of the twentieth century is far from over," Stevenson said in accepting the nomination. Eisenhower, who also had backed the decision to wage a limited war in Korea, nevertheless seemed to offer a way out of the quagmire. Two weeks before the election he said, "I shall go to Korea," and though he did not say what he would do when he got there, his pledge, coming from a man identified with victory in World War II, was a masterful stroke. Popularly regarded as the candidate best able to end the war, Eisenhower was politically irresistible. It was appropriate that the last word of his last campaign address was "peace."

The two other issues also worked to Eisenhower's benefit. Republican charges that the Truman administration was infested with Communists and that Stevenson was himself dangerously "soft" came not only from Joseph McCarthy but also from Eisenhower's running mate. Richard Nixon spoke of "Adlai the Appeaser," who lacked "backbone training" because he was a "Ph.D. graduate of Dean Acheson's cowardly college of Communist containment." Stevenson was vulnerable because he had once given a deposition attesting to Alger Hiss's good reputation. As Governor of Illinois, moreover, he had courageously vetoed a bill requiring loyalty oaths of all state employees.

The issue of corruption hammered a last nail into the Democrats' coffin. In its last years the Truman administration was plagued by scandals, many of them involving money-making schemes or influence peddling by the President's cronies. Promising to "drive the crooks and the Communists from their seats of power," Eisenhower embarked on a moral crusade for decent government. Electing a Democrat to replace Truman, an Indiana Republican suggested, would be equivalent to "putting a new pin on a soiled diaper." On the eve of the inauguration one supporter told Eisenhower that "for the first time in many years the country feels clean again."

What was striking about the election was not so much the magnitude of Eisenhower's victory—he received 55 percent of the vote and carried thirty-nine states—as the high level of voter interest. In 1948 only 51.5 percent of those eligible had voted, but in 1952 the turnout was 62.7 percent. Eisenhower broke through traditional Democratic strongholds, winning nearly half the popular vote in the South (doing particularly well in the cities) and carrying Virginia, Florida, Texas, and Tennessee. Stevenson's reluctance to campaign on the old New Deal slogans and Eisenhower's reputation as a liberal Republican combined to mute economic issues. The Republicans, therefore, did better than they had expected in working-class wards. Whether as a result of his promise to end the war, his crusade for clean government, or his reputation as a family man (in contrast to the divorced Stevenson), Eisenhower was even more popular among women (58.5 percent) than men (52.5 percent). Most significant of all was his showing among the middle class in the burgeoning suburbs. Stevenson captured New York City, Chicago, Cleveland, and Boston, but in each case Eisenhower won the surrounding suburbs by even larger pluralities, thereby offsetting the Democrats' advantage. These expanding areas also had exceedingly high turnout rates.

Critics of Eisenhower interpreted the 1952 election as a popularity contest involving no real issues beyond Ike's famous grin and twinkling blue eyes. They were mistaken. So, too, were those who saw him as a babe in the woods who did not understand politics or the use of power. If Eisenhower seemed to remain above political battles it was because he recognized that his reputation for nonpartisanship was an important political asset. As one advisor explained to him, "The people want another George Washington. They really think of you as a modern George Washington." If Eisenhower urged his program on congressional Republicans cautiously, it was because he knew that his party was torn between a liberal and conservative wing. He wanted to heal rather than widen the rift. If Eisenhower adopted a more restrained view of presidential authority than his Democratic predecessors, it was because of his belief in the separation of powers and his distaste for emotionally charged disputes. None of this, however, prevented him from manipulating his powers to influence legislation or from using patronage to reward loyal followers. He also fashioned an orderly administrative system based on a clear chain of command.

To staff his Cabinet, Eisenhower relied primarily on successful businessmen, many of whom had some political experience. Secretary of the Treasury George M. Humphrey, a staunch fiscal conservative, had headed a successful steel company in Ohio. Three other Cabinet members—Secretary of the Interior Douglas McKay, Postmaster General Arthur Summerfield, and Secretary of Defense Charles E. Wilson—had made their fortunes in the automobile industry, giving some point to Adlai Stevenson's quip that the New Dealers were making way for the car dealers. Wilson, who had served as president of General Motors since 1940, once explained his reluctance to use defense contracts for the purpose of reducing unemployment in words that few workers appreciated: "I've always liked bird dogs better than kennel dogs myself. You know, one who will get out and hunt for food rather than sit on his fanny and yell." The rhetoric of the automobile industry even crept into Cabinet discussions. On one occasion, explaining why large cuts in defense spending were necessary, Humphrey said to Wilson: "Charley, . . . you just got to get out the best damn *streamlined model* you ever did in your life. . . . This means a *brand new model*—we can't just patch up the old jalopy."

These appointments fairly reflected Eisenhower's own outlook. The new President was determined to reverse the direction taken by the New

Deal and Fair Deal, or, in his words, to remove "the Left-Wingish, pinkish influence in our life." Referring to the Tennessee Valley Authority, which symbolized such intervention in the economy, Eisenhower once blurted out: "By God, if ever we could do it, before we leave here, I'd like to see us *sell* the whole thing, but I suppose we can't go that far." The President demonstrated his economic orthodoxy by removing the moderate wage and price controls Truman had instituted, and by closing down many small federally operated establishments that appeared to compete with private business. In addition, Eisenhower cut the government payroll by two hundred thousand workers and trimmed federal spending by 10 per-cent—or $6 billion—in his first year. In 1954 Congress enacted an admin-istration measure lowering price supports for farm products.

His position on natural resource development clearly revealed Eisen-hower's desire to limit federal involvement. The President consistently favored private rather than public development of hydroelectric power plants. He reversed Truman's decision to proceed with federal construc-tion of such a plant in Hell's Canyon, Idaho, licensed a private firm to build the dams, and threatened to veto any legislation looking toward federal development. Eisenhower opposed the Tennessee Valley Authori-ty's request to build a new plant to furnish power for the Atomic Energy Commission. The AEC instead awarded the contract to a private concern known as Dixon-Yates. When a 1955 congressional investigation revealed that the consultant who advised the AEC to accept this arrangement was connected with an investment firm that marketed Dixon-Yates securities, a scandal erupted and Eisenhower had to cancel the contract. Finally, the President favored granting the states control of offshore oil deposits within their historic boundaries (usually a distance of three miles). Truman had twice vetoed such legislation on the grounds that tidelands oil belonged to the federal government. In May 1953, much to the delight of Texas, California, and Louisiana, Eisenhower signed the Submerged Lands Act, turning these rights over to the states.

But despite Eisenhower's inclination, he in fact presided over a further enlargement of the welfare state. The social security system was expanded to include more workers, to increase benefits, and to lower the age of eligibility for old-age pensions. In 1954 an additional 4 million workers were brought under the unemployment insurance program. In 1955 Con-gress raised the minimum wage from 75 cents to $1.00 an hour (although Eisenhower had favored a 90-cent limit). The administration supported, unsuccessfully, a modest program to provide $200 million over three years to assist school construction in impoverished districts. The President also won authorization for building an additional 35,000 public housing units. Finally, the Interstate Highway Act (1956) provided for the construction of a modern interstate highway system. In urging its enactment, Eisen-hower pointed out that new roads could reduce traffic accidents, relieve the massive congestion sure to develop as automobile use increased, and provide for quick evacuation "in case of an atomic attack on our key cities."

In expanding government benefits the Eisenhower administration was responding, in part, to congressional pressure. Although the Republicans won a slim victory in Congress in 1952 (they controlled the Senate by one vote and the House by ten), the Democrats recaptured control of both houses in 1954 and retained it throughout the remainder of Eisenhower's presidency. The administration was also taking account of economic realities. Sharp recessions in 1954 and 1958 led the President to abandon his budget-balancing efforts and to accelerate spending. The government therefore ran a deficit in five of his eight years in office. The people had not elected Eisenhower to dismantle the welfare state, the President's brother observed. Conveying the results of a public-opinion poll, Milton Eisenhower said: "Please note the 'new conservatism' really means that we should keep what we have, catch our breath for a while, and improve administration; it does not mean moving backward." In the main, that was the prescription the Eisenhower administration followed.

## THE WANING OF McCARTHYISM

The President was as determined to step up the campaign against internal subversion as he was to curb the expansion of the welfare state. Eisenhower succeeded in toughening the government loyalty program. He turned responsibility for loyalty investigations over to departmental security officers who evaluated all employees and submitted reports to each department head for action. The administration also introduced stricter standards for measuring loyalty. The old criteria—reasonable grounds for believing an employee disloyal (1947) or reasonable doubt as to an employee's loyalty (1951)—no longer sufficed. As of 1953 the government would dismiss any "security risk," which meant that it would seek information concerning "any behavior, activities, or associations which tend to show that the individual is not reliable or trustworthy." Partly to appease right-wing Republicans, the State Department appointed an ardent McCarthyite, Scott McLeod, as security officer. Within a year, McLeod had ousted 484 persons, including several career officials whose only crime had been to tell the truth about the relative strength of the Communist and nationalist forces in China. Even Joe McCarthy seemed satisfied, commenting that the new loyalty program was "pretty darn good, if the administration is sincere."

Perhaps the most famous alleged "security risk" was Dr. J. Robert Oppenheimer, who had headed the project to develop the atomic bomb during World War II. A man of profound intellect who exerted a charismatic hold on his fellow physicists, Oppenheimer had associated with left-wing causes and individuals during the late 1930s. The government

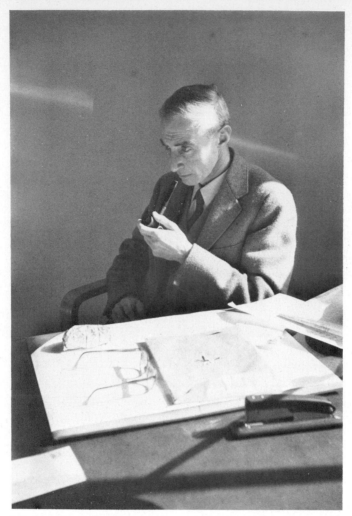

J. Robert Oppenheimer.

compiled a massive dossier on him during the war but knew him to be loyal, considered him indispensable, and regarded his activities as merely indiscreet. Disturbed by the nuclear arms race, Oppenheimer unsuccessfully opposed the decision to proceed with a hydrogen bomb in 1949. By 1953 he was head of Princeton's Institute for Advanced Study, retaining only a consultant's contract with the Atomic Energy Commission. When his old dossier was dragged out, Eisenhower directed that a "blank wall" be erected between Oppenheimer and sensitive material. When Oppenheimer refused to resign his contract, a hearing was held in the spring of 1954 that deteriorated into a judicial farce. A special panel found, by a vote of 2 to 1, that reinstating Oppenheimer's clearance would be inconsistent with national security. The AEC upheld the ruling because Oppenheimer's association with radicals had exceeded the "tolerable limits of prudence and self-restraint," because his attitude toward the hydrogen bomb was "disturbing," and because of fundamental defects in his "character." Nine years later the government implicitly conceded the injustice by presenting the Fermi Award for distinguished contributions to American science to Oppenheimer at a White House ceremony.

Congress, too, joined the continuing hunt for domestic radicals in 1954. When a conservative Republican endeavored to amend the Internal Security Act (1950) by requiring Communist-infiltrated (as well as Communist and Communist-dominated) organizations to register with the Attorney General, a liberal Democrat offered a counter proposal: that the Communist party itself be defined as an "agency of a hostile foreign power" and stripped of the privileges political groups usually enjoyed. Hubert Humphrey of Minnesota, who proposed the change, declared: "I do not intend to be a half-patriot." In the end, the Communist Control Act (1954) incorporated both provisions, and it passed the Senate with but one dissenting vote. The act asserted that the Communist party was "an instrumentality of a conspiracy to overthrow the Government" and declared that its existence constituted a "clear, present and continuing danger." The measure was seldom invoked, although it once served to deny a Communist candidate a place on the ballot in a New Jersey election.

The new security program, the Oppenheimer case, and the mood in Congress all revealed the persistence of anticommunism. But by 1954 the worst of the hysteria was beginning to fade, and with it ebbed the power of Joseph McCarthy. Eisenhower, who strongly disapproved of McCarthy's tactics, had been reluctant to challenge the junior Senator from Wisconsin. Campaigning in Wisconsin in 1952, Eisenhower had agreed not to make a speech defending General George Marshall, whom he admired greatly, on the grounds that to do so would alienate McCarthy's followers and hurt the Republican ticket. As one worried politician informed an Eisenhower aide, "When a man calls on the Pope, he doesn't tell him what a fine fellow Martin Luther was." After the election Eisenhower refused to criticize McCarthy publicly. Privately he said he would not "get into the gutter with that guy," although he confessed that "at times one feels almost like hanging his head in shame when he reads some of the unreasoned, vicious outbursts of demagoguery that appear in our public prints." Then, in 1954, McCarthy crossed swords with two institutions—the Army and the Senate—and they proved too powerful for him.

The Army seemed a most unlikely target, but McCarthy accused it of promoting and giving an honorable discharge to a dentist who, in filling out loyalty forms, had refused to answer questions about his political affiliations. McCarthy criticized the man responsible, General Ralph Zwicker, as not having "the brains of a five-year-old." The Senator warned

Secretary of the Army Robert Stevens: "I am going to kick the brains out of anyone who protects Communists!" The Army retorted that McCarthy had tried to pull strings to obtain preferential treatment for a recently inducted member of his staff. Stevens and McCarthy then lumbered toward a showdown that knowledgeable Republicans desperately wanted to avert. One Senator advised McCarthy: "Joe, you're not dealing with Dean Acheson any longer. Let's look to the future." But McCarthy would not be swayed. Congressional hearings into the controversy began before a nationwide television audience in April 1954 and continued for two months. Toward the end, enraged by the attempt of attorney Joseph Welch to poke fun at his allegations, McCarthy savagely attacked a lawyer employed by Welch's law firm for having once belonged to a left-wing organization. Welch then berated McCarthy, concluding, "Have you no sense of decency, sir, at long last? Have you left no sense of decency?" That the congressional committee found some of the Army's allegations well founded was less important than that many Americans, offended by McCarthy's tactics, had begun to ask the same question.

By hurling wild accusations, McCarthy managed to alienate almost all Senate Democrats and a considerable number of Republicans. "The hard fact is that those who wear the label—Democrat—wear with it the stain of an historic betrayal," he thundered in 1954. McCarthy called Democrat J. William Fulbright "halfbright" and termed Republican Senator Ralph Flanders "senile. I think they should get a man with a net and take him to a good quiet place." In June 1954 Flanders introduced a motion to censure McCarthy. It was referred to a special committee that in September recommended censure on two counts: showing contempt for the Senate by refusing to testify before a subcommittee investigating the use of campaign funds in 1952, and abusing General Zwicker. In December, with the midterm elections safely past, the Senate censured McCarthy on the first count only. The vote was 67 to 22, with Democrats voting unanimously for censure and Republicans dividing evenly. Terming the action a "lynch party," McCarthy apologized to the people for having supported Eisenhower two years earlier. McCarthy retained his committee assignments but suffered a great loss of prestige. His popularity continued to diminish until his death three years later.

Eisenhower made his most significant contribution to civil liberties through his Supreme Court appointments. His choice of Earl Warren to replace Fred Vinson as Chief Justice in September 1953 was especially important. In 1956 Warren delivered an opinion in which the Court ruled that the federal Smith Act preempted the field of sedition, thereby rendering state sedition laws invalid. The Court upheld a lower-court decision that overturned the conviction of a Communist sentenced to twenty years in prison for having violated a Pennsylvania ordinance. A year later the Court dealt a crippling blow to the Smith Act in *Yates* v. *U.S.* (1957). John Marshall Harlan, another Eisenhower appointee, ruled for the majority that the Smith Act's injunction against conspiring to advocate the forcible overthrow of the government applied to the advocacy of concrete actions but not abstract principles. If one did not call for direct revolutionary acts, one could lawfully urge the overthrow of the government. The *Yates* decision rendered further prosecutions under the Smith Act all but impossible.

# DESEGREGATION AND THE SOUTH

If the Supreme Court took a leading role in defending civil liberties, it came close to revolutionizing patterns of race relations. On May 17, 1954, in *Brown* v. *Board of Education,* the Court unanimously overturned the "separate but equal" doctrine. That doctrine, first elaborated in *Plessy* v. *Ferguson* (1896), had allowed states to provide segregated facilities as long as they were of the same quality. It provided the legal foundation for the intricate Jim Crow system in the South, which included everything from separate schools, hospitals, and railroad cars, to separate football fields, drinking fountains, and restrooms. By 1950, the Court had supported the right of blacks to attend white universities or law schools, but on the grounds that those facilities could not be duplicated. In the *Brown* decision, however, the Court met the issue squarely, holding that separate public schools were inherently unequal and therefore unconstitutional. Unanimity was possible only because of the influence of Chief Justice Earl Warren. One member of the Court admitted that had the decision come a year earlier, four justices would have dissented and the majority would have written separate opinions. That, he believed, "would have been catastrophic," for only a unanimous decision stood much chance of winning public approval.

To achieve unanimity, however, Warren avoided claiming that the framers of the Fourteenth Amendment had intended to bar segregated schools, for the evidence was at best "inconclusive." Instead, the Court relied on the work of sociologists and psychologists. Even though the buildings might be of similar quality, Warren asserted, racially segregated schools had a harmful effect on black children by creating "a feeling of inferiority as to their status in the community that may affect their hearts and minds in a way unlikely ever to be undone." In asserting that this conclusion was "amply supported by modern authority," the Court relied largely on studies that indicated black children often placed a higher value on white skin color than on black, thereby revealing what one psychologist termed "basic feelings of inferiority, conflict, confusion in the self-image, resentment, hostility toward himself, hostility toward whites." The Court's reliance on evidence of this kind led such critics as Senator Sam J. Ervin of North Carolina to claim that the justices had "substituted their personal political and social ideas for the established law of the land."

Recognizing that its decision required a monumental change in Southern life and was sure to provoke intense opposition, the Supreme Court decided to allow ample time for implementation. In May 1955, in a second school decision, it asked local federal courts to determine the pace of desegregation. Insisting only that a "prompt and reasonable start" be made and that desegregation proceed "with all deliberate speed," the Court acknowledged that it would take time to iron out problems relating to administration, school size, transportation, and personnel. A "declaration of unconstitutionality is not a wand by which these transformations can be accomplished," one justice noted privately. "Not even a Court can in a day change a deplorable situation into the ideal. It does its duty if it gets effectively under way the righting of a wrong." The Court, fearing that the inability to enforce a decision would discredit the judicial process, was as committed to gradualism as to integration.

Public-opinion polls indicated that most white Southerners—perhaps more than 80 percent—opposed the *Brown* ruling. In March 1956, 101 of the 128 Southern senators and congressmen echoed this sentiment by signing a "Southern manifesto," which blasted the Supreme Court. This much the Court may have anticipated, but no one was prepared for the wave of massive resistance that followed. In states of the deep South, "White Citizens' Councils" were formed that applied economic pressure on blacks (and white businessmen) who were known to favor integration. In addition, measures of "interposition" were adopted whereby the states placed their authority behind local schoolboard officials who defied federal court orders. Various states hounded the NAACP by demanding its membership lists, using such membership as a basis for dismissal from state employment, and making it a crime to incite a disturbance by attacking local segregation ordinances. In some cases, rock-throwing mobs prevented black children from attending class with whites.

Of all the techniques of evasion and defiance, none were more effective than the pupil placement laws. Enacted in many states after 1954, these laws provided for the assignment of students on an individual basis. The criteria established by Georgia were typical. They permitted school boards to consider "the psychological qualification of the pupil for the type of teaching and associations involved," "the psychological effect upon the pupil of attendance at a particular school," "the ability to accept or conform to new and different educational environments," "the morals, conduct, health, and personal standards of the pupil," and "mental energy and ability." The result was that black and white children were invariably assigned to different schools. In 1958 the Supreme Court accepted the constitutionality of such laws. Consequently, ten years after the *Brown* ruling, the vast majority of black children in the South still attended segregated schools.

Nevertheless, the forces unleashed by the Supreme Court helped inspire Southern blacks to adopt a more militant posture. In December 1955 blacks in Montgomery, Alabama began a boycott of city buses to protest

Jim Crow seating practices which required blacks to vacate seats and move to the rear to make room for whites who had boarded after them. The boycott began when seamstress Rosa Parks, a long-time NAACP member and well-known member of Montgomery's black community, was arrested for refusing a bus driver's request to vacate her seat for a white male passenger. The protesters demanded courteous treatment by bus drivers, employment of black drivers in black districts, and seating on a first-come, first-served basis with "Negroes seated from the back of the bus toward the front [and], whites seated from the front toward the back."

The boycott's leader was 27-year-old Martin Luther King, Jr., who, after having received a divinity degree and a doctorate in theology from Boston University, had become pastor of the Dexter Avenue Baptist Church. King considered his task that of "combining the militant and the moderate." He preached a philosophy of nonviolent resistance, declaring: "We must meet the forces of hate with the power of love; we must meet physical force with soul force." By arranging car and taxi pools and sometimes walking long distances, Montgomery's blacks made the boy-

Rosa Parks being fingerprinted, Montgomery, Alabama.

cott effective. They also adhered to King's teachings even when whites retaliated with mass arrests and intimidation. The movement finally achieved victory in May 1956, when a district court ruled segregation on the city buses illegal, and when the Supreme Court affirmed the ruling six months later. After another flurry of violence, beatings, and bombings, desegregation was carried out. In 1957 King also established the Southern Christian Leadership Conference, which served thereafter as his organizational base.

Turmoil in the South ultimately had repercussions in Washington. Eisenhower personally regretted the 1954 desegregation ruling, believing that law could not alter age-old customs overnight and that, in his words, "we can't demand perfection in these moral questions." The President also opposed federal infringement on states' rights. Yet in the District of Columbia, where the states'-rights problem did not arise, Eisenhower moved swiftly to comply with court orders. His administration ended segregation in Washington's restaurants, hotels, theaters, and public schools. Although Eisenhower approached the matter of legislation gingerly, he eventually concurred with Attorney General Herbert Brownell, who favored legislative action. In 1957 Congress passed the first civil rights act in eighty-two years, empowering the Justice Department to seek injunctions against interference with the right to vote and creating a Commission on Civil Rights to investigate such occurrences. Although clothed only with fact-finding powers, the commission viewed its chief task as "restoring the franchise to all American citizens." In its report, which demonstrated beyond any doubt that a pattern of discrimination barred blacks from voting in the South, the commission recommended the appointment of temporary federal registrars as a solution.

The Eisenhower administration faced its most explosive civil rights crisis in Little Rock, Arkansas. Desegregation of Central High School was scheduled to begin in September 1957. But many whites wished to obstruct the plan, and the state's ambitious governor, Orville Faubus, believed that supporting desegregation would mean political suicide. To avert violence when school opened, Faubus sent the National Guard to Little Rock with instructions to prevent integration. The guardsmen, bayonets at the ready, turned back nine blacks who sought admission and maintained segregation for nearly three weeks until a federal judge ordered them to desist. When Faubus removed the troops, a howling mob overwhelmed the police who tried to protect the black students. With the level of tension rising by the hour, the mayor appealed to Eisenhower, informing him that the "situation is out of control and police cannot disperse the mob." Eisenhower responded by sending federal troops to uphold the court order. The President told one unhappy southern senator that "failure to act in such a case would be tantamount to acquiescence in anarchy and the dissolution of the union." Troops patrolled the high school for months, but the controversy over desegregation convulsed the city for two more years.

## JACK KEROUAC AND THE BEAT GENERATION

Jack Kerouac's novel *On the Road* was published in 1957 and instantly became a best seller. It had taken Kerouac six years to find a publisher but that was hardly surprising since the manuscript, in its original form, violated all literary conventions. Typed as an unbroken, seldom-punctuated,

William Burroughs, Peter Orlovsky, Gregory Corso, and Allen Ginsberg.

single-spaced paragraph, on a 250-foot roll of shelf paper (the last six feet of which were rewritten when a pet cocker spaniel chewed them up), the novel appeared only after it had been heavily edited by the publisher. According to Kerouac's biographer, Ann Charters, *On the Road* "captured the spirit of his own generation, their restlessness and confusions in the years immediately following World War II." Centering on a series of cross-country automobile trips taken by Kerouac and his friends in the late 1940s, the novel popularized the life style associated with the major figures in the Beat Movement. The fictional characters—Sal Paradise, Dean Moriarty, Carlo Marx, and Old Bull Lee—had real-life counterparts in Kerouac, Neal Cassady, Allen Ginsberg, and William Burroughs.

To say, as one critic has, that *On the Road* depicted "an underground subculture that departed entirely from the dominant middle class mores of the fifties" is to understate the matter. Beat writers, rejecting socially prescribed roles and socially approved forms of behavior, exhibited more contempt than pity for the "square" world, for "the middleclass non-identity which usually finds its perfect expression . . . in rows of well-to-do houses with lawns and television sets in each living room with everybody looking at the same thing and thinking the same thing at the same time." The Beats most admired those who in their view were the least tied down by obligations to career or country—the poets, the hoodlums, the junkies, the hoboes, the jazz musicians, and the blacks. Those groups, generally regarded as among the most deprived in the nation, were from the Beat perspective among the most fortunate: free to take life as it came, to act with abandon, to appreciate the intensity of each experience, to "dig everything."

Though Beat writings contained a critique of conformity, technology, and mechanization, Beat writers shared no single political outlook. Allen Ginsberg (whose poem "Howl" began "I saw the best minds of my generation destroyed by madness, starving hysterical naked/dragging themselves through the negro streets at dawn looking for an angry fix") offered a thoroughly radical indictment

Jack Kerouac, 1958.

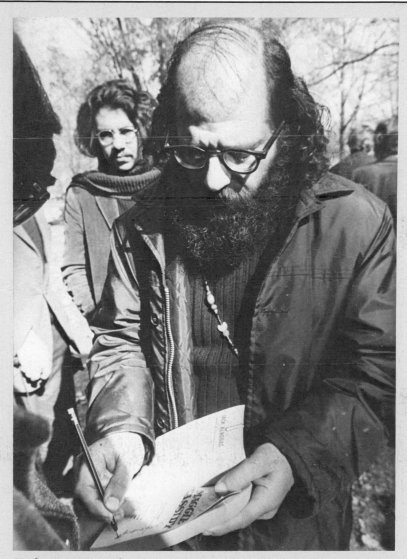

Ginsberg at Kerouac's gravesite, 1969.

of American society, its anti-Communist paranoia, and a reliance on nuclear weapons. Yet William Burroughs, the author of another Beat classic, *Naked Lunch* (1959), believed that "increased government control leads to a totalitarian state." In 1956 Kerouac declared that if he were to vote it would be for Dwight Eisenhower. The key word was *if*. What united the Beats was a conviction that politics held few answers to life's most crucial problems. Those problems required personal rather than social solutions. The characteristic Beat stance was one of political disengagement.

Beat authors received much acclaim in the 1950s (a reviewer in the *New York Times* hailed publication of *On the Road* as a "historic occasion"), but they more commonly encountered hostility. *Time* magazine, denouncing the Beats as "disorganization" men concerned only with self-gratification, labelled Ginsberg "the discount-house Whitman of the Beat Generation." Another reviewer, in a blistering assault on "the Know-Nothing Bohemians," remarked on Kerouac's "simple inability to say anything in words." The Customs Bureau seized copies of *Howl*, attempting to repress it on the grounds of obscenity. In 1957, however, a judge in San Francisco cleared the poem of those charges. William Burroughs spent years in self-imposed exile to avoid indictment for drug possession, and Neal Cassady went to jail in 1958 for marijuana possession. Kerouac, a victim of alcoholism, died at the age of 47 in 1969. He had been too ill in his final years to realize that the cultural rebellion then sweeping across the nation owed much to the Beat generation.

## ACHESON TO DULLES

As massive change began at home, so similar rumbles began to shake a world supposedly divided rigidly into only "two camps." Secretary of State John Foster Dulles had difficulty comprehending the rumbles partly because of his own unbending anti-Communist views. The deeply religious son of a Presbyterian minister, Dulles hated atheistic communism. As the senior partner of a great New York law firm, Dulles had formed ties during the interwar period with Western nations that were staunchly anti-Soviet. His diplomatic experience reached back to 1919, and this long background plus his religious beliefs led Eisenhower to remark, "To me he is like a patriarch out of the Old Testament."

Several other convictions were perhaps most important in shaping Dulles's policies. He had served under Dean Acheson, notably as the negotiator for the Japanese security treaty. As Secretary of State he carried on his predecessor's Cold War policies. If anything, Dulles believed Acheson had not been tough enough, certainly not anti-Communist enough publicly to quiet such critics as Joseph McCarthy. Dulles therefore proclaimed in 1952 that his policies would aim at "peaceful liberation" of Communist areas, not mere containment. This meant no negotiations with the Soviets. Even after Stalin's death in March 1953 and Winston Churchill's public plea for a summit conference to reduce Cold War tensions, Dulles assured Americans that he would continue to fight rather than negotiate. Churchill disgustedly remarked that Dulles was "the only bull I know who carried his china shop with him." The Secretary's belief that he had to appease McCarthy and other congressmen also resulted in a purge of Foreign Service Officers that crippled the American diplomatic corps for the next decade.

Finally, Dulles assumed that for economic and strategic reasons, the United States had to intensify Acheson's drive to integrate the "free world" within a system controlled by Americans. Dulles constantly worried that communists would gain control of such third-world areas as Southeast Asia and the Middle East, which contained rich raw materials, and thus be able slowly to strangle the United States economy.

Despite Dulles's fears, American policies were usually restrained because Eisenhower kept a firm leash on the State Department. The President once remarked, "There's only one man I know who has seen more of the world and talked with more people and knows more than [Dulles] does—and that's me." Eisenhower rejected Dulles's advice to end the Korean conflict "before all Asia . . . by giving the Chinese one hell of a licking." Instead, the President, knowing military victory impossible, obtained an armistice in mid-1953 by using a combination of diplomacy and military threat (including the deployment of atomic-tipped missiles in Korea when China and North Korea refused to make peace). Eisenhower's primary concern was to balance the budget and thereby, he believed, invigorate the economy. He cut Truman's military budget, especially the expensive ground combat forces. Informing his Cabinet that "peace rests squarely on, among other things, productivity," the President emphasized that "unless we can put things in the hands of people who are starving to death we can never lick communism." His concern heightened when in the mid-1950s Russia's economy grew at the rate of 7 percent annually while the American increased at about half that figure. Eisenhower nevertheless retained faith in the free market system, refused to inject massive governmental monies during his first term, and left office warning about the dangers of "a military-industrial complex."

Dulles's diplomacy therefore had to rely not upon conventional ground troops, but rather upon nuclear "massive retaliation," or, as he defined it, the ability "to retaliate instantly against open aggression by Red Armies . . . by means of our own choosing." Dulles and new military strategists, such as 30-year-old Henry Kissinger of Harvard, declared that atomic weapons could be refined so that they could be effectively used in conventional wars. Cheaper than troops, such weapons could give the country "more bang for a buck." Meanwhile, Dulles flew around the globe establishing new alliances with nations on the Communist borders. These countries, especially those in the Middle East (where the Central Treaty Organization, or CENTO, was formed), and in Southeast Asia (where the Southeast Asia Treaty Organization, or SEATO, developed), would, it was hoped, provide the manpower while Dulles gave atomic support if necessary. The Secretary might have proclaimed "peaceful liberation," but Eisenhower was in effect following Truman's "containment" idea.

Atomic bomb test, Yucca Flat, Nevada, 1953.

To establish these policies, Eisenhower worked effectively with Congress. Yet the new President fought back hard and successfully in 1954 when conservatives, led by Republican Senator John Bricker of Ohio, tried to pass the "Bricker Amendment" to the Constitution. This proposal gave Congress additional power over the President's constitutional right to make treaties. It especially struck at Executive agreements (those made by the President with a foreign power which would be binding only for the President's term in office, but which usually remained in effect much longer—as had Roosevelt's Executive agreements at Yalta). Eisenhower refused to compromise his power. Overcoming strong southern Democratic-Republican support for the amendment, he defeated it by a narrow margin.

## CRISES IN A THIRD CAMP: IRAN, GUATEMALA, AND SOUTHEAST ASIA

Fate tricked Eisenhower and Dulles. They were prepared to deal with Stalinist Russia, but Stalin died in March 1953. New Soviet leadership, soon headed by Nikita Khrushchev, changed some policies, concentrated on internal development, and made overtures to Tito and Mao Tse-tung— leaders whom Stalin had angered with his iron-fisted methods. Eisenhower and Dulles had also planned to concentrate on European affairs, the area they knew best. In 1954, the Secretary of State and British officials pressured France finally to agree to German rearmament and membership in NATO. The following year Dulles could claim a victory for "liberation" as Soviet troops finally left Austria after the Austrians promised they would not join any anti-Soviet alliance. Washington's European policies seemed firmly in place.

But American energies soon had to switch to the newly emerging nations. The focal point of the Cold War was changing. Dulles understood the importance of this "third camp." "To oppose nationalism is counterproductive," he declared. He worked to remove British and French colonialism from the Middle East and Asia before the foreign domination triggered further radical nationalism. But he also expected the new nations to be pro-American and anti-Communist, hence his famous remark that "neutrality . . . is an immoral and short-sighted conception." Fearing that Khrushchev's economic and ideological power might woo the Third World to the Soviets, Dulles grimly warned NATO leaders of the possible consequences: "The world ratio as between Communist dominated peoples and free peoples would change from a ratio of two-to-one in favor of freedom to a ratio of one-to-three against freedom. That," the Secretary of State emphasized, "would be an almost intolerable ratio, given the industrialized nature of the Atlantic community and its dependence upon broad markets and access to raw materials."

Within eighteen months after entering office, Eisenhower scored two triumphs in the Third World. In Iran, a nationalist government under Mohammed Mossadegh had taken over the nation's rich oil wells in 1951 from British companies that had long exploited them. Mossadegh's action set a dangerous precedent, for the Middle East held nearly 90 percent of all non-Communist oil reserves, and his success could lead to similar seizures elsewhere. In 1953 the U.S. Central Intelligence Agency worked with Iranian army officers to overthrow Mossadegh, give full powers to the friendly Shah of Iran, and restore the oil wells to the companies. But henceforth British oil firms had to share the profits with American companies.

Eisenhower performed an encore in Latin America. Since 1947 the United States had kept its southern neighbors in line by military aid, channeled through the Rio Pact of 1947 (a hemispheric military alliance that was a precursor of NATO), and the establishment of the Organization of American States in 1948. In the OAS Charter, each nation promised not to intervene in others' internal affairs, to consult frequently, and to resolve disputes peacefully. The United States, however, refused to give economic aid the Latin Americans desperately needed, particularly when their raw materials dropped steeply in price during the mid-1950s.

Guatemalan officials took matters into their own hands. In this desperately poor nation, roughly the size of Tennessee, a 1944 revolution had weakened the dictatorial rule of a few wealthy Guatemalans who had long dominated affairs. During 1953 Colonel Jacobo Arbenz Guzmán accelerated the reform, seizing vast properties held by the American-owned United Fruit Company. Dulles demanded prompt payment for the property. Guatemala was obviously unable to pay immediately. In May 1954, as U.S. threats grew more ominous, the Arbenz government received a shipment of arms from the Communist bloc. Dulles responded swiftly. In April he had obtained a general anti-Communist resolution from the OAS clearly aimed at Guatemala. Now he armed an anti-Arbenz force that had gathered in neighboring Honduras. In June 1954 this unit of Guatemalans marched into their country, overthrew Arbenz, and restored United Fruit's property. Dulles lied in publicly disclaiming any connection with the coup. He had little choice, for the United States had broken its own OAS pledge not to intervene in another nation's internal affairs. When Arbenz tried to obtain a hearing at the United Nations, Dulles blocked it. The United States had overthrown a constitutional government, and guerrilla warfare soon erupted again in Guatemala, but Eisenhower and Dulles believed that they had saved the hemisphere from communism.

The administration's next crisis was different. It occurred in Southeast Asia and required the delicate operation of removing French colonialism from Indochina (Cambodia, Laos, and Vietnam), while preventing Ho Chi Minh, who was both nationalist and communist, from obtaining power in Vietnam. Since 1950 American aid to France had multiplied until by 1953 it accounted for 80 percent of the French war budget for Indochina. France nevertheless suffered defeat after defeat at the hands of Ho's troops. In early 1954 the French made a catastrophic blunder by committing main forces to the indefensible area of Dienbienphu. Paris appealed for help. Dulles wanted to intervene, as did Vice-President Richard Nixon, and the administration even discussed the use of atomic weapons. Eisenhower's military sense stopped what could have been a tragedy. He refused to intervene with conventional forces unless congressional leaders approved and Great Britain agreed to join the effort. Neither

Dulles and Eisenhower.

would go along. The opposition of the Senate Democratic leader, Lyndon Johnson of Texas, was especially strong.

The defeated French then met with Ho's government and other interested nations at Geneva, Switzerland. Two agreements emerged in July 1954. The first, signed only by France and Ho's regime, worked out a cease-fire arrangement. To carry out this agreement, a temporary dividing line was drawn across the country at the 17th parallel. The second document, the "Final Declaration," provided for reuniting the country under procedures that were to climax with elections in 1956. It further stated that the 17th parallel line "is provisional and should in no way be interpreted as a political or territorial boundary." The United States would not directly endorse this agreement. Ho could obviously win the election (Eisenhower later estimated he would have received 80 percent of the vote), and Dulles did not want to be a party to a pact giving Vietnam to a Communist regime. Instead, Eisenhower brought in Ngo Dinh Diem to head a new South Vietnam government. Diem had been living in an American Roman Catholic seminary. Dulles and Diem readily agreed that no national elections should be held. American aid rapidly flowed to Diem, and the United States now replaced France as the key foreign power in Southeast Asia.

The American commitment was neither accidental nor abrupt. The State Department had concluded in 1951 that Indochina had to be controlled for its "much-needed rice, rubber, and tin," and because its fall "would be taken by many as a sign that the force of communism is irresistible." A secret National Security Council paper in 1952 reiterated these points, adding that the loss of Southeast Asia would "make it extremely difficult to prevent Japan's eventual accommodation to Communism." Japan, which was the centerpiece of American policies in Asia, required Southeast Asia's markets and raw materials. Eisenhower publicly warned in 1954 that if Vietnam fell, the rest of non-Communist Asia could follow like a "fallen domino."

In late 1954 Dulles tried to keep the dominoes in place by establishing the Southeast Asia Treaty Organization (SEATO). The signatories (United States, France, England, Australia, New Zealand, the Philippines, Thailand, and Pakistan) promised to "consult immediately" if aggression occurred in the area. It was a weak alliance, made weaker by India's, Indonesia's, and Burma's refusal to join, but it would provide a major pretext for the American involvement in Vietnam during the 1960s. The Senate overwhelmingly ratified the SEATO pact. Meanwhile, when Communist China threatened small islands around Formosa which it claimed were rightfully its own, Eisenhower warned that any move would be countered by the United States fleet. The President was even prepared to use nuclear weapons against China if it attacked the offshore islands. Dulles and Chiang then worked out a military alliance that assured long-term American support. To show its enthusiasm for these measures, the Senate vastly increased presidential powers by passing the "Formosa Resolution." This resolution gave Eisenhower the right to respond to crisis around Formosa without consulting Congress. To fight the Cold War more effectively, the Senate was surrendering its constitutional power to declare war.

# THE TURN: SUEZ AND HUNGARY, 1956

Centralized power had dangerous implications, particularly if it could be used irresponsibly in a world comprised not simply of "two camps," but rather of "gray areas," as the nations that disavowed both camps came to be known. The rapid emergence of such gray areas caused two momentous crises in 1956.

The first occurred early in the year when Nikita Khrushchev launched an attack against the ghost of Josef Stalin by condemning him as a

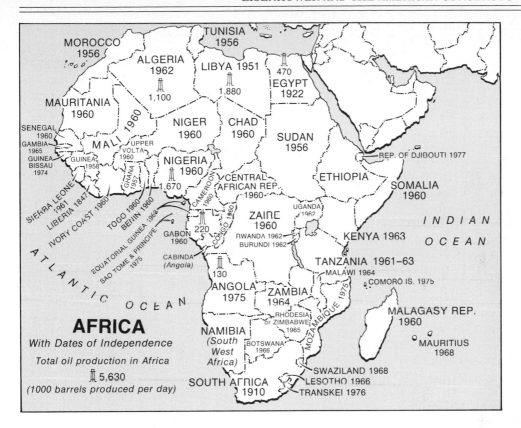

MOROCCO 1956
TUNISIA 1956
ALGERIA 1962
LIBYA 1951
470
EGYPT 1922
MAURITANIA 1960
1,100
1,880
NIGER 1960
CHAD 1960
SUDAN 1956
MALI 1960
SENEGAL 1960
GAMBIA 1965
GUINEA-BISSAU 1974
GUINEA 1958
UPPER VOLTA 1960
NIGERIA 1960
REP. OF DJIBOUTI 1977
CENTRAL AFRICAN REP. 1960
ETHIOPIA
SOMALIA 1960
SIERRA LEONE 1961
LIBERIA 1847
IVORY COAST 1960
GHANA 1957
1,670
TOGO 1960
BENIN 1960
CAMEROON 1960
UGANDA 1962
ZAIRE
KENYA 1963
INDIAN OCEAN
EQUATORIAL GUINEA 1968
SAO TOME & PRINCIPE 1975
GABON 1960
CONGO 1960
220
RWANDA 1962
BURUNDI 1962
CABINDA (Angola)
130
TANZANIA 1961–63
MALAWI 1964
COMORO IS. 1975
ANGOLA 1975
ZAMBIA 1964
MOZAMBIQUE 1975
MALAGASY REP. 1960
MAURITIUS 1968

**AFRICA**
*With Dates of Independence*

*Total oil production in Africa*
5,630
*(1000 barrels produced per day)*

NAMIBIA (South West Africa)
RHODESIA or ZIMBABWE 1965
BOTSWANA 1966
SWAZILAND 1968
LESOTHO 1966
TRANSKEI 1976
SOUTH AFRICA 1910

repressive ruler and military blunderer. Khrushchev hoped to consolidate his own power, remove Stalinists who opposed him, and gain room to carry out his own policies. The results, however, were quite different. Soviet controlled nations of Eastern Europe seized on the speech as an opportunity for throwing off Stalinist policies and seeking their own nationalistic goals. Riots occurred in Hungary and Poland as crowds demanded removal of Stalinist leaders. In early autumn, a confused Khrushchev bent to some demands, but the dissolution of the Soviet bloc continued.

Meanwhile the United States was also clashing with several of its client states. In 1952 the British had been forced by Egyptian nationalism to surrender their long hold on that country. Two years later, the government of General Abdul Nasser demanded that Britain turn over the vital Suez Canal to Egypt. Nasser's plans also included building a great Aswan dam on the Nile River to provide badly needed electric power. Dulles offered to help fund the dam, hoping that this would pull Nasser closer to the West. But Egypt then made an arms agreement with the Soviet bloc and recognized Communist China. Dulles retracted his offer, punishing Nasser before the world for dallying with the Communists. The Egyptian leader retaliated by seizing the Suez Canal in July 1956 so he could use the canal tolls to build the dam himself.

Dulles rushed across the Atlantic to work out a compromise. Before he could succeed, the British and French made a final effort in late October to restore their old imperial dreams by sending a military force into the Suez. They were joined by Israel, which hoped to improve the dangerously insecure borders it had lived with since 1948. Dulles and Eisenhower were aghast. They feared that the conflict would turn the Arabs against the West, lead to seizure of the vast Western-controlled oil resources in the area, and give Khrushchev the chance to inject Russian power into the Mediterranean theater. The United States demanded an immediate withdrawal by Anglo-French-Israeli forces and turned off large amounts of oil to England and France until they pulled back. Deserted by the Americans, the Europeans retreated, followed by the Israelis.

Khrushchev seized this opportunity to dispatch the Red Army and execution squads to end the anti-Stalinist uprisings in Hungary. Order was reimposed in Eastern Europe. The United States offered no aid to the Hungarian resistance—so ended Dulles's vaunted policy of "peaceful liberation." Russia then offered Nasser funds and experts to build the Aswan dam project. The Soviets were indeed a new presence in the Mediterranean. Equally important, Nasser had successfully defied one of the two superpowers, and the Poles, Hungarians, British, and French had vividly demonstrated that the world was no longer comprised of two monolithic camps. The second Eisenhower administration would begin in a radically altered world.

## Suggested Reading

Useful accounts of the Eisenhower administration are Herbert Parmet, *Eisenhower and the American Crusades* (1972); Peter Lyon, *Eisenhower* (1974); Charles C. Alexander, *Holding the Line: The Eisenhower Era* (1975); Douglas T. Miller and Marion Nowak, *The Fifties* (1977); Fred I. Greenstein, *The Hidden-Hand Presidency: Eisenhower as Leader* (New York, 1982); and Steven E. Ambrose's two-volume biography of *Eisenhower* (1982, 1984). On the 1952 election, consult John Bartlow Martin, *Adlai Stevenson of Illinois* (1977). An important study of Republican conservation policies is Aaron Wildavsky, *Dixon-Yates* (1962); the best account of Eisenhower and Congress is Gary Reichard, *The Reaffirmation of Republicanism* (1975).

For women's roles in the 1950s, see Betty Friedan, *The Feminine Mystique* (1963). The growth of the female labor force is described in Alice Kessler-Harris, *Out to Work: A History of Wage-Earning Women in the United States* (1982). The sociological literature on the suburbs, while uneven, is indispensable. The more valuable studies include Herbert Gans, *The Levittowners* (1967); Scott Donaldson, *The Suburban Myth* (1969); William M. Dobriner, *Class in Suburbia* (1963); Bennett M. Berger, *Working-Class Suburb* (1969); and Barry Schwartz, ed., *The Changing*

*Face of the Suburbs* (1976). Michael N. Danielson, *The Politics of Exclusion* (1976) discusses the exclusion of blacks. For conservatism, see William Newman, *The Futilitarian Society* (1961); and John P. Diggins, *Up From Communism: Conservative Odysseys in American Intellectual History* (1975).

Supreme Court decisions in the area of civil liberties are explored in Thomas Emerson, *The System of Freedom of Expression* (1970). For McCarthy's difficulties with the Army and the Senate, see Robert Griffith, *The Politics of Fear: Joseph R. McCarthy and the Senate* (1970); and Fred Cook, *The Nightmare Decade* (1971). Two fine studies of the most famous case involving science and national security are Philip Stern, *The Oppenheimer Case* (1969); and John Major, *The Oppenheimer Hearing* (1971).

For the 1954 desegregation ruling, its origins and consequences, see Richard Kluger, *Simple Justice* (1976); for a critique, see Lino A. Graglia, *Disaster by Decree* (1976). The Southern response is examined in Numan Bartley, *The Rise of Massive Resistance* (1969); and Francis M. Wilhoit, *The Politics of Massive Resistance* (1973). For Martin Luther King, Jr., and the Montgomery bus boycott, see Stephen B. Oates, *Let The Trumpet Sound: The Life of Martin Luther King, Jr.* (New York, 1982). The 1957 Civil Rights Act is examined in J. W. Anderson, *Eisenhower, Brownell, and the Congress* (1964); and Foster R. Dulles, *The Civil Rights Commission* (1968). Robert B. Burk, *The Eisenhower Administration and Black Civil Rights* (1984) is a more general account.

For further reading and research in foreign policy, one must start with R. H. Burns, ed., *Guide to American Foreign Relations Since 1700* (1983). Highly readable overviews of the era's diplomacy include Robert Divine, *Eisenhower and the Cold War* (1981); Lloyd Gardner's essay "The Perils of Liberation," in his *Covenant with Power* (1984); Alfred Grosser, *The Western Alliance: European-American Relations Since 1954* (1980); and the second volume of the Ambrose biography of Eisenhower listed above. For specific crises, the best overview of Vietnam is George Herring, *America's Longest War* (1979), and see the essays and documents in William Appleman Williams, *et al.*, *America in Vietnam* (1985); a fresh perspective on Iran is Burton I. Kaufman, *The Oil Cartel Case* (1978). See also Kaufman's *Trade and Aid, Eisenhower's Foreign Economic Policy* (1982). African policy is discussed in Madeleine Kalb, *The Congo Cables* (1982). There are several superb accounts of the Guatemalan intervention: Richard H. Immerman, *The CIA in Guatemala* (1982), which takes the story to 1961; Stephen Schlesinger and Steven Kinzer, *Bitter Fruit* (1981); and Blanche Wiessen Cook, *The Declassified Eisenhower* (1981), ranging far beyond Guatemala. For the 1956 Suez crisis, see Donald Neff, *Warriors at Suez* (1981), and the most revealing *Anthony Eden: A Biography* (1981) by David Carlton. For nuclear policy, see especially Lawrence Freedman, *The Evolution of Nuclear Strategy* (1983); and Robert Divine, *Blowing on the Wind* (1978). The shock effect of Eisenhower policies on the West and Japan is noted in Richard Barnet, *The Alliance* (1983). The Soviet view is in Nikita Khrushchev's remarkable two-volume memoir; see especially *Khrushchev Remembers* (1970).

For analyses of the Beat Generation, consult Ann Charters, *Kerouac: A Biography* (1973); and John Tytell, *Naked Angels: The Lives and Literature of the Beat Generation* (1976).

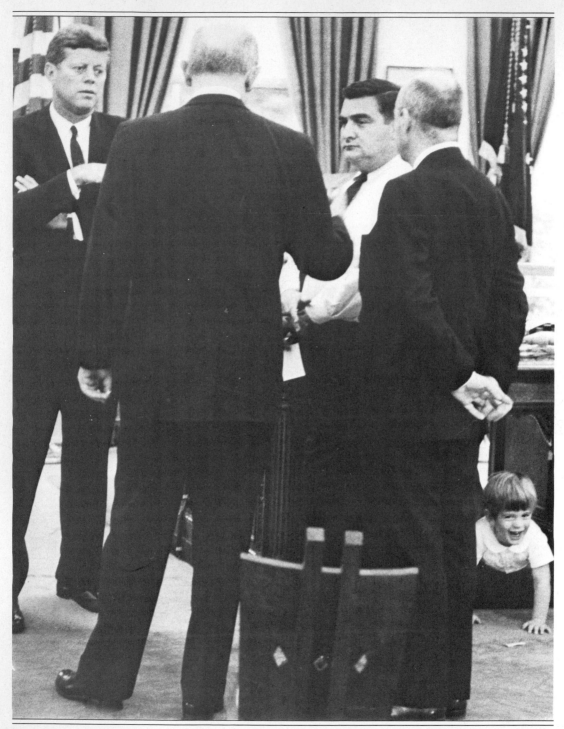

Kennedy, Pierre Salinger, and John, Jr.

# CHAPTER THIRTEEN

# 1957–1963

## New Frontiers at Home and Abroad

The Suez and Hungarian crises transformed the Cold War. They demonstrated that the two great powers no longer monopolized global affairs and especially could no longer control the newly emerging areas. Confronted with this new world, American policymakers could respond in one of two ways: either continue to focus on Europe and relationships with Russia or begin to concentrate attention on such less industrialized areas as Vietnam and Latin America. The Eisenhower administration chose the first alternative, John F. Kennedy the second. Kennedy's fateful choice determined the nation's foreign policy for the next ten years. And like the 1950s crises in foreign affairs, so too would domestic decisions of the Eisenhower years reshape the future choices in domestic politics. The Supreme Court ruling of 1954 outlawing school segregation, for example, provided a legal foundation for the massive civil rights movement of the early 1960s. Both abroad and at home Americans faced a transformed world. It remained only to be seen how they would respond to it.

## AFTER SUEZ: EUROPE

Although the Suez and Hungarian crises reshaped world affairs, the transformation did not occur overnight. The most dramatic international event in the late 1950s was the Russian-American confrontation over Berlin, a city that had long symbolized the hostility between East and West. Situated inside Communist-controlled East Germany, Berlin had been divided into Russian and Western sectors since 1945. As Khrushchev bluntly remarked, West Berlin was a "bone in my throat," for it served as a display of Western wealth and power as well as a listening post deep within the Soviet empire.

In 1958 Khrushchev decided to dislodge the bone. He believed that the launching of Sputnik in late 1957 gave him a military advantage. Projecting this earth satellite into the upper atmosphere demonstrated that Soviet missile capability was greater than the American. Moreover, in early 1958 Western Europe, with American encouragement, created a large common economic market (the European Economic Community, or EEC) by agreeing gradually to abolish tariffs and other restrictions on trade. The EEC included France, Italy, Belgium, Netherlands, Luxembourg, and—most crucial to Khrushchev—West Germany. With this decision, the Europeans had gone far to lessen the nationalisms that had produced two world wars. But they had also tied West Germany more firmly within the Western camp. Faced with a rejuvenated, pro-West Germany—always a fearful sight to Russians—and believing that his new missile capacity gave him the necessary diplomatic leverage, Khrushchev struck at the Western Powers by demanding in November 1958 that they surrender control of West Berlin. Eisenhower and the European leaders rejected the demand and stood firm.

Khrushchev backed off, proposing that visits be exchanged with Eisenhower for personal discussions. The United States eagerly accepted, particularly because a visit would allow the President to see previously closed areas of Russia and spread the Eisenhower charm. "The name Eisenhower meant so much" to the Russians, one State Department official noted. "I mean, you could send [Vice-President] Nixon over, but the average Ivan wouldn't know who the hell he was. But Eisenhower meant something. It was victory. It was World War II and all that." Khrushchev arrived in the United States in mid-1959, visiting American farms and a movie set of *Can-Can* (whose uninhibited dancing girls appalled him), and discussing foreign policy with the President. Eisenhower, however, was never to see Moscow. He had planned to do so after a summit conference in early 1960 in Paris. But before world leaders could fly to the French capital, Khrushchev angrily announced that the Soviets had shot down an American spy plane, a U-2, which had been taking aerial photographs more than a thousand miles inside Russia.

At first Washington denied involvement. Khrushchev then produced evidence that the denials were lies, and Eisenhower hastily assumed full responsibility for sending the plane over Russia. The Soviet leader heatedly refused to talk with the President. The summit was over before it had begun. The United States was embarrassed, but it is probable that neither Khrushchev nor Eisenhower had originally wanted to go to Paris, for neither side was willing to budge on the key Berlin question. Of equal significance, U-2 planes had been flying over Russia for four years. They brought back information that convinced Washington officials that despite Khrushchev's bragging about his missiles, he did not have missile superiority or even military equality with the United States. Khrushchev realized that he had been found out and therefore was not displeased to avoid talking with the President. Publicly, the Russian began softening his stand by downplaying the importance of missiles: "They are not like cucumbers, you know—you don't eat them, and more than a certain number are not required." The real loser was U-2 pilot Francis Gary Powers. He was imprisoned in Russia for two years until exchanged for a captured Soviet spy.

## AFTER SUEZ: NEWLY EMERGING AREAS

Berlin captured world attention, but the effects of the 1956 crises were already working profound changes elsewhere. For the Suez episode had demonstrated new and unexpected features of the Cold War. Despite its awesome power, the United States had been unable to control its junior partners, the British and French. The Soviets, meanwhile, had needed tanks and planes to keep its supposed ally, Hungary, within the Russian bloc. The old bipolar globe—the world divided and controlled by the two superpowers—was disappearing. This disappearance was hastened as China and Russia became enemies in 1960 because of differences over Communist ideology and their 1200-mile common boundary.

The effects of these changes were especially noticeable in the newly independent nations in Asia and Africa, which had recently freed themselves from European colonialism. The leaders of these countries often refused to join either the Soviet or American side. They instead tried to play Washington off against Moscow in order to acquire aid from both camps. This had been Nasser's policy in Egypt, and although he had suffered a military setback in 1956, he had retained control of the Suez Canal while receiving aid from both Americans and Russians. Nasser set an example that sparked nationalist revolutions in the Middle East.

Eisenhower and Dulles feared that the new nations would be unstable, anti-Western, and, therefore, pro-Communist. As Dulles had once blurted out, neutrality was "immoral." These changes in turn could threaten the supply of oil which Europe and the United States required from the Middle East. The results could be disastrous. "In my view," Dulles remarked in early 1957, "we are in a war situation right now." Consequently, in the spring of that year Congress passed a resolution proposed by Eisenhower that allowed him to commit American power to stop "overt armed aggression" by Communists in the Middle East if a nation in the area asked for such help. This "Eisenhower Doctrine" was unfortunate. It angered some Middle Eastern nations, divided others, and forced some to choose between East and West, something they did not want to do.

The Doctrine, moreover, was largely irrelevant. The area was not threatened by overt Communist invasion but by intense, internal nationalism, which the proclamation did not cover. Yet when the monarchy in Iraq was suddenly overthrown by an internal coup led by pro-Nasser nationalists in 1958, the government of neighboring Lebanon asked for American protection. No "overt" Communist threat was apparent; indeed, Eisenhower knew the Lebanese president needed help against *internal* opposition, not external. Eisenhower nevertheless immediately landed fourteen thousand American troops in Lebanon to display his muscle. The bikini-clad bathers on the shore scarcely moved as the Marines waded in, and the effect on Iraq was equally slight. Despite the Eisenhower Doctrine and the Lebanon landings, Middle Eastern nationalism continued to flourish and unsettle the area. As the Suez crisis had demonstrated, foreign troops only worsened the situation. The world could not be rolled back to the pre-1956 years.

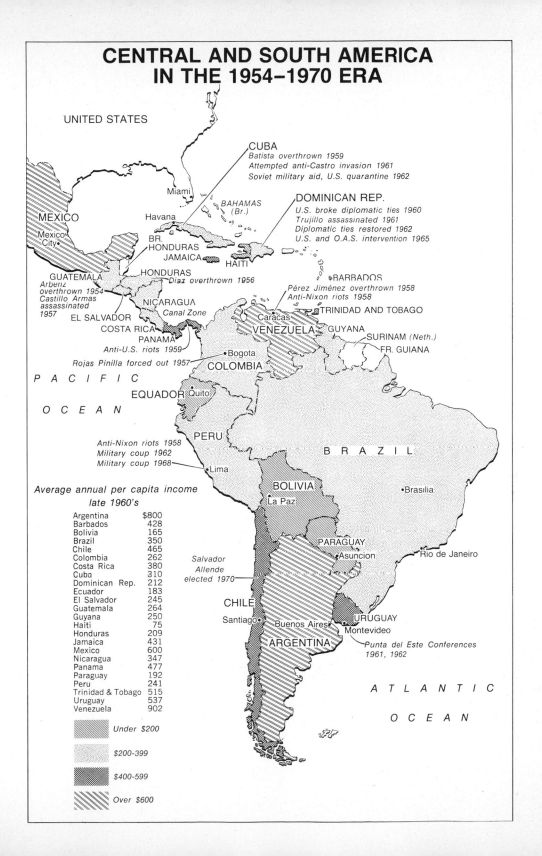

# CENTRAL AND SOUTH AMERICA
# IN THE 1954–1970 ERA

UNITED STATES

Miami

CUBA
Batista overthrown 1959
Attempted anti-Castro invasion 1961
Soviet military aid, U.S. quarantine 1962

BAHAMAS
(Br.)

DOMINICAN REP.
U.S. broke diplomatic ties 1960
Trujillo assassinated 1961
Diplomatic ties restored 1962
U.S. and O.A.S. intervention 1965

MEXICO
Mexico City

Havana

BR. HONDURAS

JAMAICA

HAITI

GUATEMALA
Arbenz overthrown 1954
Castillo Armas assassinated 1957

HONDURAS
Díaz overthrown 1956

BARBADOS

Pérez Jiménez overthrown 1958
Anti-Nixon riots 1958

EL SALVADOR

NICARAGUA
Canal Zone

TRINIDAD AND TOBAGO

COSTA RICA
PANAMA
Anti-U.S. riots 1959
Rojas Pinilla forced out 1957

Caracas

VENEZUELA

GUYANA

SURINAM (Neth.)
FR. GUIANA

Bogota

COLOMBIA

P A C I F I C

EQUADOR  Quito

O C E A N

PERU

Anti-Nixon riots 1958
Military coup 1962
Military coup 1968

Lima

B R A Z I L

Brasília

Average annual per capita income
late 1960's

BOLIVIA
La Paz

| | |
|---|---|
| Argentina | $800 |
| Barbados | 428 |
| Bolivia | 165 |
| Brazil | 350 |
| Chile | 465 |
| Colombia | 262 |
| Costa Rica | 380 |
| Cuba | 310 |
| Dominican Rep. | 212 |
| Ecuador | 183 |
| El Salvador | 245 |
| Guatemala | 264 |
| Guyana | 250 |
| Haiti | 75 |
| Honduras | 209 |
| Jamaica | 431 |
| Mexico | 600 |
| Nicaragua | 347 |
| Panama | 477 |
| Paraguay | 192 |
| Peru | 241 |
| Trinidad & Tobago | 515 |
| Uruguay | 537 |
| Venezuela | 902 |

PARAGUAY
Asuncion

Rio de Janeiro

Salvador
Allende
elected 1970

CHILE
Santiago

Buenos Aires

ARGENTINA

URUGUAY
Montevideo

Punta del Este Conferences
1961, 1962

A T L A N T I C

O C E A N

| | |
|---|---|
| ▨ | Under $200 |
| ▨ | $200-399 |
| ▨ | $400-599 |
| ▨ | Over $600 |

# THE GOOD NEIGHBOR AND A CHANGING NEIGHBORHOOD

Nationalism also threatened American policies in Latin America, where the United States had seemed to have sure control. By 1955 American companies produced 10 percent of Latin America's products, 30 percent of its export goods (and in such nations as Venezuela and Cuba two or three times that percentage), invested more that $3 billion directly, and dominated the continent's great oil and mineral resources. That domination, however, had brought no prosperity to most Latin Americans. With little industrialization, the area depended on world market prices for its oil and other raw materials, but most of these prices declined in the late 1950s. Foreign investment worsened this drain of money, for Americans took more profits out of Latin America than they put back in. This economic trap was aggravated by the highest population growth rate in the world. In other words, the key sections of Latin America's economy were largely exploited by foreign capital, and that economy was scarcely growing fast enough to keep up with the population increase.

Washington officials understood this, but since 1947 had poured their resources into Europe while taking Latin America for granted. During these years Belgium and Luxembourg alone received three times more economic aid than the twenty Latin American nations combined. Over two-thirds of the aid that did go south was for military purposes, not economic growth. The political results were all too obvious: instability, frequent changes of government, repressive right-wing dictatorships, and a heightened anti-American nationalism among intellectuals and jailed politicians. Between 1930 and 1965, 106 illegal and often bloody changes of government occurred throughout the continent. Only Mexico of all twenty Latin American governments had peaceful presidential changes through this period. (Woodrow Wilson, who had bitterly opposed the Mexican Revolution between 1913 and 1916, would doubtless have been surprised but pleased.)

Latin America differed fundamentally from Africa or Southeast Asia, for it had been free of direct colonial control for more than a century, and was politically more experienced. Latin Americans knew that their problems could not be solved by throwing off foreign rulers as Egypt, Vietnam, and others were doing, for there was no such formal colonialism in the area. Instead, they had to control and develop their internal resources, that is, loosen the economic grip that the United States held on their countries. The question was whether Washington would help or hinder that aspiration. In 1954 Dulles had given his answer by helping overthrow a nationalistic left-wing government in Guatemala. The area had then quieted somewhat. In early 1958 a high State Department official was asked whether he thought there was much anti-Yankee feeling among Latin Americans. "No sir, I do not," he promptly replied.

Two months later Vice-President Nixon traveled south. From Uruguay to Venezuela crowds hurled eggs and stones at his car, nearly tipping it over in Caracas, Venezuela. Eisenhower ordered a thousand Marines to prepare to rescue Nixon, who escaped back to Washington before the troops were dispatched. The outburst shocked the United States. The President ordered a review of Latin American policies. He finally initiated economic-aid programs, which, after 1961, the Kennedy administration would enlarge and attempt to glamorize with the title "Alliance for Progress." But this was too little and too late to prevent anti-American nationalists from working fundamental, revolutionary changes.

It was, for example, too late to insulate Cuba from such a revolution. This was striking, for nowhere had United States control been so complete. Americans controlled 80 percent of the island's utilities, 90 percent of the mines, ranches, and oil, owned half the great sugar crop, and surrounded Cuba with military might. The island had one of the highest per-capita income figures in the southern hemisphere, but the wealth fell

Castro at the United Nations, 1960.

into the hands of foreign investors and a few Cubans, while the mass of the people suffered in poverty. In 1952, Fulgencio Batista overthrew a moderately liberal regime and created a military dictatorship. He received support from highly unlikely bedfellows, the United States military (which helped train and equip Batista's forces), and a well-behaved Communist party, which sought to survive by whipping up local support for the dictator. The United States Air Force pinned the Legion of Merit on Batista's breast, calling him "a great president."

That sentiment was not shared by most Cubans. In 1953 a young, middle-class lawyer (unemployed, as were most Cuban lawyers) started a revolt. Fidel Castro was captured and imprisoned, but by 1957 he was again free, and then collected a force of peasants and middle-class Cubans that successfully chopped up the police units sent out to destroy the guerrillas. The Communists refused to cooperate with Castro until late 1958, when Batista was preparing to escape with millions from the Cuban treasury for a luxurious exile in Spain. On January 1, 1959, Castro marched triumphantly into Havana. Washington officials, an authoritative journalist reported, generally agreed that "there was no dominant Communist influence. . . . One official went so far as to say that there was very little trace of Communism in the movement."

As Castro moved to change the distribution of wealth, and especially of land ownership, his relationships with the Communists and the United States altered. The Communists provided disciplined organization and an ideology, which Castro required. When the Cuban leader visited the United States, Eisenhower left Washington to go golfing. There was little to talk about. Castro insisted that American companies and land holdings be placed in Cuban hands. He could not pay for these without borrowing money from abroad and again becoming indebted to foreigners. As the *New York Times* editorialized in mid-1960, "So long as Cuba is in the throes of a social revolution directed by her present leaders, she is going to be in conflict with the United States. We think it is wrong, but it is a fact of life. The revolution harms American interests in Cuba and in Latin America generally." Castro turned to the Soviet Union for credits, machinery, and military equipment. Eisenhower first cut back Cuban sugar imports, then authorized the secret training of 1400 anti-Castro Cubans by the Central Intelligence Agency, although the President never did decide when—or even whether—they might be used. Assuming that Castro was "beyond redemption," as a State Department official commented, the United States and Cuba broke diplomatic relations in January 1961.

## THE EISENHOWER LEGACY AND THE NEW FRONTIER

Eisenhower presided during a decade that many Americans would later recall with nostalgia. The generation that came of age during the 1950s seemed quiet, apolitical, and more concerned about personal security than international crises. It would later be tagged as "the generation that never showed up." This was how Eisenhower wanted it. Despite provocations in Korea, the Middle East, and Berlin greater than those that later faced Presidents Kennedy and Johnson, Eisenhower, unlike his successors, did not involve the country in war. His use of power was restrained. He frequently remarked that he had seen enough war. Moreover, Eisenhower cared more about balancing the budget and strengthening the American economy than he did about creating a great military force that might intervene at will in the post-1956 world.

He did not disavow anti-Communist policies, but neither did he think that those policies were worth undermining the American economic, political, and even educational systems. Between 1950 and 1960, for example, such leading universities as Harvard, Chicago, Columbia, Pennsylvania, California, and Johns Hopkins had obtained large amounts of money, both from such private foundations as Ford and Carnegie and from the federal government, to establish defense-policy centers. Instead of questioning governmental power, many American intellectuals were justifying that power. With this in mind, Eisenhower issued a warning in his Farewell Address of January 1961. He spoke of "the prospect of domination of the nation's scholars by Federal employment, project allocations, and the power of money," and noted that too often " a government contract becomes virtually a substitute for intellectual curiosity." Eisenhower believed that two "threats, new in kind or degree," had appeared:

> This conjunction of an immense military establishment and a large arms industry is new in American experience. The total influence—economic, political, even spiritual—is felt in every city, every state house, every office of the federal government. We recognize the imperative need for this development. Yet we must not fail to comprehend its grave implications. . . . In the councils of government, we must guard against the acquisition of unwarranted influence, whether sought or unsought, by the military-industrial complex. The potential for the disastrous rise of misplaced power exists and will persist. . . . We should take nothing for granted.

In part this warning expressed Eisenhower's fear that the incoming Kennedy administration would try to control world affairs by spending even greater sums on arms. His fear was well founded. In accepting the Democratic presidential nomination in 1960, John F. Kennedy called not for caution, but for "sacrifices" on "the New Frontier." He spoke in Los Angeles in late afternoon as the sun went down on what had been the last of the old American frontier territory. The New Frontier, Kennedy declared,

> sums up not what I intend to offer the American people but what I intend to ask of them. It appeals to their pride, not to their pocketbook; it holds out the promise of more sacrifice instead of more security.

> But I tell you the New Frontier is here whether we seek it or not . . . uncharted areas of science and space, unsolved problems of peace and war, unconquered pockets of ignorance and prejudice, unanswered questions of poverty and surplus.

This call to action was most eloquently stated in Kennedy's inaugural speech of January 1961. His words sharply contrasted with Eisenhower's farewell address. Kennedy proclaimed:

> Let every nation know, whether it wishes us well or ill, that we shall pay any price, bear any burden, meet any hardship, support any friend, oppose any foe to assure the survival and the success of liberty.
>
> This much we pledge—and more. . . .
>
> In the long history of the world, only a few generations have been granted the role of defending freedom in its hour of maximum danger. I do not shrink from this responsibility; I welcome it. . . .
>
> And so, my fellow Americans, ask not what your country can do for you; ask what you can do for your country.

## JOHN F. KENNEDY

In April 1960 Richard E. Neustadt, a political scientist at Columbia University, published *Presidential Power*. Neustadt believed that a strong President "contributes to the energy of government and to the viability of public policy." He attempted, therefore, to show how a chief executive could exercise power effectively. "The Sixties, it appears, will be a fighting time," Neustadt predicted. "It follows that our need will be the greater for a Presidential expert in the Presidency." Shortly after the book appeared, John F. Kennedy, the Democratic nominee for President, recruited Neustadt as an advisor. In truth, the two men held similar views. Kennedy thought that the President "must serve as a catalyst, an energizer, the defender of the public good and the public interest." He must "place himself in the very thick of the fight," for he was "the vital center of action in our whole scheme of government."

"Energy," "fight," "vitality," "public interest"—the words were temperamentally congenial to Kennedy. But while he was President his approach to domestic policies could more accurately be described by a different vocabulary: "caution," "prudence," "compromise," "interest group." Kennedy believed that politics was the art of the possible, that politicians were most likely to succeed if they dealt with concrete rather than abstract issues, and that a give-and-take process in resolving those issues was not only inevitable but also desirable. For a President to safeguard the national interest translated, in the pluralist world of American politics, into arrnaging mutually acceptable tradeoffs between such competing interest groups as business and labor, farmers and consumers, blacks and whites. "Politics and legislation," Kennedy once said, "are not matters for inflexible principles or unattainable ideals."

Kennedy was elected to the House of Representatives in 1946, to the Senate in 1952, and, at the age of 43, to the presidency. His rise to political eminence was so swift and his personal qualities were so attractive that his virtues were exaggerated by the public, by the media, and especially by his inner circle of friends and admirers. A vigorous man who enjoyed sports such as sailing, Kennedy felt it necessary to deny that he suffered from Addison's disease (an adrenal insufficiency requiring cortisone treatments) so as not to jeopardize his career. Kennedy was a naval officer in World War II who courageously rescued members of his crew after their PT boat had been sunk in the South Pacific. Although he was widely regarded as a hero, Kennedy's poor seamanship was partly responsible for the disaster. A person of impressive intellect, Kennedy was awarded a Pulitzer Prize in 1957 for *Profiles in Courage*, a book written primarily by an aide. The truth about these incidents, however, was not widely known or accepted until after Kennedy's death.

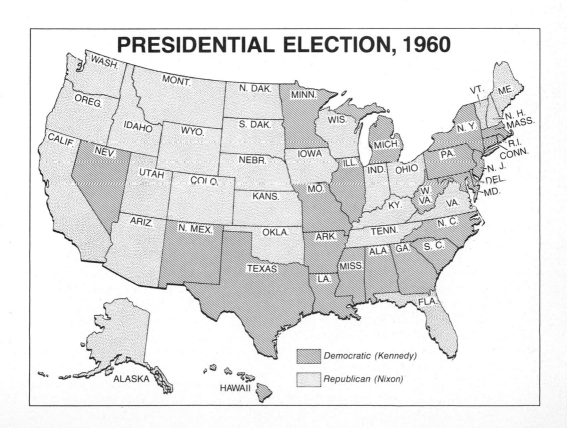

**PRESIDENTIAL ELECTION, 1960**

Democratic (Kennedy)

Republican (Nixon)

# CONGRESS AND THE NEW FRONTIER

Unlike Franklin D. Roosevelt and Dwight Eisenhower, Kennedy did not take office with a resounding popular mandate. He barely edged out Richard Nixon, winning by the smallest margin of any President in the twentieth century. Kennedy, who received 49.7 percent of the popular vote to his opponent's 49.6 percent, actually carried fewer states than did Nixon. Although Kennedy secured a 303 to 219 majority in the electoral college, had 4500 people in Illinois and 28,000 people in Texas voted Republican instead of Democratic, Nixon would have emerged the victor in the electoral college. President by a razor-thin margin, Kennedy was not in a position to make demands on Congress.

Nor could Kennedy turn for support to first-term congressmen carried into office on his coattails. In 1960 Kennedy invariably trailed the Democratic ticket; worse still, his party lost twenty-two seats in the House and two in the Senate. Although the Democrats maintained comfortable majorities in both houses of Congress, those majorities were deceptive, consisting largely of Southerners who regarded many New Frontier programs with distaste. The seniority system gave Southern Democrats representing rural constituencies control of key committees: Wilbur Mills of Arkansas headed the House Ways and Means Committee, Harry Byrd of Virginia chaired the Senate Finance Committee, and Howard Smith of Virginia ran the House Rules Committee. Kennedy barely won a bitterly contested struggle to liberalize the Rules Committee by enlarging its membership, and then only because he had the backing of Speaker Sam Rayburn of Texas. Even the Kennedy style appeared to offend some congressmen. "All that Mozart string music and ballet dancing down there," said one; "he's too elegant for me, I can't talk to him."

In some respects religion acted as another constraint on the President. Kennedy's Catholicism had played an important role in the 1960 election. Many Protestants bolted the Democratic party, but Kennedy received 80 percent of the Catholic vote (rather than the 63 percent a Democrat could ordinarily expect). On the whole, the religious issue appears to have cost Kennedy votes. However, his loss of support occurred primarily in the South, where the Democrats could afford it; meanwhile he gained support in such critical states as Illinois and Michigan. As the first Catholic President, Kennedy leaned over backwards to dispel any suspicion that he was under Church influence. He did not favor sending an American ambassador to the Vatican, and he similarly opposed "unconstitutional aid to parochial schools." It was easier to prove that a Catholic could be elected President than to convince skeptics that a Catholic President could be scrupulously fair.

The conflict over federal aid to education illustrated Kennedy's difficulties with Congress. Early in 1961 Kennedy proposed spending $2.3 billion over three years to build new schools and to raise teachers' salaries.

The wealthiest states would receive $15 per child, the poorest nearly twice that amount. A separate program to aid college students would bring the package to $5.6 billion. But federal aid to education raised divisive issues. In a vain effort to appease Southern Democrats, the administration agreed not to withhold aid from segregated school districts. The religious issue proved more difficult to resolve. Kennedy declared that the Constitution prohibited aid to parochial schools, but the Catholic Church replied that the Constitution did not prohibit long-term, low-interest loans to help such schools improve their facilities. An arrangement was seemingly worked out restricting the federal aid bill to public schools, but attaching an amendment to the National Defense and Education Act authorizing loans to parochial schools for expanding their mathematics, science, and language facilities. At the last minute, a Northern Catholic Democrat on the Rules Committee, fearing that Congress would renege on aid to religious schools, joined Republicans and Southern Democrats to oppose the education bill. In July 1961 the President watched helplessly as the Rules Committee, by a one-vote margin, buried the measure.

A second New Frontier proposal—Medicare—met a similar fate. In February 1961 Kennedy asked Congress to extend social security benefits to people over the age of 65 to cover hospital and nursing home costs. This would be financed by a small increase in the social security tax. The President pointed out that the elderly had, on the average, half the income of people under 65 but medical expenses that were twice as high. Kennedy insisted that his plan, which would not cover surgical expenses or physicians' fees, ensured "absolute freedom" in the choice of a doctor and hospital. The American Medical Association, however, viewed Medicare as a giant step toward socialized medicine. Doctors foresaw a "bureaucratic task force" invading "the privacy of the examination room." The twenty-five-member House Ways and Means Committee was the real hurdle. Its chairman, Wilbur Mills, opposed the plan, as did ten Republicans and six Southern Democrats. They easily bottled up the bill. In July 1962 the Senate defeated the measure by a vote of 52 to 48, with twenty-one Democrats opposing the administration. The limitation of presidential leadership in domestic affairs was rapidly becoming clearer.

# THE NEW ECONOMICS

Yet the picture of a stodgy, conservative Congress frustrating the hopes of an energetic, liberal President is accurate only in part. Kennedy understood the need to establish domestic priorities, and in the process he often sacrificed reform programs. This was true even in the case of Medicare, for Kennedy, recognizing that he needed Wilbur Mills's support for tax reform and trade expansion, did not press the Ways and Means Committee too hard. Moreover, to attract Southern Democratic support for economic proposals Kennedy postponed introducing civil rights legislation for as long as possible. He always put first things first, and in his view what came first was the economy. In January 1961 the nation was in the throes of a recession: unemployment stood at 5.4 million, more than 6 percent of the labor force. Kennedy's goal was to stimulate economic growth and reduce unemployment while at the same time balancing the budget and preventing inflation.

The administration applied a number of remedies to the sluggish economy. To aid jobless workers, Kennedy extracted from Congress, though usually in a diluted form, legislation that increased unemployment compensation, created manpower retraining programs, and provided for public works in depressed areas. Congress also raised the minimum wage from $1.00 to $1.25 an hour and brought an additional 3.6 million workers under the law's protection. To stimulate business expansion, Congress granted a 7 percent tax credit to firms investing in new equipment. Kennedy attached the greatest significance to the Trade Expansion Act (1962). This facilitated the export of American goods to the European Common Market by authorizing the President to arrange mutual tariff reductions of 50 percent on certain categories of goods and, in other cases, to eliminate tariffs completely. To assist industries threatened by foreign competition, the government would help businessmen change or diversify their products and retrain workers who lost their jobs.

The keys to curbing inflation were labor's willingness to limit wage demands to an amount justified by gains in productivity and industry's corresponding readiness to keep prices down. Early in 1962 Kennedy helped persuade the steelworkers to accept a noninflationary wage settlement. Then in April, U.S. Steel announced a price hike of $6 a ton, and other steel companies immediately followed suit. Furious at what he termed this "utter contempt for the public interest," Kennedy mustered every ounce of executive authority to salvage his economic program. He pressured smaller steel companies into holding the price line, threatened to take government contracts away from the offending concerns, and hinted that the Justice Department would determine whether the price increases violated the antitrust laws. Faced with massive presidential and public pressure, U.S. Steel backed down and rescinded the increase.

Kennedy's stance earned him the lasting resentment of the business community. The remark attributed to him at the time—"My father always told me that all businessmen were sons-of-bitches, but I never believed it till now"—did nothing to allay suspicion. When, in May 1962, the stock market hit the skids, dropping 35 points in a day and 100 points in two weeks, Wall Street attributed the disaster to a lack of confidence in the administration. Whatever businessmen may have thought, their fears were illogical. Not only did Kennedy's tax and trade policies favor business interests, but the administration also sponsored a plan, bitterly resented by Senate liberals, that conceded a dominant interest in the newly developed communications satellite to the American Telephone and Telegraph Company. (The satellite, launched into outer space, relayed television and radio signals around the world.) In addition to this, during his first eighteen months in office Kennedy worked hard to achieve a balanced budget. So orthodox did the New Frontier's fiscal program appear that journalist Walter Lippmann commented, "It's like the Eisenhower administration 30 years younger."

Not until late in 1962 did Kennedy endorse the planned use of budget deficits as the only certain means of spurring further economic growth. In January 1963 the President called for a $13.5 billion reduction in corporate and personal taxes over three years. With the closing of loopholes, this would inject $10 billion into the economy, but it would also produce a $12 billion deficit in a total budget of $98.8 billion. Kennedy's plan, while thoroughly Keynesian in its assumptions, did not satisfy all liberals. John Kenneth Galbraith, the Harvard economist whom Kennedy had appointed Ambassador to India, believed that "money from tax reduction goes into the pockets of those who need it least; lower tax revenues will become a ceiling on spending." Galbraith wished to create a deficit by expanding programs to aid the needy rather than by cutting taxes. On the other hand, Kennedy's proposal shocked conservatives. Dwight Eisenhower offered a homely bit of economic wisdom: "Spending for spending's sake is patently a false theory. No family, no business, no nation can spend itself into prosperity."

Unfortunately for Kennedy, more congressmen, and particularly more members of the House Ways and Means Committee, preferred Eisenhower's brand of economics to Galbraith's. Once again, as in the case of Medicare and federal aid to education, a House committee blocked consideration of a key New Frontier proposal. But by 1963 Kennedy had somewhat lowered his sights, at least with respect to domestic matters. The exercise of power proved a sobering experience. Although he never repudiated his activist view of the presidency, Kennedy came to see the office in terms of its limitations as well as its opportunities. "The problems are more difficult than I had imagined they were," he conceded. "Every President must endure a gap between what he would like and what is possible."

## KENNEDY AND CIVIL RIGHTS

The same practical considerations that modified Kennedy's view of presidential authority also affected his stand on civil rights. In 1960 Kennedy declared that the President should throw the full moral weight of his office behind the effort to end racial discrimination. "If the President does not himself wage the struggle for equal rights—if he stands above the battle—then the battle will inevitably be lost." Once in office, however, Kennedy found himself torn between the claims of white Southerners, whose support he needed, and the pressure applied by an increasingly militant civil rights movement. Not until 1963 did Kennedy cease standing above the battle, and he then acted only after segregationist resistance to demands for racial equality provoked massive turmoil.

Unlike Eisenhower, Kennedy relied heavily on the black vote. In the 1960 campaign he expressed agreement with the Supreme Court ruling on desegregation, but perhaps nothing did more to solidify his support among blacks than his intervention on behalf of Dr. Martin Luther King, Jr. Late in October a Georgia judge jailed King for taking part in a protest demonstration. In a well-publicized move, Kennedy telephoned King's wife, both to express his concern and to offer assurances regarding her husband's safety. The next day, Robert F. Kennedy, the candidate's brother, helped arrange King's release on bail. Kennedy's phone call, a symbolic act at best, nevertheless had the right personal touch. When Nixon remained silent, the Democrats printed two million copies of a pamphlet entitled *No-Comment Nixon versus a Candidate with a Heart, Senator Kennedy*. In 1960 black voters provided Kennedy's margin of victory in Texas, Illinois, New Jersey, and Michigan. Had only white people voted, Nixon would have received 52 percent of the vote and gone to the White House.

Kennedy understood this, yet he placed civil rights lower on his legislative agenda than other New Frontier measures. To introduce a civil rights bill, Kennedy believed, would alienate Southerners, split the Democratic party, snarl Congress in a filibuster, and dissipate administration energies. He considered the chance of passage too slim to justify these risks. So the President turned instead to other techniques. He issued an Executive Order designed to pressure federal agencies and government contractors into hiring more black workers. In addition, Kennedy sought to achieve through litigation what he doubted was possible through legislation. Under Attorney General Robert F. Kennedy, the Justice Department attempted to speed the pace of school desegregation by entering court cases on the side of those challenging separate facilities. The policy had some success. In Eisenhower's last three years, 49 school districts had begun the process of desegregation. In Kennedy's three years, 183 did so.

In the eyes of New Frontiersmen, the franchise held the key to racial equality. Litigation to win the vote seemed crucial, for if blacks attained political strength commensurate with their numbers, politicians would accord them justice and the Jim Crow system would topple. Many states in the Deep South systematically excluded blacks from the polls. In Mississippi, where blacks constituted over 40 percent of the population, they made up less than 4 percent of the eligible voters. To attack this system, the Justice Department utilized the Civil Rights Act of 1957, which authorized it to seek injunctions against interference with the right to vote. The Eisenhower administration had brought only ten suits under the act. The Kennedy administration filed forty-five such suits.

Yet the reliance on litigation had three fatal defects. First, it assumed that the law sanctioned racial equality, which, in much of the South, it did not. Second, it assumed a degree of judicial impartiality that did not exist. A number of judges in Southern district courts held harshly segregationist views and stymied moves toward integration. Judge Harold Cox, a Kennedy appointee, informed a Justice Department official: "I spend most of my time in fooling with lousy cases brought before me by your Department in the Civil Rights field." Cox could find no pattern of discrimination in Clarke County, Mississippi, although only one black, a high-school principal, had succeeded in registering to vote in thirty years. Another judge branded the 1954 Supreme Court ruling "one of the truly regrettable decisions of all time." Even where successful, litigation was a glacial process, and this proved to be a third source of weakness. Many blacks were no longer willing to let the law run its course. They insisted that equality was a moral as well as a legal issue. By taking direct action to end segregation, they forced Kennedy to choose sides.

The first such case involved the "freedom rides," which were themselves an offshoot of the sit-in movement. In February 1960 a group of black college students in Greensboro, North Carolina sat down at a Woolworth's lunch counter and refused to leave until served. Within a year, fifty thousand people had participated in similar demonstrations in over one hundred cities and had succeeded in desegregating many hotels, stores, theaters, and parks. The freedom ride seemed a logical extension of this tactic. In May 1961 white and black students boarded buses in Washington with plans to travel through the deep South, desegregating depots as they went. Angry mobs met the buses, though, and attacked the riders with chains and rocks. The President finally sent five hundred marshals to Montgomery, Alabama to prevent further violence. Kennedy then asked the Interstate Commerce Commission to ban segregation at all bus and train stations. In November 1961 such an edict took effect, although some Southern communities continued to evade it. The Justice Department also persuaded airlines to desegregate their terminals. The freedom riders had, in effect, created the conditions under which Kennedy was willing to employ executive authority on behalf of civil rights.

Kennedy's hand was forced a second time in September 1962 when James Meredith tried to integrate the University of Mississippi law school. The controversy originated when a U.S. Court of Appeals found that the university had rejected Meredith solely on the basis of race and ordered his admission. After a segregationist judge stayed the ruling, Supreme Court Justice Hugo Black ordered its enforcement. Meredith flew to Oxford, Mississippi in a federal plane and was escorted to the campus by federal marshals. Governor Ross Barnett tried to convince Robert Kennedy that Southern sentiment would never tolerate the integration of Ole Miss. Barnett thought Meredith was "being paid by some left-wing organization to do all this. He has two great big Cadillacs, no income, riding around here. . . . We never have trouble with our people, but the NAACP, they want to stir up trouble down here." The Attorney General responded that "if we don't follow the order of the federal court, we don't have anything in the United States." In the end, white students and outside troublemakers, massed behind Confederate battle flags, attacked the federal marshals. A fifteen-hour riot ensued in which two men were killed and the campus was shrouded in tear gas. The President dispatched thousands of federal troops to restore order, to protect Meredith's right to attend class, and to demonstrate that, in Robert Kennedy's words, only the rule of law permitted a nation "to avoid anarchy and disorder and tremendous distress."

The nine months following the Mississippi crisis saw the administration move haltingly toward an affirmative civil rights posture. In November 1962 the President issued a long-awaited Executive Order banning segregation in all new housing subsidized by the federal government. In February 1963 Kennedy introduced a civil rights bill designed to prevent biased registrars from using spurious tests to deprive blacks of the vote. The bill provided that the completion of six grades of public school would automatically constitute proof of literacy. Yet civil rights activists now considered these steps inadequate. They pointed out that the Executive Order did not affect housing that was already built or that would be privately financed. They noted that Kennedy, while favoring a civil rights bill, refused to support an effort to amend the Senate rules to make easier the termination of debate. Without such a change, a Southern filibuster seemed certain to block passage of any civil rights measure. Assessing Kennedy's record in March 1963, Martin Luther King, Jr. found that the administration had settled for "tokenism." Nearly a decade after the Supreme Court decision, only 7 percent of black children in the South attended class with white children, and two thousand districts remained segregated. King concluded: "The administration sought to demonstrate to Negroes that it has concern for them, while at the same time it has striven to avoid inflaming the opposition."

In the spring of 1963 civil rights demonstrations in Birmingham, Alabama made further fence straddling impossible. Black leaders in the city—where blacks constituted 40 percent of the population—launched a drive to end segregation in stores and to pressure businessmen to hire black sales and clerical help. Adhering to King's philosophy that "you can struggle without hating; you can fight war without violence," blacks engaged in protest marches, sit-ins, and even kneel-ins at white churches on Good Friday. The city government reacted savagely. Police Commissioner Eugene "Bull" Connor met the marchers, many of them schoolchildren, with fire hoses and snarling police dogs and threw thousands into jail. The Mayor, who had lost the previous election but was contesting the result in court, called white businessmen who favored some form of accommodation "a bunch of quisling, gutless traitors." He said of Robert Kennedy: "I hope that every drop of blood that's spilled he tastes in his throat, and I hope he chokes on it." In May, riots and bombings rocked the city. The following month, with the crisis in Birmingham still unresolved, Governor George C. Wallace challenged an attempt by two black

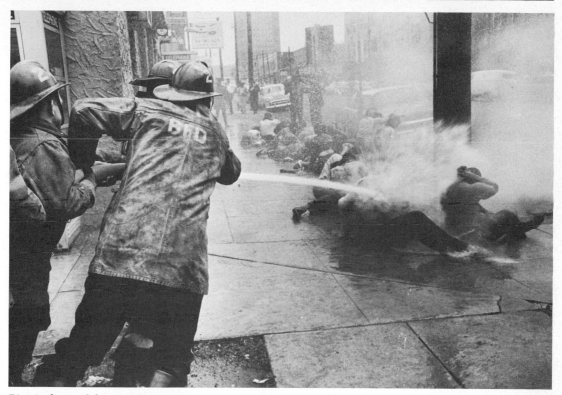

Birmingham, Alabama, 1963.

students to integrate the University of Alabama. To safeguard their entrance, the President federalized the National Guard.

In June 1963, responding directly to these events in Alabama, Kennedy endorsed a sweeping civil rights bill. It would prevent segregation in hotels, restaurants, theaters, and other public places; permit the Justice Department to file suits for school desegregation; prohibit discrimination in state programs receiving federal aid; and remove racial barriers to employment and trade-union membership. "We are confronted primarily with a moral issue," the President asserted. The demand for racial justice had grown so loud, the "fires of frustration and discord" had begun to burn so brightly, that government could no longer stand aside. Indeed, the government must prove that revolutionary changes in race relations could occur in a "peaceful and constructive" way.

In three years Kennedy had traveled a considerable distance. Yet one element remained constant: his effort to link New Frontier programs at home with initiatives abroad. In justifying his attempt to place federal authority squarely behind the movement for racial equality, Kennedy noted: "Today we are committed to a worldwide struggle to promote and protect the rights of all who wish to be free. And when Americans are sent to Vietnam or West Berlin we do not ask for whites only."

## DAVID SMITH: THE MACHINE SHOP AND SCULPTURE

David Smith transformed twentieth-century sculpture by combining the American machine shop with radical versions of modern art. Reaching the peak of his powers between 1958 and 1965, Smith's work exemplified the new American leadership in world art at precisely the same time John F. Kennedy proclaimed in his inaugural address that a "new generation" of Americans would assume world political leadership.

Smith learned about machines in Decatur, Indiana, where he was born in 1906. One of his ancestors had been a frontier blacksmith. Leaving home at 16, he enrolled briefly at Ohio State and Notre Dame before learning to weld in the Studebaker automotive works in South Bend. Smith then traveled to New York City, encountering the work of leading European artists who were fleeing Nazism to live in the United States. As these emigrés helped make New York City the center of the art world, Smith lived among them, beginning as a painter, then moving into "constructivism," whereby objects other than paint (for example, bits of newspaper, glass, or metal) were placed on the picture to change it from a painting to a construction. At that point, Smith recalled, "I was then a sculptor." To de-

David Smith welding.

David Smith with *Cubi I*, 1963.

velop his craft he believed he needed nothing "outside of factory knowledge," which he had gained as a welder.

During the late 1930s, as many artists protested the drift toward war, Smith became politically involved. He expressed his vision in fifteen horror-filled, yet magnificently designed "Medals for Dishonor" These depicted scenes of such "dishonors" as *War-Exempt Sons of the Rich, Munitions-Makers,* and *Elements Which Cause Prostitution.* In the 1940s his work became increasingly abstract, and for the first time he combined painting with sculpture so that the colors seemed to change the form of his pieces. One

*Medal for Dishonor No. 9: Bombing Civilian Populations,* 1939.

critic noted that Smith was among the first to practice "drawing in space," and called some of his work "a graceful abstract drawing that has leaped off the page into three-dimensional life."

Smith was soon exploring all forms, from overpowering monoliths to light, lyrical creations that, although made from heavy steel, seemed to float in air. His greatest work was done at his studio on the shore of Lake George in upper New York State, where he could display his works outdoors, the only place he thought large enough for them. Here he extended and transformed European art styles, particularly Cubism, which drew natural subjects in simplified lines and basic geometric shapes, usually to show the subject simultaneously from several points of view. In 1958 he began his spectacular *Cubi* series, shaping great slabs of stainless steel in pure geometrical construction and then polishing and arranging them so their three dimensions reflected changing sunlight—sometimes with dazzling intensity, sometimes with a delicacy that one critic called "purely optical poetry." In these new forms, Smith expressed the essence of Cubism. He indeed worked with steel, he declared, because it was at once "so beautiful" while "also brutal: the rapist, the

David Smith in his sculpture garden.

murderer, and the death-dealing giants are also its offspring." In *Cubi* he brought the beauty and brutality into one.

A burly man who lived life to the full, Smith had by the 1960s not only created an American sculpture, but shaped world art as well. Yet in 1965 he could declare, "I'm 20 years behind my vision." In the spring of that year he was killed in an automobile crash.

## THE WORLDWIDE NEW FRONTIER

The problems afflicting Americans at home deeply influenced Kennedy's foreign policies. His diplomacy assumed a united homefront that would unquestioningly support the President in Asia as it had in Europe, and that would see racism and poverty at home as less important than using national resources to fight communism overseas. For Kennedy, like most of his generation, was the product of World War II and the Cold War. As a young congressman in 1949, he attacked Truman for "losing" China, refused as a senator to take a public position on Senator Joseph McCarthy's vicious attacks, and in 1956 justified American support to Ngo Dinh Diem's autocratic regime in South Vietnam. By 1960, Kennedy had focused on the newly emerging areas as the key to victory in the Cold War. The new President believed that Americans must confront communism everywhere. "What is at stake in the election of 1960 is the preservation of freedom all around the globe," he proclaimed during the campaign, and he made this the central theme of his administration's foreign policy.

That remark seemed to make little-known countries in Southeast Asia, for example, as important to American interests as Western Europe. But as Kennedy saw it, the global battle would be to the finish. "Freedom and communism are locked in a deadly embrace," he believed in 1960, and later declared, "The world cannot exist half slave and half free." In a speech in May 1961 he was specific: "The great battleground for the defense and expansion of freedom today is the whole southern half of the globe—Asia, Latin America, Africa, and the Middle East—the lands of the rising peoples." His famous inaugural was a trumpet call to that battle. It was also a speech that never mentioned domestic problems. Those could be assumed as secondary to the "historic mission" of America abroad. Nor did Kennedy set any limits on that mission. "I don't believe that there is anything this country cannot do," he declared during his television debates with Vice-President Nixon in 1960.

A strong presidency was required to carry out the mission, one even stronger than that developed by Roosevelt, Truman, and Eisenhower.

Kennedy declared that the President "must be prepared to exercise the fullest powers of his office—all that are specified and some that are not." He even believed that the office not only spoke for all Americans, but represented "all of the people around the world who want to live in freedom." Kennedy established a separate foreign-affairs group in the White House under his National Security Advisor, McGeorge Bundy, former Dean of Harvard College. Bundy would be followed by Walt W. Rostow and then in 1969 by Henry Kissinger. All three used their location to drain power from the Department of State and congressional foreign-affairs committees. In diplomacy, the President had become a virtual king—only more so, for he was an elected king, complete with advisors who did not have to be responsible to Congress or to anyone but the President.

## ICBMs AND GREEN BERETS

As Commander in Chief Kennedy had at his disposal the most powerful military force in history. During the campaign he had charged Eisenhower with allowing a "missile gap" to develop in favor of the Soviets. Having seen the U-2 and other intelligence reports, Eisenhower knew that there was no gap. Kennedy also soon learned this, but refused to believe that American power was sufficient. Without evidence of Russian intentions, the new President assumed that Khrushchev would try to build new missiles as rapidly as possible. The Soviets had in fact decided to move slowly in this area, but Kennedy nevertheless accelerated American missile building. Khrushchev interpreted this to mean the Americans wanted a first-strike capability (that is, forces sufficient to wipe out Russia in one strike without fear of a return salvo), and so he ordered a step-up of Russian production and began nuclear testing at an increased rate. The most expensive arms race in history had begun, with China and France rushing to build their own nuclear weapons. Secretary of Defense Robert McNamara later believed that the Kennedy decision was "not justified" but was "necessitated by a lack of accurate information." By 1964 the United States force of 750 ICBMs (intercontinental ballistic missiles) was four times greater than that of the Soviets.

Kennedy, however, determined that since nuclear weapons would be of little use in the jungles and hamlets of the newly emerging areas, he would need conventional forces. Eisenhower, the foremost American military figure of the post-1950 era, believed that such power would be too expensive and ineffective, but Kennedy assumed that it was crucial if the new nations were to be saved from communism. He increased the number of conventional Army troops, created the Special Forces (and suggested the "Green Berets," by which they would be known) to fight guerrilla wars, and spent billions increasing the nation's helicopter and weapon capacity

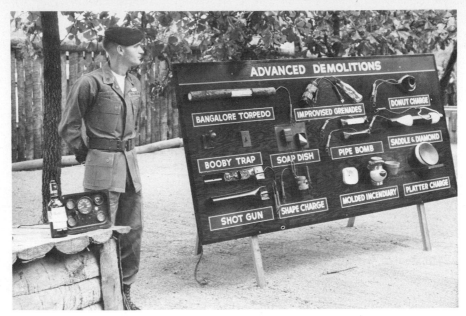

At a Green Berets training camp.

for fighting in the Third World. The Kennedy administration indeed tended to define the world primarily in military terms. Rostow told Special Forces troops in mid-1961: "I salute you, as I would a group of doctors, teachers, economic planners, agricultural experts, civil servants, or others who are now leading the way in fashioning the new nations."

## THE NEW FRONTIER CONTAINED: 1961–1962

Kennedy had determined on these policies before entering office, but in early January 1961 Khrushchev delivered a speech that spurred on the new President. The Soviet leader declared that revolutions, such as the "national liberation war" in Vietnam, were "not only admissible but inevitable." He asserted that the Communists did not have to start such wars, for nationalists within each country would fight to drive out imperialism. Communists would, however, "fully support" such conflicts. Khrushchev then focused, perhaps unfortunately, on Cuba by saying that Castro's victory was a herald of what was to come.

Kennedy interpreted this speech as a direct challenge. One reaction was to announce with great publicity the Alliance for Progress. Over a ten-year period the Alliance was to use $100 billion of United States and Latin American funds to develop and stabilize the southern continent, that is, to prevent any more Castros from appearing. The Alliance quickly encountered innumerable problems. In Washington these included bureaucratic mix-ups, lack of funds, and the growing involvement in Vietnam, which absorbed money and attention. In South America there were few funds, mistrust of Yankees, entrenched interests refusing to budge, and disputes between nations. Washington too often forgot that Latin America consisted of twenty very different countries. Worst of all, the rich in Latin America used the money to make themselves richer and the poor poorer. The gap between rich and poor widened. Political crises followed. In Central America, for example, only one revolutionary band existed in 1960. But after ten years of the Alliance for Progress, revolutions threatened El Salvador, Nicaragua, and Guatemala.

A serious blow struck the Alliance dream at the beginning when Kennedy agreed to allow the Cuban exile force, with American air cover, to invade Cuba at the Bay of Pigs in an attempt to overthrow Castro. It was a disaster from the start. Afraid that the aircraft would too deeply involve the United States, Kennedy recalled them at the last minute, leaving the small exile army at the mercy of Castro's planes and tanks. The invaders were either killed or captured. Washington had assumed that the invasion would trigger a massive uprising against Castro, but Cubans instead rallied to his side. Contrary to the expectations of the Central Intelligence Agency and the White House, there would not be a successful replay of the 1954 invasion of Guatemala. By supporting the exiles, Kennedy had broken numerous American pledges not to use force in inter-American affairs. It marked a terrible start for the Alliance and Kennedy's struggle to win the newly emerging peoples. But it redoubled his determination. He secretly ordered an immediate review of policy in other areas and soon sent five hundred more special "advisors" to Vietnam. Publicly, he tried to rebuild American prestige by announcing that the country would develop the missile and technological power to land a man on the moon within the decade. (Eight years and $24 billion later, Neil Armstrong walked on the moon, but by 1969 riots at home and interventions in newly emerging areas had nearly destroyed that prestige.)

In June 1961 Kennedy and Khrushchev met in Vienna. They worked out a ceasefire for one part of Indochina (Laos) but engaged in a heated debate on "wars of liberation." Khrushchev's next move, however, was not to support such wars, but to resolve the Berlin question. Russia had become deeply embarrassed as thousands of East Germans fled the Communist zone to find new homes in the West. Announcing that this outward flow of talent would have to stop, Khrushchev demanded an immediate Berlin settlement. Kennedy responded by adding $3 billion more to the defense budget, calling up some national reserve units to prepare for battle, and warning Americans to begin building civil-defense shelters. This last idea was questionable; there was no way to protect even half the population from being killed in a nuclear war, but Kennedy had at least replied to Khrushchev. As Russian and American tanks faced one another in Berlin, the Russians brutally solved the problem by building high concrete walls along the East German borders and ordering guards to shoot anyone who tried to escape.

# ON THE BRINK OF NUCLEAR WAR

The Berlin confrontation paled in comparison with the Cuban missile crisis of October 1962. On October 14, a U-2 plane took pictures of Soviet medium- and long-range ground-to-ground missiles being emplaced in Cuba. Why Khrushchev decided to take this step will probably never be known, but good evidence suggests several reasons. The Russian missiles in Cuba changed the military balance of power very little since the Soviets already had the capacity to destroy American targets from Russian bases. Knowing that he was behind in the missile race, Khrushchev probably thought that placing weapons ninety miles from American soil would be a political and psychological triumph. Such a success might be used to squeeze Kennedy on such international problems as Berlin. Pressures from the ruling elite in Moscow and from the Chinese Communists might also have convinced Khrushchev that he should demonstrate how tough he could be with the Americans. He could meanwhile claim publicly that the missiles protected Castro from another Washington-sponsored invasion.

Kennedy reacted with a dramatic television speech on October 22. He demanded that the ground-to-ground missiles be immediately removed, announced an American naval blockade around Cuba to search and prevent Soviet ships with missiles from reaching Havana, and warned that if any missile was fired from Cuba, the United States would fully respond—by attacking Russia. The American and Soviet forces went on full alert, with airborne bombers full of fuel and nuclear weapons. For the next six days the world was closer to nuclear obliteration than it had ever been before. Soviet ships finally turned around in mid-ocean to return to Russia, but Khrushchev refused to remove the missiles already emplaced. The fourteen-man committee advising Kennedy split. Some argued for only a blockade, others for a "surgical strike" on the missile bases (which would probably kill Russian advisors), and a few for a full-scale attack on the sites and the Castro regime. Attorney General Robert Kennedy, the President's brother, later recalled that this was "probably the brightest kind of group that you could get together," but "if six of them had been President . . . I think that the world might have been blown up."

Just hours before an American attack was planned, a deal emerged: in return for removal of the missiles, Kennedy publicly pledged not to invade Cuba, and his brother privately informed the Soviets that outdated American missiles in Turkey, on the border of Russia, would be removed.

Actually, the President had ordered the removal of the missiles in Turkey months earlier. The crisis was over. As Secretary of State Dean Rusk remarked to another committee member, "We have a considerable victory. You and I are still alive."

The reverberations of the crisis were felt long after. Kennedy emerged as a hero for facing down Khrushchev, although some suggested that the President overreacted, and not because of a military threat but for political reasons. He could not suffer another Bay of Pigs or Berlin setback, this argument went, particularly after some Republicans had warned weeks before about the Russian missiles being emplaced in Cuba. Whatever their motivations, Khrushchev and Kennedy decided to install a "hotline" telephone between Washington and Moscow so that future crises could be handled more intelligently. They next negotiated a nuclear test-ban treaty in 1963 prohibiting above-ground testing. This treaty stopped further creation of deadly radiation that was building in the earth's atmosphere from earlier tests, but it did not stop all testing. The bombs were taken underground, and more nuclear tests were conducted during the next ten years than had occurred during the previous ten. The United States military and some members of Congress demanded that Kennedy allow such expanded testing as a condition of their support of the treaty. The two great powers had nevertheless taken a first, if small, step toward arms control. One other by-product of the crisis, however, was not so constructive.

# VIETNAM

The American involvement in Vietnam had begun between 1950 and 1954. Kennedy transformed that involvement. When he became President, 675 American military advisors helped the South Vietnam government of Ngo Dinh Diem, a number that had been determined by the 1954 Geneva agreements. When Kennedy was assassinated, 17,000 American troops were in South Vietnam.

Kennedy's commitment is easily understood. He had repeatedly declared that the Cold War would be determined in the newly emerging areas, and Washington officials saw Vietnam as the key to the Asian struggle. A worse place for such a commitment could hardly be imagined, for Americans and Vietnamese lived in worlds so totally different that each easily misunderstood the other. In *Fire in the Lake,* a history of the Vietnam war, Frances FitzGerald noted, "There was no more correspondence between the two worlds than that between the atmosphere of the earth and that of the sea."

Americans thought in terms of expansion, open spaces, limitless advance, and reliance on technology. They preferred to stress the future rather than think about their past, especially if that history showed their limitations, as it often did. They liked a society that was mobile, competitive, and individualistic. But Vietnamese life depended on self-contained villages that had remained unchanged for centuries. Vietnamese considered individualism destructive to the integrated, settled, and rural life that centered on the family and the memories of ancestors. Habits were carefully handed down through generations, and when old Vietnamese died they would often be buried in the rice field to help provide sustenance for their grandchildren. Vietnam's economy depended on rice, for the country shipped large amounts to other Asian nations besides using it for its own staple diet. The people developed sophisticated growing methods, but they did not depend on technology. Change was to occur over centuries, and order, not change, was most highly desired. Otherwise the village could be disrupted, ancestral ties neglected, society torn apart. More than 80 percent of the Vietnamese were Buddhists, and their religion was tightly integrated with their everyday life.

If society did fail to work properly, if its order did disintegrate, the Vietnamese expected their leaders to step down, committing suicide if necessary, so that new leaders could make necessary changes to restore order. These changes could be radical as long as the village life retained its wholeness. For this reason, the Vietnamese could accept the revolutionary doctrines of Communist leader Ho Chi Minh, for he carefully worked through the villages to drive out French colonialism between 1946 and 1954. The Communists later used the same tactic against the Americans. The United States, on the other hand, fought Communist successes in the villages by destroying the villages. In so doing, Americans destroyed the very foundation of the society they thought they were saving.

The people of Southeast Asia had long dealt with foreign invaders. For more than a thousand years China controlled much of the area, but in the eleventh century A.D. the Chinese were driven out. During the next eight hundred years vigorous societies developed in present-day Vietnam, Laos, Cambodia, and Thailand, while the peoples continued to repulse Chinese attempts to control the area. In the nineteenth century France established a colonial empire over Cambodia, Laos, and Vietnam, but its control had been strongest in the area of South Vietnam and weakest in the north. During the 1920s a strong nationalist movement under Ho Chi Minh developed. His great opportunity appeared when Japan defeated and humiliated the French in 1940–41. With American help, French power reappeared in 1946. Ho believed that a settlement could be worked out and preferred dealing with France than with closer, more threatening neighbors: "It is better to smell the French dung for a while than eat China's all our lives." The settlement, however, broke down in late 1946, and war ensued until Ho's victory in 1954.

The Geneva Agreements of 1954 temporarily divided the country along the 17th parallel until elections could be held in 1956. Historically, South Vietnam had not been a separate nation. But with American support,

South Vietnamese President Diem, who had been installed in Saigon during late 1954 with Washington's aid, refused to hold the elections. He knew that his own weakness in the south, Ho's reputation as a nationalist, and Ho's iron hand in the north would result in a lopsided victory for the Communists. Believing that American support made his own position secure, Diem cut back drastically on promised land reforms. He concentrated power within his own family. That family was Roman Catholic, a religion adopted by only 10 percent of the Vietnamese. Elections were rigged and the South Vietnamese constitution forgotten.

Civil war finally erupted against Diem in 1958. In March 1960 the Viet Cong was organized as the Communist-led political front of the rebellion. Guerrilla warfare accelerated. In the fall of 1960 Diem's own army tried to overthrow his government but failed. As Diem approached the brink, he called for help. Kennedy responded.

## THE NEW FRONTIER IN VIETNAM: 1961–1963

The United States tried to build a nation where none had existed by supporting a ruler who was under attack by his own people. Kennedy nevertheless thought the effort necessary. Secretary of State Dean Rusk fully supported the policy. Rusk had been an army officer in Asia in 1944–45 and Assistant Secretary of State for Far Eastern affairs during the Korean War. He fervently believed that the 1960s would test whether Americans could contain communism in Asia as they had in Europe. Utterly loyal to Kennedy and, later, to President Johnson, Rusk remained dedicated to winning in Vietnam even after Kennedy's policies had failed and White House officials tried to blame their own mistakes on Rusk.

In the Department of Defense, Secretary Robert McNamara quickly built the armed force needed by Kennedy and Rusk. A brilliant product of the Harvard Business School and former president of the Ford Motor Company, McNamara employed computer and other new quantitative techniques to build and demonstrate the superiority of American power. "Every quantitative measurement we have shows we're winning this war," he declared in 1962. But in Vietnam, numbers were not enough. They could even be misleading, for the war involved a struggle in the villages that required political and cultural judgments. McNamara's computers could not make such judgments.

As a consequence, Kennedy continued to try to prop up Diem even as Diem's support was dwindling. During 1961–62, ten thousand Americans departed for Vietnam. Kennedy made the commitment even though he fully realized it was nothing more than a start. He compared aiding Diem with being an alcoholic: "The effect [of one drink] wears off and you have to take another." But given his own call to action against communism, he

McNamara, Gen. Maxwell D. Taylor, and Gen. Paul Harkins stroll by barbed-wire barricade near Saigon, South Vietnam, September 1963.

believed that he had no alternative. Diem saw clearly what was happening. The weaker he became, the more he could expect Kennedy's help. Diem could consequently pay little attention to American advice. He could do as he pleased since Kennedy had no alternative but to support the South Vietnamese regime. Meanwhile Diem's generals dreamed up statistics to feed McNamara's computers, and the computers told McNamara and Kennedy what they wanted to hear.

After the Cuban missile crisis, Kennedy's determination increased. He believed that the crisis had forced Khrushchev to retreat in the world struggle but that Russia's place would be taken by Mao Tse-tung's China. Mao, the President privately believed, was the true revolutionary, and when China developed nuclear weapons, that country would be the great threat to world stability. It was only a short step for Kennedy to conclude that since Vietnam bordered on China, and since Mao aided Ho Chi Minh, the Vietnamese struggle would decide whether Chinese communism would triumph in the newly emerging nations. All of Kennedy's assumptions were doubtful: Ho and the Vietnamese feared China and would not cooperate politically with Mao; Chinese communism had little to do with Vietnamese communism, which was highly nationalistic; and above all, Vietnamese nationalism, not communism, was the main fuel for the war against Diem. As nationalists, Vietnamese were determined to be free of all foreigners, whether French, American, or Chinese. But Kennedy, who too easily defined the world as simply "half slave and half free," seemed unable to see these differences.

Despite Washington's help, Diem's forces lost ground in 1962. Kennedy was reluctant to admit this publicly, but Americans learned of Diem's setbacks through American newspaper correspondents in Vietnam. Washington officials tried to silence these reports. The American commander in the western Pacific shouted at one critical journalist, "Why don't you get on the team?" Kennedy even privately suggested to the publisher of the *New York Times* that he give a "vacation" to one reporter who was telling the story accurately but not the way Kennedy wanted it reported. To the publisher's credit, he rejected the President's advice. American-Vietnamese relations worsened as Diem would not take United States suggestions concerning political and land reforms.

The turning point came in mid-1963. Buddhist leaders celebrated Buddha's 2587th birthday with flags and religious demonstrations. Diem had banned such displays. He ordered his troops to fire on the Buddhist leaders. Anti-Diem forces immediately rallied to the Buddhists, and civil war threatened within the principal cities. Several Buddhists responded by publicly burning themselves to death, an act that the government ridiculed as a "barbecue show." The deaths, however, dramatized the growing opposition. Kennedy decided to move.

In late August, American officials told South Vietnamese military leaders that there would be no objection if Diem were deposed. On November 1 the South Vietnamese President and his brother were captured and shot by army leaders. Although they had not known about, and indeed had disapproved of, the assassination, American officials had encouraged Diem's overthrow. In doing so, they had again demonstrated their deep involvement in the Vietnamese conflict and their determination to "save" the country even if this required helping overthrow the government. The Kennedy administration was now fully committed to the war and to a new government. What the President would have done next is unknown. On November 22, 1963, while on a political junket to Dallas, Texas, John F. Kennedy also fell victim to an assassin's bullet.

A later governmental investigation headed by Chief Justice Earl Warren concluded that the murderer was probably Lee Harvey Oswald, young, embittered, and, it seems, especially angered by Kennedy's anti-Castro policies. But Oswald never told his story, for shortly after his arrest he was shot—on national television and while surrounded by police guards—by a small-time nightclub owner, Jack Ruby. In the following years many self-appointed investigators produced evidence suggesting that Oswald was innocent, or that he was only one of several killers, or that he was the front-man for a powerful secret group still at large. Loving mysteries of this kind, especially when it involved a glamorous President,

Americans debated at length the circumstances of the tragedy. While they focused on Dallas and the shattered dreams of the Kennedy promise, a new tragedy was growing twelve thousand miles away that would destroy more than 57,000 American lives.

## Suggested Reading

For a comprehensive analysis of John F. Kennedy's career, see the two volumes by Herbert S. Parmet: *Jack: The Struggles of John F. Kennedy* (1980), and *JFK: The Presidency of John F. Kennedy* (1983). Sympathetic accounts of the New Frontier are provided in Arthur M. Schlesinger, Jr., *A Thousand Days* (1965); and Theodore Sorensen, *Kennedy* (1965). For more critical appraisals, see Henry Fairlie, *The Kennedy Promise* (1973); Bruce Miroff, *Pragmatic Illusions: The Presidential Politics of John F. Kennedy* (1976); and Garry Wills, *The Kennedy Imprisonment* (1982).

Economic policy is considered in Jim Heath, *John F. Kennedy and the Business Community* (1969); and Daniel Knapp and Kenneth Polk, *Scouting the War on Poverty: Social Reform Politics in the Kennedy Administration* (1971). Lawrence Fuchs, *John F. Kennedy and American Catholicism* (1967), is a useful work, as is David J. O'Brien, *The Renewal of American Catholicism* (1972). For a critique of the New Frontier's approach to civil rights, see Victor Navasky, *Kennedy Justice* (1971); for a more sympathetic view, Carl M. Brauer, *John F. Kennedy and the Second Reconstruction* (1977). The civil rights movement, and the response of southern whites, are considered in William H. Chafe, *Civilities and Civil Rights: Greensboro, North Carolina and the Black Struggle for Freedom* (1981); and Harris Wofford, *Of Kennedys and Kings: Making Sense of the Sixties* (1980).

On foreign policy, first consult the indexes and appropriate sections of R. H. Burns, ed., *Guide to American Foreign Relations Since 1700* (1983). Useful overviews include Warren Cohen, *Dean Rusk* (1980); Desmond Ball, *Politics and Force Levels* (1981) on the military buildup; Godfrey Hodgson, *America in Our Time* (1976), noting the transition from Eisenhower to Kennedy; and—especially crucial on economic as well as foreign policy—David Calleo, *Imperious America* (1982). For special topics see Montague Kern *et al.*, *The Kennedy Crises: The Press, the Presidency and Foreign Policy* (1983); Richard D. Mahoney, *JFK: Ordeal in Africa* (1983); George Herring, *America's Longest War* (1979) on Vietnam; Robert Kennedy, *Thirteen Days* (1969) on the missile crisis; Bernard J. Firestone, *The Quest for Nuclear Stability* (1982) on the nuclear test ban treaty; Richard Barnet, *The Alliance* (1983) on relations with Japan and Western Europe; Water LaFeber, *Inevitable Revolutions: The United States in Central America* (1985) on the Alliance for Progress.

Martin Luther King, Jr., September 1967.

# CHAPTER FOURTEEN

# 1963–1968

## The Great Society and Vietnam

John Kennedy bequeathed to Lyndon Johnson a legacy of social reform at home and a policy of military interventionism in Vietnam. That was a highly combustible mixture. Johnson, who wanted to be regarded as "president of all the people," also wanted to achieve a consensus in favor of his Great Society programs. But while he succeeded in implementing those programs in the fields of civil rights, education, and welfare, his escalation of the war in Vietnam led to unprecedented tensions and divisions. The consequences were disastrous. The war undermined social reform, stimulated the growth of irresponsible presidential power, triggered ruinous inflation, eroded fundamental civil liberties, and strained crucial diplomatic alliances. The war led, finally, to violence at home, which, if not so destructive as the violence in Vietnam, was a political turning point. It forced Johnson to withdraw from the presidential race in 1968 and paved the way for the victory of Richard M. Nixon.

## THE 1964 ELECTION

Lyndon Johnson knew as much about the exercise of political power as any American in the post-1945 era. He had grown up in central Texas, learning state and national politics during the New Deal era from such masters as fellow-Texan Sam Rayburn, Speaker of the House of Representatives. During the 1950s Johnson became leader of the Senate Democratic majority, where he wheeled and dealed, whipped and cajoled, flattered and intimidated until he became one of the strongest of all Senate leaders. Johnson often gathered votes by haranguing fellow-Senators in intense, person-to-person talks. Such encounters became known as the "treatment"; it was described by one victim as "a great overpowering thunderstorm that consumed you as it closed in around you." When he moved into the White House, Johnson was perfectly prepared to use the Executive's vast powers. Almost nothing could stop him from having his way, and he wanted his way on every issue. "When we made mistakes, I believe we erred because we tried to do too much too soon and never because we stayed away from challenge," he later wrote. "If the Presidency can be said to have been employed and to have been enjoyed, I had employed it to the utmost, and I had enjoyed it to the limit."

In the 1964 presidential campaign Johnson ran against Republican nominee Barry Goldwater, a conservative Senator from Arizona. Goldwater never had a chance. Johnson had been masterful in assuring continuity of government after Kennedy's murder. The Republicans' choice of Goldwater reflected a persistent belief in the existence of a "hidden vote," that is, a truly conservative vote that the Republican party could never obtain so long as it nominated liberal candidates. Goldwater made few concessions to Republican liberals, but he made an explicit overture to those on the right when, in accepting the nomination, he declared: "Extremism in the defense of liberty is no vice; moderation in the pursuit of justice is no virtue."

Goldwater employed several themes during the campaign. "The moral fiber of the American people is beset by rot and decay," Goldwater asserted. He traced this largely to the "political daddyism" of Lyndon Johnson and other politicians whose only concern was "the morality of get, the morality of grab." Goldwater noted ominously: "You will search in vain for *any reference* to God or religion in the Democratic platform." The Republican candidate promised to apply a carving knife to welfare state programs, thereby seeming to be cautious and negative while the Texan was pushing the country forward. "I just want to tell you this," Johnson told a cheering crowd during the campaign, "we're in favor of a lot of things and we're against mighty few."

Goldwater then made the mistake of appearing to be tougher than Johnson by asserting that the Democrats had dallied in Southeast Asia instead of winning a total victory. He further suggested that such a triumph would be hastened if military commanders in the field, rather than the President, had the final word in using nuclear weapons. Johnson effectively seized on these remarks to score Goldwater for being irresponsible and bloodthirsty. As for Vietnam, "We don't want our American boys to do the fighting for Asian boys," LBJ announced on September 25, 1964. "We don't want to get involved in a nation with 700 million people [Red China] and get tied down in a land war in Asia."

It was, therefore, as easy for the Democrats to argue that Goldwater would propel the nation into an all-out war in Vietnam as it was to portray him as an extremist on domestic issues. Johnson humiliated his opponent in the election, winning 61.1 percent of the popular vote, carrying forty-four states to Goldwater's six. One of every five people who had voted Republican in 1960 switched to the Democrats in 1964. When asked why, many said of Goldwater, "He's too radical for me." Prospects for the Johnson administration could hardly have been more promising.

## LYNDON JOHNSON AND THE GREAT SOCIETY

Lyndon Johnson had greater success than any President since Franklin Roosevelt in putting across his legislative program. After his sweeping triumph in 1964, Johnson could work with comfortable Democratic majorities in Congress. The Democrats—with majorities of 294 to 140 in the House, and 68 to 32 in the Senate—enjoyed their largest margin of control since 1937, the year Johnson had first entered Congress. The 71 freshman Democrats in the House, many of whom owed their election to the Johnson landslide, vied with one another in their willingness to cooperate with the White House. Then too, Johnson's Southern background and reputation as a moderate allowed him to enact far-reaching programs without losing his broad popular backing. Those programs often broke sharply with prevailing practice. The Revenue Act (1964) cut taxes by a whopping $11.5 billion even while the government was operating at a deficit. Advocates of an expansionary fiscal policy predicted correctly that the resulting boost in purchasing power would spur economic growth. The Housing Act (1965) providing rent supplements for low-income families displaced by urban renewal or otherwise unable to find suitable public housing. The government would subsidize that portion of their rent which exceeded 25 percent of their income. In 1965, too, Congress renovated the immigration laws, removing quotas based on race or national origin that had existed in some form for more than fifty years. The Great Society, however, channeled most of its energies into four other areas: the war on poverty, aid to education, medical care, and civil rights.

Publication of Michael Harrington's *The Other America* (1962) had done much to focus public attention on the problem of poverty. Harrington documented the existence of an "economic underworld" of some 40 to 50 million Americans, inhabited "by those driven from the land and bewildered by the city, by old people . . . and by minorities facing a wall of prejudice." He also explained how that world—which was off the beaten track of interstate turnpikes, insulated from the view of suburban commuters, and politically impotent—had become "socially invisible." Harrington believed that existing social welfare legislation bypassed the poor. Asserting that the welfare state was "not built for the desperate, but for those who are already capable of helping themselves," Harrington called for a comprehensive federal assault on poverty. This would require the extension of welfare benefits to the poor by expanding social security and minimum wage laws, providing medical care and new housing, and eliminating racial prejudice.

In January 1964 Lyndon Johnson called for an "unconditional war on poverty," and later that year Congress approved the Economic Opportunity Act as the chief weapon in that war. The measure created an Office of Economic Opportunity (OEO), which sought to provide education, vocational training, and job experience for impoverished youths. The OEO also sponsored community action programs with a view toward improving employment opportunities, health care, housing, and education in poor neighborhoods. These programs were supposed to elicit "the maximum feasible participation of residents of the areas and members of the groups served." The OEO, which spent $750 million in 1965 and $1.5 billion in 1966, succeeded in reducing poverty but not in eliminating it. Government statistics indicated that 15.4 percent of the American people lived in poverty in 1966, compared with 22.1 percent in 1959. Funds for OEO were always inadequate, and powerful local interests, anxious to get their hands on antipoverty money and patronage, often gained control of the community programs and used them for their own advancement.

The war on poverty was closely linked with federal aid to education. In the past such legislation had bogged down over the issue of assisting religious schools, but in 1965 the Johnson administration discovered an antipoverty rationale for school aid programs. The Elementary and Secondary Education Act (1965), which Congress passed in much the same form as Johnson requested, provided funds to local school districts according to a formula involving the number of children from low-income families in the county. The act also appropriated funds for the purchase of textbooks and other instructional materials that could be used by private as well as by public schools. Under this legislation, U.S. Office of Education expenditures soared from under $50 million in 1960 to $5.6 billion in 1973. Congress also followed Johnson's recommendation in approving the Higher Education Act (1965), which provided college scholarships for needy students, subsidized interest costs on loans to college students, and helped fund classroom construction.

In the case of health insurance, as in that of federal aid to education, Johnson enacted a program first proposed by Harry Truman twenty years earlier. To appease those who saw the specter of socialized medicine in any national plan, the administration tied health care to the existing social security system and allowed participating physicians to charge their "usual and customary fees" if these were reasonable. Moreover, it limited coverage to the poor and elderly, who were least able to afford medical care and least likely to be protected by private insurance plans. Medicare provided benefits covering approximately 80 percent of hospital expenses for all persons over age 65. Medicaid provided assistance in meeting doctors' bills for poor people, regardless of age, who qualified for public assistance. By July 1967, at the end of its first year of operation, 17.7 million of 19 million elderly Americans had enrolled in Medicare, one in five had entered a hospital under the law, and 12 million had used it to defray medical expenses.

Civil rights legislation rounded out the Great Society agenda. Early in 1964 the Senate passed a civil rights bill already approved by the House. The act, which grew out of John F. Kennedy's recommendations, barred discrimination on the basis of race in all public accommodations. These included restaurants, gas stations, places of entertainment, and hotels (except for private residences renting fewer than five rooms for overnight lodging). Almost all such enterprises were held to affect interstate commerce—a gas station, for example, if its customers drove across state lines. The act also authorized the Justice Department to bring suit against state facilities, such as parks and auditoriums, that remained segregated. Finally, the act included an equal opportunity clause making it unlawful for firms with more than twenty-five employees to discriminate in hiring on the grounds of race, religion, sex, or national origin.

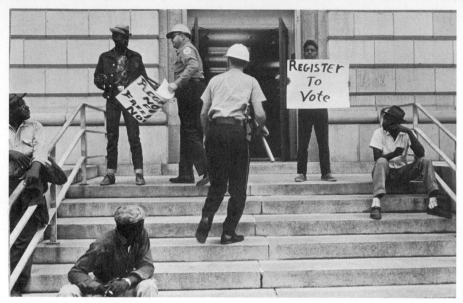

Selma, Alabama, March 1964.

The measure also included provisions to safeguard the right to vote, but these were soon superseded by the Voting Rights Act (1965), which the President urged Congress to enact after violence erupted in Alabama. Early in 1965 Dr. Martin Luther King, Jr., led a demonstration in the town of Selma, in a county where more than fifteen thousand blacks were eligible to vote but only 335 had been able to register. When state troopers attacked King's followers and extremists murdered a civil rights worker, Congress responded with a drastic measure. It affected counties that prescribed literacy or other tests for voting and contained a substantial nonwhite population, but in which relatively few blacks actually cast ballots. In those counties, located primarily but not exclusively in South Carolina, Georgia, Mississippi, Alabama, and Louisiana, the right to vote would no longer depend on literacy or character fitness. The only valid criteria would be age, residence, and citizenship. The Attorney General could appoint federal examiners to register voters, and the states, if they wished to protest, would have to appeal to a federal court in Washington, D.C.

Lyndon Johnson never passed up a chance to point out the historical significance of his legislation. To sign the education bill he traveled to the one-room schoolhouse he had attended as a child and asked his former teacher, 72-year-old "Miss Katie," to sit beside him. He journeyed to Independence, Missouri, to present the pen used to sign the Medicare bill to Harry Truman. He signed the Voting Rights Act in the same room that

Lincoln had used more than one hundred years before to free the slaves conscripted into the Confederate army. Similarly, Johnson used grandiose terms in defining his objectives. He proclaimed that the Great Society "rests on abundance and liberty for all. It demands an end to poverty and racial injustice." Despite its impressive accomplishments, few would claim that the Great Society achieved that much. Michael Harrington, whose book had inspired much of the antipoverty program, applauded Johnson's initiative but concluded sadly: "What was supposed to be a social war turned out to be a skirmish and, in any case, poverty won."

# THE WARREN COURT: JUDICIAL ACTIVISM

In seeking new remedies for the nation's problems, the President and Congress were joined by the third branch of government. Far from inhibiting reform, as it had often done in the past, the Supreme Court acted as a catalyst for social change. Of the justices most closely identified with the new activism, two—Hugo Black and William O. Douglas—had been appointed by Roosevelt; two others—Earl Warren and William Brennan— had been named by Eisenhower. The appointment of Arthur Goldberg in 1962 further tipped the scales toward judicial activism. Goldberg replaced Felix Frankfurter, who had long been the most articulate spokesman for the theory of judicial restraint. Frankfurter believed that judges must guard against the temptation to write their own biases into law and that society must not expect the Supreme Court to solve all its problems. After his retirement the Court moved boldly into areas it had once avoided.

In several important decisions, the Court curbed the erosion of civil liberties that had been under way since the 1950s. It found that membership in the Communist party did not alone constitute proof that an individual knew that the organization advocated the forcible overthrow of the government. Unless the government could demonstrate that a party member had such knowledge, conviction under the Smith Act was impossible. In 1965 the Court declared that the government could not require an individual to register as a member of a subversive organization, for to do so violated the constitutional prohibition against self-incrimination. The power of the House Un-American Activities Committee to force witnesses, under threat of contempt citation, to answer questions about their acquaintances was sharply curtailed. Finally, the Court affirmed the right of a Communist party member to obtain a passport for foreign travel. These civil liberties rulings were, ironically, among the Court's least controversial.

Following the path it had charted in the school desegregation decision of 1954, the Court threw its weight behind the civil rights movement. In 1963 the Court was forced to rule on cases stemming from a refusal to

The Supreme Court, 1965: (standing, left to right) Justices Byron R. White, William J. Brennan, Jr., Potter Stewart, and Abe Fortas; (seated, left to right) Justices Tom C. Clark, Hugo L. Black, Chief Justice Earl Warren, William O. Douglas, and John M. Harlan.

seat blacks at lunch counters. It found that local ordinances upholding segregation in private business establishments were unconstitutional, for they involved state action within the meaning of the Fourteenth Amendment. Even if no such ordinances existed, public statements upholding *de facto* segregation by city officials were held to constitute such action and were therefore enough to invalidate Jim Crow practices. In *Cox* v. *Louisiana* (1964) the Court reversed the conviction of black demonstrators in Baton Rouge who had refused to disperse when so ordered by the police. The justices decided that breach-of-the-peace laws could not serve as a pretext for preventing peaceable speech and assembly. The Court quickly sanctioned the civil rights acts of 1964 and 1965. It also ruled that delays in school desegregation were "no longer tolerable," and in *Loving* v. *Virginia* (1967) it struck down a state law barring marriage between persons of different races.

Religious dissenters, no less than civil rights workers, received new forms of legal protection. In the early 1960s, twelve states required Bible reading in public schools, and thirty others encouraged such exercises. Children in New York State recited a nonsectarian prayer: "Almighty God, we acknowledge our dependence upon Thee, and we beg Thy blessings upon us, our parents, our teachers and our country." A state court saw no objection to this. Although recitation might cause discomfort to nonbelievers, there was no need to "subordinate the spiritual needs of believers to the psychological needs of nonbelievers." But the Supreme Court, in *Engel* v. *Vitale* (1962), ruled the New York prayer unconstitutional on the grounds that it was a religious activity which placed an "indirect coercive pressure upon religious minorities." Then in 1963, the Court took up the case of Edward Schempp, a Unitarian, whose children attended a school in which biblical passages were read over the loudspeaker and students recited the Lord's Prayer. Those who did not wish to participate could wait outside the classroom. Schempp argued that this arrangement would penalize his children and make them feel like "oddballs." The Supreme Court agreed: "Through the mechanism of the State, all of the people are being required to finance a religious exercise that only some of the people want and that violates the sensibilities of others." The justices ruled that public schools could not show the slightest preference for any particular religion.

Nowhere did the Court break more decisively with the past than in the area of obscenity. In the mid-1950s, explicit sexual references in books, magazines, and motion pictures were illegal, and even such classics as D. H. Lawrence's *Lady Chatterley's Lover* were proscribed. The Supreme Court began to change all this in *Roth* v. *United States* (1957). Although ruling that obscenity did not deserve constitutional protection, the Court nevertheless felt it necessary to propose a test of obscenity, which became "whether to the average person applying contemporary community standards, the dominant theme of the material taken as a whole appeals to prurient interest." Thus began years of controversy over the meaning of such terms as "prurience." In 1961 the Court decided that a magazine could indeed appeal to prurient interest so long as it did not reveal "patent offensiveness." The justices went a step further in *Jacobellis* v. *Ohio* (1963), asserting that "material dealing with sex in a manner that advocates ideas . . . or has literary or scientific or artistic value or any other forms of social importance may not be branded as obscenity and denied the constitutional protection." In 1966 the Court extended such protection to *Fanny Hill*, an eighteenth-century novel usually considered pornographic. A book could not be banned unless "it is found to be utterly without redeeming social value." Under that standard, nearly all restrictions on the right of an adult to obtain sexually explicit material vanished.

This expansion of individual freedoms also characterized other areas of Court action. Three classic decisions revolutionized criminal justice procedures. In *Gideon* v. *Wainwright* (1963) the Court decided that an indigent person charged with a felony—in this instance, entering a pool hall and committing theft—was entitled to representation by a state-appointed attorney, although Florida law provided legal aid only for capital offenses. In *Escobedo* v. *Illinois* (1964) the Court ruled in favor of a man who, when interrogated on a murder charge, was not informed of his right to remain silent or permitted to see an attorney. Five justices believed that when the police centered their investigation on one individual and sought to extract a confession, they must allow the suspect to see a lawyer. Four members of the Court dissented: "Supported by no stronger authority than its own rhetoric, the Court today converts a routine police investigation of an unsolved murder into a distorted analogue of a judicial trial." A similarly close and bitter division prevailed in *Miranda* v. *Arizona* (1966), which involved a man who, after a two-hour interrogation, had confessed to charges of kidnapping and rape. The majority held that a confession could not be introduced as evidence unless the defendant had been informed at the outset of the interrogative process that he could see an attorney or remain silent, and that any information he provided would be used against him. The burden of proof was placed on the prosecution to show that a defendant knowingly waived the privilege against self-incrimination and the right to counsel. Four dissenting judges gravely warned that the ruling "will return a killer, a rapist or other criminal to the streets . . . to repeat his crime whenever it pleases him."

Judicial activism reached a culmination in decisions concerning legislative reapportionment. The Court in the past had skirted this issue, reasoning that if district lines were drawn unfairly, citizens should seek political, not judicial, redress. But in *Baker* v. *Carr* (1962) the Court entered the "political thicket." The case involved a resident of Memphis, Tennessee, who complained that because of malapportionment his vote for a member of the state legislature was worth less that the vote of a rural resident. The Supreme Court agreed that reapportionment was a proper question for judicial determination. Federal district judges were to set guidelines, and in 1963 the Supreme Court provided a clue as to what those guidelines should do when it overturned the county-unit voting system in Georgia, under which the candidate winning a majority in a county received all its votes. Justice William O. Douglas explained that political equality "can mean only one thing, one person, one vote." The Court applied this doctrine in *Reynolds* v. *Sims* (1964). Earl Warren, speaking for the majority, said that just as a state could not give a citizen two votes, so it could not permit any person's vote to count twice as much as anyone else's. Both houses of state legislatures had to be apportioned on the basis of population. Substantial equality, if not mathematical precision, was needed in determining the size of districts. Within a few years, the great majority of states had reapportioned their legislatures to conform with these rulings.

Most of the Warren Court's decisions sparked bitter controversy. One member of Congress called the justices an "unpredictable group of uncontrolled despots," and efforts were made to overturn certain rulings, particularly those concerning reapportionment and school prayer. In 1964 the House of Representatives passed a bill denying federal courts jurisdiction over apportionment, but the Senate refused to concur. A constitutional amendment that would have permitted the states to apportion one house of their legislatures on some basis other than population (if approved by voters in a referendum) passed the Senate in 1965 and 1966, but each time fell short of obtaining the required two-thirds majority. Similarly, in 1966 the Senate approved an amendment allowing voluntary participation in prayer in the public schools, but again by less than a two-thirds vote. Critics complained that the Supreme Court had become "a general haven for reform movements." There was, however, no minimizing the social and political impact of its rulings.

## ORIGINS OF THE NEW FEMINISM

Nor was there any minimizing the significance of the revival of feminism, inspired in part by Betty Friedan's *The Feminine Mystique*, published in 1963. The book was a powerful indictment of the "housewife-heroine" of the 1950s. After World War II, Friedan contended, women had been told that "they could desire no greater destiny than to glory in their own femininity," to seek fulfillment as wives and mothers. Instilled by women's magazines, which published such articles as "Have a Baby While You're Young," "How to Snare a Male," and "Cooking to Me is Poetry," the feminine mystique was also perpetrated by psychologists, advertisers, and educators, who dissuaded college women from seeking careers. Although women had accepted the feminine mystique because it seemed to promise a safe, secure existence, Friedan argued, it actually confined them to the home, "a comfortable concentration camp," produced feelings of emptiness, and deprived women of a sense of individualism. "I've tried everything women are supposed to do, but . . . I begin to feel I have no personality," one victim claimed. To escape the mystique, Friedan concluded, women had to develop "new life plans," establish independent careers, and pursue "goals that will permit them to find their own identity."

Betty Friedan's best seller immediately evoked a strong response from appreciative readers. "I and other women knew we were not alone," one woman wrote. "It struck at the very center of my being," wrote another. Friedan had not intended to create a new feminist movement in 1963. The publication of her book, in fact, did not immediately create one. But the civil rights struggle of the early 1960s provided another catalyst for feminist revival. First, civil rights advocates created a climate of protest that paved the way for other reform movements. Second, civil rights organizations demonstrated what committed pressure groups could accomplish through confrontation tactics and egalitarian arguments. Third, by demanding remedial legislation, the civil rights movement set a precedent for ending discrimination under law. Finally, and seemingly by accident, the Civil Rights Act of 1964 propelled a new women's movement into existence.

During congressional debate over Title VII of the civil rights bill, which prohibited discrimination in employment on grounds of race, a Virginia representative proposed an amendment that would prohibit such discrimination on grounds of sex as well. His goal was to discredit the bill, prevent its passage, and make its supporters look foolish. But once the new law was enacted, with its controversial amendment intact, the sex discrimination clause had an unexpected impact. When complaints about sex discrimination, sent to the Equal Employment Opportunity Commission (EEOC), received little attention, a small group of women's rights advocates—including Betty Friedan—tried to spur the commission to act on women's grievances. Since success seemed unlikely unless public support was mobilized, the new group took action. In 1966, twenty-eight women's rights supporters created the National Organization for Women, "to bring American women into full participation in the mainstream of American society NOW." Some NOW founders were veterans of President Kennedy's Commission on the Status of Women, formed in 1961, or of similar state commissions. Others were union leaders or professionals, like Friedan. Defining itself as a "civil rights" organization for women, NOW was the first national women's rights organization formed since 1920.

NOW's first effort was to provide the new feminist movement with an agenda. In its manifesto, NOW demanded "a truly equal partnership of the sexes, as part of the worldwide revolution of human rights." Denouncing pay disparities, employment inequities, and educational discrimination, NOW called for new types of social roles. "We reject the current assumption that a man must carry the whole burden of supporting himself, his wife, and family . . . or that marriage, home, and family are primarily woman's world and responsibility," NOW stated. While proposing a new relationship between men and women, NOW stopped short of an attack on the institution of marriage. "We believe that a true partnership between the sexes demands a different concept of marriage, an equitable sharing of the responsibilities of home and children, and of the economic burden of their support." Under the leadership of Betty Friedan, its first president, NOW became a national political pressure group, with growing numbers of local chapters. Its members sought to end sexual inequity through legislation and court decisions. They lobbied, demonstrated, filed class action suits to end discrimination in hiring and promotion, and insisted that newspapers stop publishing separate want ads for males and females.

Too radical for some, NOW proved too conservative for others. Its campaign was soon affected by the eruption of a younger, more radical, feminist wing, one that emerged from the ranks of civil rights activists.

In the early 1960s, hundreds of college students had participated in voter registration drives in the South. During these campaigns, young women developed a new consciousness of sex discrimination, both within the civil rights movement and outside it. "Assumptions of male supremacy are as . . . crippling to the woman as assumptions of white supremacy are to the Negro," one civil rights worker concluded. Similar objections to male dominance were voiced by young women who moved on to New Left community organizing projects outside the South. By 1967, radical women had developed their own brand of feminist attack, one that bore the imprint of New Left rhetoric. To radical feminists, women constituted "an oppressed class. Our oppression is total, affecting every facet of our lives. . . . We identify the enemy as man." The radical agenda, indeed, seemed to differ sharply from that of NOW. "The institution of marriage is the chief vehicle for the perpetuation of the oppression of women," the radicals contended. "It is through the role of wife that the subjugation of woman is maintained." The radical feminist recruitment technique of "consciousness raising" was also innovative. It consisted of small discussion groups, in which women reconsidered their personal experiences as political phenomena. Out of consciousness raising emerged the distinctive, all-encompassing goals of radical feminism: "women's liberation" and the eradication of "sexism." Eliminating sexism, like eliminating racism, meant changing attitudes, behavior, relationships, and institutions. The end was fundamental social change, or "revolution."

Structureless, with no headquarters, organization, or officers, women's liberation was again a contrast to NOW. "It's not a movement, it's a State of Mind," one advocate explained. But the new state of mind seemed contagious, notably among educated, younger women. During the late 1960s, women's liberation created a ferment of activity. Some radical feminists staged confrontations to gain media attention by crowning a sheep at the 1968 Miss America Pageant or invading an all-male bar in New York City. Other groups devoted their efforts to special projects—health collectives, day-care centers, abortion counseling services. Still others published "position papers" explaining their new ideology or sought to promote consciousness raising among new constituencies. While women's liberation campaigns were diffuse, NOW's goals became more specific. By 1968, the core of its legislative agenda was complete. NOW supported passage of an Equal Rights Amendment, a cause that had languished for several decades. It demanded repeal of state laws that prevented women from having abortions. And it urged the creation of government-funded day-care programs to ease the burden on working mothers.

The two feminist wings were apparently much at odds. Reform-minded NOW viewed liberationists as a lunatic fringe, given to wild pronouncements, while radical feminists denounced NOW members as bourgeois conservatives, whose equity goals were only minor. But the postures of the two wings were in fact complementary, as feminist successes in early 1970s were to prove.

# BLACK POWER AND URBAN RIOTS

The differences between radicals and reformers evident in the feminist movement were also increasingly apparent in the civil rights movement. The reformist approach, with its stress on nonviolent protest as a means and integration as an end, reached its zenith with the passage of the civil rights acts of 1964 and 1965. But the mid- and late-1960s saw the emergence of many black leaders who repudiated integration and nonviolence in favor of separatism and self-defense. The result was a fragmentation of the protest movement.

The "Black Power" slogan was coined by Stokely Carmichael, who had for several years worked with the Student Nonviolent Coordinating Committee (SNCC). This organization had helped organize the sit-ins and freedom rides. At first it endorsed Martin Luther King, Jr's, approach, but in the mid-1960s many in SNCC grew disenchanted with the existing civil rights program. They felt betrayed in 1964 when the Democratic convention refused to provide adequate representation for the Freedom Democratic party, which they had founded in Mississippi as an alternative to the lily-white state organization. SNCC workers found that turning the other cheek often created deep feelings of rage and hostility. Consequently, they became more receptive to the arguments of those, like Black Muslim leader Malcolm X, who advised: "If someone puts a hand on you, send him to the cemetery." An influx of white college students into the South to assist the civil rights movement also led some in SNCC to believe that such participation reinforced feelings of inferiority in Southern blacks. In June 1966, during a demonstration in Mississippi, Carmichael shouted: "Black Power! It's time we stand up and take over! Take over! Move on over, or we'll move on over you!"

In the following months Carmichael explained his viewpoint. Instead of seeking alliances with white liberals, who, he asserted, wished to perpetuate paternalistic control, blacks should do things for themselves. Instead of adopting nonviolent methods, "black people should and must fight back." Instead of demanding integration, which Carmichael considered "a subterfuge for the maintenance of white supremacy," blacks should develop their own cultural identity, purge their communities of outside control, and thereby achieve self-determination. Black Power looked toward the welding of blacks into a cohesive voting bloc capable of controlling political organizations inside the ghetto or of creating autonomous parties in the South. It meant establishing self-sufficient business and consumer cooperatives, and taking over public schools in black communities. "We don't need white liberals," Carmichael told a sympathetic convention of the Congress of Racial Equality (CORE). "We have to make integration irrelevant."

Not surprisingly, the sharpest critics of this doctrine were themselves veterans of the civil rights crusade. Roy Wilkins of the NAACP branded Black Power "the father of hatred and the mother of violence." Bayard Rustin, an associate of Martin Luther King, Jr., pointed out that blacks, as a minority, could not hope to achieve anything of substance without allies, particularly in the labor movement, among ethnic groups, and among poor whites. The organizations that endorsed Black Power—such as SNCC and CORE—were primarily composed of young people who disliked compromise, distrusted whites, and wanted fast results. Those that supported integration—such as the NAACP—believed that compromise was necessary, hoped to convert whites, and did not expect overnight triumphs. When Black Power advocates excluded NAACP field secretary Charles Evers from a rally in Jackson, Mississippi, he replied: "I'll be here when they're all gone."

Black Power spokesmen rejected nonviolence as well as integration. This justification of self-defense frightened many whites, but what frightened them even more were a series of explosions that rocked black ghettoes across the land. From 1964 to 1968 the United States experienced the most protracted period of domestic unrest since the Civil War. In 1964 blacks rioted in the Harlem and Bedford-Stuyvesant sections of New York City. A year later the Watts district in Los Angeles came to resemble a disaster area after a week-long riot left thirty-four dead, more than a thousand injured, and hundreds of buildings in ashes. To restore order, fifteen thousand National Guardsmen were sent to the city. In 1966 more than two dozen major riots occurred, most of them marked by looting, firebombs, and sniper fire. A study group concluded that the year's events "made it appear that domestic turmoil had become part of the American scene." Dozens of riots flared in black ghettoes in 1967. In Newark, police and guardsmen fired 13,326 rounds of ammunition in three days. In Detroit, 43 people were killed and 7200 arrested; the city was thrown into chaos. The assassination of Martin Luther King, Jr., in April 1968 led to the very thing the martyred civil rights leader most abhorred: race riots broke out in Chicago, Washington, and other cities.

These disturbances seldom involved violent clashes between whites and blacks, but rather looting, burning, and physical assaults within the ghetto's boundaries. The target might be a store owned by a white merchant, or it might be a white policeman, but the black communities themselves bore the heaviest cost. The riots did not usually occur along the points of intersection between black and white neighborhoods for, in fact, recent population shifts had done much to create two separate societies. From 1950 to 1966, 98 percent of the total black population growth

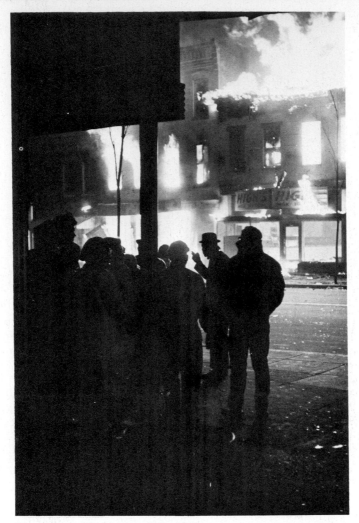

Ghetto riots: Washington, D.C., 1968.

took place in metropolitan areas, mainly in the central cities. In the same period, 78 percent of white population growth occurred in suburban areas. The National Advisory Commission on Civil Disorders, which was appointed by the President in 1967, found that the country was increasingly divided "into two societies; one, largely Negro and poor, located in the central cities; the other, predominantly white and affluent, located in the suburbs and in outlying areas."

It was this very division that the Commission, in its February 1968 report, blamed for the outbreaks. The Commission viewed the riots as a protest against conditions in the ghetto, and the ghetto as a product of white racism. The Commission pointed out that 16 to 20 percent of black city dwellers lived in "squalor and deprivation" and that 40 percent of the nation's nonwhite residents had incomes below the poverty line ($3335 for an urban family of four). It further noted that a black man was two times as likely to be unemployed as a white man, and three times as likely to be working in a low-paid or unskilled job. Chronic poverty bred disorder: "Prostitution, dope addiction, and crime create an environmental 'jungle' characterized by personal insecurity and tension. Children growing up under such conditions are likely participants in civil disorder." The Commission called for massive government programs to improve conditions in the ghettoes, but by 1968 popular support for such programs no longer existed, partly because of a backlash against the urban riots but more importantly because of the domestic costs of Lyndon Johnson's foreign policy.

## THE GLOBAL BACKGROUND TO VIETNAM

During his 1964 campaign against Barry Goldwater, Johnson had promised to pursue peace in Vietnam, but had also threatened wider war. In August he announced that two American destroyers had been attacked in international waters (the Gulf of Tonkin) by North Vietnamese torpedo boats. "The attacks were unprovoked," Johnson claimed. He ordered air strikes against North Vietnam's naval base, then urged Congress to pass a broad resolution giving him the authority to "take all necessary measures to repel any armed attack against the forces of the United States and to prevent further aggression." (It was later discovered that this resolution and the list of bombing targets had been drawn up by the White House two months before.) Democrats Wayne Morse of Oregon and Ernest Gruening of Alaska opposed the resolution. They argued that the circumstances of the attack were not clear. It seemed weird, they declared, that several small boats would challenge the strength of the United States Navy. They also believed such broad powers should not be given to the President. Senator Gaylord Nelson, Democrat of Wisconsin, urged an amendment opposing "extension of the present conflict," but this was dropped when he was assured that this was understood by Johnson. The House passed the Gulf of Tonkin Resolution 416 to 0, the Senate 88 to 2.

Four years later Secretary of Defense Robert McNamara admitted that the American people had been misled in 1964. He revealed that the American destroyers had been accompanying South Vietnamese ships and commandos that were attacking North Vietnamese bases. Shortly after the engagement, moreover, the North Vietnamese had approached the United States for peace discussions. Fearful that the South Vietnamese government was too weak even to negotiate with the North, Johnson had rejected the approach and again withheld the information from the American people.

The truth arrived much too late. Congress gave Johnson a blank check in 1964, then allowed him to cash it over and over again in the following years as he escalated the fighting into full-scale war without asking for a formal declaration of war from the legislative branch. That vital congressional restraint upon the wielding of incalculable power by a single man had disappeared. The President drew decision-making increasingly into his own hands until the fundamental choices in Vietnam—choices that would ultimately lead to hundreds of thousands of deaths—were made by four men in a regularly scheduled Tuesday luncheon group: Johnson, McNamara, Rusk, and the President's National Security Advisor, McGeorge Bundy (replaced in 1966 by Walt Whitman Rostow). There were few effective restraints on an imperial presidency during the next four years.

That presidential power was exercised in a rapidly changing world. In the Soviet Union Nikita Khrushchev fell from office in October 1964, victimized by his ineptness during the Cuban missile crisis and, more importantly, by his bungling of the Russian economy. He was replaced by two men, Aleksei Kosygin and Leonid Brezhnev, both of whom had risen to power under Stalin. They aimed at two objectives. First, they determined to mobilize Russian society for rapid economic advances. This determination and their apprenticeship under Stalin led the two leaders ruthlessly to squash any internal opposition. Dissident Soviet intellectuals, particularly Jews, were harassed, imprisoned, or declared insane. Second, the Soviets vowed to keep Chinese power contained. The two leading Communist nations were at each other throat, deeply divided over ideology and, more important, over clashing national interests. By 1965 fighting between Chinese and Soviet troops had erupted along a 1200-mile frontier. When Kosygin visited Chinese leader Mao Tse-tung in 1965, Mao said that differences between the two nations were so profound that they would last for ten thousand years. When Kosygin protested, Mao agreed to make it only nine thousand years.

These disagreements gave the Johnson administration an opportunity to reduce Cold War tensions by improving relations between the two superpowers. The Russians needed American economic aid and would welcome any easing of relations in Europe, for then they could concentrate on their more dangerous enemy in Peking. East-West trade did improve. Moscow and Washington, moreover, agreed in a Nonproliferation Treaty that they would work to prevent the spread of nuclear weapons. But no major initiative to end the Cold War occurred. American officials were too preoccupied with Vietnam. They insisted, moreover, that the Soviets were not truly mellowing. Secretary of State Rusk warned that while Americans had come to see Khrushchev as "an affable old grandfather, he was 68 and a half when he put missiles in Cuba." That perception seemed verified in August 1968, when Soviet troops suddenly marched into their satellite state of Czechoslovakia to terminate a new regime that, while remaining Communist, was nevertheless becoming more liberal and pro-Western.

As the two great powers struggled to keep the status quo, much of the rest of the world struggled to survive. In 1965 the North Atlantic nations (United States, Canada, and Western Europe) accounted for only 20 percent of the world's population but 70 percent of its income. The United States *added* as much to its income each year as Latin America had in total income, and twice as much as the total income received by Africans. Lyndon Johnson's childhood and his memories of the 1930s depression made him aware of this unequal distribution of the world's wealth. When mass starvation threatened India in 1965–67, he mobilized six hundred ships to dispatch one-fifth of the gigantic American grain crop. In one especially revealing remark the President warned Americans that "There are 3 billion people in the world and we have only 200 million of them. We are outnumbered 15 to 1. If might did make right they would sweep over the United States and take what we have. We have what they want."

In dealing with such immense problems, however, Johnson increas-

The Johnsons viewing Emanuel Leutze's *Heading West*.

ingly resorted to guns rather than food. He was not entirely free to choose. Foreign economic-aid programs had failed to work miracles in the newly emerging nations and were increasingly unpopular in Congress. Special commissions assigned to investigate the problem reported to Johnson that because government programs had failed, he should encourage private investment in Latin America, Asia, and Africa. That approach, however, was hollow. Private investors preferred to operate in secure, expanding Europe rather than in the chaotic Third World. When they did go into the newly emerging nations, their primary investment went into oil, minerals, and other raw materials, thereby further unbalancing economies that were already overly dependent on a single product.

Sometimes investors refused to move unless the American government assured their holdings. The Overseas Protection Insurance Corporation (OPIC) was thus created to insure investment against losses caused by confiscation or war. Investors who suffered such losses would be reimbursed by the United states government—that is, by the American taxpayers. Even this measure proved woefully insufficient to narrow the rapidly widening gap between the world's rich and poor. United Nations studies revealed in the mid-1960s that peoples in the newly emerging areas were closer to starvation than they were before World War II, and that their real income had shrunk so that it actually bought fewer goods than it had ten years earlier.

## LATIN AMERICA: A CASE STUDY—AND AFRICA

Latin America provided a case study of Johnson's response to these problems. United States businessmen had invested $15 billion directly into American-owned firms in these southern nations by 1965. They accounted for one-third of Latin America's industrial and mining output, one-third of its exports, and one-fifth of its taxes. These investors, however, were taking more out of Latin America than they were putting in. Between 1965 and 1970 the southern continent sent more money to Americans than it received in every year but 1967, and in 1969 the gap amounted to more than a half-billion dollars. In 1966 Latin Americans were receiving only enough development loans and grants to pay back the interest on the massive loans that they had needed during the 1955–65 period. While money for future development disappeared back into the United States, the population increased by 3 percent a year, one of the largest rates of increase in the world.

President Johnson had few remedies for these predicaments. Kennedy's Alliance for Progress was nearly dead, the victim of too little support in both North and South America. And while Johnson was devoting nearly all of his attention in foreign affairs to Vietnam, private interests lobbied in Congress to profit at Latin America's expense. For example, economic aid was given only when the recipient nation promised to spend it on American goods, regardless of the cost. Thus Bolivia had to spend American funds to buy ore carts for its vast mines from the United States even though the carts cost three times more than Belgian-made carts.

Increasing political tension resulted. The Alliance for Progress tried to build a new middle class, for such a class, in South as well as in North America, would be least likely to be revolutionary. But the middle classes were actually losing ground in Latin America by the 1960s, for their incomes were eaten by galloping inflation. "It is significant," a United Nations report observed, "that groups falling within the narrower definitions of the middle classes, such as bank employees and school teachers, have been among the most frequent and militant participants in strikes in recent years." As those middle classes grew bitter, societies polarized between very rich and very poor. Revolution grew more likely. To stop any possibility of radical change, military governments rose to power in Brazil, Bolivia, Guatemala, and Ecuador. Latin America was being torn apart.

Lyndon Johnson responded forcefully to a rebellion in Santo Domingo. In 1961 the thirty-year dictatorship of Rafael Trujillo ended with his assassination. Three years of confusion followed until the army took control. In April 1965, however, a strange combination of liberals, radicals, and low-ranking army officers tried to replace the military rulers with a more liberal government. As the military regime crumbled, it pleaded for help from President Johnson and used the bait that supporters of Fidel Castro were gaining power. Johnson immediately dispatched 22,800 American troops into the Caribbean nation to put down the rebellion. At first the President said he only wanted to assure the safety of American citizens. It soon became clear that he intended to use force to establish a stable, pro-American government. He did this even though the United States had signed the Charter of the Organization of American States (1948) which said in part, "No state or group of states has the right to intervene, directly or indirectly, for any reason whatever, in the internal or external affairs of any other state." The administration proclaimed that the troops had prevented "the Communists . . . from taking over."

No one, however, has ever been able to demonstrate that either Communists or Castroites were important in any way in the uprising. But that did not prevent the President from announcing the "Johnson Doctrine": the United States would use force, if necessary, anywhere in the hemisphere to prevent Communist governments from coming to power. The Latin Americans did not appreciate this reappearance of Theodore Roosevelt's and Woodrow Wilson's gunboat diplomacy. "It is fall here," one reporter wrote from South America, "and U.S. flags as well as leaves are being burned."

American policies in Africa (especially in those nations south of the Sahara) were not dissimilar. Between 1945 and 1970 more than forty African nations gained independence as the old European empires fragmented. Few of the new governments had the economic or political experience to hold together national, freely elected regimes. For its part, the United States provided little help. In 1965 American development aid amounted to $200 million spread among thirty-three nations. One country received $50,000. Such a program did nothing to improve conditions internally and relations with the United States externally. Eight countries fell to army coups between 1964 and 1966 as parts of the continent seemed headed toward tribal warfare. American investment meanwhile centered on two white-dominated governments, South Africa and Southern Rhodesia. In addition, South Africa received military aid because of its strategic location at the tip of the continent. Both nations appeared prosperous and stable, but appearances were at the expense of the black population, which comprised the overwhelming majority in both countries. The blacks were victimized by *apartheid*, a white-controlled system that, through legislation and violence, brutally separated and exploited the blacks.

The Johnson administration intervened directly in the former Belgian Congo. That area of 17 million blacks had suddenly become free in 1960 despite the lack of any preparation by the former Belgian rulers. Civil war erupted, but the United Nations, with American and Russian support, stabilized the area. By 1964 the United States was the dominant foreign power in the Congo, and the vast copper and diamond mines again produced their riches. Then nationalist revolts began, with rebels massacring thousands of blacks and whites. Despite help from the Central Intelligence Agency, the Congolese government could not quell the rebellion. The United States staged a paratroop strike to free a number of hostages, including sixteen Americans, whom the insurgents had threatened to kill, and by late 1965 the situation was quieted. When it flared again in 1967, President Johnson prepared large-scale military aid for the Congo, but Senate leaders, particularly conservative Democrats from the South, forced a scaling-down of the aid. The Senators argued that the administration had enough racial problems at home and enough military activity in Vietnam. The Congolese government then settled its own internal problems.

# VIETNAM ABROAD

The President's responses in Santo Domingo and the Congo differed only in degree from those in Vietnam. In each case the United States chose armed might as a solution for the social ills that generated nationalist revolts. Johnson's preoccupation with force led humorist Art Buchwald to claim that the President wanted to alert two airborne divisions, four Marine brigades, and the Atlantic fleet—before proclaiming Mother's Day. Americans would learn that military intervention often not only failed to solve the root problems but aggravated them.

The Gulf of Tonkin incidents in August 1964 were followed by five months of little fighting, but the Johnson administration was exceptionally busy. The murder of President Diem in 1963 had created political chaos. Vietnamese regimes changed so frequently that Johnson twice felt that he had to reject North Vietnamese peace overtures for fear that the American-supported regime in Saigon lacked the strength to negotiate an acceptable peace. These peace feelers were kept secret from the American people.

On February 5, 1965 (two days after the final American rejection of the second North Vietnamese peace approach), the Communists killed seven Americans at a base in Pleiku. The President immediately ordered bombing of the north in carefully selected attacks aimed at cutting off supplies flowing south to the Communist National Liberation Front of South Vietnam (the NLF). The raids were also a warning that North Vietnam should not try to escalate the pressure on the rickety regime in Saigon. South Vietnamese governments, however, had fallen owing to lack of support within the country. As for supplies coming from the north, a careful study by the Department of State, written to justify the bombings, actually revealed that of fifteen thousand weapons taken from Communist soldiers, fewer than two hundred were made in Communist factories. The remainder had been captured from South Vietnamese troops, the study concluded.

The United States escalation, therefore, was aimed less at stopping North Vietnamese intervention in the south (for in February 1965 that intervention was not significant) than at propping up Saigon regimes, which seemed incapable of defending themselves in the civil war. In March the escalation took a drastic turn. Johnson sent in Marine battalions. He thus started a build-up of American troops who were to participate directly in the combat rather than merely be "advisors" to South Vietnamese soldiers. During the summer, over one hundred thousand more Americans poured into the country. The President tried to cover these actions by declaring that the troops would only secure American and South Vietnamese bases. In a speech in April, he announced that he would enter "unconditional discussion" with North Vietnam but that the Communists would have to begin the discussions by accepting the fact of an independent South Vietnam, something the North Vietnamese would never accept. The government of Ho Chi Minh responded with its own four-point offer. It included a return to the 1954 Geneva Agreement (which stated that the boundary between north and south would only be temporary) and settlement of South Vietnam's affairs "by the South Vietnamese people themselves in accordance with the program of the [NLF] without any foreign interference." The United States replied with accelerated use of force.

With few pauses, American bombing continued for seven years. More bombs were dropped on Vietnam than on Germany, Japan, and their Axis allies during World War II. The bombing had little military effect. By 1966, eleven tough regiments of North Vietnamese troops were in the south to fight 200,000 Americans and 550,000 South Vietnamese. The Russians and Chinese supplied ever larger amounts of goods to the Communists. Most ominous of all, the North Vietnamese, who historically had fought and feared the Chinese, were necessarily moving closer to Peking in order to receive aid. The Kennedy-Johnson policy was aimed at blocking the influence of China, but the policy seemed to be producing the opposite result.

By April 1966, more Americans were being killed in action than South Vietnamese. In July, the number of American dead reached 4440, more than the number killed in the American Revolution and ten times the dead in the Spanish-American War. The results were discouraging. The South Vietnamese controlled less than 25 percent of their own 12,000 hamlets. But a stable government was finally established in Saigon by the army. Its leaders were Major-General Nguyen Van Thieu as head and, as Premier, Nguyen Cao Ky, a swashbuckling Air Force officer who had fought with the French against the Vietnamese nationalists and who had been overheard expressing admiration for Adolf Hitler.

The new regime failed to reverse the course of the war. Lieutenant Colonel John Vann, perhaps the most perceptive American advisor to serve in Vietnam, put his finger on one fundamental problem: "This is a political war and it calls for discrimination in killing. The best weapon for killing would be a knife, but I'm afraid we can't do it that way. The worst is an airplane. The next worse is artillery." Americans were not prepared either politically or militarily to fight such a war. They wanted to resort to their unimaginably powerful technology to blow up the enemy from the air or engage him in massive ground battles. The Communists actually had little to blow up (except their ports, where the presence of Russian ships made attacks dangerous), and they refused to stand still in large groups as targets for United States artillery. They fought more like George Washington's guerrilla forces of 1777 than like the Chinese in Korea during 1951. The war was confusing and frustrating both in Vietnam and, increasingly, at home. In 1966 Johnson blurted out the problem: "Most people wish we weren't there; most people wish we didn't have a war; most people don't want to escalate it, and most people don't want to get out."

## CHILD CARE: DR. SPOCK AND THE PEACE MOVEMENT

Benjamin Spock was born in 1903. He attended Yale University, cast his first vote for Calvin Coolidge in 1924 ("my father said he was the greatest president we've ever had"), attended Columbia medical school, and in 1929 began practicing pediatrics in New York City. At the time, the most popular child-raising manual was John Watson's *The Psychological Care of Infant and Child* (1928). Watson believed that every action was a response to a stimulus, that a person was "an organic machine that takes in food and lets out waste products." The chief danger facing children was that they would be smothered by parental love and, consequently, become dependent

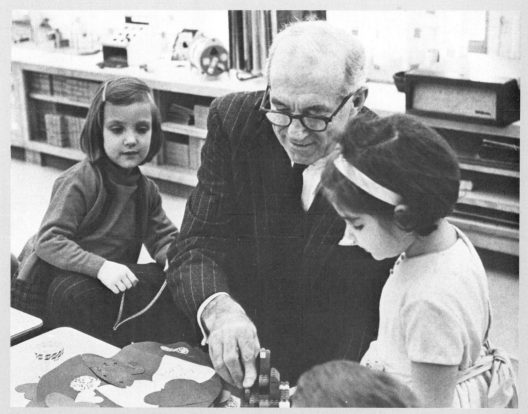

Dr. Spock with nursery-school-age children.

Dr. Spock conferring with parents.

rather than self-reliant. Warning against the "dangers lurking in the mother's kiss," Watson asserted that cuddling a child would lead to "inval-idism," the inability to cope with the harsh realities of life. Children should be treated as though they were young adults. "If you must, kiss them once on the forehead when they say good night. Shake hands with them in the morning." Watson left a professorship at Johns Hopkins to become vice-pres-ident of an advertising agency, where he applied his theory to the task of finding the right stimuli to induce consumers to respond to his clients' products.

In the 1930s and 1940s the study of child development was revolutionized by Dr. Arnold Gesell, who attempted to establish scientific norms for each stage of mental and physical growth. But it was Dr. Spock who popularized the new approach. His *Pocket Book of Baby and Child Care* (1946), written while he was serving in the U.S. Naval Reserve, contradicted Watson. Spock advised parents to relax, use their common sense, trust their own judgment, and "be flexible and adjust to the baby's needs and happiness." "Don't be afraid to love him and enjoy him. Every baby needs to be smiled at, talked to, played with, fondled—gently and lovingly—just as much as he needs vitamins and calories. That's what will make him a person who loves people and enjoys life."

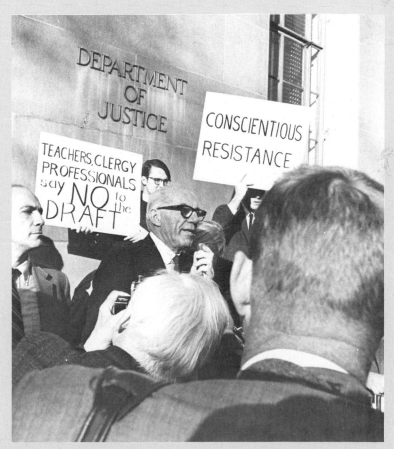

Dr. Spock at antiwar rally, 1967.

Spock, however, did not advocate total permissiveness. "Parents can't feel right toward their children in the long run unless they can make them behave reasonably, and children can't be happy unless they are behaving reasonably."

By 1963 Spock's book was selling about a million copies a year, becoming the biggest seller (next to the Bible) in American history. Spock's career took him to the Mayo Clinic in Minnesota, the medical school at the University of Pittsburgh, and Western Reserve University in Cleveland. Gradually, he turned to political action. In 1960 he supported John F. Kennedy, and in 1962, when the President resumed nuclear testing in response to Russian tests, Spock joined the peace movement. In 1964 he campaigned for Lyndon Johnson, but then became a sharp critic of the war in Vietnam. In 1967 Spock and 28,000 other people signed "A Call to Resist Illegitimate Authority," which branded the war in Vietnam illegal and unconstitutional, supported those who opposed the draft, and called on others to join in "this confrontation with immoral authority." Early in 1968 Spock and four others were indicted for conspiring to counsel violation of the Selective Service Act.

The trial, which took place in Boston, lasted nearly a month. Spock took the witness stand to explain why he opposed the war in Vietnam. "I believed that we were destroying a country that had never intended us any harm. . . . What is the use of physicians like myself trying to help parents to bring up children, healthy and happy, to have them killed in such numbers for a cause that is ignoble?" Four of the defendants, including Spock, were found guilty, fined, and sentenced to two-year prison terms. But in July 1969 a U.S. Court of Appeals reversed the convictions on the grounds that the judge's instructions to the jury were improper. The charges against Dr. Spock were dropped. He responded, "I shall redouble my efforts to free the hundreds of young men who are now serving time for resisting the war."

## VIETNAM IN THE WHITE HOUSE

Yet the President insisted on remaining in the war. Escalating troop strength to 485,000 by 1968, he committed the country to the longest and most tragic of all its wars. He did so for several reasons.

First, he believed that South Vietnam was the test of whether the United States could prevent communism—particularly the Chinese brand, which resulted from peasant revolution—from controlling all of Asia. After a fact-finding journey to Vietnam in 1961, Johnson reported to President Kennedy that since "there is no alternative to United States leadership in Southeast Asia," Americans must make a "fundamental decision whether we are to attempt to meet the challenge of Communist expansion now in Southeast Asia by a major effort . . . or throw in the towel." He never changed that view. Nor did he ever doubt that the civil war was caused not by Vietnamese nationalism but by Vietnamese who were part of a worldwide Communist movement inspired by China. The Chinese were his primary concern: "Communist China apparently desires the war to continue whatever the cost to their Allies," the President remarked on May 13, 1965. "Their target is not merely South Vietnam. It is Asia."

Second, Johnson believed that he was carrying on an essential American policy, for he was stopping communism in Asia just as President Truman had contained the Russians in Europe. He did not wish to repeat the mistake made at Munich in 1938, when England and France allowed Hitler to take Czechoslovakia and open the way for World War II. Johnson and Secretary Rusk directly compared Munich and Vietnam, a comparison that would have resulted in an instant "failure" for any college student who tried to make it in a history class. But neither Johnson nor any of his close advisors suggested that Asian economic and political conditions differed fundamentally from those of Europe, or that the United States enjoyed strong allies in Europe (allies tied together by language, culture, and wealth) whereas no such friends existed in Asia. Instead, the President attacked critics who pointed out these vital differences by calling them "special pleaders who counsel retreat in Vietnam. . . . We cannot accept their logic . . . that subjugation by an armed minority in Asia is different from subjugation by an armed minority in Europe."

Third, he claimed that he was defending commitments in Vietnam made by Eisenhower and Kennedy. His relationship with Kennedy's ghost, however, involved both love and hate. He publicly pledged to carry out the late President's policies, but privately Johnson never forgave Kennedy for relegating him into the background between 1961 and 1963. He especially grew bitter as many of Kennedy's former aides quit the foundering Johnson administration to protest against the war they had helped begin. When once reminded of a Kennedy policy, Johnson barked, "The touch football crowd isn't making decisions around here anymore." But the Texan was equally determined not to give up where Kennedy had taken the stand. He would maintain the hallowed commitment and also show the Kennedyites.

Fourth, the President believed that the commitment was consistent with American interests at home as well as abroad. He emphasized "one overriding rule: . . . that our foreign policy must always be an extension of this nation's domestic policy." This "rule" had an ironic ring in the 1960s, for the fire, rioting, and violence that ripped American cities between 1965 and 1968 mirrored the much greater destruction inflicted on Vietnam. Johnson was not, of course, referring to *that* mirror, but was pointing to the New Deal tradition, which shaped his political outlook. The New Deal had used government action in an attempt to improve living conditions for poor Americans. As President, Johnson announced a "Great Society" program to modernize and complete the New Deal. He believed that in a world made smaller by technology, Americans had to help others if they hoped to improve their own society. He proposed an Asian Development Bank and a vast plan to enrich the Mekong Valley in Southeast Asia, much as the New Deal had built the Tennessee Valley Authority. Only the Communists stood in the way. To eliminate them, however, became so costly that by 1966 Johnson was forced to cut back his Great Society at home. "Because of Vietnam," he finally admitted, "we cannot do all that we should, or all that we would like to do" in the United States.

Fifth, economic bonds between the United States and Vietnam developed, but quite differently than the administration had planned. The money pumped into the military buildup brought a rosy glow to the American economy. One economic expert concluded that American defense expenditures supported 95 percent of the employment in aircraft and missile industries, 60 percent in shipbuilding, and 40 percent in radio and communications. Including three million in the armed services, nearly seven million Americans were dependent on the Defense Department budget, and Vietnam expenditures constituted an increasingly larger proportion of that budget. When peace rumors circulated in 1965–66, the New York Stock Exchange was hit with heavy losses as investors rushed to cash in their securities before prices dropped. One broker believed that "a genuine peace offer" would "knock the market out of bed." After all, he observed, the government had scheduled a $60-billion defense budget on the assumption that the war would continue. In Vietnam itself, American oil companies and banks led the way, investing to benefit from the war and particularly from the gigantic reconstruction effort that would follow. The government encouraged such investment; its Agency for International Development (AID) provided a 100 percent guarantee against loss of money because of war or confiscation. The American business community did not turn against the war until after 1967, when the conflict began to erode rather than accelerate the economy.

Sixth, Johnson believed that he possessed the presidential power required to realize his objectives. By the mid-1960s the presidency dominated the nation in a manner undreamed of by the Founding Fathers. The Constitution's framers had feared unchecked power, and with Congress's abdication of responsibility in the Gulf of Tonkin Resolution, the President's power in foreign affairs had few limits. As journalist James Reston observed, "Something important has happened in America since Woodrow Wilson went to his grave" believing that a President's foreign policy could be paralyzed by Congress. Military efficiency as well as Congress's weakness had helped create that power. Johnson was the first president in the nation's history to enter war with a great army prepared to fight. Indeed, it was too easy to order this remarkable striking force halfway around the world.

Finally, the President had strong public support. In December 1965, as he rapidly escalated the conflict, public opinion polls indicated that 58 percent of the American people believed that increased bombing was the way to peace, and 82 percent agreed that United States troops would have to remain in Vietnam until the Communists agreed to terms. One-third of those having an opinion thought nuclear weapons should be used if they would shorten the war. (Such an opinion allowed Johnson, who opposed using nuclear weapons, to appear as a moderate as he escalated the conventional war.) Support came from all sectors. Some 477,000 students in 322 colleges gave their written commitment to the President's policies in 1966. The American Federation of Labor's national convention pledged "unstinting support" for all measures necessary "to halt Communist aggression" and bring peace to Vietnam. When antiwar spectators got in a shouting match with AFL delegates, union leader George Meany ordered that "those kookies" be thrown out of the hall. The president of the 250,000-member U.S. Jaycees—formerly the Junior Chamber of Commerce—announced a program to expose "leftists" and "peace advocates," adding that the Jaycees would work closely with the FBI. A critical newspaper suggested that the Jaycees might better sponsor discussions of the Bill of Rights.

Both the public and Congress were supporting an anti-Communist, Cold War policy that had existed since 1947. Neither was capable of questioning that policy. Nor was Johnson. "The President is still confusing popularity with policy," James Reston noted in late 1965. "And this could easily lead us deeper into the bog."

## VIETNAM AT HOME

By 1965 important segments of public opinion were beginning to change, and this change was partly inspired by intellectuals—historians, political scientists, and sociologists—who raised fundamental questions about the administration's war policy. Naturally, the questioning was loudest on college campuses, especially at "teach-ins" which began at the University of Michigan in March 1965 and then had spectacular success at other universities. But the administration refused to take its critics seriously. Although many were specialists in Asian and international affairs, Rusk disparaged their credentials, remarking "That a man knows everything there is to know about enzymes doesn't mean that he knows very much about Vietnam." Johnson simply recruited advisors from among like-minded scholars. One was Walt W. Rostow, a vocal advocate of "staying the course." Rostow, the President said, was "going to be *my* goddamned intellectual."

The war in Vietnam inspired a broader indictment of American liberalism by "new left" radicals. They drew on the work of sociologist C. Wright Mills, who had argued that American society was governed by a "power elite" composed of businessmen, military officials, and political leaders, "an elite whose power probably exceeds that of any small group of men in world history." Radicals believed that domestic reforms only propped up an immoral social system. Tom Hayden, a founder of Students for a Democratic Society (SDS), argued that many reforms were "illusory or token, serving chiefly to sharpen the capacity of the system for manipulation and oppression." According to Carl Oglesby, another SDS leader, liberals like John F. Kennedy and Lyndon Johnson were responsible for American involvement in Vietnam. "Think of the men who now engineer that war—those who study the maps, give the commands, push the buttons, and tally the dead," Oglesby said in November 1965. "They are not moral monsters. They are all honorable men. They are all liberals."

By 1967 and 1968 the rhetoric escalated with the war until it seemed the society was on the edge of a breakdown. The President implored American troops to "hang the coonskin on the wall." In Vietnam, when an army chaplain was asked to pray for a victory, he is supposed to have pleaded: "Oh, Lord, give us the wisdom to find the bastards and the strength to pile it on." After troops devastated a village allegedly controlled by the Vietcong, an American officer blurted out, "It became necessary to destroy the town in order to save it." At home, protesters chanted, "Hey, hey, LBJ, how many kids did you kill today?" as they tried to disrupt draft boards and block troop trains. One person burned himself to death at the door of the Pentagon. Students publicly set fire to their draft cards even after Congress passed a law imposing a $10,000 fine or five years in jail for such an act. Colleges were disrupted as students occupied buildings and sometimes battled police summoned to evict them.

Soon the disenchantment approached the White House itself. Senator J. William Fulbright, Democrat of Arkansas and Chairman of the powerful Senate Foreign Relations Committee, had long been a close friend of Johnson's, but turned after he discovered that the President had lied about the Gulf of Tonkin affair and the Santo Domingo intervention. Even more ominous, Secretary of Defense Robert McNamara began doubting. The President depended on him more than on any other man in the government. In August 1967, McNamara publicly called the bombing campaign a failure. Three months later Johnson sent him off to become president of the World Bank, a position that McNamara held with great distinction through the next decade as he multiplied the bank's resources for helping feed and develop newly emerging areas.

The closest American allies also fell away. Western Europeans enjoyed prosperity and new political cohesion from their European Economic Community (EEC). When it accepted Great Britain as a member in 1970, the EEC joined the United States, Russia, and Japan as the world's great economic powers. The Europeans viewed the Vietnam War as a terrible mistake, for it forced Johnson to neglect vital ties with the Atlantic nations

Tet, 1968: South Vietnamese national police chief shooting suspected North Vietnamese terrorist.

and severely weakened the American economy, the EEC's main overseas customer. Not even the British would help in Vietnam. Frustrated and angered, Secretary of State Dean Rusk exploded to a British journalist, "All we needed [from you in Vietnam] was one regiment. . . . But you wouldn't. Well, don't expect us to save you again. They can invade Sussex and we wouldn't do a damned thing about it." With few friends at home and even fewer overseas, Johnson observed that he was "in the position of a jackrabbit in a hailstorm, hunkered up and taking it."

# THE 1968 ELECTION

The worst was yet to come. Throughout 1967, American military commanders confidently predicted victory, but the bombing had not prevented the North Vietnamese from doubling their army in the south to 475,000 between 1965 to 1967. The build-up on both sides had changed a civil war within South Vietnam to a war between the United States and North Vietnam. In early February 1968, during the Tet Lunar New Year holiday, the Communists launched a devastating attack that resulted in the seizure of vital portions of the country; they even threatened the supposedly impregnable U.S. Embassy in Saigon. Because large numbers of Communists were killed in the offensive, the Johnson administration claimed victory. But the American generals then stunned Johnson by requesting another 206,000 more men to continue the war.

The President ordered an in-depth analysis of the war by experts in and out of government. They bluntly informed Johnson that he was "being led down the garden path" by the American military in Vietnam. This news was coupled with returns from the first Democratic presidential primary in New Hampshire, where Johnson barely defeated antiwar critic Senator Eugene McCarthy of Minnesota, who received a surprising 42 percent of the vote. In late March, the President dramatically announced on television that he was cutting back bombing in order to get North Vietnam to the peace table, and, so that he could concentrate on obtaining peace, he would not run for reelection in 1968.

Lyndon Johnson had become a casualty of the war. Not only had the fighting gone badly, but because the administration had underestimated war expenses in 1966–67, the economy entered a sharp inflationary spiral. It was the beginning of the worst sustained inflationary period in twentieth-century America. In April Martin Luther King's assassination set off riots in many cities, including Washington D.C., where smoke from burning buildings floated over the White House. Two months later, presidential candidate Robert Kennedy, Democratic Senator from New York, was murdered in Los Angeles. A climax to the violence occurred with the Democratic Convention in Chicago during August, when police and U.S. Army troops used tear gas to control antiwar demonstrators. Johnson could send a half-million men to Vietnam, but could not attend his own party's nominating convention. Through the smoke and the suffocatingly sweet smell of tear gas, Vice-President Hubert Humphrey was named as the Democratic nominee, and Senator Edmund Muskie of Maine the vice-presidential candidate.

The Republican ticket was headed by Richard Nixon and Spiro Agnew, governor of Maryland. Nixon had risen from the political dead after his loss in 1960 and then another defeat in the California governor's race in 1962. In the next six years he traveled widely to cement his ties with grass roots Republicans and was in the forefront of those who attacked Johnson for not ending the Vietnam war on American terms. Nixon, however, emphasized law-and-order themes during the campaign while deemphasizing the war by saying only that he had "a plan" for stopping it. Agnew was more direct, blasting Humphrey for being "soft on inflation, soft on communism, and soft on law and order."

The presence on the ballot of Governor George C. Wallace of Alabama did much to shape the outcome of the election. Formerly a Democrat, Wallace broke with the party in 1968 to run on the American Independent ticket. He adopted a hard-line anti-Communist foreign policy, even selecting retired General Curtis E. LeMay (who spoke of bombing North

Vietnam "back to the Stone Age") as his running mate. Wallace appealed to normally Democratic voters, especially in the South, who were dismayed by the breakdown of law and order and by antiwar demonstrations but who were not prepared to vote Republican. Wallace received 9.9 million votes, or 13.5 percent of the total. So Richard Nixon, with only 43.4 percent of the popular vote, eked out a victory over Hubert Humphrey by a 1-percent margin.

Although the war in Vietnam was not the only issue in 1968, it had nevertheless altered the course of American politics. In 1964 the voters had given Lyndon Johnson a dual mandate: for reform and for peace. Johnson had fulfilled the first part of the mandate, but not the second. By 1968 the war had made the return of the Republicans possible, and even the reforms so important to Johnson were placed in jeopardy.

# Suggested Reading

For political, social, and economic developments in the 1960s, consult Allen J. Matusow, *The Unraveling of America: A History of Liberalism in the 1960s* (1984); Morris Dickstein, *Gates of Eden: American Culture in the Sixties* (1977); Arthur M. Schlesinger, Jr., *Robert Kennedy and His Times* (1978); and Doris Kearns, *Lyndon Johnson and the American Dream* (1976). Great Society welfare programs are defended in Sar A. Levitan and Robert Taggart, *The Promise of Greatness* (1976) and criticized in Charles Murray, *Losing Ground: American Social Policy, 1950–1980* (1984).

Appraisals of the Supreme Court are provided in Alexander Bickel, *Politics and the Warren Court* (1965); and Philip Kurland, *Politics, the Constitution, and the Warren Court* (1970). Four judicial biographies are also informative: G. Edward White, *Earl Warren: A Public Life* (1982); Bernard Schwartz, *Super Chief: Earl Warren and His Supreme Court* (1983); James F. Simon, *Independent Journey: The Life of William O. Douglas* (1980); and Gerald T. Dunne, *Hugo Black and the Judicial Revolution* (1977). Legislative reapportionment is discussed in Richard Cortner, *The Apportionment Cases* (1970); the relationship between church and state is considered in Frank Sorauf, *The Wall of Separation* (1976).

For the resurgence of feminism in the 1960s, see Sara Evans, *Personal Politics: The Roots of Women's Liberation in the Civil Rights Movement and the New Left* (1979); Judith Hole and Ellen Levine, *Rebirth of Feminism* (1971); and Jo Freeman, *The Politics of Women's Liberation* (1979). For the civil rights movement, black power, and the ghetto riots, consult David J. Garrow, *Protest at Selma: Martin Luther King, Jr. and the Voting Rights Act of 1965* (1978); Steven F. Lawson, *Black Ballots: Voting Rights in the South, 1944–1969* (1976); Clayborne Carson, *In Struggle: SNCC and the Black Awakening of the 1960s* (1981); Robert Fogelson, *Violence as Protest* (1971); and Joe R. Feagin and Harlan Hahn, *Ghetto Revolts: The Politics of Violence in American Cities* (1973).

The antiwar movement is described in Irwin Unger, *The Movement: A History of the American New Left, 1959–1972* (1974); and Lawrence Wittner, *Rebels Against*

*War* (1984). For the 1968 election, see Lewis Chester, Godfrey Hodgson, and Bruce Page, *An American Melodrama* (1970). Marshall Frady, *Wallace* (1970) is also useful.

On foreign policy, begin with the well-annotated bibliography in R. H. Burns, ed., *Guide to American Foreign Relations Since 1700* (1983). There is no comprehensive treatment of LBJ's foreign policies, but the following are useful: Warren Cohen, *Dean Rusk* (1980); Philip L. Geyelin, *Lyndon B. Johnson and the World* (1966); George W. Ball, *The Past Has Another Pattern* (1982), a key insider who dissented; and W. W. Rostow, *Diffusion of Power, 1958–1972* (1972), another insider; as well as Johnson's own *Vantage Point* (1971). For Vietnam, begin with George Herring, *America's Longest War* (1979); William Appleman Williams, *et al., America in Vietnam; A Documentary History* (1985); Larry Berman, *Planning a Tragedy* (1982) on the pivotal 1965 decisions; and Guenter Lewy's controversial *America in Vietnam* (1978). Some of the public opinion can be gleaned from Ralph B. Levering, *The Public and American Foreign Policy, 1918–1978* (1978); and Richard Scammon and Ben Wattenberg, *The Real Majority* (1970) on the 1968 election.

Both Jessica Mitford, *The Trial of Dr. Spock* (1969), and Lynn Z. Bloom, *Dr. Spock: Biography of a Conservative Radical* (1972) are informative.

Wounded and decorated in Vietnam.

# CHAPTER FIFTEEN

# 1969–1975

## The Imperial Presidency and Watergate

Richard Nixon narrowly won the 1968 election by promising to restore law and order and to end a frustrating and unpopular war. He did neither, but nevertheless managed to attract broad new political support by adopting policies he had spent a lifetime denouncing and by exploiting ugly social divisions. In the war, he reduced American casualties through "Vietnamization." By 1972 these tactics had been so successful that Nixon won reelection by an overwhelming margin. His victory promised still further enlargement of an already bloated executive authority; indeed, a cartoon appeared with the purple-robed figure of "King Richard." But even more swiftly than Nixon had donned the robes of the imperial presidency, they were stripped from his shoulders. The Watergate scandal erupted, leading not only to Nixon's own downfall but to a widespread crisis of confidence in government. As polls showed that more people than ever before believed "there is something deeply wrong with America," new restrictions on the imperial presidency were imposed by Congress and the courts.

## THE NIXON FOREIGN POLICIES

The new President appointed Henry Kissinger, a professor of international relations at Harvard, as his National Security Advisor. The two men privately formulated their own foreign policy, neglecting Congress and the State Department, and in some instances not even bothering to keep these two bodies informed. Kissinger believed such secrecy necessary in order to carry out plans quickly and effectively. Nixon agreed, for he cared relatively little about domestic affairs (once remarking that the nation did not need a President to handle internal matters), but deeply involved himself in foreign policies. He also harbored a strong desire to have a private, shielded presidency. Before some of his most momentous decisions, Nixon would isolate himself for long periods, talking with no one.

The President slowly changed the emphases of American foreign policy. He reduced the commitment in Vietnam (and showed less interest in newly emerging areas, such as Latin America and Africa), while opening new relationships with Russia and China. Nixon responded to the new post-1956 world by deemphasizing the Kennedy-Johnson policies in the more volatile southern half of the globe and working instead for a settlement with the two great Communist powers. Several factors forced this change. Perhaps most important, Nixon understood that the world contained not two great powers but, in his words, "five economic superpowers"—the United States, Russia, Japan, China, and the EEC. Because the first two balanced one another off militarily, these five powers "will determine the economic future, and because economic power will be the key to other kinds of power," they will determine "the future of the world in other ways in the last third of this century." Russia and China, moreover, were enemies. As Kissinger noted, "The deepest international conflict in the world today is not between us and the Soviet Union but between the Soviet Union and Communist China."

All this was not new. It had been apparent since 1960, but Nixon was the first President to act upon it. He understood that this five-power world opened a marvelous opportunity for the United States to play off the other four powers against one another. He could, for example, cooperate with both the Chinese and Soviets to control the threatening economic expansion of Japan and Europe. Nixon could use American technology (such as computers) and agricultural products, which both Communist nations badly needed, to strengthen political ties and gain access for American business executives to the vast Chinese and Russian markets. Finally, if such ties were made, the United States could trade its products for Russian and Chinese help in stopping the Vietnam War so that American troops could be withdrawn on honorable terms. In all, Nixon's plans were imaginative and sweeping.

He understood, above all, that the United States had overreached itself during the 1960s with commitments that had already led to violence, inflation, and the political demise of Johnson. Thus he began by announcing a "Nixon Doctrine" in 1969 that pledged continued economic aid to allies in Asia and elsewhere but added that these allies should no longer count on the presence of American troops. He also announced that he would end the draft within two years. American troop strength would be reduced systematically in Vietnam while the South Vietnamese received more military equipment so that they could fight their own wars. This policy became known as "Vietnamization."

## THE NIXON FAILURES, 1970–1971

Vietnamization, however, was failing by early 1970. As American troops left, the South Vietnamese proved incapable of driving out Communist forces. Using bases in neighboring Cambodia, a supposedly neutral state, the North Vietnamese and NLF threatened to bring down the Saigon government. Nixon responded with heavy bombing of the Cambodian bases but kept the raids secret from everyone except a few top officials in Washington and, of course, the Cambodians and Vietnamese. On April 30, 1970, after a conservative, pro-U.S. government suddenly came to power in Cambodia, the President announced that American and South Vietnamese troops were temporarily invading Cambodia to destroy the Communist bases. Having promised to end the war, Nixon was now actually expanding it into neighboring areas. Worse, the American troops did not succeed in destroying the bases, for after they retreated, the Communists simply moved back in and then threatened to overthrow the Cambodian government itself.

The effect on the American people was electric. Colleges, including many that had remained quiet during the 1960s, erupted into antiwar violence. The nation was shaken when four students were shot to death by Ohio National Guard forces during the antiwar demonstration at Kent State University. Polls showed that half the American people disbelieved Nixon's announcement that the invasion would shorten the war. A lack of confidence in the President's foreign policy seemed to be developing, a rare event in recent American history. Henry Kissinger privately shuddered at the possible consequences, for he believed that the antiwar demonstrations were not just against Vietnam policies, but

> against authority of any kind, not just the authority of this President, but the authority of any President. . . . If confidence in him and in all institutions is systematically destroyed, we will turn into a group that has nothing left but a physical test of strength and the only outcome of this is Caesarism. . . .
> The very people who shout "Power to the People" are not going to be the people who will take over this country if it turns into a test of strength. Upper middle-class college kids will not take this country over. Some more primitive and elemental forces will do that.

But demonstrations continued, and an angry Senate finally repealed the Gulf of Tonkin Resolution. The President, however, claimed that he could continue to fight in Southeast Asia, regardless of what Congress did, in order to protect American troops already in Vietnam.

Announcing that the Cambodian invasion had been successful in removing one threat to American troops, the President further widened the war in February 1971 by invading Communist bases in Laos. This time, however, South Vietnamese rather than American troops went in; it was to be a test of Vietnamization. South Vietnam flunked the test. Meeting tough resistance, its troops scattered and ran. The Communists retained their hold on strategic areas despite an intensification of American bombing that had been carried out secretly since 1964. By mid-1971 the Communists controlled more of Laos than ever before.

The failure of Vietnamization was one of two early crises to confront Nixon. The other was a baffling economy—baffling in that, on the one hand, it was by far the world's greatest, having passed in 1970 the trillion-dollar level in annual gross national product (that is, the total product of all goods and services produced in the nation). On the other hand, it also suffered from inflation that made American goods more expensive and hence less competitive on the international market. United States products lost ground to such cheaply produced Japanese and German products as the Datsun and Volkswagen automobiles.

In 1971, for the first time since 1893, the United States suffered an overall deficit trade balance. It paid out more money to satisfy its international debts ($45.5 billion) than it received from exports and other services abroad ($42.8 billion). The world's greatest economy was sick. In August 1971 President Nixon attempted to supply a remedy by devaluing the dollar, that is, reducing each dollar's worth in gold, which is the leading international exchange standard. This act cheapened the dollar and so made American goods cheaper and easier to purchase internationally. By early 1973 the inflation and deficits continued, so the President again devalued the dollar. American exports picked up, but inflation was not halted.

## RACING TO THE MOON

Amid the gloom caused by Vietnam and the economy, the human race realized a many-thousand-year dream by sending astronauts safely to the moon and back in July 1969. That venture, the "great leap for mankind" as Neil Armstrong announced when he made the first human imprint on the moon's surface, will doubtless be remembered longer, and be of greater historical importance, than the crises that vexed the earthbound that year.

In a strict sense, space flight developed during the American Century but was the child of both Russian and American scientific breakthroughs. In 1903 a Russian, K. E. Tsiolkovsky, began making basic discoveries (including the idea for a multistage rocket, in which one stage propelled the vehicle and was then discarded as another stage took over to boost the rocket). Between 1919 and 1943, a scientist at Clark University in Massachusetts, R. H. Goddard, improved Tsiolkovsky's findings and made many of his own, especially in fuels. Goddard worked virtually alone and received little long-term support. Not even the U.S. military supported him during the 1930s because his small rockets seemed unable to carry payloads (such as explosives) of more than several pounds. Goddard, quietly experimenting at Clark or in the New Mexico desert, nevertheless developed automatic steering systems, self-cooling combustion chambers, and other discoveries that led to over two hundred patents in his name.

In the 1930s and 1940s the lone figure making basic findings on bare-bones budgets suddenly gave way to a mammoth wartime rocket project in Germany that employed twenty thousand people. By1944–45 that program produced V-2 rockets that killed thousands in England. It also produced scientists who were secretly spirited out of Germany by the victors to shape the American and Russian space programs. By 1957 the Soviets had moved ahead by launching *Sputnik*, the first artificial satellite to spin into space. They also sent the first human in a rocket beyond the earth's atmosphere. The Cold War now replaced Goddard's personal curiosity as the driving force in the discovery of space. In 1961 the United States began to catch up as Alan Shepard became the first American to travel into space. The following year John Glenn became a national hero

Dr. Robert Goddard with early space rocket.

by becoming the first American to orbit the earth. President John Kennedy committed the nation to be the first to land on the moon. The $24 billion Apollo project climaxed in 1969 when Armstrong planted the Stars and Stripes on the lunar surface, an event whose miraculousness was matched by the magic of the cameras that televised the event on earth. The Soviets meanwhile suffered fatal accidents in 1967 and 1971, then gave up their race to the moon to concentrate on learning how to live in space for long periods. Tsiolkovsky and Goddard had anticipated traveling into the new frontier of space, but not the incredible cost and deadly military competition that now resulted from their pioneering research.

## THE NIXON SUCCESSES: 1971–1972

A year before the 1972 presidential election, Nixon's misfortunes in Vietnam and with the economy hurt his chances for reelection. Any President, however, can use his control of foreign policy to make dramatic headlines

Kissinger, Nixon, and Chou En-lai, Peking, 1972.

and some political gains if he has made adequate preparation and has a sense of timing. No one knew this better than Nixon.

In August 1971 he announced that he would become the first President to travel to China. Chairman Mao Tse-tung in Peking had happily cooperated, for he hoped to use his new friendship with the United States as a weapon against his major enemy, Russia, which was massing troops along the Sino-Russian border. In an instant, twenty-two years of Sino-American enmity began to dissolve. Americans who had vocally disliked Red China for years could say little, for Richard Nixon had long been among the most vocal. Nor was there an outcry when, over United States objections, the People's Republic of China replaced Chiang Kai-shek's Taiwan government as the representative of China in the United Nations. In February 1972 Nixon dominated the television screens as he exchanged toasts with Chinese leaders. Americans overwhelmingly applauded his effort to ease tensions.

But he parlayed the journey into an even greater gain. By pitting the two enemies, Russia and China, against one another for American favors, and by sending badly needed American wheat to both, Nixon freed his hand to deal with North Vietnam without fear that the two great Communist powers might intervene. Since 1969 he had searched for an agreement with the North Vietnamese and hoped to reach one before the 1972 election, but none had been concluded. In April 1972 the North Vietnamese launched an offensive against the weakened American—South Vietnamese forces. The President responded with the heaviest bombing of the war on Hanoi, then mined North Vietnamese harbors. The mining endangered Russian ships using the harbors and was such a threatening move that Lyndon Johnson had flatly refused to do it. But now the Russians and Chinese made no active response.

Indeed, as the mines were being sown, the Russians welcomed Nixon in Moscow as the first American President to make that journey. In SALT I (Strategic Arms Limitation Talks), the United States and Soviet leaders signed an important pact limiting the number of defensive missiles each nation could possess. They also agreed to a five-year freeze on testing and deployment of intercontinental missiles. Putting Multiple Warheads (MIRVs) on the missiles, however, was not prohibited. Both nations promised that SALT I was only the first of several treaties that would reduce the number of nuclear weapons. The treaties would come none too soon, for the nuclear stockpile in the world amounted to the equivalent of fifteen tons of TNT for every man, woman, and child on earth, and it was growing steadily.

In early 1972 a majority of Americans had disliked Nixon's Vietnam policies. After he mined and bombed North Vietnam, however, and then flew to Peking and Russia, the nation approved his policies by a ratio of two to one. The President had used foreign policy much as a director uses music to build emotions to a pitch during a movie. "A lot of things are coming together at a point," said Nixon's right-hand man John Ehrlichman with a smile just before the 1972 election. "And it is a point, frankly, which we selected as a target time as a matter of enlightened self-interest."

# RICHARD NIXON AND THE NEW MAJORITY

Shortly after the 1968 election Kevin Phillips, a Nixon campaign aide, published *The Emerging Republican Majority*. The book attempted to explain why Nixon had won and how he could consolidate his position. Phillips believed that the Democrats' electoral base was shriveling while the Republicans' was expanding. The GOP had a magnificent opportunity to make further inroads among ethnic voters (particularly Irish, Polish, and Italian Catholics), the working classes, and Southern whites. George Wallace's supporters were central to this effort, for Phillips thought that they were mainly conservative Democrats in the process of abandoning their traditional allegiances and preparing to support the Republicans. They represented large numbers of people who were fed up with judicial activism, moral permissiveness, forced integration, and massive welfare spending. Phillips suggested that the Republicans could safely ignore urban blacks, youthful dissenters, and liberal intellectuals. "From space-center Florida across the booming Texas plains to the Los Angeles–San Diego suburban corridor, the nation's fastest-growing areas are strongly Republican and conservative."

Nixon's first administration, in many respects, faithfully followed Phillips's blueprint. Nixon recognized that the 1968 election left him in a precarious political position. His 43.4 percent of the vote was the smallest winning share since 1912. For the first time since Zachary Taylor's election in 1848, a first-term President failed to carry a majority in either house of Congress. The Democrats retained an edge of 58 to 42 in the Senate and 243 to 192 in the House. To ensure his reelection, Nixon, without alienating the Republican faithful, had to do several things: reassure blue-collar workers that Republicans would not dismantle the welfare state or create economic hardship; exploit social issues that could appeal to ethnic voters; and demonstrate to whites, in the South and in the suburbs, that he opposed forced integration.

In the realm of economics, the search for a new majority required considerable ideological flexibility. Nixon, an economic conservative who had always advocated a balanced budget, soon approached the problem of unemployment as if he were a liberal Democrat. Unemployment stood at 3.5 percent in December 1969, but it rose sharply to 6.2 percent in the next year. That represented the highest level of joblessness in a decade. To deal with it, the President resorted to planned budget deficits, which, he hoped, would create new jobs by pumping money into the economy. Early in 1971 he presented a "full-employment budget," one that would be balanced if the economy were operating at full tilt but that under existing circumstances would produce a $23 billion deficit. In January Nixon asserted: "I am now a Keynesian in economics." This, one observer noted, was "a little like a Christian crusader saying, 'All things considered, I think Mohammed was right.'"

Similarly, Nixon moved to an acceptance of economic controls to curb inflation. In 1969, recalling the World War II experience, he remarked: "Controls, oh my God, no! . . . They mean rationing, black markets, inequitable administration. We'll never go for controls." But by 1971, as the rate of inflation rose to 5 percent, the nation experienced a trade deficit, and the stock market tumbled, Nixon reversed fields. In August he imposed a ninety-day freeze on wages, prices, and rents. In November he established a Price Commission and Cost of Living Council to restrain both wage boosts and rent increases. The President later experimented with mandatory wage and price controls but than abandoned them in favor of voluntary compliance. Nixon always approached controls hesitantly, emphasizing the need for cooperation from business and labor. But the controls, however cautious, helped restrain inflation during 1972 and temporarily defused it as a political issue.

Nixon campaigned in 1968 against the Great Society's "welfare mess," claiming that it was "time to quit pouring billions of dollars into programs that have failed." Yet his own welfare proposals looked toward reform of the system. The Family Assistance Plan, which he proposed in 1969, would have provided a minimum income of $1600 a year for a

Spiro Agnew, Billy Graham, and Richard Nixon at the Republican Convention, 1968.

family of four, which, together with food stamps, would have meant an income of $2460. This was more than welfare systems provided in twenty states. The plan also offered income supplements for the working poor in order to reduce welfare rolls by making it more profitable to hold a job than to receive public assistance. To qualify, however, heads of households (except for the infirm and mothers with small children) would have to register for job training and accept "suitable jobs." This, Nixon said, would restore the incentive to work and identify welfare chiselers. The House enacted a version of the measure, but it died in the Senate Finance Committee. In 1970, however, the administration succeeded in federalizing the food stamp program. National criteria for eligibility were established, based on the cost of a nutritionally adequate diet, and benefits were adjusted automatically to take account of inflation.

## THE SOCIAL ISSUE AND THE
## SUPREME COURT

Nixon's economic policies were not entirely successful in checking inflation or reducing unemployment, but they preserved a level of prosperity through 1972 that enabled him to attract working-class support. Beyond this, however, the administration brilliantly exploited the "social issue"— fears that stemmed from a rising crime rate, widespread use of drugs, increasingly permissive attitudes toward sex, and growing disdain for patriotic values. The President played on these fears, which cut across usual party lines, in everything from wearing an American flag in his lapel to denouncing the "Spock-marked" generation. Vice-President Spiro Agnew did the same in his attack on student protesters (an "impudent corps of snobs") and their "effete . . . hand-wringing, sniveling" apologists.

Three issues particularly aided Nixon among working-class Catholics. The President firmly endorsed federal aid to parochial schools, informing a Catholic audience that new ways should be discovered to provide direct assistance to nonpublic schools. Nixon also entered an explosive controversy over liberalization of the New York State abortion law, which the Catholic Church bitterly opposed. He told Terence Cardinal Cooke in May 1972, "I would personally like to associate myself with the convictions you deeply feel and eloquently express." In 1970 a Commission on Obscenity and Pornography, all but one of whose members had been appointed by Lyndon Johnson, recommended that all laws "prohibiting the sale, exhibition, or distribution of sexual materials to consenting adults should be repealed." The President repudiated the Commission, and Agnew thundered, "As long as Richard Nixon is President, Main Street is not going to turn into Smut Alley."

The social issue also encompassed racial fears. The President, who had received no more than 5 percent of the black vote in 1968, had a mixed civil rights record. The administration supported the "Philadelphia plan" to eliminate discrimination on federal construction projects by establishing a quota system under which trade unions had to accept a certain number of black youths as apprentices and guarantee them union membership at the end of a training period. The plan was upheld in the courts, but implementing school desegregation was a different story. The Justice Department favored the postponement of desegregation plans in communities where strong local opposition existed. In October 1969, however, the Supreme Court upset the administration's strategy. In *Alexander* v. *Holmes County Board of Education* the Court declared unanimously that "deliberate speed" no longer sufficed; school desegregation must begin "at once."

Given existing patterns of residential segregation, this decision merely raised a more difficult question: Should children be bused to achieve racial balance in the schools? There was no more highly charged issue in the early 1970s. Public opinion polls indicated that 78 percent of the people opposed the idea of busing. In some places, attempts to introduce such plans led to violence, disorder, and school boycotts. Maintenance of the "neighborhood school" became a central concern, particularly in the South, in the suburbs, and in ethnic enclaves in the large cities. Many people had moved to the suburbs to be in better school districts. Now they faced the prospect of sending their children back into the inner cities every morning. Yet busing plans met with the approval of the Supreme Court in April 1971. In *Swann* v. *Charlotte-Mecklenburg Board of Education* the justices found that busing, even if awkward or inconvenient, was an acceptable means of integrating "schools that are substantially dispro-portionate in their racial composition."

The issue was tailor-made for a President intent on currying favor with Southern whites, suburbanites, and uneasy ethnic groups. Nixon at the same time reflected the nation's mood and contributed to its intransi-gence. In March 1970 he called for an "open society" that "does not have to be homogeneous, or even fully integrated. There is room in it for communities. . . . It is natural and right that we have Italian or Negro or Norwegian neighborhoods." He disagreed with those who said that "the only way to bring about social justice is to integrate all schools now, everywhere, no matter what the cost in the disruption of education." The President reiterated this stand during the next two years. In January 1972 a federal district judge in Richmond, Virginia ordered school boards to employ busing to eradicate racial distinctions between schools. In March, with Congress considering a constitutional amendment to forbid busing, Nixon urged the legislators to impose a moratorium on the issuance of busing orders by federal courts while a measure could be devised looking toward a permanent solution. Congress then barred the implementation of such orders until all legal appeals had been exhausted. Although the bill did not go far enough to suit him, the President signed it in the summer of 1972.

Nixon also sought to use Supreme Court appointments as part of a broader political strategy. Having pledged in 1968 to appoint strict con-structionists as a way of reversing the Court's activism, Nixon had the unusual opportunity of choosing four members in his first term. Late in 1969 he nominated Clement Haynsworth of South Carolina. Many consid-ered this a way of paying a debt to Senator J. Strom Thurmond, a staunch conservative from South Carolina. Opposition to Haynsworth quickly de-veloped when the Senate discovered that he had once acted as a judge in a case that could possibly have served his own interests. The Senate rejected the nomination by a vote of 55 to 45, with seventeen Republicans deserting the President. Nixon next sent up the name of G. Harrold Carswell of Florida. A new storm arose, primarily because an extraordinarily high number of Carswell's decisions had been reversed by higher courts. He appeared to lack any intellectual distinction, as even a supporter, Senator Roman Hruska of Nebraska, conceded: "Even if he were mediocre, there are lots of mediocre judges and people and lawyers. They are entitled to a little representation aren't they? . . . We can't have all Brandeises and Frankfurters and Cardozos and stuff like that there." The legal profession, regarding the appointment as an insult, lobbied against it, and in April 1970 the Senate turned it down. Seeking to squeeze the last ounce of political advantage from the situation, Nixon said that the issue involved "the Constitutional responsibility of the President to appoint members of the Court." Carswell's rejection, he asserted, was an act of "regional discrimination" against the South.

Ultimately Nixon appointed Harry Blackmun of Minnesota to the vacancy. The three other appointees were Lewis F. Powell, William Rehnquist, and Chief Justice Warren E. Burger. In many respects the Court veered in a more conservative direction. It ruled more frequently on behalf of the prosecution in criminal trials, declaring that a defendant who disrupted a trial by disorderly behavior could, after a warning, be removed from the courtroom or even bound and gagged. It also held that a confession extracted by unconstitutional means did not automatically invalidate a conviction where other evidence of guilt existed. The Court also made it easier for prosecutors to establish the admissibility of contested confessions. In *Miller* v. *California* (1973) the Court widened the grounds for ruling books and films obscene and expanded communities' power to ban offensive material. With respect to reapportionment, the Court softened the one-person, one-vote rule to widen somewhat the permissible disparity between voting district populations. In 1973 the Court found that schools could be financed by property taxes even though disparities resulted, for, as Justice Powell said, "at least where wealth is involved, the equal protection clause does not require absolute equality or precisely equal advantages."

Yet the Court by no means pursued a course entirely to the President's liking. In the cases involving school desegregation and busing, even some of Nixon's appointees disappointed him. In *Furman* v. *Georgia* (1972) the Court held, by a vote of 5 to 4, that the death penalty as then prescribed was imposed unfairly. It fell more heavily on the poor and violated the constitutional injunction against cruel and unusual punishment. Many states then attempted to make the death penalty mandatory for certain offenses, but the Court had greatly aided opponents of capital punishment. In 1970, in *Welsh* v. *United States*, the Court ruled that a man whose opposition to military service was rooted in a deeply held moral or ethical conviction, rather than in religious belief, could qualify for conscientious

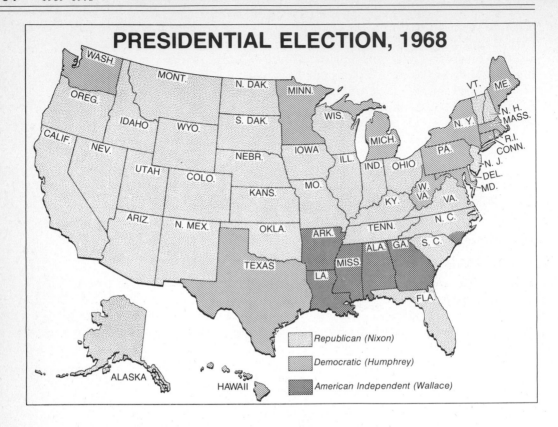

**PRESIDENTIAL ELECTION, 1968**

Republican (Nixon)

Democratic (Humphrey)

American Independent (Wallace)

objector status. Finally, the Court upheld civil liberties in two landmark decisions. In 1971 it ruled that the government could not prevent the publication of the "Pentagon Papers." On June 19, 1972, the Court rejected the Attorney General's claim that the government had the right to use wiretapping against alleged subversives or domestic radicals without first obtaining a court order. Justice Powell said: "The price of lawful public dissent must not be a dread of subjection to an unchecked surveillance power." The decision, ironically, was handed down two days after burglars working for the President's reelection were arrested in Democratic national headquarters.

## THE IMPACT OF THE WOMEN'S MOVEMENT

On August 26, 1970, thousands of women across the nation celebrated the fiftieth anniversary of the ratification of woman suffrage with parades, demonstrations, and a triumphal march down New York's Fifth Avenue.

The celebration marked a peak of feminist mobilization; the start of the 1970s was an era of women's coalitions, collectives, and caucuses. Every national network and major publication devoted time and space to the women's movement, calling on spokeswomen such as Gloria Steinem, who had just started *Ms.* magazine, or NOW's Betty Friedan, or any of a shifting galaxy of women's liberationists. An outpouring of feminist literature was also much in evidence. "What goes largely unexamined in our social order . . . is the birthright priority whereby males rule females," charged Kate Millett in *Sexual Politics* (1969). "Every avenue of power . . . is entirely in male hands." In *The Dialectic of Sex* (1970), Shulamith Firestone depicted a world of the future where adults might apply for licenses to live in "reproductive social structures," where childbirth would be "so diffused as to be practically eliminated," and where "humanity could finally revert to its naturally 'polymorphously perverse' sexuality."

But even the most far-fetched of liberationist visions served a political purpose: they made simple equity demands seem more acceptable by comparison. Or, as a suffragist had once told Charlotte Perkins Gilman, early in the century, "What you ask is so much worse than what we ask, that they will grant our demands in order to escape yours." Rapid acceptance of more moderate proposals, in fact, constituted the feminist "revolution" of the early 1970s.

The symbol of feminist success was congressional adoption of the Equal Rights Amendment, which stated that "equality of rights under the law shall not be abridged by the United States or by any state on account of sex." (The amendment prohibited sex discrimination by the government, its agencies and officers, and all institutions closely tied to the government, such as federal contractors.) An ERA had been favorably reported by the Senate Judiciary Committee since 1964 but it had then been opposed by the labor movement, the Women's Bureau, and major women's organizations, such as the League of Women Voters, all of which viewed it as a threat to protective laws. By 1970, federal courts were invalidating such laws as discriminatory to women, and the ERA's longtime opponents changed their minds. The amendment was approved by the House in 1971 and by the Senate in 1972, and it was ratified by twenty-eight states within a year. Feminists now had every hope that it would be ratified by thirty-eight states within seven years. "Our reward," Betty Friedan told a NOW convention in 1971, "is the absolute passionate excitement . . . of making history ourselves."

Not only did Congress endorse the ERA by wide margins but it seemed to make many efforts to satisfy feminist demands. Between 1971 and 1974, Congress enacted an unparalleled number of laws promoting sex equity. (The only precedent, in fact, was the Equal Pay Act of 1963, enacted before the resurgence of feminism.) During the early 1970s, for instance, Congress prohibited sex discrimination in medical training programs, enabled middle-class families to claim tax deductions for child care if both spouses worked, and extended the benefits of married women in federal service jobs. It prohibited creditors from discriminating on the basis of sex, extended the Equal Pay Act by an Educational Amendments Act, and passed a Women's Educational Equity Act, which supported training and counseling for women. The only major setback came in 1972, when President Nixon vetoed the Comprehensive Child Development bill, which would have provided a national network of day-care centers—and also would have required far more federal funding than any other equity measure. The President denounced the bill's "family-weakening implications."

Congressional efforts were complemented by a series of executive orders and labor department directives that supported feminist demands. In some cases, civil rights measures were extended to include women. In 1967, for instance, President Johnson had extended an executive order prohibiting racial discrimination by federal contractors to prevent sex discrimination as well. The order had far-flung ramifications. By 1970, the labor department issued affirmative action guidelines to all federal contractors (such as universities) to insure nondiscriminatory hiring. The same year, after a class action suit by the Women's Equity Action League, colleges and universities had to turn personnel files over to the government, so that their efforts at nondiscrimination could be validated. Feminist demands for equal opportunity rapidly had a widespread impact.

Federal court decisions, meanwhile, imposed equity in other ways. Lower courts voided protective laws, challenged sex labeling of jobs (such as "stewardess"), and reaffirmed the principle of equal pay for equal work. Even the avoidance of court decisions had results. In 1972, a sex discrimination suit against American Telephone and Telegraph was settled out of court with a multimillion dollar payment to women workers (such as operators who had been kept out of better paying jobs as linemen.) The settlement suggested that the average working woman, who was usually underrepresented in feminist organizations, might have much to gain from the women's movement.

The Supreme Court did its part as well. During the early 1970s, the Court invalidated a state law giving preference to men as executors, banned reference to sex in want ads, and equalized benefits for members of the armed services. But the Supreme Court's major decision was on the controversial issue of abortion. State abortion laws had been in effect since the late nineteenth century, prohibiting abortion in all cases except to preserve a mother's life. During the 1960s a movement grew to liberalize abortion laws by permitting abortion in other cases, such as rape and incest. By 1972, sixteen states had liberalized their laws. But feminists demanded repeal of all abortion laws, making abortion available to all women. In 1973, in *Roe* v. *Wade,* the Supreme Court declared state abortion laws unconstitutional on the grounds that they invaded the right of privacy. As legal abortion became available, maternal deaths from illegal abortion dwindled away. The Supreme Court's decision had a more far-reaching effect than any other item on the feminist agenda.

While Congress, the courts, and the executive branch transformed feminist demands into federal policy, the women's movement caused other changes as well. Public opinion polls reported significant shifts in attitudes among women and men, from disapproval of the movement to increase women's rights in the late 1960s to support for feminist planks in the early 1970s. Educational changes were widespread. Textbooks were revised to eliminate sexual stereotypes; school curricula were revised so boys and girls would not be segregated in shop and cooking classes; women's studies programs multiplied, reaching five hundred colleges by 1974; and all-male colleges rushed to welcome women (though often for financial not feminist reasons). Meanwhile, a vocational revolution seemed to have begun, as all-male or mostly male job classifications broke down. Women were becoming real estate agents, insurance adjusters, busdrivers, and bartenders; their numbers were rising as lawyers, judges, doctors, engineers, executives, ministers, and TV anchorpersons. Most significantly, they were moving into the labor force at unprecedented rates. The new entrants were mainly married women, especially those with young children at home, who seemed to be abandoning the feminist mystique with alacrity.

The widespread impact of the women's movement in the early 1970s was not absorbed without debate. A conservative backlash against women's liberation was not long in coming. "For women to announce that their very womanliness results from a bad and meretricious culture is the expression of deep self-hatred," Midge Decter charged in *The New Chastity* (1972). Working-class women and black women seemed to have little enthusiasm for feminist ideology, which in their view reflected white middle-class biases. A grass-roots middle-class aversion was visible as well, along with concern about whether or not women were acting in their own interest. "Most just trade the drudgery of housewifery for the drudgery of an office job," one woman wrote to *Time* in 1970. "Already women have more legal freedom than they know what to do with," wrote another. The most well-organized antifeminist movement, however, consisted of newly mobilized opponents of abortion rights and the ERA, who would, by the end of the 1970s, make their voices heard in public debates.

## NATIVE AMERICANS AND WOUNDED KNEE II

Of all American minorities, Indians suffered most during the 1960s and 1970s. Their population grew at four times the national rate, reaching 792,000 in 1970, but life expectancy was only 46 years (compared with the national average of 69), infant mortality rates were the nation's highest, and the suicide rate was double the country's average. Reservations lacked industry and good schools. Unemployment rates above 50 percent were not uncommon. A startling 50 percent of Native Americans on reservations, and even 20 percent of those in cities, lived below the poverty level in the late 1970s.

Indian leaders tried to deal with this tragedy, but they were divided between young and old, between those living in urban and reservation areas, and between tribes. The Kennedy, Johnson, and Nixon administrations attempted to return policy to Indian officials. This move, however, did little to dampen the anger of many Native Americans who joined militant youth groups (patterned on the black organizations of the 1960s), and, in 1968, formed the urban-based American Indian Movement (AIM). Until 1973, few whites seemed to care.

Then came the second episode of Wounded Knee (for the first, see Chapter 1). Wounded Knee was a town in the Sioux Reservation of South Dakota. The reservation, twice the size of Delaware, contained 3 million acres of which one-third was owned by whites, one-third leased by Indians to white cattlemen, and one-third used by the Sioux themselves. Seventy

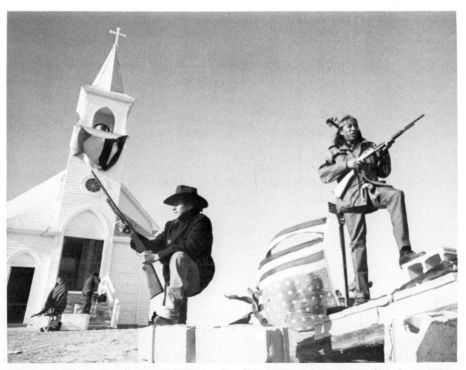

Native Americans standing guard near a church in Wounded Knee, South Dakota, 1973.

percent of the teachers on the reservation were white. Pine Ridge, the capital, was "a motley collection of shacks and houses of varying degrees of decrepitude," according to one reporter, with "a fine, tan, gritty dust . . . coating everything and getting into mouths and lungs, contributing to the hacking cough that people seem to develop rapidly here."

The reservation contained some of the nation's worst poverty: Half the families were on welfare and a moccasin factory served as the main industry. Most of the employed were mixbloods (Indians having both Indian and white blood), who controlled the reservation and worked in patronage jobs handed out by Washington officials. Full-blooded Indians lived in rural shacks where they tried to save themselves and their culture. The school dropout rate was 81 percent. Alcoholism was rampant among adult males. Considerable tension divided whites and Indians. When Raymond Yellow Thunder visited nearby Gordon, Nebraska, in 1972, he was beaten and murdered. Two white attackers were released without bail and charged only with second-degree manslaughter. Not wanting to cause further problems with the whites, neither Bureau of Indian Affairs officials nor the Sioux half-bloods controlling the reservation pushed for an investigation of the murder.

But led by women, an angry group of Sioux repudiated their leaders, whom they considered corrupt, and asked for help from AIM. In February 1973 two hundred AIM members and their supporters occupied Wounded Knee. They demanded that the government honor some 371 treaties it had broken and also insisted that the reservation's regime be radically changed. United States forces encircled the area, partly to keep the two Indian factions from attacking each other, but also to block the entry of food into the town. When AIM tried to move in reinforcements, government gunfire killed one Indian and wounded another. AIM and the Washington officials finally agreed to lift the seige and reexamine treaty obligations. The government, however, finally did little except bring suit against AIM leaders and sympathizers.

"Wounded Knee II" symbolized, but did little to help, the tragedy of the American Indian. Indeed, a white backlash erupted in the late 1970s. The backlash was notable in Congress, which had obtained almost dictatorial power over Indian affairs. White congressmen, many from Western states, proposed bills based on a ruthless policy of "termination"— that is, ending federal protection, revoking treaties, and opening Indian lands to the highest bidders. One embittered Native American spokesman believed "it all has to do with natural resources," for Congress wanted to "open up Indian lands to energy development interests, ranchers, and commercial fishermen." President Carter did little to help Indians. Despite Native American activism and a growing awareness among whites of the suffering on reservations, the supposed "reforms" of the 1960s and 1970s produced only more suffering and more hatred between Indians and whites, and among Indians themselves.

# FOOTBALL [AND POLITICS]

It began in eleventh-century England, when players representing towns pushed animal skulls, and later cow bladders, between towns that stood for "goals." King Henry II outlawed the sport in the twelfth century because its popularity interfered with archery practice needed to defend the kingdom. Reborn four hundred years later on playing fields, it became the British sport of rugby and then caught on in the United States. The first college football game was won by Rutgers' six goals to Princeton's four in 1869.

Within twenty years coaches were selecting the best players on "All-America" lists. Through the mid-1890s only one non-British name was on such lists, but Irish, Jewish, and finally Polish and Hungarian players were honored after 1900 as the new immigration from Europe created an increasingly pluralistic society. The ethnic divisions led to rules that all could understand. Thus instead of having wild scrambles (as in rugby), the game was controlled by having fixed scrimmage lines. The new rules also allowed growing numbers of spectators to learn and follow the sport. Football was nevertheless bru-

The Four Horsemen of Notre Dame, 1924.

tal. The bloody Stanford-California game of 1904 was followed by riots in San Francisco. Even Theodore Roosevelt, who prided himself on the "strenuous life," finally ordered that football be civilized or, he thundered, it would be ended by presidential proclamation.

So the forward pass was legalized in 1906 to open and speed up the game. This weapon was used by an unknown Notre Dame team to upset mighty Army in 1913. Thus began the Notre Dame tradition, for the school soon attracted the athletic sons of Ro-

man Catholic immigrants. Colleges began recruiting players in 1915, so some immigrants and other poor Americans suddenly found higher education available simply by playing football in the autumn. The sport entered glory days in the 1920s and professional teams appeared. The most renowned coach was Notre Dame's Knute Rockne, who believed that "After the Church, football is the best thing we have." His backfields moved in precise formations like the mass production assembly lines that Americans so admired. And like industry,

Knute Rockne.

Red Grange, 1925.

football became a game for specialty teams of defense, offense, and even kicking. But Americans who preached the virtues of rugged individualism could proudly point to the exploits of Red Grange ("the Galloping Ghost") of 1920s Illinois teams, Charlie ("Choo-Choo") Justice of 1940s North Carolina squads, and, in the 1960s, Joe Willie ("Broadway Joe") Namath of Alabama and O.J. ("Orange-Juice") Simpson of Southern California.

Football's popularity peaked in the 1970s. Its quick action and pageantry suited color television screens, and television in turn provided immense wealth ($13.5 million in 1973 for college games alone) for football teams and such $250,000-a-year quarterbacks as Namath. In the 1970s George Allen of the Washington Redskins symbolized the tough, disciplined life with his eighteen-hour-a-day attention to detail and his remark, "Losing is like death. If you don't win you're dead and you don't know it." Allen's good friend, President Richard Nixon, was the nation's leading fan. "The President thinks football is a way of life," Allen observed. "He is a competitor." The game provided the language for politics and diplomacy. The American bombing of North Vietnam in late 1972 was code-named "Operation Linebacker," and Nixon's code-name was "Quarterback." Conversely, such

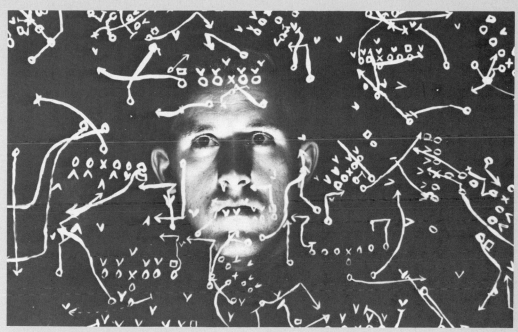

Fran Tarkenton of the Minnesota Vikings studies offensive plays, 1961.

metaphors of war as the "blitz" and the "bomb" were applied to the grid-iron.

The University of Oklahoma Athletic Director declared, "We teach a philosophy, we teach a skill, and we danged sure also teach a little bit of religion. And we teach discipline. This is one of the last areas where true discipline is taught, where love for the American flag and respect for the American President is taught, through discipline." Others, however, deplored football's commercialism and its use as an example for fighting the Cold War. Former star Dave Meggysey quit the game, claiming that he had illegally received money for playing in college and had been treated as an animal by professional coaches and owners. "Politics and pro football," Meggysey declared, "are the most grotesque extremes in the theatric of a dying empire." In the 1970s football seemed to have replaced baseball as the so-called National Pastime.

## THE ELECTION OF 1972

By 1972 the President had taken great strides toward constructing what he called a "new majority." His task was further simplified when the Democrats nominated George McGovern of South Dakota. After the upheaval at the 1968 Chicago convention, the Democrats had thoroughly revised their delegate selection procedures. In an attempt to open the party to groups that had been excluded, those procedures were democratized and rules were adopted requiring that delegations "reasonably" reflect the proportion of women, blacks, and other minorities in the population. The result was a convention unlike any seen before. Those groups with ample time, energy, and ideological fervor—such as upper middle-class activists in the antiwar, women's liberation, and civil rights movements—enjoyed greater representation than ever before. By contrast, the traditional power brokers—trade-union leaders, big-city mayors, and Southern bosses—enjoyed less.

McGovern's difficulties were compounded when it was learned that his running mate, Thomas Eagleton of Missouri, had some history of mental illness. After days of hesitation, which apparently convinced some voters that he lacked decisiveness, McGovern replaced Eagleton with Sargent Shriver, who had formerly headed the war on poverty. But McGovern's chief problem was that the Republicans succeeded in centering attention on the social issue while calling him a radical who favored "the far-out goals of the far left." The code words in 1972 were amnesty, acid, and abortion, and it made little difference that McGovern favored only the first. Condemning American involvement in the Vietnam War as immoral, he urged amnesty when the war ended for those who had fled the country to avoid the draft. McGovern did not favor legalized abortion or the use of drugs, but many Americans believed that he did or that, in any event, his supporters did. McGovern did not help his cause by stating, "Quite frankly, I am not a 'centrist' candidate." Nixon's margin of victory was decisive: 47 million votes (to McGovern's 29 million), 61.3 percent of the total vote, and a 520 to 17 electoral college majority. One Democratic campaign worker sighed, "I felt like the recreation director on the *Titanic*."

# WATERGATE AND THE PRESIDENCY

Since the era of Franklin Roosevelt, Americans had looked to the President for leadership in solving the nation's social and economic problems. When Americans were asked in the 1970s which famous people, living or dead, they would like as visitors to their homes, Lincoln was named first, four other Presidents followed, and Jesus Christ came in eleventh, just behind Harry Truman.

Such presidential popularity occurred in part because an increasingly complex society seemed to require centralized direction. More important, presidential authority was pumped up by thirty years of international crises. Throughout the Cold War, Presidents exercised powers once reserved for use in full-scale war, for many believed the executive needed a free hand to respond quickly and energetically to foreign threats. Richard Nixon carried the strong presidency to its furthest point in peacetime. Senate Democratic leader Mike Mansfeld admitted that Congress had handed much of its foreign policy power to the President "on a silver platter." Too late, Americans were learning a lesson taught more than 140 years earlier by Alexis de Tocqueville, a perceptive French visitor, in *Democracy in America:*

> No protracted war can fail to endanger the freedom of a democratic country. . . . War does not always give over democratic communities to military government, but it must invariably and immeasurably increase the powers of civil government; it must almost compulsorily concentrate the direction of all men and the management of all things in the hands of the administration. If it leads not to despotism by sudden violence, it prepares men for it more gently by their habits. All those who seek to destroy the liberties of a democratic nation ought to know that war is the surest and shortest means to accomplish it.

Tocqueville emphasized a point that Americans often failed to understand: foreign and domestic policies intertwine and shape one another.

The President and the nation learned this the hard way. In June 1972 five men connected to the Committee to Re-elect the President (CREEP) were caught trying to burglarize Democratic party headquarters in Washington's Watergate Apartments. Dismissing the break-in as a "bizarre incident," the President insisted that the White House was not involved. But in May 1973 a Senate investigation of Watergate uncovered a cesspool of illegal administration activities. Key White House aides were implicated in an attempt to cover up the burglary, and several admitted their guilt. Other revelations indicated that Nixon's campaign staff had illegally accepted large donations from corporations and individuals. In some instances the administration had apparently given the contributors political favors in return. In October 1973, with evidence accumulating that he had accepted payoffs from building contractors, Spiro Agnew resigned as Vice-President. The Justice Department permitted him to plead guilty to a charge of tax evasion. He was fined and sentenced to three years of unsupervised probation.

Nixon desperately tried to halt the rising tide of criticism, but his efforts were complicated by the discovery that an intricate recording system had for years been tape-recording almost all his White House conversations. Nixon refused to surrender these tapes. He claimed that to do so would cripple the President's authority and violate the constitutional principle of separation of powers. When the courts ruled against him, he released a few tapes. But investigators found that several contained gaps at crucial points, gaps that could not, despite the President's claims, have been caused by accident. To prove that he was, in his words, "not a crook," Nixon authorized publication of his personal tax returns. These showed that in 1970 and 1971, claiming deductions of dubious legality, he had paid a federal tax of about $800 annually on a salary of $200,000. Nixon had, moreover, paid no state income taxes since 1969 although he was a legal resident of California.

Charges were also levelled that expensive improvements on the President's oceanside residences at San Clemente, California, and Key Biscayne, Florida, had been made at the taxpayers' expense without justification. In one instance, the Secret Service claimed it had installed a $621 ice-making machine "to insure that the President was not using poisoned ice." The White House mess chief put it more directly: "The President does not like ice cubes with holes in them." An audit of his tax returns by a congressional committee added to Nixon's difficulties. The committee found that the President had improperly taken a $428,000 charitable deduction for donating his vice-presidential papers to the National Archives, had failed to report a capital gain on the sale of property, had incorrectly written off business expenses, and had failed to declare $92,298 worth of improvements made at San Clemente and Key Biscayne that were "undertaken primarily for the President's personal benefit." In April 1974, Nixon agreed to pay $444,000 in back taxes and $32,000 in interest.

The effect of these disclosures on the presidency was stunning. For years Congress had endured insults from the Nixon administration. When some members of Congress protested the continued bombing of Cambodia and North Vietnam, for example, a State Department official cynically told them that the "justification" was "the reelection of President Nixon." One newspaper observed that "By that theory he could level Boston." But the Nixon administration's arrogance, Watergate cover-up, and other illegal activities soon led the Senate and House to strike back.

They passed a landmark measure that limited presidential power to make war without Congress's assent. The War Powers Act of 1973 provided that (1) "in every possible instance" the President must consult with Congress before ordering U.S. troops into any hostilities overseas; (2) whenever the President dispatched troops to foreign lands he must, within forty-eight hours, send a full explanation to Congress; (3) he must withdraw the troops within sixty days unless Congress gave him specific authority to maintain them abroad.

To no one's surprise, Nixon vetoed the act. He argued that such a bill would have dangerously tied the President's hands during the Berlin confrontation of 1961 and the Cuban Missile crisis of 1962. Others opposed the bill for opposite reasons. They claimed it gave the President power to wage war on his own for sixty days without having to obtain congressional approval. Congress, however, believed it had found a useful middle ground, and that the measure would at least prevent future Vietnam-type interventions. The necessary two-thirds of the House and Senate voted to override Nixon's veto. That vote marked an important reversal in the thirty-year enlargement of presidential power.

Watergate not only weakened Nixon's standing with Congress, but also destroyed his ability to lead the Republican party. By 1974 even those who had stood by Nixon were shocked by each fresh disclosure. One Senator said that it was like waiting for the other shoe to drop, except "I don't know how many shoes there are to fall. I feel like I've been dealing with a centipede this past year." One poll found that only 24 percent of the voters classified themselves as Republicans, the smallest percentage identified with any major party in the twentieth century. The Democrats virtually swept the 1974 congressional elections, including such traditional Republican seats as one in Michigan that they had not held since 1932.

Watergate altered the American political landscape and undermined presidential power. In the late 1960s a majority of Americans had identified the groups dangerous to society as atheists, black militants, student demonstrators, prostitutes, and homosexuals. In 1968 and 1972, Nixon, by running on the social issue, had successfully exploited those fears. But the late 1973, pollster Louis Harris reported, none of these groups was considered harmful by a majority of people. Instead, the groups considered dangerous were people who hired political spies, generals who conducted secret bombing raids, politicians who engaged in wiretapping, businessmen who made illegal campaign contributions, and politicians who attempted to use federal investigatory agencies for partisan purposes.

# THE LOSS OF CIVIL LIBERTIES

At the same time as the Watergate scandal was unfolding, the American people learned that the federal government had, for more than a decade, systematically violated their constitutional rights. First exposed by the *New York Times* in 1974, and then confirmed over the next two years in the reports of a House committee chaired by Otis Pike (Dem.-N.Y.), a Senate committee headed by Frank Church (Dem.-Idaho), and a special committee under Nelson Rockefeller, those violations had begun even before the United States entered the war in Vietnam. But that war, and especially the turmoil and dissent accompanying it, led the Central Intelligence Agency, the Federal Bureau of Investigation, and other agencies to mount their most aggressive campaigns against civil liberties, and to do all they could to conceal their actions from Congress, the courts, and the people.

Nothing better illustrated the government's behavior than the CIA program known as "Operation CHAOS." Although the CIA was prohibited by law from spying on American citizens, the agency had begun to do so in the 1950s. In the summer of 1967, with antiwar demonstrations reaching a crescendo and with President Johnson convinced that the demonstrators were being funded by foreign powers, the CIA stepped up its activities. Although it discovered no foreign involvement, the agency nevertheless accelerated its campaign at President Nixon's behest in 1969. By 1974 the CIA had compiled dossiers on 7200 American citizens, stored the names of 300,000 individuals and groups in a computerized index file, opened 215,000 first-class letters, placed wiretaps on telephones, installed bugging devices in people's homes, and burglarized the offices of dissident groups. Speaking of the mail-opening program, one CIA official admitted, "This thing is illegal as hell." Not to be outdone by the CIA, the FBI remodeled its own counterintelligence program, COINTELPRO, and began to shift its attention to black militants, the New Left, and the antiwar movement. A House committee summarized some of the results of the FBI program: "Careers were ruined, friendships severed, reputations sullied, businesses bankrupted and, in some cases, lives endangered."

Two actions demonstrated Richard Nixon's own cavalier disregard for civil liberties. In May 1969, furious that news of the "secret" bombing of Cambodia had leaked to the press, the Nixon administration placed wiretaps on a number of government officials and newspaper reporters. For nearly two years the Justice Department monitored their phone calls although, as the President later conceded privately, the transcripts produced no evidence of subversion, but "just gobs and gobs of material: gossip and bullshitting." In July 1970 Tom C. Huston, a presidential aide, concocted a plan designed at once to expand and centralize the government's counter-intelligence operations. Proposing that surreptitious entry be used to obtain information, Huston admitted: "Use of this technique is clearly illegal: it amounts to burglary." But he explained further: "It is also the most fruitful tool and can produce the type of intelligence which cannot be obtained in any other fashion." The President approved these recommendations, but when FBI Director J. Edgar Hoover objected (primarily, it seems, because he feared their implementation would reduce the FBI's role), Nixon rescinded his approval.

The administration's contempt for civil liberties was again evident a year later. In June 1971 Dr. Daniel Ellsberg, a former Pentagon expert on Vietnam, made public the secret "Pentagon Papers," which documented American policy in Indochina between 1945 and 1968. The administration first attempted to block their publication in newspapers, but the Supreme Court ruled against prior restraint by a 6 to 3 vote. A majority of the justices found that the government had failed to prove that release of the documents would "inevitably, directly and immediately" injure the nation. Indeed, Nixon never believed that the documents jeopardized the nation's security, although he did fear their release might set a dangerous precedent. Ellsberg was then indicted for stealing government property.

At the same time the White House created a "plumbers" group of secret agents to "stop security leaks and to investigate other sensitive security matters." One of the group's first tasks was to discredit Ellsberg, and this, in turn, seemed to require a covert operation. The plumbers believed that damning evidence might be found in the office files of a Los Angeles psychiatrist whom Ellsberg had been consulting. The President's chief domestic advisor, John Ehrlichman, approved a burglary of the office as long as "it is not traceable." In September 1971 the plumbers broke into the psychiatrist's office, but failed to turn up evidence that would, in their words, "nail the guy cold."

Daniel Ellsberg's trial for espionage and the theft of government property was held in 1973. The government's behavior during the trial was consistent with its previous behavior. While the trial was in progress, John Ehrlichman offered the directorship of the FBI to the presiding judge, William Matthew Byrne, Jr. The offer, if not actually improper, was surely irregular. The administration only grudgingly confessed that it had masterminded a burglary of Ellsberg's psychiatrist's office, and then urged Judge Byrne—unsuccessfully—not to make the information public. Finally, the government did not reveal, until ordered to do so by the judge, that the wiretaps it had installed in 1969 had inadvertently picked up some of Ellsberg's conversations. Furious at this behavior, Judge Byrne declared a mistrial and dismissed the charges against Ellsberg. He noted that the circumstances in the case offended "a sense of justice." That judgment was equally applicable to CHAOS, COINTELPRO, wiretapping, the Huston plan, and, as the Watergate investigation had already begun to reveal, to a much broader range of White House activities.

## IMPEACHMENT: THE PRESIDENCY FROM NIXON TO FORD

In late 1973 the House of Representatives ordered its Judiciary Committee to determine whether Nixon had committed impeachable offenses, defined by the Constitution as "Bribery, or other high crimes and misdemeanors." During nine months of study, the Committee wavered in its view of whether the President should be impeached. Nixon's headline-making trips abroad, Americans' veneration of their President, and the memory of Nixon's triumph in the 1972 elections raised dangerous political problems for Congress. The dilemma was especially acute in an election year. By July 1974, however, the Judiciary Committee had assembled a massive amount of evidence that seemed damning to the President's case. Nor did Nixon help his cause by withholding more than 100 tapes of private conversations on the grounds of "Executive privilege," asserting that they must remain secret or otherwise the President's ability to protect the national interest would be endangered.

Three weeks in the summer of 1974 marked a turning point in American history. On July 24 the Supreme Court unanimously ordered the President to surrender sixty-four tapes to John Sirica, judge of the District Court in the District of Columbia where the Watergate trial was held. After listening to the tapes, Sirica could give all relevant portions to Special Watergate Prosecutor Leon Jaworski, who could then turn them over to Congress. The President thus had to retreat from his claim of Executive privilege for all his documents. For the first time, however, the Supreme Court also ruled that the President had the right to withhold information on the grounds of Executive privilege when the information concerned military or diplomatic matters. Since the tapes in dispute did not cover such national security issues, Nixon had to surrender them so that the courts could base their decisions on all possible evidence.

One week later, John Ehrlichman, who as the President's chief domestic affairs advisor had held great power, was found guilty of directing the break-in at the office of Daniel Ellsberg's psychiatrist. Ehrlichman was also found guilty of lying to investigators about his role in the crime. He received a sentence of twenty months to five years in prison. Four of Nixon's Cabinet officials, his two top White House assistants, and former Vice-President Agnew had now been named in criminal cases. In all, thirty-eight officials associated with the Nixon administration had either pleaded guilty or been indicted for crimes. American history offered no parallel.

On July 30 the House Judiciary Committee completed six days of public debate by recommending that the full House of Representatives approve three Articles of Impeachment. The first Article accused the President of lying about, and trying to conceal, the role of his White House staff in the Watergate break-in. The second Article alleged that Nixon had violated the constitutional rights of citizens by placing unlawful wiretaps on telephones and by using the FBI, CIA, and Internal Revenue Service to harass his political opponents. The third Article declared the President had refused to comply with congressional subpoenas for documents and taped conversations. Two other articles, one condemning Nixon's secret bombing of Cambodia in 1969–70 and another accusing him of income tax evasion and of using government monies for private gain, were rejected by the committee as inadequate reasons for impeachment.

The Judiciary Committee reached its decision after long, bitter debate and intense soul searching. Republicans and Southern Democrats were especially uncomfortable as evidence against the President accumulated. But as a leading conservative from Alabama commented: "And . . . what if we fail to impeach? Do we ingrain forever in the very fabric of our Constitution a standard of conduct in our highest office that at the least is deplorable and at the worst is impeachable?" In the end, as many as seven Republicans and all twenty-one Democrats voted for at least one of the Articles. The Committee's debate, which attracted a huge television and radio audience, had an immense political impact. Congressmen effectively used a medium that, until 1974, had been so manipulated by the White House that it had been called "Presidential television."

No one any longer doubted that the House would vote to impeach the President by a wide margin. Nixon's last hope lay in the Senate, but that hope quickly died. On August 5 he released the transcripts of three conversations he had held with his chief White House assistant, H. R. Haldeman, a few days after the June 1972 Watergate break-in. These tapes showed that Nixon had raised the possibility of getting the CIA to order the FBI to halt its investigation of the burglary. "Don't go any further into this case period!" was the language the President proposed. The President also conceded that he had kept this information from his own lawyers and from the impeachment inquiry. Granting that he had committed a "serious act of omission," and that impeachment in the House was "virtually a foregone conclusion," Nixon insisted that his behavior did not warrant a conviction in the Senate.

But the disclosure that he had obstructed justice and withheld the truth provided the "smoking pistol" for which many congressmen were searching. And the fingerprints were unmistakably clear. Support for the President evaporated overnight. Republicans began a stampede for res-

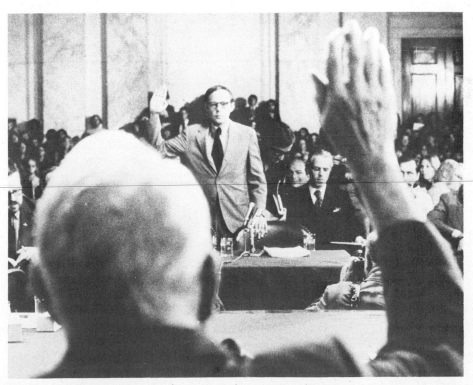

Senator Sam Ervin swears in John Dean at the Watergate hearings.

ignation or impeachment. The situation in the White House became tense. According to investigative reporters, Nixon began to roam the mansion at night, communing with the portraits of past Presidents, and at one point summoning Henry Kissinger to kneel with him in prayer. White House aides feared that if they pressured him to quit, Nixon might respond irrationally. All orders from the President to the military were carefully monitored by top civilian officials in the Pentagon.

Finally, on the night of August 7, Nixon met with two conservative Arizona Republicans, Senator Barry Goldwater and Representative John Rhodes, the House Minority Leader. They reported that the Senate would surely vote to impeach. Even the ten Republican members of the Judiciary Committee who had defended the President a few days earlier had reversed their positions. One member reportedly asked if the committee could reconvene so he could change his vote, but he was informed that "the train had left the station." Its destination became known on August 9, 1974, when for the first time in history an American President was forced to resign his office. Vice-President Gerald Ford, whom Nixon had appointed to replace Agnew, became Chief Executive.

The presidency, which had increasingly dominated foreign and domestic policies in the American Century, had finally been curbed by Congress and the Supreme Court. Yet Nixon's resignation occurred primarily because he had tape-recorded incriminating conversations and then refused advice from close friends to destroy the tapes. A disturbing question remained: whether the unconstitutional acts described in the Articles of Impeachment could have been uncovered if Nixon had not made the recordings, or if he had destroyed them before Congress learned of their existence.

Gerald Ford, moreover, unilaterally used his new power to protect Nixon from criminal prosecution. On September 8, 1974, the President said that he was pardoning Nixon for all federal crimes he "committed or may have committed" during his years in the White House. Ford's announcement set off a storm of protest since it precluded a trial and thereby undercut proper legal processes. Two years later, the pardon returned to haunt Ford. It was an important reason why many Americans preferred Jimmy Carter instead of Ford in the presidential election. The ghost of Richard Nixon continued to stalk the corridors of American politics.

## HENRY KISSINGER: FOREIGN POLICY FROM NIXON TO FORD

One official, however, emerged from the morass of Watergate with an enhanced reputation. In 1973, after having served as the President's National Security Advisor, Henry Kissinger became Secretary of State. That same year he finally succeeded in negotiating a Vietnam ceasefire with

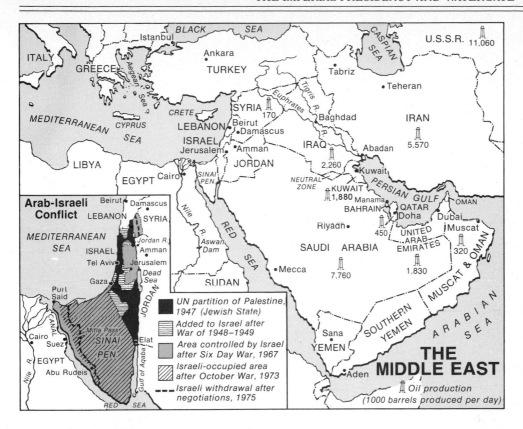

Arab-Israeli Conflict

- ■ UN partition of Palestine, 1947 (Jewish State)
- ▤ Added to Israel after War of 1948–1949
- ▦ Area controlled by Israel after Six Day War, 1967
- ▨ Israeli-occupied area after October War, 1973
- - - - Israeli withdrawal after negotiations, 1975

**THE MIDDLE EAST**

⚒ Oil production (1000 barrels produced per day)

his North Vietnamese counterpart, Le Duc Tho. The two men were rewarded with the 1973 Nobel Peace Prize. Tho refused his share, correctly asserting that war between North and South Vietnam continued. The American troops left, however, and Kissinger accepted his share of the prize. "Half a prize for half a peace seems just about right," one journalist observed.

Kissinger followed with equally successful (from his and Nixon's view), if less publicized, diplomacy in Chile. Since 1970 President Salvador Allende had turned Chile toward a more nationalist, independent course, and attempted to gain his nation's economic independence—and distribute its wealth more equitably—by seizing property owned by North American corporations and wealthy Chileans. Kissinger and Nixon secretly moved to undermine the new regime. By 1973 Allende's government suffered severely not only from its own economic errors but a cutoff of the U.S. aid on which Chile had long depended. Kissinger meanwhile strengthened Washington's ties with the Chilean army. In September 1973 the army struck. It overthrew Allende, who died in the struggle, ended all attempts at reform, established a military regime, and then tortured and murdered thousands of political prisoners. Americans both North and South were saddened by Chile's new course, but Kissinger and Nixon were pleased that they had played a major part in overthrowing a government they had always mistrusted and feared. They believed the United States had proved that it could still guide the fortunes of Third-World nations, at least those in Latin America.

Turning from Chile with satisfaction—and from Vietnam with obvious relief—Kissinger pledged his full attention to renewing frayed ties with Western Europe. This important relationship had deteriorated politically and economically. The Nixon administration placed first priority on détente with Russia and China. The policy worked well (Soviet Premier Brezhnev was so pleased that he embarrassed Kissinger by kissing him full on the mouth when they met), but relations with the Atlantic partners suffered, for they feared the superpowers might be making deals that did not consider Europeans' interests.

Before Kissinger could move to repair the Atlantic alliance, however, war in the Middle East wrecked his plans. The roots of the conflict went back to 1967 when the Egyptians blockaded several ports that were crucial for Israel's security. On June 5, 1967, the Israelis suddenly retaliated. In the "Six-Day War," they humiliated the Egyptians and their Arab allies by seizing the prized city of Jerusalem (the world home of three great religious faiths—Islam, Judaism, and Christianity), sweeping across the Sinai Desert to the Suez Canal, and wiping out large portions of the Egyptian and Syrian armies. The Arabs refused to discuss peace until Israel returned the conquered areas. The Israelis rejected this demand, claiming that the new boundaries were necessary for their security.

Re-equipped with massive Soviet aid, the Egyptians and Syrians suddenly attacked Israel in October 1973. The Egyptian army redeemed itself. Israel staved off a major setback only with a brilliant crossing of the Suez that enveloped large numbers of Egyptian troops and placed Israeli forces in Egypt itself. Kissinger flew to the Middle East five times in six months, and with cooperation from the Soviets (who feared a prolonged war would result in Egyptian defeat), brought about direct Egyptian-Israeli talks, the first since Israel was founded in 1948. A temporary settlement provided for mutual troop withdrawal and creation of a buffer zone in the Sinai Peninsula.

Although key problems remained unresolved in the Middle East, the Egyptian-Israeli disengagement gave Kissinger cause for satisfaction. The same could not be said for developments in Southeast Asia. After pulling out its combat troops, the United States cut aid to the Saigon government in 1974. During the spring of 1975, the North Vietnamese Communists launched an all-out offensive. The beleaguered Saigon regime, riddled with corruption and deserted slowly by Washington, asked desperately for American help. Investigation revealed that two years before, Nixon had secretly assured the South Vietnamese that in a such a situation the United States would use its great power to protect the South: "You can count on us," he had told them. But in April 1975, Nixon was in disgrace at San Clemente, California. Across the Pacific television cameras recorded the sordid details of U.S. officials shoving aside former Vietnamese allies so the Americans could escape by helicopter moments before the Communists seized Saigon. The long United States war in Southeast Asia was finally over.

# Suggested Reading

For Richard Nixon and his administration see Fawn M. Brodie, *Richard Nixon: The Shaping of His Character* (1981); Garry Wills, *Nixon Agonistes* (1970); Jonathan Schell, *The Time of Illusion* (1975); Rowland Evans and Robert Novak, *Nixon in the White House* (1971); and Vincent J. Burke, *Nixon's Good Deed: Welfare Reform* (1974). Leonard W. Levy, *Against the Law* (1974) is an attack on the Burger Court's approach to criminal justice. Bob Woodward and Scott Armstrong's, *The Brethren* (1979) purports to provide the inside story of the nation's highest tribunal in the Nixon and Ford years.

On the impact of the women's movement see Janet Giele, *Women and the Future: Changing Sex Roles in Modern America* (1978); and William H. Chafe, *Women and Equality: Changing Patterns in American Culture* (1977). For Native Americans consult Vine DeLoria, Jr., *Behind the Trail of Broken Treaties* (1974). The erosion of civil liberties is documented in Athan Theoharis, *Spying on Americans* (1979); Morton H. Halperin, *et al.*, *The Lawless State* (1976); David Wise, *The American Police State* (1976); David J. Garrow, *The FBI and Martin Luther King, Jr.* (1981); and Peter Schrag, *Test of Loyalty* (1974), an account of the Daniel Ellsberg case.

The literature on Watergate is extensive. Some of the more important works are J. Anthony Lukacs, *Nightmare: The Underside of the Nixon Years* (1976); Theodore H. White, *Breach of Faith: The Fall of Richard Nixon* (1975); John J. Sirica, *To Set the Record Straight* (1979); Jim Houghan, *Secret Agenda: Watergate, Deep Throat and the CIA* (1984); and James Doyle, *Not Above the Law* (1977).

On foreign policy, the key source for further research is R. H. Burns, ed., *Guide to American Foreign Policy Since 1700* (1983). Indispensable are the two-volume (and massive) memoirs by Henry Kissinger, *The White House Years* (1979) on 1969–72, and *Years of Upheaval* (1982) on 1972–73. Compare these with Nixon's own memoirs, *RN* (1978), and especially with Seymour Hersh, *The Price of Power* (1983), an astonishing attack on the Nixon-Kissinger policies; as well as with Lloyd Gardner, "The Burden of Richard Nixon," in *A Covenant With Power* (1984). John Newhouse, *Cold Dawn* (1973) covers the SALT I agreement. A good assessment on Vietnam, especially on the military side, is Timothy J. Lomperis, *The War Everyone Lost—and Won* (1984). The Soviet side is analyzed in Joseph G. Whelen, *Soviet Diplomacy and Negotiating Behavior* (1982). A fine case study of the oil crisis is Stephen G. Rabe, *The Road to OPEC: U.S. Relations with Venezuela, 1919–1976* (1982). A superb critique of the international economic policies is David Calleo, *Imperious Economy* (1982).

A place to begin in understanding football in American life is David Riesman and Reuel Denney, "Football in America," *American Quarterly* (1951), pp. 309–25. On the development of space technology, see Barton C. Hacker, "Robert H. Goddard and the Origins of Space Flight," in Carroll W. Pursell, Jr., ed., *Technology in America: A History of Individuals and Ideas* (1981).

Young urban professionals, New York City, 1984.

# CHAPTER SIXTEEN

# New Directions:

## Carter and Reagan

Vietnam and Watergate continued to influence American life long after the last soldier had returned home and the last conspirator had gone to jail. It was only logical, in the aftermath of Watergate, that successful politicians would be those who had no connection with the Washington establishment. Neither Jimmy Carter nor Ronald Reagan had held federal office, elective or appointive, before being elected President. Politics became the art of running against the government. Winning elections became the art of selling a candidate's personal integrity to the voters. It was equally logical, in the aftermath of Vietnam, that an assertive foreign policy, a promise to make America strong again, would exert a strong appeal. Although the policies that Carter and Reagan adopted differed in important respects, the differences concerned the speed at which the nation was moving more than the direction in which it was going: toward a dousing of social reform at home and a rekindling of Cold War hostilities abroad.

## JIMMY CARTER AND THE "NEW REALITIES"

In 1971, when he became governor of Georgia, Jimmy Carter regarded the presidency with "reverence." Then he had an opportunity to meet the men—Nixon and McGovern, Humphrey and Muskie, Reagan and Rockefeller—who had been contesting for the office over the years and, as Carter recalled, "I lost my feeling of awe about presidents." In early 1973, undaunted by the label applied to him by journalists—"Jimmy Who?"— Carter set out to win the Democratic nomination. By 1976, with his only political experience one term in the Georgia Senate and one term as the state's governor, Carter recognized that the Watergate backlash might do wonders for his candidacy.

He portrayed himself as an "outsider" who never had been involved in corrupt Washington politics. To voters fed up with deception in high places, he promised, "I will never lie to you." Gambling that his status as a Southerner, his image as an unknown newcomer without Washington connections, and his emphasis on personal integrity would strike responsive chords in the electorate, Carter collected Democratic delegates as a gambler gathers chips. "We figured the odds as best we could," he explained, "and then we rolled the dice."

In his speech accepting the Democratic nomination in June 1976, Carter placed himself squarely within the party's reform tradition. Calling for "an end to discrimination because of race and sex," he said: "Too many have had to suffer at the hands of a political and economic elite who have shaped decisions and never had to account for mistakes or suffer from injustice." Pledging support for a revamping of the income-tax structure, Carter lashed out at "unholy, self-perpetuating alliances . . . between money and politics." Urging enactment of new welfare programs, including a "nationwide comprehensive health program for all our people," Carter stated: "The poor, the weak, the aged, the afflicted must be treated with respect and compassion and with love." Although Carter also warned that government could not solve every problem, most of his listeners detected strong populist overtones in the speech.

Many things helped Carter in the campaign, not least President Ford's reputation as a bumbler. Ford tripped down some steps on a state occasion, cut himself diving into the White House swimming pool, and bumped his head boarding a helicopter. Newsmen adapted Lyndon Johnson's cutting remark that Ford had played too much football without a helmet, and made it crueller still: "He can't even play President without a helmet." Nor did Ford's choice of Senator Robert Dole of Kansas as his running mate help the Republicans. In a televised debate with his Democratic counterpart, Senator Walter Mondale of Minnesota, Dole charged that World War I, World War II, and Korea were "all Democrat wars." Such remarks angered Democratic moderates whom the Republicans badly needed on election day. Finally, Ford's own statement during a debate with Carter that, partly due to Republican policies, "There is no Soviet domination of Eastern Europe," cost the President crucial support from Poles, Czechs, and other Americans of Eastern European origin.

Yet the electorate, or at least the 54 percent that bothered to vote, responded to more than mishaps, mudslinging, and miscues. Ford did best among the affluent and the comfortable, Carter among the poor and disadvantaged. The vote, pollsters found, "fractured to a marked degree along the fault line separating the haves and the have-nots." Carter won about 55 percent of the Catholic and Jewish vote, but more than 90 percent of the black vote. The Georgian carried ten of the eleven southern states (all except Virginia); in seven of the ten, black voters provided his margin of victory. With a total of 40.8 million votes to Ford's 39.1 million, Carter emerged with a 297 to 241 victory in the Electoral College.

Expectations that Jimmy Carter would preside over a new era of reform were short-lived. Within 100 days of his taking office, many people thought that Carter had begun "shifting to the right." Within a year disgruntled liberals believed that Carter was the most conservative Democratic President since Grover Cleveland. Within eighteen months, critics charged that Carter "is a Democrat who often talks and thinks like a Republican." And within two years, they sneered that Carter, "a counterfeit populist," was in truth "as Republican as Gerald Ford."

Liberals centered their fire on three aspects of the President's legislative program. They claimed that his energy bill, enacted in 1978 after a fierce congressional struggle, benefited the oil companies by deregulating natural gas prices; that his tax reform measure, approved in 1977, failed to close loopholes enjoyed by the wealthy and offered little relief to middle-income individuals; and that his medical-care proposals fell far short of the comprehensive health programs supported by Senator Edward Kennedy (Dem.-Mass.). By 1978 Kennedy had begun to complain that the administration was sacrificing the needs of "the poor, the black, the sick, the young, the cities and the unemployed."

Carter's policies undoubtedly reflected his own managerial outlook, his tendency to convert social problems into engineering problems and to seek technical solutions for them. Moreover, Carter found it necessary to placate members of Congress, especially chairmen of powerful committees. Demanding modifications in the energy and tax proposals, these Democratic leaders forced Carter to retreat or even surrender. The President could no longer invoke party discipline against Democrats who increasingly divided along geographical ("sun-belt" versus "snow-belt") and ideological lines. As the party system fragmented, congressional defiance of the White House became more common. In the late 1970s power shifted dramatically up Pennsylvania Avenue to Capitol Hill.

As presidential influence over—and party discipline in—Congress declined, pressure groups rushed to fill the vacuum. Carter had promised to attack the "unholy" alliance "between money and politics," but these groups, representing virtually every important economic interest in the country, nevertheless gained tremendous influence in Congress. They multiplied "like rabbits," Senator Edward Kennedy warned, "and are doing their best to buy every senator, every representative, and every issue in sight." The groups included trade associations (as the American Medical Association and National Education Association), corporations, labor, and single-issue interests (antiabortion or anti-gun control advocates, for example). They cemented their power by giving lavishly to congressional campaigns. Not surprisingly, Congress passed laws encouraging such gifts. Labor unions had long been allowed to contribute to campaigns, but corporations had not—until, that is, new laws in the 1970s permitted them to set up political action committees (PACs) to support sympathetic politicians. The PACs transformed political fund-raising, especially since the unions' political power seemed to be fading. By 1978 a top advisor to Carter mourned, "We have a fragmented, Balkanized society," with each special economic group "interested in only one domestic program"—its own.

More than anything else, however, the nagging problem of inflation limited Carter's freedom of action. To fight inflation, he believed, it was essential to reduce the federal budget deficit. But since the President also wanted to increase spending for national defense, he recommended a moderate reduction in social welfare expenditures. Carter's proposed budget for 1980, therefore, elicited anger from liberals and cautious approval from conservatives. The Black Congressional Caucus termed the budget "immoral and unjust," while a Bank of America spokesman thought "it catches the right mood."

In January 1979 Carter's chief domestic policy advisor, Stuart E. Eizenstat, explained that the President's scaled-down domestic agenda was due to the "new realities" of the late 1970s. Those "unhappier realities" included "high inflation coupled with high unemployment, and widespread public cynicism toward the government." Such realities—combined with Carter's own managerial disposition, the erosion of presidential power, and the growing influence of interest groups—constituted the legacy of the 1970s, a legacy that would shape politics in the 1980s.

## CARTER'S FOREIGN POLICY: CONFUSION . . .

Americans not only had to deal with a fragmented society at home, but a fragmented world abroad. They faced complex problems in the newly emerging nations that had little to do with Soviet communism. Dealing with these problems frustrated Americans, who prefer their foreign relations to resemble a baseball game—that is, of short duration with clearly identified opponents and a definite winner. Foreign policy refuses to be so simple.

Jimmy Carter came to power with little knowledge of foreign policy. His colorful younger brother Billy was astonished at Jimmy's ambition to lead the world's greatest power: "My mother joined the Peace Corps when she was 70, my sister Gloria is a motorcycle racer, my other sister, Ruth, is a Holy Roller preacher, and my brother thinks he is going to be President of the United States! I'm the only normal one in the family."

The new President tried to make up for his inexperience by appointing Cyrus Vance (a New York lawyer) as Secretary of State, and Zbigniew Brzezinski (a Columbia University expert on Eastern Europe) as National Security Council Advisor. Both had extensive experience in foreign policy. But they conflicted in advising Carter. Vance hoped to be patient and conciliatory in strengthening relations with Russia. He wanted to deal with crises in the newly emerging nations not by blaming them on the Soviets, but treating them as problems of new, ambitious nationalisms. Vance received support from Andrew Young, Carter's Ambassador to the United Nations. A well-known black leader, Young believed that African problems, for example, should be dealt with by Africans; neither of the two superpowers had the understanding or power to control such affairs. (Young's approach helped resolve several African crises, especially in removing obstacles so the former British colony of Rhodesia could become the black-governed nation of Zimbabwe.) Brzezinski, on the other hand, viewed the world largely in terms of the U.S.-Soviet conflict. He saw a grim Russian face behind upheavals in Third-World countries, and increasingly urged a tough military line towards the Soviets.

Carter had to choose between the Vance-Young and Brzezinski views. The President was not well equipped for the task. Trained as an engineer at the U.S. Naval Academy, he remained, in the words of close observers, "an engineer, a manager," and a "problem-solving President" who might know "how every single engine or pump works," but had little sense of the larger structure within which machinery had to function. He had no consistent larger view of world affairs. In 1973 Brzezinski had brought Carter into the new Trilateral Commission for an education in foreign policy. Brzezinski and New York banker David Rockefeller had begun the Commission to coordinate policies among Japan, the United States, and Western Europe so these industrial powers could deal with the sudden economic and Third-World crises of the 1970s. But the trilateral approach proved disappointing. Even Brzezinski disgustedly wrote in 1976 that "neither Europe nor Japan is prepared to play a major role" in solving the crises. By 1980, indeed, the Western alliance would be in its worst shape since 1945.

The United States thus moved more and more on its own. Carter determined to restore its authority abroad (and reinvigorate Americans' faith in their own values at home), by sharply cutting the Vietnam-inflated military budget and emphasizing his support of human rights. Those rights were to include personal freedom from torture and imprisonment for political reasons. They also included access to food, shelter, medical care, and education, and the right to enjoy such liberties as free speech and assembly. Such rights, Carter declared, were "the soul of our foreign policy." He soon learned, however, that he could not practice what he preached. Some of the world's worst violators of human rights (South Korea, Argentina, Guatemala, Nicaragua, Iran) were also important allies of the United States. He therefore did little to pressure the Korean or Iranian governments. When he criticized Argentina and Guatemala, they refused to cooperate any longer with U.S. military programs. The President's policy was both needed and decent (and helped return Argentina to democratic government in 1984), but even his advisers admitted that it had never been thought through, never reconciled with the major security needs of U.S. foreign policy.

Carter's relations with the Soviets meanwhile steadily declined. When he publicly attacked Moscow's human rights violations and welcomed Soviet dissidents to the White House (a welcome that Nixon and Kissinger had refused to give), Brezhnev delivered an icy political blast. Talks aimed at slowing the runaway arms race nearly collapsed. In October 1977 one breakthrough did occur when the two superpowers agreed to work for peace in the explosive Middle East. But the possibility of a larger Russian presence frightened both Egyptians and Israelis. A firestorm of objection from U.S. friends of Israel forced Carter (in Brzezinski's words) to "walk away" from the deal. Brezhnev was outraged, but Carter managed to score a major victory in 1979 when he mediated the Camp David accords between Egypt's leader, Anwar Sadat, and Israeli Prime Minister Menachem Begin. The agreement, reached at the presidential retreat in the Maryland mountains, marked the first peace treaty between Egypt and Israel after three decades of war. Begin also pledged to return the large Sinai area to Egypt that Israel had seized in 1967. No deal, however, could be reached on the festering question of other areas claimed by both Israeli settlers and hundreds of thousands of Palestinians.

The Soviets perhaps became most disturbed when the United States announced in 1978 that it would begin formal diplomatic relations with China. The Chinese needed U.S. arms to protect the long border they shared with the Soviet Union and claimed they wanted $100 billion of outside investment to develop their economy in the 1980s. Carter was happy to open China to U.S. investors, but he severely limited any military aid out of fear of possible Russian reaction. Superpower relations further soured in 1978–79 when Soviet officials and thirteen thousand Cuban troops appeared in Ethiopia to help that East African nation in a war begun by neighboring Somalia. The region was strategically located along the oil shipping lanes of the Middle East. (See map, p. 523.) The United States consequently quickly sent aid to the Somalis.

Against this ominous background, Carter and Brezhnev met in Vienna in 1979 to negotiate SALT II (the second Strategic Arms Limitations Talks). Under the agreement, each side was to have no more than 2400 nuclear missile launchers (with that number reduced to 2250 in eighteen months). Not more than 1320 of the launchers were to be "MIRVed"—that is, have as many as ten Multiple-Independent-Reentry-Vehicle nuclear bombs that could be separated in midflight and hit individual targets. U.S. critics claimed that SALT II favored the Russians, whose nuclear force was comprised of large, single-head missiles, and hurt the U.S. force that depended more on MIRVs and other new technology weapons. These critics vowed to kill the treaty when it came before the Senate for ratification.

Carter had not been effective in dealing with Congress. Since the early 1970s, moreover, the legislative bodies had become fragmented. House and Senate leaders could no longer deliver votes for Carter as, for example, Senator Lyndon Johnson had delivered support for Eisenhower's policies in the 1950s. The Georgian had also spent much of his political capital in pushing through two treaties in 1978 that would give the Panama Canal to the Panamanians in the year 2000. The Panamanians had often rioted against the U.S.-built and controlled Canal Zone, which had split their country since 1903. U.S. military officials worried that the waterway could not be protected against future rioting. The final treaties gave the North Americans special privileges (including the right to intervene militarily to keep the canal open). But led by conservative Senators and former California Governor Ronald Reagan, opponents fought the pacts until the treaties were ratified with only a single extra vote.

## . . . TO COLD WAR

As SALT II came before the Senate, a series of events suddenly erupted and—machine gun–like—destroyed both Carter's presidency and his hope of thawing the Cold War. The blasts occurred in Iran, Central America, and Afghanistan.

In late 1978 a revolution led by Moslem religious leaders undermined the Iranian government of Shah Riza Pahlevi. The Shah was Washington's closest military ally in the Middle East. He had used his immense oil wealth to purchase billions of dollars of U.S. arms. But he had also tried to modernize his nation too rapidly. When conservative opposition appeared, especially among college-age Iranians as well as the Moslem leaders, the Shah imprisoned and killed many of his critics. As the crisis grew, Carter's advisers again split: Vance wanted to talk with the Shah's opposition, but Brzezinski considered even the use of U.S. troops to keep the Shah in power. While Americans debated, the Shah was toppled from his famous Peacock Throne in early 1979. Ayatollah Ruhollah Khomeini, the 80-year-old Moslem leader, took control.

More shocks quickly followed. The disruption of Iranian oil exports gave OPEC (the organization of Arab and other oil producers) a chance to raise their prices by 50 percent. The price rise drove up inflation in the United States until it skyrocketed from the 7 percent annual increase of 1974–78 to more than 13 percent in 1979. Alarmed Americans watched 30 billions of their dollars flow to oil producers instead of being used to pay for higher food and housing costs. (A second cause of the disastrous U.S. trade balance was the $7 billion Americans illegally spent to import cocaine.)

Nor could Carter prevent the overthrow of another U.S. friend, Anastasio Somoza, the dictator of Nicaragua. The revolutionary Sandinista Front had been fighting Somoza since the early 1960s. Named after Augusto Sandino, the guerrilla fighter who forced U.S. Marines to stop occupying Nicaragua in 1933, the Sandinistas disliked and feared the United States. Carter (as had many Presidents before him) supported Somoza, but also pushed the dictator to pursue human rights principles. That policy undercut Somoza, whose authority increasingly depended on brutality. Carter finally tried to intervene so the Sandinistas could not gain power. When not a single Latin American nation would join Carter, his efforts failed and the Sandinistas marched into the capital, Managua, in July 1979. By 1980 the new government carried on most of its trade with the United States, but increasingly dealt with Castro's Cuba to obtain educational, medical, and military help. The revolution, moreover, threatened to spread to help left-wing forces in neighboring El Salvador, but the rebels' "final offensive" was turned back by the U.S.-supplied Salvadoran army in January 1981.

The setbacks in Iran and Nicaragua were disasters for Carter. Worse, however, lay ahead. In October 1979 he decided to allow the Shah, suffering from cancer, to enter the United States for treatment. Infuriated Iranian mobs, encouraged by Khomeini, stormed the U.S. Embassy in Teheran on November 4 and seized sixty-nine American diplomats. Fifty-three of them were finally held as hostages; the rest were freed. The crisis dominated American television screens (the popular ABC late-night news show "Nightline" was born during the crisis). Unable to deal with Khomeini, Carter watched his own popularity sink to new lows. In April 1980, as the presidential election campaign intensified, Carter ordered a secret rescue mission. But several of the U.S. helicopters crashed in an Iranian desert and killed eight American soldiers. Vance resigned after the President overruled his opposition to the mission. (Only after months of secret talks and U.S. economic pressure were the hostages released in January 1981.)

As Americans were preoccupied with the Iranian crisis, the Soviet Union invaded its southern neighbor Afghanistan in late December 1979. It marked the first time in the post-1945 era that Russian troops had launched an invasion outside their East European bloc. Afghanistan was a strategic gateway both for the Soviets' southern borders and the Middle East oilfields. In 1978–1979 the pro-Russian Afghan government had become wobbly. Moscow officials also feared that Khomeini's Moslem fanaticism (in which communism was hated as much as U.S. capitalism) would spread over Afghanistan. They therefore dispatched eighty thousand troops to take control. Poorly armed Afghan guerrillas fought back with surprising effectiveness and tied down the Russians in a long, bloody struggle. A stunned Carter, who in 1977 had declared his policies would not be shaped by "the inordinate fear of Communism," had become consumed by the fear. He sent arms to the Afghan rebels and then stopped shipment of 17 million tons of U.S. wheat promised to the Soviets. The Russians badly needed the grain because of their own failed agricultural system, but they quickly obtained supplies elsewhere, especially from Argentina and Canada. American farmers bitterly attacked Carter for the loss of the Russian market, and George Shultz (Nixon's former Secretary of the Treasury) condemned the President for turning vital trade "on and off like a light switch."

The President then dramatically announced a "Carter doctrine": the United States would, if necessary, unilaterally use force to prevent any further Russian encroachment in the Middle East–Southwest Asia region. He backed up his doctrine with a military budget (which he had promised in 1976 to cut by $5 billion) that now rose $20 billion to a record peacetime high of $106 billion. Carter thus helped prepare the way for Ronald Reagan's massive military build-up. But the Georgian also prepared the way for Reagan's 1980 election triumph with his ineffectual responses to the crisis of SALT II (which died without a vote in the Senate), the economy, the overthrow of Somoza and the Shah, and the Soviet invasion of Afghanistan. *Business Week* caught the nation's mood: "The country is entering the decade of the 1980s as a wounded, demoralized colossus."

## POLITICAL EVANGELICALISM AND THE MORAL MAJORITY

American politics in the 1980s were influenced not only by these reversals but also by the impact of evangelical Christianity. The word *evangelical* derives from the Greek for "good news," and evangelicals devoted themselves to spreading the good news that Jesus had come into the world to save sinners and make them whole. Evangelicals emphasized the responsibility of each person, believing an individual could be redeemed only by being "born again"—that is, confessing one's sins, accepting a resurrected Jesus as a "personal savior," and leading a new life. Jimmy Carter was born again after listening to a sermon entitled "If you were arrested for being a Christian, would there be any evidence to convict you?"

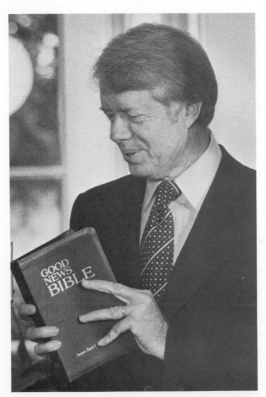

Jimmy Carter with a gift from the American Bible Society, 1977.

Although he was already a Sunday school teacher and deacon in his church, Carter decided that "if arrested and charged with being a committed follower of God, I could probably talk my way out of it! It was a sobering thought." Carter then began to search "for a closer relationship with God," to devote himself to religious concerns, and to witness publicly. His election gave born-again Christianity wider visibility and recognition.

George Gallup, Jr. termed 1976 "the year of the evangelical," and the late 1970s and early 1980s saw a burgeoning of the movement. Books by evangelical authors became best sellers. Billy Graham's *How To Be Born Again* (1977) had an initial printing of eight hundred thousand copies, the largest for any hardcover book ever published, and another five hundred thousand copies were soon needed. Widely sold in supermarkets and drugstores, evangelical books became so successful that, as one critic noted, "customers could find books on Christian weight loss and Christian money management." In many large cities, there were "Christian Yellow Pages," directories that would only sell space to an advertiser who "accepts Jesus Christ as . . . personal Lord and Savior and acknowledges Jesus as the Son of God." One million school children were soon attending five thousand Christian elementary and high schools where subjects were taught from an evangelical perspective. In Christian night clubs patrons could order grape juice cocktails and listen to gospel songs. By 1978 there were 1300 radio stations—one out of every seven in the country—that were Christian owned and operated, and one new such station was being added every week.

But television, not radio, became the chief medium for spreading the new message. Pat Robertson's "700 Club," aired on his Christian Broadcasting Network from Virginia Beach, Virginia, was a pioneering venture. Viewers could phone an operator who would take a pledge and then pray with the caller. One of the regulars on the show, Jim Bakker, eventually decided to create his own program—the PTL, or Praise the Lord, Club. Bakker's program, televised from Charlotte, North Carolina, combined sermons, inspirational conversation, faith healing, speaking in tongues, and entertainment. Bakker made the "PTL Club" the most-viewed daily television program in the world, one observer noted, by adopting a format used on secular nighttime talk shows: "the major star with an opening monologue, a co-host to feed the star straight lines, guest celebrities giving brief but fervent testimonials, guest singers, or instrumentalists." The new "electronic church" and the "televangelists" had many critics in the mainstream religious community, but by 1978 Robertson was receiving $30 million a year in contributions, and Bakker, at $25 million, was not far behind.

The new evangelicalism was characterized by social conservatism and political activism. Born-again Christians attacked "secular humanism," by which they meant the view that all truths are relative, all moral values situational, and all ethical judgments tentative. They supported the "right-to-life" movement and condemned legalized abortion. They opposed the Equal Rights Amendment (ERA) and other feminist demands. They attacked court decisions that they claimed legalized pornography. They blasted the gay rights movement on the grounds that homosexuality was sinful. Just as many of their demands focused on the family and sex roles, so others focused on the public schools. Evangelicals favored reintroducing prayer, teaching "scientific creationism" as an alternative to the theory of evolution, and imposing stricter discipline on students. To a considerable extent, they attributed permissiveness and moral decay to the behavior of politicians who were insensitive to family values.

It was, then, only a short step to full-fledged political action. Many recognized the truly awesome potential of the movement, with its captive television audience and appealingly simple message, but none more clearly than the Reverend Jerry Falwell. Minister for many years of the Thomas Road Baptist Church in Lynchburg, Virginia, Falwell had taken a congregation of thirty-five souls (who met "in the former plant of the Donald Duck Bottling Company") and built it into one of seventeen thousand. He had his own television program, "The Old Time Gospel Hour," which raised more money each year than Robertson's or Bakker's. In July 1979 Falwell founded the Moral Majority and within two years was claiming 4 million members. Combining the old time religion with the most sophisticated computer technology, Falwell not only targeted potential contributors but also evaluated candidates for office on the basis of their votes on such issues as the ERA, federal funding for abortions, and school prayer. In 1980, after developing a "hit list" of liberal Senators and Congressmen, the Moral Majority mailed more than one billion pieces of literature to selected voters. "What can you do from the pulpit?" Falwell asked. "You can register people to vote. You can explain the issues to them. And you can endorse candidates, right there in church on Sunday morning."

In 1980 there was never any doubt which presidential candidate Falwell or most other evangelicals would endorse. Democrat Jimmy Carter, Republican Ronald Reagan, and independent John Anderson were all born-again Christians (as was one voter in every three), but Carter's brand of evangelicalism, and Anderson's, were distinctly too liberal for the Moral Majority. Richard Viguerie, one of the new breed of conservative fund raisers, wrote in *The New Right: We're Ready to Lead* (1980): "Not only has the Carter administration ignored the born-again Christians, it has actively and aggressively sought to hurt the Christian movement in America." Ronald Reagan said that he deplored the "wave of humanism and hedonism in the land. I think there is a hunger in this land for a spiritual revival, a return to a belief in moral absolutes." He was talking Jerry Falwell's language. As the Republicans looked for a vice-presidential candidate in 1980 Falwell let it be known he would support Reagan "even if he has the devil running with him." To consolidate his hold on the

Rev. Jerry Falwell, 1984.

religious right, Reagan appointed Reverend Bob Billings, the first executive director of the Moral Majority, as his campaign's religious advisor.

Evangelicals were fond of quoting a verse from the book of Proverbs: "Righteousness exalteth a nation; but sin is a reproach to any people." Righteousness and sin, however, could be defined in different ways. Evangelicalism could be, and for a minority of believers was, hospitable to ideals of reform, social justice, and disarmament. There were born-again Christians who asserted that Scripture "is clearly and emphatically on the side of the poor, the exploited and the victimized," who spoke out against nuclear proliferation and pledged themselves "to non-cooperation with our country's preparation for nuclear war. On all levels—research, development, testing, production, deployment, and actual use of nuclear weapons—we commit ourselves to resist in the name of Jesus Christ.'' Yet as the Reagan era dawned, the majority of evangelicals had lined up solidly behind a conservative social agenda and a President committed to cutting social welfare expenditures and building up the military. In the 1980 election, Ronald Reagan received 51 percent of the popular vote, but 63 percent of the votes of white born-again Christians.

## THE REAGAN REDIRECTION

The contours of Reagan's victory were also shaped by the large number of eligible voters who did not bother to vote. The turnout—52 percent— was the lowest in a presidential election since 1948. As a group, those who actually voted were older, whiter, and wealthier than the eligible voters, since young, black, and poor people have the lowest turnout rates. This worked to Reagan's advantage. He was supported by 55 percent of voters who were 45 years or older, by 55 percent of voters who were white, and by 63 percent of voters earning over $50,000 a year. Carter did well but not as well as necessary among traditional Democrats. Trade union households, for example, gave him only a 3-point margin over Reagan compared to a 20-point margin over Ford four years earlier. Although polling experts noted that the election represented "a strong call for moderate change," the outcome was widely construed as a mandate for conservatism because of Reagan's electoral college margin (489 to 49) and his party's congressional gains. Republicans took control of the Senate for the first time since 1954.

An avowed conservative, Ronald Reagan for much of his life had been a staunch liberal. In 1932, at the age of 21, he had supported Franklin D. Roosevelt, and he remained a Democrat, actively involved in liberal causes, through the 1940s. Reagan described himself then as a "very emotional New Dealer" and a "near hopeless, hemophilic liberal." But by 1947 he feared that communists were attempting to infiltrate the motion picture industry and that liberals were ignoring the danger. "Light was dawning in some obscure region of my head," Reagan wrote in his autobiography, *Where's The Rest of Me?* (1965). He began to move to the right, a move sharply accelerated by his marriage in 1952 to Nancy Davis, herself a dedicated conservative. During the 1950s and 1960s, as a popular speaker for General Electric, Reagan asserted that the welfare state was "the most dangerous enemy ever known to man," the progressive income tax was an invention of Karl Marx, and unemployment insurance often amounted to "a prepaid vacation plan for freeloaders." In 1962 he formally changed his party affiliation, and in 1964 endorsed the candidacy of Barry Goldwater who, he later said, "was possibly a little ahead of his time." Elected governor of California in 1966 and then reelected in a landslide,

Ronald Reagan in "Law and Order," 1953.

he sought the Republican presidential nomination in 1968 and 1976, and finally obtained it in 1980.

Reagan's critics, before his election and after, disparaged his abilities by poking fun at his alleged shallowness, superficiality, and inattention to detail. "You can wade through Ronald Reagan's deepest thoughts and not get your ankles wet," said one pundit; Reagan was "the president with the seven-minute attention span," said another. Indeed, Reagan was known on occasion to confuse Afghanistan with Pakistan, to forget the name of a Cabinet member, or to watch movies instead of reading briefing papers. Yet it was all too easy to underrate his political ability. Reagan understood that the public cared less whether a president had all the facts at his fingertips than whether an administration had an overall sense of direction. He used television more successfully than any of his predecessors to convey his message to the public. He recognized the importance of finding talented administrators and of delegating authority to them. He knew which voters had elected him, and what he had to do (and what he did not have to do) to be reelected.

In 1980 the presidency was widely thought to have entered its "post-imperial" phase: Gerald Ford claimed it was "imperiled, not imperial," and Walter Mondale called it "the fire hydrant of the nation." Ronald Reagan set out to refurbish executive authority, and to a considerable extent he succeeded by reasserting influence over Congress, centralizing the budget-making process, bringing the bureaucracy to heel, and, according to pollsters, persuading most Americans that he had "strong qualities of leadership." The expansion of executive authority, however, was designed to curtail rather than to expand the scope of government. Federal programs to combat poverty, to advance civil rights, to protect the environment, and to safeguard consumers were so well entrenched after years of steady growth that it would take an activist in the White House to trim them back. As an Urban Institute study put it, "Reagan found it necessary to adopt the approach of Wilson and Roosevelt in order to pursue the objectives of Coolidge and Harding."

In truth, Reagan endeavored to reverse the direction social policy had taken ever since the New Deal, but especially since the Great Society, and to turn the welfare state clock back—if not to the 1920s then perhaps to the 1950s. Liberals, who thought they had been unhappy with Jimmy Carter as president, discovered in 1981 the true meaning of the word unhappiness. The Reagan administration announced that it was prepared to slice federal welfare spending and adopt "supply-side economics." Supply siders held that the government could stimulate business growth, create new jobs, and ensure widespread prosperity by giving everyone greater incentives—by rewarding entrepreneurial risk taking, by increasing opportunities for profit making, by enlarging take-home pay—in short, by expanding the supply of goods, which would then create a greater demand for them. The centerpiece of supply-side economics was, from a political standpoint, almost too good to be true: a whopping tax cut.

In 1981 the administration won Congressional approval for just such a massive tax cut, providing for across-the-board reductions of 5 percent the first year and an additional 10 percent in each of the succeeding two years. The measure was undeniably popular. In a nationwide television address, Reagan asked viewers: "Are you entitled to the fruits of your own labor or does government have some presumptive right to spend and spend and spend?" Public pressure on Congress became irresistible, and as it appeared a bill would, in fact, pass, a multitude of interests clamored for special breaks: accelerated depreciation, lucrative write-offs, near-elimination of the estate tax. An exasperated Democrat finally announced, "the auction is over." But Reagan's own budget chief, David Stockman, offered the most candid description of what had happened: "Do you realize the greed that came to the forefront? The hogs were really feeding. The greed level, the level of opportunism, just got out of control."

Tax reduction benefited all taxpayers, but not all equally. The Treasury Department's estimates showed that, over the three years, 9 percent of the total relief would go to those earning under $15,000, and 36 percent to those earning more than $50,000. There were 162,000 families with incomes of $200,000 or more; their taxes were cut by $3.6 billion. There were 31,700,000 families who earned $15,000 or less; they realized a saving of $2.9 billion. The administration's overall policies reflected a similar distribution of benefits. Real disposable family income (adjusted for taxes and inflation) fell in 1981 and 1982, then rose in 1983 and 1984 until it was, on the average, 3.5 percent higher than in 1980. But averages could be deceiving. Over the four-year period, the real disposable income of the poorest fifth of American families declined by nearly 8 percent, while that of the middle fifth rose by about 1 percent and that of the wealthiest fifth jumped by almost 9 percent. The Reagan administration presided over a major redistribution of income away from the poor and toward the rich.

Many economists had predicted that a tax cut coupled with increased outlays for defense would produce record deficits. The predictions soon came true. As military spending soared (from $133 to $246 billion) and annual budget deficits approached $200 billion, the total national debt, which stood at $800 billion in Fiscal Year 1981, grew to $1.5 trillion in Fiscal Year 1985. Nearly as much debt accumulated in Reagan's first administration as in the nation's entire history prior to his election. As the administration understood, such deficits threatened to produce sky-high interest rates and eventually retard economic growth. As some scholars pointed out, however, those deficits were also "a means of advancing the Reagan revolution." A colossal national debt—by 1985 one dollar in every seven spent by the federal government went to pay interest on that debt—created permanent pressure to reduce federal spending for social programs.

One of Reagan's purposes was to cut taxes even if it meant creating deficits; a second was to curb inflation even if it meant temporarily increasing unemployment. The inflation rate in 1980, more than 12 percent, had proven politically fatal for Jimmy Carter. Like Carter, Reagan knew that the surest way to reduce inflation was to permit unemployment to rise, but unlike his predecessor he was willing to do it. The unemployment rate was about 7 percent in November 1980; two years later it was 10.8 percent, the highest level since the late 1930s. Not only were 12 million people jobless, but 1.6 million were too discouraged to look for work and 6.5 million were working fewer hours a week than they wanted. "The current recession," Reagan's top economic advisor at the time commented, "is an unavoidable cost of slowing inflation." The inflation rate indeed fell to about 4 percent in 1983 and 1984, and as the recession ended the unemployment rate returned to about the level it had been under Carter.

A third objective of the Reagan administration was to cut welfare spending even if it increased the number of people who lived in poverty. The President proposed reducing social programs by a considerably larger margin than Congress would approve. He asked Congress to appropriate $75 billion less for these purposes over a four-year period than would have been spent at prevailing levels; this would have amounted to a 17 percent reduction. Congress grudgingly granted a little more than half of what the President wanted, agreeing to a cutback of $38 billion, or 9 percent. Significantly, the administration requested the most Draconian reductions—totaling 28 percent—in programs that directly benefited the poor, such as Food Stamps, Aid to Families with Dependent Children, school lunches, housing assistance, and Medicaid. The administration sought only an 11 percent reduction in Social Security, Medicare, and unemployment insurance, many of whose beneficiaries were not poor. When Ronald Reagan took office, 11.7 percent of Americans had incomes that placed them below the poverty level. The figure had remained steady for about a decade, but by 1982 it had risen to 15 percent, the highest since Lyndon Johnson had launched the war on poverty.

## THE POOR AND THE YUPPIES

That antipoverty crusade had been inspired, in part, by the appearance of Michael Harrington's *The Other America* in 1962. Harrington's *The New American Poverty*, published in 1984, met a chillier response. Harrington pointed out that government social programs primarily aided those who were not poor rather than those who were. The chief beneficiaries were not welfare recipients but rather the aged, who were entitled to Medicare and Social Security. "The welfare state in the United States is primarily for people over sixty-five," he wrote, "most of whom are not now, and for a long time have not been, poor." Harrington described the new poor—the "uprooted" and the "superfluous," the homeless men and women sleeping in doorways, the deinstitutionalized mental patients roaming the streets aimlessly, the black teenagers facing unemployment, the illegal aliens toiling in sweatshops, and the Indians, "the poorest of the poor in a land that was once their own." Harrington called for expanded welfare services, for a full-employment program, and for "a new campaign for social decency."

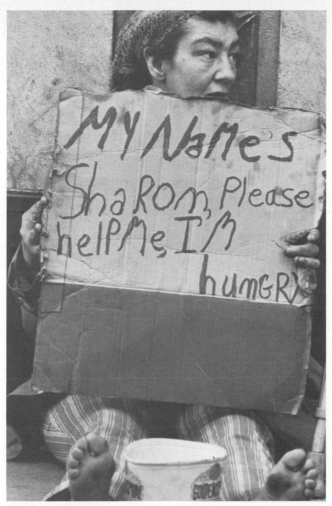

Homeless Woman, New York City, 1979.

Harrington also said that it was the young in particular who "need a vision that transcends the mindless hedonism of so much of contemporary life." But according to *Newsweek* magazine, which dubbed 1984 "the year of the Yuppie," a new class of young urban professionals could not get enough of hedonism, mindless or otherwise. Yuppies were characterized by their age (which ranged from the early twenties to late thirties), their income (which began at $40,000 but seemed not to have an upper limit), and their occupations (which cut across the professional and managerial worlds), but especially by their concern with "lives, careers, apartments and dinners," by their willingness to "define themselves by what they own." They joined expensive fitness clubs, exchanged business cards at "networking" parties, shopped at gourmet food stores, wore designer-label clothing, and lived, when they could, in newly "gentrified" districts. *Newsweek* concluded that millions of Yuppies, who were generally conservative on economic issues but liberal on social issues, voted for Ronald Reagan in 1984. One who did not, a 25-year-old woman who was an advertising executive, liked Reagan "for financial reasons" but disliked his stand on abortion. "I knew Reagan would win easily anyway," she explained. "I had the best of both worlds. I could vote my conscience and still come out ahead financially."

In 1984 Reagan not only captured a large share of the Yuppie vote but also consolidated his hold on a very different constituency: evangelical Christians. The President, who effected virtually all of his economic policies, instituted virtually none of the Moral Majority's social program. Reagan first deferred congressional consideration of antiabortion and school prayer proposals so his tax and budget policies could be enacted. By 1983, when the administration got around to supporting the measures, it could not muster the necessary support in Congress. In March 1984 the Senate turned down a Constitutional amendment permitting voluntary individual or group prayer in the public schools. The vote, fifty-six in favor and forty-four opposed, fell eleven short of the needed two-thirds majority; of the opponents, twenty-six were Democrats and eighteen Republicans. One Reagan aide, asked what the administration planned to give the Moral Majority, replied "symbolism." The President granted a White House audience to right-to-life marchers, supported tax-exempt status for Christian schools that barred blacks, pronounced 1983 "the year of the Bible," and endorsed the entire evangelical platform. He told the National Religious Broadcasters early in 1984 that "the spectacular growth of C.B.N. and P.T.L." proved that "so many millions hunger for your product: God's good news." In the election, exit polls indicated, Reagan was the choice of 80 percent of white born-again Christians.

# AFFIRMATIVE ACTION AND UNDOCUMENTED ALIENS: DILEMMAS OF RACE AND ETHNICITY

The problems of "affirmative action" and "undocumented aliens," which plagued Ronald Reagan's administration as they had Jimmy Carter's, were in a sense legacies of the 1960s. The Civil Rights Act of 1964 had barred discrimination on the basis of race or sex, and the Equal Employment Opportunity Commission thereafter instituted policies to ensure that all federal contractors, city and state governments, and colleges and universities established goals or timetables for the hiring and promotion of members of minority groups. The purpose was to remedy years of discrimination by acting affirmatively in behalf of blacks, women, Hispanics, Native Americans, and Asian Americans, but the method sparked bitter controversy. Similarly, the Immigration Reform Act of 1965 had abolished the discriminatory policy of admitting people on the basis of their national origins, but established, for the first time, numerical limits on immigration from nations in the Western Hemisphere. As population pressures mounted in Mexico, Central America, and South America, millions of illegal or undocumented aliens entered the United States. Their presence posed a dilemma that was as much political as it was legal.

Carter approached the problem of affirmative action cautiously because the issue was one on which Democrats sharply disagreed. Civil rights organizations viewed all-out support for affirmative action, including the setting of "quotas," as a litmus-paper test of an administration's commitment to racial justice, but such quotas offended other important elements in the Democratic coalition, especially labor unions, whose members felt threatened, and Jews, who historically had been victimized by quotas. These differences were evident in 1977 when the administration decided to file a brief in the case of Allan Bakke, who was challenging "race-conscious" admissions policies at the medical school of the University of California at Davis. The Department of Justice first circulated a brief which defended the principle of affirmative action but opposed actual quotas. When civil rights leaders and the Black Congressional Caucus protested strongly, Carter came to believe that submitting the brief would be politically disastrous. So the Department prepared a new statement which omitted any condemnation of quotas, thereby mollifying some groups while antagonizing others.

In June 1978 the Supreme Court handed down its ruling in the Bakke case. Bakke, having twice been turned down by the medical school at Davis, in 1973 and 1974, had obtained a court order admitting him. The school then reserved sixteen of one hundred places in its entering class for "disadvantaged students"—blacks, Chicanos, American Indians, and Asian Americans. Bakke had a better academic record than those admitted under this minority quota, and so he claimed he had been denied the equal protection of the law. By a 5 to 4 margin the Supreme Court ruled in his favor: The use of an "explicit racial classification," in situations where no former discriminatory behavior had been demonstrated, violated the Fourteenth Amendment. At the same time, however, the Court approved, by another 5 to 4 vote, programs that used race as "simply one element in the admissions process." Justifying such "race-conscious programs," Justice Harry A. Blackmun said: "In order to get beyond racism, we must first take account of race."

The Reagan administration took a much dimmer view of affirmative action programs than had the Carter administration. Reagan called quotas "reverse discrimination," a "federal distortion of the principle of equal rights." The assistant attorney general for civil rights in the Department of Justice, William Bradford Reynolds, echoed these sentiments. The government would not "in any respect support the use of quotas or any other numerical or statistical formulas," Reynolds said, for they subverted "the color-blind ideal of equal opportunity for all." When the Detroit and the New Orleans police departments established quotas for promoting blacks, the administration interceded to overturn the agreements, which had been entered into voluntarily. This opposition to affirmative action had much to do with the widespread perception among blacks that the Reagan administration was hostile to their best interests. Blacks, who had given Reagan only 11 percent of their votes in 1980, gave him a minuscule 9 percent in 1984.

The Supreme Court also began to edge away even from its very limited endorsement of affirmative action in the Bakke case. In 1980 the Memphis fire department had agreed to fill one half of all new vacancies with blacks (and upgrade many black employees), but in 1981, city agencies, facing financial difficulties, were forced to cut back. To preserve seniority rights, the fire department began laying off the recently hired blacks. Black firefighters obtained an injunction to stop the department from implementing this policy, the union fought back, and the Supreme Court, in June 1984, ruled that the injunction had been improperly granted. A six-member majority declared that it was not permissible to give preferential treatment to black firefighters who had not themselves been discriminated against. The Court declared that Congress had not intended, in passing the Civil Rights Act of 1964, to fix racial quotas. The majority included President Reagan's appointee, Sandra Day O'Connor. The prospect of additional Supreme Court appointments in the President's second term gave little comfort to those who supported what the minority in the Memphis case called "race-conscious remedies to correct patterns of discrimination."

Patterns of discrimination—less familiar, perhaps, but no easier to erase—also affected millions of undocumented aliens. Calculations of the number of people who were, by the mid-1980s, living and working in the United States illegally, varied widely, but the lowest figure anyone cited was 4 million, and some observers thought 6 or 8 million were better estimates. The Census Bureau indicated that 45 percent of the undocumented aliens came from Mexico, 17 percent from countries of Central and South America, and the remainder from Asia, Africa, and Europe. Most of the illegal aliens worked at hot, dirty jobs for minimum, or below-minimum wages, doing the kind of work for the kind of pay that American citizens would not do. The states with large numbers of illegal aliens—California, Texas, Florida—were those with low rates of unemployment. Although undocumented aliens paid Social Security taxes, income taxes, and sales taxes, they were not eligible for Food Stamps, Aid to Families with Dependent Children, Medicaid, or school lunch programs. They often did not make use of social services for which they were eligible for fear of being discovered and deported.

Surveillance of the Mexican border through an infrared sighting device, 1983.

As public awareness of the problem increased, Carter and Reagan appointed special commissions to devise a solution. The commissions made three recommendations: "amnesty" for illegal aliens who had resided continuously in the United States for a certain period; stiff sanctions for employers who knowingly hired illegal aliens; and a system of national identification to permit employers to distinguish between citizens and others. These proposals formed the basis of the Simpson-Mazzoli bill, a bipartisan measure, which was passed by the Senate in 1982 and 1983, and then by the House in 1984. The bill then went to a conference committee, but the conferees were unable to agree on an acceptable version. The measure died a silent death, deserted by conservatives who feared it was too costly and liberals who feared it would constitute a "major step toward a police state."

The Reagan administration, which had originally supported Simpson-Mazzoli, withdrew its support when it realized the potential cost of the amnesty provisions. The House version would have granted permanent resident alien status to those who had resided in the United States since January 1, 1977, and temporary status to those who had lived in the country since January 1, 1980. These people would eventually become eligible for citizenship and, consequently, for federal welfare benefits. Depending on the number of illegal aliens who actually applied for citizenship, the cost, according to the administration, could come to $12 billion over five to six years. So it urged the Senate and House conferees to impose a limit of $1 billion on federal welfare expenditures under the measure, and the conferees refused. At the same time, Democratic Senators Edward M. Kennedy and Alan Cranston, civil liberties groups, and Hispanic organizations condemned the employer-sanction and national-identification provisions of Simpson-Mazzoli. They argued that employers would seek to avoid any risk of prosecution by refusing to hire Hispanics, even citizens or legal aliens.

In the meantime, one of the most crucial rights enjoyed by illegal aliens—the right of their children to attend the public schools—was preserved by the narrowest of margins. In June 1982, by a vote of 5 to 4, the Supreme Court declared that a Texas ordinance that denied funding for the education of children who had entered the country illegally violated the equal protection clause of the Fourteenth Amendment. To deny these children a public education, the majority said, deprived them of "the ability to live within the structure of our civic institutions" and "does not comport with fundamental conceptions of justice." Chief Justice Warren Burger wrote the minority opinion, and was joined by Justice O'Connor. Burger conceded that the Texas statute was wrongheaded, even harmful. But he did not believe that the Supreme court had "the authority to strike down laws because they do not meet our standards of desirable social policy, 'wisdom,' or 'common sense.'" Burger went on: "The Constitution does not provide a cure for every social ill, nor does it bestow judges with a mandate to try to remedy every social problem." With Congress and the President unable to agree about amnesty or employer sanctions, with the Supreme Court one appointment away from validating a Texas-type discriminatory statute, it was not clear who would accept a mandate to try to remedy one of the most serious social problems the nation faced.

## FEMINIZATION OF POVERTY, THE ERA, AND THE GENDER GAP

The first fifteen years of feminism were characterized by crucial changes in women's lives. In 1960, 35 percent of American women were in the labor force; by 1980, over half were wage earners. In the past, only a minority of married women worked outside the home, and they tended to enter the job market after their children were grown. By 1980, three out of every five married women with school-age children had joined the work force, as had half of married women with children under six. Women's private lives had also changed. In 1960, under one-third of women aged 20 to 24 were unmarried; by 1980, half were unmarried. Prospects for motherhood were different too. In 1960, just after the peak of the baby boom, a woman might expect to have 3.61 children; by 1980, she was having only 1.86, less than the number needed for a no-growth population rate. Finally, family life became less stable. The divorce rate rose to record levels, doubling between 1960 and 1980. During the 1970s, the number of families headed by women had almost doubled, as had the number of women living alone.

Whether women were finally "free to become themselves," as Betty Friedan had hoped, remained uncertain. But it was clear that women's roles were in a state of flux. Some statistics suggested indisputable advances. By 1980, for instance, women were a majority of the college population; they entered prestigious and profitable vocations; record numbers ran for public office, and many won, especially on the state and local level. But other developments were less auspicious, such as the rapid rise of the female-headed family and the consequent "feminization of poverty." By 1980, two out of three female-headed families received child welfare, and two-thirds of the long-term poor were women. Due in part to the rise in separation and divorce, the feminization of poverty was also a result of the massive increase of babies born to never-married mothers. During the 1970s, the number of families headed by unwed mothers increased over 400 percent. Half of all illegitimate births were to teenagers.

While the illegitimacy rate rose most rapidly among whites, it was highest among blacks. By the start of the 1980s, 55 percent of all black children were born to unwed mothers, 85 percent of black teenage mothers were unmarried, and 47 percent of black families with children were headed by women (compared to 21 percent in 1960). In 1983, the NAACP warned that "deterioration of the black family" threatened to negate all the social and economic advances blacks had made since 1960. The National Urban League blamed the deterioration on "steady attrition" in the numbers of black men who could support families. In 1984, almost 30 percent of black men 20 to 60 years old were unemployed or not seeking work. Since 1960, the League pointed out, the black divorce rate had increased by 400 percent, and by 1984, the rate at which black couples separated was five times as great as that among white couples.

Concern over women's roles within the family and outside it was reflected in the major issues of the women's movement. During the late 1970s, an antifeminist backlash gained momentum. The "Stop ERA" campaign, led by Phyllis Schlafly, lobbied in state legislatures to prevent ERA ratification; the deadline had been extended by Congress until June 1982. Schlafly argued that the ERA would cause "radical loosening of the legal bonds that keep the family together." NOW contended that the ratification battle was a referendum over sex discrimination. When the amendment failed, three votes short of ratification, Schlafly claimed that feminists had "shot themselves in the foot"; NOW vowed to continue the campaign. The ERA was not the sole source of controversy. The "right-to-life" movement that began in the 1970s advocated a constitutional amendment that would reverse federal policy and prohibit all abortions. Life, it contended, began at conception. In June 1983 the Senate defeated the antiabortion amendment and the Supreme Court confirmed women's constitutional right to abortion by upsetting city ordinances that limited access to it. But both controversies, over the ERA and abortion, were destined to continue. Feminist causes had become a permanent part of the political agenda.

According to opinion polls of the early 1980s, a majority of both men and women supported the ERA and abortion rights. But a "gender gap" had developed on other issues. It first appeared in the 1980 presidential election, where women provided a far larger proportion of the Carter vote (58 percent) than the Reagan vote (49 percent): Subsequent opinion polls and the 1982 congressional vote suggested that more women than men favored Democratic candidates and Democratic policies on employment, inflation control, and staying out of war. Pollsters also discovered that the greatest contributors to the gender gap were wage-earning women and women under 45, two categories of voters that were expected to grow. As the election of 1984 approached, Democratic presidential candidates tried to capitalize on the new trends in voting behavior, while Republicans either denied that a gender gap existed or declared that it was based on a misreading of Republican policies.

## THE 1984 ELECTION

When Democratic candidate Walter Mondale chose New York representative Geraldine Ferraro as his running mate at the 1984 Democratic convention, it seemed as if the gender gap might be put to the test. Describing herself as a "housewife from Queens," Ferraro had spent three terms in the House and served as head of the 1984 Democratic Platform Committee. Her candidacy was the result of a combination of circumstances. First, there were no self-evident competing choices for the Vice-Presidential spot, especially since the runner-up in the primaries, Gary Hart, seemed to be incompatible with nominee Mondale. In addition, Mondale was under pressure from NOW, which had given him its support early on (and some of whose members briefly threatened to withdraw their support were a woman not chosen). More effective was Betty Friedan's argument that selecting a woman would represent a commitment to expansion of opportunity for all, a theme Mondale wished to stress. Among women candidates, Ferraro appeared to be the most promising because of her potential appeal to an ethnic vote—Catholic, Italian-American, and working-class—as well as to other traditional Democrats. The daughter of immigrants, she had worked her way up in the world as teacher, lawyer, and public prosecutor. Married for twenty-four years, she had been a full-time housewife for many of them, and had raised three children. Ferraro also had much support from important politicians such as New York's Governor Cuomo and House Speaker Thomas ("Tip")

Geraldine Ferraro, 1984.

O'Neill, who found her "spunky and game." Finally, there was the feeling within the Mondale camp that a bold, unconventional step was needed, both to energize the campaign and to prove that the candidate could take strong, decisive action.

Ferraro's historic nomination generated widespread enthusiasm, drew an outpouring of volunteers, and represented a triumph to feminists. Republicans criticized the nomination as tokenism. "I would like it better if she were a candidate, and not a woman candidate," said former Maine Senator Margaret Chase Smith, when interviewed in retirement. "Now, I was never a woman candidate." No sooner had the campaign started than a furor erupted over whether Ferraro would reveal the entirety of her family finances beyond the income tax statements required by law. To do so, as the press demanded, meant a public airing of her husband's finances, a possible source of irregularities, as well as her own. No comparable concern over a spouse's finances had arisen before a woman candidate ran for Vice-President. That Ferraro finally released the information demanded by the press and handled the situation with aplomb won her acclaim. But the controversy hurt the Democratic campaign.

When votes were counted, the gender gap seemed to have all but vanished. President Reagan won 57 percent of the women's vote, as opposed to 42 percent for Mondale. (The male vote was 61 percent to 37 percent). All nine women challengers for Senate seats lost, as did thirty-nine of forty-one women challengers for House seats. Recriminations about the women's vote were rampant in the Democratic camp. "The party got a gun put to its head . . . to choose a woman for Vice President," a Mondale staff member told the press. "They didn't bring in anything. Women vote for President just like men do." Feminists were "remote from the women's vote," a top Democratic consultant charged. "These people can't deliver their sisters." With an 18-point gap between the candidates, Democratic women pointed out, the gender gap could not be expected to have had much impact. "We didn't invent defeat," said Ann Lewis, political director of the Democratic National Committee. "White men have been losing elections for years." The power of the gender gap, it seemed, and that of NOW to represent women voters, would have to be proven in a future election.

The extent to which Ronald Reagan had succeeded in altering the political agenda was evident in the kind of general campaign waged by the Democrats. Walter Mondale represented a traditional brand of Democratic liberalism, but his speech accepting the nomination called for a well-managed, not merely a well-meaning, government, a president who could say "no" to special-interest groups, a strong military posture with no major cuts in defense spending, policies to ensure private-, not public-sector, economic growth, and the maintenance of family values. "I will cut the deficit by two-thirds," the liberal Democrat promised; "we must cut spending and pay as we go." Mondale did attack Reagan for pandering to the rich and powerful, but the Democrat said little or nothing about social welfare, racial justice, or immigration reform. In November, Reagan captured 59 percent of the popular vote and carried forty-nine of fifty states. Ronald Reagan had established the terms of political debate for the 1980s as surely as Franklin Roosevelt had for the 1930s.

# NEW DIRECTIONS IN U.S. FOREIGN POLICY? (OR: THE GREAT DEBATE OVER THE USE OF FORCE)

Reagan's foreign policy enjoyed fewer successes than his domestic initiatives. Critics claimed that he indeed scored only one victory during his first term: invading the tiny Caribbean island of Grenada in 1983 and overthrowing a pro-Cuban government. The action proved costly as eighteen U.S. soldiers died during a six-day fight against Cubans (many of whom were working as engineers and technical advisers) and a few Grenadans. Reagan claimed a major victory, especially in demonstrating that the "Vietnam syndrome" no longer prevented the application of American military power. There were, however, no other Granadas available. Other foreign policy problems in the Middle East, Central America, and with the Soviet Union were more complex and less easily managed.

Nor could these problems be resolved simply by carrying out Reagan's 1980 campaign promise of "rearming America" by raising defense spending until it amounted to $1.5 trillion over five years. The President soon learned that a defense budget, no matter how large, could not solve the problems that had vexed Jimmy Carter. Such spending was useful only when it served a coherent foreign policy, that is, a view of U.S. interests in the world that realistically assessed what was important, what was possible, and what Americans would support. The administration could not develop such a coherent view. Defense Department statements instead pledged to defend freedom everywhere. Such an objective was unrealistic; no one, for example, argued that U.S. troops should fight alongside Afghanistan guerrillas against the Soviet invaders. But when uniformed military leaders saw such statements, they warned that considerably more than even $1.5 billion would be required to carry out such a global policy. The American economy, even after it regained much of its health in 1983–84, faced huge deficits that required cutting expenditures—including the 10 to 13 percent increase in the rate of military spending demanded by Reagan. Budget restraints forced the President to accept half that increase, and thus the defense budget growth rate approximated that proposed by Jimmy Carter in 1980.

Reagan's problems also resembled Carter's in another respect: his advisers differed sharply over policy, and the President often proved unable to reconcile the differences. Caspar Weinberger, the Secretary of Defense, led the drive for huge military budgets, but he was also quite reluctant to use that force. In late 1984 Weinberger delivered a remarkable speech that listed the conditions that prevented the deployment of U.S. troops. It marked the first time in history that an American official publicly told potential enemies the exact conditions that had to be met before the country would go to war. Two of Weinberger's conditions were shaped by the Vietnam experience: the need for strong support from the American people and the need for military commanders in the field to be assured they would be allowed to "win" wars. In virtually all of Reagan's foreign policy problems, from guerrilla wars in Central America to fighting a nuclear war against the Soviets, these two conditions were not likely to be met. Yet the uniformed military for whom Weinberger spoke insisted on the conditions. They remained bitter over the humiliation and frustration they encountered in fighting an unwinnable and little-supported war in Vietnam, and they vowed never again to put U.S. soldiers in such a trap.

On the other hand, Reagan's two Secretaries of State, Alexander Haig (1981–82) and George Shultz, were more willing to use force. Shultz even publicly answered Weinberger with a speech declaring that "power and diplomacy'' were inseparable. He implied that successful diplomacy could not be conducted without use of the U.S. military machine. In one vital area, the Middle East, Shultz had partially gotten his way. The results had not been happy. In 1982 Israeli armies struck at their leading enemy, the Palestinian Liberation Front (PLO) that had bases in neighboring Lebanon. Lebanese groups armed by Syria (that was in turn aided by the Soviets) struck back and bogged down the Israeli force. Shultz proposed a peace plan and sent 1500 U.S. troops to help pacify the area. West European allies also sent in token units. The Americans, however, encamped in an indefensible position in the Lebanese capital of Beirut and became the target of Lebanese bombs. One explosive killed 240 U.S. soldiers in late 1983. Pro-Israeli and pro-American factions in Lebanon proved weak. Shultz had underestimated both their strength and U.S. ability to make peace among the devastation and senseless killing in Beirut. Reagan nevertheless declared that U.S. troops would remain because pulling them out would amount to ''surrender'' to the pro-Soviet Syrian-Lebanese groups. But as more Americans were killed, the policy became unpopular, the 1984 election approached, and Reagan quietly reversed himself and withdrew the troops.

## CENTRAL AMERICA

Perhaps because of that experience, Shultz was more cautious in dealing with revolutions that seemed to be expanding across Central America. The centers of the problem were Nicaragua and El Salvador. Both were small countries in a region long dependent on U.S. wishes, but their actions inflamed North American opinion in a way unmatched since the Vietnam debate a decade earlier.

From the start Reagan had mistrusted the revolutionary Sandinista government in Nicaragua, especially its close economic and military ties with Cuba, its aid to the revolution in El Salvador, and its reluctance to hold elections. Secretary of State Haig even declared that it might be necessary to ''go to the source'' (that is, Cuba) to destroy the threats posed by the Sandinistas. Unable, or unwilling, to devise a political solution, and refusing to work with the friendly democratic nations in the region who criticized his military approach, Reagan chose to try to overthrow the Sandinistas with force. Working through the Central Intelligence Agency, the administration armed a force of anti-Sandinista Nicaraguans (soon known as contras) that by 1985 numbered fifteen thousand troops. This force used U.S.-created camps in Honduras as bases for their attacks into northern Nicaragua.

The contras, however, were so ineffective that the CIA decided to take charge. It directed attacks deep into Nicaragua, flew accompanying air missions, and then aided in the mining of Nicaraguan harbors. The mining proved to be a mistake. Neutral ships suffered damages, and in late 1984 an outraged U.S. Congress, following vocal groups in public opinion, stopped all government aid to the contras. The aid, however, was replaced by more than $5 million of supplies sent by private American groups in 1984–85. The CIA also continued to be active in the region. The Sandinistas meanwhile conducted an election in late 1984 that consolidated their hold on the country, although it also brought a strong opposition minority group into the government.

Perhaps more important, Reagan's military policies produced results opposite from those he intended. To meet the U.S. pressure, the Sandinistas doubled their army between 1980 and 1985 to fifty thousand regular troops, armed over one hundred thousand civilians to fight invaders, tightened their control over the country, and moved closer to Cuba and the Communist bloc for help. The President responded with maneuvers of up to thirty thousand troops in Honduras that threatened the Sandinistas, and permanently stationed U.S. warships off Nicaraguan coasts. The contra attacks meanwhile destroyed millions of dollars of property and further worsened an already desperate economic situation in Nicaragua. More than four thousand lives had been lost in the fighting by 1985. As the war intensified, so did the U.S. debate over Reagan's policy, especially as the President suddenly shut off U.S. trade with Nicaragua in 1985 in an effort to bring down that nation's economy.

Washington officials claimed greater success in El Salvador, but that claim was also challenged. The smallest country in the region, El Salvador suffered one of the widest gaps between the few rich (the so-called forty families) and the millions of poor. In 1979 some army officers tried to stop a spreading revolution by seizing power and promising reforms. But little happened. Instead the army split between right-wing leaders, who frequently murdered civilians whom they suspected of "liberal" tendencies, and the moderates, who became politically isolated. Between 1979 and 1985 the right-wing "death squads" killed more than forty thousand civilians. But the terror only strengthened the revolutionaries who controlled much of the eastern part of El Salvador, and it sickened U.S. public opinion.

To check the revolution, Washington officials began a massive training program for Salvadoran troops (including instruction on treating civilians more humanely). Reagan also picked José Napoleon Duarte, a U.S.-educated politician, to create a government that could effectively wage war but also impress North Americans with its moderation. In 1984 Duarte won the presidency in an election heavily influenced by millions of dollars sent into El Salvador by the Reagan administration. U.S. officials and key Salvadoran army officers accelerated the war in the belief that total military victory was possible.

Many critics disagreed with that policy. They claimed no military victory was in sight and that the Reagan administration, in both Nicaragua and El Salvador, was willing to "fight to the last Central American" while understanding that U.S. troops could not be directly used. The wars meanwhile devastated the already poor countries. El Salvador was completely dependent for its survival on U.S. aid. Central Americans fled northward to escape the terror. One of every eight Salvadorans lived in the United States by 1985, and the overwhelming majority did so illegally. When the Reagan administration cracked down and tried to return some of these Salvadorans to their own country, U.S. church leaders began a "sanctuary movement" that defied Reagan on the grounds that the Salvadorans' return to their homeland meant their death. Washington officials responded with a number of arrests, including the arrest of priests and nuns, but the sanctuary movement nevertheless spread—along with the instability, poverty, terror, and revolution in Central America.

## NEGOTIATING WITH "THE EVIL EMPIRE"

In 1980 Reagan had directly blamed the Russians for all the world's problems, even those in the newly emerging nations. After entering the White House he often denounced the Soviet Union as "the evil empire" with which diplomatic talks were fruitless. Soviet leaders, he claimed, "reserve unto themselves the right to commit any crime, to lie, to cheat." The Russians responded in kind. Their policies, moreover, became more unpredictable and threatening when death struck their aged leadership. Four men, Leonid Brezhnev, Yuri Andropov, 73-year-old Konstantin Chernenko, and, finally, Mikhail Gorbachev—a well-educated 54-year old who belonged to a new generation of Russian leaders—led the Soviet Union within just three years. Russian leadership (and the economy) became less stable as Reagan appeared more aggressive. Relations between the two superpowers sank to the lowest level since the worst days of the Cold War in the early 1950s.

As Reagan began his military build-up, he nevertheless agreed to talk with the Soviets about controlling both strategic (or long-range) nuclear weapons and intermediate missile forces. Talks continued until 1983 when the Russians walked out because the United States began placing new intermediate-range missiles in Western Europe. The emplacement was a U.S. response, begun by Jimmy Carter, to similar missiles installed by the Soviets after 1977 in Eastern Europe. The talks had actually been of little use. The Soviets used them in an unsuccessful effort to halt the installation of the new U.S. missiles. For their part, American officials were bitterly divided between Pentagon leaders, who wanted no arms control treaty that could restrain their arms build-up, and State Department officers, who believed that a treaty could make U.S.-Soviet relations less threatening and more manageable.

Reagan could not make a clear choice between the two American policies. He was ignorant of basic facts about the arms race (he wrongly believed, for example, that the Soviet SS-19 missile was larger than the SS-18 because 19 is larger than 18), and was not overly interested in a deal. The Pentagon position thus won by default, at least until the 1984 presidential campaign began. Polls revealed that the President's popularity was weakest on arms issues. Many Americans feared that the President, and especially some of his advisors, did not properly dread the destruction made possible by nuclear weapons. That fear did not diminish when word leaked in 1982 that Reagan and Weinberger had approved a policy to fight and "win" a protracted nuclear war. Democratic Party leaders joined the "nuclear freeze" movement that aimed at freezing the number of missiles in both Russia and the United States until a treaty could be negotiated. To undercut this threat to both his arms buildup and reelection plans, Reagan suddenly lowered his anti-Soviet rhetoric, met with Soviet officials in mid-1984, and pledged new arms talks. The new discussions indeed began at Vienna in early 1985.

By then, however, a new problem appeared. In a national television speech, Reagan announced that possible scientific breakthroughs could lead to a virtually foolproof defense against a missile attack. He urged Congress to begin a multibillion dollar research program on this Strategic Defense Initiative (SDI), or "Star Wars," as his critics quickly labeled it. The proposed system depended on technology that, in the words of one expert, required new discoveries equal to those of eight of the projects that sent men to the moon. (The moon, moreover, had not put up any resistance; the Soviets would try to counter each American discovery.) Even if those problems were solved, the SDI would be so complicated that it could only be run by computers that were a thousand times faster—and many times more dependable—than present systems, which had malfunctioned and caused a number of false nuclear alerts. Even if it could be deployed, at incredible cost, the SDI would not protect the United States against new Russian "cruise" missiles that delivered nuclear bombs in the atmosphere—that is, below the proposed "Star Wars" system. But Reagan insisted on going ahead. The SDI threatened to carry the superpower military struggle fully into space.

Foreign policy had little effect on the 1984 election. In the months before the balloting Reagan had withdrawn U.S. forces from the Middle East. He also temporarily pulled some American troops out of Central America and so drove that explosive question off the front newspaper pages. In dealing with the Soviets he had talked tough and then promised to negotiate on arms control, but continued his military build-up and his push for "Star Wars." The President's foreign policies had largely been failures, but his political strategy brilliantly hid those failures from most American voters.

## THE COMPUTER REVOLUTION—AFTER FOUR CENTURIES OF EVOLUTION

*Time* magazine annually chooses a "Man" or "Woman of the Year." Churchill, Hitler, Queen Elizabeth II of England, and the astronauts have been acclaimed. In 1983, however, an object—the computer—won for the first time. As *Time* explained, the computer had revolutionized American life for it "can send letters at the speed of light, diagnose a sick poodle . . . , test recipes for beer," and be used by the rock group Earth, Wind, and Fire to explode smoke bombs at precise moments in concert. A California high school programmed a computer that at 5:15 P.M. each day phoned parents of absent students. The truancy rate in the school dropped 64 percent in one year.

The machine's effect on the ex-change of information—especially the printing of newspapers, book publishing, and the writing of college term papers and laboratory reports—had no parallel since Gutenberg first used movable type in Germany during the 1450s. More than half of all employed Americans in the 1980s made their living not by making products but by exchanging information. This rapidly growing part of the work force depended on computers whose disk memory was small enough to be carried in a handbag but contained the equivalent of more than one thousand books. With lightning speed, the machine carried out its two basic functions: computing numbers and the storing and retrieval of information.

Most Americans encountered the

A ten-year-old student using a computer, 1985.

computer only in the 1970s and 1980s, but some of its basic principles date back to the seventeenth century when the great French philosopher, Pascal, devised the first machine that could multiply as well as add. At about the same time a mathematician, John Napier, invented logarithms that allowed complex figures to be adapted easily to computing machines. The next key step occurred two centuries later when an eccentric British inventor, Charles Babbage (who also devised the speedometer) spent forty years building a huge, incredibly complex machine that contained nearly all the main features of the modern computer. It could even be programmed.

Americans then stepped in to make the Pascal-Babbage inventions more practical. Herman Hollerith was an engineer working with the U.S. Census of 1880 when he borrowed Babbage's device of putting information on punched cards and then retrieving it with spring-loaded pins that corresponded to the holes of the cards holding the information wanted. The 1890 Census results were consequently tabulated in one-third the time spent on the 1880 survey. Hollerith quit government to build a fortune with his now-famous punch-card system. In this first great era of American corporate development and mergers (the 1890s through the 1920s), Hollerith's Tabulating Machine Company became in 1924 International Business Machines (IBM).

Within a decade, IBM dominated the business machine industry. Over the next sixty years it became the most glamorous and successful of American corporations. But IBM's initial successes came from fast-talking salesmen, not technical breakthroughs. Important scientific innovations began in the 1940s and were

Automatic Sequence Control Calculator, 1944.

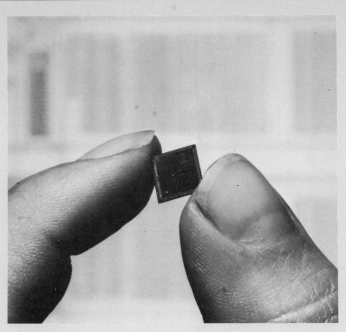

Microchip.

spurred on by U.S. military needs in the early Cold War years. Scientists at the University of Pennsylvania built the ENIAC, whose thirty tons, 18,000 vacuum tubes, and 6,000 switches performed 5,000 computations a second to target artillery fire. Sperry-Rand Corporation's UNIVAC of 1951 first used modern programming, including magnetic tape instead of punched cards. UNIVAC helped make computers famous by accurately predicting Dwight Eisenhower's triumph in the 1952 presidential elections.

American scientists were now making breathtaking discoveries. In 1947 researchers at Bell Telephone Laboratories had developed the transistor. This device used semiconduct-ing materials (as silicon, for example) to control electrical currents, and it did so more rapidly, cheaply, and with cooler temperatures than could vacuum tubes. Within a decade transistors were being printed on silicon pieces to become "microchips," or integrated circuits for computers. In the early 1970s engineers succeeded in putting the machine's entire processing unit on a single silicon chip. The chip thus became a "microprocessor." As one observer summarized the change in computer technology by the 1980s, "if the automobile business had developed like the computer business, a Rolls-Royce would now cost $2.75 and run 3 million miles on a gallon of gas."

In the early 1980s small, pioneering businesses, led by Apple, Hewlett-Packard, and only later by IBM, developed desk-top-size computers that cost under $1000 and could be used in the home or office. Experts estimated that by 1990 offices would have more computers than typewriters. The American industrial revolution had thus come full circle. The single craftsman in his eighteenth-century cottage had become the centralized giant corporation producing iron, steel, and automobiles in the early 1900s. But now, as the twentieth century came to a close, the "electronic cottage," as futurist Alvin Toffler called it, created new possibilities for decentralization and individual enterprise.

## TRADITION, SCIENCE, AND THE AMERICAN CENTURY

Reagan's success was acknowledged even by one of his most vigorous critics, Speaker of the House of Representatives Thomas ("Tip") O'Neill, an old-style New Deal Democrat from Massachusetts. "In my fifty years of public life," O'Neill privately admitted to Reagan after the President's 1984 election triumph, "I've never seen a man more popular than you are with the American people."

The President's immense popularity could be explained by his own friendly personality and eternal optimism, his ingenious use of the media, the economic upturn that peaked as he ran for reelection, and the inability of his Democratic Party opponents to wage an effective campaign. But something strange also seemed to be happening. Contradictions abounded, contradictions that could not be explained easily, only observed and studied.

Reagan, for example, received strong support from those Americans who professed to value religion and family above all else. But he was the first divorced person to be elected President, his relations with his own children were poor, and he admitted that he seldom attended church. He had come out of (and retained many close friends in) a society in Hollywood whose moral values were not usually equated by Reagan's evangelical and middle-class supporters with the values of the New Testament. During an age in which knowledge was power, and information became ever more complex and extensive, Reagan prided himself on not knowing details of policy. In 1980 he had run for the White House by promising he would get the government "off the backs of the people," and repeated that theme in 1984. But his administration imposed censorship on information, unknown since the crisis of World War II, and his economic policies actually *increased* the government's share of the nation's gross national product from 23 percent in 1980 to 25 percent in 1983. In all, he preached traditional values in a nation whose space voyages, computer industry, motion pictures, literature, and chemical products (such as the "pill") made it perhaps the least traditional society in recorded history.

The radical nature of the American Century was nowhere better demonstrated than in the field of biotechnology, the new industry that by combining discoveries in biology and technology gave scientists almost godlike power over human life. For three centuries researchers had known that cells formed the foundation blocks of life, but not until the 1830s, when the first powerful microscopes appeared, could the body's cells be closely examined. By the 1930s European scientists argued that the cell was an invisible mass of chemicals that was the pilot of human and plant life. When cells changed, for example, disease occurred. Electron microscopes helped California researchers discover in 1951 the spiral shape of the protein molecules that make up most of a cell. Two British scientists then took the crucial step of finding the specific molecules in the cell that carry genetic information (hair and eye color, height, and so on) from one generation to the next. Once it was understood how genes were made up (that is, in long chains of DNA, or deoxyribonucleic acid), and how the long chains worked, the genes could be manipulated. "Gene machines" could even synthesize different parts of the chain.

In a mere thirty years after the discoveries of the 1950s, this international scientific effort produced "genetic engineering" that could, for example, transplant genes into a patient's cells to make the patient immune to certain diseases. Such research developed new medicines, seeds, foods, even animals. New species of grain were formed that miraculously gathered nitrogen from the air (thus making fertilizers unnecessary), were immune to insect pests, and needed little water. But playing with nature's basic tool posed great, even unknown, dangers. One laboratory used genetic engineering to produce a bacteria that could prevent a potato crop from being destroyed by frost. A judge, however, refused to allow the bacteria to be spread because no one knew what else the bacteria might do once it was released in the air. An uproar ensued in 1982 when a biotech report noted the possibility of creating a disease-resistant person "which has only in part human attributes." Leading Protestant, Jewish, and Roman Catholic leaders warned that unless such work was closely controlled, biotechnology could lead to the horrors glimpsed in Nazi Germany:

> History has shown us that there will always be those who believe it appropriate to "correct" our mental and social structures by genetic means, so as to fit their vision of humanity. . . . Those who would play God will be tempted as never before.

In 1976 a government agency, the National Institutes of Health (NIH), had agreed with such views and issued national guidelines for the splicing of genes. In 1985 the NIH extended the guidelines. It did so a week after Reagan's second inagural address, which again called for a reaffirmation of traditional values so that "history" could "say of us, these were golden years."

Similar contradictions were evident in the President's plan, unveiled in May 1985, to restructure the nation's tax system through a "peaceful revolution." Appealing to old-fashioned virtues of "fairness" and "simplicity," the President proposed to replace the existing fourteen-bracket system with a three-bracket system, with a rate of 15 percent on taxable incomes of $4,000-$29,000, 25 percent on the amount from $29,000-$70,000, and 35 percent on the amount over $70,000. The plan would eliminate deductions for state and local income taxes, thereby penalizing states (especially in the industrial northeast) which funded health, welfare, and education programs. Because it would lower tax rates on the poor and eliminate some glaring loopholes, Reagan's plan was widely perceived as one that would attract broad popular support. Yet the plan retained accelerated depreciation writeoffs, capital-gains breaks, and depletion allowances for oil and gas producers, all of which added up to lucrative windfalls for the wealthy. The President promised that certain proposals, such as increasing the dependency exemption to $2,000, would strengthen the traditional family. Again, as critics noted, "This is government social engineering, of the sort Reaganites are supposed to eschew in general and especially when done through the tax code."

Contradictions between the President's appeal to traditional values and his actual policies also appeared in foreign policy. Since 1776 Americans professed to believe that "all men are created equal." After 1954, U.S. federal officials enforced new, far-reaching court decisions and laws to end racial segregation. But in South Africa, Reagan supported a government that enforced the brutal policy of *apartheid*—state enforced segregation in which a minority white government used force to deprive blacks (who made up 73 percent of the country's population) of nearly all political, economic, and other personal rights. The Reagan officials had pursued a policy of "constructive engagement"—that is, a policy of remaining friendly with the white regime while trying to pressure it gently and quietly to end *apartheid* and make peace with surrounding black African states. But reform and peace did not appear. In early 1985, blacks began violently resisting *apartheid*. The white government declared martial law. In battles between blacks and the police, some 600 people, nearly all black, were killed in a period of four months. Many Americans, including a number of Reagan's conservative supporters, strongly protested *apartheid*. Congress threatened to pass legislation that imposed economic sanctions on South Africa unless police brutalities stopped and the white government opened talks with black leaders (most of whom had been jailed). Reagan, despite his appeal to traditional American values, threatened to veto any such legislation, although, bowing to political pressure, he did prove willing to impose a few of the sanctions with which Congress threatened South Africa.

The President's policy towards South Africa, his tax reform proposal, the NIH guidelines on biotechnology, the "Star Wars" program—all raised fundamental questions. In reality, how traditional were Reagan's "new directions"? And were the traditional values that the President appealed to in his speeches appropriate to deal with the new technological, economic, and foreign policy dilemmas that appeared as the American Century approached the year 2000?

## Suggested Reading

For Jimmy Carter's political career, see James Wooten, *Dasher: The Roots and the Rising of Jimmy Carter* (1976); and Jules Witcover, *Marathon: The Pursuit of the Presidency, 1972–1976* (1977). On the evangelicals, consult Erling Jorstad, *Evangelicals in the White House* (1981); Robert C. Liebman and Robert Wuthnow eds., *The New Christian Right* (1983); David F. Wells and John D. Woodbridge, *The Evangelicals* (1975); and Jeremy Rifkin with Ted Howard, *The Emerging Order* (1979). The Reagan administration is discussed in Laurence I. Barrett, *Gambling with History: Reagan in the White House* (1983); Robert Dallek, *Ronald Reagan: The Politics of Symbolism* (1984); Lou Cannon, *Reagan* (1982); Ronnie Dugger, *On Reagan: The Man and His Presidency* (1983); and John L. Palmer and Isabel V. Sawhill, eds., *The Reagan Record* (1984), an assessment by the Urban Institute.

The controversy over affirmative action is discussed in Allan P. Sindler, *Bakke, DeFunis, and Minority Admissions* (1978); and Joel Dreyfuss and Charles Lawrence III, *The Bakke Case: The Politics of Inequality* (1979). For the background of the controversy over undocumented aliens, see Richard Polenberg, *One Nation Divisible: Class, Race, and Ethnicity in the United States since 1938* (1980). The feminization of poverty is examined in Ken Auletta, *The Underclass* (1982). For women's political activism, see Ethel Klein, *Gender Politics* (1984).

On foreign policy, a good overview is Seyom Brown, *The Faces of Power* (1983) that covers the years from Truman through part of Reagan's first term. The key books on Carter's diplomacy are three "inside" accounts: Carter's own *Keeping Faith* (1982); Cyrus Vance, *Hard Choices* (1983); and the most revealing, Zbigniew Brzezinski, *Power and Principle* (1983). Human rights policies are analyzed in Lars Schoultz, *Human Rights and U.S. Policy Towards Latin America* (1981). A useful account of the Iranian crisis is Barry Rubin, *Paved with Good Intentions* (1980). On Reagan, the Cannon, Barrett, and Dallek biographies listed above are useful, and Alexander M. Haig's *Caveat* (1984) revealing on 1980 to early 1982. The two indispensable books on the Reagan administration's view of the Soviets, and especially arms negotiations, are Strobe Talbott, *Deadly Gambits* (1984); and Robert Scheer, *With Enough Shovels* (1982). Defense policy is critiqued in Ronald V. Dellums, R. H. Miller, and H. Lee Halterman, *Defense Sense* (1983). Central American policy for both the Carter and Reagan years is analyzed in Robert S. Leiken, ed., *Central America: Anatomy of Conflict* (1984); the readings in Marvin Gettleman et al., *El Salvador* (1982); and the expanded edition of Walter LaFeber, *Inevitable Revolutions* (1984). The Reagan view is in *The Report of the President's National*

*Bipartisan Commission on Central America* (1984), which was chaired by Henry Kissinger. On the Middle East, see Itamar Rabinovich, *The War for Lebanon, 1970–1983* (1984).

The following are useful for understanding the historical meaning of the computer's development: Robert Sobel, *IBM* (1981); T. S. Reid, *The Chip* (1985); and David F. Noble, *Forces of Production: A Social History of Industrial Automation* (1984).

# PHOTO CREDITS

**Chapter 10: Opener** UPI/Bettmann Newsphotos **317** Robert Capa/Magnum, courtesy of Life Magazine **318** Dwight D. Eisenhower Library **329** Culver Pictures **330** Margaret Bourke-White, Life Magazine © 1943 Time Inc. **331** Margaret Bourke-White, Life Magazine © 1940 Time Inc. **332** Margaret Bourke-White, Life Magazine © 1941 Time Inc. **333** Margaret Bourke-White, Life Magazine © 1945 Time Inc. **341** George C. Marshall Research Foundation Photo

**Chapter 11: Opener** Library of Congress **349** Walter Sanders, Life Magazine © 1948 Time Inc. **351** Wallace Kirkland, Life Magazine © 1948 Time Inc. **352** Leonard McCombe, Life Magazine © 1970 Time Inc. **353** UPI/Bettmann Newsphotos **356** AP/Wide World Photos **362** AP/Wide World Photos **364** AP/Wide World Photos **379** UPI/Bettmann Newsphotos

**Chapter 12: Opener** Joe Scherschel, Life Magazine © 1958 Time Inc. **388** above, Burton Glinn/Magnum, courtesy of Life Picture Service; below, Ralph Crane, Life Magazine © 1956 Time Inc. **396** H. Cartier-Bresson/Magnum **401** AP/Wide World Photos **403** Burt Glinn/Magnum **404** UPI/Bettmann Newsphotos **405** Peter Siion/ Stock, Boston **408** J. R. Eyerman, Life Magazine © 1953 Time Inc. **411** Dwight D. Eisenhower Library

**Chapter 13: Opener** Library of Congress **423** UPI/Bettmann Newsphotos **435** Charles Moore/Black Star **436** Dan Budnik/Woodfin Camp & Associates **437** Dan Budnik/Woodfin Camp & Associates **438** Estate of David Smith, Courtesy of M. Knoedler and Company, New York **439** Dan Budnik/Woodfin Camp & Associates **442** Bruno Barbey/Magnum **448** UPI/Bettmann Newsphotos

**Chapter 14: Opener** Benedict J. Fernandez **458** Danny Lyon/Magnum **459** Fred Ward/Black Star **468** Burt Glinn/Magnum **471** AP/Wide World Photos **477** H. Hammid/Photo Researchers **478** H. Hammid/Photo Researchers **479** Henry Wilhelm/ Black Star **485** AP/Wide World Photos

**Chapter 15: Opener** Philip Jones Griffiths/Magnum **496** NASA **497** AP/Wide World Photos **500** Ken Regan/Camera 5 **508** UPI/Bettmann Newsphotos **510** Library of Congress **511** Culver Pictures **512** Culver Pictures **513** Myron Davis, Life Magazine © 1961 Time Inc. **521** UPI/Bettmann Newsphotos

**Chapter 16: Opener** Melchior DiGiacomo/The Image Bank **536** UPI/Bettmann Newsphotos **539** Art Stein/Photo Researchers **541** Courtesy of Ludlow Sales Corporation **545** John Veltri/Rapho-Photo Researchers **549** J. P. Laffont/Sygma **553** D. Goldberg/Sygma **561** Above, Jeffrey W. Myers/Stock, Boston; below, courtesy of IBM **562** Charles Feil/Stock, Boston

# INDEX

# ABOUT THE AUTHORS

**Walter LaFeber** is the Marie Underhill Noll Professor of History at Cornell University. His publications include *The New Empire: An Interpretation of American Expansion, 1865-1898* (1963), for which he received the Beveridge Prize of the American Historical Association; *Inevitable Revolutions: The United States and Central America* (1983, 1984); *The Panama Canal: The Crisis in Historical Perspective* (1978, 1979); *America, Russia, and the Cold War, 1945-1984* (1985); and *America in Vietnam: A History with Documents* (1985), also a coauthored work. In addition, Professor LaFeber won the first Clark Award for undergraduate teaching at Cornell.

**Richard Polenberg** is Professor of American History at Cornell University. He is the author of *Reorganizing Roosevelt's Government, 1936-1939* (1966); *War and Society: The United States, 1941-1945* (1972); and *One Nation Divisible: Class, Race, and Ethnicity in the United States Since 1938* (1980). He is the editor of *America at War: The Home Front, 1941-1945* (1968); and *Radicalism and Reform in the New Deal* (1972). He served as chairman of the History Department at Cornell from 1977 to 1980, and is a recipient of the Clark Award for Distinguished Teaching.

**Nancy Woloch** is the author of *Women and the American Experience* (1984).

## *A Note on the Type*

The text of this book was set on the Linotype in Aster, a type face designed by Francesco Simoncini (born 1912 in Bologna, Italy) for Ludwig and Mayer, the German type foundry. Starting out with the basic old-face letter forms that can be traced back to Francesco Griffo in 1495, Simoncini emphasized the diagonal stress by the simple device of extending diagonals to the full height of the letter forms and squaring off. By modifying the weights of the individual letters to combat this stress, he has produced a type of rare balance and vigor. Introduced in 1958, Aster has steadily grown in popularity.